MEET THE SOUTHERN LIVING® FOODS STAFF

On these pages we invite you to meet the *Southern Living* Foods Staff (left to right unless otherwise noted).

Denise Gee, Associate Foods Editor; Susan Hawthorne Nash, Foods Editor; Donna Florio, Associate Foods Editor; Andria Scott Hurst, Associate Foods Editor

(front) Kaye Mabry Adams, Executive Editor; (back) Wanda Stephens, Administrative Assistant; Vicki Poellnitz, Editorial Assistant

Assistant Foods Editors: (front) Peggy Smith, Cynthia Briscoe; (back) Monique Hicks, Patty Vann, Lynnmarie Cook

Test Kitchens Staff: Vanessa McNeil, Vie Warshaw, Jan Moon

(front) Judy Feagin, Assistant Test Kitchens Director; (back) Vanessa Taylor Johnson, Test Kitchens Director; Margaret Monroe, Test Kitchens Staff; Mary Allen Perry, Test Kitchens Staff

Photographers and Photo Stylists: (front) Mary Lyn Jenkins, Charles Walton IV, Tina Cornett; (back) William Dickey, Cindy Manning Barr, Ralph Anderson, Buffy Hargett

Lemon Meringue Cake,
page 118

Southern Living®

1999 ANNUAL RECIPES

Oxmoor House®

© 1999 by Oxmoor House, Inc.
Book Division of Southern Progress Corporation
P.O. Box 2463, Birmingham, Alabama 35201

Southern Living®, Summer Suppers®, and *Holiday Dinners®* are
federally registered trademarks of Southern Living, Inc.

Library of Congress Catalog Number: 79-88364
ISBN: 0-8487-1904-2
ISSN: 0272-2003

Printed in the United States of America
First printing 1999

WE'RE HERE FOR YOU!

We at Oxmoor House are dedicated to serving you
with reliable information that expands your imagination
and enriches your life. We welcome your comments and
suggestions. Please write us at:

Oxmoor House, Inc.
Editor, *Southern Living® Annual Recipes*
2100 Lakeshore Drive
Birmingham, AL 35209

To order additional publications, call 1-205-877-6560.

We Want Your
FAVORITE RECIPES!

Southern Living cooks are the best cooks of all, and we
want your secrets! Please send your favorite original
recipes for main dishes, desserts, and everything in
between, along with any hands-on tips and a sentence
about why you like each recipe. We can't guarantee we'll
print them in a cookbook, but if we do, we'll send you
$20 and a free copy of the cookbook. Send each recipe
on a separate page with your name, address, and day-
time phone number to:

Cookbook Recipes
Oxmoor House
2100 Lakeshore Drive
Birmingham, AL 35209

Southern Living®

Executive Editor: Kaye Mabry Adams
Foods Editor: Susan Hawthorne Nash
Associate Foods Editors: Donna Florio, Denise Gee,
    Andria Scott Hurst
Assistant Foods Editors: Cynthia Briscoe, Lynnmarie P.
    Cook, Monique Hicks, Peggy Smith, Patty M. Vann
Test Kitchens Director: Vanessa Taylor Johnson
Assistant Test Kitchens Director: Judy Feagin
Test Kitchens Staff: Vanessa A. McNeil, Margaret Monroe,
    Jan Moon, Mary Allen Perry, Vie Warshaw
Administrative Assistant: Wanda T. Stephens
Editorial Assistant: Vicki Poellnitz
Director of Photography and Color Quality: Kenner Patton
Senior Foods Photographer: Charles Walton IV
Photographers: Ralph Anderson, Tina Cornett,
    William Dickey
Senior Photo Stylist: Cindy Manning Barr
Photo Stylists: Buffy Hargett, Mary Lyn H. Jenkins
Photo Services: Tracy Duncan
Production Manager: Vicki Weathers
Editorial Coordinator: Bradford Kachelhofer
Production Assistant: Nicole Johnson

Oxmoor House, Inc.

Editor-in-Chief: Nancy Fitzpatrick Wyatt
Senior Editor, Copy and Homes: Olivia Kindig Wells
Art Director: James Boone

Southern Living® 1999 Annual Recipes

Senior Foods Editor: Susan Payne Stabler
Associate Editor: Keri Bradford Anderson
Copy Editor: Catherine Ritter Scholl
Director, Production and Distribution: Phillip Lee
Associate Production Manager: Theresa L. Beste
Production Assistant: Faye Porter Bonner

CONTRIBUTORS
Designer: Carol Middleton
Indexer: Mary Ann Laurens
Editorial Consultant: Jean Wickstrom Liles

Cover: *Holiday Lane Cake, page 306*
Back Cover: *Sweet Corn Soup With Shiitakes and Shrimp,
    page 168; Jalapeño Grilled Pork, Aztec Gold, page 160;
    1-2-3 Blackberry Sherbet, page 130; Wild Rice-Shrimp
    Salad, Asparagus and Tomatoes With Herb Vinaigrette,
    Orange-Pecan Muffin, pages 55 and 56*
Page 1: *Company Pork Roast, page 276; Snap Peas With Roasted
    Garlic Dressing, page 269; Apple-Cranberry Pie, page 269*
Page 4: *Lemon Meringue Cake, page 118*

CONTENTS

OUR YEAR AT SOUTHERN LIVING.

Dear Friends,

Our twenty-first volume of *Southern Living® Annual Recipes* epitomizes one of the South's most treasured customs: sharing the joys of food. You, our readers, are the inspiration for these pages of recipes, entertaining ideas, and creative suggestions.

We stay in touch with you—and you with us—via e-mail, telephone, and mail. For all of you—well-seasoned cooks, kitchen newcomers, veteran recipe contributors, and first-time readers—time is critical, great flavor is important, and your love of our region is precious.

In 1999, we traveled the South to bring you a taste of its diverse cuisine. We shared with you sizzling cast-iron cooking techniques from Alligator, Mississippi, native Jack Butler (page 32). We treated you to terrific new spins on vegetable side dishes by Nashville native Martha Phelps Stamps (page 243). And we showcased the culinary bounty of North Carolina's landmark Biltmore Estate (page 230).

We also took you into our Test Kitchens for a hands-on cooking experience ("Ready, Set, Go!," page 14). We delivered help in planning menus ("Four Meals Made Easy," page 60). And we provided high-flavor, healthy options on our *Living Light* pages.

Along the way you invited us into your kitchens to sample heartwarming soups (page 20), velvety gravies (page 34), and glorious new ways to preserve summer's best produce in colorful pickles and preserves (page 170). Your recipes made it possible for us to deliver simple dinnertime solutions each month through *Quick & Easy* and *What's for Supper?* And many of your ideas found their way into our popular *Dessert of the Month* feature.

As we look ahead toward the next century of food, tell us

what you'd like to see on the Southern Living *table.*

We always want to hear from you, so speak up. Introduce us to a great cook in your area, ask us to feature a particular food from your region, or lend some help with a kitchen dilemma. Your thoughts are most welcome.

Thank you for making our annual recipe collection a part of your culinary library. Please stay in touch with us.

Susan Hawthorne Nash
Foods Editor

Susan joined the Foods Staff of Southern Living *in 1992 and has worked on the magazine in several different capacities, including Editorial Coordinator, before being named to the position of Foods Editor in 1997. She is a member of the International Association of Culinary Professionals and the Association of Food Journalists.*

BEST RECIPES OF 1999

Members of our Foods Staff gather almost every day to taste-test and assign recipes an in-house rating based on taste, overall appeal, ease of preparation, and even cost. Here we share this year's highest-rated recipes.

■ **MARGARET'S CREAMY GRITS** *(page 18):* One taste of these rich grits, and you'll leave the usual plain-grits-with-a-pat-of-butter behind forever. The secret to this recipe's creamy decadence? Half-and-half and two kinds of cheese.

■ **KAHLÚA BEVERAGE SIPPER** *(page 27):* Kahlúa provides a coffee flavor to this smooth concoction, while egg yolks, milk, and half-and-half give it a velvety texture.

■ **RASPBERRY SHORTBREAD** *(page 29):* These classic Scottish butter cookies will win you over with their melt-in-your-mouth appeal. Real butter contributes to their tender, crumbly texture, and raspberry jam and a powdered sugar glaze add an irresistible sweetness.

■ **APRICOT-ALMOND SHORTBREAD** *(page 29):* Try this variation of Raspberry Shortbread for a delicious change of taste. In this version, apricot jam and almonds add their distinct flavors to the same basic shortbread recipe, demonstrating shortbread's versatility.

■ **PIÑA COLADA CAKE** *(page 117):* This stately six-layer sensation begins with our definitive white cake as its foundation. It gets a tropical flair from the Piña Colada Filling that's spread between its layers and from its Rum Buttercream Frosting sprinkled with flaked coconut.

■ **ORANGE CREAM CAKE** *(page 118):* This cake uses the same white cake layers as Piña Colada Cake, but the flavor similarities end there. Orange Cream Filling and Orange Buttercream Frosting give it a refreshing citrus accent perfect for a springtime celebration.

■ **1-2-3 BLACKBERRY SHERBET** *(page 130):* This recipe reminds us that sometimes the simple things are also the best. Three ingredients—fresh blackberries, sugar, and buttermilk—are all you need to create this divine dessert.

■ **BLACKBERRY COBBLER** *(page 131):* Few things taste better than homemade blackberry cobbler in summer, and this home-style favorite will have you longing for the taste of the amethyst and garnet berries all year long.

■ **GRILLED SUMMER SQUASH AND TOMATOES** *(page 144):* This simple side celebrates two Southern favorites: green tomatoes and yellow squash. Slice and marinate the vegetables; then grill. Summer cooking couldn't be easier.

■ **WATERMELON SORBET** *(page 166):* This sweet sorbet showcases the refreshing late-summer melon at its best. Its delicate taste is a delight—as are its four simple ingredients.

■ **LEMON POUND CAKE WITH MINT BERRIES AND CREAM** *(page 183):* A luscious lemon cream and fresh strawberries add the finishing touches to Lemon Pound Cake, making it a dreamy ending to any summer menu.

■ **HONEY GRAHAM BREAD** *(page 211):* Golden honey lends a touch of sweetness to this wholesome loaf bread. Slice and eat it unadorned, or slather it with your favorite flavored butter.

■ **HONEY-PECAN TART** *(page 212):* Honey, whipping cream, butter, and pecans come together to create this rich, decadent tart. Drizzle melted chocolate over the baked tart for a sensational finale for any meal.

■ **PARMESAN CHEESE BITES** *(page 221):* These cheesy snacks spiked with red pepper are perfect for impromptu parties. Just make and freeze them up to a month ahead to have delicious appetizers ready at a moment's notice.

■ **LAMB CHOPS WITH MINTED APPLES** *(page 230):* Guests will applaud when you serve this impressive entrée from Biltmore Estate. A dry rub made with rosemary, sage, and other herbs and spices seasons succulent lamb, which is complemented perfectly by Minted Apples.

■ **FRIED GREEN TOMATO NAPOLEONS** *(page 230):* If you love tomatoes, you'll adore this savory twist on traditional Napoleons. Stack fried green tomatoes with yellow and red pear tomatoes, and top with chopped plum tomatoes for an unforgettable, elegant appetizer.

■ **VEAL SCALLOPINI WITH SHIITAKES** *(page 232):* You'll relish every bite of this easy entrée, another favorite from Biltmore Estate. A buttery wine sauce coats tender veal and fresh shiitake mushrooms.

■ **CLEAR-THE-CUPBOARD COOKIES** *(page 278):* This recipe takes the best of what you probably already have in your pantry—coconut, oats, flour, sugar, cereal—and creates cookies that kids and adults alike will devour.

■ **CINNAMON ROLLS** *(page 284):* These tender Cinnamon Rolls were made for the holidays. Just make and freeze them ahead; then follow the directions for gift-giving.

■ **BLUE CHEESE TERRINE WITH TOMATO-BASIL VINAIGRETTE** *(page 288):* Tangy blue cheese takes center stage in this savory dish accented by roasted bell peppers and a wonderful Italian-inspired vinaigrette.

■ **PRALINE-CRUSTED CHEESECAKE** *(page 295):* This cheesecake's dense, creamy filling is attraction enough for cheesecake enthusiasts. But it's the Pralines embellishing the crust and top that make it an irresistible dessert for all.

HOLIDAY RECIPE CONTEST WINNERS

We received nearly 5,500 entries in our third-annual Holiday Recipe Contest. Here are the winning recipes by category.

GREAT BEGINNINGS

■ **CRAB CAKES WITH MAUI SAUCE** *(page 310):* Grand Prizewinner. A four-ingredient sauce and sautéed spinach leaves add flair to this easy-but-impressive appetizer.

■ **TORTILLA SOUP** *(page 310):* Runner-up. Cilantro, cumin, and garlic season this Southwestern chicken soup topped with fried tortilla strips and shredded Monterey Jack cheese.

■ **CHICKEN-AND-BRIE QUESADILLAS WITH CHIPOTLE SALSA** *(page 311):* Runner-up. These quesadillas call for Brie instead of the traditional Cheddar or Monterey Jack cheese and feature a fresh salsa of chipotle chiles and plum tomato.

BY POPULAR DEMAND

■ **AMARETTO-WALNUT BROWNIES** *(page 311):* Grand Prizewinner. Almond liqueur, toasted walnuts, and chocolate deliver simple satisfaction in these rave-winning fudgy squares.

■ **SAUSAGE, SPINACH, AND BEAN SOUP** *(page 311):* Runner-up. Italian sausage, spinach, and cannellini beans make this a hearty soup perfect for cold winter evenings.

■ **ROSEMARY ROASTED TURKEY** *(page 312):* Runner-up. Butter, white Zinfandel, and orange juice keep this turkey moist and juicy while it roasts. Fresh rosemary sprigs lend it a piney, lemony scent.

EASYGOING ENTRÉES

■ **HEARTY TEX-MEX SQUASH-CHICKEN CASSEROLE** *(page 312):* Grand Prizewinner. Spinach, yellow squash, and red bell pepper provide healthy goodness for this comforting one-dish meal.

■ **SAVANNAH SEAFOOD PARMESAN** *(page 312):* Runner-up. Shrimp and crabmeat team up with bow tie pasta, pimiento, and Parmesan cheese to create this satisfying meal-in-itself.

■ **APPLE-BACON STUFFED CHICKEN BREASTS** *(page 313):* Runner-up. Chicken breast halves take on a new flavor dimension when stuffed with a mixture of apple, cranberries, bacon, and cinnamon.

ALL-STAR SIDE DISHES

■ **SAVORY SPINACH-GORGONZOLA CUSTARDS** *(page 313):* Grand Prizewinner. Custard cups give shape to these baked custards crowned with caramelized onion and pungent Gorgonzola cheese.

■ **DIVINE MACARONI AND CHEESE** *(page 314):* Runner-up. Four cheeses—Parmesan, cream cheese, mascarpone, and Gorgonzola—create the creamiest macaroni and cheese you'll ever taste.

■ **POTATO-HORSERADISH GRATIN WITH CARAMELIZED ONIONS** *(page 314):* Runner-up. Potato slices bake in a creamy horseradish sauce before being topped with sweet caramelized onions.

SWEET REWARDS

■ **FIG CAKE** *(page 314):* Grand Prizewinner. Fig preserves and applesauce supply sweet moistness to this classic cake. Cinnamon, cloves, and nutmeg add the spice.

■ **TOASTED ALMOND-BUTTER CAKE** *(page 315):* Runner-up. Toasted slivered almonds and almond extract contribute their characteristic slightly sweet nut flavor to this buttery three-layer cake.

■ **FUDGE TRUFFLE-PECAN TART** *(page 315):* Runner-up. This easy tart takes just 10 minutes to prepare and bakes for just 20 minutes—a small time investment for such a nutty, fudgy confection.

JANUARY

January offers a welcome respite from the whirlwind of the holiday season, and "Soup's On!" provides you with the perfect recipes for cozy nights at home. Chunky Italian Soup, Creamy Chicken Noodle Soup, Sausage-Tortellini Soup . . . what could be more satisfying on a cold winter night?

Two Southern favorites—country ham and grits—step into the spotlight in "Slice of Heaven" and "Grits—A Southern Staple." Tuck slivers of Country Ham into your favorite home-made biscuits for a savory treat any time of day. Margaret's Creamy Grits will also have you coming back for more.

READY, SET, GO!

Join us for some fun as our Foods staff turns a sack of everyday ingredients into a bounty of great recipes. Editors and kitchen staffers were asked to stretch their ingenuity to produce a recipe in a limited amount of time using a grocery bag full of familiar items. Here are some of our favorite creations from that day.

CHICKEN WONTONS WITH HOISIN PEANUT DIPPING SAUCE

Asian inspiration turns a handful of pantry ingredients into neatly wrapped wontons in about 30 minutes.

Prep: 20 minutes
Cook: 10 minutes

1 cup diced cooked chicken
4 green onions, diced
1 cup finely shredded cabbage
2 tablespoons chopped fresh cilantro
2 teaspoons brown sugar
1 tablespoon hoisin sauce
1 teaspoon sesame oil
36 wonton wrappers
Peanut oil
Hoisin Peanut Dipping Sauce

• **Stir** together first 7 ingredients. Spoon 1 teaspoon mixture onto center of each wonton wrapper.
• **Moisten** wonton wrapper edges with water. Bring corners together, pressing to seal.
• **Pour** oil to a depth of 3 inches into a Dutch oven; heat to 375°. Fry wontons in batches until golden, turning once. Drain on wire racks over paper towels. Serve immediately with Hoisin Peanut Dipping Sauce. **Yield:** 3 dozen.

Hoisin Peanut Dipping Sauce

Prep: 10 minutes
Cook: 2 minutes

½ cup chicken broth
2 tablespoons hoisin sauce
2 tablespoons sesame oil
2 tablespoons soy sauce
1 tablespoon creamy peanut butter
1 teaspoon cornstarch

• **Bring** all ingredients to a boil in a small saucepan, whisking constantly; boil 1 minute. **Yield:** about ¾ cup.

PORK CHOPS WITH CORNBREAD-APPLE STUFFING

Prep: 35 minutes
Cook: 47 minutes

¼ cup butter or margarine, divided
2 celery ribs, chopped
1 medium-size sweet onion, chopped
1 cooking apple, chopped
1 (14½-ounce) can chicken broth, divided
1 tablespoon chopped fresh or 1 teaspoon dried sage
1 (8-ounce) package cornbread stuffing mix
8 (¾- to 1-inch-thick) boneless pork chops (2 pounds)
1 teaspoon salt
¼ teaspoon pepper
¼ cup vegetable oil, divided
1 cup dry white wine, divided
3 tablespoons all-purpose flour
Cranberry-Orange Relish

• **Melt** 2 tablespoons butter in a large skillet over medium heat; add celery and onion, and sauté until tender. Add apple, and sauté 1 minute. Add 1 cup broth; remove from heat, and stir in sage and cornbread stuffing mix.
• **Butterfly** pork chops by making a lengthwise cut down center of 1 edge, cutting to within ½ inch of opposite edge. Open chops, pressing with hand to flatten; sprinkle with salt and pepper. Spoon ½ cup stuffing mixture onto each chop. Roll up, and tie with string.
• **Brown** pork chops, 4 at a time, in 2 tablespoons hot oil in large skillet, turning once.
• **Transfer** chops to a lightly greased rack in a broiler pan. Pour ½ cup wine into pan.
• **Bake** at 375° for 20 to 30 minutes or until done; cool slightly. Remove string, and cut pork into 1-inch-thick slices.
• **Melt** remaining 2 tablespoons butter in skillet over medium heat; whisk in flour, and cook, whisking constantly, 1 minute.
• **Whisk** in remaining chicken broth and remaining ½ cup wine, and cook over medium heat, whisking constantly, until

thickened. Spoon over pork slices, and serve with Cranberry-Orange Relish. **Yield:** 8 servings.

Cranberry-Orange Relish

Prep: 5 minutes
Chill: 2 hours

1 (16-ounce) can whole-berry
    cranberry sauce
1 (11-ounce) can mandarin
    oranges, drained and chopped

• **Stir** together cranberry sauce and oranges. Cover and chill 2 hours. **Yield:** about 2 cups.

MOROCCAN GARLIC CHICKEN

Prep: 25 minutes
Cook: 30 minutes

4 skinned and boned chicken
    breast halves
½ teaspoon salt
½ teaspoon pepper
1 tablespoon butter or margarine
1 medium onion, sliced
2 garlic cloves, pressed
1 medium zucchini, chopped
10 ounces uncooked couscous
½ cup raisins (optional)
1 tablespoon chopped fresh or
    1 teaspoon dried basil
½ teaspoon ground saffron

• **Cut** chicken into bite-size pieces, and sprinkle with salt and pepper.
• **Melt** butter in a large nonstick skillet over medium heat; add onion and garlic, and sauté until tender.
• **Add** chicken, and cook, stirring often, 8 minutes or until done.
• **Add** zucchini, and sauté 3 minutes or until tender. Remove from heat.
• **Prepare** couscous according to package directions; stir in raisins, if desired. Cover and remove from heat. Let stand 5 minutes or until liquid is absorbed. Stir in basil and saffron. Let stand 5 minutes.
• **Stir** couscous mixture into chicken mixture; cook over medium-high heat 2 minutes or until thoroughly heated. Serve immediately. **Yield:** 4 servings.

A recent creative planning meeting offered us a refreshing departure—an opportunity to spend a day together in the kitchens.

Most weeks in the Foods department, editors are researching and writing stories and scouring recipe files to find your best ideas. In the same week, kitchen staff members are preparing close to 100 appetizers, entrées, side dishes, salads, and desserts for rating and photography.

When we took a day to stray from our routines and to try on different hats in the kitchen, we had some tasty results.

"Through all the good-natured competition and teasing among the teams, we all turned out great food that we were proud of," says Associate Foods Editor Donna Florio.

The best part of the culinary calisthenics? "Sampling all of the good things we prepared," votes Test Kitchens staff member Vie Warshaw.

"Friendly competition and great teamwork," says Margaret Monroe of her day of trading places.

A panel of editorial "foodies" tasted the results, naming the recipes on pages 14 through 17 the winners. We hope you agree.

ITALIAN STUFFED SANDWICH

Prep: 25 minutes
Bake: 25 minutes
Cook: 20 minutes

1 (16-ounce) Italian bread loaf
8 bacon slices, chopped
⅔ cup chopped onion
2 garlic cloves, pressed and divided
1 (14-ounce) can quartered
    artichoke hearts, drained and
    coarsely chopped
¾ cup shredded Parmesan cheese,
    divided
⅓ cup mayonnaise
¼ cup minced fresh parsley,
    divided
¼ teaspoon pepper
1 (16-ounce) jar marinara sauce
⅓ cup dry white wine (optional)

• **Cut** off top one-third of bread loaf, and set aside. Scoop out remaining bread, leaving a ¼-inch-thick shell.
• **Tear** bread into small pieces; set aside.
• **Cook** bacon in a large skillet until crisp; remove bacon, reserving 1 tablespoon drippings in skillet.
• **Sauté** onion and 1 garlic clove in hot bacon drippings until tender.
• **Stir** in bread pieces, bacon, artichoke, ½ cup cheese, mayonnaise, 2 tablespoons parsley, and pepper.
• **Spoon** artichoke mixture into bread shell; cover with bread top. Wrap in aluminum foil.
• **Bake** at 375° for 20 minutes. Open foil, and sprinkle sandwich with remaining ¼ cup Parmesan cheese. Bake sandwich, uncovered, 5 more minutes. Slice.
• **Bring** remaining 1 garlic clove and marinara sauce to a boil in skillet. Reduce heat, and simmer, stirring occasionally, 10 minutes.
• **Stir** in wine, if desired; simmer 5 minutes. Remove mixture from heat, and stir in remaining 2 tablespoons parsley. Serve sauce with sandwich. **Yield:** 4 to 6 servings.

SOUTHWESTERN ROLL WITH CILANTRO HOLLANDAISE SAUCE

Prep: 25 minutes
Bake: 25 minutes

½ pound ground chuck
1 small onion, chopped
2 garlic cloves, minced
3 tablespoons chopped fresh
    cilantro, divided
¼ cup salsa
½ teaspoon salt
¼ teaspoon pepper
1 (7-ounce) jar roasted sweet red
    peppers
1 (11-ounce) can refrigerated
    crusty French bread loaf
½ (12-ounce) package frozen
    spinach soufflé, thawed
1 (0.9-ounce) envelope
    hollandaise sauce mix
Salsa

• **Cook** first 3 ingredients in a large non-stick skillet, stirring until beef crumbles and is no longer pink; drain. Return to skillet, and stir in 1 tablespoon cilantro and next 3 ingredients.
• **Drain** red peppers, and pat dry with paper towels. Cut peppers into thin strips.
• **Roll** dough to a 14- x 10-inch rectangle on a lightly greased baking sheet. Spoon soufflé over dough, spreading to within 1 inch of edges. Top with pepper strips.
• **Spoon** ground chuck mixture lengthwise down center of dough. Roll up, starting at a long edge; place, seam side down, on a lightly greased baking sheet.
• **Bake** at 350° for 20 to 25 minutes or until bread is golden. Slice.
• **Prepare** hollandaise sauce according to package directions; stir in remaining 2 tablespoons cilantro. Serve over roll with salsa. **Yield:** 6 servings.

ROASTED POTATO PIZZAS

These individual flatbreads received our highest rating—and the grand prize in our contest. Add sautéed garlic and onion to bottled pasta sauce to shave 30 minutes off your time in the kitchen.

Prep: 35 minutes
Cook: 35 minutes
Bake: 32 minutes

2 bacon slices
1 garlic clove, minced
½ (8-ounce) package fresh
    mushrooms, chopped
1 (15-ounce) can tomato sauce
1 teaspoon dried Italian seasoning
6 dried tomatoes, chopped
1 teaspoon salt, divided
1 teaspoon freshly ground pepper,
    divided
6 small red potatoes, thinly sliced
1 small onion, sliced
1 tablespoon olive oil
1 teaspoon chopped fresh or dried
    rosemary
1 (8-ounce) can refrigerated
    crescent rolls
1 (3-ounce) package shredded
    Parmesan cheese

• **Cook** bacon in a large skillet until crisp; remove bacon, reserving 2 tablespoons drippings. Crumble bacon, and set aside.
• **Sauté** garlic and mushrooms in 1 tablespoon reserved drippings in skillet. Stir in tomato sauce, Italian seasoning, dried tomatoes, ¼ teaspoon salt, and ¼ teaspoon pepper. Cook over medium heat, stirring occasionally, 30 minutes. Set aside.
• **Combine** potato, onion, remaining 1 tablespoon drippings, oil, remaining ¾ teaspoon salt, remaining ¾ teaspoon pepper, and rosemary in a roasting pan.
• **Bake** at 450° for 18 to 20 minutes, stirring once. Set aside.
• **Unroll** crescent rolls, and separate into 8 triangles; shape each triangle into a 4-inch circle, and place on ungreased baking sheets.
• **Bake** at 375° for 6 minutes. Top with tomato sauce mixture, potato mixture, bacon, and Parmesan cheese. Bake 5 to 6 more minutes. **Yield:** 8 servings.

B.Y.O.B.

Ask couples to bring their 10 favorite ingredients in a paper bag. Divide into teams, give each team a bag, and challenge them to create a recipe using at least half the items. Here's a sample of some ingredients that would work well.

- shredded Cheddar cheese
- refrigerated piecrusts
- marinara sauce
- black beans
- mayonnaise
- white wine
- bacon
- Italian bread
- celery
- artichoke hearts

FARMER'S BEANS AND RICE WITH ROSEMARY BISCUITS

Prep: 20 minutes
Cook: 30 minutes

2 cups chopped cooked ham
1 cup chopped carrot
1 medium onion, chopped
1 tablespoon vegetable oil
2 (14½-ounce) cans chicken
    broth
2 (14½-ounce) cans Cajun-style
    stewed tomatoes, undrained
2 (15-ounce) cans black-eyed
    peas with pork, rinsed and
    drained
1 teaspoon Creole seasoning
1 cup uncooked long-grain rice
Rosemary Biscuits

• **Sauté** first 3 ingredients in hot oil in a Dutch oven until tender; stir in broth and next 3 ingredients. Bring to a boil; boil 10 minutes.
• **Stir** in rice. Cover, reduce heat, and simmer 20 minutes or until rice is tender. Serve mixture with Rosemary Biscuits. **Yield:** 10 cups.

Rosemary Biscuits

Prep: 6 minutes
Bake: 10 minutes

1 (3-ounce) package cream cheese, softened
1¾ cups biscuit mix
½ cup milk
2 teaspoons chopped fresh or dried rosemary

• **Cut** cream cheese into biscuit mix with a pastry blender or fork until mixture is crumbly; add milk and rosemary, stirring just until dry ingredients are moistened.
• **Turn** biscuit dough out onto a lightly floured surface, and knead 3 or 4 times.
• **Pat** or roll dough to ¾-inch thickness; cut diagonally with a knife into 1-inch diamonds. Place on a baking sheet.
• **Bake** at 400° for 10 minutes or until lightly browned. **Yield:** 2 dozen biscuits.

CHEESY MINESTRONE

Prep: 25 minutes
Cook: 30 minutes

1 pound smoked sausage, sliced
1 small onion, chopped
2 tablespoons all-purpose flour
1 (3.5-ounce) package chicken flavor ramen noodle soup mix
1 quart water
1 (14½-ounce) can chicken broth
1 (16-ounce) package frozen whole kernel corn, thawed
1 medium zucchini, coarsely chopped
1 (10-ounce) can diced tomatoes and green chiles, undrained
1 (19-ounce) can cannellini beans, rinsed and drained
2 tablespoons chopped fresh basil or 2 teaspoons dried basil
1 cup (4 ounces) shredded mozzarella cheese
Tortilla-Lime Crackers

• **Sauté** sausage and onion in a Dutch oven over medium-high heat until onion is tender; stir in flour, and cook, stirring constantly, 2 minutes.
• **Remove** seasoning packet from soup mix. Set noodles aside.
• **Add** seasoning packet, 1 quart water, and next 5 ingredients to sausage mixture; bring to a boil. Reduce heat, and simmer 5 to 7 minutes.
• **Stir** in noodles and basil; cook, stirring occasionally, 3 minutes.
• **Sprinkle** each serving with cheese; serve with Tortilla-Lime Crackers. **Yield:** about 8 cups.

Tortilla-Lime Crackers

Prep: 6 minutes
Bake: 7 minutes

4 (8-inch) flour tortillas
2 tablespoons butter or margarine, melted
1 tablespoon lime juice

• **Brush** tortillas evenly with butter; cut each tortilla into 8 wedges. Sprinkle wedges evenly with lime juice, and place on a baking sheet. Bake at 375° for 7 minutes. **Yield:** 32 crackers.

GRITS—A SOUTHERN STAPLE

Grits are to the South what rice is to Asia—a soothing accompaniment, a cultural statement on a plate.

As comforting as they are with a pat of butter, grits welcome embellishment. Add cheese or cream for a blanket of richness; add hot sauce or black pepper for a blast of heat. Grits become mini cakes when cooled in a shallow pan and cut into shapes.

Grits are corn kernels that have been ground to a coarse, medium, or fine consistency. And (for your next crossword puzzle) groats are the hulled, crushed kernels of grains.

GRITS WITH GRILLED CHICKEN AND ONIONS

Prep: 20 minutes
Cook: 1 hour and 18 minutes
Chill: 1 hour (optional)

2⅔ cups uncooked stone-ground grits
5⅓ cups water
2 cups (8 ounces) shredded Cheddar cheese, divided
¼ cup butter or margarine, divided
1 teaspoon salt, divided
¾ teaspoon pepper, divided
2 large onions, cut into ½-inch slices
2 tablespoons bourbon or apple juice
4 skinned and boned chicken breast halves
½ cup barbecue sauce

• **Rinse** grits according to package directions. Bring 5⅓ cups water to a boil in a Dutch oven; gradually stir in grits. Reduce heat, and simmer, stirring occasionally, 25 minutes.
• **Stir** in ½ cup cheese, 2 tablespoons butter, ½ teaspoon salt, and ¼ teaspoon pepper. Keep warm, or spread into a greased 11- x 7-inch baking dish; cover and chill at least 1 hour, and cut into 2-inch-square cakes.
• **Melt** remaining 2 tablespoons butter in a large skillet over medium heat; add onion, remaining ½ teaspoon salt, and remaining ½ teaspoon pepper.
• **Cook,** stirring often, 30 minutes or until onion is caramel colored. Add bourbon; cook, stirring constantly, 1 minute. Keep warm.
• **Grill** chicken, or cook in skillet over medium heat (300° to 350°) 6 minutes on each side or until done. Cool slightly; shred. Stir together chicken and barbecue sauce.
• **Top** grits evenly with chicken mixture, onion mixture, and remaining 1½ cups cheese. **Yield:** 6 to 8 servings.

STONE-GROUND GRITS

Grits purchased from the grocery store are usually hominy grits—degerminated corn that has been finely ground on steel rollers.

Stone-ground grits are simply whole-grain corn ground very coarsely on stones. The key is whole grain.

If you can't find stone-ground grits locally, order them by mail. But because the cost of shipping is often more than the price of the grits, these purveyors suggest you order with a friend and buy grits in quantity. (Grits freeze very well.)

Callaway Gardens Country Store: 1-800-280-7524. Cost is $12.95 plus shipping for three 2-pound bags.

Falls Mill & Country Store: (931) 469-7161. Cost is $5 plus shipping for a 5-pound bag (10-pound minimum order).

Hoppin' Johns: 1-800-828-4412. Cost is $4.50 plus shipping for a 2-pound bag.

Sellwood Farm: 1-800-522-0403. Cost is $2.75 plus shipping for a 1-pound bag.

stiff peaks form. Fold one-fourth of egg white mixture into grits. Fold grits into remaining egg white mixture. Pour into a greased and floured 2-quart soufflé dish; sprinkle with paprika.
• **Bake** at 400° for 45 minutes or until puffed and lightly browned. **Yield:** 6 servings.

Elizabeth R. Drawdy
Spindale, North Carolina

SLICE OF HEAVEN

Country ham is a dry-cured Southern delicacy. With these recipes you can try it whole, in an excellent bread, and tucked into a biscuit for a taste of the good ole days.

MARGARET'S CREAMY GRITS

In the Test Kitchens, we stood in line for a bowlful of this decadent dish created by Margaret Monroe, one of our culinary experts.

Prep: 10 minutes
Cook: 22 to 25 minutes

2 quarts half-and-half or whipping cream
1 teaspoon salt
½ teaspoon granulated garlic
½ teaspoon pepper
2 cups uncooked quick-cooking grits
1 (8-ounce) package cream cheese, cubed
1 (12-ounce) package shredded sharp Cheddar cheese
1 teaspoon hot sauce

• **Bring** first 4 ingredients to a boil in a Dutch oven; gradually stir in grits. Return to a boil; cover, reduce heat, and simmer, stirring occasionally, 5 minutes or until thickened.
• **Add** cream cheese, Cheddar cheese, and hot sauce, stirring until cheeses melt. **Yield:** 12 cups.

GARLIC-CHEESE GRITS SOUFFLÉ

Prep: 30 minutes
Bake: 45 minutes

2 tablespoons butter or margarine
2 garlic cloves, minced
4 cups water
¾ teaspoon salt
½ teaspoon pepper
¼ teaspoon dry mustard
¼ teaspoon ground turmeric
1 cup uncooked regular grits
4 large eggs, separated
2 cups (8 ounces) shredded sharp Cheddar cheese
⅛ teaspoon hot sauce
¼ teaspoon cream of tartar
Paprika

• **Melt** butter in a medium saucepan over medium heat; add garlic, and sauté until tender.
• **Stir** in 4 cups water and next 4 ingredients; bring to a boil. Gradually stir in grits. Reduce heat, and simmer, stirring occasionally, 15 to 20 minutes or until thickened. Remove from heat; stir in egg yolks, cheese, and hot sauce.
• **Beat** egg whites and cream of tartar at high speed with an electric mixer until

COUNTRY HAM BREAD WITH HERB BUTTER

Prep: 25 minutes
Rise: 2 hours and 30 minutes
Bake: 30 to 40 minutes

1 (¼-ounce) envelope active dry yeast
½ cup warm water (100° to 110°)
1 cup cornmeal
3 tablespoons sugar
2 cups buttermilk
1 large egg, lightly beaten
3 tablespoons butter or margarine, melted
2 teaspoons ground black pepper
½ teaspoon ground red pepper
5½ to 6 cups all-purpose flour
2½ cups cooked, ground country ham
Cornmeal
Herb Butter

• **Combine** yeast and warm water in a large bowl; let stand 5 minutes.
• **Stir** in cornmeal and next 6 ingredients; stir in enough flour to make a stiff

dough. Turn dough out onto a lightly floured surface.

• **Knead** in ham until dough is smooth and elastic (about 10 minutes). Place in a well-greased bowl, turning to grease top.

• **Cover** and let rise in a warm place (85°), free from drafts, 2 hours or until doubled in bulk.

• **Grease** 2 (9-inch) round cakepans; sprinkle with cornmeal. Punch dough down; divide in half. Shape each half into a round loaf. Place in cakepans; brush with water.

• **Cover** and let rise in a warm place, free from drafts, 30 to 40 minutes or until doubled in bulk.

• **Bake** at 375° for 30 to 40 minutes or until loaves sound hollow when tapped. Remove from pans immediately. Serve warm with Herb Butter. **Yield:** 2 loaves.

Herb Butter

Prep: 5 minutes

½ cup butter or margarine, softened
½ cup chopped fresh chives
¼ cup minced fresh parsley
1 tablespoon lemon juice
Dash of pepper

• **Stir** together all ingredients; cover and chill. **Yield:** ½ cup.

COUNTRY HAM

Prep: 15 minutes
Soak: 24 hours
Cook: 2 to 3 hours
Stand: 2 hours

1 (10- to 12-pound) uncooked country ham
2 cups cider vinegar
2 cups apple juice
1 cup sugar
1½ cups fine, dry or soft breadcrumbs
1 cup firmly packed dark brown sugar
2 tablespoons pepper

• **Scrub** ham in warm water with a stiff brush, and rinse well.

• **Place** ham in a large nonaluminum stockpot. Cover with water; add vinegar, and let soak 24 hours.

• **Drain** ham, and rinse; return to stockpot. Insert a meat thermometer into ham, making sure it does not touch fat or bone. Add water to cover, apple juice, and sugar. Bring to a boil; reduce heat, and simmer, uncovered, 2 hours or until thermometer registers 140°, adding hot water as needed to keep ham covered. Remove from heat; let stand 2 hours.

• **Drain** ham; trim skin, leaving a thin layer of fat. Stir together breadcrumbs, brown sugar, and pepper; press over ham. Cool completely.

• **Cut** ham into very thin slices, reserving any breadcrumb mixture that detaches; serve ham and breadcrumb mixture in biscuits. **Yield:** 30 servings.

John Egerton
Nashville, Tennessee

COUNTRY HAM WITH RAISIN SAUCE

Prep: 15 minutes
Soak: 24 hours
Bake: 5 hours

1 (15- to 20-pound) uncooked country ham
1 tablespoon all-purpose flour
1 (23½- x 19-inch) oven cooking bag
2 (12-ounce) cans cola soft drink
Raisin Sauce

• **Place** ham in a large container. Cover with water, and let soak 24 hours. Drain. Scrub ham in warm water with a stiff brush, and rinse well.

• **Add** flour to oven cooking bag; twist end of bag, and shake to coat.

• **Place** ham, fat side up, in oven bag. Place bag in a 2-inch-deep roasting pan.

• **Pour** cola over ham. Insert a meat thermometer into ham, making sure it does not touch fat or bone. Close bag with tie; cut 6 (½-inch) slits in top of bag. Cover with aluminum foil.

• **Bake** at 325° for 4 hours. Remove foil, and bake 1 more hour or until meat thermometer registers 140°. Remove from oven, and cool slightly. Slice ham,

and serve with Raisin Sauce. **Yield:** 45 servings.

Note: Do not use diet cola soft drink for this recipe.

Raisin Sauce

Prep: 10 minutes
Cook: 45 minutes

2 cups raisins
1½ cups water
Pinch of salt
2 cups sugar
1 tablespoon cornstarch
1 tablespoon grated orange rind
3 tablespoons fresh orange juice
½ cup chopped walnuts or pecans

• **Bring** first 3 ingredients to a boil in a saucepan; reduce heat, and simmer 30 minutes. Combine sugar and next 3 ingredients; stir into raisin mixture. Return to a boil, stirring constantly. Boil, stirring constantly, 1 minute. Stir in walnuts. **Yield:** 2 cups.

Teresa Nobles
Clarkson, Kentucky

HANDLING HAM

Rufus Brown of Johnston County Hams offers these tips for careful ham handling.

■ Store uncooked country ham by hanging it unopened in a cool dark place. Cook it within six months.

■ Refrigerate vacuum-sealed cooked country ham. Once the seal is broken, use ham within a month.

The best country hams are available from small companies such as Johnston County Hams located in Smithfield, North Carolina. If you want one of theirs, call (919) 934-8054. Their 10-pound cooked country ham costs $62; a 14-pound uncooked country ham costs $46.

SOUP'S ON!

Nothing is more chill-chasing than a bowl of steaming noodle soup. You can substitute your favorite pasta and vegetables in any of these recipes.

CHUNKY ITALIAN SOUP
(pictured on page 38)

Hot, buttered cornbread makes this soup a meal.

Prep: 20 minutes
Cook: 45 minutes

1 pound lean ground beef or beef tips
1 medium onion, chopped
2 (14.5-ounce) cans Italian-style tomatoes
1 (10¾-ounce) can tomato soup with basil, undiluted
4 cups water
2 garlic cloves, minced
2 teaspoons dried basil
2 teaspoons dried oregano
1 teaspoon salt
½ teaspoon pepper
1 tablespoon chili powder (optional)
1 (16-ounce) can kidney beans, drained
1 (16-ounce) can Italian-style green beans, drained
1 carrot, chopped
1 zucchini, chopped
8 ounces rotini pasta, cooked
Grated Parmesan cheese

• **Cook** beef and onion in a Dutch oven over medium heat, stirring until beef crumbles and is no longer pink; drain. Return to pan. Stir in tomatoes, next 7 ingredients, and, if desired, chili powder; bring to a boil. Reduce heat; simmer, stirring occasionally, 30 minutes.
• **Stir** in kidney beans and next 3 ingredients; simmer, stirring occasionally, 15 minutes. Stir in pasta. Sprinkle each serving with cheese. **Yield:** 10 cups.

Alice Pahl
Raleigh, North Carolina

SAUSAGE-TORTELLINI SOUP

Prep: 25 minutes
Cook: 46 minutes

1 pound Italian sausage
1 large onion, chopped
1 garlic clove, pressed
3 (14½-ounce) cans beef broth
2 (14½-ounce) cans diced tomatoes, undrained
1 (8-ounce) can tomato sauce
1 cup dry red wine
2 carrots, thinly sliced
1 tablespoon sugar
2 teaspoons dried Italian seasoning
2 small zucchini, sliced
1 (9-ounce) package refrigerated cheese-filled tortellini
½ cup shredded Parmesan cheese

• **Discard** sausage casings.
• **Cook** sausage, onion, and garlic in a Dutch oven over medium-high heat, stirring until sausage crumbles and is no longer pink; drain and return to pan.
• **Stir** in broth and next 6 ingredients; bring to a boil. Reduce heat; simmer 30 minutes. Skim off fat.
• **Stir** in zucchini and tortellini; simmer 10 minutes. Sprinkle each serving with cheese. **Yield:** 10 cups.

Louise Bodziony
Gladstone, Missouri

CREAMY CHICKEN NOODLE SOUP

Prep: 20 minutes
Cook: 55 minutes

1 tablespoon butter or margarine
1 large onion, chopped
3 cups chopped cooked chicken
3 (14½-ounce) cans chicken broth
1 (10¾-ounce) can cream of mushroom soup, undiluted
1 (10¾-ounce) can cream of chicken soup, undiluted
1 (8-ounce) package spaghetti, broken into 2-inch pieces
7 celery ribs, diced
6 medium carrots, diced
1 teaspoon poultry seasoning
1 teaspoon pepper
1 teaspoon grated lemon rind
2 cups milk
2 cups (8 ounces) shredded sharp Cheddar cheese

• **Melt** butter in a Dutch oven over medium heat; add onion, and sauté until tender. Stir in chicken and next 9 ingredients; bring to a boil. Reduce heat, and simmer 45 minutes.
• **Stir** in milk, and return to a simmer. Remove from heat; let stand 10 minutes. Sprinkle with cheese. **Yield:** 12 cups.

Mary M. Huie
Anniston, Alabama

SIZING UP PASTA

■ Two ounces (just over ½ cup dry) short pasta such as elbow macaroni, shells, or spirals will yield 1 cup cooked pasta.

■ Two ounces long pasta (½-inch-diameter bunch dry) such as spaghetti, angel hair, or linguine will make 1 cup cooked pasta.

■ Two ounces uncooked medium egg noodles will yield ½ cup cooked pasta.

PASS THE CHICKEN

These recipes offer you terrific ways to serve chicken, and each has a preparation time of 30 minutes or less.

CREAMY CHICKEN-RICE CASSEROLE

Chopped cooked chicken streamlines meal preparation in this casserole.

Prep: 30 minutes
Bake: 30 minutes

1 (6-ounce) package long-grain and wild rice mix
3 to 4 cups chopped cooked chicken
1 small onion, chopped
1 (2-ounce) jar diced pimiento, drained
1 (16-ounce) package frozen French-style green beans, thawed
1 (6-ounce) jar sliced mushrooms, drained
1 (8-ounce) can sliced water chestnuts, drained
1 (10¾-ounce) can cream of celery soup, undiluted
1 (8-ounce) container sour cream
½ teaspoon salt
½ teaspoon pepper
1 cup (4 ounces) shredded Swiss or fontina cheese

• **Cook** rice according to package directions. Combine rice, chicken, and next 9 ingredients; spoon into a greased shallow 3-quart baking dish. Top with cheese.
• **Bake** at 350° for 30 minutes or until casserole is bubbly around edges. **Yield:** 6 to 8 servings.

Note: Freeze the casserole up to 1 month, if desired. Thaw in refrigerator 24 hours; let stand at room temperature 30 minutes before baking.
Daphne K. Harbinson
Fairview, North Carolina

DIJON CHICKEN

Prep: 5 minutes
Cook: 30 minutes

1 (6-ounce) jar marinated artichoke hearts
2 skinned and boned chicken breast halves
⅛ teaspoon salt
⅛ teaspoon pepper
1 tablespoon olive oil
½ cup dry white wine or chicken broth
2 tablespoons Dijon mustard

• **Drain** artichoke hearts; cut hearts into fourths, and set aside.
• **Sprinkle** chicken breast halves with salt and pepper.
• **Brown** chicken in hot oil in a skillet over medium-high heat.
• **Combine** wine and mustard; pour over chicken. Add artichoke; cover and cook over medium heat 10 minutes. **Yield:** 2 servings.
Delana W. Pearce
Lakeland, Florida

FREEZING CHICKEN

■ Cook 1 pound of boneless chicken breasts or thighs to get 2 cups chopped; or cook 1 (3½-pound) whole chicken to get 3 cups chopped. Freeze chopped cooked chicken up to one month. You can also check your local grocery store for frozen chopped cooked chicken.

■ To freeze uncooked chicken, place chicken pieces in individual zip-top plastic bags; then place individual packages in a large heavy-duty zip-top plastic freezer bag, and label. Freeze chicken pieces up to six months and whole chickens up to one year.

GLAZED CHICKEN AND PEARS

Prep: 10 minutes
Cook: 1 hour

1 (16-ounce) can pear halves in heavy syrup
2 teaspoons cornstarch
½ teaspoon dry mustard
¼ teaspoon salt
¼ teaspoon pepper
1 cup water
¼ teaspoon grated lemon rind
2 tablespoons fresh lemon juice
2 teaspoons soy sauce
4 bone-in chicken breast halves, skinned
2 tablespoons vegetable oil

• **Drain** pears, reserving liquid; set pears aside.
• **Whisk** together pear liquid, cornstarch, and next 7 ingredients.
• **Brown** chicken in hot oil in a skillet over medium-high heat.
• **Add** pear liquid mixture; bring to a boil. Cover, reduce heat, and simmer 45 minutes. Remove chicken from skillet, reserving drippings; keep warm.
• **Add** pears to drippings in skillet; cook, stirring often, over medium-high heat until liquid is reduced by half. Spoon over chicken. **Yield:** 4 servings.
Nancy B. Hall
Calvert City, Kentucky

Start the Year Light

Do you have to loosen your belt after overindulging during the holiday season? To help, we offer recipes that will make you feel as though you are being naughty when you're not. Remember that taking the time to plan meals will help you stick to your New Year's goal to eat more healthfully. A weekly shopping trip will allow you to keep fresh ingredients on hand.

CHICKEN WITH MUSHROOM SAUCE

Prep: 10 minutes
Cook: 25 minutes

6 skinned and boned chicken breast halves
3 tablespoons all-purpose flour, divided
Vegetable cooking spray
1 (8-ounce) package fresh mushrooms, sliced
3 tablespoons chopped purple onion
1 garlic clove, minced
1 cup low-sodium, fat-free chicken broth
½ cup dry white wine
2 tablespoons light soft cream cheese
1 teaspoon dried basil
½ teaspoon dried thyme
¼ teaspoon salt
¼ teaspoon pepper
3 cups hot cooked rice

• **Place** chicken between 2 sheets of heavy-duty plastic wrap, and flatten to ¼-inch thickness using a meat mallet or rolling pin.

• **Dredge** flattened chicken in 2 tablespoons flour.
• **Brown** chicken, in batches, in a large nonstick skillet coated with cooking spray over medium heat. Remove chicken from skillet.
• **Add** mushrooms, onion, and garlic to skillet, and sauté over medium heat 1 minute.
• **Whisk** in remaining 1 tablespoon flour, and cook, whisking constantly, 1 minute.
• **Stir** in broth and next 6 ingredients; bring to a boil. Cover, reduce heat, and simmer 10 minutes. Add chicken; cover and cook 5 minutes. Uncover and simmer 5 minutes.
• **Spoon** chicken and sauce over hot cooked rice. **Yield:** 6 servings.

♥ Per serving: Calories 289
Fat 3.2g   Cholesterol 70mg
Sodium 505mg

RED BEANS AND COUSCOUS
(pictured on page 39)

You can have this hot and on the table with the opening of a few cans and minimal cooking time.

Prep: 10 minutes
Cook: 15 minutes

1 (14½-ounce) can low-sodium, fat-free chicken broth
1 (14½-ounce) can diced tomatoes, undrained
1 teaspoon salt
½ teaspoon dried crushed red pepper
½ teaspoon dried basil
½ teaspoon dried oregano
10 ounces quick-cooking couscous
1 (15.5-ounce) can red kidney beans, rinsed and drained
2 tablespoons olive oil
4 green onions, diced
½ cup diced green bell pepper
¼ cup chopped fresh parsley
1 celery rib, diced
2 garlic cloves, pressed

• **Bring** first 6 ingredients to a boil in a large saucepan over medium-high heat; remove from heat.
• **Stir** in couscous; let stand 10 minutes. Fluff mixture with a fork.
• **Stir** in kidney beans and remaining ingredients. Serve hot or slightly chilled. **Yield:** 8 servings.

Roxanne E. Chan
Albany, California

♥ Per serving: Calories 215
Fat 3.8g   Cholesterol 0mg
Sodium 391mg

MOCHA MARBLE POUND CAKE

Prep: 20 minutes
Bake: 1 hour

¼ cup margarine, softened
1 cup sugar
1 teaspoon vanilla extract
½ cup egg substitute
1 (8-ounce) container coffee
    low-fat yogurt, divided
2 cups all-purpose flour
2 teaspoons baking powder
1 teaspoon baking soda
½ teaspoon salt
⅓ cup cocoa, divided
Vegetable cooking spray
½ cup sifted powdered
    sugar
½ to 1 teaspoon fat-free
    milk

• **Beat** margarine at medium speed with an electric mixer until creamy; gradually add sugar, beating 5 to 7 minutes. Add vanilla and egg substitute, beating just until blended.
• **Reserve** 1½ tablespoons yogurt in a small bowl.
• **Combine** flour and next 3 ingredients. Add flour mixture to margarine mixture alternately with remaining yogurt, beginning and ending with flour mixture. Beat at low speed just until blended after each addition.
• **Divide** batter in half; stir ¼ cup cocoa into 1 portion. Alternately spoon batters into a 9- x 5-inch loafpan coated with cooking spray; swirl gently with a knife to create a marbled effect.
• **Bake** at 325° for 55 to 60 minutes or until a wooden pick inserted in center of cake comes out clean.
• **Cool** cake in pan on a wire rack 10 minutes; remove from pan, and cool on wire rack.
• **Whisk** remaining cocoa and powdered sugar into reserved yogurt; add milk, as needed, for desired consistency. Pour mixture over cooled cake. **Yield:** 12 servings.

Judy Warren
Charlotte, North Carolina

❤ Per serving: Calories 226
Fat 4.7g Cholesterol 2mg
Sodium 361mg

PACKETS OF FLAVOR

Just as the Academy Award envelopes reveal triumphs, seasoning packets deliver winning flavors. For years we have used the familiar packages for dressings and soups, but these recipes open the envelopes to new taste sensations.

For Crawfish Delicacy, you'll find crawfish frozen in 1-pound packages at most supermarkets. Thaw them in your refrigerator overnight, or run cold water over the unopened package. Do not drain; the juice is very flavorful.

SWISS STEAK MONTEREY

Prep: 8 minutes
Cook: 25 minutes

⅓ cup all-purpose flour
½ teaspoon garlic salt
¼ teaspoon pepper
2 pounds cubed round or sirloin
    steak
3 tablespoons vegetable oil
2 (8-ounce) cans tomato sauce
1 (1.3-ounce) envelope dry onion
    soup mix
1 (8-ounce) container sour
    cream

• **Combine** first 3 ingredients. Dredge cubed steak in flour mixture.
• **Brown** steak, in batches, in hot oil in a Dutch oven. Return all steak to pan.
• **Stir** in tomato sauce and soup mix; bring to a boil. Cover, reduce heat, and simmer 15 minutes. Remove steak, reserving liquid in pan; keep warm.
• **Stir** sour cream into tomato mixture; simmer, stirring constantly, until heated. (Do not boil.) Serve over steak. **Yield:** 6 to 8 servings.

Bebe May
Pensacola, Florida

CRAWFISH DELICACY

Prep: 15 minutes
Cook: 44 minutes

½ cup vegetable oil
1 small onion, chopped
½ small green bell pepper,
    chopped
1 celery rib, chopped
2 pounds frozen cooked, peeled
    crawfish tails, thawed
3 tablespoons all-purpose flour
1 (1.5-ounce) envelope beef stew
    seasoning mix
4 green onions, chopped
¼ cup chopped fresh parsley
3 cups hot water
½ teaspoon salt
¼ teaspoon ground red pepper
¼ teaspoon ground black pepper
Dash of garlic powder
Hot cooked rice
Garnish: fresh parsley sprigs

• **Microwave** first 4 ingredients in a 13- x 9-inch microwave-safe dish at HIGH 6 to 8 minutes or until tender. Stir in crawfish; microwave at HIGH 6 minutes. Stir in flour and next 8 ingredients.
• **Microwave,** uncovered, at HIGH 15 minutes, stirring twice. Cover; microwave at MEDIUM (50% power) 15 minutes, stirring twice. Serve over hot cooked rice; garnish, if desired. **Yield:** 8 servings.

Chicken Delicacy: Substitute 4 cups chopped cooked chicken for frozen crawfish tails.

Note: To prepare on cooktop, sauté onion, bell pepper, and celery in hot oil in a large saucepan. Stir in crawfish and next 9 ingredients; bring to a boil. Reduce heat; simmer, stirring occasionally, 30 minutes.

Deborah Donahoe
Metairie, Louisiana

CHEESE SPREAD

Prep: 5 minutes
Chill: 2 hours

1   (8-ounce) package cream
      cheese, softened
½   cup sour cream
1   (0.7-ounce) envelope Italian-
      style dressing mix
1   cup (4 ounces) shredded
      Cheddar cheese

• **Beat** cream cheese at medium speed with an electric mixer until fluffy; add sour cream and dressing mix, beating until blended. Reserve 1 tablespoon Cheddar cheese; stir remaining Cheddar cheese into cream cheese mixture.
• **Spoon** into a bowl; cover and chill 2 hours. Sprinkle with reserved Cheddar; serve with crackers. **Yield:** 1½ cups.

Maia L. Artman
Norman, Oklahoma

GLAZED GEMS

Glazing is a simple way to add a touch of glamour to some vegetables and fruits. Read the box at right for tips; then try these examples of glazing at its best.

BROWN SUGAR-GLAZED CARROTS

These wonderfully flavorful carrots received our highest rating.

Prep: 5 minutes
Cook: 35 minutes

1   pound medium carrots
¾   teaspoon salt, divided
2   tablespoons butter or margarine
½   cup minced onion
1½ tablespoons dark brown sugar
⅔   cup apple juice
¼   teaspoon pepper

• **Cut** carrots diagonally into ¼-inch-thick slices. Cook in boiling water to cover with ½ teaspoon salt 5 minutes or until crisp-tender. Drain and rinse with cold water. Pat dry with paper towels.
• **Melt** butter in a large skillet over low heat; add onion, and cook, stirring constantly, 10 minutes.
• **Add** brown sugar; cook, stirring constantly, 5 minutes. Add apple juice; cook, stirring occasionally, 10 minutes.
• **Stir** in carrot, remaining ¼ teaspoon salt, and pepper. **Yield:** 6 servings.

Renie Steves
Fort Worth, Texas

ORANGE-GLAZED BEETS

Glazing adds an extra dimension to the rich color of beets.

Prep: 10 minutes
Cook: 30 to 40 minutes

5   small beets with tops (1½
      pounds) *
⅓   cup sugar
1½ tablespoons cornstarch
1   teaspoon grated orange rind
¼   cup fresh orange juice
1   tablespoon red wine vinegar
1   teaspoon salt

• **Cut** tops from beets, leaving a 1-inch stem. Cook beets in boiling water to cover in a medium saucepan 35 minutes or until tender; drain, reserving ½ cup liquid. Peel beets, and cut into ¼-inch-thick slices.
• **Stir** together reserved liquid, sugar, and next 5 ingredients in saucepan. Bring to a boil, stirring occasionally. Boil, stirring constantly, 1 minute. Add beets. **Yield:** 4 servings.

* Substitute 1 (16-ounce) can sliced beets for fresh, if desired. Drain canned beets, reserving ½ cup liquid. Omit cooking in boiling water.

Dorsella Utter
Louisville, Kentucky

GLAZED ONIONS

This recipe employs a simplified method of glazing—baking in the oven. Butter, brown sugar, and lemon juice give these onions a subtle sheen.

Prep: 10 minutes
Bake: 15 minutes

1   (16-ounce) package boiling
      onions, peeled
2   tablespoons butter or margarine,
      melted
2   tablespoons light brown
      sugar
2   tablespoons lemon juice
1   tablespoon chopped fresh
      parsley
½   teaspoon salt

• **Place** onions in an 8-inch square pan.
• **Stir** together butter and next 4 ingredients; pour over onions.
• **Bake** at 425° for 15 minutes. **Yield:** 4 to 6 servings.

SHINE ON

Bring out the best flavors of vegetables and fruits by glazing them. It's easy—just follow these simple instructions.

Simmer carrots, winter squash, apples, or other produce until just tender, and remove from the cooking liquid. Add sugar or brown sugar to the liquid, and boil until the mixture is syrupy. Return the vegetables or fruits to the syrup, stirring until they are glazed and warm. Or try oven glazing, as we do with Glazed Onions.

For an instant glaze, melt a small amount of jelly or preserves, and pour over cooked, drained vegetables. Try orange marmalade over carrots or winter squash, or apple jelly over onions.

1998 Top-Rated Recipes

Thirty-eight recipes received our top rating last year. Here's a sampling.

Want to taste the rest of 1998's best? For a copy of all 38 top-rated recipes, just send a self-addressed, stamped, business-size envelope to Year's Best Recipes Editor, *Southern Living,* P.O. Box 523, Birmingham, AL 35201. You can also find all of the recipes in *Southern Living® 1998 Annual Recipes* (pages 11 and 12).

SAUSAGE-FILLED CRÊPES

1 pound ground pork sausage
1 small onion, diced
2 cups (8 ounces) shredded
   Cheddar cheese, divided
1 (3-ounce) package cream cheese
½ teaspoon dried marjoram
Crêpes
½ cup sour cream
¼ cup butter or margarine,
   softened
¼ cup chopped fresh parsley
Sliced tomato

• **Cook** sausage and onion in a large skillet over medium heat, stirring until sausage crumbles and is no longer pink; drain well. Return sausage to skillet.
• **Add** 1 cup Cheddar cheese, cream cheese, and marjoram, stirring mixture until cheeses melt. Spoon 3 tablespoons filling down center of each Crêpe.
• **Roll** up; place, seam side down, in a lightly greased 13- x 9-inch baking dish.
• **Bake,** covered, at 350° for 15 minutes. Stir together sour cream and butter; spoon over Crêpes. Bake 5 more minutes. Sprinkle with remaining 1 cup Cheddar cheese and parsley. Serve with sliced tomato. **Yield:** 6 to 8 servings.

Note: Assemble Sausage-Filled Crêpes ahead and freeze, if desired. When ready to serve crêpes, let stand at room temperature 30 minutes. Bake, covered, at 350° for 40 minutes. Proceed with sour cream, butter, cheese, and parsley as directed.

Crêpes

3 large eggs
1 cup milk
1 tablespoon vegetable oil
1 cup all-purpose flour
½ teaspoon salt
Melted butter

• **Beat** first 3 ingredients at medium speed with an electric mixer until blended. Gradually add flour and salt, beating until smooth. Cover; chill 1 hour.
• **Coat** bottom of a 7-inch nonstick skillet with melted butter; place skillet over medium heat until hot.
• **Pour** 3 tablespoons batter into skillet; quickly tilt in all directions so batter covers bottom of skillet.
• **Cook** 1 minute or until crêpe can be shaken loose from skillet. Turn crêpe over, and cook about 30 seconds. Place on a cloth towel to cool. Repeat procedure with remaining batter. Stack crêpes between sheets of wax paper. **Yield:** 12 crêpes.

Beth Ann Stein
Apple Valley, Minnesota

CARROT SOUFFLÉ

1½ pounds carrots, sliced
½ cup butter or margarine
3 large eggs
¼ cup all-purpose flour
1½ teaspoons baking powder
1½ cups sugar
¼ teaspoon ground cinnamon

• **Cook** carrot in boiling water to cover 20 to 25 minutes or until tender; drain.
• **Process** carrot, butter, and remaining ingredients in a food processor until smooth, stopping to scrape down sides. Spoon into a lightly greased 1½-quart soufflé dish.
• **Bake** at 350° for 1 hour and 10 minutes or until set. **Yield:** 6 servings.

Kathy Johns
Sulphur, Louisiana

CORN FLAN

The secret to this delectable flan is straining the mixture before baking.

4 cups fresh corn kernels (8 ears)
1½ cups half-and-half
6 large eggs
1 teaspoon salt
½ teaspoon freshly ground
   pepper
2 (1.2-ounce) envelopes
   demi-glace sauce mix
1 cup chopped fresh Italian
   parsley
⅓ cup olive oil

• **Process** corn kernels in a blender until smooth, stopping to scrape down sides.
• **Add** half-and-half and next 3 ingredients; process until smooth.
• **Pour** corn mixture through a wire-mesh strainer into a bowl, discarding solids.
• **Pour** corn mixture into 8 (6-ounce) buttered custard cups or ramekins. Place custard cups in a 13- x 9-inch baking dish. Add hot water to dish to a depth of 1 inch.
• **Bake** at 350° for 25 minutes or until set. Remove custards from water, and cool 5 minutes on a wire rack. Invert onto serving plates.
• **Prepare** demi-glace sauce according to package directions.
• **Process** parsley and olive oil in blender until smooth. Serve demi-glace sauce and parsley oil with flan. **Yield:** 8 servings.

Note: For testing purposes only, we used Knorr brand demi-glace sauce mix.

Executive Chef Rick Small
Keswick Hall, Virginia

APPLESAUCE PIE

You can create this filling of luscious homemade applesauce with just five basic ingredients: apples, lemon, sugar, butter, and vanilla.

10 large Granny Smith apples, peeled and chopped
1 large lemon, sliced and seeded
2½ cups sugar
3 tablespoons butter or margarine
1 teaspoon vanilla extract
1 (15-ounce) package refrigerated piecrusts
Spiced Ice Cream (optional)

• **Cook** first 3 ingredients in a Dutch oven over medium heat, stirring often, 35 minutes or until thickened. Remove from heat. Discard lemon slices. Stir in butter and vanilla. Cool.
• **Fit** 1 piecrust into a 9-inch pieplate according to package directions. Pour in applesauce filling.
• **Roll** remaining piecrust to press out fold lines; cut into ½-inch strips. Reserve 4 strips. Arrange remaining strips in a lattice design over applesauce filling; fold edges under, and crimp.
• **Cut** reserved pastry strips in half lengthwise. Lay halves side by side, and twist; arrange around inner edge of pie to form a border.
• **Bake** on lowest oven rack at 425° for 30 to 35 minutes or until golden, shielding with aluminum foil to prevent excessive browning, if necessary. Serve with Spiced Ice Cream, if desired. **Yield:** 1 (9-inch) pie.

Spiced Ice Cream

2 pints vanilla ice cream, softened
1 teaspoon ground cinnamon
½ teaspoon ground nutmeg

• **Stir** together all ingredients; cover and freeze. **Yield:** 2 pints.

BRIGHT WINTER SALADS

Serving salad is an easy way to complete your meals. You can make most of these recipes in 10 minutes or less; others you can prepare quickly and chill before serving them. Cover them tightly so that they won't dry out or pick up flavors from other items in the refrigerator.

CITRUS-AND-AVOCADO SALAD

Prep: 15 minutes

2 avocados, peeled and sliced
¼ cup lemon juice
2 large pink grapefruit, sectioned *
3 oranges, peeled and sliced
Leaf lettuce
Dressing
Garnish: chopped dates

• **Toss** together avocado slices and lemon juice.
• **Arrange** avocado, grapefruit sections, and orange slices on lettuce leaves. Serve with Dressing; garnish, if desired. **Yield:** 6 servings.

* Substitute 1 (26-ounce) jar grapefruit sections, drained, for fresh grapefruit, if desired.

Dressing

Prep: 15 minutes

1 (8-ounce) container sour cream
8 pitted dates
½ teaspoon grated orange rind
1½ tablespoons fresh orange juice
¼ teaspoon salt

• **Process** all ingredients in a blender until smooth, stopping to scrape down sides. **Yield:** 1 cup.

Gayle Millican
Rowlett, Texas

CARROT-BROCCOLI SALAD

Prep: 10 minutes
Chill: 1 hour

½ cup mayonnaise
2 tablespoons red wine vinegar
⅛ teaspoon salt
¼ teaspoon pepper
1½ cups small broccoli flowerets
1 cup shredded carrot
1 medium-size red apple, cut into chunks
½ cup walnuts, toasted and chopped
¼ cup raisins
Leaf lettuce (optional)

• **Stir** together first 4 ingredients in a large bowl; add broccoli and next 4 ingredients, tossing well. Cover and chill 1 hour. Serve on lettuce leaves, if desired. **Yield:** 4 servings.

Nora Henshaw
Okemah, Oklahoma

PINEAPPLE SLAW

Prep: 10 minutes
Chill: 8 hours

1 (15-ounce) can pineapple chunks, undrained
3 tablespoons olive oil
2 tablespoons white balsamic vinegar
½ teaspoon grated orange rind
½ teaspoon celery seeds
¼ teaspoon salt
¼ teaspoon dry mustard
1 (10-ounce) package shredded cabbage
2 large oranges, peeled and sectioned *
1 large apple, cut into small chunks

• **Drain** pineapple, reserving ⅓ cup juice.
• **Whisk** together reserved ⅓ cup pineapple juice, oil, and next 5 ingredients in a large bowl until well blended.

• **Add** pineapple, cabbage, orange, and apple; toss gently. Cover and chill 8 hours. **Yield:** 6 servings.

* Substitute 1 (11-ounce) can mandarin oranges, drained, for 2 large oranges, if desired.

LaJuan Coward
Jasper, Texas

GREEN SALAD WITH LEMON-DILL VINAIGRETTE

Prep: 10 minutes

1 (14.8-ounce) jar hearts of palm, drained
1 purple onion
1 roasted red bell pepper, drained
6 cups mixed baby lettuces
Lemon-Dill Vinaigrette
Shaved Parmesan cheese

• **Cut** hearts of palm into ½-inch slices. Cut onion in half lengthwise; slice and separate into strips. Cut bell pepper into thin strips.
• **Combine** baby lettuce, hearts of palm, onion, and pepper in a large salad bowl; toss with Lemon-Dill Vinaigrette. Top with Parmesan cheese, and serve immediately. **Yield:** 6 servings.

Lemon-Dill Vinaigrette

Prep: 5 minutes

¼ cup lemon juice
1 teaspoon dried dillweed
1 teaspoon garlic salt
½ cup olive oil

• **Whisk** together all ingredients in a bowl. **Yield:** ⅔ cup.

GLORY OF CUSTARDS

Eggs, milk, and sugar form the foundation for all custards, and the amount of cornstarch determines the thickness. These stirred desserts require a saucepan, a whisk, low heat, and a steady stirring hand.

VANILLA CUSTARD

Prep: 10 minutes
Cook: 22 minutes
Chill: 2 hours

½ cup sugar
3 tablespoons cornstarch
½ teaspoon salt
4 egg yolks
3 cups milk
2 tablespoons butter or margarine
2 teaspoons vanilla extract

• **Bring** first 5 ingredients to a boil in a heavy saucepan over medium heat (about 20 minutes), whisking constantly; boil, whisking constantly, 1 minute or until thickened. Remove mixture from heat.
• **Stir** in butter and vanilla. Place heavy-duty plastic wrap directly on surface of custard (to keep "skin" from forming); chill 2 hours. **Yield:** 4 cups.

Nancy Woodall
Bellaire, Texas

Vanilla Custard Sauce: *(pictured on page 113)* Decrease cornstarch to 1 tablespoon; prepare as directed. Serve with strawberries or cake. **Yield:** 4 cups.

Chocolate Custard Tart: *(pictured on page 113)* Stir 2 (4-ounce) bittersweet chocolate bars, chopped, into sugar mixture; prepare custard as directed. Fit 1 refrigerated piecrust into a 9- x 2-inch

tart pan according to package directions; trim off excess pastry along edges, and prick bottom and sides of piecrust with a fork. Bake at 425° for 12 minutes or until browned. Cool on a wire rack. Pour custard into tart shell. Place heavy-duty plastic wrap directly on surface of custard; chill 2 hours. Top with sweetened whipped cream and, if desired, chocolate curls. **Yield:** 1 (9-inch) tart.

Spanish Cream: Omit milk and butter. Sprinkle 1 envelope unflavored gelatin over ¼ cup cold water; set aside. Cook sugar, cornstarch, salt, egg yolks, and 2¾ cups whipping cream in a saucepan over medium-low heat, whisking constantly, until mixture is thickened and coats a spoon. Stir in gelatin mixture until dissolved. Remove from heat, and stir in vanilla. Pour into 8 lightly greased ½-cup molds. Cover and chill 2 hours or until set. Unmold and serve with fresh fruit. **Yield:** 8 servings.

Kahlúa Beverage Sipper: *(pictured on page 113)* Omit cornstarch, salt, and butter; decrease milk to 2 cups and vanilla to 1 teaspoon. Increase yolks to 5. Whisk together sugar, milk, 2 cups half-and-half, and egg yolks; prepare according to directions. Stir in ½ cup coffee liqueur and vanilla. Serve warm or cold. Garnish with cinnamon sticks. **Yield:** 5 cups.

THE LAST COURSE

When you crave a sweet ending, reach for winter-fresh apples and pears or a convenient can of crushed pineapple. Select McIntosh or Rome apples for tarts and Anjou pears for cooking in gently bubbling liquid. Preparation of these desserts is speedy, but allow time for chilling and baking.

POACHED PEARS WITH WHITE CARAMEL SAUCE

To core whole fruit, insert an apple corer into the bottom, cutting to but not through the stem end, and twist.

8 cups water
¾ cup sugar
6 small firm pears, peeled and
    cored
White Caramel Sauce
Garnishes: chocolate sauce, fresh
    mint sprigs

• **Bring** 8 cups water and sugar to a boil in a Dutch oven. Add cored pears; cover, reduce heat, and simmer 12 to 15 minutes or until tender. Remove from heat; uncover and cool.
• **Cover** pears; chill 8 hours, if desired.
• **Drain** pears, and cut into thin slices, keeping stems intact. Serve with White Caramel Sauce; garnish, if desired. **Yield:** 6 servings.

White Caramel Sauce

¾ cup sugar
⅓ cup water
1⅓ cups whipping cream
2 tablespoons vanilla extract
¾ cup butter or margarine

• **Cook** sugar and ⅓ cup water in a heavy saucepan over medium heat, stirring often, about 15 minutes or until reduced to 6 tablespoons.
• **Add** cream and vanilla. (Mixture will be lumpy.) Cook over medium heat, stirring often, 15 minutes or until reduced to 1 cup. Remove from heat.
• **Stir** in butter. Cover sauce, and chill up to 3 days, if desired. Serve warm. **Yield:** 1½ cups.

PINEAPPLE RIGHT-SIDE-UP SNACK CAKE

1 (8-ounce) can crushed
    pineapple, undrained
2½ cups all-purpose flour
1 tablespoon baking powder
¼ teaspoon salt
¾ cup sugar
⅓ cup milk
⅓ cup butter or margarine, melted
2 large eggs, lightly beaten
½ teaspoon vanilla extract
⅓ cup firmly packed brown sugar

• **Drain** pineapple, reserving ⅓ cup juice; set both aside.
• **Combine** flour and next 3 ingredients; make a well in center. Combine reserved juice, milk, and next 3 ingredients; add to dry ingredients, stirring just until dry ingredients are moistened. Spoon into a greased 9- x 9-inch square pan. Top with pineapple and brown sugar.
• **Bake** at 350° for 25 to 30 minutes or until a wooden pick inserted in center comes out clean. Cool in pan on a wire rack 10 minutes. **Yield:** 15 servings.

BRANDIED APPLE TARTS

1 (10-ounce) package frozen puff
    pastry shells
1 cup sugar
6 cooking apples, thinly sliced
¼ teaspoon ground cinnamon
½ cup brandy
Vanilla ice cream

• **Bake** shells according to package directions. Remove tops and soft pastry underneath, discarding tops. Set aside.
• **Cook** sugar in a large skillet over medium heat, stirring constantly, until golden. Stir in apple and cinnamon; cook, stirring often, until tender. Remove apple with a slotted spoon.
• **Stir** brandy into sugar mixture; cook, stirring often, 10 to 15 minutes or until thickened. Fill shells with apple; top with ice cream. Drizzle with brandy mixture. Serve immediately. **Yield:** 6 servings.

GIFTED SHORTBREAD

Most of us love shortbread's indulgently buttery flair. What most don't realize is how colorful and flavorful it can be. Use the real thing—butter—for the best taste.

BUTTER-MINT SHORTBREAD

Prep: 10 minutes
Bake: 25 minutes

1 cup butter, softened
¾ cup powdered sugar
½ teaspoon mint extract
½ teaspoon vanilla extract
2 cups all-purpose flour
Powdered sugar

• **Beat** butter and ¾ cup sugar at medium speed with an electric mixer until light

and fluffy. Add flavorings, beating until blended. Gradually add flour, beating at low speed until blended. Press into an ungreased 15- x 10-inch jellyroll pan.
• **Bake** at 325° for 25 minutes or until golden. Cool in pan on a wire rack 10 minutes. Cut into squares; sprinkle with powdered sugar. Remove from pan; cool on wire rack. **Yield:** 3 dozen.

Edwina Gadsby
Great Falls, Montana

MARBLE-TOPPED HAZELNUT SHORTBREAD

Prep: 15 minutes
Bake: 30 minutes
Cool: 40 minutes

½ cup chopped hazelnuts or macadamia nuts
2 cups sifted cake flour
¾ cup powdered sugar
¼ teaspoon salt
1 cup butter, softened
4 (1-ounce) semisweet chocolate squares
1 (2-ounce) vanilla candy coating square

• **Bake** hazelnuts in a shallow pan at 350°, stirring occasionally, 5 to 10 minutes or until toasted; set aside. Reduce oven temperature to 325°.
• **Combine** flour, sugar, and salt; add butter, and beat at low speed with an electric mixer until blended. Press into an aluminum foil-lined 10-inch round cakepan. Bake at 325° for 25 to 30 minutes or until lightly browned.
• **Microwave** semisweet chocolate squares in a small microwave-safe bowl at HIGH, stirring twice, 1 minute or until melted. Spread over shortbread.
• **Place** vanilla candy coating in a small heavy-duty zip-top plastic bag; seal. Submerge in hot water until melted.
• **Snip** a tiny hole in 1 corner of bag, and drizzle lines ¾ inch apart over chocolate. Swirl melted coating and chocolate with a wooden pick. Sprinkle with nuts.
• **Cool** in pan on a wire rack 40 minutes. Cut into wedges. **Yield:** 16 servings.

Lucy Marie Duncan
Willis, Virginia

RASPBERRY SHORTBREAD

These cookies received our highest Test Kitchens rating.

Prep: 15 minutes
Bake: 20 minutes

1 cup butter, softened
⅔ cup sugar
2½ cups all-purpose flour
1 (10-ounce) jar seedless raspberry jam, divided *
1½ cups powdered sugar
3½ tablespoons water
½ teaspoon almond extract

• **Beat** butter and ⅔ cup sugar at medium speed with an electric mixer until light and fluffy. Gradually add flour, beating at low speed until blended.
• **Divide** dough into 6 equal portions; roll each portion into a 12- x 1-inch strip. Place strips on lightly greased baking sheets.
• **Make** a ½-inch-wide by ¼-inch-deep indentation down center of strips using the handle of a wooden spoon. Spoon half of jam evenly into indentations.
• **Bake** at 350° for 15 minutes. Remove from oven; spoon remaining jam into indentations. Bake 5 more minutes or until lightly browned.
• **Whisk** together powdered sugar, water, and almond extract; drizzle over warm shortbread. Cut each strip diagonally into 1-inch slices. Cool in pans on wire racks. **Yield:** 6 dozen.

* Substitute any flavor jam or 1 (11¼-ounce) jar lemon curd for raspberry jam, if desired.

Apricot-Almond Shortbread: Gently coat unbaked shortbread strips with ¾ cup finely chopped almonds, pressing in gently. Make and fill indentations, substituting apricot jam for raspberry jam. Bake as directed.

Lynne Chatellier
Summerville, South Carolina

COZY BEVERAGES

Surprise your guests with these spirited concoctions. From the comforting warmth of a Cappuccino Sipper to the fruitiness of Champagne Punch, these beverages allow you to celebrate all year long.

CAPPUCCINO SIPPER

Prep: 5 minutes
Cook: 5 minutes

½ cup sugar
3 cups brewed coffee
3 cups half-and-half
¼ to ½ cup rum
¼ to ½ cup brandy
Sweetened whipped cream
Ground cinnamon (optional)

• **Bring** first 5 ingredients to a boil in a large saucepan over medium heat, stirring constantly. Remove from heat.
• **Top** each serving with sweetened whipped cream and, if desired, cinnamon. **Yield:** 7 cups.

Paula McCollum
Springtown, Texas

APRICOT COOLERS

Prep: 3 minutes

2 cups apricot nectar, chilled
2 cups unsweetened pineapple juice, chilled
⅓ cup lemon juice
1 (12-ounce) can ginger ale, chilled

• **Stir** together all ingredients. Serve immediately over ice. **Yield:** 6 cups.

Teresa Hubbard
Russellville, Alabama

ORANGE BRANDY SMASH

Lace your glass with long strips of orange rind before adding this frozen beverage.

Prep: 3 minutes
Freeze: 8 hours

9 cups water
2 cups brandy
1 (12-ounce) can frozen lemonade
    concentrate
1 (12-ounce) can frozen orange
    juice concentrate
Garnish: orange rind strips

● **Stir** together first 4 ingredients in a 1-gallon container until concentrates thaw. Cover and freeze 8 hours, stirring occasionally. Spiral rind strips into glasses, if desired. Spoon frozen mixture into glasses. Serve immediately. **Yield:** 3½ quarts.

Fran Pointer
Kansas City, Missouri

CHAMPAGNE PUNCH

Prep: 5 minutes

3 cups red fruit punch, chilled
3 cups unsweetened pineapple
    juice, chilled
3 cups white grape juice, chilled
1 (750-milliliter) bottle pink
    champagne, chilled *

● **Stir** together all ingredients. Serve immediately. **Yield:** 12 cups.

* Substitute 2 (12-ounce) cans ginger ale, chilled, for pink champagne, if desired.

Note: For testing purposes only, we used Hawaiian Punch brand red fruit punch.

Judi Grigoraci
Charleston, West Virginia

FROM OUR KITCHEN TO YOURS

No-recipe suppers are easy on the cook. You can turn an ordinary hot dog into a Mexican dog with hot salsa, shredded cheese, and sour cream.

Or you can bake or microwave a large sweet potato. Top the hot potato with butter and a little cinnamon. Toss a bag of mixed salad greens with your favorite dressing. Supper will be filling, nourishing, and even taste a little like dessert.

TIMELY ADDITIONS

To help you plan your time in the kitchen, we've added two extra ingredients to most of our recipes—preparation time and cooking time. Prep time refers to chopping, slicing, mixing, stirring, blending, and marinating—however long it takes to prepare the ingredients for cooking. Our Test Kitchens staff may chop, slice, and dice a bit faster, so your prep time may vary by a minute or two. Cook time refers to the time the recipe actually bakes, simmers, broils, or grills. Add the cook time and the prep time to determine how long it takes to get a recipe from our pages to your table.

JANUARY MENUS

Try some of these appetizing combinations from this month's pages for family dinners and entertaining.

■ Serve Grits With Grilled Chicken and Onions (page 17) with Citrus-and-Avocado Salad (page 26). Add your favorite crusty rolls.

■ Crawfish Delicacy (page 23) needs just a tossed salad to complete the meal.

■ For breakfast, brunch, or dinner, Margaret's Creamy Grits (page 18) beg for Country Ham (page 19) and your favorite hot buttermilk biscuits.

IN YOUR WINEGLASS

From time to time we'll make wine suggestions, but you have the final choice. Whenever you can, try two or three different brands of the same variety to enjoy the subtle—or sometimes dramatic—differences. Remember that a wine is good only if you like it.

■ Try a slightly tart Sauvignon Blanc with Grits With Grilled Chicken and Onions (page 17).

■ A crisp, spicy Gewürztraminer will complement the flavors of Crawfish Delicacy (page 23).

TIDBITS

■ Sprinkle beef and chicken strips lightly with 1 or 2 tablespoons cornstarch before you stir-fry them. It helps the meat to brown beautifully and quickly. The velvety texture of the completed recipe is a bonus.

■ Microwave ovens can hold and sometimes transfer stale cooking odors. If your microwave has bad breath, place a few sheets of newspaper inside the *cold* oven. Close the door, and leave it there overnight. You'll wake to a fresh-smelling appliance. Discard the paper, and you're in business again. We don't know how or why it works; we're just glad it does.

FEBRUARY

Come along as we visit novelist and cast-iron enthusiast Jack Butler in "Jack's Skillet," and discover why a recipe's most important ingredient might be the skillet itself. After a taste of Jack's Catfish, Hush Puppies, and Fruit Cobbler, you'll become a cast-iron devotee as well. "From Our Kitchen to Yours" follows up with tips on seasoning cast iron.

Novice and experienced cooks alike will find a gravy to crave in "Good Gravy." Never made a gravy? We'll show you how. Make the best in town? Taste and compare. These recipes offer you a choice, from Country Ham With Red-Eye Gravy to Tomato Gravy to Chocolate Gravy. Making them is easy; choosing your favorite may take a little more time.

JACK'S SKILLET

*Cooking isn't just a hobby for Jack Butler—
it's an ironclad passion. This novelist and Mississippi
native uses cast-iron pieces during his daily ritual of
cooking dinner. Here the seasoned cook shares some
of his tastiest treasures from the skillet.*

OLD-FASHIONED FISH FRY
Serves Four

Jack's Catfish
Coleslaw
Hush Puppies or Buttermilk Biscuits
Fruit Cobbler

JACK'S CATFISH

Prep: 5 minutes
Cook: 12 minutes

2 **pounds catfish fillets**
½ **teaspoon salt**
½ **teaspoon pepper**
¾ **cup all-purpose flour**
½ **cup vegetable oil**

● **Sprinkle** fish with salt and pepper.
● **Place** flour in a heavy-duty zip-top plastic bag; add 2 or 3 fillets at a time. Seal and shake to coat. Remove fish, shaking to remove excess flour. Set aside ½ cup remaining flour mixture for Hush Puppies, if desired.
● **Pour** oil into a 10-inch cast-iron skillet; heat to 375°. Fry fish in batches 3 minutes on each side or until fish flakes with a fork. Drain on paper towels. **Yield:** 4 servings.

Jack Butler
Alligator, Mississippi

HUSH PUPPIES

Prep: 10 minutes
Cook: 12 minutes

½ **cup reserved flour from Jack's Catfish or ½ cup all-purpose flour**
½ **cup yellow cornmeal**
½ **teaspoon salt**
¼ **teaspoon baking soda**
½ **teaspoon freshly ground pepper**
1 **large egg**
½ **cup buttermilk**
¼ **cup minced onion**
2 **cups vegetable oil**

● **Combine** first 5 ingredients in a bowl; make a well in center of mixture.
● **Stir** together egg and buttermilk; add to dry ingredients, stirring just until dry ingredients are moistened. Stir in onion.
● **Pour** oil into a 10-inch cast-iron skillet, and heat to 375°.
● **Drop** batter by tablespoonfuls into oil, and fry in batches 3 minutes on each side or until golden. Drain hush puppies on paper towels, and serve immediately. **Yield:** 4 servings.

Jack Butler
Alligator, Mississippi

BUTTERMILK BISCUITS

Prep: 10 minutes
Bake: 20 minutes

2 **cups all-purpose flour**
4 **teaspoons baking powder**
¼ **teaspoon baking soda**
Pinch of salt
¼ **cup butter or margarine**
¾ **to 1 cup buttermilk**
2 **tablespoons butter or margarine**
2 **tablespoons butter or margarine, melted**

● **Stir** together first 4 ingredients in a large bowl.
● **Cut** ¼ cup butter into flour mixture with a pastry blender until crumbly; add buttermilk, stirring just until dry ingredients are moistened.
● **Turn** dough out onto a lightly floured surface, and pat or roll to ½-inch thickness; cut with a 2½-inch round cutter.
● **Place** 2 tablespoons butter in a 10½-inch cast-iron skillet. Place skillet in 350° oven 5 minutes or until butter melts. Remove skillet from oven, and add biscuits.
● **Bake** at 350° for 20 minutes or until golden. Brush biscuits with 2 tablespoons melted butter. **Yield:** 1 dozen.

Jack Butler
Alligator, Mississippi

FRUIT COBBLER

Prep: 12 minutes
Bake: 58 minutes

1½ recipes Universal Black Iron
        Skillet Piecrust
1 tablespoon butter or margarine
½ cup all-purpose flour
1 cup sugar, divided
4 to 5 cups fresh or frozen
        blueberries, peaches, or
        blackberries
Sugar

• **Roll** piecrust to ¼-inch thickness. Fit into a 10-inch cast-iron skillet. Trim excess pastry along edges, reserving trimmings. Prick bottom and sides of piecrust with a fork.
• **Bake** at 375° for 8 minutes. Remove from oven. Set aside.
• **Cut** butter into flour with a pastry blender until crumbly; add ½ cup sugar.
• **Place** one-third of blueberries in piecrust; sprinkle with about one-third of remaining ½ cup sugar.
• **Sprinkle** with one-third of flour mixture. Top with one-third of pastry trimmings. Repeat layers twice. Sprinkle with additional sugar.
• **Bake** at 375° for 50 minutes or until crust is lightly browned. **Yield:** 8 to 10 servings.

Universal Black Iron Skillet Piecrust

Prep: 15 minutes

2 cups all-purpose flour
Pinch of salt
⅔ cup butter or margarine
½ cup cold water

• **Combine** flour and salt; cut in butter with a pastry blender until mixture is crumbly. Sprinkle water, 1 tablespoon at a time, evenly over surface; stir with a fork just until dry ingredients are moistened. **Yield:** pastry for 1 (10-inch) pie.

Jack Butler
Alligator, Mississippi

> *"We don't talk nonstick in polite company. . . . A well-cured iron skillet is as slippery as anything needs to get."*
>
> *Jack Butler*

He moves comfortably around his kitchen, preparing to fry catfish in a large cast-iron skillet. He mixes flour, salt, and pepper for breading the fish, working with the confidence of someone who cooks regularly and without recipes. And for Jack Butler, cooking is a passion.

He sandwiches time in the kitchen between his career as a writer (*Living in Little Rock with Miss Little Rock, Dreamer, Jujitsu for Christ*) and his job as director of creative writing at the College of Santa Fe.

"My whole family was used to being around good, down-home food," he says, sliding two plump, flour-dusted fillets into the pan. "And as a Baptist preacher's son, I frequently went with my father into the homes of church members, and we had really great food there."

Leaving home brought a new appreciation for those meals. "When I was first married, I tried to re-create the stuff I grew up with so we could eat decently. It took two or three years to learn those things," Jack says with a wry smile. "Before that, I'd assumed knowing how to cook was a birthright." He turns over a fillet, which sizzles fiercely as its crusty golden side appears just above the oil.

Years of improvising in the kitchen led to a food column for the weekly *Arkansas Times.* The column led to a book, *Jack's Skillet: Plain Talk and Some Recipes from a Guy in the Kitchen* (Algonquin Books of Chapel Hill, 1997). In it, Jack displays an unvarnished passion for cast-iron cookery and fresh food as well as a thoughtful, witty style.

"Now my favorite way to unwind after work is to spend an hour in the kitchen," he writes, "an icy martini at hand, things bubbling or sizzling while I wash and peel and chop yet other things or roll out a rich crust leaving . . . floury fingerprints on my cold and beaded glass."

The catfish is done, delicately browned and crisp. Jack places it on paper bags to drain, and he begins to mix up batter for the hush puppies. As the fritters drop into the oil and bob back to the surface, he pulls coleslaw from the refrigerator and places it on the table. He piles a platter high with fish and hush puppies next to it. We sample the products of Jack's skillet and pronounce them to be mighty fine.

Jack smiles modestly and raises a small toast. "You can't do any better in this life," he says, "than to put something delicious in a friend's mouth."

For tips on seasoning cast iron, see "From Our Kitchen to Yours" on page 50.

GOOD GRAVY

No doubt about it—Southerners are crazy for gravy. Sometimes the gravy is even more important than the main course.

From breakfast to dinner, red-eye to chocolate, gravy enriches biscuits, pastas, grits, and even ice cream. If you're a gravy craver, get ready to mop your plate. And don't think that gravy making is an arduous task. You can make most of these recipes without preparing a meat. If you're an old hand at gravy making, ladle up these reader ideas next to yours.

COUNTRY HAM WITH RED-EYE GRAVY

A dose of strong black coffee, this recipe's key ingredient, will keep many people awake, hence the name Red-Eye Gravy.

Prep: 5 minutes
Cook: 15 minutes

3 (¼- to ½-inch-thick) country ham slices
¼ cup butter or margarine
¼ cup firmly packed light brown sugar (optional)
1 cup strong brewed coffee

• **Make** cuts in fat to keep ham slices from curling.
• **Melt** butter over low heat in a heavy skillet; add ham, and cook 5 minutes on each side or until lightly browned. Remove ham from skillet, and keep warm.
• **Stir** brown sugar into hot drippings until dissolved, if desired.
• **Add** coffee, and bring to a boil; reduce heat, and simmer 5 minutes. Serve with ham or with ham and biscuits. **Yield:** 1 cup gravy.

CHICKEN GRAVY

Prep: 2 minutes
Cook: 5 minutes

2 tablespoons butter or margarine
2 tablespoons all-purpose flour
1 (10½-ounce) can chicken broth, undiluted
½ cup milk
2 teaspoons dried minced onion
⅛ teaspoon pepper

• **Melt** butter in a large skillet over medium-high heat. Whisk in flour, and cook, whisking constantly, 1 minute.
• **Whisk** in broth and remaining ingredients. Cook over medium heat, whisking constantly, 2 minutes or until mixture thickens. **Yield:** 1½ cups.

Note: To serve gravy over chicken, sprinkle 4 skinned and boned chicken breast halves with ¼ teaspoon salt and ¼ teaspoon pepper. Melt 2 tablespoons butter in skillet over medium-high heat; add chicken, and cook 6 to 7 minutes on each side or until done. Serve chicken with gravy.

MUSHROOM GRAVY

Prep: 10 minutes
Cook: 10 minutes

1 medium onion, minced
3 garlic cloves, minced
2 tablespoons olive oil
1 (8-ounce) package sliced fresh mushrooms
1 (10½-ounce) can beef broth, undiluted
1 tablespoon soy sauce
2 tablespoons cornstarch
¾ cup water
¼ teaspoon salt
½ teaspoon pepper

• **Sauté** onion and garlic in hot oil in a medium saucepan over medium-high heat until tender; add mushrooms, and sauté 5 minutes.
• **Stir** in beef broth and soy sauce. Stir together cornstarch and ¾ cup water; gradually stir into broth mixture. Bring to a boil over medium heat, stirring constantly; boil, stirring constantly, 1 minute.
• **Stir** in salt and pepper. Serve gravy over meat loaf or mashed potatoes. **Yield:** 3 cups.

Karen C. Greenlee
Lawrenceville, Georgia

SOUTHWESTERN GRAVY

This yummy gravy sparks almost any dish. We loved it right out of the bowl.

Prep: 5 minutes
Cook: 35 minutes

¼ cup vegetable oil
¼ cup all-purpose flour
2 medium onions, chopped
2 cups hot water
1 (14½-ounce) can diced tomatoes, undrained
1 (10-ounce) can diced tomatoes and green chiles
1 (6-ounce) can tomato paste
1 teaspoon Worcestershire sauce
4 beef bouillon cubes
¼ teaspoon sugar
¼ teaspoon pepper

• **Whisk** together oil and flour in a large skillet; cook over medium heat, whisking constantly, until roux is caramel colored (about 20 minutes).
• **Add** onion, and cook, stirring often, 5 minutes.
• **Stir** in 2 cups hot water and remaining ingredients; bring to a boil. Reduce heat, and simmer 5 minutes. Serve with grits, eggs, chicken, pork, or black-eyed peas. **Yield:** 6½ cups.

Martha Smith Vaughn
Tarrant, Alabama

TOMATO GRAVY

An old-fashioned favorite steps up to the contemporary plate.

Prep: 5 minutes
Cook: 8 minutes

2 tablespoons butter or margarine
2 tablespoons minced shallots
1 (14½-ounce) can diced
   tomatoes, undrained
½ cup whipping cream
1 teaspoon chicken bouillon
   granules
½ teaspoon sugar
¼ teaspoon pepper

• **Melt** butter in a large skillet over medium heat; add shallots, and sauté until tender. Stir in tomatoes; bring to a boil. Reduce heat; simmer, stirring constantly, 2 to 3 minutes.
• **Stir** in whipping cream and remaining ingredients; simmer, stirring often, 3 minutes or until thickened. Serve with pasta, potatoes, or veal. **Yield:** 2 cups.

Jeanne Elwood
Birmingham, Alabama

CHOCOLATE GRAVY

A must-have recipe for chocolate lovers.

Prep: 5 minutes
Cook: 5 minutes

⅓ cup sugar
1½ tablespoons all-purpose
   flour
1½ tablespoons cocoa
½ cup milk
½ cup water
¼ cup butter or margarine
1 teaspoon vanilla extract

• **Whisk** together first 5 ingredients in a small saucepan. Bring to a boil over medium heat, whisking constantly.
• **Boil,** stirring often, until thickened and bubbly. Stir in butter and vanilla. Serve over biscuits, shortbread, or ice cream. **Yield:** 1¼ cups.

Sandi Pichon
Slidell, Louisiana

HOT PASTAS

There's just something comforting about a dough that cradles flavor—and cooks in a flash. These days a tempting assortment of pastas is available in both dried and refrigerated varieties, so have fun exercising your options for the best look and flavor.

BEANS AND PASTA

Prep: 10 minutes
Cook: 42 minutes

1 large onion, sliced
1 small red bell pepper, cut into
   thin strips
1 small yellow bell pepper, cut into
   thin strips
2 garlic cloves, minced
2 tablespoons olive oil
1 (8-ounce) package sliced fresh
   mushrooms
2 (14.5-ounce) cans Italian-style
   diced tomatoes
1 (15-ounce) can black beans,
   rinsed and drained
1 (15¼-ounce) can kidney beans,
   rinsed and drained
1 (3.5-ounce) jar capers, drained
1 (2¼-ounce) can sliced ripe
   olives, drained
¼ teaspoon salt
½ teaspoon pepper
8 ounces angel hair pasta, cooked
⅓ cup crumbled feta cheese or
   shredded Parmesan cheese

• **Sauté** first 4 ingredients in hot oil in a large skillet over medium-high heat 3 minutes; add sliced mushrooms, and sauté 4 minutes.
• **Stir** in tomatoes and next 6 ingredients; bring to a boil. Reduce heat, and simmer, stirring occasionally, 25 minutes. Serve over hot cooked pasta, and sprinkle with cheese. **Yield:** 6 servings.

Anna Johnson
Buies Creek, North Carolina

ITALIAN BEEF STIR-FRY
(pictured on page 39)

Refrigerated pasta freezes beautifully in its airtight package up to four months.

Prep: 10 minutes
Cook: 11 minutes

1 pound flank steak
1 tablespoon olive oil
½ teaspoon salt
¼ teaspoon pepper
2 small zucchini, thinly sliced
2 garlic cloves, pressed
1 cup cherry tomato halves
¼ cup Italian dressing
1 (9-ounce) package refrigerated
   linguine, cooked
½ cup shredded Parmesan cheese

• **Cut** flank steak diagonally across the grain into thin slices; cut each slice in half crosswise.
• **Heat** oil in a large skillet or wok at medium-high heat 2 minutes. Stir-fry steak 1 to 1½ minutes or to desired degree of doneness; sprinkle with salt and pepper. Remove from skillet with a slotted spoon.
• **Add** zucchini and garlic, and stir-fry 2 to 3 minutes or until crisp-tender.
• **Add** steak, tomato, and dressing; stir-fry 1 minute or until thoroughly heated. Serve over hot cooked pasta; sprinkle with cheese. **Yield:** 4 servings.

Lilann Taylor
Savannah, Georgia

CREATIVE WITH CANS

You won't be sacrificing nutrition when you make these recipes using canned ingredients. "Canning . . . preserves nutritional value and provides a healthy, tasty, and convenient alternative to fresh and frozen products," says Dr. Barbara Klein, professor of Food and Nutrition at the University of Illinois at Urbana. Just open the cans, dump, stir, and cook. It's that easy!

MARINATED VEGETABLES

Prep: 10 minutes
Chill: 8 hours

3 tablespoons red wine vinegar
¼ cup vegetable oil
2 garlic cloves, pressed
1 teaspoon dried oregano
½ teaspoon salt
½ teaspoon ground cumin
½ teaspoon curry powder
½ teaspoon pepper
1 (15.5-ounce) can garbanzo beans
1 (16-ounce) can kidney beans
1 (15.5-ounce) can pinto beans
1 (15.25-ounce) can whole kernel corn
3 green onions, chopped
3 celery ribs, chopped
¼ cup chopped fresh parsley

• **Whisk** together first 8 ingredients in a large bowl.
• **Rinse** and drain garbanzo beans and next 3 ingredients; add to red wine vinegar mixture.
• **Add** green onions, celery, and parsley; toss mixture to coat. Cover and chill 8 hours. **Yield:** 8 to 10 servings.

Suzan L. Wiener
Spring Hill, Florida

GREEN BEAN-AND-CORN CASSEROLE

Prep: 15 minutes
Bake: 30 minutes

1 (14½-ounce) can French-style green beans, rinsed and drained
1 (11-ounce) can white shoepeg corn, rinsed and drained
1 (10¾-ounce) can cream of celery soup, undiluted
3 celery ribs, chopped
1 small onion, chopped
½ cup (2 ounces) shredded Cheddar cheese
1 (8-ounce) container sour cream
¼ teaspoon salt
¼ teaspoon pepper
22 round buttery crackers, crushed
1 (2-ounce) package sliced almonds
¼ cup butter or margarine, melted

• **Stir** together first 9 ingredients in a large bowl.
• **Pour** green bean mixture into a lightly greased 11- x 7-inch baking dish.
• **Stir** together cracker crumbs, almonds, and melted butter, and sprinkle over casserole.
• **Bake** at 350° for 30 minutes or until bubbly. **Yield:** 6 servings.

Heather Jean Reames
Greenville, South Carolina

TACO SOUP
(pictured on page 38)

Prep: 5 minutes
Cook: 40 minutes
Bake: 8 minutes

1 pound ground beef
1 (15.5-ounce) can pinto beans
1 (15.25-ounce) can whole kernel corn
1 (14.5-ounce) can green beans
1 (15-ounce) can Ranch beans, undrained
1 (14.5-ounce) can stewed tomatoes
1 (12-ounce) can beer
1 (10-ounce) can diced tomatoes and green chiles
1 (1¼-ounce) envelope taco seasoning mix
1 (1-ounce) envelope Ranch dressing mix
5 (6-inch) corn tortillas
Salt

• **Brown** beef in a stockpot, stirring until it crumbles and is no longer pink; drain. Return beef to pot.
• **Rinse** and drain pinto beans, corn, and green beans; stir into beef. Stir in Ranch beans and next 5 ingredients; bring to a boil. Reduce heat; simmer 30 minutes.
• **Cut** tortillas into ¼-inch strips. Place on a baking sheet; coat with cooking spray. Sprinkle with salt.
• **Bake** at 400° for 5 to 8 minutes. Ladle soup into bowls, and top with tortilla strips. **Yield:** 10 cups.

Janet Rash
Carrollton, Texas

Eye of Round Roast,
page 60

Chunky Italian Soup, page 20

Taco Soup, page 36

Red Beans and Couscous, page 22

Italian Beef Stir-Fry, page 35

Enticing Enchiladas, page 57

Caramelized Onion Tart, page 96

SUCCULENT QUAIL

Quail are lean, juicy little game birds. Wild ones have a subtle, gamey taste; domestic birds are milder. If you are a quail lover, here are some new ways to serve it. If you haven't tried quail because you have not been sure how to handle it, look to the box on this page. We also tested these recipes with chicken, so even if quail is not on your menu you can enjoy these wonderful flavors.

QUAIL STROGANOFF

Prep: 10 minutes
Cook: 3 minutes
Bake: 55 minutes

8 quail, dressed
2 tablespoons butter or margarine
1 medium onion, chopped
1 (8-ounce) package sliced fresh
    mushrooms
½ cup dry white wine
1 (10¾-ounce) can cream of
    mushroom soup, undiluted
½ teaspoon dried oregano
½ teaspoon dried rosemary
¼ teaspoon pepper
1 (8-ounce) container sour cream
Hot cooked egg noodles

• **Place** quail in a lightly greased 13- x 9-inch baking dish. Melt butter in a skillet over medium heat; add onion and mushrooms. Sauté until tender. Add wine and next 4 ingredients; pour over quail.
• **Bake,** covered, at 350° for 45 minutes. Remove from oven; remove quail with tongs. Stir sour cream into drippings, and return quail to mixture.
• **Bake,** uncovered, 10 more minutes or until done. Serve over hot cooked egg noodles. **Yield:** 4 servings.

Chicken Stroganoff: Substitute 4 bone-in chicken breast halves for quail.
Hazel Sellers
Albany, Georgia

QUAIL SMOTHERED IN GRAVY

Prep: 10 minutes
Cook: 31 minutes

½ cup all-purpose flour
¾ teaspoon salt
¾ teaspoon pepper
6 quail, dressed
½ cup vegetable oil
2 cups water

• **Combine** first 3 ingredients; dredge quail in flour mixture, reserving remaining flour mixture. Brown quail in hot oil in a heavy skillet over medium-high heat; drain on paper towels, reserving 2 tablespoons drippings in pan.
• **Whisk** reserved flour mixture into drippings; cook over medium heat 3 minutes or until dark brown. Whisk in water until smooth. Add quail; cover and reduce heat. Simmer, stirring occasionally, 20 minutes or until quail is done. Serve with potatoes. **Yield:** 2 to 3 servings.

Chicken Smothered in Gravy: Substitute 8 chicken legs or thighs for quail.
Betty Cameron
Aliceville, Alabama

QUAIL P'S AND Q'S

Getting into the game is easy when you know the etiquette for quail. Eat as much of the breast meat as you can using your knife and fork. The rest is finger food. It is quite acceptable—and almost necessary—to pick up the legs and wings with your thumb and index finger. When serving quail as an entrée, allow two large birds per person. For an appetizer serving, one is appropriate.

Look for quail in the frozen meats section of the grocery store. Or call Good Heart Specialty Meats in San Antonio, Texas, toll-free at 1-888-466-3992.

ASIAN GRILLED QUAIL

Prep: 20 minutes
Chill: 30 minutes
Cook: 45 minutes

¼ cup hoisin sauce
2 tablespoons sesame seeds
3 tablespoons chile-garlic sauce
3 tablespoons dark sesame oil
3 tablespoons honey
1 teaspoon ground ginger
8 quail, dressed
1 (14½-ounce) can chicken broth
2 teaspoons cornstarch
Garnishes: sliced green onions or
    green onion curls

• **Combine** first 6 ingredients in a shallow dish or large heavy-duty zip-top plastic bag, gently squeezing to blend; add quail. Cover or seal; chill 30 minutes, turning occasionally.
• **Remove** quail from marinade, reserving marinade.
• **Prepare** fire by piling charcoal or lava rocks on 1 side of grill, leaving the other side empty. Place rack on grill. Arrange quail over empty side; grill, covered with grill lid, 30 minutes or until done.
• **Pour** reserved marinade into a small saucepan. Reserve ¼ cup chicken broth, and add remaining chicken broth to marinade. Bring mixture to a boil over medium-high heat; boil, stirring occasionally, 5 minutes.
• **Whisk** together cornstarch and reserved ¼ cup chicken broth until smooth. Whisk into marinade mixture; boil, whisking constantly, 1 minute. Serve with quail; garnish, if desired. **Yield:** 4 servings.

Asian Grilled Cornish Hens: Substitute 4 (1- to 1½-pound) Cornish hens for quail. Grill as directed 45 to 50 minutes or until done.

QUAIL AND DRESSING

Prep: 15 minutes
Cook: 25 minutes
Bake: 1 hour and 5 minutes

1 (5.9-ounce) package cornbread
   mix (4 cups)
1 medium onion, diced
½ cup diced celery
1 garlic clove, minced
2 tablespoons vegetable oil,
   divided
1 cup uncooked long-grain rice
2 (14.5-ounce) cans reduced-fat
   chicken broth
2 white bread slices, torn
1 teaspoon rubbed sage
1 teaspoon pepper
8 quail, dressed

• **Prepare** cornbread according to package directions; cool and crumble.
• **Sauté** onion, celery, and garlic in 1 tablespoon hot oil in a large skillet over medium-high heat until tender.
• **Add** rice, and sauté 1 minute. Add broth, and bring to a boil. Cover, reduce heat, and simmer 20 minutes.
• **Stir** in cornbread, white bread, sage, and pepper. Spoon into a lightly greased 13- x 9-inch baking dish.
• **Brown** quail 2 minutes on each side in remaining 1 tablespoon hot vegetable oil over medium-high heat. Place quail over dressing.
• **Bake,** covered, at 350° for 45 minutes or until quail is done. **Yield:** 4 servings.

Chicken and Dressing: Substitute 4 bone-in chicken breast halves for quail.
Gail Ladner Eaves
Louisville, Mississippi

FAT TUESDAY ON THE LIGHT SIDE

For those unable to visit the Big Easy during Mardi Gras, we bring a taste of New Orleans to you. Chef Dominique Macquet of Dominique's at the Maison Dupuy Hotel shares some treasures from his menu. You can savor these simplified recipes without leaving the comforts of home.

FIRE-ROASTED SHRIMP WITH ORZO

Pair this with Mantanzas Creek Sauvignon Blanc 1997.

Prep: 45 minutes
Chill: 1 hour
Cook: 30 minutes

1 pound unpeeled, jumbo fresh
   shrimp
2 teaspoons hot chili-sesame oil
6 tablespoons chopped fresh
   cilantro, divided
¾ teaspoon salt
1½ cups uncooked orzo
1 small carrot, chopped
1 celery rib, chopped
1 large shallot, chopped
2 garlic cloves, minced
1 teaspoon canola oil
2 cups water
½ stalk lemongrass, diced
¼ teaspoon curry powder
2 tablespoons coconut milk
1 tablespoon lite soy sauce
1 teaspoon grated fresh ginger
Crunchy Vegetables

• **Peel** shrimp, leaving tails on; reserve shells. Devein shrimp, if desired.
• **Toss** together shrimp, chili-sesame oil, 2 tablespoons cilantro, and salt in a large bowl. Cover and chill 1 hour.

• **Cook** orzo according to package directions; drain. Spoon hot orzo into 4 lightly greased 6-ounce custard cups, pressing lightly with back of a spoon. Set aside.
• **Sauté** carrot and next 3 ingredients in hot canola oil in a large nonstick skillet over medium-high heat 3 minutes. Add 2 cups water; bring to a boil.
• **Add** reserved shrimp shells, lemongrass, and curry powder. Reduce heat, and simmer 20 minutes. Remove from heat; cool slightly.
• **Process** shell mixture in a food processor. Pour through a fine wire-mesh strainer into a saucepan, pressing with the back of a spoon. Discard solids.
• **Stir** coconut milk, soy sauce, ginger, and remaining 4 tablespoons cilantro into shell mixture; bring to a boil. Remove from heat.
• **Heat** a large nonstick skillet over high heat; add shrimp, and cook 3 minutes or just until shrimp turn pink.
• **Unmold** orzo onto plates. Spoon coconut milk mixture around orzo. Arrange shrimp around orzo; serve with Crunchy Vegetables. **Yield:** 4 servings.

Note: Lemongrass is an herb used in Asian cooking; it has a sour lemon flavor. You can find it in large supermarkets and Asian markets.

Crunchy Vegetables

Prep: 15 minutes

1 tablespoon lime juice
1 teaspoon hot chili-sesame oil
1 teaspoon sugar
2 small zucchini, cut into thin strips
1 large carrot, cut into thin strips
1 yellow squash, cut into thin strips
¼ teaspoon freshly ground pepper

• **Whisk** together first 3 ingredients in a large bowl. Add zucchini, carrot, and squash; toss. Sprinkle vegetables with pepper. **Yield:** 4 servings.

Chef Dominique Macquet
Dominique's at the Maison Dupuy Hotel
New Orleans, Louisiana

❤ Per serving: Calories 428
Fat 9.1g Cholesterol 129mg
Sodium 721mg

GOAT CHEESE WRAPPED IN PHYLLO

Pair this with Mantanzas Creek Chardonnay 1995.

Prep: 1 hour and 10 minutes
Bake: 12 minutes

1 tablespoon light butter
4 small white onions, chopped
1 teaspoon sugar
½ cup balsamic vinegar
⅓ cup honey
1 teaspoon chopped fresh thyme
4 frozen phyllo sheets, thawed
Butter-flavored vegetable cooking spray
1 (3-ounce) goat cheese log, crumbled
Garnish: fresh thyme sprigs

• **Melt** butter in a large nonstick skillet over medium heat; add onion and sugar, and cook, stirring often, 30 minutes or until caramel colored.
• **Add** vinegar and honey to onion mixture. Cook over medium heat, stirring occasionally, 15 to 20 minutes or until

mixture is thickened. Stir in chopped fresh thyme.
• **Stack** phyllo, coating each layer with cooking spray. Cut phyllo stack into 6 (5-inch) squares. Spoon onion mixture evenly onto centers of phyllo squares. Top evenly with goat cheese.
• **Lift** corners of phyllo squares, and twist together. Place packets on a lightly greased baking sheet; coat each packet with cooking spray.
• **Bake** phyllo packets at 375° for 12 minutes or until golden; garnish, if desired. **Yield:** 6 servings.

Chef Dominique Macquet
Dominique's at the Maison Dupuy Hotel
New Orleans, Louisiana

❤ Per serving: Calories 202
Fat 6.9g Cholesterol 10mg
Sodium 129mg

PASS THE PANCAKES

Pancakes from scratch can be deliciously simple: Just cook them ahead, store in your refrigerator up to two days, and reheat on a wire rack at 350°. These versions are just as tasty when made with egg substitute; we tested them both ways.

FEATHERWEIGHT PANCAKES

Prep: 8 minutes
Cook: 12 minutes

3 large eggs, separated *
¾ cup large-curd cottage cheese
¼ cup all-purpose flour
¼ teaspoon salt
Powdered sugar

• **Beat** egg whites at high speed with an electric mixer until stiff peaks form.

• **Beat** egg yolks at high speed until thick and pale; stir in cottage cheese, flour, and salt. Fold in egg whites.
• **Pour** about ¼ cup batter for each pancake onto a hot, lightly greased griddle. Cook until tops are covered with bubbles and edges look cooked; turn and cook other side. Dust with powdered sugar; serve with syrup. **Yield:** 1 dozen.

* Substitute ¾ cup egg substitute for 3 eggs, if desired. Whisk together egg substitute, cottage cheese, flour, and salt. Cook as directed.

Carrie Treichel
Johnson City, Tennessee

TOASTED PECAN PANCAKES

Prep: 5 minutes
Cook: 10 minutes

½ cup all-purpose flour
⅓ cup whole wheat flour
¼ cup uncooked quick-cooking oats
2 tablespoons yellow cornmeal
1 tablespoon sugar
1 teaspoon baking powder
½ teaspoon baking soda
½ teaspoon salt
¼ cup chopped pecans, toasted
1 large egg *
1 cup buttermilk
2 tablespoons vegetable oil

• **Stir** together first 9 ingredients; make a well in center of mixture.
• **Stir** together egg, buttermilk, and oil; add to dry ingredients, stirring just until moistened.
• **Pour** about 2 tablespoons batter for each pancake onto a hot, lightly greased griddle. Cook until tops are covered with bubbles and edges look cooked; turn and cook other side. Serve with syrup. **Yield:** 14 pancakes.

* Substitute ¼ cup egg substitute for 1 egg, if desired.

Vivian Smith
Wesley Chapel, Florida

LEMON PANCAKES WITH STRAWBERRY BUTTER

Prep: 8 minutes
Cook: 12 minutes

3 large eggs, separated *
¼ teaspoon cream of tartar
¾ cup ricotta cheese
⅓ cup cake flour
¼ cup butter or margarine, melted
2 tablespoons sugar
1 tablespoon grated lemon rind
⅛ teaspoon salt
Strawberry Butter
Garnish: fresh mint sprigs

• **Beat** egg whites and cream of tartar at high speed with an electric mixer until stiff peaks form.
• **Beat** egg yolks, ricotta cheese, and next 5 ingredients at medium speed of mixer until smooth. Fold in egg whites.
• **Pour** about ¼ cup batter for each pancake onto a hot, lightly greased griddle. Cook until tops are covered with bubbles and edges look cooked; turn and cook other side. Serve with Strawberry Butter; garnish, if desired. **Yield:** 1 dozen.

* Substitute ¾ cup egg substitute for 3 eggs, if desired. Whisk together egg substitute, cream of tartar, and next 6 ingredients. Cook as directed.

Strawberry Butter

Prep: 5 minutes

½ cup butter or margarine, softened
¼ cup strawberry preserves

• **Stir** together butter and preserves until blended. **Yield:** ¾ cup.

Helen H. Maurer
Christmas, Florida

TENDERLOIN TRIO

Delicious all year, fresh pork is most plentiful and reasonably priced from October to February. Here we offer you three ways to prepare the succulent tenderloin. All of them are company—and pocketbook—pleasers.

PORK TENDERLOIN WITH ONION-BALSAMIC SAUCE

2 tablespoons balsamic vinegar
1 garlic clove, pressed
1 small onion, diced
2 (¾-pound) pork tenderloins, trimmed
Onion-Balsamic Sauce

• **Combine** first 3 ingredients in a shallow dish or large heavy-duty zip-top plastic bag; add tenderloins. Cover dish, or seal bag; chill 2 hours, turning meat occasionally.
• **Remove** tenderloins from marinade, discarding marinade.
• **Grill** tenderloins, covered with grill lid, over high heat (400° to 500°) 6 to 7½ minutes on each side or until a meat thermometer inserted into thickest portion of meat registers 160°. Slice and serve tenderloins with Onion-Balsamic Sauce. **Yield:** 6 servings.

Onion-Balsamic Sauce

3 large purple onions, coarsely chopped
½ cup firmly packed light brown sugar
1 cup dry red wine
1 tablespoon balsamic vinegar
1 beef bouillon cube

• **Cook** onion in a skillet coated with cooking spray over medium heat, stirring occasionally, 15 minutes.
• **Stir** in sugar; cover and cook, stirring occasionally, 10 minutes.

• **Add** wine, vinegar, and bouillon cube to onion mixture; cook, uncovered, stirring occasionally, until liquid is reduced by half. Serve sauce with tenderloin. **Yield:** 1 cup.

Shannon Ritchie
Birmingham, Alabama

PORK TENDERLOIN WITH APRICOT SAUCE

2 tablespoons dried rosemary
½ teaspoon salt
½ teaspoon freshly ground pepper
1 cup orange juice
3 tablespoons apricot preserves
2 tablespoons raspberry vinegar
1 teaspoon ground ginger
2 garlic cloves, minced
2 (¾-pound) pork tenderloins, trimmed
Garnish: Italian parsley sprigs

• **Combine** first 8 ingredients. Pour half of mixture into a shallow dish, reserving remaining mixture; add pork tenderloins to dish. Cover and chill 1 hour, turning occasionally.
• **Remove** pork from marinade, discarding marinade; place pork on a rack in a broiler pan.
• **Broil** 5 inches from heat (with electric oven door partially open) 15 minutes or until a meat thermometer inserted into thickest portion registers 160°, turning and basting with reserved apricot mixture. Slice and serve with pan juices. Garnish, if desired. **Yield:** 6 servings.

SOUTHERN-STYLE STUFFED PORK TENDERLOIN

1 (1-pound) pork tenderloin, trimmed
½ teaspoon salt
½ teaspoon freshly ground pepper
½ cup chopped cooked collard greens
¼ cup (1 ounce) shredded Cheddar cheese
2 tablespoons diced red bell pepper
1 tablespoon vegetable oil
Sweet Potato Chutney

• **Slice** pork tenderloin lengthwise down center, cutting to but not through bottom. Place between 2 sheets of heavy-duty plastic wrap, and flatten to ¼-inch thickness using a meat mallet or rolling pin. Sprinkle with salt and pepper.
• **Stir** together collard greens, cheese, and bell pepper. Spoon over tenderloin, spreading to within ¼ inch of edges. Roll tenderloin up, jellyroll fashion, starting with a short side; secure with wooden picks.
• **Brown** tenderloin in hot oil in a large ovenproof skillet over medium-high heat 2 minutes on each side.
• **Place** skillet in oven, and bake at 350° for 25 minutes. Let stand 5 minutes before slicing. Serve with Sweet Potato Chutney. **Yield:** 4 servings.

Sweet Potato Chutney

1 large sweet potato, cooked, peeled, and diced
1 large apple, diced
3 small green onions, minced
3 tablespoons chopped fresh parsley
1 celery rib, chopped
2 tablespoons minced crystallized ginger
1 teaspoon grated fresh ginger
¼ teaspoon pepper
2 tablespoons cider vinegar
2 tablespoons frozen apple juice concentrate, thawed

• **Stir** together all ingredients in a bowl. **Yield:** 2½ cups.

Roxanne E. Chan
Albany, California

MONEY-SAVING MEAL

Cutting food costs is easier than you think. Follow these simple steps to help trim your family's food bill: Look over food ads for specials, clip coupons, and take advantage of good buys by being flexible with menus and the shopping list. Here's a menu perfect for your family. When we priced this menu at our market, it cost less than $3 a serving. Turn the page for a complete grocery list.

𝒢OOD CENTS MENU
Serves Six

Hamburger Steak
Whipped Celery Potatoes
Garlic Broccoli
Parmesan-Garlic Breadsticks

HAMBURGER STEAK

Prep: 8 minutes
Cook: 26 minutes

2 pounds ground chuck
½ teaspoon salt
½ teaspoon pepper
1 tablespoon vegetable oil
1 large onion, chopped
1 medium-size green bell pepper, chopped
2 (8-ounce) cans tomato sauce
2 tablespoons Worcestershire sauce
½ teaspoon dry mustard

• **Combine** first 3 ingredients in a large bowl; shape into 6 patties.
• **Cook** patties in hot oil in a large non-stick skillet over medium-high heat 2 minutes on each side or until browned.

• **Drain** beef patties, and remove from skillet.
• **Sauté** onion and bell pepper in skillet over medium-high heat 2 minutes or until tender.
• **Stir** in tomato sauce, Worcestershire sauce, and dry mustard; bring to a boil.
• **Add** beef patties to skillet; cover, reduce heat, and simmer 15 minutes. Uncover and cook 5 more minutes or until patties are no longer pink. **Yield:** 6 servings.

Carrie Treichel
Johnson City, Tennessee

WHIPPED CELERY POTATOES

Prep: 10 minutes
Cook: 40 minutes

2 pounds red potatoes
3½ cups water
1¾ teaspoons salt, divided
1 cup butter or margarine, divided
3 celery ribs, chopped
1 small onion, diced
¼ cup milk
⅛ teaspoon pepper

• **Bring** potatoes, 3½ cups water, and 1½ teaspoons salt to a boil in a large saucepan. Cover, reduce heat, and simmer 30 minutes or until tender; drain and cool 5 minutes.
• **Peel** potatoes, if desired; place potatoes in a bowl.
• **Melt** 2 tablespoons butter in saucepan; add celery and onion, and sauté until tender.
• **Add** celery mixture to potatoes; beat at low speed with an electric mixer until blended.
• **Add** remaining butter, milk, remaining ¼ teaspoon salt, and pepper to potato mixture; beat at high speed until mixture is fluffy (do not overbeat). Serve immediately. **Yield:** 6 to 8 servings.

GARLIC BROCCOLI

Prep: 5 minutes
Cook: 7 minutes

1 (16-ounce) package broccoli
     flowerets
2 teaspoons dark sesame oil
2 teaspoons vegetable oil
2 garlic cloves, pressed
¼ cup lite soy sauce
1 tablespoon sugar
1 tablespoon balsamic
     vinegar
1 tablespoon water

• **Arrange** broccoli in a steamer basket over boiling water.
• **Cover** broccoli, and steam 5 minutes or until crisp-tender. Transfer to a serving bowl; keep warm.
• **Heat** sesame oil and vegetable oil in a small saucepan over medium heat 1 minute or until hot. Remove saucepan from heat.
• **Add** garlic and next 4 ingredients to saucepan, stirring until sugar dissolves. Pour garlic mixture over broccoli, tossing to coat. Serve immediately. **Yield:** 6 servings.

PARMESAN-GARLIC BREADSTICKS

Prep: 8 minutes
Bake: 15 minutes

2¼ cups biscuit mix
½ cup grated Parmesan
     cheese
1 tablespoon butter or margarine,
     melted
¼ teaspoon garlic powder
⅔ cup milk

• **Combine** first 4 ingredients in a large bowl; stir in milk until blended.
• **Roll** dough into a 10- x 9-inch rectangle on a lightly floured surface. Cut dough into 10 (1-inch) strips; place on a lightly greased baking sheet. Bake at 400° for 13 to 15 minutes. **Yield:** 10 breadsticks.

Julia McLeod
Hendersonville, North Carolina

"MONEY-SAVING MEAL" MARKET ORDER

STAPLES ON HAND
Salt
Pepper
Dry mustard
Sugar
Vegetable oil
Lite soy sauce
Worcestershire sauce
Garlic powder

GROCERY LIST
Produce
1 garlic bulb
1 bunch celery
1 medium-size green bell pepper
1 (16-ounce) package broccoli
   flowerets
2 pounds red potatoes
1 large onion
1 small onion

Dairy
½ cup grated Parmesan cheese
1 cup milk
3 sticks butter

Meat
2 pounds ground chuck

General
Dark sesame oil
Balsamic vinegar
2¼ cups biscuit mix
2 (8-ounce) cans tomato sauce

SIDEKICKS

Have you planned your favorite entrée but need new ideas for the rest of the dinner plate? Try these short and versatile recipes.

HERBED VEGETABLE MEDLEY

2 tablespoons butter or vegetable
     oil
3 garlic cloves, pressed
2 medium carrots, cut into thin
     strips
1 teaspoon salt
1 teaspoon lemon pepper
3 small zucchini, cut into thin
     strips
3 small yellow squash, cut into
     thin strips
1 medium-size red bell pepper, cut
     into thin strips
⅓ cup chopped green onions
2 tablespoons chopped fresh basil
     or 1 teaspoon dried basil

• **Heat** butter in a large skillet over medium-high heat; add garlic, and sauté 1 to 2 minutes.
• **Add** carrot, salt, and lemon pepper; sauté 2 to 3 minutes. Add zucchini and remaining ingredients; sauté 3 to 4 minutes or until vegetables are crisp-tender. **Yield:** 8 servings.

LEMONY RICE

2 tablespoons butter or margarine
1¼ cups uncooked long-grain rice
2½ cups chicken broth
1½ teaspoons grated lemon rind
2 tablespoons fresh lemon juice
½ teaspoon salt
¼ teaspoon ground white pepper
2 tablespoons chopped fresh
     parsley

• **Melt** butter in a medium saucepan over medium-high heat; add rice, and

sauté 2 minutes or until rice is lightly browned.
- **Stir** chicken broth and next 4 ingredients into browned rice; bring mixture to a boil. Cover, reduce heat, and simmer 20 minutes or until rice is tender. Stir in chopped parsley, and serve immediately. **Yield:** 6 servings.

Tracee Flaherty
Brunswick, Maine

BREADS IN A FLASH

In 30 minutes or less you'll be welcoming family or friends to your table with the enticing aroma of these hot baked treats. You'll need to allow rising time for Onion-Bacon Rolls, but while you're waiting, you can prepare the rest of the meal and set the table.

ITALIAN PARKER HOUSE ROLLS

Prep: 10 minutes
Bake: 12 minutes

2 (12-ounce) cans refrigerated
   buttermilk biscuits
¾ cup Italian dressing
3 tablespoons grated Parmesan
   cheese
½ teaspoon poppy seeds
½ teaspoon sesame seeds

- **Separate** biscuits, and dip each in Italian dressing. Fold biscuits in half. Place 2 biscuits, seam side down, in each of 10 lightly greased muffin pans.
- **Combine** cheese, poppy seeds, and sesame seeds; sprinkle on biscuits.
- **Bake** at 400° for 10 to 12 minutes or until golden. **Yield:** 10 rolls.

Barbara Operschall
St. Louis, Missouri

PECAN CRESCENT TWISTS

Prep: 15 minutes
Bake: 12 minutes

2 (8-ounce) cans refrigerated
   crescent rolls
6 tablespoons butter or margarine,
   melted and divided
½ cup chopped pecans
¼ cup sugar
1 teaspoon ground cinnamon
⅛ teaspoon ground nutmeg
½ cup powdered sugar
2 tablespoons maple syrup or
   milk

- **Unroll** crescent rolls, and separate each can into 4 rectangles, pressing perforations to seal. Brush evenly with 4 tablespoons melted butter.
- **Stir** together pecans and next 3 ingredients; sprinkle 1 tablespoon mixture onto each rectangle, pressing in gently.
- **Roll** up, starting at a long side, and twist. Cut 6 shallow ½-inch-long diagonal slits in each roll.
- **Shape** rolls into rings, pressing ends together; place on a lightly greased baking sheet. Brush rings evenly with remaining 2 tablespoons butter. Bake at 375° for 12 minutes or until golden.
- **Stir** together powdered sugar and syrup until glaze is smooth; drizzle over warm twists. **Yield:** 8 servings.

Nancy Matthews
Grayson, Georgia

HERBED FRENCH BREAD

Prep: 10 minutes
Bake: 10 minutes

½ cup butter or margarine,
   softened
¼ cup grated Parmesan cheese
1 teaspoon dried basil
1 teaspoon dried rosemary
1 teaspoon garlic powder
1 (16-ounce) French bread
   loaf, cut into ¾-inch-thick
   slices

- **Stir** together first 5 ingredients. Spread 1 side of bread slices evenly with butter mixture, and place, buttered side up, on baking sheets.
- **Bake** bread slices at 425° for 9 to 10 minutes or until lightly browned. Serve immediately. **Yield:** 8 servings.

Laurie Garvie
Dallas, Texas

ONION-BACON ROLLS

Prep: 15 minutes
Rise: 30 minutes
Bake: 15 minutes

8 bacon slices
1 small onion, diced
1 small green bell pepper, diced
½ teaspoon dried dillweed
½ teaspoon pepper
1 (16-ounce) package frozen roll
   dough, thawed
¼ cup milk
1 teaspoon poppy seeds
1 teaspoon sesame seeds

- **Cook** bacon in a large skillet until crisp; remove bacon, reserving 1 tablespoon drippings in skillet. Crumble bacon.
- **Sauté** onion and bell pepper in bacon drippings until tender; remove with a slotted spoon, and drain on paper towels. Place mixture in a small bowl; stir in bacon, dillweed, and pepper.
- **Pat** each roll into a 3-inch circle; spoon 1 tablespoon bacon mixture onto center. Bring up edges, pinching to seal; place, seam side down, into lightly greased muffin pans.
- **Brush** rolls with milk; sprinkle with poppy seeds and sesame seeds. Cover and let rise in a warm place (85°), free from drafts, 30 minutes or until doubled in bulk.
- **Bake** at 375° for 15 minutes or until golden. **Yield:** 2 dozen.

Helen Goggans
Kingsland, Arkansas

GOING BANANAS

Every generation has a passion for these sweet and slender fingers of the tropics. This pair of treats delivers nothing short of rich banana flavor. For peak taste, use only ripe fruit. Bananas are nutritious and economical, so buy them by the bunch.

BANANA SPLIT CAKE

Prep: 30 minutes
Bake: 1 hour and 15 minutes

3 cups all-purpose flour
1 teaspoon baking soda
¼ teaspoon salt
2 cups sugar
3 large eggs, lightly beaten
1 cup vegetable oil
½ cup buttermilk
2 cups mashed banana (5 medium)
1 cup chopped pecans
1 cup flaked coconut
1½ teaspoons vanilla extract
1 (20-ounce) can crushed
    pineapple, undrained
1 (16-ounce) jar maraschino
    cherries, drained
1 (8-ounce) package cream cheese,
    softened
1½ cups powdered sugar
Garnishes: toasted flaked coconut,
    long-stemmed maraschino
    cherries, grated milk chocolate,
    chopped pecans, hot fudge
    sauce

• **Combine** first 4 ingredients in a large bowl. Stir together eggs, oil, and buttermilk. Add egg mixture to flour mixture, stirring just until dry ingredients are moistened. Stir in banana and next 3 ingredients.
• **Drain** pineapple, reserving 2 tablespoons juice. Chop cherries. Gently press pineapple and maraschino cherries between layers of paper towels. Stir pineapple and cherries into banana mixture. Spoon into a greased and floured 10-inch tube pan.
• **Bake** at 350° for 1 hour and 15 minutes or until a wooden pick inserted in center comes out clean. Cool in pan on a wire rack 10 to 15 minutes; remove from pan, and cool on wire rack.
• **Beat** cream cheese at medium speed with an electric mixer until smooth. Gradually add powdered sugar, beating at low speed until blended. Stir in reserved pineapple juice. Pour over cake; garnish, if desired. **Yield:** 1 (10-inch) cake.

JoAnn Mayfield
Paducah, Kentucky

CHOCOLATE-WRAPPED BANANA CHEESECAKE

Prep: 30 minutes
Bake: 1 hour
Chill: 8 hours

3 medium-size ripe bananas
2 teaspoons lemon juice
2 (8-ounce) packages cream
    cheese, softened
1 cup sugar
1 cup mascarpone cheese *
4 large eggs
1 tablespoon vanilla extract
Peanut-Graham Crust
1 cup milk chocolate morsels
1 tablespoon butter or
    margarine
Caramelized Bananas

• **Mash** bananas with a fork; stir in lemon juice until blended. Set aside.
• **Beat** cream cheese and sugar at medium speed with an electric mixer until light and fluffy.
• **Add** mascarpone to cream cheese mixture, beating until smooth.
• **Add** eggs, 1 at a time, beating well after each addition.
• **Stir** in banana and vanilla. Pour into Peanut-Graham Crust.
• **Bake** at 325° for 1 hour (center will be slightly soft). Remove cheesecake from oven; run a knife around edge to loosen sides. Cool on a wire rack; cover and chill 8 hours.
• **Microwave** chocolate morsels and butter in a 1-quart microwave-safe bowl at HIGH 1 minute; stir until smooth. Let mixture stand 30 minutes.
• **Remove** sides of springform pan from cheesecake. Spread three-fourths of melted chocolate around sides of cheesecake.
• **Arrange** Caramelized Bananas on top; drizzle with remaining chocolate. **Yield:** 12 servings.

* Substitute 1 (8-ounce) package cream cheese, 2½ tablespoons sour cream, and 2 tablespoons whipping cream for mascarpone cheese, if desired. Beat ingredients well at medium speed with an electric mixer. Use 1 cup mixture for cheesecake recipe, reserving remainder for another use.

Peanut-Graham Crust

2 cups graham cracker crumbs
1 cup finely chopped dry-roasted
   peanuts
½ cup sugar
½ cup butter or margarine,
   melted

• **Stir** together all ingredients; press onto bottom and 1 inch up sides of a 9-inch springform pan.
• **Bake** at 375° for 10 to 12 minutes. Cool on a wire rack. **Yield:** crust for 1 (9-inch) cheesecake.

Caramelized Bananas

4 medium-size bananas
½ cup firmly packed light brown
   sugar
¼ cup butter or margarine

• **Cut** bananas diagonally into ⅓-inch-thick slices.
• **Cook** brown sugar and butter over high heat in a small skillet, stirring constantly, 5 minutes or until thickened. Remove from heat; stir in banana. Cool. **Yield:** 1¼ cups.

BANANA POWER

■ Purchase yellow bananas that have green tips, and ripen at room temperature for two to three days. When bananas achieve a golden color and a moist, slightly sticky flesh, use them immediately to make breads and cakes.

■ To speed ripening, place bananas in a brown paper bag with an apple. To slow the ripening process, place in the crisper bin of the refrigerator. The thick skin will turn brown, but the inside will remain firm until ready to use.

■ Sprinkle banana flesh with lemon juice to prevent darkening.

VALENTINE TEA

Share an afternoon tea with your sweetheart. Swirl flavored butters on Cherry-and-Cream Scones, or present a tray of unusual Almond Cookies. These recipes will also enhance your favorite brunch menu.

CHERRY-AND-CREAM SCONES

Prep: 15 minutes
Bake: 15 minutes

2 cups all-purpose flour
1 tablespoon baking powder
¼ teaspoon salt
⅓ cup sugar
⅓ cup butter or margarine
1½ cups whipping cream, divided
1 (3-ounce) package dried
   cherries
2 tablespoons sugar

• **Combine** first 4 ingredients; cut in butter with a pastry blender until crumbly.
• **Add** 1¼ cups whipping cream and cherries, stirring just until dry ingredients are moistened.
• **Turn** dough out onto a lightly floured surface; knead 5 or 6 times.
• **Pat** or roll dough to ½-inch thickness; cut with a 5-inch heart-shaped cutter, and place on a lightly greased baking sheet. Brush dough with remaining ¼ cup whipping cream; sprinkle evenly with 2 tablespoons sugar.
• **Bake** at 375° for 12 to 15 minutes or until scones are golden. Serve warm. **Yield:** 1 dozen.

Note: Cut dough with a 2-inch round cutter, if desired. **Yield:** 1 dozen.

STRAWBERRY SPARKLER

Prep: 10 minutes

1 (10-ounce) package frozen
   strawberries, thawed
2 cups cranberry juice, chilled
1 (750-milliliter) bottle
   champagne, chilled *

• **Process** strawberries in a blender until smooth; pour into a pitcher. Stir in cranberry juice and champagne, and serve immediately. **Yield:** 6 cups.

* Substitute 1 (1-liter) bottle sparkling water, chilled, for champagne, if desired.
Deborah Eichhorn
Dayton, Ohio

ALMOND COOKIES

Prep: 20 minutes
Bake: 1 hour and 20 minutes

3 cups slivered almonds,
   toasted
4 egg whites
1½ cups sugar
1 teaspoon powdered sugar
1 teaspoon almond liqueur *
Sugar

• **Process** slivered almonds in a food processor until finely ground. (Do not overprocess to a powder.)
• **Beat** egg whites at high speed with an electric mixer until stiff peaks form. Fold in ground almonds, 1½ cups sugar, powdered sugar, and liqueur.
• **Drop** by rounded teaspoonfuls onto parchment paper-lined baking sheets; sprinkle with additional sugar.
• **Bake** at 300° for 20 minutes or until golden; remove to wire racks to cool. **Yield:** about 4 dozen.

* Substitute ½ teaspoon almond extract for liqueur, if desired.
Mitchelann Rayas
Gainesville, South Carolina

FROM OUR KITCHEN TO YOURS

FREEZE FRAME

Do you know what's in your freezer and do you know how long it's been there? It's time to take inventory. The freezer is an easy holding bin for food you'll never eat but don't have the heart to throw away. Rule number one: If it's not dated, don't plate it.

■ Store new purchases toward the bottom; bring older items to the surface.

■ Take the freezer's temperature. Every 10 degrees over 0°F cuts food storage time in half. Cool food to room temperature before freezing, and freeze only a few items at a time if space is limited. Overloading the compartment can slow the process—food frozen too slowly will lose quality and may spoil.

■ Be on the lookout for freezer burn—a dry surface of gray-white spots. Improperly packaged food lets in air and moisture causing the unsightly splotches. Freezer burned food won't harm you, but most of it tastes awful.

■ Thaw food in the refrigerator. Thawing food at room temperature invites bacteria.

■ Freeze and thaw food one time; textures change when food is thawed and refrozen. Vegetables get mushy, meats get tough, and casseroles get soggy.

TIDBITS

Don't throw away that outdated yeast. It won't rise to lofty heights, but it will add grand flavor to pancake and waffle batter, muffin mixes, and biscuit dough.

When accidents in our Test Kitchens result in burns, we use Cumarindine Ointment. It's available in 1.6-, 3.2-, and 13.1-ounce jars and is distributed by Terrell Laboratories, Inc., 1900 Dee Hicks Road, Altoona, AL 35952; call (205) 589-6429.

PUT OUT THE FIRE

In his book *The Gadget Guru's Guide to the Kitchen,* Andy Pargh reminds us to keep several fire extinguishers handy and to choose them carefully. The ABCs of extinguishers refers to the kind of fire each is designed to put out. Class A is specially formulated for wood, paper, rubber, and most plastics. Class B is for oil, solvents, grease, and other flammable liquids. Class C is for electrical fires. Classes B and C are filled with dry chemicals.

Multipurpose extinguishers, known as the ABC type, are recommended for the kitchen and most other locations in the house. If there's a fire, you don't have to wonder if you have the right class.

If you have a fire in a pan, don't move the pan. Instead, follow these tips: Turn off the burner and the range fan. Carefully slide a lid over the pan to smother the flames (do not just pop the top on the pan). If the fire has spread to the cooktop already, turn off the burners and the range fan. Pour baking soda on the fire until the fire is out. If baking soda doesn't work, then go for the multipurpose extinguisher.

SEASONING CAST IRON

Read all about Jack Butler's passion for cast-iron cookery in "Jack's Skillet" on pages 32 and 33. Pull out your cast iron, old or new, and try Jack's recipes. Kitchen shops feature wonderful selections of cast iron in all shapes and sizes. However, don't limit your search to retail stores; yard sales and flea markets are home to some fantastic finds.

When you buy a new piece of cast iron, it's neither shiny nor black, and it's definitely not ready to use. But give cast iron a little attention and you're set for years of good cooking.

■ For new pieces, scrub with steel wool soap pads and hot water; then hand-wash with a mild detergent and dry thoroughly. Iron left uncoated will rust, so immediately spread solid vegetable shortening on the inside, including the underside of the lid (do not use butter or margarine). Place in a 250° to 300° oven 15 minutes; remove from the oven, and wipe any excess grease around the interior to evenly coat the surface. Return to the oven, and bake 1½ to 2 more hours. Remove from the oven, and let cool to room temperature. Repeat this procedure two or three times.

■ For old pieces, scrub and dry thoroughly. If cast iron is badly caked, run it through a cycle in your self-cleaning oven. When pieces are clean, follow the seasoning process described in the previous paragraph.

■ Never place cast iron in a dishwasher. The harsh detergent, water jets, and humid, hot environment are damaging. Never marinate food in cast iron; acidic mixtures will ruin the cast-iron seasoning you've worked hard to achieve.

■ Remove food from cast iron after cooking; do not use for storing leftovers. Clean thoroughly with a nylon scouring pad after each use (steel wool soap pads are not recommended for regular cleaning).

MARCH

Having dinner on the table without a lot of fuss is a snap this month. "Four Meals Made Easy" provides you with four simple weeknight menus along with a complete grocery list and menu plan. Offer your family recipes such as Eye of Round Roast and Chicken Tetrazzini, and take-out food will become a thing of the past. Find other simple dinner options in "What's for Supper?: Solutions for Yesterday and Today." Two of our long-time readers share their favorite time-tested casseroles.

For dessert, turn to "Dessert of the Month: Look What's Brewing." These mouthwatering treats—Mocha Torte, Coffee Tart, and Coffee Buttons—deliciously demonstrate that coffee's popularity needs no justification.

WHAT A CATCH

We've discovered that many of you—our readers— and quite a few of our region's chefs enjoy showcasing the distinctive, sweet flavor of trout. Reel these wonderful recipes into your collection.

SWEET ONION-STUFFED TROUT

Prep: 50 minutes
Cook: 24 minutes

8 medium-size red potatoes, cubed
16 bacon slices, divided
4 baby Vidalia onions, sliced
1 cup whipping cream
2 tablespoons butter or margarine
2 teaspoons salt, divided
2 teaspoons pepper, divided
4 (12-ounce) butterflied trout
2 cups all-purpose flour
¼ cup olive oil
Vidalia Onion Sauce

• **Cook** potato in boiling water to cover 10 minutes or until tender; drain.
• **Chop** 8 bacon slices. Cook chopped bacon in a skillet over medium-high heat, stirring often, 10 minutes. Add onion; sauté 10 minutes or until tender.
• **Add** potato to skillet, and mash with a fork. Stir in whipping cream, butter, ½ teaspoon salt, and ½ teaspoon pepper; cook, stirring constantly, until thoroughly heated.
• **Sprinkle** trout with ½ teaspoon salt and ½ teaspoon pepper.
• **Spoon** stuffing evenly on 1 side of each trout; fold other side of each trout over stuffing.
• **Wrap** 2 bacon slices around each trout, securing with wooden picks.

• **Stir** together flour, remaining 1 teaspoon salt, and remaining 1 teaspoon pepper in a shallow dish. Dredge fish in flour mixture.
• **Fry** 2 trout at a time in hot oil in a skillet over medium-high heat 6 minutes on each side or until fish flakes with a fork. Serve with Vidalia Onion Sauce. **Yield:** 4 servings.

Vidalia Onion Sauce

Prep: 5 minutes
Cook: 25 minutes

2 baby Vidalia onions, sliced
1 tablespoon olive oil
2 cups whipping cream
¼ teaspoon salt
¼ teaspoon pepper

• **Sauté** onion in a large skillet in hot oil over medium-high heat 10 minutes or until tender.
• **Stir** in whipping cream. Reduce heat, and simmer 15 minutes or until liquid is reduced by half. Stir in salt and pepper. **Yield:** about 3 cups.

Executive Chef Robert Stricklin
Big Cedar Lodge
Ridgedale, Missouri

CORNMEAL-CRUSTED TROUT

Prep: 45 minutes
Cook: 24 minutes

2 bacon slices, chopped
2 tablespoons olive oil, divided
½ purple onion, diced
½ green bell pepper, diced
3 garlic cloves, minced
¼ cup fresh or frozen whole corn kernels
2 cups crumbled cornbread
2 ounces fresh lump crabmeat, drained
2 tablespoons chopped fresh cilantro
1 jalapeño pepper, seeded and chopped
1 large egg, lightly beaten
1 teaspoon salt, divided
1 teaspoon ground black pepper, divided
4 (12-ounce) butterflied trout
2 cups cornmeal
2 teaspoons ground red pepper
1 teaspoon salt
1 teaspoon garlic powder
8 bacon slices
Picante Aïoli

• **Cook** chopped bacon in 1 tablespoon hot oil in a large skillet over medium-high heat 8 to 10 minutes.
• **Stir** in onion and next 3 ingredients, and sauté 5 minutes or until tender. Remove from heat; stir in cornbread, next 4 ingredients, ½ teaspoon salt, and ½ teaspoon pepper.
• **Sprinkle** trout with remaining ½ teaspoon salt and remaining ½ teaspoon pepper. Spoon one-fourth of cornbread mixture on 1 side of each trout. Fold other side over stuffing.
• **Stir** together cornmeal and next 3 ingredients; dredge trout in mixture. Wrap 2 bacon slices around each trout, securing with wooden picks.
• **Cook** 2 trout at a time in remaining 1 tablespoon hot oil 6 minutes on each side or until fish flakes with a fork. Serve immediately with Picante Aïoli. **Yield:** 4 servings.

Picante Aïoli

Prep: 3 minutes
Chill: 30 minutes

1 cup mayonnaise
⅓ cup picante sauce
3 garlic cloves, minced
¼ teaspoon salt
¼ teaspoon pepper

• **Combine** all ingredients. Cover and chill at least 30 minutes. **Yield:** 1⅓ cups.
Executive Chef Robert Stricklin
Big Cedar Lodge
Ridgedale, Missouri

TROUT AMANDINE
(pictured on page 77)

Prep: 15 minutes
Cook: 16 minutes

2 tablespoons butter
⅓ cup sliced almonds, toasted
½ cup milk
1 egg yolk
½ teaspoon hot sauce
1 cup all-purpose flour
1 teaspoon salt
1 teaspoon pepper
6 (12-ounce) trout fillets
Vegetable oil
Lemon Cream Sauce

• **Melt** butter in a large heavy skillet over low heat; add almonds. Sauté almonds until golden; remove from skillet, and drain on paper towels. Wipe skillet clean.
• **Whisk** together milk, egg yolk, and hot sauce in a shallow dish. Stir together flour, salt, and pepper in a shallow bowl. Dredge trout fillets in flour mixture; dip in egg yolk mixture. Dredge trout fillets again in flour mixture, shaking to remove any excess flour mixture.
• **Pour** oil into skillet to a depth of ¼ inch; heat to 375°. Fry trout in batches in oil 3 to 4 minutes on each side or until golden. Serve with Lemon Cream Sauce; sprinkle with almonds. **Yield:** 6 servings.

Note: To keep cooked fish warm while others fry, place on a wire rack in a shallow pan. Place pan in a 200° oven.

Fishing the South's great trout streams will have you hooked.

Mention the words "fly fishing" to people who love the sport, and you'll see their consciousness shift to another realm—a watery world where all that matters are the pleasures of exploring clear streams and waving a rod through the air in hopes of reeling in a trophy fish. And fishing is just part of the adventure. The aroma of cornmeal-crusted fish frying streamside in an ebony skillet adds to the experience.

THE FISHING HOLE
   Every trout fisherman has a favorite fishing spot. Here are a few we've enjoyed.

Blackberry Farm, Walland, Tennessee: A posh mountain club and inn near Knoxville, this retreat keeps its Singing Brook Trout Pond well stocked for guests. Executive Chef John C. Fleer terms his trout specialties "foothills cuisine," recipes that artfully balance the fancy with the familiar; call (423) 984-8166 for reservations and information, or fax (423) 983-5708.

Brigadoon Lodge, Soque River, North Georgia: Near Clarkesville, Georgia, Brigadoon Lodge offers catch-and-release guided fishing. Limited overnight accommodations and meals are also available to guests; call (706) 754-1558 or toll free at 1-888-427-4423. You can also find them on the Internet at www.brigadoonlodge.com.

Dogwood Canyon, Ridgedale, Missouri: This 10,000-acre private wilderness nature park is 25 minutes from Big Cedar Lodge resort. Fishing experiences include guided trophy trout fishing, catch and release, and catch and keep; call (417) 335-2777.

Hiwassee River, Benton, Tennessee: Orvis-endorsed Dry Flyer Outfitters provides everything you'll need for a great day on the river—guides, equipment, flies, and lunch; call (423) 338-6263. A wonderful cabin set on 150 acres at Windswept Farm offers comfortable, thoughtfully appointed lodging; call (423) 263-0440.

Lemon Cream Sauce

Prep: 5 minutes
Cook: 15 minutes

½ cup butter or margarine
2 tablespoons all-purpose
     flour
1 (14½-ounce) can chicken broth
2 garlic cloves, pressed
1 tablespoon lemon juice
⅓ cup whipping cream
¼ cup white wine Worcestershire
     sauce
¼ teaspoon salt
½ teaspoon hot sauce

• **Melt** butter in a large skillet over medium heat; whisk in flour. Cook, whisking constantly, 1 minute.
• **Whisk** in broth, garlic, and lemon juice; bring mixture to a boil, whisking constantly. Reduce heat, and simmer, whisking constantly, 5 minutes.
• **Whisk** in whipping cream and remaining ingredients; cook, whisking constantly, 5 minutes or until sauce is thickened. **Yield:** 1¼ cups.
Ann Albritton
Montgomery, Alabama

BACON-WRAPPED TROUT STUFFED WITH CRAWFISH

Prep: 30 minutes
Cook: 22 minutes

¾ cup butter or margarine, divided
1 medium onion, diced
3 celery ribs, diced
½ red bell pepper, diced
2 garlic cloves, minced
8 ounces uncooked, peeled crawfish tails
¼ cup dry white wine
1 teaspoon salt, divided
1 teaspoon pepper, divided
8 (8-ounce) dressed trout
16 bacon slices

• **Melt** 2 tablespoons butter in a large skillet over medium heat.
• **Add** onion and next 3 ingredients; sauté 10 minutes.
• **Add** crawfish; cook, stirring constantly, 5 minutes.
• **Add** wine to skillet; stir to loosen particles from skillet. Add ½ cup butter, ½ teaspoon salt, and ½ teaspoon pepper, stirring until butter melts. Cool mixture slightly.
• **Remove** heads from trout, leaving tails intact. Spoon crawfish mixture evenly into trout cavities. Sprinkle outside of fish evenly with remaining ½ teaspoon salt and remaining ½ teaspoon pepper.
• **Wrap** 2 bacon slices around each trout; secure with wooden picks.
• **Melt** remaining 2 tablespoons butter in a large skillet over medium-high heat; add trout in batches, and cook 2 minutes on each side.
• **Transfer** trout to a 15- x 10-inch jelly-roll pan or roasting pan.
• **Bake** at 350° for 8 minutes or until fish flakes with a fork. **Yield:** 8 servings.
Executive Chef John C. Fleer
Blackberry Farm
Walland, Tennessee

TROPHY TROUT

Careful handling of fresh trout is the first step in preparing a great recipe. Here are some tips.

■ Do not keep your catch in wicker creel more than three hours on a warm day.

■ Clean trout quickly and put it in a watertight plastic bag or container to keep trout cool and dry until you reach home.

■ Prepare trout at cleaning time according to the way you'll be cooking it.

■ Freeze trout in a quantity suitable for one meal. Place fish in large container and cover with water; then freeze.

■ Thaw frozen trout under cold running water. Thaw quickly but never at room temperature or in warm water. Do not refreeze.

■ For information on shopping for trout, see "From Our Kitchen to Yours" on page 68.

GREAT GRUB FROM MCGUIRE'S

There are two things you don't expect to find in Irish pubs—a full menu of high-quality food and a comprehensive wine list. But at McGuire's Irish Pub in Pensacola, Florida, you'll get both. McGuire and Molly Martin started the pub in 1977. He did the cooking; she did the singing. Now their son, Jim, a Culinary Institute of America-trained chef, oversees the kitchen. In a celebration of St. Patrick's day, we adapted two of their recipes—a soup and a bread—from *McGuire's Irish Pub Cookbook*.

IRISH POTATO SOUP

Prep: 15 minutes
Cook: 1 hour and 5 minutes

½ cup unsalted butter
1 medium onion, thinly sliced
3 leeks, sliced
3 large baking potatoes, peeled and cut into ¼-inch-thick slices
3 (14½-ounce) cans chicken broth
1 teaspoon salt
¼ teaspoon pepper
Toppings: shredded Cheddar cheese, crumbled cooked bacon, chopped fresh chives

• **Melt** butter in a large saucepan over low heat; stir in onion and leek. Cover and cook 20 minutes. Stir in potato; cover and cook 15 minutes. Stir in broth, salt, and pepper; bring to a boil. Reduce heat, and simmer 30 minutes or until potato is tender. Remove from heat, and cool slightly.
• **Process** soup in batches in a blender until smooth, stopping to scrape down sides; return to saucepan, and cook over medium heat until heated. Serve with desired toppings. **Yield:** 11 cups.
McGuire's Irish Pub Cookbook
(Jessie Tirsch, Pelican Publishing Company, 1998)

ONION-RYE BREAD

Prep: 2 hours and 30 minutes
Bake: 30 minutes

¾ cup minced onion
2 tablespoons vegetable oil,
 divided
½ cup milk
¼ cup water
1¼ cups bread flour, divided
¾ cup rye flour, divided
1 tablespoon sugar
1 teaspoon salt
1 (¼-ounce) envelope active dry
 yeast
1 tablespoon caraway seeds
1 large egg
1 teaspoon water

• **Sauté** onion in 1 tablespoon hot oil in a small skillet over medium-high heat 4 to 5 minutes or until golden. Set aside.
• **Combine** remaining 1 tablespoon oil, milk, and ¼ cup water in a saucepan; heat to 120° to 130°.
• **Stir** together ¾ cup bread flour, ¼ cup rye flour, sugar, salt, and yeast in a large mixing bowl; make a well in center of mixture.
• **Stir** in milk mixture with a wooden spoon. Stir in remaining ½ cup rye flour, onion, and caraway seeds. Gradually stir in enough remaining bread flour to make a stiff dough.
• **Turn** dough out onto a floured surface, and knead until smooth (about 8 minutes). Place in a well-greased bowl, turning to grease top.
• **Cover** and let rise in a warm place (85°), free from drafts, 1 hour or until doubled in bulk.
• **Punch** dough down, and turn out onto a lightly floured surface; let stand 5 minutes. Shape into a loaf, and place in a greased 9- x 5-inch loafpan.
• **Cover** and let rise in a warm place, free from drafts, 45 minutes or until doubled in bulk. Stir together egg and 1 teaspoon water; brush over loaf.
• **Bake** at 375° for 30 minutes or until loaf sounds hollow when tapped. Remove from pan immediately, and cool on a wire rack. **Yield:** 1 loaf.

McGuire's Irish Pub Cookbook
(Jessie Tirsch, Pelican Publishing
Company, 1998)

CELEBRATE SPRING

This menu is perfect for every occasion—
a wedding party, a celebration of spring's arrival, or
a simple outdoor gathering. If you're the host,
you won't be exhausted with last-minute preparations.
Just before serving, drizzle the dressing over the
asparagus and tomatoes.

A SPRING CELEBRATION
Serves Four

Wild Rice-Shrimp Salad
Asparagus and Tomatoes With
Herb Vinaigrette
Orange-Pecan Muffins

WILD RICE-SHRIMP SALAD
(pictured on page 78)

Prep: 40 minutes
Chill: 5 hours

6 cups water
1½ pounds unpeeled, medium-size
 fresh shrimp
1 (6-ounce) package long-grain
 and wild rice mix
1 (7-ounce) jar marinated
 artichoke quarters
4 green onions, sliced
½ cup chopped green bell pepper
12 ripe olives, sliced
1 celery rib, sliced
⅓ cup mayonnaise
¾ teaspoon curry powder
Leaf lettuce

• **Bring** 6 cups water to a boil; add shrimp, and cook 3 to 5 minutes or just until shrimp turn pink. Drain and rinse with cold water.
• **Peel** 16 shrimp, leaving tails on; set aside. Peel remaining shrimp; devein, if desired, and chop.
• **Cook** rice according to package directions. Drain artichokes, reserving 3 tablespoons liquid. Stir together rice, chopped shrimp, artichokes, green onions, and next 3 ingredients.
• **Stir** together reserved artichoke liquid, mayonnaise, and curry powder; toss with rice mixture. Cover and chill 5 hours. Serve on lettuce-lined plates; top each serving with 4 whole shrimp. **Yield:** 4 servings.

Wild Rice-Chicken Salad: Substitute 2 cups chopped cooked chicken for chopped shrimp. Omit whole shrimp.
Celia Alison
Selma, Alabama

ASPARAGUS AND TOMATOES WITH HERB VINAIGRETTE

(pictured on page 78)

Prep: 15 minutes
Cook: 3 minutes
Chill: 3 hours

1 pound fresh asparagus
⅓ cup olive oil
¼ cup red wine vinegar
1 tablespoon chopped fresh
   chives
2 teaspoons dried oregano,
   crushed
¼ teaspoon salt
¼ teaspoon pepper
4 to 6 plum tomatoes, sliced
Garnish: chopped fresh chives

• **Snap** off tough ends of asparagus. Cook in boiling water to cover 3 minutes or until crisp-tender; drain. Plunge asparagus into ice water to stop the cooking process; drain. Cover; chill 3 hours.
• **Whisk** together oil and next 5 ingredients. Drizzle vinaigrette over asparagus and tomato slices; garnish, if desired. **Yield:** 4 servings.

Margaret Best
Vine Grove, Kentucky

ORANGE-PECAN MUFFINS

(pictured on page 78)

Prep: 20 minutes
Bake: 22 minutes

1 (3-ounce) package cream
   cheese, softened
¾ cup sugar
1 large egg
3 cups biscuit mix
1¼ cups orange juice
½ cup chopped pecans, toasted
1 teaspoon grated orange rind

• **Beat** cream cheese at medium speed with an electric mixer until fluffy; gradually add sugar, beating well. Add egg, beating until blended.
• **Add** biscuit mix to cream cheese mixture alternately with orange juice, beginning and ending with biscuit mix and beating after each addition.

• **Stir** in pecans and orange rind. Spoon batter into greased muffin pans, filling two-thirds full.
• **Bake** at 375° for 22 minutes or until muffins are golden. Remove muffins from pans. **Yield:** 20 muffins.

Mary Cunnyngham
Cleveland, Tennessee

SPILLIN' THE BEANS

Both dried and canned black beans are assets to any kitchen pantry. You can tuck dried beans away in an airtight container up to one year. If you substitute canned beans for dried beans, just remember that 1 cup uncooked dried beans equals about 2 (15-ounce) cans beans, drained. Two cups uncooked dried beans yield 6 cups cooked beans.

CUBAN BLACK BEANS

Prep: 20 minutes
Soak: 8 hours
Cook: 1 hour

1 (16-ounce) package dried
   black beans *
1 medium onion, chopped
1 small green bell pepper,
   chopped
3 garlic cloves, pressed
3 tablespoons olive oil
2 quarts water
1 tablespoon white vinegar
1½ teaspoons salt
¼ teaspoon pepper
1 bay leaf
Hot cooked rice
Chopped green onions

• **Place** beans in a Dutch oven; cover with water 2 inches above beans. Soak beans 8 hours. Drain.

• **Sauté** onion, bell pepper, and garlic in hot oil in Dutch oven over medium-high heat until tender.
• **Add** beans, 2 quarts water, and next 4 ingredients; bring to a boil. Cover, reduce heat, and simmer 1 hour or until beans are tender. Discard bay leaf. Serve black bean mixture over hot cooked rice; sprinkle with chopped green onions. **Yield:** 9 cups.

* Substitute 3 (15-ounce) cans black beans, undrained, for dried beans, if desired. Omit 2 quarts water, and reduce simmering time to 15 to 20 minutes.

Dolores Cruz
Pomona Park, Florida

PLEASING PASSOVER

Passover is a time of recounting the ancient Israelites' exodus from Egypt. Family stories, ceremonial foods, synagogue service, and songs are also part of this observance. Enjoy these traditional recipes along with a bit of history.

BROWNIES FOR PASSOVER

½ cup butter or margarine,
   softened
2 cups sugar
4 large eggs
1 cup matzo cake meal
½ cup cocoa
⅓ cup potato starch
¼ teaspoon salt
½ cup water
1 teaspoon vanilla extract
1 cup chopped walnuts
Powdered sugar (optional)

• **Beat** butter at medium speed with an electric mixer until creamy; gradually

add sugar, beating well. Add eggs, 1 at a time, beating until blended after each addition. Add matzo cake meal and next 6 ingredients; stir well.
- **Spoon** batter into a greased 13- x 9-inch baking dish.
- **Bake** at 350° for 30 to 35 minutes or until a wooden pick inserted in center comes out clean. Cool on a wire rack; cut into squares. Sprinkle with powdered sugar, if desired. **Yield:** 2 dozen.

SOLUTIONS FOR YESTERDAY AND TODAY

Worried about what to put on the table tonight?
Follow the lead of two of our readers, and prepare casseroles.
These recipes are time-tested family pleasers.

MANDEL BREAD

Mandel bread, or mandelbrot, is a crisp cookie similar in texture to biscotti.

4 large eggs
1½ cups sugar, divided
½ cup vegetable oil
1 tablespoon grated lemon rind
1 tablespoon fresh lemon juice
¼ teaspoon almond extract
½ cup potato starch
½ cup matzo cake meal
½ teaspoon salt
½ cup chopped walnuts
1 tablespoon ground cinnamon

- **Beat** together eggs and 1 cup sugar at medium speed with an electric mixer until blended.
- **Combine** oil and next 3 ingredients; gradually add to egg mixture, beating until fluffy.
- **Stir** together potato starch, cake meal, and salt; fold into egg mixture. Stir in walnuts, and pour batter into 2 greased and floured 9- x 5-inch loafpans.
- **Bake** at 350° for 25 minutes or until a wooden pick inserted in center comes out clean. (Loaves will be about 1 inch thick.) Cool in pans on wire racks 10 minutes; remove from pans, and cool completely on wire racks.
- **Stir** together remaining ½ cup sugar and cinnamon; set aside.
- **Cut** each loaf into ½-inch-thick slices; place slices on an ungreased baking sheet. Sprinkle with cinnamon mixture.
- **Bake** at 325° for 35 minutes or until golden and crisp. **Yield:** 2 dozen.

In the '70s, Juanita McMillon's dinners consisted of casseroles, earning her the title of "Casserole Queen" from her teenage children. With ground chuck and noodles on hand, a variety of casseroles were oven-ready in 40 minutes. Turn the page to find two of her favorites.

Today's timesaving ingredients allow Cecelia Shepherd of South Carolina to prepare a Tex-Mex dinner before her daughter finishes watching her favorite show. These enchiladas and beans are ready for baking in just 20 minutes.

ENTICING ENCHILADAS
(pictured on page 39)

Prep: 20 minutes
Bake: 20 minutes

1 pound ground chuck
1 small onion, chopped
1 cup cream-style cottage cheese
1 (10-ounce) can diced tomatoes and green chiles, undrained
1 (8-ounce) can tomato sauce
1 (4.5-ounce) can chopped green chiles (optional)
10 (6-inch) flour tortillas
2 cups (8 ounces) shredded Mexican cheese blend
Garnish: chopped fresh parsley

- **Cook** beef and onion in a large skillet over high heat, stirring until beef crumbles and is no longer pink; drain. Return to skillet; stir in cottage cheese. Set aside.
- **Process** diced tomatoes and tomato sauce in a food processor until smooth, stopping to scrape down sides. Stir in chopped chiles, if desired.
- **Spoon** 2 to 3 tablespoons beef mixture down the center of each tortilla; top each with 2 tablespoons tomato mixture and 1½ tablespoons shredded cheese.
- **Roll** up tortillas, and place, seam side down, in a lightly greased 13- x 9-inch baking dish. Pour remaining tomato mixture over top; sprinkle with remaining shredded cheese. Bake at 350° for 20 minutes or until bubbly. Garnish, if desired. **Yield:** 4 to 6 servings.
Cecelia Shepherd
Mount Pleasant, South Carolina

EASY REFRIED BEANS

Prep: 5 minutes
Bake: 20 minutes

1 (10-ounce) can diced tomatoes and green chiles, undrained
2 (16-ounce) cans refried beans
1 (1¼-ounce) envelope taco seasoning mix
1 cup (4 ounces) shredded Mexican cheese blend
Garnish: fresh parsley sprig

- **Stir** together first 3 ingredients; spoon into a lightly greased 2-quart baking dish. Sprinkle with cheese. Bake at 350° for 20 minutes or until thoroughly heated. Garnish, if desired. **Yield:** 4 to 6 servings.
Cecelia Shepherd
Mount Pleasant, South Carolina

BEEF, CHEESE, AND NOODLE CASSEROLE

Prep: 40 minutes
Bake: 30 minutes

6   ounces wide egg noodles, cooked
6   green onions, chopped
2   pounds ground chuck
1   (14½-ounce) can diced tomatoes
1   (15-ounce) can tomato sauce
1   teaspoon sugar
1   teaspoon salt
¼   teaspoon garlic salt
½   teaspoon pepper
1   (16-ounce) loaf process cheese spread
1   (8-ounce) container sour cream
1   (8-ounce) package cream cheese, softened

• **Stir** together egg noodles and green onions; set aside.
• **Cook** ground beef in a large skillet over medium heat, stirring until it crumbles and is no longer pink; drain and return to skillet. Stir in diced tomatoes and next 5 ingredients.
• **Cut** cheese spread into ½-inch cubes; reserve 1 cup. Stir together remaining cheese spread, sour cream, and softened cream cheese.
• **Spoon** one-third of ground beef mixture into a 13- x 9-inch baking dish; top with half of noodle mixture and half of sour cream mixture. Repeat layers once.
• **Spoon** remaining one-third of ground beef mixture over sour cream mixture, and sprinkle evenly with reserved 1 cup cubed cheese.
• **Bake** at 350° for 30 minutes or until cheese is melted and bubbly. **Yield:** 6 to 8 servings.

Juanita F. McMillon
DeKalb, Texas

HAMBURGER-CORN BAKE

Prep: 40 minutes
Bake: 45 minutes

1½   pounds ground chuck
1   large onion, chopped
6   ounces medium egg noodles, cooked
1   (10¾-ounce) can cream of chicken soup, undiluted
1   (10¾-ounce) can cream of mushroom soup, undiluted
1   (15¼-ounce) can whole kernel corn, drained
1   (2-ounce) jar diced pimiento, drained
1   (8-ounce) container sour cream
1   cup fine, dry breadcrumbs
2   tablespoons butter or margarine, cut up

• **Cook** beef and onion in a large skillet over medium heat, stirring until ground beef crumbles and is no longer pink; drain. Return beef mixture to skillet; stir in noodles and next 5 ingredients.
• **Spoon** into a lightly greased 13- x 9-inch baking dish. Sprinkle with breadcrumbs, and dot with butter. Bake at 350° for 45 minutes or until breadcrumb topping is golden. **Yield:** 8 servings.

Juanita F. McMillon
DeKalb, Texas

BRINGING HOME THE BEEF

■ Wash hands right before and after working with uncooked beef.

■ Refrigerate uncooked ground beef up to two days, or freeze in the original packaging up to two weeks.

■ For longer storage, wrap in aluminum foil, plastic wrap, or freezer paper; freeze up to four months.

■ Thaw ground beef in the refrigerator, and never refreeze uncooked ground beef.

ON YOUR SIDE

Side dishes don't have to have minor roles in meals—fresh ideas can make them standouts. Impress your family and friends by serving any of these with roast chicken, steaks, or chops.

MUSHROOM BREAD PUDDING

Prep: 15 minutes
Chill: 8 hours
Bake: 45 minutes

2   tablespoons unsalted butter
2   tablespoons olive oil
3½   cups (10 ounces) sliced shiitake mushrooms
1   small onion, chopped
2   garlic cloves, minced
1   teaspoon ground black pepper
½   teaspoon dried thyme
1   (16-ounce) Italian bread loaf
2   large eggs
2   cups milk
1   teaspoon salt
⅛   teaspoon ground red pepper
2   tablespoons grated Parmesan cheese

• **Melt** butter with oil in a large skillet over medium-high heat; add mushrooms, and sauté 2 minutes. Add onion and next 3 ingredients, and sauté 5 minutes or until onion is tender.
• **Remove** crust from bread loaf. Cut loaf into 1-inch cubes.
• **Place** half of bread cubes in a lightly greased 2-quart baking dish; top with mushroom mixture. Cover with remaining bread cubes.
• **Whisk** together eggs, milk, and salt; pour over bread. Cover and chill 8 hours.
• **Sprinkle** bread pudding mixture with ground red pepper and cheese.
• **Bake** at 350° for 45 minutes or until set. **Yield:** 6 servings.

Ellen Burr
Truro, Massachusetts

CAULIFLOWER AU GRATIN

Prep: 22 minutes
Bake: 1 hour

1 head cauliflower, cut into
   flowerets
1 teaspoon salt, divided
¼ cup butter or margarine, melted
24 saltine crackers, crushed
1 tablespoon sugar
½ teaspoon pepper
½ cup diced green bell pepper
1 (14½-ounce) can diced tomatoes
1 medium onion, chopped
1½ cups (6 ounces) shredded
   sharp Cheddar cheese, divided

• **Cook** cauliflower in boiling water to cover with ½ teaspoon salt 5 minutes; drain.
• **Combine** remaining ½ teaspoon salt, butter, and next 3 ingredients; stir in cauliflower, diced bell pepper, tomatoes, onion, and 1¼ cups cheese. Spoon into a lightly greased 2-quart baking dish. Sprinkle with remaining cheese.
• **Bake** at 350° for 1 hour. Serve immediately. **Yield:** 6 servings.

Clairiece Gilbert Humphrey
Charlottesville, Virginia

TOMATO-FETA GREEN BEANS

Tomato, lemon juice, olive oil, feta, and pine nuts give these beans a Greek twist.

Prep: 10 minutes
Bake: 8 minutes
Cook: 10 minutes

¼ cup pine nuts *
2 (16-ounce) packages frozen
   French-style green beans,
   thawed
2 garlic cloves, minced
2 teaspoons dried Italian
   seasoning
1 tablespoon olive oil
4 plum tomatoes, chopped
2 tablespoons lemon juice
1 teaspoon salt
½ teaspoon pepper
1 (4-ounce) package crumbled
   feta cheese

• **Bake** pine nuts in a shallow pan at 350° for 6 to 8 minutes or until toasted. Set aside.
• **Drain** green beans well, pressing between layers of paper towels to remove excess moisture.
• **Sauté** garlic and Italian seasoning in hot oil in a large skillet over medium heat 1 minute; add green beans, and sauté 5 to 7 minutes.
• **Stir** in tomato, and cook, stirring constantly, 2 minutes or until thoroughly heated. Stir in lemon juice, salt, and pepper. Sprinkle with cheese and pine nuts. **Yield:** 6 servings.

* Substitute ¼ cup chopped toasted walnuts for pine nuts, if desired.

Penny Nichols
Baton Rouge, Louisiana

ZESTY FRIES

French fries are fine one by one, but they're better eaten by the handful. When cut from knobby, brown-skinned potatoes, home fries sizzle to a golden color with or without their peels. For crispier fries, slice the potatoes early, cover with cool water, and chill several hours. Drain well, and blot moisture before frying.

FRENCH FRIES

Our editor's wife, Pam Floyd, places a peeled onion in the cooking oil for flavor.

Prep: 15 minutes
Cook: 36 minutes

4 pounds Idaho potatoes
Vegetable oil
Salt

• **Cut** potatoes into ½-inch-wide strips. Pour vegetable oil to a depth of 4 inches in a Dutch oven, and heat to 375°. Fry potato strips in small batches in hot oil 12 minutes or until golden. Drain on paper towels. Sprinkle with salt to taste. **Yield:** 8 to 10 servings.

Crinkle-Cut Fries: Cut potatoes into ½-inch-wide strips using a waffle cutter. Fry as directed.

Waffle Chips: Cut potatoes into ¼-inch-thick slices using a waffle cutter. Fry 10 to 12 minutes.

Note: For testing purposes only, we used Wesson vegetable oil.

Pam Floyd
Trussville, Alabama

SHAKE AND DIP 'EM

Season fries while they are hot from the pot. Open the spice cabinet, use your imagination, and shake. If salt and ketchup are your usual fry sides, try one of these new seasoning or topping combinations. Whatever shape your French fries, try these inventive flavor accents.

■ Thousand Island dressing with
   horseradish

■ Hickory salt with barbecue sauce

■ Popcorn salt with cheese spread

■ Cajun seasoning with ketchup
   and hot pepper sauce

FOUR MEALS MADE EASY

Our menus for four feature carefully chosen ingredients to stretch your budget and save time. Total cost per person for each meal was less than $4.50 with groceries purchased at our local supermarkets. If you shop for sales, you might reduce the cost even further.

MONDAY'S MENU
Serves Four

Chicken-Vegetable Soup
Garlic Crisps
Coleslaw

Timetable: Prepare soup and crisps.
Toss coleslaw with dressing.

CHICKEN-VEGETABLE SOUP

Prep: 15 minutes
Cook: 38 minutes

4 cups chicken broth
1 (28-ounce) can crushed
    tomatoes, undrained
1 (16-ounce) can diced tomatoes,
    undrained
1 (10-ounce) can diced tomatoes
    and green chiles, undrained
1 small onion, chopped
3 small carrots, sliced
3 celery ribs, sliced
1 garlic clove, minced
3 to 4 cups chopped cooked
    chicken
1 small zucchini, diced
2 teaspoons sugar
½ teaspoon salt
½ teaspoon pepper
4 chicken bouillon cubes
2 tablespoons all-purpose flour
¼ cup water

• **Bring** first 8 ingredients to a boil in a Dutch oven; cover, reduce heat, and simmer 30 minutes. Stir in chicken and next 5 ingredients.
• **Stir** together flour and ¼ cup water until smooth. Stir into chicken mixture; bring to a boil. Cover, reduce heat, and simmer, stirring often, 6 to 8 minutes or until thickened. **Yield:** 12 cups.

GARLIC CRISPS

Prep: 4 minutes
Bake: 12 minutes

4 (8-inch) flour tortillas
Butter-flavored vegetable cooking
    spray
1 teaspoon garlic salt

• **Cut** tortillas into quarters. Coat with cooking spray; sprinkle with garlic salt. Place tortilla quarters on an ungreased baking sheet.
• **Bake** at 350° for 12 minutes or until golden. Cool. Store in an airtight container. **Yield:** 16 crisps.

TUESDAY'S MENU
Serves Four

Eye of Round Roast
Roasted Potatoes
Zucchini-Carrot Casserole

Timetable: Bake roast; add potatoes
after 20 minutes. Prepare casserole.

EYE OF ROUND ROAST
(pictured on page 37)

Prep: 15 minutes
Chill: 8 hours
Bake: 45 minutes

1 (4½-pound) eye of round roast
1 (4-ounce) jar Chinese sweet-hot
    mustard
3 tablespoons olive oil
2 garlic cloves, pressed
2 teaspoons lite soy sauce
1 teaspoon Worcestershire sauce
Roasted Potatoes, uncooked

• **Place** roast on an 18- x 11-inch piece of heavy-duty aluminum foil. Combine mustard and next 4 ingredients; spread over roast. Fold foil over roast to seal. Place in a shallow roasting pan; chill 8 hours.
• **Remove** roast from foil; place in roasting pan. Cover; bake at 450° for 20 minutes. Arrange potatoes around roast. Bake, uncovered, 25 minutes or until potatoes are tender and a meat thermometer inserted into roast registers 145°. Cover. Let stand 15 minutes; slice. (Chop and chill 2 cups roast for Beef Hash in Thursday's menu.) **Yield:** 4 servings.

Roasted Potatoes

4 potatoes, each cut into 8 wedges
2 tablespoons olive oil
2 garlic cloves, pressed
1 teaspoon salt
½ teaspoon pepper

• **Toss** together all ingredients. Bake as directed. **Yield:** 4 servings.

Pam R. Gorham
Naples, Florida

ZUCCHINI-CARROT CASSEROLE

Prep: 15 minutes
Bake: 20 minutes

2 tablespoons butter or margarine
2 medium zucchini, sliced
2 carrots, sliced
1 small onion, chopped
1 (8-ounce) container sour cream
1 cup (4 ounces) shredded
    Cheddar cheese
½ teaspoon salt
½ teaspoon pepper
2 tablespoons Italian-seasoned
    breadcrumbs

• **Melt** butter in a skillet over medium heat; add zucchini, carrot, and onion. Sauté 8 to 10 minutes or until tender. Remove from heat; stir in sour cream and next 3 ingredients.
• **Spoon** into a lightly greased 1-quart baking dish. Sprinkle with breadcrumbs.
• **Bake** at 350° for 20 minutes or until heated. **Yield:** 4 servings.

Agnes L. Stone
Ocala, Florida

HERE'S THE PLAN

Organize your time each day with a few simple steps. Turn the page to find a complete grocery list for the week's menus.

Monday: Quarter chickens, and cook in boiling water to cover 25 minutes; chop chicken, reserving broth. Set aside half of chopped chicken for Wednesday's menu. Set aside 6 flour tortillas for Thursday's menu. Marinate Eye of Round Roast for baking on Tuesday.

Tuesday: Bake roast; reserve 2 cups chopped roast for Thursday's menu.

Wednesday: Reserve half of the French bread for Thursday's menu.

WEDNESDAY'S MENU
Serves Four

Chicken Tetrazzini
Green Salad and Dressing
Parmesan Cheese Bread

Timetable: Bake tetrazzini and cheese bread. Chop 3 plum tomatoes, and slice 2 carrots; add to salad greens. Serve with dressing.

CHICKEN TETRAZZINI

Prep: 35 minutes
Bake: 25 minutes

3 tablespoons butter or
    margarine
1 medium onion, chopped
1 green bell pepper,
    chopped
1 garlic clove, pressed
3 tablespoons all-purpose
    flour
2 cups milk
7 ounces spaghetti, cooked
3 cups chopped cooked
    chicken
1 cup (4 ounces) shredded
    Cheddar cheese, divided
1 (10¾-ounce) can cream
    of mushroom soup,
    undiluted
¼ cup dry white wine
1 (4-ounce) can sliced
    mushrooms, drained
1 (2-ounce) jar diced pimiento,
    drained
½ cup grated Parmesan
    cheese
2 tablespoons chopped fresh
    parsley
1 teaspoon salt
½ teaspoon pepper

• **Melt** butter in a large skillet over medium heat; add onion, bell pepper, and garlic. Sauté until tender.
• **Stir** in flour; cook, stirring constantly, 1 minute. Gradually stir in milk; cook over medium heat, stirring constantly, until thickened and bubbly.
• **Stir** in pasta, chicken, ¾ cup Cheddar cheese, and next 8 ingredients. Spoon mixture into a lightly greased shallow 2-quart baking dish.
• **Bake** at 350° for 20 minutes; sprinkle with remaining ¼ cup Cheddar cheese, and bake 5 more minutes. **Yield:** 4 to 6 servings.

Note: To make ahead, cover and chill. Let stand 30 minutes; uncover and bake 35 minutes or until casserole is thoroughly heated.

Millie Ebel
Louisville, Kentucky

PARMESAN CHEESE BREAD

Prep: 5 minutes
Bake: 10 minutes

1 (16-ounce) French bread
    loaf
1 garlic clove, halved
3 tablespoons olive oil
¼ cup grated Parmesan
    cheese

• **Split** bread loaf horizontally; reserve top half for Thursday's menu.
• **Rub** cut side of bottom half of bread with garlic, and place bread on a baking sheet. Brush with oil, and sprinkle with Parmesan cheese.
• **Bake** at 350° for 10 minutes or until toasted; cut into 2-inch slices. **Yield:** 4 servings.

Marie A. Davis
Charlotte, North Carolina

GROCERY LIST

STAPLES ON HAND
Lite soy sauce
Worcestershire sauce
Olive oil
Vegetable oil
Butter or margarine
Italian-seasoned breadcrumbs
All-purpose flour
Sugar
Brown sugar
Chicken bouillon cubes
Beef bouillon cubes
Garlic cloves
Cornstarch
Dry white wine
Grated Parmesan cheese
Butter-flavored vegetable
    cooking spray
Salt and pepper
Garlic salt
Ground cinnamon

PRODUCE
4 pounds medium potatoes
2 medium onions
2 small onions
1 bunch fresh parsley
2 (1-pound) packages carrots
1 bunch celery
1 (16-ounce) package mixed salad
    greens
3 zucchini
1 green bell pepper
3 plum tomatoes
Coleslaw mix

GENERAL
1 (4-ounce) jar Chinese sweet-hot
    mustard
1 (16-ounce) French bread
    loaf
1 (13.5-ounce) package 8-inch flour
    tortillas
1 (8-ounce) jar honey
1 (2-ounce) jar diced pimiento
1 (4-ounce) can sliced mushrooms
1 (10¾-ounce) can cream of
    mushroom soup
1 (16-ounce) can diced tomatoes
1 (28-ounce) can crushed tomatoes
1 (10-ounce) can diced tomatoes
    and green chiles
1 (21-ounce) can apple fruit filling
1 (7-ounce) package spaghetti
Salad dressing
Coleslaw dressing
1 pint orange juice

DAIRY
1 pint milk
1 (8-ounce) container sour cream
1 (8-ounce) package shredded
    Cheddar cheese

MEAT
4- to 6-pound eye of round roast
2 (2½- to 3-pound) whole
    chickens

THURSDAY'S MENU
Serves Four

Beef Hash
Honey-Glazed Carrots
Buttered French Bread
Apple Enchiladas

Timetable: Prepare enchiladas. Prepare hash and carrots. Slice and butter reserved French bread; bake with enchiladas.

BEEF HASH

Prep: 10 minutes
Cook: 30 minutes

1   cup hot water
1   beef bouillon cube
3   medium potatoes, peeled and
      cubed (1½ pounds)
1   medium onion, chopped
1   garlic clove, minced
2   tablespoons vegetable oil
2   cups chopped cooked eye of
      round roast
½   teaspoon salt
1   teaspoon pepper
2   tablespoons chopped fresh
      parsley (optional)

• **Stir** together 1 cup hot water and beef bouillon cube until cube dissolves.
• **Sauté** potato, onion, and garlic in hot oil in a large skillet over medium-high heat 10 minutes.
• **Add** beef to skillet; cover, reduce heat, and cook, stirring occasionally, 15 minutes or until potato is tender.
• **Stir** in bouillon mixture, salt, pepper, and, if desired, parsley; cover and simmer 5 minutes. **Yield:** 4 servings.

Suzan L. Weiner
Spring Hill, Florida

HONEY-GLAZED CARROTS

Prep: 10 minutes
Cook: 16 minutes

1 pound carrots, cut into 1-inch
   pieces
1 cup boiling water
¼ teaspoon salt
½ cup orange juice
2 teaspoons cornstarch
2 tablespoons butter or margarine
2 tablespoons honey

• **Cook** carrot pieces in 1 cup boiling
water with salt in a medium saucepan
10 minutes or until tender; drain carrot,
and place in a serving bowl.
• **Stir** together orange juice and cornstarch in a small saucepan until smooth.
• **Stir** in butter and honey; cook over
medium heat, stirring constantly, 4 minutes or until thickened. Pour over carrot, and toss to coat. **Yield:** 4 servings.
Carrie Treichel
Johnson City, Tennessee

APPLE ENCHILADAS

Prep: 45 minutes
Bake: 20 minutes

1 (21-ounce) can apple fruit
   filling
6 (8-inch) flour tortillas
1 teaspoon ground cinnamon
⅓ cup butter or margarine
½ cup sugar
½ cup firmly packed light brown
   sugar
½ cup water

• **Spoon** fruit filling evenly down centers of tortillas; sprinkle with cinnamon.
Roll up, and place, seam side down, in a
lightly greased 2-quart baking dish.
• **Bring** butter and next 3 ingredients to
a boil in a medium saucepan; reduce
heat, and simmer, stirring constantly, 3
minutes. Pour over enchiladas; let stand
30 minutes.
• **Bake** at 350° for 20 minutes. **Yield:** 4
to 6 servings.
Gayle Millican
Rowlett, Texas

THE LIGHT STUFF

*Stuffing isn't just for the holiday turkey anymore.
Add dimension to meats and vegetables with these innovative
mixtures. We've expanded the idea to include sides and
main dishes. Most recipe preparation times are under
40 minutes. Combine pantry staples with a few fresh
ingredients to create these impressive dishes.*

CARROT-AND-CABBAGE STUFFED PEPPERS
(pictured on page 75)

*These stuffed peppers are as flavorful
as they are colorful.*

Prep: 20 minutes

3 red, green, or yellow bell peppers
3 tablespoons olive oil
3 tablespoons cider vinegar
1½ teaspoons sugar
1 teaspoon Herb Seasoning
1 (10-ounce) bag shredded
   cabbage
3 carrots, shredded
1 small sweet onion, diced
1 teaspoon poppy seeds
Garnish: fresh basil sprigs

• **Cut** bell peppers in half lengthwise;
remove seeds.
• **Whisk** olive oil and next 3 ingredients
in a large bowl; add cabbage and next 3
ingredients, and toss. Spoon mixture into
pepper halves. Garnish, if desired. **Yield:**
6 servings.

♥ Per serving: Calories 113
Fat 7.3g Cholesterol 0mg
Sodium 23mg

Herb Seasoning

1 tablespoon garlic powder
1 tablespoon onion powder
1 tablespoon dried basil
1 tablespoon dried marjoram
1 tablespoon dried thyme
1 tablespoon dried parsley flakes
1 tablespoon dried savory
1 tablespoon ground mace
1 tablespoon freshly ground black
   pepper
1 tablespoon ground sage
½ teaspoon ground red pepper

• **Stir** together all ingredients. Freeze
mixture in an airtight container up to 6
months. **Yield:** ⅓ cup.
Hilda Marshall
Culpeper, Virginia

SPINACH-STUFFED SHELLS

(pictured on page 75)

*Serve these shells with a tossed
salad, fat-free dressing, and breadsticks
for a complete meal.*

*Prep: 40 minutes
Bake: 30 minutes*

2 (10-ounce) packages frozen
    chopped spinach, thawed
1 pound extra-lean ground
    beef
¼ teaspoon ground nutmeg
½ teaspoon salt, divided
½ teaspoon pepper, divided
1 (16-ounce) jar marinara
    sauce
1 (16-ounce) container 1%
    low-fat cottage cheese
1 large egg, lightly beaten
¼ cup grated Parmesan cheese
18 jumbo shells, cooked

• **Drain** spinach well, pressing between
layers of paper towels. Set aside.
• **Cook** beef in a large skillet, stirring
until it crumbles and is no longer pink.
Drain and pat dry with paper towels.
Wipe pan drippings from skillet with a
paper towel.
• **Return** beef to skillet; stir in nutmeg,
¼ teaspoon salt, ¼ teaspoon pepper,
and marinara sauce. Set aside.
• **Stir** together spinach, cottage cheese,
egg, Parmesan cheese, remaining ¼ teaspoon salt, and remaining ¼ teaspoon
pepper. Spoon evenly into shells.
• **Spread** half of sauce mixture in a
lightly greased 13- x 9-inch baking dish.
Arrange shells over sauce; pour remaining sauce over shells.
• **Bake,** covered, at 350° for 30 minutes.
Yield: 6 servings.

Note: Freeze shells and sauce before
baking, if desired. To bake, thaw in refrigerator overnight. Let stand at room
temperature 30 minutes. Bake as directed above.

*Regina Esslinger
Hunt Valley, Maryland*

❤ Per serving: Calories 450
Fat 14.4g Cholesterol 83mg
Sodium 802mg

HAWAIIAN STUFFED CHICKEN BREASTS

*Prep: 35 minutes
Bake: 30 minutes*

1 (8¼-ounce) can crushed
    pineapple
6 skinned and boned chicken
    breast halves
2 tablespoons margarine
½ medium-size green bell
    pepper, chopped
½ medium-size red bell pepper,
    chopped
⅔ cup hot water
1 (6-ounce) package chicken-
    flavored stuffing mix
2 tablespoons brown sugar
2 tablespoons white vinegar
1 tablespoon grated fresh
    ginger

• **Drain** pineapple, reserving juice. Set
aside.
• **Place** chicken between 2 sheets of
heavy-duty plastic wrap, and flatten to
¼-inch thickness using a meat mallet or
rolling pin.
• **Melt** margarine in a large nonstick
skillet over medium-high heat; add
chopped bell peppers, and sauté 5 minutes or until tender.
• **Stir** in ⅔ cup hot water and seasoning
packet from stuffing mix. Stir in stuffing
mix and pineapple.
• **Spoon** about ½ cup stuffing mixture
onto each chicken breast; roll up, securing with wooden picks, and place in a
lightly greased 11- x 7-inch baking dish.
• **Stir** together reserved pineapple juice,
brown sugar, vinegar, and ginger; drizzle
evenly over chicken.
• **Bake** at 400° for 25 to 30 minutes or
until chicken is done. **Yield:** 6 servings.

*Vikki D. Sturm
Rossville, Georgia*

❤ Per serving: Calories 311
Fat 6.3g Cholesterol 67mg
Sodium 552mg

STUFFED ARTICHOKES

*Prep: 20 minutes
Cook: 30 minutes*

4 large artichokes
Lemon wedges
½ cup grated Parmesan
    cheese
¼ cup Italian-seasoned
    breadcrumbs
2 garlic cloves, pressed
½ teaspoon coarsely ground
    pepper
4 teaspoons olive oil
4 celery ribs, halved
4 carrots, halved

• **Cut** off stem ends so that artichokes
will sit upright. Trim about ½ inch from
artichoke tops. With scissors, trim away
one-fourth of each outer leaf. Rub leaf
edges with lemon. Spread leaves gently
to reach center; snip around fuzzy this-
tle (choke), and remove with a spoon.
• **Stir** together cheese and next 3 ingredients; spoon evenly between artichoke
leaves. Drizzle evenly with oil.
• **Place** celery and carrot in bottom of a
Dutch oven. Pour in water to a depth of
1 inch. Arrange artichokes over vegetables. Bring to a boil over medium heat.
Cover, reduce heat, and simmer 30 minutes. Discard celery and carrot. **Yield:** 4
servings.

*Gwen Louer
Roswell, Georgia*

❤ Per serving: Calories 160
Fat 5.7g Cholesterol 8mg
Sodium 485mg

Stand-up Starters

Master this selection of delicious appetizers, and discover their versatility. Prepare several dips—including Pizza Dip, Beef-and-Spinach Dip, and Monterey Shrimp Dip—and offer your favorite tortilla chips for the start of a great cocktail party. Or choose any of them to brighten and extend an everyday meal with your family.

PIZZA DIP

Prep: 15 minutes
Bake: 20 minutes

1 (8-ounce) package light
    cream cheese, softened
½ cup light sour cream
¼ teaspoon dried oregano
¼ teaspoon garlic powder
¼ teaspoon ground red
    pepper
¾ cup pizza sauce
½ cup chopped pepperoni
¼ cup chopped green
    onions
1 cup (4 ounces) shredded
    mozzarella cheese
Tortilla chips

• **Beat** first 5 ingredients at medium speed with an electric mixer until well blended; spread in a lightly greased 9-inch pieplate.
• **Spoon** pizza sauce evenly over cream cheese mixture; sprinkle with pepperoni, and top with green onions.
• **Bake** at 350° for 10 minutes. Sprinkle dip with mozzarella cheese, and bake 10 more minutes or until mozzarella cheese melts. Serve with tortilla chips.
Yield: 4 servings.

Angela Randle
Cordova, Tennessee

BEEF-AND-SPINACH DIP

Prep: 10 minutes
Cook: 20 minutes

1 pound lean ground beef
1 small onion, chopped
1 (8-ounce) package cream
    cheese, softened
2 (9-ounce) packages frozen
    creamed spinach, thawed
1 to 1½ teaspoons hot sauce
¼ teaspoon ground nutmeg
⅓ cup refrigerated shredded
    Parmesan cheese
Tortilla chips

• **Cook** ground beef and onion in a large skillet, stirring until beef crumbles and is no longer pink; drain beef mixture, and return to skillet.
• **Stir** in softened cream cheese and next 3 ingredients, and cook mixture over low heat, stirring often, until cream cheese melts.
• **Sprinkle** dip with shredded Parmesan cheese, and serve with tortilla chips.
Yield: 4 cups.

MONTEREY SHRIMP DIP

Prep: 10 minutes
Cook: 3 minutes

1 (8-ounce) package Monterey
    Jack cheese with peppers,
    shredded
2 (4-ounce) cans shrimp,
    drained
1 (2¼-ounce) can sliced ripe
    olives, drained
¾ cup mayonnaise
¼ cup chopped green onions
Tortilla chips

• **Stir** together first 5 ingredients in a 1-quart microwave-safe dish.
• **Microwave** at HIGH 3 minutes or until cheese melts, stirring after each minute. Serve immediately with tortilla chips.
Yield: 3¼ cups.

Debra Newlin
Pensacola, Florida

PARMESAN-BACON STICKS

Prep: 15 minutes
Bake: 1 hour

15 bacon slices, cut in half
    lengthwise (about 1 pound)
1 (3-ounce) package thin
    breadsticks (30 breadsticks)
½ to ⅔ cup grated Parmesan
    cheese

• **Wrap** bacon around breadsticks; roll in Parmesan cheese, and place on baking sheets.
• **Bake** at 250° for 1 hour. Serve immediately. **Yield:** 2½ dozen.

Note: For testing purposes only, we used Alessi Thin Breadsticks.

Tracy K. Morgan
Knoxville, Tennessee

LOOK WHAT'S BREWING

Savoring the robust taste and aroma of coffee is a morning ritual. When used in desserts, coffee heightens flavors. Make these treats ahead to let the flavors mellow before serving.

MOCHA TORTE

Prep: 25 minutes
Bake: 18 minutes

1¼ cups water
¼ cup instant coffee granules, divided
1 (18.25-ounce) package devil's food cake mix with pudding
1 cup butter or margarine, softened
2 cups powdered sugar
2 tablespoons cocoa
2 tablespoons whipping cream
¼ cup coffee liqueur (optional)
Mocha Frosting

• **Stir** together 1¼ cups water and 2 tablespoons instant coffee granules until dissolved.
• **Prepare** cake mix according to package directions, substituting coffee mixture for water.
• **Pour** batter into 3 greased and floured 8-inch round cakepans.
• **Bake** at 350° for 18 minutes or until a wooden pick inserted in center comes out clean. Cool in pans on wire racks 10 to 15 minutes; remove from pans, and cool completely on wire racks.
• **Beat** butter at medium speed with an electric mixer until creamy; gradually add powdered sugar, beating at low speed until blended.
• **Add** remaining 2 tablespoons coffee granules, cocoa, and whipping cream, beating until blended.
• **Brush** cake layers evenly with coffee liqueur, if desired.
• **Spread** cocoa mixture between cake layers. Spread Mocha Frosting on top and sides of cake. **Yield:** 1 (3-layer) cake.

Mocha Frosting

Prep: 10 minutes

3 cups powdered sugar
¼ cup cocoa
2 tablespoons instant coffee granules
½ cup butter or margarine, softened
1 tablespoon vanilla extract
1 tablespoon coffee liqueur *

• **Stir** together first 3 ingredients.
• **Beat** butter at medium speed with an electric mixer until creamy; gradually add powdered sugar mixture, beating until spreading consistency. Stir in vanilla and coffee liqueur. **Yield:** 3 cups.

* Substitute 1 tablespoon whipping cream for liqueur, if desired.

COFFEE BUTTONS

Prep: 30 minutes
Freeze: 30 minutes

2 tablespoons instant coffee granules
½ cup butter or margarine, softened
3 cups powdered sugar, divided
2 to 3 tablespoons coffee liqueur
Powdered sugar
8 (2-ounce) vanilla candy coating squares
2 (2-ounce) chocolate candy coating squares

• **Crush** instant coffee granules with back of a spoon or with a mortar and pestle to make coffee powder.
• **Beat** butter at medium speed with an electric mixer until creamy; gradually add 1½ cups powdered sugar, beating until smooth.
• **Add** 2 tablespoons liqueur and coffee powder; beat until blended. Add remaining 1½ cups powdered sugar, beating at low speed until blended. Shape mixture into 1-inch balls; roll in powdered sugar. Place on a baking sheet. Flatten to ¼-inch thickness; freeze at least 30 minutes.
• **Melt** vanilla candy coating in a saucepan over low heat; remove from heat. Place coffee rounds on tines of a fork; dip rounds in coating, letting excess drip. Return to baking sheet, and let stand 25 minutes.
• **Place** chocolate coating in a heavy-duty zip-top plastic bag; seal. Submerge in hot water until chocolate melts.
• **Snip** a tiny hole in 1 corner of bag; drizzle chocolate over rounds. Let stand 10 minutes. Store in an airtight container or freeze up to 3 weeks. **Yield:** 2½ dozen.

Tamy White
Hartwell, Georgia

COFFEE TART

Prep: 35 minutes
Cook: 8 minutes
Chill: 2 hours

½ cup slivered almonds,
    toasted
20 chocolate wafer cookies
1 cup sugar, divided
⅓ cup butter or margarine,
    melted
½ cup butter or margarine
2 tablespoons instant coffee
    granules
3 (4-ounce) bittersweet
    chocolate bars, coarsely
    chopped
6 egg yolks
2 cups whipping cream
Garnishes: chocolate-covered
    coffee beans, whipped
    cream

• **Process** almonds, cookies, and ¼ cup sugar in a food processor until ground; stir in ⅓ cup melted butter. Press into a 10-inch tart pan.
• **Bake** at 350° for 10 minutes. Cool completely on a wire rack.
• **Cook** remaining ¾ cup sugar, ½ cup butter, coffee granules, and chocolate in a heavy saucepan over low heat, stirring constantly, until smooth.
• **Beat** egg yolks until thick and pale. Gradually stir about one-fourth of hot chocolate mixture into yolks; add to remaining hot mixture, stirring constantly. Cook over medium heat, stirring constantly, 1 to 2 minutes or until mixture reaches 160°. Remove from heat. (Mixture will be very thick.)
• **Spread** two-thirds of chocolate mixture into crust.
• **Cool** remaining chocolate mixture 30 minutes.
• **Beat** whipping cream at high speed with an electric mixer until soft peaks form. Stir one-third of whipped cream into remaining chocolate mixture until smooth. Fold in remaining whipped cream. Spread over chocolate layer.
• **Cover** tart, and chill 2 hours or until firm. Garnish, if desired. **Yield:** 1 (10-inch) tart.

SEASON FOR PEAS

A bowl of fresh peas makes a bright, sweet announcement that spring is here. Enjoy this vegetable the simplest and best way of all—barely cooked and tossed with a nugget of butter. Or dress up peas, even the frozen variety, in these recipes.

PEA SOUP

2 pounds fresh, unshelled sweet
    green peas
2 tablespoons chopped fresh mint
    leaves
2 tablespoons butter or margarine
2 garlic cloves, chopped
2 shallots, chopped
2 cups whipping cream
1 teaspoon salt
½ teaspoon pepper

• **Shell** peas, reserving pods; set peas aside. Bring pods and water to cover to a boil in a large Dutch oven; cover, reduce heat, and simmer 45 minutes. Drain, reserving ¼ cup liquid.
• **Process** pods and reserved liquid in a food processor until smooth, stopping to scrape down sides.
• **Pour** pod mixture through a wire-mesh strainer into a large saucepan; cook over medium-high heat, stirring occasionally, until reduced to 2 cups. Set aside.
• **Bring** peas and water to cover to a boil in Dutch oven; reduce heat, and simmer 5 minutes. Drain; reserve ½ cup peas. Process remaining peas and mint in food processor until smooth, stopping to scrape down sides. Set aside.
• **Melt** butter in Dutch oven over medium-high heat; add garlic and shallots, and sauté until tender.
• **Stir** pea mixture, garlic mixture, whipping cream, salt, and pepper into pod mixture. Cover and chill. Garnish with reserved ½ cup peas. **Yield:** 8 cups.

PEAS AND POTATOES WITH DILL

1½ pounds new potatoes
2 cups fresh, shelled sweet
    green peas
¾ cup whipping cream
3 tablespoons chopped fresh
    dill
2 tablespoons butter or
    margarine
1 teaspoon salt

• **Cook** new potatoes in boiling water to cover in a large Dutch oven 15 minutes.
• **Add** green peas to Dutch oven; cover and cook 5 minutes or until potatoes are tender. Drain.
• **Stir** in whipping cream and remaining ingredients. Serve immediately. **Yield:** 6 to 8 servings.

PEAS, PLEASE

If you're not lucky enough to have a garden, a generous friend with a garden, or a produce market that peddles peas, you can have fresh peas delivered to your door.

Order them from Diamond Organics by calling toll free 1-888-674-2642 for $4 per pound. One pound of sweet green peas yields about 1 cup of shelled peas.

PEAS AND PASTA

1 cup fresh, shelled sweet green peas
2 tablespoons butter or margarine
1 garlic clove, minced
¼ cup dry sherry
¾ cup whipping cream
¾ cup grated Parmesan cheese
4 ounces linguine, cooked
2 ounces thinly sliced prosciutto or country ham, cut into thin strips
¼ teaspoon freshly ground pepper

• **Cook** peas in boiling water to cover 5 minutes or until crisp-tender; drain. Plunge into ice water to stop the cooking process; drain.
• **Melt** butter in a large skillet over medium-high heat; add garlic, and sauté 2 minutes or until tender. Stir in sherry, and cook 5 minutes or until reduced by half. Reduce heat to medium; stir in whipping cream, and bring to a simmer. Whisk in cheese until smooth; stir in linguine, peas, prosciutto, and pepper. Serve immediately. **Yield:** 2 servings.

FROM OUR KITCHEN TO YOURS

Just like fresh: Christopher Ranch has packed the fresh flavors of garlic and ginger in 4.25-ounce jars. Look for them in the produce section near the fresh garlic. Refrigerate these products after opening and they will hold their fresh flavor up to three months. Remember these conversions: 1 teaspoon chopped garlic equals 2 to 3 garlic cloves, and 1 teaspoon chopped ginger equals 2 teaspoons freshly grated ginger.

PERFECT IN POUCHES

We were very happy with the results when we tried Reynolds Hot Bags. They are extra heavy-duty aluminum foil cooking bags that are presealed on three sides to form a large pouch. They can be used on the grill or in the oven. We got great oven-baked ribs without the hassle of tending or turning. And the best part was the easy cleanup. To receive a free packet of brochures and more recipes, call 1-800-745-4000. Here's a no-fuss recipe that uses the product.

BARBECUE RIBS

2½ to 3 pounds spareribs, cut in half
1½ teaspoons seasoned salt
½ teaspoon pepper
1 large aluminum foil baking bag
1½ cups barbecue sauce
1 tablespoon all-purpose flour

• **Sprinkle** ribs with salt and pepper; place in a single layer in foil bag.
• **Stir** together barbecue sauce and flour; spread over ribs. Seal bag, and place in a 15- x 10-inch jellyroll pan.
• **Bake** ribs at 450° for 1 hour and 15 minutes or until tender. **Yield:** 6 servings.

A BAKER'S DREAM

If you're a baker, try a bread and pizza baking stone. The clay stones heat evenly and absorb moisture, producing baked goods with crisp crusts and light textures. We baked pizza and cookies that were crisp and perfectly browned. Try these cookies, adapted from "The Pampered Chef," on a baking stone—they're great.

CHOCOLATE CHIP-PEANUT BUTTER COOKIES

½ cup chunky peanut butter
¾ cup shortening
½ cup firmly packed light brown sugar
½ cup sugar
1 large egg
½ teaspoon vanilla extract
1¼ cups all-purpose flour
½ teaspoon baking soda
¼ teaspoon salt
1 cup (6 ounces) semisweet chocolate morsels

• **Beat** first 6 ingredients at medium speed with an electric mixer until creamy.
• **Stir** together flour, soda, and salt. Gradually add to peanut butter mixture, beating at low speed until blended; stir in semisweet chocolate morsels. Drop batter by rounded tablespoonfuls onto a baking stone.
• **Bake** cookies at 375° for 10 to 15 minutes. Let stand 2 minutes. Remove cookies to wire racks, and cool completely. **Yield:** 4 dozen.

TROUT FISHING

After you drool over the trout recipes on pages 52 through 54, here's what to look for when you shop. Trout is available fresh and frozen, and you can buy fish whole or cut it into fillets. Unless you catch the fish yourself, you'll want to buy farm-raised trout. Look for shiny, bright skin; firm flesh; and a clean scent. Some markets have tanks of live trout; choose the alert swimmers for best flavor and texture.

When you select wines to pair with some of the trout dishes, try a French white Burgundy with Sweet Onion-Stuffed Trout (page 52). A crisp Sauvignon Blanc tastes great with the Bacon-Wrapped Trout Stuffed With Crawfish (page 54). If you're a Chardonnay lover, the Trout Amandine (page 53) or the Cornmeal-Crusted Trout (page 52) are delicious complements. Another full-bodied white wine that's great with trout is Viognier [VEE-on-YEA].

APRIL

Journey across the South in search of home this month in "Reunions '99: Homeplaces." Travel to King Ranch in Texas for a taste of the King family's rich, down-home cooking, or gather at the banks of the Shenandoah for a riverside picnic. You'll find a common love of good food in all of these stories. Turn through the pages to find plenty of family-pleasing recipes, including Smoked Pork, Golden Cheddar Cheese Scones, and Apple Charlotte.

"Novel Teas" and "Dessert of the Month: Fresh From the Churn" offer new options for two trusted food traditions. Tea proves to be more than just a beverage in Tea Pound Cake and in Red Zinger Jelly, while buttermilk adds its distinctive flavor to pralines, fudge, and even sherbet.

DINING OUT

Welcome springtime with good friends and great food. Serve supper on the patio, the deck, or near the garden, and let nature be your decorator.

SUPPER FOR SIX

Southern Fresh Fruit Punch

Goat Cheese Dumplings With Roasted Bell Pepper Vinaigrette

Roasted Chicken With Poblano Vinaigrette and Corn Pudding

Steamed Sugar Snap Peas

Poppy Seed Rolls

Molded French Cream

SOUTHERN FRESH FRUIT PUNCH

Prep: 40 minutes
Chill: 2 hours

6 to 8 large lemons
4 to 6 large oranges
2 quarts water
1½ cups sugar
8 regular-size tea bags
1 cup diced fresh pineapple

• **Peel** lemons and oranges; carefully remove and discard pith, reserving rind.
• **Squeeze** juice from lemons to measure 1½ cups; squeeze juice from oranges to measure 2 cups. Set juices aside.
• **Bring** 2 quarts water and sugar to a boil in a large saucepan, stirring often; boil 1 minute. Pour over tea bags and reserved rind; cover and steep 20 minutes.
• **Discard** tea bags and rind, squeezing tea bags gently. Stir in juices and pineapple. Cover and chill at least 2 hours. Serve over ice. **Yield:** about 3 quarts.
Mrs. E. O'Brien
Richmond, Virginia

GOAT CHEESE DUMPLINGS
(pictured on page 76)

Prep: 30 minutes
Cook: 6 minutes

¼ cup diced dried tomatoes in oil, drained
¾ cup (6 ounces) goat cheese
2 garlic cloves, minced
2 tablespoons chopped fresh parsley
3 tablespoons chopped fresh basil
½ teaspoon freshly ground pepper
16 wonton wrappers
Vegetable oil
Roasted Bell Pepper Vinaigrette
Garnish: whole chile peppers

• **Stir** together first 6 ingredients in a medium bowl.
• **Place** 1 tablespoon cheese mixture in center of each wonton wrapper. Moisten wonton edges with water; fold in 2 opposite sides over filling. Fold over remaining sides, overlapping edges and pressing to seal.

• **Pour** oil to a depth of 3 inches into a heavy saucepan; heat to 350°.
• **Fry** dumplings in batches 2 to 3 minutes or until golden (do not overcook); drain on paper towels. Serve immediately with Roasted Bell Pepper Vinaigrette. Garnish, if desired. **Yield:** 6 to 8 servings.

Roasted Bell Pepper Vinaigrette

Prep: 20 minutes

2 large red bell peppers
¼ cup red wine vinegar
¼ cup chopped fresh cilantro
2 garlic cloves
1 tablespoon sugar
½ teaspoon salt
½ teaspoon pepper
½ cup vegetable oil
Garnish: fresh basil sprig

• **Place** bell peppers on an aluminum foil-lined baking sheet.
• **Broil** 5 inches from heat (with electric oven door partially open) 5 minutes on each side or until blistered.
• **Place** bell peppers in a large heavy-duty zip-top plastic bag; seal and let stand 10 minutes to loosen skins. Peel bell peppers; discard seeds.
• **Process** bell pepper, vinegar, and next 5 ingredients in a blender until smooth, stopping once to scrape down sides. Turn blender on high; add oil in a slow, steady stream. Cover and chill, if desired. Garnish, if desired. **Yield:** about 1⅔ cups.

Note: You can also serve the dumplings on a mixed green salad. Top with grilled chicken, and drizzle with Roasted Bell Pepper Vinaigrette.

ROASTED CHICKEN WITH POBLANO VINAIGRETTE AND CORN PUDDING

Prep: 15 minutes
Bake: 20 minutes

1 teaspoon ground cinnamon
1 teaspoon chili powder
1 teaspoon brown sugar
½ teaspoon salt
½ teaspoon pepper
½ teaspoon cocoa
1 tablespoon olive oil
1 teaspoon balsamic
   vinegar
6 skinned and boned chicken
   breast halves
Poblano Vinaigrette
Corn Pudding
Garnishes: tomatillos, fresh
   cilantro sprigs

• **Stir** together first 8 ingredients; rub over chicken. Place chicken in a lightly greased 15- x 10-inch jellyroll pan.
• **Bake** at 400° for 15 minutes. Drizzle 1 tablespoon Poblano Vinaigrette over each chicken breast; bake 5 more minutes or until done. Serve with remaining Poblano Vinaigrette and Corn Pudding. Garnish, if desired. **Yield:** 6 servings.

Poblano Vinaigrette

Prep: 25 minutes

2 poblano chile peppers
6 tomatillos
½ small onion
2 garlic cloves
1½ cups fresh cilantro leaves
3 tablespoons olive oil
2 tablespoons lime juice
1 teaspoon brown sugar
½ teaspoon pepper

• **Place** peppers on an aluminum foil-lined baking sheet.
• **Broil** 5 inches from heat (with electric oven door partially open) about 5 minutes on each side or until blistered.
• **Place** chile peppers in a heavy-duty zip-top plastic bag; seal and let stand 10 minutes to loosen skins.
• **Peel** chile peppers; remove and discard seeds.

• **Place** tomatillos, onion, garlic, and water to cover in a saucepan; bring to a boil over medium-high heat. Reduce heat; simmer 10 minutes. Drain and cool.
• **Process** tomatillo mixture, chile peppers, cilantro, and remaining ingredients in a blender or food processor 30 seconds or until minced. **Yield:** 6 servings.

Note: Poblano peppers, known as ancho peppers when dried, are dark green, tapered chile peppers, about 3 inches wide and 4 to 5 inches long. They have a sweet, smoky flavor. Find them fresh in the produce section. They're also available canned or dried.

Corn Pudding

Prep: 10 minutes
Cook: 20 minutes

2 cups milk
½ cup yellow cornmeal
1 (16-ounce) package frozen
   whole kernel corn, thawed
½ teaspoon salt
2 tablespoons whipping cream

• **Bring** milk to a boil in a heavy saucepan; gradually add cornmeal, stirring until blended after each addition. Cook, stirring constantly, just until mixture begins to boil. Reduce heat; cook, stirring constantly, until thickened.
• **Add** corn, stirring until mixture is consistency of whipped potatoes. Stir in salt and whipping cream. Yield: 6 servings.

LaJuan Coward
Jasper, Texas

STEAMED SUGAR SNAP PEAS

Prep: 5 minutes
Cook: 4 minutes

4 cups sugar snap peas, trimmed
3 tablespoons butter or margarine,
   melted
½ teaspoon salt
¼ teaspoon pepper
Garnish: edible flowers

• **Arrange** peas in a steamer basket over boiling water. Cover and steam 3 to 4 minutes or until crisp-tender. Toss with butter, salt, and pepper. Garnish, if desired; serve peas immediately. **Yield:** 6 servings.

TOAST TOPPERS

Step aside, plain bread and butter. Let's toast the bread for crunch and add these toppers for quick, zesty meals.

MOLDED FRENCH CREAM

This silky smooth dessert received our highest rating. See "From Our Kitchen to Yours" on page 100 for preparation tips and directions for crystallizing the violas and fresh mint leaves.

Prep: 15 minutes
Chill: 4 hours

2 (8-ounce) containers sour cream
3 cups whipping cream, divided
1½ cups superfine sugar
2 envelopes unflavored gelatin
½ cup cold water
2 (8-ounce) packages cream
    cheese, softened
2 teaspoons vanilla extract
1 tablespoon superfine sugar
Garnishes: crystallized violas,
    crystallized fresh mint leaves

• **Whisk** together sour cream and 2 cups whipping cream in a medium saucepan; gradually add 1½ cups sugar, whisking with each addition. Cook over low heat, whisking often, until warm.
• **Sprinkle** gelatin over ½ cup cold water in a saucepan; let stand 1 minute. Cook over medium heat, stirring until gelatin dissolves. Add to sour cream mixture.
• **Beat** cream cheese at medium speed with an electric mixer fitted with whisk attachment until light and fluffy. Gradually add sour cream mixture and vanilla, beating until smooth.
• **Pour** into a lightly greased 8-cup mold or 2-quart bowl; chill until firm, or, if desired, up to 2 days. Unmold onto a serving platter.
• **Beat** remaining 1 cup whipping cream until foamy; add 1 tablespoon sugar, beating until soft peaks form. Spoon whipped cream into a pastry bag fitted with a star-shaped tip. Pipe whipped cream around base of mold. Garnish, if desired. **Yield:** 16 servings.

AVOCADO DELUXE SANDWICHES

Prep: 20 minutes

8 thin avocado slices
¼ cup Italian dressing
1 tablespoon mayonnaise
4 oatmeal or whole wheat bread
    slices, toasted
4 (1-ounce) process American
    cheese slices
8 thin tomato slices
1 cup alfalfa sprouts

• **Toss** avocado slices gently with Italian dressing; drain well, reserving dressing.
• **Spread** mayonnaise evenly over 1 side of bread slices. Top bread slices evenly with avocado, cheese, tomato, and alfalfa sprouts.
• **Drizzle** sandwiches with reserved Italian dressing, and serve immediately. **Yield:** 4 servings.

STICKY BUN TOAST TOPPER

Prep: 5 minutes
Cook: 1 minute

2 tablespoons brown sugar
1 tablespoon butter or margarine
1 tablespoon light corn syrup
¼ teaspoon ground cinnamon
4 white bread slices, toasted
¼ cup chopped pecans, toasted

• **Combine** first 4 ingredients in a l-cup glass measuring cup. Microwave at HIGH 1 minute; stir and spread evenly over toast slices. Sprinkle with pecans. **Yield:** 4 servings.

Jennifer Simpson
Brownwood, Texas

TOMATO-CHEESE-BACON MELTS

Prep: 10 minutes
Bake: 6 minutes

1 (16-ounce) garlic bread loaf,
    split lengthwise
2 tablespoons mayonnaise
3 plum tomatoes, sliced
½ teaspoon salt
½ teaspoon pepper
1 (16-ounce) package bacon,
    cooked and crumbled
1 (8-ounce) package shredded
    Cheddar cheese

• **Cut** each bread half into 3 pieces. Place, cut side up, on a baking sheet.
• **Bake** at 450° for 4 minutes or until toasted. Spread mayonnaise evenly over 1 side of bread pieces.
• **Top** with tomato; sprinkle with salt and pepper. Top with bacon; sprinkle with cheese. Bake 2 more minutes or until cheese melts. **Yield:** 6 servings.

Jill Ann Kelley
Essex, Missouri

MANGO-CRAB SALAD SANDWICHES

Prep: 15 minutes

¼ cup mayonnaise
1 tablespoon finely chopped celery
1 tablespoon chopped fresh
    cilantro
2 teaspoons lemon juice
1 teaspoon minced jalapeño
    pepper
⅔ cup peeled, chopped mango
1 (14¼-ounce) can crabmeat,
    rinsed and drained
4 lettuce leaves
2 English muffins, split and toasted
1 tablespoon slivered almonds,
    toasted

• **Combine** first 5 ingredients in a large bowl, stirring until blended. Add mango and crabmeat; toss gently to coat.
• **Arrange** 1 lettuce leaf on each muffin half; top evenly with crabmeat mixture.
• **Sprinkle** each sandwich with slivered almonds. **Yield:** 2 servings.

*Grilled Asparagus
Salad With Orange
Vinaigrette, page 102*

Crawfish Risotto, page 120

Carrot-and-Cabbage Stuffed Peppers, page 63

Spinach-Stuffed Shells, page 64

Apricot Bellini,
page 145

Goat Cheese Dumplings With Roasted Bell
Pepper Vinaigrette, page 70

Trout Amandine, page 53

Wild Rice-Shrimp Salad,
Asparagus and Tomatoes
With Herb Vinaigrette,
Orange-Pecan Muffin,
pages 55 and 56

Chicken-Black Bean
Salad, page 124

Joy's Potato Salad, page 83

Warm Apple-Buttermilk
Custard Pie, page 98

HOMEPLACES

For many Southerners, home means a place of memory. For some,
it's a lovingly preserved house built by an ancestor. Others gather at churches,
farms, or campgrounds where great-grandparents worshiped and toiled.
Within these pages, we meet families who come together at their special homeplaces
to break bread, laugh, remember, and explore their common histories.

SETTLED BY SIGHTLERS

The Sightler family and Gaston, South Carolina, share a 243-year history. George Sightler started it all when he settled near Gaston in 1756. And the town and the family grew together in direct proportion to each other. Last year the family celebrated its 50th annual family reunion.

"The true identity of a town must be found in those who proudly and unceasingly declare it home; and eight generations of the Sightler family have faithfully lived their lives in Gaston," reads a proclamation by the Gaston Town Council naming the third weekend in July as Sightler Family Weekend.

Lots of hugs, laughs, and good food fuel the gathering. This family of great cooks produced a cookbook as one of the 50th reunion souvenirs. Here's a sample of some of their terrific recipes.

SMOKED PORK

We adapted this family recipe
for smaller cuts of meat.

Prep: 1 hour
Cook: 6 hours

Hickory wood chunks
2 cups prepared mustard
1½ cups ketchup
¾ cup cider vinegar
2 tablespoons sugar
2 tablespoons Worcestershire
    sauce
1 tablespoon hot sauce
2 tablespoons butter or
    margarine
1 (5- to 6-pound) Boston butt
    pork roast
5 garlic cloves, chopped
2 tablespoons salt
1 tablespoon pepper

• **Soak** hickory wood chunks in water 1 hour.
• **Cook** mustard and next 6 ingredients in a saucepan over low heat, stirring often, 20 minutes; set aside.
• **Cut** deep slits in roast using a paring knife. Stir together garlic, salt, and pepper; rub on all sides of roast.
• **Prepare** charcoal fire in smoker; let burn 15 to 20 minutes.
• **Drain** wood chunks, and place on coals. Place water pan in smoker; add water to depth of fill line.
• **Place** roast on lower food rack, and top with 1 cup mustard mixture.
• **Cook,** covered, 6 hours or until a meat thermometer inserted into thickest portion of roast registers 165°. Remove from smoker; cool slightly. Chop and serve with remaining mustard sauce.
Yield: 8 to 10 servings.

Jay Poole
Gaston, South Carolina

GOLDEN CHEDDAR CHEESE SCONES

Prep: 11 minutes
Bake: 15 minutes

4 cups all-purpose flour
2 tablespoons baking powder
½ teaspoon baking soda
2 teaspoons salt
¼ cup sugar
2 cups (8 ounces) shredded
    Cheddar cheese
2 large eggs
1 (8-ounce) container sour
    cream
½ cup vegetable oil
⅓ cup milk

• **Combine** first 5 ingredients; stir in cheese.
• **Combine** eggs and next 3 ingredients; add to flour mixture, stirring just until moistened.
• **Knead** dough 10 to 12 times on a lightly floured surface. Roll or pat to ¾-inch thickness.
• **Cut** dough with a 3-inch round cutter; place on a lightly greased baking sheet.
• **Bake** at 400° for 15 minutes. **Yield:** 1 dozen.

Melba Sightler Lucas
Gaston, South Carolina

Two Centuries of Tradition

In Stanley, North Carolina, the Rhyne family will soon celebrate their 200th year. Richard and Barbara Rhyne have no doubt about the date the ancestral home was completed—1799 is spelled in brick on the outside of the home. All of these recipes are family favorites, a tasty collection of the Rhynes' bicentennial bounty.

WIXIE'S REFRIGERATOR ROLLS

Prep: 1 hour and 10 minutes
Chill: 8 hours
Bake: 15 minutes

½ cup shortening
3½ to 4 cups all-purpose flour
1 (¼-ounce) envelope active dry
    yeast
⅓ cup sugar
1¼ teaspoons salt
1½ cups warm water (100° to 110°)
¼ cup butter or margarine,
    melted

• **Cut** shortening into 3½ cups flour with a pastry blender until crumbly. Combine yeast and next 3 ingredients; let stand 5 minutes. Gradually stir in flour mixture to make a soft dough, adding more flour if necessary. Cover and chill 8 hours.
• **Turn** dough out onto a lightly floured surface; knead until smooth and elastic (1 to 2 minutes). Shape dough into 1½-inch balls; place in a lightly greased 13-x 9-inch pan. Cover and let rise in a warm place (85°), free from drafts, 1 hour or until doubled in bulk.
• **Bake** at 450° for 12 to 15 minutes or until golden; brush with butter. **Yield:** 2 dozen.

Ruth Rhyne Smull
Alexandria, Virginia

AUNT BEULAH'S COLESLAW WITH COOKED DRESSING

Prep: 1 hour and 25 minutes
Chill: 1 hour

1 large cabbage, shredded (12
    cups)
1 small onion, chopped
1 teaspoon salt
Cooked Dressing
2 tablespoons mayonnaise
½ cup sugar
¼ teaspoon pepper
1 tablespoon white vinegar

• **Place** cabbage and onion in a bowl; sprinkle with salt. Cover with ice cubes.

Let stand 1 hour; drain. Combine dressing and next 4 ingredients; toss with cabbage mixture. Chill 1 hour. **Yield:** 10 cups.

Cooked Dressing

Prep: 5 minutes
Cook: 5 minutes

3 tablespoons sugar
1½ tablespoons all-purpose
    flour
1 teaspoon dry mustard
1 large egg
¾ cup milk
¼ cup white vinegar
1 tablespoon butter or margarine

• **Cook** first 6 ingredients in a heavy saucepan over low heat, stirring constantly, 5 minutes or until thickened; stir in butter, and cool. **Yield:** 2 cups.

Helen Rhyne Lieurance
Mount Holly, North Carolina

EGG CUSTARD PIE

Prep: 15 minutes
Bake: 22 minutes

2 (9-inch) frozen deep-dish
    piecrusts
1½ teaspoons ground nutmeg,
    divided
2½ cups milk
1 (12-ounce) can evaporated
    milk
6 large eggs
1 cup sugar
1 tablespoon vanilla extract
¼ teaspoon salt

• **Sprinkle** piecrusts evenly with ½ teaspoon nutmeg. Bake at 475° for 2 minutes. Remove from oven. Gently press crusts down while warm.
• **Heat** 2½ cups milk and evaporated milk in a large saucepan over medium heat. (Do not boil.)
• **Process** eggs, next 3 ingredients, and remaining 1 teaspoon nutmeg in a blender until smooth. Turn blender on high; gradually add half of hot mixture

in a slow, steady stream. Stir egg mixture into remaining hot milk mixture. Pour evenly into piecrusts.
• **Bake** at 475° for 5 minutes. Reduce oven temperature to 425°; bake 15 more minutes. (Pies will not be set.) Cool pies on wire racks 45 minutes. Chill. **Yield:** 2 (9-inch) pies.

Barbara Lowe Rhyne
Mount Holly, North Carolina

No Place Like Home

Joberta Wells had dreamed of restoring and retiring to her grandparents' 1895 farmhouse. When she discovered the structure couldn't be saved, the Yosemite, Kentucky, woman did the next best thing: She tore it down and built a new one exactly like it.

Taylors of Tabernacle

Since 1826, the descendants of the Rev. Howell Taylor have gathered at the Tabernacle Methodist Church campground to worship, swap tales, and feast. For last year's Taylor reunion, more than 500 family members came from as far as Ireland and as near as Memphis for six days of meetings, memories, and meals. Try this Taylor family recipe for a sample of their favorite fare.

SHARPE BAKED APPLES

Prep: 15 minutes
Bake: 35 minutes

12 **medium Granny Smith or other cooking apples, cored**
6 **tablespoons butter, divided**
½ **cup water**
¾ **cup sugar**

• **Cut** 1 inch of peel from tops of apples. Place apples in a greased 13- x 9-inch pan. Place 1½ teaspoons butter into each cavity; sprinkle evenly with ½ cup water and sugar. Bake at 350°, basting often, 35 minutes. **Yield:** 12 servings.

Martha Sharpe
Humboldt, Tennessee

To celebrate the new home, Joberta and her sister held a family reunion there, the first since 1949. Just as in 1949, the food was served from a flatbed farm wagon under an oak tree. For Joberta and family, it was like being home again.

BARBARA SUE'S SPOONBREAD

Prep: 25 minutes
Bake: 1 hour

1 **quart milk**
1 **cup white cornmeal**
¼ **cup butter or margarine**
4 **large eggs, lightly beaten**
¼ **cup sugar**
2 **teaspoons salt**

• **Heat** milk in a small saucepan over low heat 10 to 12 minutes or until almost boiling; stir in cornmeal. Cook over low heat, stirring occasionally, 5 minutes or until thickened; stir in butter. Remove from heat, and beat with a wooden spoon 1 minute.
• **Stir** one-fourth of hot mixture into eggs; add to remaining hot mixture, stirring constantly. Stir in sugar and salt. Pour into a lightly greased 2-quart baking dish.
• **Bake** spoonbread at 350° for 1 hour. **Yield:** 6 servings.

Barbara Sue Sweeney Griffin
Liberty, Kentucky

JOY'S POTATO SALAD
(pictured on page 79)

Prep: 30 minutes
Cook: 20 minutes
Chill: 8 hours

2 **pounds small new potatoes**
2 **teaspoons salt, divided**
1 **medium-size green bell pepper, diced**
12 **cherry tomatoes, halved**
½ **small purple onion, diced**
3 **tablespoons minced fresh basil**
⅓ **cup red wine vinegar**
½ **teaspoon pepper**
2 **teaspoons sugar**
½ **cup olive oil**
Red leaf lettuce

• **Cook** potatoes in boiling water to cover and 1 teaspoon salt 15 to 20 minutes or until tender; drain. Plunge into ice water to stop the cooking process; drain. Peel potatoes, and cut in half.
• **Place** potato, bell pepper, and next 3 ingredients in a large bowl.
• **Process** remaining 1 teaspoon salt, vinegar, pepper, and sugar in a blender until smooth. Turn blender on high; add oil in a slow, steady stream. Pour over potato mixture; toss gently to coat.
• **Cover** and chill 8 hours. Drain; serve in a lettuce-lined bowl. **Yield:** 6 to 8 servings.

Joy Wells Tarter
Dunnville, Kentucky

KING RANCH ROUNDUP

When Capt. Richard King's great-great-grandchildren and their children plan a get-together, they often head for the large white homeplace at the family's ranch. They look forward to a taste of the rich heritage they share and to reminders of the ties that bind them to their colorful forefather. This recipe sampling captures some of the best flavors of the ranch.

APPLE CHARLOTTE

Prep: 40 minutes
Bake: 1 hour

1 (24-ounce) day-old sliced white sandwich bread loaf
1 cup butter or margarine, softened
8 large Granny Smith apples
2 cups ice water
¼ cup lemon juice
1 cup sugar
1 teaspoon ground cinnamon
1 teaspoon ground allspice
1 tablespoon vanilla extract
3 tablespoons butter or margarine
Vanilla ice cream

• **Trim** crusts from bread. Spread 1 cup butter evenly on both sides of slices. Cut slices in half lengthwise. Cover bottom and sides of a buttered 2½-quart soufflé dish with bread pieces, reserving remaining pieces.
• **Peel** apples, and cut into thin wedges. Place wedges in a large shallow dish; cover with 2 cups ice water and lemon juice. Let stand 5 minutes; drain.
• **Combine** sugar and next 3 ingredients; add apple, tossing to coat. Place in dish over buttered bread; dot with 3 tablespoons butter. Arrange reserved bread pieces on top; drizzle with any remaining liquid from tossing apples. Place dish on a baking sheet.
• **Bake** at 425° for 1 hour or until apple is tender and bread is browned. Serve warm or cool with vanilla ice cream. **Yield:** 8 servings.

GUACAMOLE

Prep: 15 minutes

8 ripe avocados, peeled
1 medium-size ripe tomato, diced
1 small onion, minced
½ teaspoon salt
⅛ teaspoon pepper
1 to 1½ tablespoons lemon juice
3 tablespoons minced fresh cilantro
1 tablespoon hot sauce (optional)

• **Mash** avocados with a fork until smooth; stir in tomato, next 5 ingredients, and, if desired, hot sauce. Serve immediately; or cover and chill up to 2 hours. Serve with tortilla chips. **Yield:** about 5 cups.

BROCCOLI SALAD

Prep: 17 minutes

1 cup mayonnaise
2 tablespoons sugar
2 tablespoons red wine vinegar
1 (16-ounce) package broccoli flowerets, chopped
5 bacon slices, cooked and crumbled
½ cup raisins
¼ cup chopped onion

• **Stir** together first 3 ingredients in a large bowl; add broccoli and remaining ingredients, tossing well. **Yield:** 8 to 10 servings.

TEXAS CAVIAR

Prep: 30 minutes
Chill: 2 hours

1 (15-ounce) can black-eyed peas, rinsed and drained
1 (15½-ounce) can white hominy, drained
2 tomatoes, seeded and chopped
4 green onions, thinly sliced
2 garlic cloves, minced
1 medium-size green bell pepper, diced
1 small onion, chopped
¼ cup chopped fresh cilantro
1 (8-ounce) jar hot picante sauce
2 tablespoons lime juice (optional)

• **Combine** first 9 ingredients, and, if desired, lime juice.
• **Cover** and chill at least 2 hours. Serve with tortilla chips, or wrap in flour tortillas. **Yield:** 4 cups.

SHALL WE GATHER AT THE RIVER

For Tammy Goff, beside the Shenandoah River is the only place to hold her family's annual summer picnics. "My family has lived in the valley [Toms Brook, Virginia] for generations," she says, "and we still carry on traditions started centuries ago." They gather to feast all day on home cooking and to talk, swim, and play volleyball.

Attachment to this land goes deep, and though Tammy now lives in Norfolk, her love for the homeplace is obvious. "Nothing can stop our coming home for family picnics," she says. "We never miss a chance to get back to the river."

You'll enjoy Tammy's home-style recipes as much as we did.

SUMMER SAUSAGE

Prep: 15 minutes
Chill: 3 days
Bake: 5 hours

5 pounds ground beef
¼ cup meat cure mix
2½ tablespoons mustard seeds
2 tablespoons garlic powder
2½ tablespoons cracked black pepper
1 tablespoon hickory salt
1 tablespoon mesquite liquid smoke
1 (0.6-ounce) envelope zesty Italian dressing mix

• **Combine** all ingredients in a large bowl until blended; cover and chill 3 days, stirring occasionally.
• **Shape** mixture into 4 (10-inch) logs; place on a rack in a broiler pan.
• **Bake** at 225° for 5 hours, turning once. Drain on paper towels; cool completely on a wire rack. Store in refrigerator up to 3 weeks, or freeze up to 2 months. Thinly slice before serving. **Yield:** 4 (10-inch) logs.

Note: For testing purposes only, we used Morton Tender Quick meat cure mix, located in the spice section of the supermarket.

Tammy Goff
Norfolk, Virginia

MARZETTI'S SPAGHETTI

This is Tammy's version of Johnny Marzetti Casserole, a popular school lunchroom dish in the 1950s.

Prep: 20 minutes
Cook: 25 minutes

3 pounds ground beef
3 large onions, chopped
3 (14.5-ounce) cans diced tomatoes
3 (10¾-ounce) cans cream of mushroom soup, undiluted
1 (46-ounce) can tomato juice
3 tablespoons Worcestershire sauce
1 teaspoon salt
1½ teaspoons hot sauce
1 (16-ounce) loaf process cheese spread, cubed
1 (8-ounce) loaf process cheese spread, cubed
16 ounces spaghetti, cooked

• **Cook** ground beef and onion in a stockpot over medium heat, stirring until beef crumbles and is no longer pink; drain and return to pot.
• **Stir** in tomatoes and next 5 ingredients; bring to a boil. Reduce heat, and simmer 15 to 20 minutes. Stir in process cheese spread until melted. Serve over spaghetti. **Yield:** 12 servings.

Tammy Goff
Norfolk, Virginia

COMING HOME TO THE PLAYHOUSE

Neighbors and family of Mary Frances Cull come to celebrate at Prancy's Playhouse, a small white house adjacent to her home in Alabama. Dress up for a tea party of your own and savor these small delights.

VEGEWICHES

Prep: 25 minutes

1 (8-ounce) package cream cheese, softened
¼ cup chopped green bell pepper
½ cup chopped cucumber
¼ cup chopped green onions
2 celery ribs, chopped
1 tablespoon lemon juice
¼ teaspoon salt
¼ teaspoon pepper
22 white or wheat bread slices

• **Beat** cream cheese at medium speed with an electric mixer until creamy. Stir in bell pepper and next 6 ingredients. Spread on half of bread slices; cover with remaining bread slices.
• **Trim** crusts from sandwiches. Cut sandwiches into fourths. Serve immediately, or store, covered with damp paper towels, in an airtight container in refrigerator. **Yield:** 44 sandwiches.

Marion Dinan
Birmingham, Alabama

PIMIENTO CHEESE FINGER SANDWICHES

Prep: 10 minutes

12 ounces sharp Cheddar cheese, shredded
½ cup mayonnaise
1 (7-ounce) jar diced pimiento, drained
⅛ teaspoon ground red pepper
¼ teaspoon salt
20 thin white or wheat bread slices

• **Process** first 5 ingredients in a food processor until smooth, stopping to scrape down sides.
• **Spread** cheese mixture on half of bread slices; cover with remaining bread slices. Trim crusts from sandwiches. Cut each sandwich into 4 strips. **Yield:** 40 sandwiches.

Note: Be sure to shred your own cheese. Preshredded cheese is not recommended for this recipe.

Bebe Buchanan
Birmingham, Alabama

TURKEY TEA SANDWICHES

Prep: 10 minutes

2 (8-ounce) packages petite dinner rolls, split
Honey Mustard-Butter Spread or Cranberry-Butter Spread
1 pound thinly sliced cooked turkey, cut into 2-inch squares

• **Spread** cut sides of rolls with Honey Mustard-Butter Spread or Cranberry-Butter Spread. Place turkey evenly on bottom halves; cover with tops. **Yield:** 50 sandwiches.

Honey Mustard-Butter Spread

Prep: 5 minutes

½ cup butter or margarine, softened
¼ cup honey
2 teaspoons prepared mustard

• **Beat** all ingredients at medium speed with an electric mixer until light and fluffy. **Yield:** 1 cup.

Cranberry-Butter Spread

This spread is great on any rolls.

Prep: 25 minutes

1 cup sugar
½ cup water
1¼ cups cranberries
½ cup butter or margarine, softened
1 tablespoon powdered sugar

• **Bring** 1 cup sugar and water to a boil in a small saucepan over medium heat, stirring until sugar dissolves. Stir in berries; bring to a boil. Reduce heat; simmer, stirring occasionally, 10 to 15 minutes or until thickened. Remove from heat; cool.
• **Press** through a fine mesh strainer; discard solids. Beat butter at medium speed with an electric mixer until fluffy; add powdered sugar and cranberry mixture, beating until blended. **Yield:** 1 cup.

Bebe Buchanan
Birmingham, Alabama

PRANCY'S PLAYHOUSE

Mary Frances Cull moves around her yard like a butterfly. Her yard overflows with friends and family, all in their Sunday best. Children dance around the tables in dresses and trousers too pretty for playing in the grass. Ladies don white gloves as novel as the playhouse they've come to celebrate.

"They've called me Prancy for years, my brothers and sisters," Mary Frances says, shaking her head. "They say I was spoiled rotten, that my feet never touched the ground. I was the youngest of five children, and Daddy built that playhouse for me." She flips through an album of photographs, mostly black-and-white pictures of the five Montalbano brothers and sisters. They stand like dominoes in front of the small white house their father, Sam, built 45 years ago.

Sam's wife, Mary, 92, remembers well the path of the playhouse. "It moved here and there over the years. It's even been to the lake. We used it to store skis, if you can believe it. When we sold the lake house, we brought it to Mary Frances' house."

Mary lives on 22 acres in Shelby County, Alabama, and is surrounded by four of her children. Other family members are scattered. Mary Frances' playhouse tea party is an excuse to gather together. Her brother Dickey lives in Coral Springs, Florida, and loves having a reason to come home.

Now her great-granddaughters spend most of the day cooking imaginary food inside Prancy's Playhouse, whose walls have heard the secrets of three generations of children.

BUILDING MEMORIES

Marion and Frankie Greer's Kentucky farm serves as a loving memorial to the couple. With wooded campsites for 200 family members and a pavilion for activities, the Kings Mountain site is perfect for the Greer descendants' annual reunion. Family members rotate duties for the theme, decorations, and activities. Everyone helps with meals, contributing favorite dishes.

At the end of the three-day reunion, they part with waves of goodbye and memories tucked away until next year. Dig in to some of the reunion fare.

FREEZER CUCUMBER PICKLES

Prep: 30 minutes
Chill: 48 hours

3½ cups thinly sliced cucumber
2 small onions, sliced and
     separated into rings
1 tablespoon salt
1 cup sugar
½ cup white vinegar
3 tablespoons water

• **Combine** first 3 ingredients in a large bowl; set aside.
• **Cook** sugar, vinegar, and 3 tablespoons water in a saucepan over medium heat, stirring until sugar dissolves. Pour over cucumber mixture.
• **Cover** and chill 48 hours.
• **Spoon** into half-pint jars or freezer containers; seal, label, and freeze pickles up to 6 months. Thaw in refrigerator before serving; use thawed pickles within a week. **Yield:** about 3 pints.

Darlene Brunson
Bossier City, Louisiana

TINY HAM-AND-CHEESE SANDWICHES

Prep: 10 minutes

1 (3-ounce) package cream cheese,
     softened
¾ cup (3 ounces) shredded sharp
     Cheddar cheese
1½ tablespoons mayonnaise
2 teaspoons Worcestershire
     sauce
2 teaspoons lemon juice
Dash of ground red pepper
Dash of hot sauce
Dash of garlic salt
Dash of ground black pepper
2 (7½-ounce) packages party
     rolls, split
1 pound sliced cooked ham, cut
     into 2-inch squares

• **Beat** first 9 ingredients at medium speed with an electric mixer until creamy.
• **Spread** cut sides of rolls with cream cheese mixture.
• **Place** a ham piece on bottom halves of each roll; cover with tops.
• **Serve** sandwiches immediately, or store, covered with damp paper towels, in an airtight container in refrigerator. **Yield:** 4 dozen.

Mary Frances Cull
Birmingham, Alabama

THREE-BEAN BAKE

Prep: 15 minutes
Bake: 55 minutes

½ pound ground chuck
1 small onion, chopped
6 bacon slices, chopped
1 (15-ounce) can pork and beans,
    undrained
1 (15¼-ounce) can lima beans,
    rinsed and drained
1 (15-ounce) can kidney beans,
    rinsed and drained
½ cup firmly packed brown sugar
½ cup ketchup
½ cup barbecue sauce
1 teaspoon dry mustard

• **Cook** first 3 ingredients in a large skillet, stirring until beef crumbles and is no longer pink. Drain and return to skillet. Stir in pork and beans and remaining ingredients. Pour into a greased 1½-quart baking dish. Bake at 400° for 45 to 55 minutes. **Yield:** 6 servings.

Slow Cooker Three-Bean Bake: Brown first 3 ingredients; drain. Place in a 5-quart slow cooker; stir in remaining ingredients. Cook, covered, on HIGH 2½ to 3 hours.
Margie Lou Greer
Collinsville, Illinois

CHOCOLATE GRAVY

Prep: 10 minutes
Cook: 25 minutes

1 cup sugar
3 tablespoons all-purpose flour
3 tablespoons cocoa
2 cups milk
2 egg yolks, lightly beaten
2 teaspoons vanilla extract

• **Stir** together first 3 ingredients in a saucepan; stir in milk and yolks. Cook over low heat, stirring constantly, 25 minutes or until thickened. Stir in vanilla. Serve with biscuits. **Yield:** 2¾ cups.
Thelma Greer
Stanford, Kentucky

MEET ME IN . . .

Picking the perfect location is one of the most important parts of a successful reunion. Here are a few popular places for reunions around the South. Read the box at right to find some strategies for planning a reunion.

Town Creek, Alabama: Doublehead Resort, 1-800-685-9267. Take advantage of boat rentals and horseback rides. Rates: $200 per night for two people in a three-bedroom, two-bath cottage (Memorial Day-Labor Day); $10 for each additional person (10 people maximum).

Vero Beach, Florida: Disney's Vero Beach Resort, 1-800-359-8000. Treasure hunts, kayaking excursions, and tons of fun at Walt Disney World are only two hours away. Rates: rooms and villas $140-$450 per night.

Pine Mountain, Georgia: Callaway Gardens, 1-800-225-5292. Enjoy a wildlife preserve, golf, hiking, bicycling, and tennis. Rates: villas $210-$560 per night.

Jamestown, Kentucky: Lake Cumberland Resort State Park, (502) 343-3111. Pumpkin Creek Lodge offers a quiet retreat with full amenities. Rates: rooms and cabins $44-$120 per night.

Vacherie, Louisiana: Oak Alley Plantation, (504) 265-2151. Turn-of-the-century Creole cottages, perfect for a small reunion. Rates: $95-$125 per night.

Natchez, Mississippi: Monmouth Plantation, (601) 442-5852. Antebellum plantation on 26 acres, with croquet and fishing. Rates: rooms and cottages $140-$355 per night.

Ridgedale, Missouri: Big Cedar Lodge, (417) 335-2777. A fishing paradise, with miniature golf, swimming, and tennis. Rates: rooms and cabins $79-$349; rates vary with season.

Maggie Valley, North Carolina: Cataloochee Ranch, (828) 926-1401. Horseback rides through the Smoky Mountains and shopping in town. Rates: $95-$275 per night.

Kingston, Oklahoma: Lake Texoma State Resort Park, 1-800-528-0593. Golf, fishing, and a variety of children's activities. Rates: $57-$150 per night.

Nashville, Tennessee: Opryland Hotel, (615) 889-1000. Visit the Grand Ole Opry or ride on the *General Jackson* riverboat to restaurants and shops. Rates: $165-$205 per night.

Bandera, Texas: Mayan Dude Ranch, (830) 796-3312. Tennis and tubing on the Medina River. Rates: $104-$130 per night.

Pembroke, Virginia: Mountain Lake Resort, (540) 626-7121. Open May through October. Fishing, boating, golf, and tennis. Rates: $135-$650 (latter rate for eight guests) per night.

REUNION SURVIVAL TIPS

■ Simplify bookkeeping by choosing one person to pay the deposit in advance and the balance upon arrival.

■ Spread the fun around; have each family prepare a meal and bring a snack and dessert to share.

■ Find out what special events are in the area. Also, family talent shows and sing-alongs help pass the time. And don't forget the baseballs and mitts for outdoor games.

■ A group that arrives early can call others to request last-minute or forgotten items.

NOVEL TEAS

If we love tea over ice, why not in ice cream?
We decided to use this year-round elixir in some of our
favorite dishes. We discovered tea—in its many forms and
flavors—deserves much more than sipping respect.
As an ingredient, it's easy to use, affordable, and on every
pantry shelf. It shines in jelly, adds mystery to pound cake,
and nicely tames the ever-popular mint julep.

SALAD GREENS WITH HERBED EARL GREY VINAIGRETTE

This recipe makes 1½ cups
vinaigrette; store the remainder in
the refrigerator for another use.

Prep: 45 minutes

⅓ cup white wine vinegar
2 regular-size Earl Grey tea bags
1 teaspoon Dijon mustard
½ teaspoon salt
½ teaspoon freshly ground pepper
1 cup canola oil
¼ cup minced fresh basil
9 cups mixed salad greens
Prosciutto Croutons

• **Bring** vinegar to a boil. Pour over tea bags; cover and steep 30 minutes. Discard tea bags.
• **Process** vinegar mixture, mustard, salt, and pepper in a blender until smooth. Turn blender on high; add oil in a slow, steady stream. Stir in basil.
• **Toss** greens with about ¾ cup vinaigrette. Spoon evenly onto 6 salad plates; top evenly with Prosciutto Croutons. Serve immediately. **Yield:** 6 servings.

Prosciutto Croutons

Prep: 15 minutes
Cook: 3 minutes

2 (3-ounce) goat cheese logs
18 paper-thin prosciutto or other ham slices, cut into strips (about 6 ounces)
2 tablespoons butter or margarine

• **Shape** cheese into 18 balls. Wrap each ball with prosciutto strips, covering cheese completely.
• **Melt** butter in a large skillet over medium-high heat; add cheese balls, and sauté 1 to 2 minutes, turning often, or until cheese is warm. Serve immediately. **Yield:** 18 croutons.

RED ZINGER JELLY

Prep: 25 minutes
Cook: 10 minutes

1¾ cups water
12 regular-size red zinger tea bags
¼ cup fresh orange juice
3 cups sugar
2 tablespoons grated orange rind
2 teaspoons orange liqueur (optional)
1 (3-ounce) package liquid pectin

• **Bring** 1¾ cups water to a boil in a large saucepan; pour water over tea bags. Cover and steep 20 minutes. Discard tea bags.
• **Pour** orange juice through a fine wire-mesh strainer into saucepan, discarding pulp. Stir in brewed tea, sugar, orange rind, and, if desired, liqueur; bring to a boil. Boil, stirring constantly, 2 minutes. Remove from heat, and cool 5 minutes.
• **Stir** liquid pectin into tea mixture; return to a boil; boil, stirring constantly, 1 minute. Remove from heat, and skim off foam with a metal spoon.
• **Pour** hot jelly into hot, sterilized jars, filling to ¼ inch from top; wipe jar rims. Cover at once with metal lids, and screw on bands.
• **Process** in boiling-water bath 5 minutes, or store in refrigerator up to 3 months. **Yield:** 12 (½-cup) jars.

WILD RASPBERRY TEA GRANITA

Prep: 25 minutes
Freeze: 8 hours

6 cups cranberry juice drink
⅔ cup sugar
10 regular-size raspberry tea bags

• **Bring** cranberry juice drink and sugar to a boil in a saucepan, stirring until sugar dissolves; pour over tea bags. Cover and steep 20 minutes; discard tea bags. Pour into a 13- x 9-inch pan.
• **Freeze** 8 hours. Remove from freezer 20 minutes before serving. Break into pieces; serve immediately. **Yield:** 6 cups.

TEA POUND CAKE

Prep: 20 minutes
Bake: 1 hour and 35 minutes

1   cup butter, softened
½   cup shortening
3   cups sugar
5   large eggs
3   cups all-purpose flour
½   teaspoon baking powder
¼   teaspoon salt
½   cup unsweetened instant tea
     powder
1   cup milk
1   teaspoon vanilla extract

• **Beat** butter and shortening at medium speed with an electric mixer 2 minutes or until creamy. Gradually add sugar, beating 5 to 7 minutes. Add eggs, 1 at a time, beating just until yellow disappears.
• **Combine** flour and next 3 ingredients; add to butter mixture alternately with milk, beginning and ending with flour mixture. Beat at low speed just until blended after each addition. Stir in vanilla. Pour batter into a greased and floured 12-cup Bundt pan or 10-inch tube pan.
• **Bake** at 325° for 1 hour and 35 minutes or until a wooden pick inserted in center comes out clean. Let cool in pan 10 minutes; remove from pan. Cool completely on a wire rack. **Yield:** 1 (10-inch) cake.

TEA JULEPS

Prep: 5 minutes
Chill: 2 hours

1   (0.24-ounce) package sugar-free
     iced tea mix
¼   cup peppermint schnapps
¼   cup bourbon

• **Prepare** tea according to package directions; stir in schnapps and bourbon. Cover and chill 2 hours. Serve over ice. **Yield:** 2 quarts.

Note: For testing purposes only, we used Crystal Light iced tea mix.
Maugie Pastor
Aaah! T'Frere's House and Garçonniere
Lafayette, Louisiana

ORANGE PEKOE-CHOCOLATE ICE CREAM

Prep: 55 minutes
Chill: 2 hours
Freeze: 15 minutes

1   medium orange
1   quart whipping cream
1   quart half-and-half
10 regular-size orange pekoe tea
     bags
6   egg yolks
½   cup sugar
1   (4-ounce) dark sweet chocolate
     bar, chopped
2   teaspoons vanilla extract

• **Peel** orange with a paring knife, making sure not to include white portion of rind; reserve orange for another use.
• **Bring** orange rind, whipping cream, and half-and-half to a boil in a Dutch oven; add tea bags. Reduce heat, and simmer 20 minutes. Remove tea bags and rind with a slotted spoon; discard.
• **Beat** egg yolks and sugar until yolks are thick and pale. Gradually stir about one-fourth of hot mixture into yolks; add to remaining hot mixture, stirring constantly.
• **Bring** to a boil over medium-high heat, stirring constantly; reduce heat, and simmer, stirring constantly, 10 minutes or until thickened. Remove from heat.
• **Add** chocolate and vanilla, stirring until chocolate melts.
• **Pour** through a wire-mesh strainer into a large bowl, discarding any lumps; cover and chill 2 hours.
• **Pour** mixture into freezer container of a 4-quart electric freezer; freeze according to manufacturer's instructions. **Yield:** 2 quarts.

Note: For testing purposes only, we used Lipton tea bags.

OVEN-BAKED FISH

If grilling fresh fish is not your cooking style, try these fast-to-fix oven recipes and the menu suggestions.

CRISPY BAKED FILLETS

Menu Suggestion: sautéed yellow squash, garlic bread, and sliced tomato, onion, and cucumber

Prep: 8 minutes
Bake: 10 minutes

2   tablespoons mayonnaise
½   teaspoon dried Italian
     seasoning
¼   teaspoon salt
¼   teaspoon pepper
1   pound orange roughy fillets
½   cup fine cornflake crumbs

• **Stir** together first 4 ingredients; brush over fillets. Dredge fillets in cornflake crumbs, and place on a lightly greased baking sheet.
• **Bake** at 450° for 10 minutes or until fish flakes with a fork. **Yield:** 4 servings.

SPICY MUSTARD FISH

Menu Suggestion: steamed green beans, glazed carrots, and crusty dinner rolls

Prep: 6 minutes
Bake: 12 minutes

30 round buttery crackers
2   tablespoons Dijon mustard
½   teaspoon dried basil, crushed
½   teaspoon hot sauce
¼   teaspoon pepper
1⅓ pounds orange roughy fillets
Lime wedges (optional)

• **Process** crackers in a food processor until finely ground.

- **Stir** together mustard and next 3 ingredients; brush over fillets. Dredge fillets in cracker crumbs, and place on a lightly greased rack in a broiler pan.
- **Bake** at 450° for 12 minutes or until fish flakes with a fork. Serve with lime wedges, if desired. **Yield:** 4 servings.

Helen H. Maurer
Christmas, Florida

CATFISH PARMESAN

Menu Suggestion: oven-fried potatoes, coleslaw, and fresh pineapple

Prep: 15 minutes
Bake: 25 minutes

1 cup fine, dry breadcrumbs
⅓ cup grated Parmesan cheese
1 teaspoon salt
½ teaspoon pepper
½ teaspoon paprika
2 tablespoons chopped fresh parsley (optional)
½ teaspoon chopped fresh oregano (optional)
6 (8-ounce) catfish fillets
½ cup butter or margarine, melted
Garnishes: lemon wedges, fresh oregano sprigs

- **Stir** together first 5 ingredients and, if desired, parsley and chopped oregano.
- **Dip** catfish in butter; dredge in bread-crumb mixture, and place on a parchment paper-lined baking sheet.
- **Bake** at 375° for 25 minutes or until fish flakes with a fork. Garnish, if desired. **Yield:** 6 servings.

Linda M. Bevill
Monticello, Arkansas

HEAVENLY BROILED GROUPER

Menu Suggestion: broiled tomatoes, steamed broccoli, and breadsticks

Prep: 10 minutes
Broil: 10 minutes

2 pounds grouper fillets
½ cup grated Parmesan cheese
1 tablespoon butter or margarine, softened
3 tablespoons reduced-fat mayonnaise
3 tablespoons chopped green onions
1 garlic clove, pressed
¼ teaspoon salt
Dash of hot sauce

- **Place** fillets in a single layer in a lightly greased 13- x 9-inch pan.
- **Stir** together Parmesan cheese and next 6 ingredients; spread mixture over fillets.
- **Broil** 6 inches from heat (with electric oven door partially open) 10 minutes or until lightly browned and fish flakes with a fork. **Yield:** 6 to 8 servings.

Note: Do not broil closer to heat than 6 inches or topping may burn before fish is done.

CURRY ADDS CHARACTER

Amber-hued curry packs a wallop of flavor. This mighty spice blend meshes the sweetness of ground cinnamon, cloves, and nutmeg with zesty red and black pepper, cumin, and golden turmeric. Opt for a generous pinch of the exotic powder and take familiar seafood and sauces or your favorite chicken salad on a rousing adventure.

VEGETABLE CURRY

Prep: 10 minutes
Cook: 21 minutes

3 cups broccoli flowerets
1 small green bell pepper
1 small red bell pepper
1 small yellow bell pepper
3 carrots
¼ cup butter or margarine
1 small onion, diced
2 tablespoons all-purpose flour
1½ tablespoons curry powder
½ teaspoon salt
¼ teaspoon ground red pepper
1 (14½-ounce) can chicken broth
½ cup coconut milk *
½ pound small fresh green beans
Hot cooked rice
Garnishes: roasted peanuts, fresh cilantro sprigs

- **Cook** broccoli in boiling water to cover 3 minutes; drain and set aside. Cut bell peppers into thin strips; thinly slice carrots.
- **Melt** butter in a large skillet over medium heat; add onion, and sauté until tender.
- **Stir** in flour and next 3 ingredients. Cook, stirring constantly, 1 minute. Gradually stir in broth; bring to a boil. Reduce heat, and simmer, stirring constantly, 8 minutes or until thickened.
- **Stir** in broccoli, bell pepper, carrot, coconut milk, and green beans; cook, stirring constantly, 3 minutes or just until vegetables are crisp-tender. Serve over rice; garnish, if desired. **Yield:** 4 servings.

* Substitute ½ cup half-and-half for coconut milk, if desired.

Shrimp Curry: Omit broccoli flowerets, carrots, bell peppers, and green beans. Stir ¾ pound peeled, medium-size fresh shrimp into sauce with coconut milk; serve as directed.

QUICK CURRIED CHICKEN

Prep: 15 minutes
Cook: 25 minutes

2 tablespoons butter or margarine
1 large onion, chopped
1 large green bell pepper, chopped
2 garlic cloves, pressed
2 (10¾-ounce) cans cream of
    celery soup, undiluted
1 (12-ounce) can evaporated
    milk
4 cups chopped cooked chicken
1 (2-ounce) jar diced pimiento,
    drained
1 tablespoon curry powder
1 tablespoon chopped fresh ginger
1 tablespoon Worcestershire sauce
¼ teaspoon salt
¼ teaspoon ground red pepper
Hot cooked rice
Toppings: chutney, chopped roasted
    peanuts, crumbled cooked
    bacon

• **Melt** butter in a large saucepan over
medium heat; add onion, bell pepper,
and garlic. Sauté until tender.
• **Stir** in soup and next 8 ingredients;
cook over low heat, stirring constantly,
15 minutes or until thoroughly heated.
Serve over rice with desired toppings.
Yield: 8 servings.

Ingeborg Sears
Wilmington, North Carolina

INDIAN OMELET

Prep: 5 minutes
Cook: 10 minutes

3 large eggs
2 tablespoons whipping cream
¼ teaspoon salt
¼ teaspoon pepper
2 tablespoons butter or margarine
1 (5-ounce) can white chicken
    in water, drained and flaked
1 tablespoon chopped green
    onions
Curry Sauce

• **Whisk** together first 4 ingredients in a
bowl; set aside.

• **Melt** butter in a 10-inch omelet pan or
nonstick skillet over medium heat; add
chicken and green onions, and sauté 2
minutes or until onions are tender.
• **Add** egg mixture to pan. As mixture
starts to cook, gently lift edges with a
spatula, and tilt pan so uncooked portion flows underneath.
• **Fold** omelet in half; serve immediately
with Curry Sauce. **Yield:** 2 servings.

Curry Sauce

Prep: 5 minutes
Cook: 5 minutes

2 tablespoons butter or margarine
2 tablespoons all-purpose flour
2 teaspoons curry powder
⅔ cup chicken broth
½ cup whipping cream
⅛ teaspoon salt
⅛ teaspoon pepper

• **Melt** butter in a saucepan over low
heat; whisk in flour and curry powder.
Cook, whisking constantly, 1 minute.
Gradually add broth; cook over medium
heat, whisking constantly, 1 minute or
until thickened.
• **Whisk** in whipping cream, salt, and
pepper; cook, whisking occasionally, 2
minutes or until thoroughly heated.
Yield: 1 cup.

Note: Store sauce in refrigerator up to 3
days, if desired. Reheat in a heavy
saucepan over low heat, stirring constantly. Serve over cooked vegetables, if
desired.

Mildred Anderson
Conway, Arkansas

TAKE A POWDER

Curry powder comes in two styles:
standard and Madras, a hotter
blend. Protect curry's pungency
by storing it in an airtight container
in a cool, dry place up to two
months.

TOAST TO SPRING

There's no better sound than the slam of
a screened door, echoing the arrival of
spring. Step onto the porch and welcome the season with a cool beverage
and quick snack from this fine selection.

SMOKED SALMON
CHEESECAKE

Prep: 30 minutes
Bake: 1 hour and 40 minutes
Chill: 8 hours

3 tablespoons fine, dry
    breadcrumbs
5 tablespoons shredded Parmesan
    cheese, divided *
3 tablespoons butter or
    margarine
1 small onion, chopped
½ small green bell pepper,
    chopped
3 (8-ounce) packages cream
    cheese, softened
½ (8-ounce) package cream
    cheese, softened
4 large eggs
½ cup whipping cream
½ cup (2 ounces) shredded
    Jarlsberg cheese
5 ounces smoked salmon,
    chopped **
1 teaspoon hot sauce

• **Stir** together breadcrumbs and 2
tablespoons Parmesan cheese; sprinkle
in a buttered 8-inch springform pan. Set
pan on a large sheet of aluminum foil,
allowing at least 4 inches around edges;
pull up edges, covering sides. Set pan
aside.
• **Melt** butter in a large skillet over
medium-high heat; add onion and bell
pepper, and sauté until tender.
• **Beat** cream cheese, eggs, and whipping cream at medium speed with an
electric mixer until creamy. Add remaining Parmesan, sautéed vegetables, and
Jarlsberg cheese, beating until blended.

• **Stir** in salmon and hot sauce. Pour into prepared pan. Place pan in a roasting pan; add hot water to roasting pan to a depth of 2 inches. Bake at 300° for 1 hour and 40 minutes. Turn oven off. Let cheesecake stand in closed oven 1 hour.
• **Remove** cheesecake from water bath; cool on a wire rack. Chill at least 8 hours. Serve with assorted crackers. **Yield:** 14 to 16 appetizer servings.

✱ Substitute 5 tablespoons shredded Romano cheese for Parmesan cheese, if desired.

✱✱ Substitute 5 ounces smoked trout for smoked salmon, if desired.

Note: Jarlsberg is a mild Swiss-style cheese with large, irregular holes. Swiss may be substituted.

Judith Smith-Ille
Watkinsville, Georgia

ANCHO CHILE BUTTER

Prep: 30 minutes

½ cup butter, softened and
    divided
1 shallot, minced
1 teaspoon ancho chile
    powder
Pinch of salt
Pinch of freshly ground
    pepper
2 teaspoons lemon juice
Additional ancho chile powder

• **Melt** 1 teaspoon butter in a small skillet over medium-high heat; add shallot, and sauté 2 minutes.
• **Stir** together shallot, remaining butter, 1 teaspoon ancho powder, and next 3 ingredients. Shape into a 4-inch log; wrap in plastic wrap. Chill until firm. Sprinkle with ancho powder; serve on crackers, breads, meat, or vegetables. **Yield:** ½ cup.

Renie Steves
Fort Worth, Texas

CUCUMBER-YOGURT DIP

Prep: 15 minutes
Chill: 8 hours

4 small cucumbers
1 (32-ounce) container plain
    nonfat yogurt
3 garlic cloves, minced
3 tablespoons olive oil
1½ tablespoons minced fresh
    dill
1½ tablespoons red wine
    vinegar
1 teaspoon salt

• **Peel,** seed, and grate cucumbers; place in a colander lined with 2 layers of cheesecloth. Place colander in a bowl. Spoon yogurt over cucumber; cover and chill 8 hours.
• **Spoon** cucumber and yogurt into a medium bowl; stir in garlic and remaining ingredients. Serve with toasted pita wedges. **Yield:** about 2 cups.

Kimberly R. Diamondidis
Germantown, Maryland

CITRUS WINE COCKTAIL

Prep: 5 minutes

1 (750-milliliter) bottle dry white
    wine, chilled
½ cup orange liqueur
¼ cup sugar
1 (10-ounce) bottle club soda,
    chilled

• **Stir** together first 3 ingredients in a large pitcher until sugar dissolves; stir in club soda. Serve over ice, if desired. **Yield:** 5½ cups.

Note: For testing purposes only, we used Triple Sec liqueur.

CRANBERRY-GINGER FIZZ

Prep: 20 minutes

Rind of 1 orange, cut into strips
1¼ cups cranberry juice drink
1 cup water
½ cup orange juice
⅓ cup sugar
3 fresh ginger slices
1 teaspoon vanilla extract
2⅔ cups soda water, chilled

• **Bring** first 6 ingredients to a boil in a saucepan; reduce heat, and simmer 10 minutes.
• **Pour** mixture through a wire-mesh strainer into a 2-quart pitcher, discarding solids. Stir in vanilla; cool.
• **Stir** in soda water; serve over ice. **Yield:** 5⅓ cups.

Madeline Gibbon
Sherwood, Arkansas

PATIO BLUSH

Prep: 5 minutes

1 (6-ounce) can frozen orange
    juice concentrate, thawed
    and undiluted
¼ cup lemon juice
¼ cup honey
¼ cup maraschino cherry juice
1 pint pineapple sherbet
1 (2-liter) bottle ginger ale, chilled

• **Stir** together first 4 ingredients; pour into 6 (16-ounce) glasses. Top each with a scoop of sherbet; fill with ginger ale. **Yield:** 6 servings.

TEXAS FIRECRACKERS

Prep: 45 minutes
Bake: 25 minutes

2 skinned and boned chicken breast halves
24 pepperoncini salad peppers
6 ounces Monterey Jack cheese with peppers, cut into 24 strips
12 frozen phyllo pastry sheets, thawed
½ cup butter or margarine, melted

• **Cook** chicken in boiling water to cover 20 minutes or until done; drain. Cut into 2- x ½-inch pieces.
• **Cut** tops from peppers; remove seeds. Stuff each pepper with 1 chicken piece and 1 cheese strip.
• **Stack** 3 phyllo sheets on a large cutting board, brushing each with melted butter. Keep remaining sheets covered with a slightly damp towel to keep from drying out.
• **Cut** phyllo stack crosswise into thirds; cut in half lengthwise. Place a stuffed pepper 1 inch from short edge; roll up, and twist ends of phyllo.
• **Repeat** procedure with remaining phyllo, butter, and stuffed peppers. Place on baking sheets coated with cooking spray.
• **Bake** at 375° for 20 to 25 minutes or until golden. **Yield:** 2 dozen appetizers.

Carol Barclay
Portland, Texas

FIELDS OF FLAVOR

Fans of sweet onions eagerly await their arrival in supermarkets each spring—or order them by mail. Read on and join us as we sample the harvest with these savory recipes.

ONION RISOTTO

Serve risotto as a side dish with grilled chicken or fish, or as a light main course with salad.

Prep: 10 minutes
Cook: 45 minutes

1 pound fresh asparagus
2 pounds sweet onions, cut in half and thinly sliced
2 garlic cloves, pressed
2 teaspoons salt
2 tablespoons olive oil
1 (16-ounce) package Arborio rice
8 cups warm chicken broth
1 cup dry white wine
½ cup shredded Parmesan cheese

• **Snap** off tough ends of asparagus; cut asparagus into 2-inch pieces. Set aside.
• **Sauté** onion, garlic, and salt in hot oil in a Dutch oven until tender.
• **Add** rice; cook, stirring constantly, 2 minutes. Reduce heat to medium; add 1 cup chicken broth. Cook, stirring often, until liquid is absorbed.
• **Repeat** procedure with remaining broth, 1 cup at a time. (Cooking time is about 30 minutes.)
• **Add** asparagus and wine; cook, stirring gently, until liquid is absorbed. Stir in cheese; serve immediately. **Yield:** 6 servings.

CORN WITH BACON AND CARAMELIZED ONION

Adapted from a recipe by Chef Bob Waggoner of the Charleston Grill

Prep: 20 minutes
Cook: 25 minutes

4 ears fresh corn
6 bacon slices, chopped
2 medium-size sweet onions, cut into thin strips
2 tablespoons light molasses
¼ teaspoon salt
¼ teaspoon pepper

• **Cut** corn from cob; set corn aside.
• **Cook** bacon in a heavy skillet until crisp; remove bacon, reserving 1 tablespoon drippings in skillet. Crumble bacon, and set aside.
• **Add** onion to reserved drippings in skillet; cook over medium-high heat, stirring often, 15 minutes or until onion is caramel colored.
• **Add** corn, and cook, stirring often, 8 minutes. Stir in molasses, salt, and pepper; place in a serving dish, and sprinkle with bacon. **Yield:** 4 servings.

In Georgia, they call them Vidalias. In Texas, they're 1015s. By any name, the South's sweet onions are just plain good. Onion lovers just can't seem to get enough of the mild flavor.

SWEET GEORGIA VIDALIAS

R. T. Stanley strides across a long field, his heavy work boots sinking into the freshly furrowed, sandy soil. He pulls an onion out of the ground, clips the spidery roots and the green top, then slices it in half with his pocketknife.

"Now *this* is what we're looking for," he says, displaying the onion's shiny heart. The concentric rings are moist, firm, and almost perfectly round. "If all my onions could be like this, I would be real pleased."

With that, the farmer raises the onion to his lips and takes a big, juicy bite. "Boy, that's good," he says with a smile.

R. T., along with his brother and sons, grows some thousand acres of the flavorful vegetable on his farm in Vidalia, Georgia, the area that gave rise to the popularity of the sweet onion. It all started back in 1931, when Vidalia resident Mose Coleman planted onions in his vegetable garden. When he tasted them, they were sweet instead of hot. Mose started selling the onions, and over the years, demand grew. Today, few vegetables have the popularity Vidalias enjoy.

A Granex-type onion derived from yellow Bermudas, Vidalias are large and slightly squatty. Only those specimens grown in specially designated areas of southeast Georgia can be called Vidalias, and growers must be registered. These stringent guidelines are designed to protect the flavor that made these onions famous. "A Vidalia onion is the sweetest onion you can get," R. T. brags.

Could be. But there are more than 100 farmers over in Texas who might take issue with that assertion.

TEXAS 1015s

In the Rio Grande Valley, Bob Peterson oversees the last of his 1015 Supersweet onion harvest. Texas' answer to the Vidalia is a jumbo planted on October 15 of each year—hence the name 1015 (ten fifteen). The early planting date yields an earlier harvest, giving the state's growers a jump on the market.

Dr. Leonard Pike of Texas A&M University developed the 1015 while trying to produce a uniform, disease-resistant onion suited to Texas growing conditions. The result was a very large onion—the average 1015 weighs ¾ of a pound—that was also exceptionally mild.

"1015s put us on the map, so to speak," Bob explains, tipping his hat to Dr. Pike's discovery. "They were something we could rally behind, wave the flag, and let the industry know we were in business—the sweet onion business."

Bob grew up on an onion farm and remembers loading regular yellow onions into closed vans as a youngster. "We just had to stop and cry—tears just running down our faces as we worked," he says. "1015s are not that way."

While Vidalias and 1015s are the best-known of the South's sweet onions, Florida and North Carolina also produce small crops of the mild bulbs. Harvests range from April to June, but these beloved vegetables are available much of the year thanks to controlled-atmosphere storage.

Both types of sweet onions have low levels of sulfur, the compound that leads to strong flavors and stinging eyes. But even the experts disagree somewhat on whether it's genetics or environment that makes the onions sweet.

Others may try to grow sweet onions, R. T. says, but they just won't have the same results. It takes the right combination of soil, water, and temperature. But a lack of these elements doesn't keep people from trying.

"We had one man come from Little Rock, Arkansas, and buy a pickup load of our soil from right out of this field and carry it back to grow onions in it," R.T. says incredulously. "But I figured since we never did hear anything from him he didn't have any success."

CARAMELIZED ONION TART

(pictured on page 40)

This rustic tart defines simplicity. Serve it as a sophisticated first course.

Prep: 45 minutes
Bake: 25 minutes

3 **pounds large sweet onions, sliced**
2 **tablespoons olive oil**
1 **teaspoon salt**
½ **(17¼-ounce) package frozen puff pastry sheets, thawed**
½ **cup shredded Parmesan cheese**
Garnish: fresh rosemary sprigs

• **Cook** onion in hot oil in a large skillet over low heat, stirring often, 30 to 35 minutes or until onion is caramel colored. Stir in salt, and set aside.
• **Unfold** pastry sheet; fit into a 9-inch square tart pan.
• **Bake** at 400° for 15 to 20 minutes or until browned. Remove from oven. Press pastry with the back of a spoon to flatten. Top with caramelized onion; sprinkle with Parmesan cheese. Bake 5 more minutes. Garnish, if desired. **Yield:** 6 servings.

GRILLED ONION SALAD

Serve this salad as a main dish.

Prep: 20 minutes
Chill: 2 hours
Grill: 15 minutes

4 **large sweet onions**
⅓ **cup balsamic vinegar**
2 **tablespoons walnut oil**
2 **tablespoons honey**
1 **teaspoon salt**
8 **cups mixed salad greens**
¼ **cup chopped fresh parsley**
¼ **cup chopped pecans, toasted**

• **Peel** onions, leaving root end intact. Cut each onion vertically into quarters, cutting to within ½ inch of root end. Cut each quarter vertically into thirds. Place in a shallow dish.

• **Whisk** together vinegar and next 3 ingredients. Pour over onions; cover and chill 2 hours.
• **Drain** onions, reserving vinaigrette mixture.
• **Grill** onions, covered with grill lid, over medium-high heat (350° to 400°) 10 to 15 minutes or until tender. Place each onion on 2 cups salad greens; drizzle with reserved vinaigrette. Sprinkle with parsley and pecans. **Yield:** 4 servings.

ONION SOUP

Prep: 20 minutes
Cook: 1 hour and 17 minutes

4 **pounds large sweet onions**
2 **garlic cloves, minced**
2 **tablespoons vegetable oil**
2 **tablespoons all-purpose flour**
1 **(14½-ounce) can chicken broth**
1 **cup water**
1 **teaspoon pepper**
1 **tablespoon chopped fresh rosemary**
¼ **teaspoon salt**
3 **(14½-ounce) cans beef broth**
1 **cup Merlot wine**
6 **baguette slices, toasted**
6 **(1-ounce) slices farmers cheese**

• **Cut** onions in half; cut halves into slices.
• **Cook** onion and garlic in hot oil in a Dutch oven over low heat, stirring often, 40 to 45 minutes or until onion is caramel colored.
• **Stir** in flour; cook, stirring constantly, 2 minutes.
• **Stir** in chicken broth and next 4 ingredients; cook, stirring to remove particles from bottom of Dutch oven.
• **Stir** in beef broth and wine; bring to a boil. Reduce heat, and simmer 20 to 30 minutes or until thickened.
• **Top** each serving with a bread slice and a cheese slice. **Yield:** 12 cups.

MINTED PORK LOIN

Prep: 25 minutes
Cook: 1 hour and 20 minutes

3 **medium-size sweet onions, chopped**
3 **garlic cloves, minced**
1 **tablespoon olive oil**
¼ **cup fresh mint, chopped**
½ **cup orange juice**
2½ **teaspoons salt, divided**
½ **teaspoon pepper**
1 **(4-pound) pork loin roast**
1 **tablespoon black peppercorns**
1 **tablespoon fresh rosemary**
½ **medium-size sweet onion**

• **Sauté** chopped onion and garlic in hot oil in a large skillet 5 minutes.
• **Stir** in mint, orange juice, ½ teaspoon salt, and pepper; cook, stirring constantly, until orange juice evaporates.
• **Butterfly** roast by making a lengthwise cut down center to within ½ inch of other side. Open roast, and place between 2 sheets of heavy-duty plastic wrap; flatten to ½-inch thickness using a mallet or rolling pin.
• **Spread** mint mixture over roast; roll up; tie at 1-inch intervals with string.
• **Process** peppercorns, rosemary, ½ onion, and remaining 2 teaspoons salt in a food processor until ground. Spread over pork.
• **Prepare** fire by piling charcoal or lava rocks on 1 side of grill, leaving the other side empty. Place rack on grill. Place pork loin over empty side, and grill, covered with grill lid, over medium-high heat (350° to 400°) 1 hour.
• **Grill** pork over direct heat 4 minutes on each side or until a meat thermometer inserted into thickest portion registers 160°. Let stand 10 minutes before slicing. **Yield:** 6 servings.

Hearty Vegetable Entrées

Meat with every meal isn't the rule of thumb anymore, and passing on meat doesn't necessarily mean relying on tofu in your diet. You can have a satisfying and healthy dinner without beef, poultry, pork, or seafood. If you are afraid your family will turn up their noses at such a notion, don't tell until after they've feasted on any of these recipes.

VEGGIE PIZZAS

Prep: 12 minutes
Bake: 8 minutes

½ cup dried tomatoes
1 small purple onion, thinly sliced
2 garlic cloves, minced
1 (14-ounce) can artichoke hearts, drained
1 (4-ounce) jar sliced mushrooms, drained
2 tablespoons balsamic vinegar
¼ cup chopped fresh basil
4 (7-inch) pizza crusts
1 cup (4 ounces) shredded reduced-fat mozzarella cheese

• **Let** tomatoes stand in water to cover 10 minutes; drain well, pressing between layers of paper towels. Chop tomatoes.
• **Stir** together onion and next 5 ingredients. Sprinkle tomato over pizza crusts; top evenly with onion mixture. Sprinkle evenly with cheese. Place pizzas on baking sheets.
• **Bake** at 400° for 6 to 8 minutes or until cheese melts. **Yield:** 4 servings.

❤ Per serving: Calories 521
Fat 11.9g Cholesterol 0mg
Sodium 827mg

QUICK BEAN SOUP

Prep: 15 minutes
Cook: 15 minutes

1 large onion, chopped
1 small green bell pepper, chopped
2 teaspoons vegetable oil
1 (16-ounce) can kidney beans, rinsed and drained
1 (15-ounce) can pinto beans, rinsed and drained
1 (15-ounce) can black beans, rinsed and drained
2 (14½-ounce) cans no-salt-added stewed tomatoes, undrained
1 (14½-ounce) can low-sodium fat-free chicken broth
1 cup picante sauce
1 teaspoon ground cumin

• **Sauté** onion and bell pepper in hot oil in a large saucepan until tender.
• **Add** kidney beans and remaining ingredients, and bring to a boil. Cover, reduce heat, and simmer 10 minutes. **Yield:** 10 cups.

Tara Herrenbruck
Independence, Missouri

❤ Per cup: Calories 180
Fat 1.5g Cholesterol 0mg
Sodium 534mg

VEGETABLE LASAGNA

Although this lasagna has more than 30 percent of its calories from fat, it is well worth the splurge.

Prep: 40 minutes
Bake: 25 minutes

1 (8-ounce) package light cream cheese, softened
¾ cup light ricotta cheese
½ cup light sour cream
1 large egg
¼ cup grated Parmesan cheese
2 teaspoons dried Italian seasoning
1 (14½-ounce) can diced tomatoes with basil, garlic, and oregano, undrained
1 (6-ounce) can no-salt-added tomato paste
¼ cup chopped fresh parsley
¼ cup balsamic vinegar
½ teaspoon pepper
1 medium onion, chopped
1 (8-ounce) package sliced fresh mushrooms
1 large zucchini, chopped
4 garlic cloves, pressed
Vegetable cooking spray
6 lasagna noodles, cooked
1 (8-ounce) package shredded reduced-fat mozzarella cheese

• **Beat** cream cheese at medium speed with an electric mixer until creamy. Add ricotta cheese and next 4 ingredients; beat until smooth. Set aside.
• **Bring** tomatoes and next 4 ingredients to a boil; cover, reduce heat, and simmer 10 minutes. Set aside.
• **Sauté** onion and next 3 ingredients in a large nonstick skillet coated with cooking spray until tender.
• **Layer** half each of noodles, cream cheese mixture, onion mixture, and tomato mixture in a lightly greased 13- x 9-inch baking dish. Repeat layers once. Sprinkle with mozzarella cheese.
• **Bake,** covered, at 350° for 25 minutes. Let stand 10 minutes before serving. **Yield:** 10 servings.

❤ Per serving: Calories 219
Fat 8.7g Cholesterol 34mg
Sodium 441mg

Fresh From the Churn

Southerners delight in the tang of a glass of cold buttermilk, while cooks savor the buttery flavor and tenderness that it contributes to cakes and pies. If you don't have it on hand, substitute ⅔ cup plain low-fat or nonfat yogurt mixed with ⅓ cup milk for each cup buttermilk needed. Powdered buttermilk, found at your local grocery, is shelf stable and is an excellent choice for baking. (Mix according to package directions.)

BUTTERMILK POUND CAKE

Prep: 20 minutes
Bake: 1 hour and 5 minutes

1 cup butter or margarine, softened
2 cups sugar
4 large eggs
1 teaspoon vanilla extract
1 teaspoon lemon extract
3 cups all-purpose flour
½ teaspoon baking soda
½ teaspoon baking powder
¼ teaspoon salt
1 cup buttermilk
Buttermilk Glaze

• **Beat** butter at medium speed with an electric mixer 2 minutes or until creamy. Gradually add sugar, beating 5 to 7 minutes. Add eggs, 1 at a time, beating just until yellow disappears. Stir in flavorings.
• **Combine** flour and next 3 ingredients; add to butter mixture alternately with buttermilk, beginning and ending with flour mixture. Beat at low speed just until blended after each addition. Pour batter into a greased and floured 12-cup Bundt pan.
• **Bake** at 325° for 1 hour and 5 minutes or until a wooden pick inserted in center comes out clean. Cool in pan on a wire rack 10 to 15 minutes; remove from pan, and cool on wire rack. Pour Buttermilk Glaze over warm cake. **Yield:** 1 (10-inch) cake.

Mae Moore
Arlington, Virginia

Buttermilk Glaze

We couldn't resist this glaze, an old favorite of ours, over this cake.

Prep: 15 minutes

2 tablespoons buttermilk
¼ cup sugar
2 tablespoons butter or margarine
¾ teaspoon cornstarch
⅛ teaspoon baking soda
¾ teaspoon vanilla extract

• **Bring** first 5 ingredients to a boil in a small saucepan over medium heat, stirring constantly; remove from heat, and cool mixture slightly. Stir in vanilla. **Yield:** ½ cup.

WARM APPLE-BUTTERMILK CUSTARD PIE
(pictured on page 80)

The combination of a buttery fruit filling and a crumbly cinnamon topping makes this apple pie a dessert delight.

Prep: 30 minutes
Bake: 1 hour and 10 minutes
Stand: 1 hour

½ (15-ounce) package refrigerated piecrusts
½ cup butter or margarine, divided
2 Granny Smith apples, peeled and sliced
½ cup sugar
¾ teaspoon ground cinnamon, divided
1⅓ cups sugar
4 large eggs
2 tablespoons all-purpose flour
1 teaspoon vanilla extract
¾ cup buttermilk
3 tablespoons butter or margarine, softened
¼ cup sugar
¼ cup firmly packed light brown sugar
½ cup all-purpose flour

• **Fit** piecrust into a 9-inch pieplate according to package directions; fold edges under, and crimp.
• **Melt** ¼ cup butter in a large skillet over medium heat; add apple slices, ½ cup sugar, and ½ teaspoon cinnamon. Cook, stirring occasionally, 3 to 5 minutes or until apple slices are tender; set aside.
• **Beat** ¼ cup butter and 1⅓ cups sugar at medium speed with an electric mixer until creamy.
• **Add** eggs, 1 at a time, beating just until yellow disappears.
• **Add** 2 tablespoons flour and vanilla, beating until blended.
• **Add** buttermilk, beating until smooth.
• **Spoon** apple mixture into piecrust; pour buttermilk mixture over apple mixture.
• **Bake** at 300° for 30 minutes.
• **Stir** together 3 tablespoons butter, ¼ cup sugar, brown sugar, ½ cup flour,

and remaining ¼ teaspoon cinnamon until crumbly. Sprinkle over pie.
• **Bake** 40 more minutes or until a knife inserted in center comes out clean. Let stand 1 hour before serving. **Yield:** 1 (9-inch) pie.

Patricia A. Harmon
Baden, Pennsylvania

BUTTERMILK PRALINES

Have a friend help drop these pralines because they harden quickly.

Prep: 20 minutes
Cook: 20 minutes

2 cups sugar
1 teaspoon baking soda
⅛ teaspoon salt
1 cup buttermilk
2 tablespoons butter or margarine
1 tablespoon light corn syrup
2½ cups pecan halves

• **Bring** first 4 ingredients to a boil in a heavy 4-quart saucepan, stirring constantly. Boil, stirring constantly, 5 minutes or until a candy thermometer registers 210°.
• **Stir** in butter, corn syrup, and pecans; return to a boil, and boil, stirring constantly, 5 minutes or until thermometer registers 232° (thread stage).
• **Remove** from heat, and beat with a wooden spoon 1 to 2 minutes or just until mixture begins to thicken. Quickly drop by tablespoonfuls onto wax paper; let stand until firm. Store in an airtight container. **Yield:** 2½ dozen.

Lynne Teal Weeks
Columbus, Georgia

BUTTERMILK SHERBET

Prep: 5 minutes
Freeze: 8 hours

2 cups buttermilk
1 (8-ounce) can crushed pineapple, undrained
¾ cup sugar

• **Stir** together all ingredients until sugar dissolves.
• **Freeze** in a shallow airtight container 8 hours, stirring twice. **Yield:** 3 cups.

Jan Griffin
Charleston, West Virginia

BUTTERMILK FUDGE SQUARES

Prep: 20 minutes
Bake: 20 minutes

1 cup butter or margarine
¼ cup cocoa
1 cup water
½ cup buttermilk
2 large eggs
1 teaspoon baking soda
1 teaspoon vanilla extract
2 cups sugar
2 cups all-purpose flour
½ teaspoon salt
Chocolate-Buttermilk Frosting

• **Cook** first 3 ingredients in a small saucepan over low heat, stirring constantly, until butter melts and mixture is smooth; remove from heat.
• **Beat** buttermilk and next 3 ingredients at medium speed with an electric mixer until smooth. Add butter mixture to buttermilk mixture, beating until blended.
• **Combine** sugar, flour, and salt; gradually add to buttermilk mixture, beating until blended.
• **Pour** mixture into a greased 15- x 10-inch jellyroll pan.
• **Bake** at 350° for 15 to 20 minutes or until cake is set.
• **Spread** Chocolate-Buttermilk Frosting over warm cake.
• **Cut** into squares while warm. Cool before serving. **Yield:** 2 dozen.

Chocolate-Buttermilk Frosting

Prep: 15 minutes

1 cup butter or margarine
¼ cup cocoa
⅓ cup buttermilk
1 (16-ounce) package powdered sugar
1 teaspoon vanilla extract
¼ cup chopped pecans

• **Cook** first 3 ingredients in a medium saucepan over medium heat, stirring constantly, until butter melts and mixture is smooth.
• **Remove** butter mixture from heat; stir in powdered sugar, vanilla, and pecans. **Yield:** about 2½ cups.

Marie Davis
Charlotte, North Carolina

MORE WAYS WITH BUTTERMILK

■ For a tangy flavor, try buttermilk in biscuits, cornbread, or mashed potatoes.

■ Soak chicken or catfish in buttermilk before dredging in flour to fry.

■ Extend dressings by adding a dab of buttermilk.

■ Drizzle buttermilk over baked apples.

From Our Kitchen to Yours

MARKET FRESH

Sweet, juicy strawberries are at their peak and priced right in the produce section. The California Strawberry Commission offers quick ways to enjoy them.

For a fresh strawberry sauce: Stem and halve berries; process berries in a food processor or blender until almost smooth. Mix in a little sugar, and season with a teaspoon or two of lemon juice. Serve over ice cream, pudding, or pound cake.

For a luscious dip: Beat softened light cream cheese with enough fat-free milk to reach dipping consistency. Mix in finely crumbled blue cheese; add a dash of coarsely ground black pepper. Serve with whole strawberries for dipping.

For a mild, flavorful salsa: Coarsely chop 3 cups whole strawberries, 1 mango, 1 avocado, and ¼ cucumber, and place in bowl. Stir in ½ cup chopped fresh cilantro and 1 tablespoon lemon juice. Chill at least 20 minutes. Serve with blue corn tortilla chips.

For more ideas and strawberry facts, contact the California Strawberry Commission, (831) 724-1301; Web site: www.calstrawberry.com; Florida Strawberry Growers Association, P.O. Drawer 2550, Plant City, FL 33564; (813) 752-6822 or www.straw-berry.org.

TIPS AND TIDBITS

Serve the Caramelized Onion Tart on page 96 with a chilled Sauvignon Blanc for an appetizing evening opener.

Want dinner in a hurry? The National Potato Promotion Board has created a new recipe brochure—"Speed Spuds! A Whole New Way to Do Dinner." It features quick-cooking techniques for potatoes that yield a complete meal in less than 30 minutes. To receive a free copy, send a self-addressed, stamped (66 cents), business-size envelope to SPEEDSPUDS! RECIPE BROCHURE, 5105 East 41st Avenue, Denver, CO 80216.

CRYSTALLIZED FLOWERS

To crystallize the violas and mint leaves for the Molded French Cream, rinse flower petals and mint leaves; let dry on paper towels.

Beat 2 cups powdered sugar, 1 tablespoon meringue powder, and ⅓ cup water at low speed with an electric mixer until blended; beat at high speed 4 to 5 minutes or until fluffy.

Brush powdered sugar mixture on all sides of flower petals and mint leaves; sprinkle petals and leaves with 1 cup superfine sugar. Let stand on wire racks 24 hours to dry.

MOLDS FOR FRENCH CREAM

Jan Moon of our Test Kitchens staff used an 8-cup mold for the dessert on page 72. If you don't have a mold identical to the one she used, don't fret. The shape of the mold won't affect the flavor. Make yours tall and slim or short and wide. When a large dessert is more than you need, use two 4-cup molds; serve one and give one to a friend.

A SPLASH OF VINEGAR

A little distilled white vinegar goes a long way. Keep it on hand for the following uses.

- Remove spaghetti sauce stains from plastic containers.

- Make vinegar ice cubes to clean and deodorize garbage disposal.

- Make crystal glasses sparkle.

- Remove coffee and tea stains from pots and cups.

- Loosen burned food from pans.

- Use it as a substitute for lemon juice in recipes.

- Sprinkle it on fish fillets to make them firmer and whiter.

- Add a dash to mashed potatoes to make them creamier.

- Revive wilted vegetables with a tablespoon of vinegar when rinsing.

- Rub onto cheese to prevent drying out and molding.

- Cut grease during cleanup.

- Clean sponges.

- Add 2 teaspoons vinegar when cooking dried beans to make them tender and easier to digest.

- Keep fresh beets from fading by adding a little vinegar to the water when cooking.

- Add 1 tablespoon vinegar to the water when steaming or boiling cauliflower to improve appearance and taste.

Source: Vim & Vinegar *by Melodie Moore, Harper Perennial*

May

Satisfy your sweet tooth with this month's irresistible desserts. In "Triple Crown Cakes," the cake batter is the same for the three cakes, but the fillings vary. They're all so delicious, you won't be able to pick a favorite (we couldn't). "Old-Fashioned Fudge Cake" offers you a chocolate-lover's delight with Hot Fudge Cake. In just 10 minutes, you can have it ready to bake. Scoop into the dessert hot from the oven, and give in to your natural instincts . . . top it with ice cream.

If cookies and candies are more your style, turn to "Dessert of the Month: Hip Chips." Chocolate-Brickle Cookies, White Chocolate Chip-Oatmeal Cookies, and Chocolate-Cherry Cordial Truffles take advantage of the wonderful variety of baking chips available today.

GREAT TIPS FOR SPRING

Asparagus is among the most eagerly awaited seasonal vegetables. The elegant green spears herald months of fresh produce to come. Find asparagus from late February into summer.

GRILLED ASPARAGUS SALAD WITH ORANGE VINAIGRETTE
(pictured on page 73)

Prep: 35 minutes
Chill: 1 hour
Grill: 10 minutes

1 pound fresh asparagus
1 tablespoon grated orange rind
¼ cup fresh orange juice
⅓ cup olive oil
¼ cup balsamic vinegar
1 teaspoon Dijon mustard
½ teaspoon salt
¼ teaspoon pepper
1 pound mixed gourmet salad
    greens
4 cooked bacon slices, crumbled
    (optional)
Orange rind strips

• **Snap** off tough ends of asparagus; place asparagus in a shallow dish.
• **Combine** grated rind and next 6 ingredients in a jar; cover tightly. Shake jar vigorously. Pour one-third of vinaigrette over asparagus; cover and chill 1 hour. Drain. Set aside remaining vinaigrette.
• **Grill** asparagus, covered with grill lid, over medium-high heat (350° to 400°) 8 to 10 minutes or until crisp-tender; cool.
• **Combine** greens, remaining vinaigrette, and, if desired, bacon; mound onto 4 plates. Tie asparagus into 4 bundles with string; place over greens. Cover string with rind strips. **Yield:** 4 servings.

WARM ASPARAGUS SANDWICH

Prep: 15 minutes
Cook: 9 minutes

1 pound fresh asparagus
¼ teaspoon salt
2 tablespoons butter or margarine,
    melted
1 (16-ounce) French bread loaf,
    split horizontally
3 to 4 plum tomatoes, sliced
½ teaspoon salt
⅛ teaspoon pepper
4 thin prosciutto slices
½ pound fontina cheese,
    shredded

• **Snap** off tough ends of asparagus; cut asparagus into 4-inch pieces. Cook in boiling water to cover with ¼ teaspoon salt 5 to 6 minutes or until crisp-tender; drain.
• **Brush** melted butter on cut sides of bread; place, cut side up, on baking sheets.
• **Broil** 5½ inches from heat (with electric oven door partially open) 1 minute. Remove from oven; arrange tomato on bottom half of bread.
• **Sprinkle** with ½ teaspoon salt and pepper; top with prosciutto and asparagus. Sprinkle with cheese. Broil bottom half 2 more minutes or until cheese melts. Replace top half, and cut into 4 sections. Serve immediately. **Yield:** 4 servings.

ASPARAGUS MORNAY

Prep: 25 minutes
Cook: 25 minutes

1½ pounds fresh asparagus
½ teaspoon chicken bouillon
    granules
2 tablespoons hot water
1 tablespoon butter or margarine
1 tablespoon all-purpose flour
1 cup half-and-half
⅛ teaspoon ground nutmeg
⅛ teaspoon salt
½ cup (2 ounces) shredded Swiss
    cheese
2 round buttery crackers, crumbled

• **Snap** off tough ends of asparagus. Cook asparagus in boiling water to cover 8 to 10 minutes or until crisp-tender; drain and pat dry with paper towels. Arrange in a greased 11- x 7-inch pan.
• **Stir** together bouillon granules and 2 tablespoons hot water until granules are dissolved.
• **Melt** butter in a small saucepan over low heat. Whisk in flour until smooth. Cook, whisking constantly, 1 minute. Gradually whisk in bouillon, half-and-half, nutmeg, and salt; cook over medium heat, whisking constantly, until thickened and bubbly. Remove from heat; stir in cheese until melted. Pour mixture over asparagus; sprinkle with cracker crumbs.
• **Broil** 6 inches from heat (with electric oven door partially open) 5 minutes or until lightly browned. **Yield:** 4 servings.

Ellie Wells
Lakeland, Florida

ASPARAGUS TIPS

Choose spears with tightly closed, unbruised tips. Early varieties tend to be slender and more tender than later ones. Peel sturdier stalks up to the tip with a vegetable peeler before cooking in boiling, salted water. This will yield tender vegetables without overcooking.

BREAKFAST IN A HURRY

These handheld starters offer nutritious and flavorful alternatives to sweet morning cereals. Add a juice box for the perfect send-off. Don't limit these recipes to sunup only—you can reheat them in the microwave for an afternoon snack.

BREAKFAST BURRITOS

Prep: 10 minutes
Cook: 16 minutes

5 (12-inch) flour tortillas
1½ cups frozen hash browns, thawed
3 tablespoons vegetable oil
1 small green bell pepper, chopped
1 small red bell pepper, chopped
6 large eggs, lightly beaten
¼ cup chopped fresh cilantro
½ teaspoon salt
¼ to ½ teaspoon pepper
Toppings: picante sauce, sour cream

• **Heat** tortillas according to package directions; keep warm.
• **Sauté** hash browns in hot oil in a large skillet 6 to 8 minutes; add bell peppers, and sauté 5 minutes or until tender. Add eggs, and cook, stirring occasionally, 3 minutes or until eggs are done. Stir in cilantro, salt, and pepper.
• **Spoon** egg mixture evenly down centers of tortillas; roll up. To serve, wrap individually in wax paper or aluminum foil. Serve with desired toppings. **Yield:** 5 servings.

Note: Chill leftover burritos up to 4 hours. To reheat, microwave 1 wax paper-wrapped burrito at HIGH 30 seconds or bake aluminum foil-wrapped burritos at 350° for 20 to 25 minutes.
Kimberly Emeric
Huntsville, Alabama

BEST BISCUITS WITH SAUSAGE

Prep: 15 minutes
Bake: 14 minutes

4 cups biscuit mix
¾ cup lemon-lime soft drink
1 (8-ounce) container sour cream
12 sausage patties

• **Stir** together first 3 ingredients in a medium bowl until mixture forms a dough. Turn dough out onto a lightly floured surface; knead 3 or 4 times.
• **Divide** dough into 12 portions; flatten each portion slightly with hands, and arrange in a lightly greased 9-inch round cakepan.
• **Bake** at 425° for 12 to 14 minutes or until golden. Split biscuits.
• **Cook** sausage patties according to package directions. Drain patties on paper towels.
• **Place** 1 patty between each biscuit, and serve immediately. **Yield:** 1 dozen.

Note: Refrigerate leftover biscuits with sausage overnight. To reheat, bake aluminum foil-wrapped sausage biscuits at 350° for 5 to 10 minutes or until heated.

Note: For testing purposes only, we used Sprite for lemon-lime soft drink.
Pam Welch
El Dorado, Arkansas

PEANUT BUTTER ROLLUPS

Prep: 10 minutes
Bake: 14 minutes

12 white bread slices
¼ cup creamy peanut butter
¼ cup sugar
2 tablespoons ground cinnamon
2 tablespoons butter or margarine, melted

• **Cut** crusts from bread slices, and reserve for another use. Roll bread slices with a rolling pin to ⅛-inch thickness.
• **Spread** 1 teaspoon peanut butter on 1 side of each bread slice. Stir together sugar and cinnamon; sprinkle evenly over peanut butter.

• **Roll** up slices, jellyroll fashion; place, seam side down, on a lightly greased baking sheet. Brush with melted butter. (Rolls may be frozen at this point.)
• **Bake** at 350° for 7 minutes on each side or until rolls are light golden. **Yield:** 6 servings.

Note: Freeze unbaked rolls up to 1 week, if desired. Thaw at room temperature, and bake as directed.
Edith Askins
Greenville, Texas

SUNRISE CANADIAN BACON SQUARES

Prep: 20 minutes
Bake: 30 minutes

1 teaspoon butter or margarine
1 (6-ounce) package Canadian bacon slices, cut into thin strips
½ cup (2 ounces) shredded Swiss cheese
¼ cup grated Parmesan cheese
2 tablespoons chopped fresh parsley
2⅓ cups biscuit mix
1 large egg, lightly beaten
1 cup milk
⅓ cup mayonnaise
1 egg yolk, lightly beaten

• **Melt** butter in a large skillet over medium heat; add bacon, and sauté 6 minutes. Stir in cheeses and parsley.
• **Stir** together biscuit mix and next 3 ingredients until blended; spread half of mixture in a greased 8-inch square pan.
• **Top** with Canadian bacon mixture, and cover with remaining biscuit mixture. Brush with beaten egg yolk.
• **Bake** at 350° for 25 to 30 minutes. Cool in pan on a wire rack; cut into squares. **Yield:** 16 squares.

Note: If desired, bake squares ahead of time and chill. To reheat 1 square in microwave, wrap with a paper towel, and microwave at HIGH 25 seconds. To reheat in oven, wrap in aluminum foil; bake at 350° for 15 minutes or until heated.
Marge Clyde
San Antonio, Texas

BACKYARD BARBECUE

Make your first warm-weather party a classic with this menu. Not only is it easy to prepare, but it's also light. You can even make most of the recipes ahead. So spend more time joining the celebration—and less time cooking.

SPRING BARBECUE
Serves Eight

Pork Chops With Tangy Barbecue Sauce
Dill Potato Salad
Marinated Vegetables
Molasses Baked Beans
Barbecue Bread
Tropical Ice

Tangy Barbecue Sauce, Molasses Baked Beans, and Tropical Ice can be prepared ahead so you can spend time with guests. The Marinated Vegetables and Dill Potato Salad are better if made in advance and allowed to chill. That leaves grilling the Barbecue Bread and pork chops, reheating the baked beans, and enjoying the day's outdoor activities.

PORK CHOPS WITH TANGY BARBECUE SAUCE

Prep: 5 minutes
Grill: 14 minutes

8 (4-ounce) boneless pork loin
    chops (½ inch thick)
Tangy Barbecue Sauce

• **Grill** pork chops, covered with grill lid, over medium-high heat (350° to 400°) 7 minutes on each side, basting often with 1 cup Tangy Barbecue Sauce. Serve with remaining 1 cup Tangy Barbecue Sauce. **Yield:** 8 servings.

Tangy Barbecue Sauce

Prep: 15 minutes
Cook: 1 hour

1 cup white vinegar
½ cup ketchup
¼ cup firmly packed light brown
    sugar
¼ cup lemon juice
2 tablespoons low-sodium
    Worcestershire sauce
1 tablespoon prepared mustard
1 teaspoon ground black
    pepper
1 teaspoon ground red pepper
1 teaspoon lite soy sauce
½ green bell pepper, chopped

• **Bring** all ingredients to a boil in a small saucepan, stirring occasionally.

Reduce heat, and simmer, stirring occasionally, 45 minutes. **Yield:** 2 cups.

John Pelham
Birmingham, Alabama

♥ Per serving: Calories 250
Fat 11.3g   Cholesterol 77mg
Sodium 300mg

DILL POTATO SALAD

Prep: 15 minutes
Cook: 25 minutes
Chill: 2 hours

2 pounds small new potatoes, cut
    into wedges
1 (10-ounce) package frozen
    tiny sweet green peas,
    thawed and drained
½ cup reduced-fat mayonnaise
½ cup plain low-fat yogurt
1 tablespoon Dijon mustard
½ teaspoon garlic powder
¼ teaspoon salt
¼ teaspoon pepper
1 small sweet onion, chopped
3 tablespoons minced fresh
    dill
Garnish: fresh dill sprigs

• **Cook** potato wedges in boiling water to cover in a saucepan 25 minutes or until tender; drain and add peas.
• **Stir** together mayonnaise and next 7 ingredients in a large bowl. Add potato mixture; toss to coat. Cover and chill at least 2 hours. Garnish, if desired. **Yield:** 8 servings.

Judy Hasselkus
Indianapolis, Indiana

♥ Per serving: Calories 178
Fat 5.1g   Cholesterol 7mg
Sodium 279mg

MARINATED VEGETABLES

Prep: 15 minutes
Chill: 4 hours

1½ cups tarragon vinegar *
1 cup water
½ cup sugar
2 tablespoons chopped fresh or
    2 teaspoons dried basil
½ teaspoon salt
½ teaspoon pepper
6 medium tomatoes, cut into
    wedges
4 cucumbers, sliced
2 medium-size purple onions,
    thinly sliced
3 carrots, thinly sliced
Garnish: fresh basil leaves

• **Whisk** together first 6 ingredients in a large bowl.
• **Add** tomato and next 3 ingredients; toss to coat. Cover and chill at least 4 hours. Drain vegetables, or serve with a slotted spoon. Garnish, if desired. **Yield:** 8 servings.

* Substitute 1½ cups white wine vinegar for tarragon vinegar, if desired.

Patty McCoy Horton
Demopolis, Alabama

♥ Per serving: Calories 109
Fat 0.6g   Cholesterol 0mg
Sodium 169mg

MOLASSES BAKED BEANS

Prep: 15 minutes
Bake: 3 hours

1 large onion, chopped
1 large green bell pepper,
    chopped
4 garlic cloves, minced
1 tablespoon olive oil
4 (14½-ounce) cans diced
    tomatoes, drained
1 (14½-ounce) can low-sodium,
    fat-free chicken broth
1 cup molasses
3 (15.5-ounce) cans great Northern
    beans, rinsed and drained
1 teaspoon freshly ground pepper

• **Sauté** first 3 ingredients in hot oil in a Dutch oven until tender.
• **Stir** in diced tomatoes and remaining ingredients.
• **Bake,** uncovered, at 375°, stirring occasionally, 3 hours. **Yield:** 8 servings.

♥ Per serving: Calories 358
Fat 2.4g   Cholesterol 0mg
Sodium 638mg

BARBECUE BREAD

Prep: 35 minutes
Cook: 2 minutes

1 garlic bulb
8 thick white bread slices
Butter-flavored vegetable cooking
    spray

• **Cut** off pointed end of garlic bulb; place garlic on a piece of aluminum foil. Fold foil to seal. Bake at 425° for 30 minutes; let garlic cool. Squeeze pulp from 4 cloves; reserve remaining garlic cloves for another use.
• **Lightly** coat bread slices with vegetable cooking spray.
• **Grill,** without grill lid, over medium heat (300° to 350°) 1 minute on each side or until toasted. Rub with roasted garlic. **Yield:** 8 servings.

♥ Per serving: Calories 79
Fat 1.9g   Cholesterol 0mg
Sodium 135mg

TROPICAL ICE

Prep: 5 minutes
Freeze: 4 hours

1 (26-ounce) jar sliced mangoes,
    drained
1 (15¼-ounce) can crushed
    pineapple in juice,
    undrained
3 tablespoons sugar
3 tablespoons lime juice

• **Process** all ingredients in a blender until mixture is smooth; pour into an 8-inch square pan. Freeze 3 to 4 hours or until firm, stirring 2 or 3 times. Let stand 5 minutes before serving. **Yield:** 8 servings.

♥ Per ½ cup: Calories 112
Fat 0.3g   Cholesterol 0mg
Sodium 2mg

OLD-FASHIONED FUDGE CAKE

There's a reason this recipe will soon be batter stained: In just 10 minutes the basic ingredients are mixed and the pudding-like cake is baking. Yes, after the hot mixture is poured over the prepared cake mix, it looks strange. But the finished product comes out of the oven a tender cake hiding a dark chocolate pudding. It's best served warm with ice cream.

HOT FUDGE CAKE

1 (18.25-ounce) package devil's
    food cake mix without
    pudding
1 cup sugar
¼ cup cocoa
2 cups hot water
1 teaspoon vanilla extract
Vanilla ice cream
Toasted chopped pecans

• **Prepare** cake batter according to package directions. Pour into a lightly greased 13- x 9-inch pan.
• **Stir** together sugar and next 3 ingredients; pour over batter (it will sink to bottom of pan). Do not stir.
• **Bake** at 350° for 45 minutes. Let stand 10 minutes. Serve with vanilla ice cream and chopped pecans. **Yield:** 12 to 15 servings.

Marie A. Davis
Charlotte, North Carolina

Perky Pimiento Cheese

Be prepared to pass out recipes next time you serve pimiento cheese—these ideas add new spunk to the old spread. Mix diced pimiento with your favorite cheese, and then jazz it with jalapeños, splash it with sherry, or give it texture with dry-roasted peanuts. Or pair the goodness of Granny Smith apples with piquant olives and tangy feta.

PIMIENTO CHEESE SPREAD

Prep: 15 minutes

2 cups (8 ounces) shredded extra-sharp Cheddar cheese
1 (2-ounce) jar diced pimiento, drained
⅔ cup mayonnaise
⅓ cup chopped pecans, toasted
6 small pimiento-stuffed olives, diced
¼ teaspoon hot sauce
¼ teaspoon pepper
1 tablespoon dry sherry (optional)

• **Stir** together first 7 ingredients, and, if desired, dry sherry. Cover and chill, if desired. **Yield:** 2 cups.

WHITE CHEDDAR PIMIENTO CHEESE

Prep: 6 minutes

1 (8-ounce) block sharp white Cheddar cheese, softened
1 (4-ounce) jar diced pimiento, drained
1 jalapeño pepper, seeded and minced
¼ cup mayonnaise

• **Cut** cheese into ½-inch cubes. Process cheese in a food processor until smooth, stopping to scrape down sides. Add remaining ingredients, and process until blended. Cover and chill, if desired. **Yield:** 1½ cups.

Maria Heldreth
Louisville, Kentucky

FOUR-CHEESE SPREAD

Prep: 15 minutes

1½ (8-ounce) blocks white Cheddar cheese, finely shredded
1 (8-ounce) block mild Cheddar cheese, finely shredded
½ cup finely shredded Parmesan cheese
½ cup feta or Gorgonzola cheese
¾ cup mayonnaise
1 (4-ounce) jar diced pimiento, undrained
2 teaspoons sweet pickle juice
2 teaspoons mustard-mayonnaise sauce

• **Stir** together all ingredients. Cover and chill, if desired. **Yield:** 4 cups.

Raleigh McDonald Hussung
Nashville, Tennessee

SPLENDID SPREADS

A coffeepot survey of our staffers revealed some curious pimiento cheese combos.

■ "I love it finely shredded, with lots of garlic salt."

■ "We mix in crumbled bacon or chopped dill pickles."

■ "I fire it up with jalapeño or serrano peppers."

■ "Slather it on a ripe tomato sandwich, or layer it in a BLT."

CHEDDAR-SWISS SPREAD

Prep: 10 minutes

1 cup (4 ounces) shredded Cheddar cheese
½ cup (2 ounces) shredded Swiss cheese
½ cup chopped dry-roasted peanuts
½ cup mayonnaise
1 (2-ounce) jar diced pimiento, undrained
1 tablespoon minced onion
1 teaspoon prepared mustard
¼ teaspoon pepper

• **Stir** together all ingredients. Cover and chill, if desired. **Yield:** 1 cup.

Jan Downs
Shreveport, Louisiana

FETA-AND-APPLE SPREAD

Prep: 7 minutes

2 (4-ounce) packages crumbled feta cheese
1 medium Granny Smith apple, diced
½ cup sour cream
¼ cup chopped kalamata olives or pitted ripe olives
1 medium carrot, shredded
1 tablespoon chopped fresh parsley
1 (4-ounce) jar diced pimiento, drained

• **Stir** together all ingredients. Cover and chill, if desired. **Yield:** 3 cups.

Note: For convenient sandwiches, serve spread in quartered pita rounds.

Mary Pappas
Richmond, Virginia

FOREVER GREENS

An artful blend of fresh greens sparked with crunchy vegetables and a savory dressing can be as satisfying as any complicated entrée or fancy dessert.

EIGHT-LAYER SALAD

Prep: 40 minutes
Chill: 8 hours

1 head iceberg lettuce, torn
1 bunch green onions, chopped
½ green bell pepper, chopped
1 celery rib, chopped
½ red bell pepper, chopped
1 (10-ounce) package frozen sweet
      green peas, thawed
1 cup dry-roasted peanuts
1 cup (4 ounces) shredded
      Monterey Jack cheese
1 cup mayonnaise
2 tablespoons sugar
8 bacon slices, cooked and crumbled

• **Layer** first 8 ingredients in a large bowl. Spread mayonnaise over cheese; top with sugar and bacon. Cover and chill at least 8 hours. Toss before serving. **Yield:** 12 servings.

Marie A. Ippolito
Indianapolis, Indiana

ORANGE-ALMOND SALAD

Prep: 15 minutes

⅔ cup sliced almonds
⅓ cup sugar
8 cups mixed salad greens
1 (15-ounce) can mandarin
      oranges, drained and chilled
Vinaigrette

• **Cook** almonds and sugar in a large non-stick skillet over medium heat, stirring often, 5 to 7 minutes or until almonds are browned and sugar is melted. Spoon onto wax paper; cool. Break into small pieces. Toss together salad greens, oranges, almonds, and Vinaigrette. **Yield:** 4 to 6 servings.

Vinaigrette

Prep: 5 minutes
Chill: 2 hours

⅔ cup olive oil
⅓ cup cider vinegar
⅓ cup sugar
1 tablespoon chopped fresh parsley
1 teaspoon salt
¼ teaspoon ground black pepper
¼ teaspoon dried crushed red
      pepper

• **Combine** all ingredients in a jar; cover tightly, and shake vigorously. Chill 2 hours. **Yield:** 1¼ cups.

Janie Baur
Spring, Texas

MIXED GREENS WITH WALNUTS

Prep: 45 minutes

1 small head Boston lettuce
1 small head Bibb lettuce
1 small head romaine lettuce
1¼ cups coarsely chopped walnuts
2 tablespoons butter or margarine
1¾ teaspoons salt, divided
2 large shallots, halved
2 tablespoons white wine vinegar
2 teaspoons sugar
½ teaspoon ground white pepper
1 teaspoon Dijon mustard
1 cup olive oil
2 (8-ounce) packages sliced fresh
      mushrooms

• **Rinse** lettuces, and separate leaves. Let leaves stand in cold water to cover in a large bowl 30 minutes. Drain well, and pat dry with paper towels. Tear leaves into bite-size pieces.
• **Bake** walnuts in a shallow pan at 350° for 10 minutes or until toasted. Stir in butter and ½ teaspoon salt.
• **Pulse** shallots in a food processor until minced. Add remaining 1¼ teaspoons salt, vinegar, and next 3 ingredients.

With processor running, pour oil through food chute. Add ¼ cup walnuts, and process until smooth.
• **Toss** lettuce and mushrooms with ½ cup vinaigrette; top salad with remaining 1 cup walnuts. Serve with remaining vinaigrette, if desired. **Yield:** 8 servings.

Shirley Corriher
Atlanta, Georgia

TOSSING AND TURNING

Gentle handling and proper storage are the keys to putting together a great mix of greens. In her award-winning book *CookWise*, Atlanta's noted food scientist Shirley Corriher shares her wisdom on keeping salad greens crisp for weeks.

■ Chill greens and other produce right after purchasing them.

■ Limit oxygen supply for greens by storing in a zip-top plastic bag after squeezing out all the air.

■ Soak greens in cold water 10 to 30 minutes before storing.

■ For shorter storage, wrap greens in damp paper towels, and place in a zip-top plastic bag.

■ For longer storage, remove as much surface water as possible by spinning greens in a salad spinner before wrapping in dry paper towels and storing in a zip-top plastic bag.

■ Add dressing in small amounts to greens just before serving. Less is best when adding dressing. Toss only a small amount of dressing into a salad. Taste and add more, if desired.

■ Serve salads on cold plates to keep greens crispier. Chill plates in freezer 10 minutes before serving.

ASIAN SLAW

Prep: 15 minutes
Chill: 24 hours

2 (3-ounce) packages beef-
　flavored ramen noodle
　soup mix
2 (8.5-ounce) packages slaw
　mix
1 cup sliced almonds, toasted
1 cup sunflower kernels
1 bunch green onions, chopped
½ cup sugar
¾ cup vegetable oil
⅓ cup white vinegar

• **Remove** flavor packets from soup mix, and set aside; crush noodles. Place noodles in bottom of a large bowl. Top with slaw mix; sprinkle with almonds, sunflower kernels, and green onions.
• **Whisk** together contents from flavor packets, sugar, oil, and vinegar; pour over slaw. Cover and chill 24 hours. Toss before serving. **Yield:** 8 to 10 servings.

Janice Watson
Birmingham, Alabama

WHAT'S FOR SUPPER?

WRAPPED WITH FLAVOR

The term "meal-in-one" takes on new meaning when you add "no pots to clean." Easy cleanup is only one of the merits of cooking in foil packets. It's also easier to customize each serving for picky eaters' tastes.

If you prefer oven baking, bake at 450° for 3 to 5 minutes longer than grilling the recipe requires. Remember to use oven mitts or tongs to remove the foil packets from the grill or oven. Open packets carefully to prevent burns from the hot steam.

MEXICAN PORK CHOPS

Prep: 10 minutes
Grill: 40 minutes

4 (½-inch-thick) boneless pork
　loin chops
½ teaspoon salt
1 teaspoon chili powder
1 (30-ounce) jar mild chunky
　salsa
1 (15¼-ounce) can kidney beans,
　rinsed and drained
1 (10-ounce) package frozen
　whole kernel corn, thawed
½ cup uncooked long-grain rice
1 cup (4 ounces) shredded
　Mexican cheese blend

• **Tear** off 4 (18- x 12-inch) heavy-duty aluminum foil sheets.
• **Place** 1 chop in center of each foil sheet. Sprinkle pork chops with salt and chili powder.
• **Stir** together salsa and next 3 ingredients; spoon evenly over chops.
• **Bring** up 2 sides of each foil sheet, and double-fold with about 1-inch-wide folds. Double-fold each end to form a packet, leaving room for heat circulation inside packet.
• **Grill,** covered with grill lid, over medium-high heat (350° to 400°) 30 to 40 minutes or until done. Sprinkle evenly with cheese before serving. **Yield:** 4 servings.

BARBECUE HOBO SUPPER

Prep: 12 minutes
Grill: 30 minutes

1½ pounds ground round
½ cup barbecue sauce
½ teaspoon salt
½ teaspoon pepper
½ pound baby carrots
1 pound new potatoes, cut
　in half
1 medium onion, cut into 8 wedges
1 large red or green bell pepper,
　cut into 8 wedges

• **Tear** off 4 (18- x 12-inch) heavy-duty aluminum foil sheets.

• **Combine** ground round and ¼ cup barbecue sauce; shape into 4 patties.
• **Place** 1 patty in center of each foil sheet; sprinkle evenly with salt and pepper. Top evenly with remaining ¼ cup barbecue sauce, baby carrots, and remaining ingredients.
• **Bring** up 2 sides of each aluminum foil sheet, and double-fold with about 1-inch-wide folds. Double-fold each end to form a packet, leaving room for heat circulation inside packet.
• **Grill,** covered with grill lid, over medium-high heat (350° to 400°) 12 to 15 minutes on each side or until ground beef is no longer pink and vegetables are tender. **Yield:** 4 servings.

Bill Garner
Birmingham, Alabama

FOIL-WRAPPED CHICKEN

Prep: 10 minutes
Grill: 35 minutes

2 medium zucchini, sliced
2 carrots, sliced
1 (14-ounce) can baby corn,
　drained
8 chicken thighs, skinned
2 green onions, sliced
1 tablespoon sesame seeds,
　toasted and divided
⅓ cup soy sauce
3 tablespoons hoisin sauce
1 tablespoon minced fresh ginger
1 garlic clove, pressed

• **Tear** off 4 (18- x 12-inch) heavy-duty aluminum foil sheets.
• **Place** first 3 ingredients evenly in the center of each sheet; top each with 2 chicken thighs. Sprinkle with green onions.
• **Stir** together 2 teaspoons sesame seeds and next 4 ingredients; spoon evenly over chicken.
• **Bring** up 2 sides of each foil sheet, and double-fold with about 1-inch-wide folds. Double-fold each end to form a packet, leaving room for heat circulation inside packet.
• **Grill,** covered with grill lid, over medium-high heat (350° to 400°) about 35 minutes or until chicken is done.

Sprinkle with remaining 1 teaspoon sesame seeds before serving. **Yield:** 4 servings.

Note: Find hoisin sauce in the Asian section of your grocery store or in an Asian market.

CARIBBEAN FISH

Prep: 10 minutes
Grill: 15 minutes

4 (6-ounce) orange roughy fillets
½ teaspoon salt
¼ teaspoon pepper
¼ to ½ teaspoon Cajun seasoning
2 medium-size yellow squash, sliced
1 medium-size red bell pepper, cut into strips
4 teaspoons butter or margarine
4 teaspoons grated lime rind
4 teaspoons fresh lime juice
4 teaspoons chopped fresh parsley
1 (2-ounce) package sliced almonds, toasted

• **Tear** off 4 (18- x 12-inch) heavy-duty aluminum foil sheets.
• **Place** a fillet in center of each foil sheet; sprinkle evenly with salt, pepper, and Cajun seasoning. Top evenly with squash and bell pepper; dot with butter. Sprinkle evenly with lime rind and remaining ingredients.
• **Bring** up 2 sides of each foil sheet, and double-fold with about 1-inch-wide folds. Double-fold each end to form a packet, leaving room for heat circulation inside packet. Place packets on a baking sheet.
• **Grill,** covered with grill lid, over medium-high heat (350° to 400°) 15 minutes or until fish flakes easily. **Yield:** 4 servings.

Glennette Lewis
Decatur, Texas

PICK OF THE CHICK

Eating healthy often carries a hefty price tag, so don't pass the grocery store special on whole chickens or chicken pieces. With a little extra work in the kitchen, you can afford to indulge in these succulent pieces.

SALSA RICE AND CHICKEN

Prep: 30 minutes
Bake: 1 hour and 15 minutes

1⅓ cups uncooked rice
1 (24-ounce) jar salsa
1 (10¾-ounce) can reduced-fat, low-sodium cream of chicken soup, undiluted
1 (8-ounce) container fat-free sour cream
⅓ cup water
¼ teaspoon pepper
Vegetable cooking spray
1 (3-pound) chicken, cut up and skinned
2 teaspoons paprika

• **Stir** together first 6 ingredients. Spoon into a 13- x 9-inch baking dish coated with cooking spray. Place chicken on top, pressing gently into rice. Coat chicken with cooking spray; sprinkle with paprika.
• **Bake,** covered, at 350° for 45 minutes; uncover and bake 30 more minutes or until chicken is done. **Yield:** 6 servings.

Note: For testing purposes only, we used Campbell's Healthy Request Cream of Chicken Soup.

Paula Joye
Goose Creek, South Carolina

♥ Per serving: Calories 456
Fat 10.5g   Cholesterol 103mg
Sodium 814mg

LEMON-MUSTARD CHICKEN

Prep: 10 minutes
Marinate: 2 hours
Grill: 50 minutes

1 tablespoon grated lemon rind
¾ cup fresh lemon juice
⅓ cup Dijon mustard
¼ cup chopped fresh basil
4 (6-ounce) bone-in chicken breast halves, skinned
Vegetable cooking spray

• **Stir** together first 4 ingredients; reserve ½ cup.
• **Place** chicken in a large heavy-duty zip-top plastic bag; add remaining lemon juice mixture. Seal and chill 1 to 2 hours, turning chicken occasionally.
• **Coat** grill rack with cooking spray; place on grill.
• **Remove** chicken from marinade, discarding marinade. Place chicken, bone side up, on grill.
• **Grill,** covered with grill lid, over medium-high heat (350° to 400°) 10 minutes. Turn chicken, and baste with reserved ½ cup lemon mixture. Grill 30 to 40 more minutes or until done, turning and basting with lemon mixture every 5 minutes. **Yield:** 4 servings.

Jessica King
Richmond, Virginia

♥ Per serving: Calories 169
Fat 4.2g   Cholesterol 69mg
Sodium 648mg

MAPLE-GLAZED CHICKEN WINGS

Prep: 30 minutes
Marinate: 4 hours
Grill: 30 minutes

2½ pounds chicken wings,
   skinned
¾ cup maple syrup
½ cup chili sauce
1 small onion, diced
2 tablespoons Dijon mustard
2 teaspoons low-sodium
   Worcestershire sauce
¼ to ½ teaspoon dried crushed
   red pepper

• **Cut** off wingtips, and discard; cut wings in half at joint.
• **Stir** together syrup and next 5 ingredients. Reserve 1 cup syrup mixture; cover and chill.
• **Place** chicken in a heavy-duty zip-top plastic bag; pour remaining syrup mixture over chicken. Seal; chill 4 hours, turning chicken occasionally.
• **Remove** chicken from marinade, discarding marinade.
• **Grill** chicken, without grill lid, over medium-high heat (350° to 400°) 30 minutes or until done, turning and basting occasionally with reserved 1 cup syrup mixture. **Yield:** 8 appetizer servings.

Note: To bake this recipe, place chicken in a 15- x 10-inch jellyroll pan coated with cooking spray. Bake at 375° for 45 minutes or until done, turning and basting with reserved 1 cup syrup mixture every 10 minutes.

Ellie Wells
Lakeland, Florida

♥ Per serving: Calories 271
Fat 6.9g   Cholesterol 68mg
Sodium 421mg

BAKED HONEY CHICKEN

Sprinkle the chicken with paprika and coat with vegetable cooking spray to aid in browning.

Prep: 30 minutes
Marinate: 1 hour
Bake: 1 hour and 30 minutes

¼ cup honey
¼ cup lite soy sauce
⅓ cup minced onion
2 tablespoons grated fresh
   ginger
2 garlic cloves, minced
1 (3-pound) whole chicken,
   skinned
Vegetable cooking spray
2 teaspoons paprika
Garnishes: gourmet salad greens,
   lemon slices

• **Combine** first 5 ingredients in a large heavy-duty zip-top plastic bag; add chicken. Seal and chill 1 hour, turning occasionally.
• **Coat** a rack in a roasting pan with cooking spray.
• **Remove** chicken from marinade, and place, breast side up, on rack. Pour marinade over chicken. Tuck wings under.
• **Bake,** covered with aluminum foil, at 375° for 45 minutes. Uncover and coat chicken with cooking spray; sprinkle with paprika.
• **Bake,** uncovered, 45 more minutes or until a meat thermometer inserted into chicken thigh registers 180°, basting occasionally. Remove from oven; let stand 15 minutes. Transfer to a serving dish; garnish, if desired. **Yield:** 6 servings.

Mary Frances Lanning
The Woodlands, Texas

♥ Per serving: Calories 218
Fat 6.7g   Cholesterol 73mg
Sodium 422mg

BREADED CHICKEN DRUMSTICKS

Prep: 30 minutes
Bake: 1 hour

½ cup fine, dry breadcrumbs
2 teaspoons onion powder
2 teaspoons curry powder
½ teaspoon dry mustard
¼ teaspoon salt
¼ teaspoon garlic powder
¼ teaspoon paprika
¼ to ½ teaspoon ground red
   pepper
12 chicken drumsticks, skinned
   (3 pounds)
¼ cup fat-free milk
Vegetable cooking spray
Garnish: fresh parsley sprigs

• **Combine** first 8 ingredients in a shallow dish.
• **Dip** chicken in milk; coat with crumb mixture, and place in a 13- x 9-inch baking dish coated with cooking spray. Coat chicken with cooking spray.
• **Bake** at 375° for 1 hour or until done. Garnish, if desired. **Yield:** 6 servings.

Nora Henshaw
Okemah, Oklahoma

♥ Per serving: Calories 204
Fat 6.6g   Cholesterol 80mg
Sodium 263mg

CHICKEN BY THE NUMBERS

Compare fat grams of roasted chicken pieces with and without the skin.

1 breast half with skin...............8g
1 breast half without skin...........3g
2 wings with skin......................13g
2 wings without skin..................3g
1 drumstick with skin................6g
1 drumstick without skin...........2g
1 thigh with skin......................10g
1 thigh without skin..................6g

Not Your Usual Spread

Peanut butter is not just for kids' sandwiches. Use it—creamy or crunchy—to add depth to soups, salads, and sauces. The lunchbox staple stylishly goes beyond two slices of soft white bread.

THAI GREEN APPLE SALAD

4 large Granny Smith apples
¼ cup lemon juice
3 garlic cloves, minced
2 onions, thinly sliced
1 tablespoon vegetable oil
½ pound ground pork
¼ cup crunchy peanut butter
2 tablespoons fish sauce
1 tablespoon sugar
½ teaspoon ground white pepper
1 jalapeño pepper, seeded and minced
6 cups torn leaf lettuce

• **Peel** apples; cut into thin wedges. Toss with lemon juice. Set aside.
• **Sauté** garlic and onion in hot oil in a large skillet until tender; remove with a slotted spoon.
• **Add** pork to skillet; cook, stirring constantly, 4 to 5 minutes or until no longer pink; drain and return to skillet.
• **Stir** in peanut butter and next 4 ingredients; cook, stirring often, until thoroughly heated. Drain apple. Stir apple and garlic mixture into pork mixture. Serve over lettuce. **Yield:** 6 servings.

Valerie Payne
Johnson City, Tennessee

PEANUT BUTTER BREAD

Prep: 10 minutes
Bake: 1 hour

2 cups all-purpose flour
½ cup sugar
2 teaspoons baking powder
1 teaspoon salt
¾ cup creamy or crunchy peanut butter
1 large egg
1 cup milk

• **Stir** together first 4 ingredients in a medium bowl; cut in peanut butter with a fork or pastry blender until crumbly.
• **Stir** together egg and milk; stir into dry ingredients just until moistened. Pour batter into a greased 9- x 5-inch loafpan. Bake at 350° for 1 hour or until a wooden pick inserted in center comes out clean. Remove from pan immediately, and cool on a wire rack. **Yield:** 1 (9-inch) loaf.

Peanut Butter Muffins: Spoon batter into greased muffin pans, filling two-thirds full. Stir together ½ cup uncooked regular oats; 2 tablespoons golden raisins, chopped; 2 tablespoons honey; and 1 tablespoon butter or margarine, melted. Spoon mixture evenly over batter. Bake at 350° for 25 to 30 minutes. **Yield:** 1 dozen.

Agnes L. Stone
Ocala, Florida

NUTTY CHICKEN STRIPS

Prep: 30 minutes
Bake: 20 minutes

6 skinned and boned chicken breast halves
2 cups lightly salted dry-roasted peanuts, finely chopped
1 cup fine, dry breadcrumbs
1 cup crunchy peanut butter
¼ cup sesame oil
1 tablespoon soy sauce
¼ teaspoon ground red pepper

• **Cut** chicken into ¼-inch strips. Stir together chopped peanuts and crumbs.

Stir together peanut butter and next 3 ingredients; add chicken. Toss to coat. Dredge chicken in crumb mixture; place on 2 greased 15- x 10-inch jellyroll pans.
• **Bake** at 425° for 10 minutes; turn chicken over; bake 5 to 10 minutes. Let stand 10 minutes. **Yield:** 6 to 8 servings.

Weeknight Standbys

Expand the variety of your weeknight menus with versatile side dishes. You can use frozen vegetables instead of fresh in both of these recipes.

SAVORY SQUASH

Prep: 35 minutes
Bake: 30 minutes

10 to 12 large yellow squash, sliced
1 large onion, sliced
1 (8-ounce) container sour cream
½ teaspoon salt
¼ teaspoon pepper
1½ cups (6 ounces) shredded Cheddar cheese
2 cups cornflakes cereal, crushed
3 tablespoons butter, melted

• **Cook** squash and onion in boiling water to cover 20 minutes; drain well, pressing between paper towels.
• **Stir** together squash mixture, sour cream, salt, and pepper. Spoon into a lightly greased 13- x 9-inch baking dish. Top with cheese.
• **Stir** together cornflake crumbs and melted butter; sprinkle over casserole.
• **Bake** at 350° for 30 minutes. **Yield:** 8 to 10 servings.

Valerie Hallman
Casseroles Etc.
Hoover, Alabama

GREEN BEAN BAKE

Prep: 25 minutes
Bake: 20 minutes

1 pound fresh green beans,
   trimmed
2 small purple onions, chopped
1 tablespoon olive oil
1 tablespoon brown sugar
2 tablespoons butter or margarine
2 tablespoons all-purpose flour
2 cups milk
½ cup grated Parmesan cheese
½ teaspoon salt
¼ teaspoon pepper
½ cup slivered almonds

• **Cook** green beans in boiling water to cover in a large saucepan 3 minutes or until crisp-tender; drain. Rinse with cold water to stop the cooking process; drain.
• **Sauté** onion in hot oil in saucepan over medium-high heat 5 minutes. Reduce heat to medium. Stir in brown sugar; cook, stirring often, 15 minutes or until caramel colored. Remove from pan, and set aside.
• **Melt** butter in saucepan over low heat; whisk in flour.
• **Cook,** whisking constantly, 1 minute. Gradually whisk in milk; cook over medium heat, whisking constantly, until thickened and bubbly. Remove from heat; stir in cheese, salt, and pepper until smooth.
• **Stir** in green beans and onion. Spoon into a greased 1½-quart baking dish. Top with almonds.
• **Bake** at 350° for 20 minutes or until almonds are lightly browned. **Yield:** 4 to 6 servings.

Danielle Bergmooser
Rocklin, California

SERVED STRAIGHT UP

Dust off your martini glasses, but hold the ice cubes. The shapely beverage classic beautifully displays food. Here we toast the shrimp cocktail—with two tantalizing sauces—and an easy-yet-elegant dessert.

DOUBLE-DIP SHRIMP

Prep: 30 minutes
Chill: 1 hour

20 unpeeled, jumbo fresh shrimp
   (about 1 pound)
Paprika
Lemon wedges
¾ cup ketchup
3 tablespoons prepared
   horseradish
2 tablespoons lemon juice,
   divided
1 teaspoon Worcestershire sauce
¾ cup sour cream
¼ cup Dijon mustard
2 tablespoons chopped fresh
   parsley
Garnishes: lemon slices, fresh
   parsley sprigs

• **Cook** shrimp in boiling water 3 to 5 minutes or just until shrimp turn pink; drain. Peel shrimp, leaving tails intact; devein, if desired. Chill 1 hour.
• **Sprinkle** paprika in a saucer. Rub rims of 4 chilled martini glasses with lemon wedges; dip edges in paprika.
• **Stir** together ketchup, horseradish, 1 tablespoon lemon juice, and Worcestershire sauce. Cover and chill, if desired.
• **Stir** together remaining 1 tablespoon lemon juice, sour cream, mustard, and chopped parsley. Cover sauce, and chill, if desired.
• **Place** a spatula in center of a martini glass. Spoon 2 tablespoons of first sauce on 1 side of spatula; spoon 2 tablespoons of second sauce on other side. Carefully remove spatula. Repeat procedure with remaining sauces and glasses. Arrange shrimp around edge of glasses. Garnish, if desired. **Yield:** 4 servings.

INDIVIDUAL RASPBERRY TRIFLES

Prep: 20 minutes

1 (3.9-ounce) package vanilla
   instant pudding mix
2 cups fresh raspberries *
½ cup seedless raspberry jam
½ (10.75-ounce) pound cake, cut
   into ½-inch cubes
½ cup whipping cream
1 tablespoon sugar

• **Prepare** pudding according to package directions.
• **Stir** together raspberries and jam. Spoon ¼ cup raspberry mixture into 4 martini glasses.
• **Top** with ¼ cup pudding. Top with pound cake. Spoon remaining raspberry mixture over cake; top with remaining pudding. Chill, if desired.
• **Beat** whipping cream and sugar at high speed with an electric mixer until soft peaks form. Dollop on trifles. **Yield:** 4 servings.

* Substitute 2 cups individually frozen raspberries, thawed and drained, for fresh, if desired.

Vanilla Custard Sauce to serve over Fresh Strawberries or Pound Cake; Kahlúa Beverage Sipper; Chocolate Custard Tart, page 27

Blackberry Custard, page 132;
Blackberry Cobbler, page 131

1-2-3 Blackberry Sherbet, page 130

Cherry Cobbler, page 156

Cappuccino Mousse Cake,
White Chocolate Mousse Torte,
page 154

TRIPLE CROWN CAKES

*The fillings and frostings are exquisite, but
the foundation of these cakes is equally fine.
"The definitive white cake" was our Test Kitchens'
consensus. We think you'll agree.*

Does someone you know love piña coladas? Here's a way to enjoy that tropical taste with a fork. Is there a lemon meringue pie fancier in your life? Celebrate his or her birthday with a Lemon Meringue Cake. Do you love the sweet taste of fresh peeled oranges? Then bite into a slice of Orange Cream Cake.

BASIC WHITE CAKE BATTER

½ cup butter, softened
½ cup shortening
2 cups sugar
3 cups cake flour
4 teaspoons baking powder
½ teaspoon salt
⅔ cup milk
⅔ cup water
2 teaspoons vanilla extract
¾ teaspoon almond extract
6 egg whites

• **Beat** butter and shortening at medium speed with an electric mixer until creamy; gradually add sugar, beating mixture well.
• **Combine** flour, baking powder, and salt; add to butter mixture alternately with milk and water, beginning and ending with flour mixture. Beat at low speed until blended after each addition. Stir in flavorings.
• **Beat** egg whites at high speed with an electric mixer until stiff peaks form; fold about one-third of egg whites into batter. Gradually fold in remaining egg whites. **Yield:** about 7 cups.

PIÑA COLADA CAKE

*Prep: 15 minutes
Bake: 35 minutes
Chill: 4 hours*

1 recipe Basic White Cake
    Batter (see recipe at left)
Piña Colada Filling
Rum Buttercream Frosting
2 cups flaked coconut

• **Pour** cake batter into 3 greased and floured 8-inch round cakepans.
• **Bake** at 325° for 30 to 35 minutes or until a wooden pick inserted in center comes out clean. Cool in pans on wire racks 10 minutes; remove from pans, and cool layers completely on wire racks.
• **Split** layers horizontally. Spread Piña Colada Filling evenly between layers (not on top); cover and chill at least 4 hours.
• **Spread** Rum Buttercream Frosting on top and sides of cake; sprinkle top and sides evenly with flaked coconut, pressing in gently.
• **Store** cake in refrigerator. (Cake may be frozen up to 1 month.) **Yield:** 1 (6-layer) cake.

Piña Colada Filling

*Prep: 5 minutes
Cook: 10 minutes
Chill: 4 hours*

1 (10½-ounce) can frozen piña
    colada mix concentrate,
    thawed and undiluted
¼ cup cornstarch
6 egg yolks
1½ cups half-and-half
3 tablespoons butter or margarine,
    cut up
1 cup flaked coconut
1 teaspoon vanilla extract

• **Bring** first 4 ingredients to a boil in a 3-quart saucepan over medium heat, whisking constantly.
• **Boil,** whisking constantly, 1 minute. Remove from heat; whisk in remaining ingredients.
• **Pour** mixture into a bowl. Cover and chill at least 4 hours. **Yield:** 3¾ cups.

Rum Buttercream Frosting

Prep: 10 minutes

½ cup butter, softened
1 (16-ounce) package powdered
    sugar
3 tablespoons rum
3 tablespoons milk
1 teaspoon vanilla extract

• **Beat** butter at medium speed with an electric mixer until creamy; gradually add 1 cup powdered sugar, beating at low speed until blended.
• **Add** rum, milk, and vanilla, beating until blended. Gradually add remaining powdered sugar. **Yield:** 2½ cups.

Vanilla Buttercream Frosting: Substitute 3 tablespoons milk for rum for a total of 6 tablespoons milk.

Orange Buttercream Frosting: Substitute 3 tablespoons orange liqueur for rum, and add 2 tablespoons grated orange rind, 1 drop of red liquid food coloring, and 1 drop of yellow liquid food coloring.

LEMON MERINGUE CAKE
(pictured on page 4)

Prep: 30 minutes
Bake: 32 minutes
Chill: 4 hours

1 recipe Basic White Cake
   Batter (see recipe on previous
   page)
Lemon Filling
Meringue Frosting
**Garnish: assorted fresh edible
   flowers, lemon rind curls**

• **Pour** Basic White Cake Batter evenly into 3 greased and floured 10-inch round cakepans.
• **Bake** at 325° for 18 to 22 minutes or until a wooden pick inserted in center comes out clean. Cool in pans on wire racks 10 minutes; remove from pans, and cool on wire racks. (Cake layers may be frozen up to 1 month.)
• **Spread** Lemon Filling between layers (not on top), placing cake on an oven-proof platter. Cover; chill at least 4 hours.
• **Spread** Meringue Frosting on top and sides of cake.
• **Bake** at 425° for 10 minutes or until golden. (Top will brown more than sides.) Garnish, if desired. Serve immediately. **Yield:** 1 (3-layer) cake.

Lemon Filling

Prep: 20 minutes
Cook: 10 minutes
Chill: 4 hours

1½ cups sugar
½ cup cornstarch
¼ teaspoon salt
6 egg yolks
2½ cups half-and-half
¼ cup butter or margarine,
   cut up
1 tablespoon grated lemon
   rind
¾ cup fresh lemon juice

• **Bring** first 5 ingredients to a boil in a 3-quart saucepan over medium heat, whisking constantly.
• **Boil,** whisking constantly, 1 minute or until thickened. Remove from heat; whisk in butter and lemon rind. Gradually whisk in lemon juice until smooth; pour into a bowl. Cover and chill at least 4 hours. **Yield:** 4 cups.

Meringue Frosting

Prep: 10 minutes

3 tablespoons meringue powder
½ cup water
¼ teaspoon cream of tartar
½ cup sugar

• **Beat** meringue powder and ½ cup water at high speed with an electric mixer until foamy.
• **Add** cream of tartar, beating until soft peaks form. Gradually add sugar, 1 tablespoon at a time, beating until stiff peaks form. **Yield:** about 4½ cups.

Note: Find meringue powder at cake-decorating and crafts stores.

ORANGE CREAM CAKE

Prep: 15 minutes
Bake: 30 minutes
Chill: 4 hours

1 recipe Basic White Cake Batter
   (see recipe on previous page)
Orange Cream Filling
1 recipe Orange Buttercream
   Frosting (see recipe variation
   on previous page)
**Garnishes: Cream Cheese Eggs,
   sugared grapes, fresh edible
   flowers**

• **Pour** cake batter into 3 greased and floured 9-inch round cakepans.
• **Bake** at 325° for 25 to 30 minutes or until a wooden pick inserted in center comes out clean. Cool in pans on wire racks 10 minutes; remove from pans, and cool on wire racks.
• **Spread** Orange Cream Filling between cake layers (not on top). Cover and chill at least 4 hours.
• **Spread** Orange Buttercream Frosting on top and sides of cake. Garnish, if desired. Store in refrigerator. (Freeze up to 1 month, if desired.) **Yield:** 1 (3-layer) cake.

Orange Cream Filling

Prep: 15 minutes
Cook: 8 minutes
Chill: 4 hours

½ cup sugar
¼ cup cornstarch
6 egg yolks
2 cups half-and-half
3 tablespoons butter, cut up
3 tablespoons orange liqueur or
   orange juice concentrate
2 tablespoons grated orange
   rind
1 teaspoon vanilla extract

• **Bring** first 4 ingredients to a boil in a 3-quart saucepan over medium heat, whisking constantly.
• **Boil,** whisking constantly, 1 minute or until thickened. Remove from heat; whisk in butter and remaining ingredients until smooth. Pour into a bowl; cover and chill at least 4 hours. **Yield:** 3 cups.

Cream Cheese Eggs

Prep: 1 hour
Stand: 8 hours

1 (3-ounce) package cream cheese,
   softened
3 drops of blue liquid food coloring
1 drop of yellow liquid food coloring
1 teaspoon vanilla extract
½ teaspoon almond extract
1 (16-ounce) package powdered
   sugar
1 tablespoon milk
¼ cup finely chopped toasted
   pecans
½ cup sugar

• **Beat** first 5 ingredients at medium speed with a heavy-duty electric mixer until creamy. Gradually add 2 cups powdered sugar and milk, beating until smooth. Add remaining powdered sugar; beat to form a stiff dough. Knead in pecans. Shape into 1½-inch-long eggs; roll in granulated sugar. Let stand at room temperature 8 hours to dry. **Yield:** 4 dozen.

Note: Store Cream Cheese Eggs in the freezer, if desired.

CELEBRATE CINCO DE MAYO

The bright colors and unique flavors of these recipes suggest a lively time is at hand. It's Cinco de Mayo, a May holiday commemorating Mexico's independence from France.

Enjoy this menu for a light fiesta lunch or dinner. To save you time, the recipes include some make-ahead tips.

FLAVORFUL FIESTA
Serves Six to Eight

Colorful Salsa

Creamy Guacamole

Tortilla Chips

Taco-Chicken Skewers

Mexican Pizza

Mock Margaritas

COLORFUL SALSA

Prep: 15 minutes
Chill: 1 hour

3 large tomatoes, chopped
2 (4.5-ounce) cans chopped
  green chiles
1 small onion, finely chopped
¼ cup chopped ripe olives
⅓ cup chopped fresh cilantro
3 tablespoons fresh lime
  juice
2 garlic cloves, pressed
½ teaspoon salt
½ teaspoon pepper
1 jalapeño pepper, seeded and
  chopped (optional)

• **Stir** together first 9 ingredients in a medium bowl. Stir in jalapeño pepper, if desired; cover salsa, and chill at least 1 hour. Serve salsa with tortilla chips.
Yield: 3 cups.

Debra A. Hall
Alexandria, Virginia

CREAMY GUACAMOLE

Prep: 15 minutes

4 ripe avocados, peeled and
  seeded
1 (8-ounce) package light cream
  cheese, softened
½ cup picante sauce
2 tablespoons lemon juice
1 teaspoon garlic salt
Garnish: chopped tomato

• **Mash** avocados and cream cheese with a fork or potato masher.
• **Stir** in picante sauce, lemon juice, and garlic salt.
• **Cover** and chill up to 2 hours, if desired. Garnish, if desired. Serve with tortilla chips. **Yield:** 3 cups.

Virginia McGonigal
Bakersfield, California

TACO-CHICKEN SKEWERS

Prep: 10 minutes
Cook: 8 minutes

1 (8-ounce) container sour
  cream
1 (7-ounce) jar green salsa
2 tablespoons chopped fresh
  cilantro
1 (1¼-ounce) envelope taco
  seasoning mix, divided
4 skinned and boned chicken
  breast halves, cut into 1-inch
  pieces
Garnish: fresh cilantro leaves

• **Combine** first 3 ingredients and 1 teaspoon taco seasoning mix in a bowl, stirring well. Cover and chill up to 8 hours, if desired.
• **Toss** chicken with remaining taco seasoning mix. Cook chicken in a large nonstick skillet coated with vegetable cooking spray over medium-high heat 6 to 8 minutes or until done. Serve immediately, or cover and chill up to 2 hours. Serve on skewers with salsa mixture. Garnish, if desired. **Yield:** 6 to 8 appetizer servings.

Frank Lindstrom III
Birmingham, Alabama

MEXICAN PIZZA

Prep: 20 minutes
Bake: 15 minutes

1 (15-ounce) can kidney beans,
  rinsed and drained
2 teaspoons vegetable oil
¼ teaspoon ground cumin
¼ teaspoon chili powder
1 garlic clove, pressed
1 (4.5-ounce) can chopped green
  chiles
8 (8-inch) flour tortillas
½ cup salsa
1 small onion, diced
½ green bell pepper, diced
3 tablespoons sliced ripe olives
1 cup (4 ounces) shredded
  mozzarella cheese
Garnish: fresh cilantro leaves

• **Mash** beans with a fork; stir in oil and next 4 ingredients. Place 4 tortillas on greased baking sheets; spread with bean mixture.
• **Top** each with 1 tablespoon salsa; sprinkle with onion and bell pepper. Top with remaining tortillas, spreading each with 1 tablespoon salsa; sprinkle with olives and cheese.
• **Bake** at 400° for 12 to 15 minutes. Cut into wedges; garnish, if desired. **Yield:** 4 main-dish servings or 10 to 12 appetizer servings.

Dick Sidnam
Bradenton, Florida

MOCK MARGARITAS

Prep: 10 minutes
Freeze: 2 hours

1 (12-ounce) can frozen lemonade
   concentrate, thawed
1 (12-ounce) can frozen limeade
   concentrate, thawed
1 cup powdered sugar
6 cups crushed ice
Lime wedges
Coarse salt
1 (1-liter) bottle club soda,
   chilled

• **Process** half of first 4 ingredients in a blender until smooth. Pour into a 4-quart plastic container. Repeat procedure. Freeze until firm; remove from freezer 30 minutes before serving. Rub lime over rims of stemmed glasses. Place salt in a saucer; spin rim of each glass in salt. Stir soda into frozen mixture until slushy; pour into glasses. **Yield:** about 3 quarts.

Margaritas: Stir 1 cup tequila into mixture before freezing.

RAPID RISOTTO

"Make risotto?" you might ask. "I'll be stirring all day." Not with these recipes. Count on these risottos for easy side dishes or entrées.

EASY BAKED RISOTTO

Prep: 10 minutes
Bake: 30 minutes

1 tablespoon butter or margarine
1 small onion, minced
¾ cup uncooked Arborio rice
1 (14½-ounce) can chicken broth
½ teaspoon dried Italian seasoning
¼ teaspoon salt
¼ teaspoon pepper

• **Melt** butter in a 10-inch ovenproof skillet over medium heat; add onion, and sauté until tender.
• **Add** rice, and cook, stirring constantly, 3 minutes. Stir in broth, and bring to a boil. Stir in remaining ingredients.
• **Bake,** covered, at 350° for 30 minutes or until liquid is absorbed. **Yield:** 4 servings.

CRAWFISH RISOTTO
(pictured on page 74)

Prep: 20 minutes
Cook: 1 hour and 15 minutes

¾ cup butter or margarine
1 medium onion, diced
1 poblano chile pepper, seeded and
   diced
4 garlic cloves, pressed
2 pounds uncooked Arborio rice
3 quarts chicken broth
2 pounds cooked, peeled crawfish
   tails *
8 ounces Monterey Jack cheese
   with peppers, shredded
2 tablespoons Creole seasoning
Garnishes: shredded Parmesan
   cheese, fresh Italian parsley
   sprigs

• **Melt** butter in a Dutch oven over medium heat; add onion, poblano chile, and garlic, and sauté until tender.
• **Add** rice, and cook, stirring constantly, 5 to 7 minutes. Add 1 cup chicken broth; cook, stirring constantly, until liquid is absorbed.
• **Repeat** procedure with remaining broth, ½ cup at a time. (Cooking time is about 1 hour.)
• **Stir** in crawfish; cook, stirring constantly, 4 minutes. Add Monterey Jack cheese and Creole seasoning, stirring until cheese melts. Garnish, if desired. **Yield:** 12 servings.

* Substitute 2 pounds cooked, peeled, medium-size fresh shrimp for crawfish, if desired.

Chef Gus Martin
Palace Cafe
New Orleans, Louisiana

BROCCOLI RISOTTO WITH PARMESAN

Prep: 10 minutes
Cook: 45 minutes

6½ cups chicken broth
1 medium onion, chopped
2 tablespoons olive oil
1½ cups uncooked Arborio rice
1 (16-ounce) package broccoli
   flowerets
1 cup shredded Parmesan
   cheese
¼ teaspoon salt
¼ teaspoon pepper
Shredded Parmesan cheese

• **Bring** broth to a boil in a saucepan; remove from heat, and keep warm.
• **Sauté** chopped onion in hot oil in a saucepan over medium-high heat until tender.
• **Add** rice; cook, stirring constantly, 2 minutes. Reduce heat to medium; add ¾ cup broth, and cook, stirring constantly, until absorbed.
• **Repeat** procedure with 4½ cups hot broth, ¾ cup at a time. Add broccoli and remaining 1¼ cups hot broth, ½ cup at a time.
• **Cook,** stirring constantly, until liquid is absorbed and rice is creamy. (Cooking time is about 30 minutes.) Stir in 1 cup cheese, salt, and pepper. Serve with additional cheese. **Yield:** 8 servings.

Penny Montalbano
Coral Springs, Florida

NOW THAT'S ITALIAN

Risotto (rih-SAW-toh) gets its soft, creamy texture from the key ingredient: Italian-grown Arborio rice. When heated and stirred, the high starch level in this plump, short-grain rice breaks down, causing each kernel to stick together and form a creamy base. Just about any ingredient can be added for texture, flavor, or international flair.

COOKING FOR MOM

For Clint Hayes of Birmingham, Alabama, cooking for his mother, Wilsie, comes naturally. "Mom didn't cook much when we were growing up," he says, "and I started cooking in high school while working in a greasy spoon. Now we have her over once or twice a month."

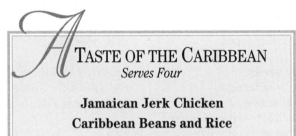

A TASTE OF THE CARIBBEAN
Serves Four

Jamaican Jerk Chicken
Caribbean Beans and Rice
Fried Plantains

JAMAICAN JERK CHICKEN

Prep: 10 minutes
Marinate: 24 hours
Cook: 55 minutes

½ cup chopped green onions
2 habanero chile peppers, seeded
    and chopped *
2 garlic cloves, pressed
1 tablespoon chopped fresh or
    2 teaspoons dried thyme
1 teaspoon salt
¼ teaspoon ground nutmeg
¼ teaspoon ground allspice
¼ teaspoon ground cinnamon
¼ teaspoon pepper
3 tablespoons red wine vinegar
2 tablespoons lime juice
1 tablespoon orange juice
1 teaspoon vegetable oil
1 (4-pound) whole chicken,
    cut up **

• **Combine** first 13 ingredients in a shallow dish or heavy-duty zip-top plastic bag; add chicken. Cover or seal; chill 24 hours.
• **Remove** chicken from marinade, discarding marinade.
• **Prepare** fire by piling charcoal or lava rocks on 1 side of grill, leaving the other side empty. Place rack on grill. Arrange chicken over empty side, and grill, covered with grill lid, over medium-high heat (350° to 400°) 25 minutes. Place chicken in a 13- x 9-inch baking dish.
• **Bake,** covered, at 350° for 30 minutes or until done. **Yield:** 4 servings.

* Substitute 1 tablespoon habanero hot sauce for 2 habanero chile peppers, if desired.
** Substitute 4 pounds chicken pieces for whole chicken, if desired.

CARIBBEAN BEANS AND RICE

Prep: 10 minutes
Soak: 8 hours
Cook: 1 hour and 20 minutes

1 cup dried kidney beans
½ pound salt pork
4½ cups water
1 (14-ounce) can coconut milk
1½ cups uncooked long-grain rice
½ habanero chile pepper, seeded *
1 garlic clove, pressed
1 tablespoon chopped fresh or 1
    teaspoon dried thyme
1 teaspoon pepper
½ teaspoon salt
3 green onions, chopped

• **Place** beans in a Dutch oven; add water to 2 inches above beans. Soak 8 hours. Drain and rinse.
• **Bring** beans, salt pork, 4½ cups water, and coconut milk to a boil in Dutch oven. Cover, reduce heat, and simmer 45 minutes or until beans are tender.
• **Add** rice and next 5 ingredients; return to a boil. Cover, reduce heat, and simmer 25 minutes or until rice is tender. Remove and discard pork; stir in green onions. **Yield:** 7 cups.

* Substitute 2 teaspoons habanero hot sauce for ½ habanero chile pepper, if desired.

FRIED PLANTAINS

Prep: 5 minutes
Cook: 10 minutes

3 large plantains
¼ cup butter or margarine
1 tablespoon sugar
½ teaspoon ground cinnamon

• **Cut** each plantain in half crosswise; cut each half lengthwise into ¼-inch-thick slices.
• **Melt** butter in a large skillet over medium heat. Add plantains; sprinkle with sugar and cinnamon. Cook 3 to 4 minutes on each side or until golden; drain on paper towels. **Yield:** 4 servings.

SOFT ON ROUGHY

Orange roughy is a chameleon of sorts: Its pearl-white complexion, tender texture, and mild, nonfishy flavor allow it to quickly take on whatever seasoning comes its way. And this boneless New Zealand fish fillet—always flash-frozen for the ultimate freshness—is ideal for fast grilling, frying, stuffing . . . you name it. Catfish fillets make a nice substitute in these recipes.

TROPICAL ORANGE ROUGHY WITH CRAB STUFFING

Prep: 25 minutes
Marinate: 20 minutes
Bake: 20 minutes

2 cups orange juice
¼ cup dry white wine
2 tablespoons lite soy sauce
2 tablespoons Dijon mustard
1 teaspoon lime juice
¼ teaspoon minced fresh ginger
⅛ teaspoon ground cinnamon
4 (6- to 8-ounce) orange roughy
    fillets
2 (6-ounce) cans lump crabmeat,
    drained
1 large egg
1 small onion, diced
½ cup Italian-seasoned
    breadcrumbs
2 tablespoons cornstarch
¼ cup coconut milk

• **Combine** first 7 ingredients in a large heavy-duty zip-top plastic bag; add fillets. Seal and chill 15 to 20 minutes.
• **Remove** fillets from marinade. Place marinade in a small saucepan, and set aside.
• **Stir** together crabmeat and next 3 ingredients; spoon evenly onto fillets.
• **Roll** up each fillet, securing with wooden picks. Place, seam side down, in a lightly greased 11- x 7-inch baking dish.
• **Bake** at 350° for 15 to 20 minutes or until fish flakes easily with a fork.

• **Stir** together cornstarch and coconut milk until smooth; stir into reserved marinade. Bring to a boil over medium heat, stirring constantly; boil, stirring constantly, 1 minute or until thickened. Spoon over fish. **Yield:** 4 servings.
Pamela Trige Caracozza
Charlotte, North Carolina

ASIAN-INSPIRED ORANGE ROUGHY

Serve this teriyaki-enhanced treat with ramen noodles and vegetables.

Prep: 10 minutes
Cook: 6 minutes

¼ cup sesame seeds
1½ cups soft breadcrumbs
⅓ cup teriyaki sauce
2 tablespoons white wine vinegar
1½ tablespoons minced fresh
    ginger
½ teaspoon sugar
¼ teaspoon dried crushed red
    pepper
2 large eggs, lightly beaten
½ teaspoon salt
4 (6- to 8-ounce) orange roughy
    fillets
½ cup cornstarch
Vegetable oil
Garnish: sliced green onions

• **Cook** sesame seeds in a large heavy skillet over medium heat, stirring constantly, until golden; cool and stir in breadcrumbs.
• **Bring** teriyaki sauce and next 4 ingredients to a boil in a small saucepan; remove from heat, and keep warm.
• **Stir** together eggs and salt. Dredge fish in cornstarch; dip in egg mixture. Press breadcrumb mixture onto fish.
• **Pour** oil to a depth of ¼ inch into large heavy skillet.
• **Fry** fish in hot oil 3 minutes on each side or until fish flakes easily with a fork. Drain on paper towels. Spoon teriyaki mixture over fish; garnish, if desired. **Yield:** 4 servings.

GO FISH

A 3-ounce T-bone steak contains 8.6 grams of saturated fat. The same amount of orange roughy—which is rich in omega-3 fish oil, calcium, iron, protein, and vitamins B and D—has zero fat.

Follow these basic tips for buying and handling seafood.

■ Buy fish that has a moist, firm, elastic flesh and translucent sheen.

■ Purchase fish that has a clean, mild odor.

■ Refrigerate fish immediately in the coldest part of the refrigerator; use it within a day or two.

ORANGE ROUGHY DIJON

Prep: 10 minutes
Bake: 10 minutes

4 (6- to 8-ounce) orange roughy
    fillets
½ teaspoon salt
¼ teaspoon pepper
¼ cup butter or margarine,
    softened
2 tablespoons Dijon mustard
1 tablespoon lemon juice
2 teaspoons Worcestershire
    sauce
1 garlic clove, minced
½ cup fine, dry breadcrumbs

• **Sprinkle** fish with salt and pepper; place in a lightly greased 13- x 9-inch baking dish. Combine butter and next 4 ingredients; spread on fish. Top with breadcrumbs.
• **Bake** at 450° for 10 minutes or until fish flakes easily with a fork. **Yield:** 4 servings.

PAN-FRIED ROUGHY WITH TOMATO-BASIL SALSA

Prep: 20 minutes
Cook: 15 minutes

4 (6- to 8-ounce) orange roughy
   fillets
1 cup yellow cornmeal
½ cup butter or margarine
1 medium-size sweet onion,
   chopped
2 tablespoons olive oil
1 large tomato, chopped
2 tablespoons chopped fresh or
   2 teaspoons dried basil
2 tablespoons lemon juice
¼ teaspoon salt
¼ teaspoon pepper

• **Coat** fish with cornmeal.
• **Melt** butter in a large skillet over medium-high heat; add fillets, and cook 4 minutes on each side or until fish flakes with a fork. Remove from skillet, and keep warm. Pour off drippings; wipe skillet with a paper towel.
• **Sauté** onion in hot oil in skillet over medium-high heat 4 minutes or until tender.
• **Add** tomato and basil, and cook, stirring often, 3 minutes; drain. Stir in lemon juice, salt, and pepper. Spoon salsa over fish. **Yield:** 4 servings.

Peggo Duquemin Rogers
Jacksonville, North Carolina

HELPING OUT THE HELPERS

No need to apologize for bringing out packaged products—these timesaving treasures are great when time is short and dinner is late. But tonight, try adding a dash of ingenuity to tried-and-true flavors to make a good thing even better. With these recipes you can create family favorites that cook in 50 minutes or less.

SKILLET SAUSAGE CASSEROLE

Prep: 20 minutes
Cook: 30 minutes

1 (6-ounce) package long-grain
   and wild rice mix
1 pound ground pork sausage
4 to 5 green onions, chopped
2 celery ribs, chopped
1 (2.1-ounce) package chicken
   noodle soup mix
2½ cups water
1 cup (4 ounces) shredded
   Cheddar cheese

• **Cook** wild rice mix according to package directions.
• **Cook** sausage, green onions, and celery in a large skillet, stirring until sausage crumbles and is no longer pink; drain and return to skillet.
• **Stir** in rice, soup mix, and water; bring to a boil. Reduce heat, and simmer, uncovered, 15 minutes. Remove from heat; sprinkle with cheese. **Yield:** 8 servings.

Note: For testing purposes only, we used Uncle Ben's Long Grain & Wild Rice mix and Lipton Chicken Noodle Cup a Soup.

Chris Bates
Monaca, Pennsylvania

HOT STUFFED JALAPEÑOS

Prep: 20 minutes
Bake: 25 minutes

1 (12-ounce) jar whole jalapeño
   peppers, rinsed and drained
2 (8-ounce) packages shredded
   sharp Cheddar cheese
1 pound ground pork sausage
1½ cups biscuit mix
2 large eggs, lightly beaten
1 (6-ounce) package seasoned
   coating
Ranch-style dressing

• **Cut** peppers lengthwise down 1 side, leaving other side intact; remove seeds. Stuff each pepper with 1 teaspoon cheese; pinch edges to close.

• **Combine** sausage, biscuit mix, and remaining cheese; divide into 16 portions. Wrap each portion around a stuffed pepper. Dip peppers in egg; coat with coating mix. Place on a greased rack in a 13- x 9-inch pan.
• **Bake** at 350° for 25 minutes. Serve with dressing. **Yield:** 16 appetizers.

Note: For testing purposes only, we used Shake 'N Bake Seasoned Coating Mix for seasoned coating.

Courtney Bush
Austin, Texas

BACON, ZUCCHINI, AND CORNBREAD BAKE

Prep: 25 minutes
Bake: 50 minutes

6 bacon slices
1 medium onion, chopped
½ red bell pepper, chopped
½ green bell pepper, chopped
3 celery ribs, chopped
2 garlic cloves, minced
1 (6-ounce) package cornbread
   stuffing mix
1 cup milk
3 large zucchini, shredded
1 large egg, lightly beaten
½ cup (2 ounces) shredded
   Cheddar cheese

• **Cook** bacon in a large skillet over medium heat until crisp; remove bacon, reserving 2 teaspoons drippings in skillet. Crumble bacon, and set aside.
• **Sauté** onion and next 4 ingredients in reserved drippings over medium-high heat until tender.
• **Stir** together stuffing mix, seasoning packet, and milk; let stand 10 minutes.
• **Stir** in bacon, sautéed vegetables, zucchini, and egg; spoon into a lightly greased 11- x 7-inch baking dish.
• **Bake** at 350° for 30 minutes; sprinkle with cheese. Cover and bake 20 more minutes. **Yield:** 8 servings.

Note: For testing purposes only, we used Stove Top Stuffing Mix for Chicken.

Karen Martis
Merrillville, Indiana

CHICKEN SALAD FOR A CHANGE

Save this collection of fresh ways with chicken salads for your casual entertaining. Our readers share some terrific variations on the theme. Lots of ingredients mean loads of flavor, not necessarily lots of work.

WARM BARBECUE CHICKEN SALAD

Prep: 40 minutes
Bake: 35 minutes

3 cups shredded cooked chicken
Barbecue Dressing
1 cup frozen whole kernel corn, thawed
2 bacon slices, cooked and crumbled
6 cups torn leaf lettuce (about 1 head)
4 plum tomatoes, chopped
⅓ large purple onion, sliced and separated into rings
⅔ cup shredded mozzarella cheese

• **Stir** together chicken and 1 cup Barbecue Dressing in a lightly greased 9-inch square pan.
• **Bake,** covered, at 350° for 35 minutes or until warm.
• **Cook** corn in boiling water to cover 3 to 4 minutes; drain.
• **Toss** together corn, bacon, and next 3 ingredients. Top with warm chicken mixture, and sprinkle with cheese. Serve immediately with remaining 2 cups dressing. **Yield:** 6 servings.

Barbecue Dressing

Prep: 10 minutes
Cook: 20 minutes

1 (18-ounce) bottle barbecue sauce
⅓ cup firmly packed light brown sugar
½ cup honey
⅓ cup ketchup
1 tablespoon butter or margarine
1 tablespoon Worcestershire sauce
½ teaspoon seasoned salt
1 teaspoon lemon pepper

• **Bring** all ingredients to a boil in a saucepan; reduce heat, and simmer, stirring occasionally, 10 minutes. Store in refrigerator up to 3 months, if desired. **Yield:** 3 cups.

Sonja Kelly
Lake Charles, Louisiana

CHICKEN-BLACK BEAN SALAD
(pictured on page 79)

Prep: 30 minutes

3 tablespoons olive oil
1 tablespoon lemon juice
3 garlic cloves, minced
2 jalapeño peppers, chopped
2 tablespoons chopped fresh oregano
1½ teaspoons ground cumin
½ teaspoon salt
½ teaspoon pepper
3 cups chopped cooked chicken
1 (15-ounce) can black beans, rinsed and drained
1 cup frozen whole kernel corn, thawed
1 large tomato, diced
3 tablespoons chopped fresh cilantro
1 (4.2-ounce) package rectangular taco shells
6 to 8 cups shredded lettuce
Garnish: fresh cilantro sprigs

• **Whisk** together first 8 ingredients in a large bowl. Add chicken and next 4 ingredients, tossing to coat. Cover and chill, if desired.
• **Heat** taco shells according to package directions. Fill taco shells with lettuce; top evenly with chicken mixture. Garnish, if desired. **Yield:** 6 servings.

Nancy Banks
Atlanta, Georgia

ASIAN CHICKEN SALAD

Prep: 25 minutes
Chill: 30 minutes

1 pound fresh asparagus spears
3 cups chopped cooked chicken
Walnut Dressing
1 cup chopped walnuts, toasted
8 ounces oyster or shiitake mushrooms, sliced
½ cup chopped fresh chives
1 cup chow mein noodles

• **Snap** off tough ends of asparagus; remove scales from stalks with a vegetable peeler, if desired. Cut asparagus

into 1-inch pieces. Arrange asparagus in a steamer basket over boiling water. Cover and steam 1 to 2 minutes or until crisp-tender.
• **Toss** together chicken and Walnut Dressing; cover and chill 30 minutes.
• **Add** asparagus, walnuts, mushrooms, and chives to chicken mixture; toss well. Cover and chill, if desired. Sprinkle with chow mein noodles just before serving. **Yield:** 6 servings.

Walnut Dressing

Prep: 10 minutes

¼ cup rice vinegar
1 teaspoon wasabi powder *
1 garlic clove, pressed
1 tablespoon chopped fresh
    cilantro
¾ cup walnut oil
¼ cup light sesame oil
1 teaspoon grated fresh
    ginger
¾ teaspoon salt
¼ teaspoon ground red pepper

• **Process** first 4 ingredients in a food processor until blended. With processor running, pour oils through food chute in a slow, steady stream.
• **Add** ginger, salt, and red pepper; pulse 2 or 3 times to blend. Store dressing in refrigerator up to 2 weeks, if desired. **Yield:** 1¼ cups.

* Substitute grated fresh or prepared horseradish for wasabi powder, if desired.

Note: Wasabi powder is horseradish powder found in the Asian section of supermarkets.

Wendy Hansford
El Paso, Texas

HOISIN CHICKEN-AND-PASTA SALAD

Prep: 20 minutes
Cook: 30 minutes

16 ounces penne pasta,
    cooked
½ cup vegetable oil, divided
1 garlic clove, pressed
4 skinned and boned chicken
    breast halves
½ cup chicken broth
½ cup Hoisin Mixture
2 celery ribs, sliced
2 green onions, sliced
1 small cucumber, peeled, seeded,
    and sliced
½ small red bell pepper, cut into
    thin strips
¾ teaspoon salt
¾ teaspoon pepper
2 teaspoons sesame seeds,
    toasted

• **Toss** together pasta and 3 tablespoons oil in a Dutch oven.
• **Heat** remaining 5 tablespoons oil in a large skillet over medium heat; add garlic, and sauté 1 minute.
• **Add** chicken; cook 4 minutes on each side or until done. Remove chicken from skillet, and set aside.
• **Stir** chicken broth into skillet; bring to a boil. Reduce heat, and simmer 10 minutes or until reduced to ⅓ cup; remove from heat, and stir in Hoisin Mixture. Toss with pasta.
• **Cut** chicken into ½-inch cubes. Add chicken, celery, and next 5 ingredients to pasta mixture; toss well. Sprinkle with sesame seeds. Serve immediately. **Yield:** 6 servings.

Hoisin Mixture

Prep: 5 minutes

1 (7.25-ounce) jar hoisin
    sauce
1½ tablespoons sugar
2 tablespoons pale dry sherry
2 tablespoons sesame oil
1½ tablespoons rice vinegar

• **Stir** together all ingredients until sugar dissolves. Store in refrigerator up to 3

months. (Mixture also adds great flavor to stir-fry vegetables.) **Yield:** 1¼ cups.

Note: Find hoisin sauce and sesame oil in the Asian section of supermarkets.
Amy Klaren
Louisville, Kentucky

COOL GELATIN DESSERTS

Gelatin dishes rose to fame in school cafeterias, at ladies' luncheons, and at children's birthday parties. But we have discovered three cool, quivering desserts that are worthy of your next fancy dinner party.

To get the most effervescence in the new sparkling gelatins, prepare your dish the same day you plan to serve it.

GINGER ALE AMBROSIA

Prep: 15 minutes
Chill: 6 hours and 45 minutes

2 (3-ounce) packages sparkling
    white grape gelatin
1½ cups boiling water
1 (12-ounce) can ginger ale
3 oranges, peeled and sectioned
1 banana, sliced
½ cup flaked coconut

• **Stir** together gelatin and 1½ cups boiling water 2 minutes or until gelatin dissolves.
• **Stir** in ginger ale, and chill 45 minutes or until consistency of unbeaten egg white. Stir in orange, banana, and coconut. Pour into a 4-cup mold, and chill 6 hours or until firm. **Yield:** 8 servings.

SHERRIED GEL WITH STIRRED CUSTARD

Prep: 10 minutes
Chill: 8 hours

2 envelopes unflavored gelatin
½ cup cold water
1¼ cups water
⅔ cup sugar
¾ cup cream sherry
⅓ cup lemon juice
Stirred Custard

• **Sprinkle** gelatin over ½ cup cold water in a small bowl; stir mixture, and let stand 1 minute.
• **Bring** 1¼ cups water and sugar to a boil in a saucepan, stirring constantly until sugar dissolves.
• **Add** gelatin mixture, stirring until dissolved. Stir in cream sherry and lemon juice; pour into a lightly oiled 4-cup mold or glass bowl. Chill 8 hours.
• **Unmold** gelatin, and serve with Stirred Custard. **Yield:** 6 servings.

Stirred Custard

Prep: 18 minutes
Chill: 2 hours

3 cups milk
2 large eggs
⅔ cup sugar
1½ tablespoons all-purpose flour
1 teaspoon vanilla extract

• **Cook** milk in a heavy saucepan over medium heat, stirring often, until thoroughly heated.
• **Beat** eggs at medium speed with an electric mixer until frothy.
• **Add** sugar and flour, beating until thickened. Gradually stir in about 1 cup hot milk; add to remaining hot milk, stirring constantly.
• **Cook** over low heat, stirring occasionally, until mixture coats a spoon (about 10 minutes). Remove from heat; stir in vanilla. Chill 2 hours. **Yield:** 3½ cups.

Mrs. A. Mayer
Richmond, Virginia

COFFEE-AND-CREAM CHILL

Prep: 20 minutes
Chill: 4 hours

2 envelopes unflavored gelatin
½ cup cold water
½ cup sugar
1½ cups water
2 tablespoons instant coffee granules
1 cup whipping cream
2 tablespoons sugar
2 tablespoons coffee liqueur
Garnish: grated chocolate

• **Sprinkle** gelatin over ½ cup cold water in a small saucepan; let stand 1 minute.
• **Cook** over low heat, stirring until gelatin dissolves (about 2 minutes).
• **Stir** in ½ cup sugar, 1½ cups water, and coffee granules until dissolved. Pour into a 1-quart bowl. Chill 4 hours or until mixture is firm.
• **Beat** whipping cream at medium speed with an electric mixer until foamy; gradually add 2 tablespoons sugar and coffee liqueur, beating until soft peaks form.
• **Pull** a fork through gelatin to break into small pieces.
• **Spoon** ½ cup gelatin into each of 4 parfait glasses; top evenly with half of whipped cream. Repeat procedure with remaining gelatin and whipped cream. Garnish, if desired. **Yield:** 4 servings.

Diane R. Locklair
Decatur, Georgia

EDNA'S LEGACY

When Edna Eaton retired last year from Saint Mary's School in Raleigh, students and staff members sadly said goodbye to their longtime head cook. After 18 years at the school, she'd earned the right to hang up her apron.

But school officials knew they couldn't do without her fried chicken. Even Raleigh residents made visits to campus for "fried chicken day." So Edna continued to oversee preparation of her famous dish once or twice a month. Soon she was back at Saint Mary's part time.

Edna says the secret to her chicken is "soaking it with vinegar and salt. This gets the juice off and gives the right mixture for the batter." Taste for yourself.

EDNA'S FRIED CHICKEN

Prep: 55 minutes
Cook: 40 minutes

2 (2½-pound) whole chickens, cut up
¼ cup cider vinegar
¼ cup salt
3 cups all-purpose flour
2 teaspoons salt
½ teaspoon garlic salt
1 tablespoon seasoned salt
½ teaspoon poultry seasoning
2 teaspoons paprika
1 teaspoon pepper
Vegetable oil

• **Place** chicken in a large bowl; add water to cover. Add vinegar and ¼ cup salt; let stand 30 minutes. Drain well.
• **Stir** together flour and next 6 ingredients; dredge chicken in flour mixture, shaking off excess flour mixture.
• **Pour** oil to a depth of 2 inches into a Dutch oven; heat to 350°. Fry chicken, in batches, 9 to 10 minutes on each side or until done. Drain on paper towels. **Yield:** 8 servings.

Edna Eaton
Raleigh, North Carolina

Hip Chips

Remember when candy baking chips came in only one flavor (semisweet chocolate) and one size (small)? Today a parade of flavored candy chips makes baking more fun than ever. Tear open bags of chips, chunks, and morsels in butterscotch, white chocolate, peanut butter, and—one of our favorites—almond brickle, and substitute them in your recipes. Look at all the choices before you buy the same chips off the old block.

WHITE CHOCOLATE CHIP-OATMEAL COOKIES

Prep: 20 minutes
Bake: 12 minutes per batch

1 cup butter or margarine, softened
1 cup firmly packed light brown sugar
1 cup sugar
2 large eggs
2 teaspoons vanilla extract
3 cups all-purpose flour
1 teaspoon baking soda
1 teaspoon baking powder
1 teaspoon salt
1½ cups uncooked regular oats
2 cups (12 ounces) white chocolate morsels
1 cup coarsely chopped pecans

• **Beat** butter at medium speed with an electric mixer until creamy; gradually add sugars, beating well.
• **Add** eggs, 1 at a time, beating just until yellow disappears after each addition. Stir in vanilla.
• **Combine** flour and next 3 ingredients; gradually add to butter mixture, beating until blended.
• **Stir** in oats, morsels, and pecans. Drop by tablespoonfuls onto greased baking sheets.

• **Bake** at 350° for 12 minutes. Cool on baking sheets 3 minutes; remove to wire racks to cool completely. **Yield:** 6½ dozen.

Diana B. Salter
Birmingham, Alabama

CHOCOLATE-BRICKLE COOKIES

Prep: 10 minutes
Bake: 10 minutes per batch

1 cup butter or margarine, softened
1½ cups sugar
2 large eggs
1 teaspoon vanilla extract
2 cups all-purpose flour
¾ teaspoon baking soda
¼ teaspoon salt
⅔ cup cocoa
1 (7.5-ounce) package almond brickle chips
1 (2.25-ounce) package sliced almonds

• **Beat** butter at medium speed with an electric mixer until creamy; gradually add sugar, beating until blended. Add eggs, 1 at a time, beating until blended. Stir in vanilla.
• **Combine** flour and next 3 ingredients; gradually add to butter mixture, beating at low speed until blended. Stir in brickle chips and almonds. Drop by rounded teaspoonfuls onto ungreased baking sheets.
• **Bake** at 350° for 10 minutes. (Cookies will be soft.) Cool on baking sheets 2 minutes; remove to wire racks to cool. **Yield:** 6 dozen.

Note: For testing purposes only, we used Heath Bits 'O Brickle for almond brickle chips; find them in the baking section near the chocolate morsels in supermarkets.

CHOCOLATE-CHERRY CORDIAL TRUFFLES

Prep: 1 hour and 50 minutes
Chill: 2 hours
Cook: 10 minutes

⅓ cup dried cherries
¼ cup cherry brandy
2 cups (12 ounces) semisweet chocolate morsels
4 egg yolks
⅓ cup butter or margarine
⅓ cup sifted powdered sugar
¼ teaspoon cherry extract
8 (2-ounce) chocolate candy coating squares

• **Stir** together cherries and cherry brandy; let stand 1 hour.
• **Melt** chocolate morsels in a heavy saucepan over low heat, stirring until smooth. Remove from heat.
• **Beat** egg yolks at medium speed with an electric mixer until thick and pale. Gradually stir about one-fourth of melted chocolate into beaten egg yolks; add to remaining chocolate, stirring constantly.
• **Cook** mixture over medium heat, stirring constantly, 6 minutes or until a candy thermometer registers 160°. Remove from heat; add dried cherry mixture, butter, sugar, and cherry extract, stirring until butter melts and mixture is blended. Cover and chill 1 hour.
• **Shape** cherry mixture into 1-inch balls. Cover and chill 1 hour.
• **Place** coating in top of a double boiler; bring water to a boil. Reduce heat to low; cook, stirring constantly, until coating melts. Remove from heat, leaving coating over hot water.
• **Dip** balls in coating; place on wax paper. Let stand until firm. Store in refrigerator. **Yield:** 2 dozen.

Diane Sparrow
Osage, Indiana

FROM OUR KITCHEN TO YOURS

Is it still good? Labels on fresh meat, poultry, and dairy products have a "sell by" date and a "use by" date. It can be confusing. During a seminar with representatives from Tyson Foods, Inc., we learned some guidelines.

According to Sue Quillin, Tyson's fresh chicken products have a 10-day retail shelf life for maximum flavor and safety. She suggests we use the "sell by" date as the time to cook or freeze fresh chicken. If you buy chicken on May 10 with a "sell by" date of May 12, it's safe to cook or freeze it by the 12th.

Milk and most other dairy products have factored in additional "use by" time of up to seven days past the "sell by" date. Therefore, it is perfectly safe to buy milk on the "sell by" date of May 10 and use it up to seven days later.

CHEERS

You can serve wine or beer to complement the "Backyard Barbecue" recipes on pages 104 and 105. The light, fruity taste of Cabernet Franc is a winner with barbecued pork and spicy side dishes. If you prefer frosty mugs of beer, select a pale ale.

Accompany dessert with your favorite champagne or sparkling wine. Aria is a refreshing blizzard of bubbly and a great buy in our local market for $11.

A CRAFTY COOK

Sue Wiener of Springhill, Florida, writes that she has found a way to keep a cake from cracking as it cools.

"If it looks like it might [crack], I just hold it over a very low flame for a few seconds. Works great." The additional warmth allows the cake to cool more slowly without it pulling apart in the center.

SQUISHY CLEAN

Martha M. Doss of Lexington, Virginia, writes, "When I finish cleaning up, I put the wet and soapy sponge (no metal on it, of course) on a paper towel in the microwave for one minute on HIGH. When it's done, I use the wet paper towel to clean the microwave oven, which kills two birds with one shot. The sponge is now clean, and the oven is clean and odor free."

WONDROUS TOFU

We've received numerous letters from readers about the benefits of including tofu (soybean curd) in women's diets. Here's what we have learned. *American Health* magazine reports soy is a fantastic source of vegetable protein and contains a compound called phytoestrogen, which might block cancer-causing substances, reduce symptoms of menopause, and protect against heart disease.

We tested several recipes using tofu and found cooking with it to be easy and fast. If you're looking for ways to add soy to your diet, cook dried soybeans and add them to soups and salads. Use thin strips of firm tofu instead of chicken in stir-fry recipes. To make a dip for raw vegetables, process soft tofu with herbs and lemon juice. Tofu takes on the flavor of whatever you season it with, so get creative and let us know what develops. If you're serious about soy, call (757) 824-0500 or access www.tofu.com for a copy of *The Book of Tofu* ($5.95 plus shipping and handling).

MORE FOOD ON OUR WEB SITE

Look us up at southernliving.com, where we expand on the Foods stories included in each issue of our magazine.

DOUBLING UP ON DIPS

Show off your garnishing finesse when dishing up individual servings of two dips or spreads (like the recipe for Double-Dip Shrimp on page 112). Place a spatula in the center of a wide-rimmed, shallow glass, like a martini glass. Spoon desired amount of first sauce on one side of the spatula; spoon an equal amount of the second sauce on the other side. Carefully remove the spatula. Then arrange the dippers around the edge of the glass (as in the case of the shrimp recipe) or on a small plate that holds the glass (when serving chips or cut vegetables).

A BAKER'S ESSENTIALS

Test Kitchens staffer Mary Allen Perry is our queen of cakes. She bakes creations that are light as air and perfect every time. See her latest confections beginning on page 117. "I like to work with Wilton cakepans," says Mary Allen. "They're multifunctional because of their depth. I can bake thin or thick layers in the same set." A few basic pans yield good results from your favorite recipes. You'll need two 8-inch round cakepans as well as two 9-inch round cakepans.

■ Use flat, shallow baking sheets for cookies. A pan with raised sides (sometimes called a jellyroll pan) is best for thin cakes. In *Baking with Julia,* Julia Child suggests that a baker's kitchen should have two to four baking sheets. Two can be in the oven while the others are being readied. Look for the heaviest baking sheets available; they distribute heat evenly and won't warp. Cookies baked on air-cushioned baking sheets don't brown well.

■ Add two 9- x 5-inch loafpans, two 9-inch square cakepans, and a 9-inch springform pan to your list of basics, and you're ready for any recipe. These don't have to be nonstick. If they're used for baked goods only, little scouring is needed. Don't use dark-colored pans; baked goods get overly brown and burn easily. Clean pans well to prevent buildup of cooking spray. Dry them completely to preserve the surfaces.

JUNE

Dust off your favorite warm-weather memories and get ready to create new ones with some of summer's best pickings—blackberries. "Summer on the Vine" brings you a harvest of new, streamlined dessert classics, from Blackberry Custard to Blackberry Cobbler to 1-2-3 Blackberry Sherbet. And Blackberry Lemonade is the perfect elixir to quench your thirst on sultry afternoons.

Fried green tomatoes are another Southern seasonal standby, and "A Firm Believer" offers you one of our favorite versions: Blue Willow Fried Green Tomatoes. But this versatile vegetable is for more than just frying, as you'll discover when you taste novelties like Peachy Green Tomato Salsa and Pickled Green Tomatoes.

SUMMER ON THE VINE

Spend a sunny morning harvesting your own crop of blackberries right off the vine at a pick-your-own farm, or buy the gems at a nearby market or roadside stand. No matter where you choose to harvest, these berry creations put summer's sweet glory within easy reach.

BLACKBERRY LEMONADE

Prep: 10 minutes

3 cups fresh blackberries
7 cups water
¼ cup sugar
¼ (1.9-ounce) package sugar-free
    pink lemonade drink mix
Garnishes: fresh mint sprigs, lemon
    slices

• **Process** blackberries in a blender until smooth, stopping to scrape down sides.
• **Pour** through a fine wire-mesh strainer into a 2-quart pitcher, discarding solids.
• **Stir** in 7 cups water, sugar, and drink mix. Serve over ice; garnish, if desired. **Yield:** 2 quarts.

Note: For testing purposes only, we used Crystal Light pink lemonade drink mix.

Keith Haney
Madison, Alabama

BLACKBERRIES CHANTILLY

Prep: 20 minutes

1 cup crushed fresh blackberries
½ cup sugar, divided
1 cup whipping cream
½ teaspoon vanilla extract
2 tablespoons blackberry schnapps
    (optional)
1 (10.5-ounce) angel food cake
    loaf, sliced

• **Stir** together blackberries and ⅓ cup sugar; let stand 10 minutes or until sugar dissolves, stirring occasionally.
• **Beat** whipping cream at medium speed with an electric mixer until foamy; gradually add remaining sugar, vanilla, and, if desired, blackberry schnapps, beating until soft peaks form. Fold into blackberry mixture. Serve over angel food cake slices. **Yield:** 8 servings.

Anna Robinson
Oak Ridge, Tennessee

1-2-3 BLACKBERRY SHERBET
(pictured on page 115)

Our Test Kitchens awarded its highest mark to this simply sensational dessert. Just three ingredients give it its frosty flair.

Prep: 15 minutes
Freeze: 11 hours

4 cups fresh blackberries
2 cups sugar
2 cups buttermilk
Garnishes: fresh blackberries,
    fresh mint sprig

• **Stir** together 4 cups blackberries and sugar in a bowl; let mixture stand 30 minutes.
• **Process** blackberry mixture in a food processor or blender until smooth, stopping to scrape down sides.
• **Pour** through a fine wire-mesh strainer into a 9-inch square pan, discarding solids; stir in buttermilk. Cover; freeze 8 hours.
• **Break** frozen mixture into chunks, and place in a bowl; beat at medium speed with an electric mixer until smooth. Return to pan; cover and freeze 3 hours or until firm. Garnish, if desired. **Yield:** 1 quart.

Kitchen Express: Double the ingredient amounts and combine blackberry juice and buttermilk in freezer container of a 4-quart electric freezer. Freeze according to manufacturer's instructions. Pack freezer with additional ice and rock salt, and let stand 1 hour before serving.

Arlene P. Rogers
Louisville, Kentucky

BLACKBERRY COBBLER

(pictured on page 114)

Blackberry Syrup (bottom right of this page) is the perfect accompaniment for this home-style favorite.

Prep: 25 minutes
Bake: 50 minutes

8 cups fresh blackberries
2¼ cups sugar
⅓ cup all-purpose flour
1 teaspoon lemon juice
Pastry, divided
¼ cup butter or margarine, cut up
Sugar (optional)

• **Stir** together first 4 ingredients; let mixture stand 10 minutes or until sugar dissolves.
• **Roll** half of Pastry to ¼-inch thickness; cut into 1½-inch-wide strips. Place on a lightly greased baking sheet.
• **Bake** at 425° for 10 minutes or until lightly browned. Remove to a wire rack to cool. Break strips into pieces.
• **Spoon** half of blackberry mixture into a lightly greased 13- x 9-inch baking dish; top with baked pastry pieces. Spoon remaining blackberry mixture over pastry; dot with butter.
• **Roll** remaining Pastry to ¼-inch thickness; cut into 1-inch strips, and arrange in a lattice design over filling. Sprinkle with sugar, if desired. Place cobbler on a baking sheet.
• **Bake** at 350° for 50 minutes or until golden. Serve with vanilla ice cream and Blackberry Syrup, if desired. **Yield:** 8 servings.

Pastry

Prep: 5 minutes

2½ cups all-purpose flour
1¾ teaspoons baking powder
¾ teaspoon salt
½ cup shortening
⅔ cup milk

• **Stir** together first 3 ingredients in a medium bowl. Cut shortening into flour mixture with a pastry blender until mixture is crumbly.

Full of plump, fresh blackberries, Blackberry Cobbler has been a favorite of the Flournoy family for years. Take a taste, and it might become yours, too.

Carolyn Flournoy first tasted blackberry cobbler more than 50 years ago as a new bride at Sunday dinners with her husband's Louisiana family. "We enjoyed it all summer long," she remembers. "My mother-in-law always served her cobbler with ice cream and a pitcher of blackberry syrup."

The pastry-filled cobbler recipe Carolyn inherited is still in demand. "Our son Craig and daughter Kate both celebrate June birthdays," Carolyn says. "And many years they request this cobbler instead of cake." Try her Blackberry Cobbler, and create some new family traditions of your own.

• **Add** milk, stirring with a fork until dry ingredients are moistened and mixture forms a soft ball.
• **Turn** dough out onto a floured surface, and knead 6 to 8 times. **Yield:** pastry for 1 (13- x 9-inch) cobbler.

Carolyn Flournoy
Shreveport, Louisiana

BLACKBERRY JAM

Prep: 5 minutes
Cook: 23 minutes

½ to 1 cup sugar
4 cups fresh blackberries
1 teaspoon lemon juice

• **Place** sugar in a 2-quart microwave-safe bowl; microwave at HIGH 2 minutes or until sugar is warm.
• **Stir** in blackberries; cover with plastic wrap, folding back 1 edge to allow steam to escape.
• **Microwave** at HIGH 3 minutes or until sugar dissolves, stirring twice. Microwave, covered, at HIGH 10 minutes. Uncover and microwave 8 minutes or until thickened. Stir in lemon juice; cool. Store in refrigerator. **Yield:** 1⅔ cups.

Nora Henshaw
Okemah, Oklahoma

BLACKBERRY SYRUP

Prep: 10 minutes
Cook: 5 minutes

3 cups fresh blackberries
1¼ cups sugar
¼ cup light corn syrup
1 teaspoon cornstarch

• **Process** blackberries in a blender until smooth, stopping to scrape down sides.
• **Pour** through a fine wire-mesh strainer into a medium saucepan, discarding solids.
• **Stir** in remaining ingredients; bring mixture to a boil over medium heat, stirring occasionally.
• **Boil,** stirring occasionally, 1 minute. Remove from heat; cool. Serve with cobbler, pound cake, fruit, pancakes, or ice cream. **Yield:** 1⅔ cups.

BLACKBERRY CUSTARD
(pictured on page 114)

This chilled, berry-topped custard was another winner of top honors in our kitchens.

Prep: 15 minutes
Cook: 7 minutes
Chill: 2 hours

¾ cup sugar
⅓ cup all-purpose flour
Dash of salt
4 egg yolks
2 cups milk
½ teaspoon vanilla extract
1 cup whipping cream
2 tablespoons sugar
2 cups fresh blackberries
Garnish: fresh mint sprigs

• **Combine** first 3 ingredients in a heavy saucepan; whisk in egg yolks and milk.
• **Cook** over medium heat, whisking constantly, 5 to 7 minutes or until thickened. Remove from heat; stir in vanilla. Pour into a serving dish; cool. Cover and chill 2 hours.
• **Beat** whipping cream at medium speed with an electric mixer until foamy; gradually add 2 tablespoons sugar, beating until soft peaks form.
• **Spread** whipped cream over custard. Top with blackberries; garnish, if desired. **Yield:** 4 servings.

$\mathcal{I}$CY TREATS

On hot, humid days dash to the freezer for homemade ice pops. You're never too old to appreciate something cool, so we offer flavors for adults, too. Molds, ice cube trays, and small paper cups all hold these colorful creations well. Some commercial molds have their own handles, so you won't need wooden sticks. If the pops don't slide right out, give them a quick dip in lukewarm water.

PURPLE PEOPLE EATER POPS

Prep: 10 minutes
Freeze: 5 hours and 30 minutes

1 (12-ounce) can frozen grape juice concentrate, thawed and undiluted
1½ cups ginger ale
½ cup seedless purple grapes, sliced
12 wooden craft sticks

• **Stir** together juice concentrate, ginger ale, and grapes.
• **Spoon** evenly into ⅓-cup molds; freeze 30 minutes or until firm. Insert wooden sticks, and freeze at least 5 hours. **Yield:** 12 servings (4 cups).

ORANGE FLOAT POPS

Prep: 4 minutes
Freeze: 5 hours and 30 minutes

1 quart orange sherbet, softened
1 cup orange soft drink
20 wooden craft sticks

• **Stir** together sherbet and orange soft drink. Spoon evenly into ¼-cup molds; freeze 30 minutes or until firm. Insert wooden sticks, and freeze at least 5 hours. **Yield:** 20 servings (5 cups).

Note: For testing purposes only, we used Minute Maid soft drink.

STRAWBERRY-CINNAMON POPS

Prep: 5 minutes
Freeze: 5 hours and 30 minutes

¼ cup red cinnamon candies
4 cups boiling water
1 (4-ounce) package strawberry drink mix
1 (6-ounce) package strawberry gelatin
15 wooden craft sticks

• **Dissolve** cinnamon candies in 4 cups boiling water.
• **Add** drink mix and gelatin, stirring 2 minutes or until gelatin dissolves.
• **Pour** evenly into ⅓-cup molds; freeze 30 minutes or until firm. Insert wooden sticks, and freeze at least 5 hours. **Yield:** 15 servings (5 cups).

Note: For testing purposes only, we used Kool-Aid drink mix.

BERRY POPS

Adapted from a recipe by Mrs. William Yoder Jr. of Montezuma, Georgia

Prep: 10 minutes
Freeze: 5 hours and 30 minutes

1 (4.3-ounce) package berry punch mix
1 (3-ounce) package berry blue gelatin
½ cup sugar
2 cups boiling water
2 cups cold water
20 wooden craft sticks

• **Stir** together first 4 ingredients 2 minutes or until gelatin dissolves; stir in 2 cups cold water.
• **Pour** mixture evenly into ¼-cup molds; freeze 30 minutes or until firm. Insert wooden sticks, and freeze at least 5 hours. **Yield:** 20 servings (5 cups).

Note: For testing purposes only, we used Kool-Aid drink mix.

HANDHELD TIPS

■ Remove frozen treats from molds; store in heavy-duty zip-top plastic bags in freezer.

■ For icy cubes to serve with fruit juices, pour pop mixture into ice trays, and freeze. Two cups liquid fills approximately one ice cube tray.

■ Three-ounce disposable paper cups or muffin pans with paper liners are simple and inexpensive alternatives to molds. Just peel off the paper and lick.

SANGRÍA POPS

Prep: 10 minutes
Freeze: 5 hours and 30 minutes

1 (12-ounce) can frozen lemonade concentrate, thawed and undiluted
½ cup orange juice
3 tablespoons fresh lime juice
¾ cup sugar
2 cups dry white wine
20 wooden craft sticks

• **Stir** together first 5 ingredients until sugar dissolves.
• **Pour** evenly into ¼-cup molds; freeze 30 minutes or until firm. Insert wooden sticks, and freeze at least 5 hours. **Yield:** 20 servings (5 cups).

Note: For testing purposes only, we used Gewürztraminer or Riesling wine.

KIWI MARGARITA POPS

Prep: 10 minutes
Freeze: 5 hours and 30 minutes

6 kiwifruit, peeled and cut into chunks
⅔ cup tequila
¼ to ½ cup orange liqueur
¼ cup fresh lime juice
¼ cup sugar
11 wooden craft sticks

• **Process** first 5 ingredients in a food processor until smooth.
• **Spoon** mixture evenly into ¼-cup molds; freeze 30 minutes or until firm. Insert wooden sticks, and freeze at least 5 hours. **Yield:** 11 servings (2¾ cups).

Note: For testing purposes only, we used Triple Sec liqueur.

POP GOES THE SANDWICH

The dairy case is always full of surprises; you never know what'll pop up. A quick bread could inspire you to try terrific new twists on familiar sandwiches. These hearty handfuls are easy to create—just pair a filling with pop-open dough. Try ours for starters, or experiment with your own savory stuffings. The fun is in letting your imagination unfold.

EASY CALZONES

Prep: 15 minutes
Bake: 15 minutes

¾ pound ground round
¼ cup chopped onion
3 garlic cloves, minced
1 (14-ounce) jar chunky spaghetti sauce, divided
½ teaspoon dried Italian seasoning
1 (11-ounce) can refrigerated French loaf
4 (1-ounce) mozzarella cheese slices

• **Cook** first 3 ingredients in a large skillet over medium heat until ground beef crumbles and is no longer pink; drain well. Return to skillet; stir in ½ cup spaghetti sauce and Italian seasoning.
• **Unroll** French loaf; roll into a 16-inch square. Cut into 4 squares; spoon ½ cup ground beef mixture onto center of each square. Top each square with a slice of mozzarella cheese. Fold over to form a triangle, pressing edges to seal. Place on a lightly greased baking sheet.
• **Bake** at 400° for 12 to 15 minutes or until browned. Serve with remaining spaghetti sauce. **Yield:** 4 servings.

Note: For testing purposes only, we used Ragú Mushroom & Green Pepper Chunky Gardenstyle pasta sauce for spaghetti sauce.

PIG-IN-A-BLANKET BREAD

Prep: 30 minutes
Bake: 30 minutes

½ pound ground pork sausage
½ cup chopped green bell
  pepper
¼ cup chopped onion
1 garlic clove, minced
½ cup sliced fresh mushrooms
1 (11-ounce) can refrigerated
  French loaf
½ cup (2 ounces) shredded
  mozzarella cheese
½ cup grated Parmesan cheese
1 egg white
1 teaspoon water
1½ tablespoons cornmeal

• **Cook** first 4 ingredients in a large skillet over medium-high heat, stirring until sausage crumbles and is no longer pink. Add mushrooms; sauté until tender. Drain and cool.
• **Unroll** French loaf; spoon sausage mixture down center of bread dough, leaving a ½-inch border on all sides; sprinkle with mozzarella and Parmesan cheeses.
• **Stir** together egg white and 1 teaspoon water. Brush edges of loaf with egg white mixture; roll up, starting at a long edge, pressing edges to seal.
• **Sprinkle** a lightly greased baking sheet with cornmeal; place loaf on baking sheet. Brush with egg white mixture.
• **Bake** at 375° for 25 to 30 minutes or until golden. Let stand 10 minutes; cut into 1-inch slices. **Yield:** 8 servings.

Linda Adams
North Little Rock, Arkansas

GOOD-START SANDWICHES

Prep: 30 minutes
Bake: 12 minutes

2 tablespoons butter or
  margarine
9 large eggs
½ teaspoon salt
¼ teaspoon pepper
½ (8-ounce) package cream
  cheese, cut into ¼-inch cubes
  and softened
1 (11.3-ounce) can refrigerated
  large biscuits
8 bacon slices, cooked and
  crumbled
1 cup (4 ounces) shredded sharp
  Cheddar cheese

• **Melt** butter in a large nonstick skillet over medium heat. Whisk together eggs, salt, and pepper; pour into skillet, and sprinkle with cream cheese cubes.
• **Cook** over medium heat, without stirring, until eggs begin to set on bottom. Draw a spatula across bottom of skillet to form large curds; continue cooking until eggs are thickened but still moist (do not stir constantly). Remove from heat, and cool.
• **Pat** or roll each biscuit on a lightly floured surface into a 6-inch circle.
• **Spoon** egg mixture evenly onto each biscuit, and sprinkle evenly with bacon and Cheddar cheese. Brush edges with water; fold biscuits over filling, gently pressing edges with tines of a fork to seal. Place sandwiches on a lightly greased baking sheet.
• **Bake** at 375° for 10 to 12 minutes or until golden. **Yield:** 8 servings.

Note: For testing purposes only, we used Pillsbury (8-count) Grands! Flaky Biscuits.

THAI FOR TWO

Sparked by zesty Peanut Sauce, this dish from Southeast Asia provides a perfect international dinner for two. It is delicious paired with minted iced tea.

CHICKEN SATÉ

1 garlic clove, minced
3 tablespoons soy sauce
2 tablespoons lemon juice
1 teaspoon curry powder
½ teaspoon pepper
2 skinned and boned chicken breast
  halves, cut into 1-inch pieces
Hot cooked rice
Peanut Sauce

• **Combine** first 5 ingredients in a shallow dish or heavy-duty zip-top plastic bag; add chicken. Cover or seal; let stand 30 minutes.
• **Soak** 6-inch wooden skewers in warm water 30 minutes. Remove chicken from marinade, discarding marinade; thread onto skewers. Grill, covered with grill lid, over medium-high heat (350° to 400°), turning occasionally, about 8 minutes or until done. Serve over hot cooked rice with Peanut Sauce. **Yield:** 2 servings.

Peanut Sauce

1 small sweet onion, chopped
1 teaspoon minced fresh ginger
½ to ¾ teaspoon ground red pepper
1 teaspoon corn oil
½ cup creamy peanut butter
1 cup water
1 tablespoon soy sauce
¼ teaspoon salt

• **Sauté** first 3 ingredients in hot oil in a saucepan 1 minute; stir in peanut butter. Gradually stir in water, soy sauce, and salt; bring to a boil. Cook, stirring constantly, 3 minutes or until thickened. **Yield:** 2 cups.

Dave Cristy
Pine Mountain, Georgia

ETTER ON A BUN

A variety of buns makes these sandwiches all the better, and these innovative ingredients might make you forget those plain beef burgers. Follow our serving suggestions, or prepare your favorite sides.

SPINACH-FETA BURGERS

The key to shaping this mixture into patties is drying the spinach completely before adding the other ingredients.

Prep: 10 minutes
Chill: 30 minutes
Cook: 10 minutes

2 (10-ounce) packages frozen
   chopped spinach, thawed
2 (4-ounce) packages crumbled
   feta cheese
1 cup Italian-seasoned breadcrumbs
1 medium onion, diced
4 garlic cloves, minced
1 large egg, lightly beaten
½ teaspoon salt
1 teaspoon ground black pepper
¼ teaspoon ground red pepper
   (optional)
1 tablespoon vegetable oil
6 whole wheat buns, toasted

• **Drain** spinach well, pressing between layers of paper towels.
• **Combine** spinach, cheese, ¾ cup breadcrumbs, next 5 ingredients, and, if desired, red pepper; shape into 6 patties. Coat patties with remaining ¼ cup breadcrumbs; cover and chill 30 minutes.
• **Cook** patties in hot oil in a large non-stick skillet over medium heat 5 minutes on each side; drain on paper towels. Serve on buns with reduced-fat Ranch-style dressing, purple onion slices, tomato slices, pasta salad, and fresh fruit. **Yield:** 6 servings.

Shannon Farho
Baton Rouge, Louisiana

MUSHROOM BURGERS

If you don't want to fire up the grill, use a heavy grill skillet.

Prep: 5 minutes
Chill: 30 minutes
Grill: 6 minutes

4 portobello mushroom caps
1 cup Italian dressing
4 sourdough buns
4 Muenster or Gruyère cheese
   slices
Romaine lettuce leaves

• **Combine** mushrooms and Italian dressing in a shallow dish or large heavy-duty zip-top plastic bag, turning to coat. Cover or seal; chill 30 minutes, turning occasionally. Remove mushrooms, discarding dressing.
• **Grill** mushroom caps, covered with grill lid, over medium-high heat (350° to 400°) 2 to 3 minutes on each side.
• **Grill** buns, cut sides down, 1 minute or until toasted. Place mushrooms, cheese, and lettuce on buns; serve immediately with melon wedges and grilled or sautéed squash. **Yield:** 4 servings.

Adelyne Smith
Dunnville, Kentucky

GARLIC TURKEY BURGERS

You can make and chill the sauce for these burgers 8 hours ahead.

Prep: 6 minutes
Cook: 10 minutes

1 pound ground turkey
½ cup wheat germ
1 small onion, diced
2 garlic cloves, minced
1 teaspoon dried oregano
½ teaspoon fennel seeds, crushed
½ teaspoon salt
½ teaspoon pepper
6 onion buns, toasted
Dried Tomato Sauce

• **Combine** first 8 ingredients. Shape mixture into 6 patties; place on a rack in a broiler pan.
• **Broil** 4 to 5 inches from heat (with electric oven door partially open) 4 to 5 minutes on each side or until centers are no longer pink.
• **Serve** on buns with Dried Tomato Sauce, lettuce, tomato slices, French fries, and, if desired, coleslaw. **Yield:** 6 servings.

Dried Tomato Sauce

Prep: 5 minutes

⅓ cup minced dried tomatoes
   packed in oil, drained
⅓ cup plain nonfat yogurt
1½ teaspoons dried basil

• **Stir** together all ingredients until well blended; cover and chill, if desired. **Yield:** about ½ cup.

Helen Maurer
Christmas, Florida

FLAVOR TO SPARE

We've got a bone to pick with these perfect-for-summer ribs: We can't keep our hands off them. Jan Cuddington's Maple Spareribs are a prime example. The Floridian wins raves not just for her flavorful recipe, but also for being a member of "The Taste of *Southern Living* Ladies," a group of the Tallahassee Women's Newcomer's Club who enjoy discussing the flavor and ease of all our recipes. Jan, we think yours is tops.

MAPLE SPARERIBS

Prep: 35 minutes
Bake: 1 hour

3 to 4 pounds pork spareribs
1 cup maple syrup
⅓ cup soy sauce
3 tablespoons sweet cooking
    rice wine
1 tablespoon garlic powder
2 teaspoons salt
½ teaspoon sugar

• **Bring** ribs and water to cover to a boil in a large Dutch oven; reduce heat, and simmer 30 minutes. Drain. Place ribs in a lightly greased 13- x 9-inch pan.
• **Stir** together maple syrup and next 5 ingredients; pour over ribs. Bake at 325° for 1 hour. **Yield:** 2 to 3 servings.

Grilled Maple Spareribs: Boil ribs as directed; drain. Prepare fire by piling charcoal or lava rocks on 1 side of grill, leaving other side empty. Coat rack with cooking spray; place on grill. Arrange ribs over empty side, and grill, covered with grill lid, 1 hour and 30 minutes, basting occasionally with sauce. Prep: 35 minutes; Grill: 1 hour and 30 minutes.

Note: For testing purposes only, we used Kikkoman Aji-Mirin Sweet Cooking Rice Wine.

Jan Cuddington
Tallahassee, Florida

SPARERIBS IN PLUM SAUCE

Prep: 40 minutes
Grill: 1 hour and 30 minutes

4 pounds pork spareribs
2 tablespoons butter or margarine
1 medium onion, diced
3 (4-ounce) jars plum baby food
1 (6-ounce) can frozen lemonade
    concentrate, thawed and
    undiluted
¼ cup chili sauce
¼ cup soy sauce
1 tablespoon salt
1 teaspoon ground ginger
1 teaspoon Worcestershire sauce
2 teaspoons prepared mustard
2 drops of hot sauce

• **Bring** ribs and water to cover to a boil in a large Dutch oven; reduce heat, and simmer 30 minutes. Drain.
• **Melt** butter in a saucepan over medium-high heat; add onion. Sauté until golden.
• **Add** baby food and next 8 ingredients. Bring to a boil; reduce heat. Simmer 15 minutes. Remove 1 cup sauce for basting.
• **Pile** charcoal or lava rocks on 1 side of grill, leaving other side empty. Coat food rack with cooking spray; place on grill.
• **Arrange** ribs over empty side, and grill, covered with grill lid, 1 hour and 30 minutes, basting occasionally with 1 cup sauce. Serve with remaining sauce. **Yield:** 2 to 3 servings.
Clairiece Gilbert Humphrey
Charlottesville, Virginia

TANGY RIBS AND ONIONS

Prep: 10 minutes
Bake: 1 hour and 30 minutes

4 pounds pork spareribs
1 teaspoon salt
½ teaspoon pepper
2 medium-size sweet onions, sliced
1 cup ketchup
¾ cup water
2 tablespoons white vinegar
2 tablespoons Worcestershire sauce
1 teaspoon chili powder
1 teaspoon paprika
½ teaspoon ground red pepper

• **Arrange** spareribs in a shallow roasting pan; sprinkle with salt and pepper, and top with onion.
• **Bake,** covered, at 350° for 30 minutes; drain. Stir together ketchup and next 6 ingredients; pour over ribs.
• **Bake,** covered, at 350° for 45 minutes. Uncover and bake 15 more minutes. **Yield:** 2 to 3 servings.

Ellie Wells
Lakeland, Florida

NO SMALL POTATOES

Next time you sign up to tote potato salad to the neighborhood supper, show your flair for creative combinations. With a dab of curry, a hint of horseradish, a sprinkle of raisins, or the zing of salami, this standby will become a standout.

CREOLE POTATO SALAD

3 pounds red potatoes, cubed
½ cup mayonnaise
½ cup Creole mustard
1 tablespoon red wine vinegar
1 teaspoon salt
1 teaspoon prepared horseradish
½ teaspoon dried thyme
¼ teaspoon garlic powder
¼ teaspoon ground red pepper
6 hard-cooked eggs, chopped
1 medium-size sweet onion, diced

• **Cook** potato in boiling salted water to cover 12 minutes or until tender; drain and cool slightly.
• **Stir** together mayonnaise and next 7 ingredients in a large bowl; add potato, egg, and onion, tossing gently. Serve at room temperature or chilled. **Yield:** 8 servings.

Rose Turner Pate
Pittsboro, North Carolina

SOUR CREAM POTATO SALAD

7 medium baking potatoes
3 hard-cooked eggs
1 cup mayonnaise
½ cup sour cream
⅓ cup Italian dressing
1½ teaspoons horseradish
     mustard
½ teaspoon salt
¼ teaspoon celery seeds
2 celery ribs, sliced
3 green onions, sliced

• **Cook** baking potatoes in boiling water to cover 25 to 30 minutes or until tender; drain and cool. Peel and slice potatoes; set aside.
• **Chop** egg whites. Press yolks through a wire sieve into a bowl; set aside.
• **Stir** together mayonnaise and next 5 ingredients in a large bowl; add potato, chopped egg white, celery, and green onions, tossing gently.
• **Sprinkle** egg yolk over salad. Cover and chill, if desired. **Yield:** 8 servings.

Mrs. H. W. Walker
Richmond, Virginia

FOR THE LOVE OF SPUDS

■ New potatoes and boiling potatoes hold their shape better than russets do.

■ Cook potatoes unpeeled to lock in their flavor and nutrients. Once they're boiled, you can slip the skins off easily, if you wish.

■ The potato cooking water makes a delicious soup base or a liquid in moist, nutritious breads.

■ Potatoes for salads absorb more flavors if you dress them while they're hot, then chill them.

CURRIED POTATO SALAD

Though the ingredient list is long, you probably have most of these items on hand.

2 pounds medium-size red
     potatoes
¼ cup diced green onions
2 tablespoons olive oil
2 teaspoons curry powder
½ teaspoon ground allspice
¼ teaspoon dried crushed red
     pepper
½ cup sliced celery
½ cup shredded carrot
5 thin salami slices or pepperoni
     slices, cut into strips
2 tablespoons chopped
     pimiento-stuffed olives
1 tablespoon chopped fresh
     parsley
½ cup sour cream
¼ cup chopped golden raisins
¾ teaspoon seasoned salt

• **Cook** potatoes in a Dutch oven in boiling water to cover 25 to 30 minutes or until tender; drain and cool. Peel and cut into cubes.
• **Sauté** green onions in hot oil in Dutch oven 2 minutes.
• **Stir** in curry powder, allspice, and crushed red pepper; remove from heat. Add potato, tossing gently to coat. Stir in celery and next 4 ingredients.
• **Stir** together sour cream, raisins, and salt; pour over potato mixture, and toss gently. Transfer to a large bowl. Cover and chill. **Yield:** 5 cups.

Janet Bean
Charlotte, North Carolina

SKINNY DIP

It's shorts-and-swimsuit season. And if you're like most people, the more you contemplate cutting calories, the hungrier you become. Good news—you don't have to skip snack time. These dips and homemade chips (see "Little Dippers" in the box on next page) will satisfy your between-meal cravings. And best of all, these worry-free snacks are ready to chill in less than a half hour. (Chilling allows the flavors to mellow.)

LOW-FAT HUMMUS

Tahini is a paste of ground sesame seeds. Find it in large supermarkets and specialty food stores.

Prep: 12 minutes
Chill: 4 hours

1 (16-ounce) can chickpeas,
     rinsed and drained
3 garlic cloves, minced
¼ cup warm water
¼ cup lemon juice
1 tablespoon chopped fresh
     parsley
1 tablespoon tahini
1 tablespoon olive oil
½ teaspoon cumin seeds
¼ teaspoon salt
¼ teaspoon ground red pepper

• **Process** chickpeas in a food processor until smooth, stopping to scrape down sides.
• **Add** garlic and remaining ingredients; pulse until blended. Cover and chill 4 hours. **Yield:** 1½ cups.

Jo Walters
Miami, Florida

♥ Per tablespoon: Calories 26
Fat 1.1g   Cholesterol 0mg
Sodium 83mg

PINE NUT-SPINACH DIP

*You can easily double this recipe
to serve a crowd.*

*Prep: 23 minutes
Chill: 1 hour*

1 (10-ounce) package frozen
    chopped spinach, thawed
¼ cup pine nuts *
1 medium-size purple onion,
    chopped
2 garlic cloves, pressed
½ teaspoon dried thyme
    (optional)
1 teaspoon olive oil
1 cup fat-free cottage cheese
½ (8-ounce) package fat-free
    cream cheese, softened
¼ cup diced ripe olives
1 tablespoon lemon juice
¼ teaspoon salt
⅛ teaspoon pepper
Garnish: purple onion fan

• **Drain** spinach well, pressing between
layers of paper towels. Set aside.
• **Cook** pine nuts in a small nonstick
skillet over medium-high heat, stirring
occasionally, 3 minutes or until toasted.
Remove from skillet, and set aside.
• **Sauté** onion, garlic, and, if desired,
thyme in hot oil in skillet 2 minutes. Add
spinach, and sauté 3 minutes.
• **Process** cottage cheese and cream
cheese in a food processor until smooth,
stopping to scrape down sides.
• **Stir** in pine nuts, onion mixture, olives,
and next 3 ingredients. Cover and chill 1
hour. Garnish, if desired; serve with raw
vegetables. **Yield:** 3 cups.

* Substitute ¼ cup slivered almonds for
pine nuts, if desired.
*Caroline Wallace Kennedy
Newborn, Georgia*

❤ Per tablespoon: Calories 14
Fat 0.6g   Cholesterol 0mg
Sodium 53mg

CURRY DIP

*Use any leftover dip as a dressing
for chicken salad.*

*Prep: 10 minutes
Chill: 4 hours*

1 cup fat-free sour cream
½ cup fat-free mayonnaise
2 tablespoons minced fresh
    parsley
1 tablespoon minced fresh chives
2 tablespoons grated onion
2 tablespoons lemon juice
1 teaspoon curry powder
2 teaspoons prepared mustard
½ teaspoon paprika
½ teaspoon dried tarragon

• **Stir** together all ingredients. Cover
and chill at least 4 hours. Serve with raw
vegetables. **Yield:** 1½ cups.
*Gladys E. Armstrong
Amarillo, Texas*

❤ Per tablespoon: Calories 13
Fat 0.1g   Cholesterol 0mg
Sodium 76mg

CHICKPEA-AND-RED PEPPER DIP

*Prep: 5 minutes
Chill: 1 hour*

1 (16-ounce) can chickpeas, rinsed
    and drained
1 (7-ounce) jar roasted sweet red
    peppers, drained
½ cup fat-free sour cream
1 garlic clove, minced
¼ teaspoon salt
¼ teaspoon pepper
Garnish: fresh parsley sprig
**Baked Pita Chips (see recipe in
    box below)**

• **Process** first 6 ingredients in a food
processor until smooth, stopping to
scrape down sides. Cover and chill 1
hour. Garnish, if desired; serve with
Baked Pita Chips. **Yield:** 3 cups.
*Judy Carter
Winchester, Tennessee*

❤ Per tablespoon: Calories 11
Fat 0.1g   Cholesterol 0mg
Sodium 51mg

LITTLE DIPPERS

Baked Wonton Chips: Cut 56 (2-inch-square) wonton skins in half diagonally. Arrange in a single layer on ungreased baking sheets, and spray lightly with water. Bake at 375° for 8 minutes or until lightly browned. **Yield:** about 9 dozen.

❤ Per chip: Calories 12
Fat 0.1g   Cholesterol 0mg
Sodium 23mg

Baked Pita Chips: Separate each of 3 (6-inch) whole wheat pita rounds into 2 rounds. Cut into 8 wedges to make 48 triangles. Arrange in a single layer on ungreased baking sheets. Coat with butter-flavored cooking spray. Bake at 350° for 15 minutes. **Yield:** 4 dozen.

❤ Per chip: Calories 13
Fat 0.3g   Cholesterol 0mg
Sodium 20mg

GINGER DIP

Prep: 10 minutes
Chill: 1 hour

1 cup reduced-fat mayonnaise
1 cup fat-free sour cream
¼ cup minced onion
¼ cup whole water chestnuts, drained and chopped
¼ cup chopped fresh parsley
2 garlic cloves, minced
2 tablespoons crystallized ginger, chopped
1 tablespoon lite soy sauce

• **Stir** together all ingredients until blended. Cover and chill 1 hour. Serve with assorted crackers. **Yield:** 2¼ cups.
Sherry Jennings
Clarksdale, Mississippi

♥ Per tablespoon: Calories 28
Fat 2g Cholesterol 3mg
Sodium 67mg

KAHLÚA DIP

Prep: 5 minutes
Chill: 1 hour

1 teaspoon instant coffee granules
2 teaspoons lemon juice
1 (8-ounce) package light cream cheese, softened
¼ cup Kahlúa
3 tablespoons powdered sugar

• **Stir** together coffee granules and lemon juice until granules dissolve.
• **Beat** coffee mixture, cream cheese, Kahlúa, and powdered sugar at medium speed with an electric mixer until smooth. Cover and chill 1 hour. Serve with strawberries. **Yield:** 1 cup.

♥ Per tablespoon: Calories 51
Fat 2.4g Cholesterol 8mg
Sodium 80mg

ℐAVORY CHEESECAKES

Bring the creaminess of cheesecakes to the dinner plate with this luscious collection of recipes. Sugar is nowhere to be found. Instead, we've folded in an array of familiar ingredients ideal for entrée or appetizer servings. Three-Layer Cheesecake requires no baking and yields an airy texture perfect for crackers or a sandwich. A trio of cheeses—cream, ricotta, and feta—graces a crust studded with pine nuts in Spinach-Herb Cheesecake.

SPINACH-HERB CHEESECAKE
(pictured on page 151)

Prep: 25 minutes
Bake: 45 minutes

2 large tomatoes, sliced
¾ teaspoon salt, divided
¾ teaspoon pepper, divided
¼ cup pine nuts or pecan pieces, toasted
¼ cup Italian-seasoned breadcrumbs
2 tablespoons butter or margarine, melted
3 (8-ounce) packages cream cheese, softened
1 (15-ounce) container ricotta cheese
1 (8-ounce) package feta cheese, crumbled
3 large eggs
4 cups loosely packed shredded spinach
2 garlic cloves, pressed
2 tablespoons all-purpose flour
1 tablespoon chopped fresh dill
Garnish: fresh dill sprigs

• **Sprinkle** tomato slices with ¼ teaspoon salt and ¼ teaspoon pepper. Drain on paper towels 10 minutes.
• **Process** pine nuts in a food processor until ground. Stir together pine nuts, breadcrumbs, and melted butter. Press into bottom of a 9-inch springform pan.
• **Bake** at 350° for 10 minutes. Cool in pan on a wire rack.
• **Beat** cream cheese at medium speed with an electric mixer until creamy; add ricotta cheese, feta cheese, and eggs, beating until blended.
• **Stir** in spinach, next 3 ingredients, remaining ½ teaspoon salt, and remaining ½ teaspoon pepper. Pour into crust.
• **Bake** at 325° for 15 minutes. Top with tomato slices, and bake 30 more minutes or until set. Turn oven off; leave cheesecake in oven 20 minutes.
• **Cool** on a wire rack 10 minutes. Gently run a knife around edge of cheesecake, and release sides; cool 10 more minutes. Garnish, if desired; serve warm or cold. **Yield:** 12 appetizer or 8 main-dish servings.

ROASTED VEGETABLE CHEESECAKE
(pictured on page 151)

Serve with a green salad and crackers.

Prep: 1 hour
Bake: 50 minutes

2 large tomatoes, halved
1 red bell pepper, sliced
1 yellow squash, sliced
2 tablespoons olive oil, divided
1 medium-size sweet onion, sliced
2 garlic cloves, peeled
1 tablespoon butter or margarine
½ cup uncooked long-grain rice
1 cup water
1 teaspoon vegetable broth concentrate
3 (8-ounce) packages cream cheese, softened and divided
4 large eggs, divided
⅓ cup firmly packed fresh basil leaves
8 ounces fontina or Monterey Jack cheese, shredded and divided
½ teaspoon salt, divided
½ teaspoon pepper, divided
1 (8-ounce) container sour cream
1 tablespoon all-purpose flour
Garnish: fresh basil sprigs

• **Arrange** tomato halves, cut side down, on an aluminum foil-lined 15- x 10-inch jellyroll pan.
• **Toss** together bell pepper, squash, and 1 tablespoon olive oil; place on jellyroll pan next to tomato halves.
• **Toss** together onion, garlic, and remaining 1 tablespoon oil; place on jellyroll pan next to bell pepper mixture.
• **Bake** at 425° for 25 minutes, stirring occasionally; cool.
• **Melt** butter in a medium saucepan over medium-high heat; add rice, and sauté 3 minutes.
• **Stir** in 1 cup water and broth concentrate; bring to a boil. Cover, reduce heat, and simmer 10 minutes or until rice is tender. Cool slightly.
• **Press** rice into bottom of a 9-inch springform pan.
• **Process** 1½ packages cream cheese, 2 eggs, ⅓ cup basil, tomato, red bell pepper, and squash in a food processor until blended.

• **Add** 1 cup fontina cheese, ¼ teaspoon salt, and ¼ teaspoon pepper; pulse until blended. Pour over rice in pan.
• **Process** remaining 1½ packages cream cheese, remaining 2 eggs, and onion mixture in food processor until blended.
• **Add** remaining 1 cup fontina cheese, remaining ¼ teaspoon salt, and remaining ¼ teaspoon pepper. Pour over tomato mixture.
• **Bake** at 350° for 40 minutes. Stir together sour cream and flour. Spread over cheesecake, and bake 10 more minutes. Cool on a wire rack 20 minutes. Gently run a knife around edge of cheesecake, and release sides. Garnish, if desired. Serve warm or chilled. **Yield:** 12 appetizer or 8 main-dish servings.

Note: For testing purposes only, we used Knorr Concentrated Vegetable Broth.

THREE-LAYER CHEESECAKE
(pictured on page 151)

Serve over mixed greens with assorted crackers.

Prep: 20 minutes
Chill: 3 hours

3 (8-ounce) packages cream cheese, softened and divided
3 tablespoons chopped pimiento-stuffed green olives
2 teaspoons olive juice
1 tablespoon mayonnaise
1 cup (4 ounces) shredded sharp Cheddar cheese
1 (2-ounce) jar diced pimiento, drained
1 teaspoon grated onion
¼ cup butter or margarine, softened
2 garlic cloves, pressed
1 teaspoon dried Italian seasoning

• **Beat** 1 package cream cheese at medium speed with an electric mixer until creamy; stir in olives and olive juice.
• **Spread** olive mixture into bottom of a plastic wrap-lined 8- x 4-inch loafpan.

• **Beat** 1 package cream cheese at medium speed until creamy; add mayonnaise and Cheddar cheese, beating until blended. Stir in pimiento and onion; spread over olive mixture.
• **Beat** remaining package cream cheese and butter at medium speed until creamy; add garlic and Italian seasoning, beating until blended.
• **Spread** garlic mixture over pimiento mixture. Cover and chill at least 3 hours or until firm. **Yield:** 8 appetizer servings.

DELICIOUS DILL

Feathery fresh dill adds color and piquant flavor to a wide variety of food—from crisp, pungent pickles to comforting potato chowders. Use it in these recipes, or add it to quiche, potato salad, and deviled eggs. As with most herbs, substitute 1 teaspoon dried dillweed for 1 tablespoon of fresh.

SMOKED SALMON CANAPÉS

Prep: 15 minutes
Bake: 5 minutes

1 baguette
8 ounces thinly sliced smoked salmon
1 (8-ounce) package cream cheese, softened
½ cup sour cream
24 fresh dill sprigs

• **Cut** baguette into 24 (½-inch-thick) slices, and place on a baking sheet.
• **Bake** at 400° for 5 minutes or until lightly toasted; remove slices to wire racks to cool.
• **Cut** salmon into 24 pieces. Spread baguette slices evenly with cream cheese, and top evenly with salmon and sour cream. Place a dill sprig on each canapé. **Yield:** 2 dozen.

POTATO CHOWDER WITH HAM

Prep: 15 minutes
Cook: 15 minutes

4 bacon slices, chopped
1 small onion, chopped
2 cups half-and-half
1 (16-ounce) can low-sodium, fat-free chicken broth
3½ cups firmly packed frozen mashed potatoes, thawed
2 cups cubed cooked ham
1 tablespoon chopped fresh thyme
¼ teaspoon pepper
2 tablespoons chopped fresh parsley
2 to 3 teaspoons chopped fresh dill

• **Cook** bacon in a Dutch oven until crisp; remove bacon, reserving 1 tablespoon drippings in pan. Crumble bacon.
• **Sauté** onion in reserved drippings over medium heat until tender.
• **Stir** in half-and-half and next 5 ingredients; bring to a boil. Reduce heat, and simmer 5 minutes. Stir in parsley and dill. Sprinkle with bacon. **Yield:** 7 cups.

GREEN BEANS WITH LEMON-DILL BUTTER

Prep: 10 minutes
Cook: 5 minutes

2 pounds fresh green beans
1½ teaspoons salt, divided
⅓ cup butter or margarine
2 garlic cloves, cut into thin strips
½ teaspoon grated lemon rind
2 teaspoons fresh lemon juice
1 tablespoon chopped fresh dill
Garnish: fresh dill sprigs

• **Cook** green beans and 1 teaspoon salt in boiling water to cover in a large saucepan 2 minutes or until crisp-tender; drain.
• **Melt** butter in saucepan over medium heat; add garlic, and sauté 30 seconds.
• **Stir** in remaining ½ teaspoon salt, lemon rind, and lemon juice. Add green beans and chopped dill, tossing to coat. Garnish, if desired. **Yield:** 8 servings.

Victoria Miller
Charleston, South Carolina

DILLED SHRIMP WITH FETTUCCINE

Prep: 25 minutes
Marinate: 30 minutes
Cook: 20 minutes

½ pound unpeeled, large fresh shrimp
¼ cup olive oil, divided
2 tablespoons lemon juice
½ teaspoon salt
½ teaspoon pepper
¾ pound baby carrots
2 yellow squash, sliced
1 (8-ounce) package fresh mushrooms, sliced
9 ounces refrigerated fettuccine, cooked
4 garlic cloves, cut into thin strips
¼ cup all-purpose flour
⅔ cup chicken broth
½ cup dry white wine
¼ cup milk
½ cup whipping cream
2 tablespoons Dijon mustard
3 tablespoons chopped fresh or 1 tablespoon dried dillweed

• **Peel** shrimp; devein, if desired.
• **Toss** together shrimp, 2 tablespoons oil, lemon juice, salt, and pepper; cover and chill 30 minutes.
• **Remove** shrimp from marinade, discarding marinade.
• **Sauté** carrots, squash, and mushrooms in 1 tablespoon hot oil in a large skillet over medium heat 6 to 7 minutes.
• **Add** shrimp, and sauté 3 to 4 minutes or just until shrimp turn pink. Spoon over hot cooked pasta, and keep warm.
• **Sauté** garlic in remaining 1 tablespoon hot oil in skillet over medium-high heat 30 seconds.
• **Whisk** in flour; cook, whisking constantly, 1 minute.
• **Whisk** in broth, wine, and milk; bring to a boil. Reduce heat, and simmer, whisking constantly, 4 minutes or until thickened and bubbly.
• **Whisk** in whipping cream and mustard; cook, whisking constantly, 1 minute. Stir in dill. Pour over shrimp mixture. **Yield:** 4 servings.

Christine Leonardi-Evans
McKean, Pennsylvania

FEATS OF FLANK

Thin is in when it comes to flank steak. It's versatile, delicious, and, best of all, affordable. The unassuming flank steak—once a wallflower among rib-eyes and tenderloins—is now the belle of the meat case. With the at-home popularity of fajitas and stir-fries, this flat, lean cut is catching our eye. Its tough-as-nails reputation is history, thanks to the all-conquering marinade (necessary for flavor and tenderness).

BASIC MARINADE

Prep: 5 minutes

1 small onion, diced
3 garlic cloves, minced
½ cup olive oil
¼ cup lemon juice *
2 tablespoons Worcestershire sauce
2 teaspoons sugar
1 teaspoon salt
1 teaspoon pepper

• **Stir** together all ingredients in a bowl. **Yield:** 1¼ cups.

* Substitute white wine vinegar for lemon juice, if desired.

Southwestern Marinade: Substitute ¼ cup lime juice for lemon juice. Add 2 tablespoons chopped fresh cilantro and 1 teaspoon ground cumin.

Asian Marinade: Substitute ½ cup peanut oil for olive oil, ¼ cup rice wine vinegar for lemon juice, and 2 tablespoons soy sauce for Worcestershire sauce. Add 1 teaspoon grated fresh ginger.

STEAK WITH PASTA AND SESAME-GINGER BUTTER

Prep: 15 minutes
Chill: 8 hours
Cook: 20 minutes

1 (2-pound) flank steak
1 recipe Asian Marinade (see recipe variation on previous page)
8 ounces angel hair pasta, cooked
Sesame-Ginger Butter, divided
¼ teaspoon salt
½ teaspoon dried crushed red pepper
¼ cup cornstarch
¼ cup dark sesame oil, divided
¾ pound sugar snap peas, sliced
2 bunches green onions, sliced
1 red bell pepper, cut into thin strips
2 carrots, halved lengthwise and sliced

• **Place** steak in a heavy-duty zip-top plastic bag; add Asian Marinade. Seal and chill 8 hours, turning occasionally.
• **Toss** pasta with ½ cup Sesame-Ginger Butter, salt, and crushed red pepper; keep warm.
• **Remove** steak from marinade; drain well, discarding marinade. Cut steak diagonally across grain into ⅛-inch-thick slices. Toss with cornstarch.
• **Heat** 1½ tablespoons sesame oil in a skillet over high heat; add half of steak. Cook 8 minutes or until browned. Remove from skillet. Repeat with 1½ tablespoons oil and remaining steak.
• **Heat** remaining 1 tablespoon oil in skillet. Add peas and next 3 ingredients; sauté 5 minutes or until crisp-tender. Toss vegetables with remaining ½ cup Sesame-Ginger Butter. Serve steak and vegetables over pasta. **Yield:** 6 servings.

Sesame-Ginger Butter

Prep: 10 minutes
Cook: 3 minutes

½ cup butter or margarine
2 tablespoons grated fresh ginger
2 tablespoons dark sesame oil
2 tablespoons chunky peanut butter
2 tablespoons brown sugar
1 tablespoon soy sauce

• **Cook** all ingredients in a saucepan over low heat, stirring constantly, until blended. **Yield:** 1 cup.

CHICKEN-FRIED STEAK FINGERS WITH CREOLE MUSTARD SAUCE

Prep: 17 minutes
Chill: 4 hours
Cook: 30 minutes

2 teaspoons Cajun seasoning
1 recipe Basic Marinade (see recipe on previous page)
1 (2-pound) flank steak
2 large eggs
2 tablespoons hot sauce
1 cup all-purpose flour
½ cup fine, dry breadcrumbs
1 tablespoon Cajun seasoning
¼ teaspoon ground red pepper
Vegetable oil
Creole Mustard Sauce

• **Stir** Cajun seasoning into Basic Marinade until blended. Place steak in a heavy-duty zip-top plastic bag; add marinade mixture. Seal; chill 3 hours, turning occasionally. Remove steak from marinade, discarding marinade. Cut steak in half lengthwise; cut halves diagonally across the grain into ½-inch-thick strips.
• **Whisk** together eggs and hot sauce. Combine flour and next 3 ingredients. Dip strips into egg mixture; dredge in flour mixture. Cover and chill 1 hour.
• **Pour** oil to a depth of 4 inches into a Dutch oven; heat to 375°. Fry steak strips in batches 10 minutes or until golden. Serve with Creole Mustard Sauce. **Yield:** 8 appetizer servings or 4 to 6 main-dish servings.

Creole Mustard Sauce

Prep: 5 minutes

1 (8-ounce) container sour cream
¼ cup Creole mustard
1 tablespoon cider vinegar
1 teaspoon Cajun seasoning
⅛ teaspoon ground red pepper

• **Stir** together all ingredients; cover and chill. **Yield:** about 1¼ cups.

GRILLED FLANK STEAK WITH APPLE-BOURBON SAUCE AND ROASTED VEGETABLES

Prep: 10 minutes
Chill: 8 hours
Grill: 20 minutes

1 (2-pound) flank steak
1 recipe Southwestern Marinade (see recipe variation on previous page)
Apple-Bourbon Sauce
Roasted Vegetables
Garnish: fresh Italian parsley sprigs

• **Place** steak in a heavy-duty zip-top plastic bag.
• **Add** Southwestern Marinade. Seal bag, and chill 8 hours, turning steak occasionally.
• **Remove** steak from marinade, discarding marinade.
• **Grill** steak, covered with grill lid, over medium-high heat (350° to 400°) 8 to 10 minutes on each side or to desired degree of doneness.
• **Cut** steak diagonally across the grain into thin strips. Serve steak with Apple-Bourbon Sauce and Roasted Vegetables. Garnish, if desired. **Yield:** 6 servings.

Apple-Bourbon Sauce

Prep: 15 minutes
Cook: 20 minutes

2 cups barbecue sauce
2 medium Granny Smith apples, peeled and diced
1 small onion, diced
3 tablespoons cider vinegar
⅛ to ¼ teaspoon ground red pepper
¼ cup bourbon or apple juice concentrate

• **Bring** first 5 ingredients to a boil in a medium saucepan over medium heat; reduce heat, and simmer, stirring occasionally, 15 minutes. Remove mixture from heat, and stir in bourbon. **Yield:** 3 cups.

Note: For testing purposes only, we used KC Masterpiece Original Barbecue Sauce.

Roasted Vegetables

Prep: 10 minutes
Bake: 40 minutes

3 medium onions, cut into wedges
6 small red potatoes, halved
2 medium-size sweet potatoes, peeled and cut into ¼-inch-thick slices
2 tablespoons olive oil
1 teaspoon salt
½ teaspoon pepper

• **Toss** together all ingredients; place on an aluminum foil-lined baking sheet.
• **Bake** at 450° for 30 to 40 minutes or until onion and potatoes are tender. **Yield:** 6 servings.

A FIRM BELIEVER

Just because green tomatoes don't blush doesn't mean they're not worth looking into. They aren't just for frying. These tart, firm, citrusy fruits of summer have preripened personality all their own and are actually quite versatile. "Greenies" make colorful, crisp, sprightly additions to salsas and relishes, kabobs and gazpachos, savory breads, and more.

PICKLED GREEN TOMATOES

Prep: 30 minutes
Process: 10 minutes

8 cups white vinegar (5% acidity)
4 cups sugar
¼ cup mustard seeds
1 tablespoon celery seeds
1 teaspoon ground turmeric
4 pounds green tomatoes, cut into ¼-inch-thick slices
4 medium onions, sliced
1 medium-size red bell pepper, chopped

• **Bring** first 5 ingredients to a boil in a Dutch oven, stirring often. Boil, stirring often, until sugar melts. Remove mixture from heat.
• **Pack** tomato and onion into hot jars; top evenly with bell pepper. Cover vegetables with hot syrup, filling to ½ inch from top.
• **Remove** air bubbles, and wipe jar rims. Cover at once with metal lids, and screw on bands.
• **Process** in a boiling-water bath 10 minutes. **Yield:** 12 pints.

Gwen Louer
Roswell, Georgia

BLUE WILLOW FRIED GREEN TOMATOES

This recipe garnered our Test Kitchens' best marks. Topped with ripe Tomato Chutney, the Blue Willow Inn's fried green tomatoes—consumed like there's no tomorrow in Social Circle, Georgia—are a divine treat.

Prep: 10 minutes
Cook: 20 minutes

1½ cups self-rising flour, divided
1½ cups buttermilk
2 large eggs
1 teaspoon salt, divided
1 teaspoon pepper, divided
3 green tomatoes, each cut into 4 slices
2 cups vegetable oil
Tomato Chutney (optional)

• **Whisk** together 1 tablespoon flour, buttermilk, eggs, ½ teaspoon salt, and ½ teaspoon pepper in a small bowl.
• **Stir** together remaining flour, ½ teaspoon salt, and ½ teaspoon pepper in a shallow bowl.
• **Dip** tomato slices in buttermilk mixture; dredge in flour mixture.
• **Heat** oil in a heavy 10-inch skillet to 350°. Fry tomato slices 2½ minutes on each side or until golden.
• **Drain** tomato slices on paper towels. Serve fried tomatoes immediately with Tomato Chutney, if desired. **Yield:** 6 servings.

Tomato Chutney

Prep: 15 minutes
Cook: 1 hour and 30 minutes to 2 hours

2 (14½-ounce) cans diced tomatoes, undrained
1 cup firmly packed light brown sugar
½ cup sugar
2 small green bell peppers, diced
1 medium onion, diced
2 tablespoons ketchup
1 teaspoon pepper
⅛ to ¼ teaspoon hot sauce

• **Bring** all ingredients to a boil in a medium saucepan, stirring occasionally; reduce heat, and simmer, stirring occasionally, 1½ to 2 hours or until thickened. **Yield:** 5 cups.

Billie and Louis Van Dyke
Blue Willow Inn
Social Circle, Georgia

PEACHY GREEN TOMATO SALSA
(pictured on page 149)

Serve with grilled or fried chicken, catfish, or pork.

Prep: 20 minutes
Chill: 1 hour

4 green tomatoes, chopped
2 large peaches, chopped
6 green onions, sliced
½ cup olive oil
¼ cup white wine vinegar
2 tablespoons minced fresh cilantro
2 tablespoons lemon juice
1 tablespoon liquid from hot peppers in vinegar
1 tablespoon honey
1 teaspoon salt
Garnish: fresh cilantro sprigs

• **Stir** together first 10 ingredients. Cover and chill 1 hour. Garnish, if desired. **Yield:** 6 cups.

Freddie Lee Gee
Sun City Center, Florida

GRILLED SUMMER SQUASH AND TOMATOES

This little ditty of a recipe received top votes for ease and flavor.

Prep: 5 minutes
Chill: 30 minutes
Grill: 10 minutes

¼ cup olive oil
2 tablespoons balsamic
    vinegar
1 teaspoon salt
½ teaspoon pepper
4 garlic cloves, minced
4 medium-size green tomatoes,
    cut into ¼-inch-thick
    slices
1 pound yellow squash, cut
    diagonally into ½-inch-thick
    slices

• **Combine** first 5 ingredients in a shallow dish or heavy-duty zip-top plastic bag; add tomato and squash. Cover or seal; chill 30 minutes.
• **Remove** vegetables from marinade, reserving marinade.
• **Grill** vegetables, covered with grill lid, over medium-high heat (350° to 400°) 10 minutes, turning vegetables occasionally. Toss with reserved marinade. **Yield:** 6 servings.

MARINATED PORK TENDERLOINS

Marinating is a perfect way to impart additional flavor to pork. To speed up the process, pierce tenderloins with a fork. Robin Kline of the National Pork Council gives us some tips. "Always make sure the internal temperature reaches 160°, medium doneness, not the way grandmother used to cook it. And if you plan to baste pork with marinade during cooking, make additional or set some aside before adding raw pork."

PINEAPPLE-PORK KABOBS

Menu suggestion: steamed rice and soft breadsticks

Prep: 12 minutes
Marinate: 30 minutes
Grill: 25 minutes

1½ pounds pork tenderloins
3 medium zucchini
1 green bell pepper
1 medium onion
1 (8-ounce) can pineapple chunks,
    undrained
⅓ cup dark corn syrup
¼ cup soy sauce
1 tablespoon prepared mustard
1 garlic clove, pressed
½ teaspoon cracked pepper

• **Cut** pork into 1-inch cubes; cut zucchini into 1-inch slices and green bell pepper into 1-inch squares. Quarter onion. Set aside.
• **Drain** pineapple chunks, reserving juice. Set pineapple aside.
• **Stir** together reserved pineapple juice, dark corn syrup, and next 4 ingredients in a shallow dish or heavy-duty zip-top plastic bag; remove ⅓ cup marinade, and set aside. Add pork and zucchini to remaining marinade, turning to coat. Cover or seal; let stand at room temperature 30 minutes, or chill 2 hours.
• **Remove** pork and zucchini from marinade, discarding marinade. Thread pork, zucchini, bell pepper, onion, and pineapple loosely onto 8 (12-inch) skewers.
• **Grill,** covered with grill lid, over medium-high heat (350° to 400°) 22 to 25 minutes or until a meat thermometer registers 160°, turning and basting occasionally with remaining ⅓ cup marinade. **Yield:** 4 servings.

Margaret Jahns
Tarpon Springs, Florida

CORIANDER-PEPPER PORK TENDERLOIN

Menu suggestion: mashed potatoes and mixed salad greens

Prep: 5 minutes
Marinate: 30 minutes
Grill: 24 minutes

2 garlic cloves, pressed
1 tablespoon coriander seeds, crushed
1 tablespoon coarsely ground pepper
1 tablespoon brown sugar
3 tablespoons soy sauce
1½ pounds pork tenderloins

• **Combine** first 5 ingredients in a heavy-duty zip-top plastic bag; remove 2 tablespoons marinade, and set aside.
• **Prick** pork tenderloins several times with a fork, and place in plastic bag with remaining marinade. Seal, turning to coat; let stand at room temperature 30 minutes, or chill 2 hours.
• **Remove** pork from marinade, discarding marinade.
• **Grill,** covered with grill lid, over medium-high heat (350° to 400°) 12 minutes on each side or until a meat thermometer registers 160°, basting with remaining 2 tablespoons marinade. **Yield:** 3 to 4 servings.

APPLE BUTTER PORK TENDERLOIN

Menu suggestion: rice pilaf and steamed zucchini

Prep: 5 minutes
Marinate: 30 minutes
Bake: 30 minutes

1½ pounds pork tenderloins
½ teaspoon salt
2 cups apple juice
½ cup apple butter
¼ cup firmly packed brown sugar
2 tablespoons water
½ teaspoon ground cinnamon
¼ teaspoon ground cloves

• **Prick** tenderloins several times with a fork; sprinkle with salt, and place in an 11- x 7-inch baking dish. Add apple juice; cover and let stand at room temperature 30 minutes, or chill 2 hours.
• **Bake** at 350° for 15 minutes, and drain.
• **Stir** together apple butter and next 4 ingredients. Brush over pork; bake 15 more minutes or until a meat thermometer inserted into thickest portion registers 160°. Let stand 15 minutes before slicing. **Yield:** 4 servings.

Note: If tenderloins are chilled 2 hours, let stand at room temperature 30 minutes before baking.

Jane Nicol Schatzman
Winston-Salem, North Carolina

PORK TENDERLOIN WITH MUSTARD SAUCE

Menu suggestion: garlic-roasted new potatoes, steamed broccoli, and rolls

Prep: 10 minutes
Marinate: 30 minutes
Grill: 24 minutes

¼ cup soy sauce
¼ cup bourbon or apple juice
2 tablespoons brown sugar
1½ pounds pork tenderloins
⅓ cup sour cream
⅓ cup mayonnaise
1 tablespoon dry mustard
1 tablespoon minced onion
1½ teaspoons white vinegar

• **Stir** together first 3 ingredients in a shallow dish or heavy-duty zip-top plastic bag. Set aside.
• **Prick** pork tenderloins several times with a fork, and place in marinade. Cover or seal, turning to coat; let stand at room temperature 30 minutes, or chill 8 hours.
• **Remove** pork from marinade, discarding marinade.
• **Grill,** covered with grill lid, over medium-high heat (350° to 400°) 12 minutes on each side or until a meat thermometer inserted into thickest portion registers 160°.

• **Stir** together sour cream and next 4 ingredients; serve with pork. **Yield:** 4 servings.

Kathy Sellers
Nashville, Tennessee

ALLURING APRICOTS

Apricots are at their peak in June and July. To enjoy these recipes throughout the year, try our substitution suggestions. For maximum sweetness, select plump but firm apricots that are uniform in color. Because fresh apricots are highly perishable, store them in a plastic bag in your refrigerator up to five days.

APRICOT BELLINIS
(pictured on page 76)

Prep: 10 minutes

6 fresh apricots, halved (about ½ pound) *
1 (11-ounce) can apricot nectar
¼ cup sugar
1½ cups champagne **
Crushed ice
Garnishes: fresh apricot slices, fresh mint sprigs

• **Process** first 3 ingredients in a blender until smooth, stopping to scrape down sides. Stir in champagne, and serve immediately over crushed ice. Garnish, if desired. **Yield:** 4 cups.

* Substitute 1 (17-ounce) can apricot halves, drained, for fresh, if desired.
** Substitute 1 (12-ounce) can ginger ale for champagne, if desired.

APRICOT FLAN

Prep: 15 minutes
Bake: 1 hour
Chill: 8 hours

½ cup sugar
12 fresh apricots, halved (about 1 pound) *
2 (14-ounce) cans sweetened condensed milk
1 cup half-and-half
½ cup apricot preserves
3 large eggs
3 egg yolks
1 teaspoon vanilla extract
Garnishes: fresh apricot slices, fresh mint sprigs

• **Sprinkle** sugar in a 10-inch round cakepan; place over medium heat, and cook, shaking pan constantly, until sugar melts and turns a light golden brown. Remove from heat. Place apricot halves, cut side up, in caramelized sugar; set aside. (Sugar may crack slightly as it cools.)
• **Process** sweetened condensed milk and next 5 ingredients in a blender until smooth, stopping to scrape down sides. Pour over apricots in pan. Cover with aluminum foil; place in a roasting pan. Add hot water to pan to a depth of 1 inch.
• **Bake** at 350° for 1 hour or until a knife inserted in center comes out clean. Remove cakepan from water, and uncover; cool in cakepan on a wire rack 30 minutes. Cover and chill at least 8 hours.
• **Run** a knife around edge of flan to loosen; invert onto a serving plate. Garnish, if desired. **Yield:** 1 (10-inch) flan.

* Substitute 1 (17-ounce) can apricot halves, drained, for fresh, if desired.
Traci Storch
Birmingham, Alabama

QUICK-COOKED APRICOT JAM

To produce a fine jam, use only fresh apricots.

Prep: 20 minutes
Cook: 15 minutes

6 cups chopped fresh apricot (4 pounds)
3½ cups sugar, divided
1 (1¾-ounce) package powdered pectin
2 tablespoons lemon juice
1 teaspoon ascorbic-citric powder

• **Bring** apricot, ¼ cup sugar, and next 3 ingredients to a boil in a Dutch oven, stirring constantly.
• **Add** remaining 3¼ cups sugar, and boil, stirring constantly, 1 minute. Remove from heat, and skim off foam with a metal spoon.
• **Pour** hot jam into hot, sterilized jars, filling to ¼ inch from top; wipe jar rims. Cover at once with metal lids; screw on bands. Process in boiling-water bath 5 minutes. **Yield:** 3 pints.
Dorie Cochran
Rockville, Maryland

APRICOT RICE PILAF

Prep: 40 minutes
Cook: 27 minutes

1 cup uncooked long-grain rice
2½ cups chicken broth, divided
¼ cup butter or margarine
1 small onion, chopped
2 celery ribs, chopped
1 cup chopped fresh apricot *
¼ cup chopped fresh parsley
¼ cup raisins
1 tablespoon brown sugar
1 teaspoon salt
½ teaspoon pepper
½ teaspoon curry powder

• **Cook** rice in 2 cups broth according to package directions, omitting salt.

• **Melt** butter in a large skillet over medium-high heat; add onion and celery, and sauté 5 minutes or until tender. Stir in rice, remaining ½ cup broth, apricot, and remaining ingredients. **Yield:** 4 to 6 servings.

* Substitute 1 cup dried apricots for fresh, if desired. Soak the dried apricots in 1 cup water for 30 minutes; then drain.
Sue George
Birmingham, Alabama

APRICOT ICE CREAM

Prep: 15 minutes
Freeze: 45 minutes
Stand: 1 hour

2½ cups sugar
4 cups half-and-half
2 cups whipping cream
3 cups chopped fresh apricot (2½ to 3 pounds) *
2 teaspoons vanilla extract
¼ teaspoon salt

• **Stir** together all ingredients; pour mixture into freezer container of a 4-gallon electric freezer, and freeze according to manufacturer's instructions.
• **Pack** freezer with additional ice and rock salt, and let stand 1 hour before serving. **Yield:** 14 cups.

* Substitute 2 (17-ounce) cans apricot halves, drained, for fresh, if desired.

ICE CREAM SANDWICHES

Join us in sampling a rainbow of flavors sandwiched between shortbread cookies and rolled in candies and sprinkles. Our grown-up version is splashed with liqueur and served on a plate with a fork. Store extra cookies in the freezer. If desired, assemble the sandwiches ahead and freeze. Out of ice cream? Substitute frozen yogurt or serve these cookies alone with a beverage.

ICE CREAM SANDWICHES

16 (3-inch) Shortbread Cookies or Kahlúa Wafers (see recipes at right)
2 pints desired ice cream, softened
Decorations: candy-coated chocolate pieces, semisweet chocolate mini-morsels, chopped toasted nuts, toasted flaked coconut, nonpareils, ice cream syrups and toppings
Additional ice cream syrup and toppings (optional)

• **Top** each of 8 cookies with ½ cup ice cream, spreading to fit; cover each with another cookie. Decorate, if desired, and freeze until firm.
• **Drizzle** or serve sandwiches with additional syrup and toppings, if desired. **Yield:** 8 servings.

Note: For convenience, peel off round ice cream container and cut each pint crosswise into 4 rounds. Use 1 round for each sandwich.

SHORTBREAD COOKIES

Prep: 15 minutes
Bake: 20 minutes

2 cups butter, softened
1 cup powdered sugar
4 cups all-purpose flour
½ teaspoon baking powder
¼ teaspoon salt

• **Beat** butter at medium speed with an electric mixer until creamy; gradually add sugar, beating well.
• **Combine** flour, baking powder, and salt; add to butter mixture, beating at low speed until blended.
• **Turn** dough out onto a lightly floured surface; roll to ⅛-inch thickness. Cut with a floured 3-inch round cutter, and place 1 inch apart on parchment paper-lined baking sheets.
• **Bake** at 300° for 20 minutes or until edges are lightly browned; remove to wire racks to cool. **Yield:** 16 cookies.

Chocolate Shortbread Cookies: Reduce flour to 3⅓ cups. Add ⅔ cup cocoa to flour mixture, and proceed as directed.

KAHLÚA WAFERS

Prep: 15 minutes
Bake: 7 minutes

¾ cup butter, softened
¾ cup sugar
3 tablespoons Kahlúa
2 tablespoons instant coffee granules
1 teaspoon vanilla extract
2 cups all-purpose flour
¼ teaspoon baking powder
½ teaspoon salt

• **Beat** butter at medium speed with an electric mixer until creamy; gradually add sugar, beating well.
• **Stir** together Kahlúa, instant coffee granules, and vanilla until coffee granules dissolve.
• **Add** Kahlúa mixture to butter mixture, beating until blended.
• **Combine** flour, baking powder, and salt in a medium bowl; add to butter mixture, beating at low speed just until blended.
• **Turn** dough out onto a lightly floured surface, and roll to ⅛-inch thickness.
• **Cut** dough with a floured 3-inch round cutter, and place 1 inch apart on lightly greased baking sheets.
• **Bake** at 375° for 7 minutes or until cookies are lightly browned; remove to wire racks to cool completely. **Yield:** 16 cookies.

From Our Kitchen to Yours

GRILLING SAFELY

Some of us are traditionalists, cooking over a carefully laid bed of glowing coals. Others opt for the speed and convenience of gas. Whichever method you prefer, safe grilling involves both operating the equipment properly and handling the food with care.

Use long-handled tools for handling the meat, and use a mitt for additional protection. An apron will protect your clothes from splatters, but make sure that the apron strings don't hang into the fire.

Keep the grill clean. Replace greasy lava rocks or ceramic briquettes to reduce the risk of a flare-up. Keep a box of baking soda handy to put out any flames.

Hamburgers, hot dogs, steaks, chops, and fish fillets should be cooked by direct grilling over hot coals. Meats that require longer cooking times, such as roasts, ribs, whole fish, or turkeys, should be cooked by indirect grilling, with the meat positioned so it is not directly above the coals.

Minimum Safe Meat Temperatures

Ground meat and pork	160° F
Poultry (dark meat)	180° F
Poultry (white meat)	170° F
Roasts (beef, lamb, veal)	145° F

WHERE TO GRILL

Regardless of the type of grill you use, it should be located outside, well away from any combustible material. Avoid an area with overhanging trees or roof. Do not grill in the garage, carport, or porch.

Ideally, you should not grill with charcoal on a wood deck, because hot embers falling out of the bottom of the grill could set the deck on fire. One solution is to place a layer of brick atop the deck in the area beneath the grill. Make sure that the grill is level and located well away from play areas.

FOOD SAFETY

No matter what you are cooking or what kind of grill you are using, safe handling of food is important. Here are some recommendations.

■ Store raw meat in the refrigerator until you are ready to grill it.

■ Trim excess fat from meat to avoid flare-ups.

■ Make sure the grill is hot before placing meat on it. Allow about 10 minutes for a gas grill to heat up and 30 to 40 minutes if you are using charcoal briquettes.

■ Use a meat thermometer to make sure that the meat has reached a safe internal temperature. (The instant-read types are easiest to use.) Color and feel are not accurate ways to check doneness. Make sure the thermometer isn't touching any bone, as this could give a false reading.

■ Use clean plates and utensils for serving. If plates, bowls, or utensils touch raw meat, do not use them with the cooked meat.

■ Boil unused marinade that touched raw meat for at least one minute before reusing.

■ Never use vegetable cooking sprays near a lit grill.

■ Refrigerate leftovers promptly.

TIPS AND TIDBITS

Presentation is everything, and temperature is vital. Cold salad on warm plates or hot pasta on cold plates—well, you get the picture. Wrap salad plates or bowls in a damp towel and chill until ready to use. The cool plates will enhance fresh, crisp greens and dressings. For serving hot foods, wrap microwave-safe dinner plates in a damp towel and stack them in the microwave. When ready to use, microwave the plates on HIGH for 1 to 2 minutes (depending on the number of plates).

Whenever a recipe calls for alcohol, we like to list alternatives. As you adapt other recipes, here are some general guidelines for substitutions. Fruit juices, such as apple, cranberry, and white grape, are excellent substitutes for wine. If a recipe calls for a fruit-flavored liqueur, use the fruit nectar instead. Sparkling juices are good substitutes for champagne. The integrity of the recipe will remain intact as long as you use the specified amount.

BERRY TREASURES

After savoring the recipes on pages 130-132, follow our hand-picked hints for more blackberry enjoyment.

■ Check the bottom of commercial berry containers for berries that might be crushed, bruised, or starting to mold. If the container is cardboard, make certain it's not stained with juice, which indicates berries that are crushed or spoiled.

■ Store berries in a single layer on paper towel-lined shallow pans, covered lightly, in your refrigerator.

■ Wash berries just before using.

■ To freeze, arrange washed berries in a single layer in a shallow pan; once they are frozen, transfer them to a heavy-duty zip-top plastic bag.

■ You can freeze berries up to nine months.

Peachy Green Tomato Salsa
Over Fried Catfish, page 143

Garlic-Herb Steak,
Tabbouleh, Fudge Cake,
pages 175 and 176

150

Three-Layer Cheesecake, page 140

Roasted Vegetable Cheesecake, page 140; Spinach-Herb Cheesecake, page 139

Jalapeño Grilled Pork, Aztec Gold,
page 160

JULY

Juicy, ripe red tomatoes and summertime go hand in hand, and "Tomatoes From the Vine" provides you with cool tomato recipes—Tomato-Gruyère-Basil Salad, Zippy 'Maters, and Classic Tomato Gazpacho. Make and chill them ahead of time—you won't even need to turn on the oven.

You'll find plenty of other summer favorites in our annual "Summer Suppers®" special section. When you travel to the beach, turn to "Surfside With Style" for a complete grocery list and menu plan for five easy meals, including Peppery Grilled Flank Steak, Chicken Fajitas, and Savory Summer Pie. "Frosty Drinks" helps take the heat out of steamy late afternoons with beverages such as Amaretto-Coffee Freeze and Banana Punch.

ENCHANTING WHITE CHOCOLATE

Layers of angel food cake and silky mousse are topped with a velvety buttercream in these spectacularly easy desserts. Our secrets to effortless elegance? Cake mix and a two-ingredient filling.

WHITE CHOCOLATE MOUSSE TORTE
(pictured on page 116)

Prep: 20 minutes
Bake: 25 minutes
Chill: 4 hours

1 (16-ounce) package angel food
    cake mix
White Chocolate Mousse (see
    recipe on facing page)
Almond Buttercream Frosting (see
    recipe on facing page)
Garnishes: Candied Rose Petals
    and Mint Leaves (see recipe on
    facing page), white chocolate
    shavings

• **Prepare** cake batter according to package directions.
• **Spread** batter in a wax paper-lined 15- x 10-inch jellyroll pan.
• **Bake** at 350° for 20 to 25 minutes or until golden. Cool in pan on a wire rack. Loosen edges of cake from pan with a knife.

• **Cut** cake lengthwise into thirds with a serrated knife, cutting through wax paper.
• **Invert** 1 cake layer onto a serving plate, and remove wax paper. Spread layer with half of White Chocolate Mousse.
• **Repeat** procedure with remaining cake layers and mousse, ending with a cake layer. Cover torte tightly with plastic wrap, and chill at least 4 hours. Remove torte from refrigerator, and unwrap.
• **Spread** Almond Buttercream Frosting on top and sides of torte. Store in refrigerator. (Freeze up to 1 month; thaw 8 hours in refrigerator.) Garnish, if desired. **Yield:** 1 (3-layer) torte.

Note: For testing purposes only, we used Duncan Hines cake mix.

STRAWBERRY-STUDDED WHITE CHOCOLATE MOUSSE CAKE

Prep: 40 minutes
Bake: 25 minutes
Chill: 4 hours

1 (16-ounce) package angel food
    cake mix
White Chocolate Mousse (see
    recipe on facing page)
Almond Buttercream Frosting (see
    recipe on facing page)
2 quarts strawberries
12 ounces vanilla candy coating,
    melted (optional)

• **Prepare** cake batter according to package directions. Spread in a wax paper-lined 15- x 10-inch jellyroll pan.
• **Bake** at 350° for 20 to 25 minutes. Cool in pan on a wire rack; cut in half crosswise, forming 2 (10- x 7½-inch) rectangles and cutting through wax paper. Invert 1 layer onto a plate; spread with White Chocolate Mousse. Cover with remaining cake layer. Chill at least 4 hours.
• **Spread** half of Almond Buttercream Frosting on top and sides of cake.
• **Pipe** remaining frosting around top using a star tip. Chill. Dip berries in candy coating, if desired. Place on top and around sides of cake. **Yield:** 12 to 15 servings.

Note: For testing purposes only, we used Duncan Hines cake mix.

CAPPUCCINO MOUSSE CAKE
(pictured on page 116)

Prep: 20 minutes
Bake: 25 minutes
Chill: 4 hours

1 (16-ounce) package angel food
    cake mix
White Chocolate Mousse (see
    recipe on facing page)
2 recipes Coffee Buttercream
    Frosting (see recipe variation
    on facing page)
1 teaspoon ground cinnamon
Garnish: vanilla candy-coated
    cinnamon sticks

- **Prepare** cake batter according to package directions, substituting cold brewed coffee for water.
- **Spoon** batter into 3 wax paper-lined 9-inch round cakepans.
- **Bake** at 350° for 20 to 25 minutes. Cool in pans on wire racks.
- **Invert** 1 layer onto a serving plate; remove wax paper, and spread layer with half of White Chocolate Mousse. Repeat procedure with remaining cake layers and mousse, ending with a cake layer. Cover and chill at least 4 hours.
- **Spread** half of Coffee Buttercream Frosting on top and sides of cake. Using a medium star tip, pipe border around cake bottom with remaining frosting; pipe large dollops around top of cake. Sift cinnamon over cake. (Freeze cake up to 1 month; thaw 8 hours in refrigerator.) Garnish, if desired. **Yield:** 1 (3-layer) cake.

Note: For testing purposes only, we used Duncan Hines cake mix.

WHITE CHOCOLATE MOUSSE

Prep: 10 minutes
Chill: 25 minutes

1¾ cups whipping cream
4 (4-ounce) white chocolate bars, chopped

- **Heat** cream in a heavy saucepan over low heat. (Do not boil.)
- **Place** white chocolate in a 3-quart metal mixing bowl. Add cream to white chocolate; stir until smooth. Place bowl in a larger bowl filled with ice. Let stand 25 minutes, stirring every 5 minutes. (Mixture must be ice cold and have the consistency of a custard sauce).
- **Beat** chilled mixture at medium speed with an electric mixer just until stiff peaks form. (Do not overbeat or mixture will curdle.) **Yield:** about 5 cups.

Note: For testing purposes only, we used Ghirardelli Classic White Confection for white chocolate bars.

Quick White Chocolate Mousse: Omit white chocolate bars. Increase whipping cream to 2 cups, and beat at low speed with an electric mixer until frothy; gradually add 1 (3.3-ounce) package white chocolate instant pudding mix, beating 1 minute or until mixture is smooth and stiff peaks form. **Yield:** about 5 cups.

ALMOND BUTTERCREAM FROSTING

Prep: 10 minutes

½ cup butter, softened
1 (16-ounce) package powdered sugar
⅓ cup milk
1 teaspoon vanilla extract
½ teaspoon almond extract

- **Beat** butter and 1 cup powdered sugar at low speed with an electric mixer until blended.
- **Add** remaining sugar alternately with milk, beating until blended. Add flavorings. Beat frosting at medium speed until spreading consistency. **Yield:** about 3 cups.

Coffee Buttercream Frosting: Substitute ⅓ cup Kahlúa for milk.

CANDIED ROSE PETALS AND MINT LEAVES

These can be done the day before and stored in an airtight container at room temperature. Use firm rose petals that haven't been treated with chemicals.

Prep: 30 minutes

36 small rose petals
6 fresh mint leaf clusters
2 cups sifted powdered sugar
1 tablespoon meringue powder
⅓ cup water
1 cup superfine sugar

- **Rinse** petals and mint leaves; let dry on paper towels.
- **Beat** powdered sugar, meringue powder, and ⅓ cup water at low speed with an electric mixer until blended; beat at high speed 4 to 5 minutes or until fluffy.
- **Brush** powdered sugar mixture on all sides of petals and leaves; sprinkle with superfine sugar. Let stand on wire racks 24 hours. Use to decorate any cake. **Yield:** 3 dozen petals, 6 mint leaf clusters.

CHERRIES AT THEIR PEAK

Cherries are at their peak from the end of June to the beginning of August. Not only are they colorful and sweet, but one serving of fresh cherries is a fair source of dietary fiber, potassium, and vitamin C. If you have an abundance of these gems, freeze them.

To freeze cherries, select firm, ripe cherries; rinse, pat dry, arrange in a single layer on a baking sheet, and freeze until firm. Pack into freezer containers or plastic freezer bags; remove excess air before sealing.

CHERRY SALSA

Prep: 45 minutes
Chill: 1 hour

2 cups pitted fresh cherries, chopped (about 1 pound)
1 small yellow bell pepper, chopped
4 green onions, chopped
2 small jalapeño peppers, seeded and minced
¼ cup lime juice
½ teaspoon salt
2 to 3 tablespoons chopped fresh cilantro
1 tablespoon honey

• **Stir** together all ingredients. Cover and chill 1 hour. Serve with grilled chicken or pork. **Yield:** 3 cups.

CHERRY ICE CREAM

Prep: 35 minutes
Cook: 10 minutes
Stand: 1 hour

2 cups sugar
¼ cup all-purpose flour
Dash of salt
3 cups milk
4 large eggs
3 cups pitted fresh cherries (about 1¼ pounds)
3 cups whipping cream
1 teaspoon almond extract

• **Stir** together first 3 ingredients in a heavy saucepan; gradually whisk in milk until smooth. Cook over medium heat, whisking constantly, 8 minutes or until slightly thickened.
• **Beat** eggs until thick and pale. Whisk about one-fourth of hot mixture into eggs; add to remaining hot mixture, whisking constantly. Cook, stirring constantly, 1 minute. Cool.
• **Pulse** half of cherries in a food processor until finely chopped; remove. Pulse remaining cherries until coarsely chopped. Stir cherries, whipping cream, and almond extract into custard.
• **Pour** mixture into freezer container of a 1-gallon electric freezer. Freeze according to manufacturer's instructions.
• **Pack** freezer with additional ice and rock salt, and let stand 1 hour before serving. **Yield:** 9 cups.

CHERRY COBBLER
(pictured on page 115)

This cobbler will receive top honors with or without ice cream.

Prep: 30 minutes
Bake: 45 minutes
Cool: 20 minutes

6 cups pitted fresh cherries (about 2½ pounds) ✲
1½ cups sugar, divided
3 tablespoons cornstarch
½ cup water
½ teaspoon red liquid food coloring (optional)
3 tablespoons butter or margarine
1 tablespoon grated lemon rind
¼ teaspoon almond extract
1 cup all-purpose flour
1 teaspoon baking powder
½ teaspoon salt
½ cup milk
¼ cup butter or margarine
1 teaspoon vanilla extract
1 large egg
Ice cream (optional)

• **Bring** cherries, ¾ cup sugar, cornstarch, ½ cup water, and, if desired, food coloring to a boil in a medium saucepan, stirring constantly. Boil, stirring constantly, 1 minute. Remove from heat; stir in 3 tablespoons butter, lemon rind, and almond extract. Pour into a lightly greased 11- x 7-inch baking dish.
• **Combine** remaining ¾ cup sugar, flour, baking powder, and salt in a large bowl. Add milk, ¼ cup butter, and vanilla; beat at medium speed with an electric mixer 2 minutes. Add egg; beat 2 minutes. Spoon over cherry mixture.
• **Bake** at 350° for 40 to 45 minutes or until golden, shielding with aluminum foil during the last 10 minutes to prevent excessive browning, if necessary. Cool in dish on a wire rack 15 to 20 minutes. Serve warm with ice cream, if desired. **Yield:** 6 servings.

✲ Substitute 3 (14.5-ounce) cans pitted tart red cherries, if desired. Drain cherries, reserving ½ cup juice. Substitute reserved juice for ½ cup water.

Pat Boschen
Ashland, Virginia

Summer Suppers®

𝒮URFSIDE WITH STYLE

Summer vacation is the time to leave our culinary cares behind. (After all, we go to bask in the warmth of the sun, not in the radiant heat of an oven.) But how do we eat well at the beach without blowing our budget on takeout or our diet on chips and dip? Here's how: Follow the strategy on the next few pages for five satisfying meals that feed six and are easy to prepare.

PEPPERY GRILLED FLANK STEAK

This recipe makes enough flank steak for two of your week's meals. On this first night, you might add steamed zucchini and grilled corn on the cob.

Prep: 10 minutes
Chill: 8 hours
Grill: 16 minutes

⅔ cup dry white wine
¼ cup olive oil
2½ tablespoons cracked pepper
4 teaspoons sugar
2 garlic cloves, pressed
2 red bell peppers, cut into thin strips
2 yellow bell peppers, cut into thin strips
2 (1½-pound) flank steaks, trimmed
Tomato-Cheese Bread

• **Combine** first 7 ingredients in a shallow dish or large heavy-duty zip-top plastic bag; add steaks. Cover or seal, and chill mixture 8 hours, turning steak occasionally.
• **Remove** steaks and bell pepper strips from marinade, discarding marinade. Place bell pepper strips in a grill basket.
• **Grill** steaks and bell pepper strips, covered with grill lid, over high heat (400° to 500°) 8 minutes on each side or to desired degree of doneness.
• **Cut** 1 steak diagonally across the grain into thin strips. Cover and chill remaining steak for Beef Salad Niçoise (page 159). Serve sliced steak and bell pepper strips with Tomato-Cheese Bread. **Yield:** 6 servings.

Tomato-Cheese Bread

Prep: 8 minutes
Bake: 5 minutes

1 (8-ounce) container soft cream cheese
¼ cup shredded Parmesan cheese
1 garlic clove, pressed
2 tablespoons chopped fresh basil
¼ teaspoon salt
⅛ teaspoon pepper
1 (16-ounce) French bread loaf
2 plum tomatoes, sliced

• **Microwave** cream cheese in a 1-quart microwave-safe bowl at HIGH 20 seconds. Stir in Parmesan cheese and next 4 ingredients. Cut bread in half lengthwise; spread cream cheese mixture over cut sides of bread. Top with tomato. Place on a baking sheet, cut side up.
• **Broil** 5½ inches from heat (with electric oven door partially open) 4 to 5 minutes. Cut into slices. **Yield:** 6 servings.

CHICKEN FAJITAS
(pictured on page 187)

Roll up Chicken Fajitas and tuck them two to a tumbler to take on an impromptu picnic. Don't forget frosty drinks, fiery salsa, and a decadent dessert for an evening on the beach.

Prep: 10 minutes
Chill: 2 hours
Grill: 25 minutes

1 cup vegetable oil
½ cup lime juice
½ cup chopped fresh cilantro
4 garlic cloves, pressed
2 teaspoons salt
1½ tablespoons pepper
12 skinned and boned chicken breast halves
12 (6-inch) flour tortillas
1 avocado, peeled and sliced
2 cups (8 ounces) shredded Monterey Jack cheese
1 red bell pepper, cut into strips
1 yellow bell pepper, cut into strips
12 romaine lettuce leaves
Sour cream
Salsa

• **Whisk** together first 6 ingredients in a shallow dish or large heavy-duty zip-top plastic bag; add chicken. Cover or seal; chill 1 to 2 hours, turning occasionally.
• **Remove** chicken from marinade, discarding marinade.
• **Grill,** covered with grill lid, over medium-high heat (350° to 400°) 20 to 25 minutes or until done. Cut 8 chicken breast halves into thin strips. Cover and chill remaining 4 chicken breast halves, reserving for Quick Chicken Tostadas (facing page).
• **Top** tortillas evenly with chicken, avocado, and next 4 ingredients; roll up, and serve with sour cream and salsa.
Yield: 6 servings.

Mildred Bickley
Bristol, Virginia

FIVE SUPPERS

As you plan your trip, use our shopping list to pack your pantry staples; then take the list to your market to shop for perishables. En route, pick up produce from roadside stands, or keep an eye out for pick-your-own fields. Add your choice of cool drinks, fruit, and bake-shop treats to round out each meal. Once you arrive, with the shopping complete, you can focus on the fun.

The first two days you'll grill enough meat and poultry for the entire week. Afterward, you can switch the order of the meals to suit your schedule and taste.

Day 1: Peppery Grilled Flank Steak With Tomato-Cheese Bread
Day 2: Chicken Fajitas
Day 3: Savory Summer Pie
Day 4: Beef Salad Niçoise
Day 5: Quick Chicken Tostadas

WHAT YOU'LL NEED
Here's a list of ingredients you'll need to prepare the five suppers.

From Your Pantry
6 tablespoons olive oil
1 cup vegetable oil
Salt and pepper
2½ tablespoons cracked pepper
4 teaspoons sugar
9 garlic cloves
⅔ cup dry white wine
Paprika (optional)

A Trip to the Market
12 skinned and boned chicken breast halves

2 (1½-pound) flank steaks
1 (16-ounce) French bread loaf
18 (6-inch) flour tortillas
½ (15-ounce) package refrigerated piecrusts
1 (8-ounce) bottle peppercorn Ranch-style dressing
1 (8-ounce) jar salsa
¾ cup niçoise olives
1 (4.5-ounce) can chopped green chiles
1 bunch fresh cilantro
1 bunch fresh basil
⅔ cup shredded Parmesan cheese
4½ cups (18 ounces) shredded Monterey Jack cheese
½ cup (2 ounces) shredded Cheddar cheese
1 (8-ounce) container soft cream cheese
4 large eggs
1 cup half-and-half
1 (16-ounce) container sour cream
2 tablespoons butter or margarine

From the Produce Stand
3 limes
17 plum tomatoes
2 medium tomatoes
1 pound fresh green beans
6 small new potatoes
3 purple onions
3 green onions
1 bunch romaine lettuce
9 to 12 cups gourmet mixed greens
3 yellow bell peppers
4 red bell peppers
1 avocado

SAVORY SUMMER PIE
(pictured on page 185)

Round out the meal with sliced fresh melon, a bowlful of berries, and tangy lemonade.

Prep: 20 minutes
Bake: 1 hour

½ (15-ounce) package refrigerated piecrusts
1 small red bell pepper, chopped
½ purple onion, chopped
2 garlic cloves, minced
2 tablespoons olive oil
2 tablespoons chopped fresh basil
4 large eggs
1 cup half-and-half
1 teaspoon salt
½ teaspoon pepper
2 cups (8 ounces) shredded Monterey Jack cheese
⅓ cup shredded Parmesan cheese
3 plum tomatoes, cut into ¼-inch-thick slices

• **Fit** piecrust into a 9-inch deep-dish tart pan; prick bottom and sides of piecrust with a fork.
• **Bake** at 425° for 10 minutes. Remove from oven; set aside.
• **Sauté** bell pepper, onion, and garlic in hot oil in a large skillet 5 minutes or until tender; stir in basil.
• **Whisk** together eggs and next 3 ingredients in a large bowl; stir in sautéed vegetables and cheeses. Pour into crust; top with tomato.
• **Bake** at 375° for 45 to 50 minutes or until set, shielding edges with strips of aluminum foil after 30 minutes to prevent excessive browning. Let stand 5 minutes before serving. **Yield:** 8 servings.

BEEF SALAD NIÇOISE
(pictured on page 186)

Ripe summer produce and succulent steak make Beef Salad Niçoise a satisfying meal. Serve with crusty baguettes and red wine or sparkling water.

Prep: 25 minutes

1 pound fresh green beans, trimmed
6 small new potatoes, cut in half
1 grilled flank steak (see Peppery Grilled Flank Steak on page 157)
9 to 12 cups gourmet mixed greens
2 purple onions, cut in half and sliced
12 plum tomatoes, quartered
¾ cup niçoise olives
Peppercorn Ranch-style dressing

• **Cook** green beans in boiling water in a saucepan 5 minutes or until beans are crisp-tender; drain. Plunge into ice water to stop the cooking process; drain and set aside.
• **Cook** potato in boiling water to cover in saucepan 15 minutes or until tender; drain and cool slightly. Cut potato into quarters.
• **Cut** flank steak diagonally across the grain into thin strips.
• **Mound** steak strips in center of a lettuce-lined platter.
• **Arrange** green beans, potato, onion, tomato, and olives around flank steak. Serve with peppercorn Ranch-style dressing. **Yield:** 6 to 8 servings.

QUICK CHICKEN TOSTADAS

Accompany these tostadas with apple and orange wedges, salsa-spiked refried beans, and refreshing rainbow sherbet.

Prep: 15 minutes
Bake: 9 minutes

6 (6-inch) flour tortillas
2 tablespoons butter or margarine, melted
4 grilled chicken breast halves, chopped (see Chicken Fajitas on facing page)
2 tomatoes, chopped
1 (4.5-ounce) can chopped green chiles
½ cup (2 ounces) shredded Monterey Jack cheese
½ cup (2 ounces) shredded Cheddar cheese
3 green onions, chopped
Paprika (optional)
Sour cream

• **Place** tortillas in a single layer on baking sheets; brush with butter.
• **Bake** at 400° for 4 to 5 minutes or until lightly browned.
• **Combine** chicken, tomato, and chiles; spoon evenly onto tortillas. Top evenly with cheeses and green onions; sprinkle with paprika, if desired.
• **Bake** 3 to 4 more minutes or until cheeses melt. Serve with sour cream. **Yield:** 6 servings.

Carolyn Griffith
Roby, Texas

FIRE AND ICE

Here's a meal that will tease your taste buds with temperature extremes. Chili powder stokes the fire in Herbed Garbanzo Bean Spread, but it's easily soothed with a sip of Aztec Gold. The main course brings a singe of Jalapeño Grilled Pork, accompanied by a cool and colorful fruit salad. Prepare a package of Mexican cornbread, and cool it all off with scoops of your favorite ice cream.

MEXICAN MENU
Serves Eight

Herbed Garbanzo Bean Spread

Assorted Crackers

Jalapeño Grilled Pork

Minted Fruit Toss

Mexican Cornbread

Aztec Gold

Ice Cream

HERBED GARBANZO BEAN SPREAD

Prep: 6 minutes

1 (15.5-ounce) can garbanzo
   beans, drained
1 garlic clove, chopped
1½ tablespoons fresh lemon
   juice
1 tablespoon olive oil
2 teaspoons chopped fresh or
   ¾ teaspoon dried oregano
2 teaspoons chopped fresh or
   ¾ teaspoon dried thyme
½ teaspoon chili powder
¼ teaspoon salt
¼ teaspoon freshly ground pepper

• **Process** all ingredients in a food processor until smooth, stopping to scrape down sides. Serve with crackers. **Yield:** 1⅓ cups.

Jane Woods
Boca Raton, Florida

JALAPEÑO GRILLED PORK
(pictured on page 152)

Prep: 35 minutes
Chill: 8 hours
Grill: 40 minutes

5 or 6 jalapeño peppers, divided
2 garlic cloves, minced
1 plum tomato, peeled, seeded,
   and diced
¼ cup lime juice
2 tablespoons chopped fresh
   cilantro
1¼ teaspoons salt, divided
1 (3-pound) boneless pork loin
   roast
¼ cup butter or margarine
Gourmet salad greens

• **Seed** and chop 3 jalapeño peppers. Stir together chopped pepper, garlic, next 3 ingredients, and ¼ teaspoon salt.
• **Butterfly** roast by making a lengthwise cut down center of 1 flat side, cutting to within ½ inch of bottom. From bottom of cut, slice horizontally to ½ inch from left side; repeat procedure to right side. Open roast, and place between 2 sheets of heavy-duty plastic wrap; flatten to ½-inch thickness using a meat mallet or rolling pin.
• **Spread** pepper mixture over roast. Roll up, and tie at 1-inch intervals with string. Place, seam side down, in a lightly greased 11- x 7-inch dish; cover and chill 8 hours.
• **Seed** and chop remaining 2 or 3 jalapeño peppers. Combine peppers, butter, and remaining 1 teaspoon salt. Grill pork, covered with grill lid, over medium-high heat (350° to 400°) 40 minutes or until a meat thermometer inserted into thickest portion registers 160°, turning and basting often with butter mixture. Slice; serve with salad greens. **Yield:** 8 servings.

MINTED FRUIT TOSS

Prep: 20 minutes
Chill: 2 hours

¼ cup chopped fresh mint
¼ cup orange juice
3 tablespoons raspberry vinegar
3 tablespoons walnut oil or
   vegetable oil
2 tablespoons honey
2 (16½-ounce) cans pitted Bing
   cherries, drained
2 (11-ounce) cans mandarin
   orange sections, drained
2 apples, cubed
1 banana, sliced
4 kiwifruit, peeled and sliced
1 cup seedless green grapes

• **Stir** together first 5 ingredients in a large bowl; add cherries and remaining ingredients, tossing to coat. Cover and chill 2 hours. **Yield:** about 8 cups.

Mary B. Quesenberry
Dagspur, Virginia

AZTEC GOLD
(pictured on page 152)

This spirited apple-flavored thirst quencher is a perfect complement to Jalapeño Grilled Pork.

Prep: 10 minutes
Chill: 1 hour

1 (12-ounce) can frozen apple
   juice concentrate, undiluted
3 whole cloves
¼ teaspoon ground cinnamon
1 tablespoon honey
2 cups tonic water, chilled
6 tablespoons vodka, chilled
   (optional)

• **Cook** first 4 ingredients in a small saucepan over medium heat, stirring occasionally, 5 minutes or until thoroughly heated. Remove from heat; cool. Chill 1 hour, or freeze 15 minutes. Stir in tonic water and, if desired, vodka; serve immediately over ice. **Yield:** 4 cups.

ℱROSTY DRINKS

*It's no wonder we imagined being on an island
every time we tasted these beverages.
Tim Duffy, owner of Duffy's Love Shack
in St. Thomas, Virgin Islands, shared
two of his recipes with us—Pirate's Painkiller
and Funky Monkey.*

PIRATE'S PAINKILLER

Prep: 10 minutes

3 tablespoons dark rum
2 tablespoons pineapple juice
2 tablespoons cream of coconut
2 tablespoons orange juice
1 cup ice cubes
1 tablespoon orange liqueur
**Garnishes: ground nutmeg, ground
    cinnamon, maraschino
    cherries, kiwifruit slices**

• **Process** first 4 ingredients in a blender
until smooth. Serve over ice; top each
serving with orange liqueur. Garnish, if
desired. **Yield:** 1½ cups.

*Tim Duffy
Duffy's Love Shack
St. Thomas, Virgin Islands*

FUNKY MONKEY

Prep: 5 minutes

½ ripe banana
1 tablespoon butterscotch liqueur
2 tablespoons banana liqueur
2 tablespoons Irish cream
1 tablespoon gold rum
1 tablespoon Simple Syrup
Ice cubes

• **Process** first 6 ingredients in a blender
until smooth. Add ice to 1½-cup level;
process until slushy. Serve immediately.
Yield: 1½ cups.

Simple Syrup

*Prep: 2 minutes
Cook: 5 minutes*

½ cup water
½ cup sugar

• **Bring** water and sugar to a boil in a
saucepan, stirring until sugar dissolves;
boil 1 minute. Remove from heat; cool.
Store in refrigerator. **Yield:** ¾ cup.
(enough for 12 drinks).

*Tim Duffy
Duffy's Love Shack
St. Thomas, Virgin Islands*

BANANA PUNCH

*Prep: 10 minutes
Cook: 5 minutes
Freeze: 2 hours*

6 cups water
3 cups sugar
3 (32-ounce) cans unsweetened
    pineapple juice
1 (6-ounce) can frozen orange
    juice concentrate, undiluted
½ cup lemon juice
3 cups mashed ripe bananas
    (about 9)
3 (1-liter) bottles ginger ale,
    chilled

• **Bring** 6 cups water and sugar to a boil
in a Dutch oven, stirring until sugar dissolves. Remove from heat.
• **Stir** pineapple juice and next 3 ingredients into sugar mixture. Pour into a 2-
gallon container. Freeze 2 hours or until
mixture is firm.
• **Let** stand at room temperature 45 minutes before serving.
• **Pour** ginger ale over banana mixture,
stirring until slushy. Serve immediately.
Yield: 7 quarts.

*Georgia Bell
Guntown, Mississippi*

AMARETTO-COFFEE
FREEZE

Prep: 10 minutes

½ cup almond liqueur
¼ cup coffee liqueur
1 quart frozen vanilla yogurt,
    softened

• **Process** half each of all ingredients in
a blender until smooth, stopping to
scrape down sides. Pour into serving
glasses. Repeat procedure with remaining ingredients. Serve immediately.
Yield: 5½ cups.

*Caroline Kennedy
Lighthouse Point, Florida*

Cold Cooking

For Toni Reed Rashid of Altadena, Alabama, summer entertaining isn't too hot to handle when the party's on ice. Toni chooses a menu or variety of appetizers that are served cold. Start with these make-ahead recipes and add your cool favorites. Make the evening simple or grand, for a few or a crowd. Either way, you'll have time to kick back and chill out before the guests arrive.

Cool Summer Menu
Serves Six

Smoked Oyster Mousse   **Assorted Crackers**
Grilled Corn Salsa   **Tortilla Chips**
Apricot-Chicken Salad
Iced Tea

SMOKED OYSTER MOUSSE

Prep: 10 minutes
Cook: 8 minutes
Chill: 8 hours

1 (3.7-ounce) can smoked
    oysters
2 envelopes unflavored gelatin
½ cup cold water
1 (8-ounce) package cream cheese,
    softened
1 (10¾-ounce) can cream of
    mushroom soup, undiluted
1 cup mayonnaise
2 teaspoons dried parsley
    flakes
1 teaspoon Worcestershire sauce
3 drops of hot sauce

• **Drain** oysters well. Place in a large saucepan; mash and set aside.
• **Sprinkle** gelatin over ½ cup cold water, and stir.
• **Add** cream cheese and next 5 ingredients to oysters; cook over medium heat, stirring constantly, until thoroughly heated (do not boil). Stir in gelatin mixture until dissolved.
• **Pour** into a lightly oiled 4-cup mold; cover and chill 8 hours or up to 2 days. Serve with crackers. **Yield:** 3⅔ cups.

Karen Etheredge
Newton, Georgia

GRILLED CORN SALSA

Toni likes to serve colorful tortilla chips with this multicolored salsa.

Prep: 20 minutes
Grill: 10 minutes
Chill: 2 hours

3 ears fresh corn
1 large sweet onion, cut into
    ½-inch-thick slices
1 red bell pepper, halved
2 large tomatoes, seeded and
    chopped
2 jalapeño peppers, seeded and
    minced
2 garlic cloves, minced
¼ cup chopped fresh cilantro
½ teaspoon salt
¼ teaspoon ground cumin
1 tablespoon olive oil
1 tablespoon lime juice
Garnish: fresh cilantro sprig

• **Grill** first 3 ingredients, covered with grill lid, over medium-high heat (350° to 400°) 8 to 10 minutes or until tender, turning occasionally.
• **Cut** corn kernels from corn cobs. Coarsely chop onion and red bell pepper halves.
• **Combine** grilled vegetables, tomato, and next 7 ingredients in a large bowl; cover and chill 2 hours or up to 2 days. Garnish, if desired. Serve salsa with tortilla chips, grilled chicken, fish, or beef. **Yield:** 5 cups.

Toni Reed Rashid
Altadena, Alabama

APRICOT-CHICKEN SALAD

Prep: 25 minutes

½ cup plain yogurt
¼ cup mayonnaise
3 tablespoons apricot preserves
2 teaspoons grated fresh ginger
½ teaspoon salt
½ teaspoon freshly ground pepper
1 cup sliced almonds, toasted
1 (6-ounce) package dried apricots, chopped
3 cups chopped cooked chicken
¾ cup sliced celery
Bibb lettuce leaves

• **Whisk** together first 6 ingredients in a large bowl.
• **Add** almonds and next 3 ingredients, tossing gently. Serve on Bibb lettuce-lined plates. **Yield:** 6 servings.
Toni Reed Rashid
Altadena, Alabama

MAKE-AHEAD TIPS

■ Prepare salsa and mousse up to two days ahead, and refrigerate in airtight containers.

■ Make chicken salad on the day before the party.

A HINT OF MINT

Fresh mint adds a cooling touch to a variety of warm-weather dishes. Just ask Pete and Caroline Madsen of Pete's Herbs outside Charleston, South Carolina. "Mint is known for its pleasing aroma—smell a sprig, and it will raise your spirits," says Caroline.

"Don't be afraid to experiment with herbs. You'll find some terrific combinations," says Pete.

Spearmint is a fine complement to salads and marinades; peppermint is ideal in chocolate desserts and coffees.

WHEAT SALAD WITH CITRUS AND MINT

Prep: 55 minutes
Chill: 2 hours

1 cup bulgur wheat
2 cups boiling water
½ cup loosely packed minced fresh mint *
¼ cup lemon juice
3 tablespoons olive oil
½ teaspoon salt
½ teaspoon pepper
3 cups mixed salad greens
2 oranges, peeled and sectioned
2 pink grapefruit, peeled and sectioned
½ purple onion, sliced and separated into rings
1 (4-ounce) package crumbled feta cheese
Garnish: fresh mint sprigs

• **Stir** together bulgur wheat and 2 cups boiling water; let stand 30 minutes. Drain.
• **Stir** together ½ cup mint and next 4 ingredients in a large bowl; let stand 20 minutes. Stir in bulgur wheat; cover and chill 2 hours.
• **Arrange** salad greens on a platter; spoon bulgur wheat mixture over salad greens. Arrange orange and grapefruit sections over bulgur; top with onion, and sprinkle with feta. Garnish, if desired. **Yield:** 6 servings.

* Substitute lime mint or orange mint for regular mint, if desired.
Caroline Park Madsen
Johns Island, South Carolina

MINT-CRUSTED LAMB

Prep: 30 minutes
Bake: 45 minutes

2 (8-rib) lamb rib roasts (1½ pounds each), trimmed
1 teaspoon salt
½ teaspoon pepper
2 cups French bread cubes
¼ cup butter or margarine, softened
¼ cup lemon juice
¼ cup chopped fresh parsley
½ cup chopped fresh mint
2 garlic cloves, minced
¼ cup stone-ground mustard

• **Sprinkle** lamb with salt and pepper. Cook lamb in a large nonstick skillet over medium-high heat 3 to 4 minutes on each side or until browned.
• **Process** bread cubes and next 5 ingredients in a food processor until coarsely ground.
• **Brush** mustard over lamb; press breadcrumb mixture over mustard. Place lamb on a lightly greased rack in a broiler pan.
• **Bake** at 400° for 40 to 45 minutes or until a meat thermometer inserted into thickest portion registers 145°.
• **Remove** lamb from oven, and let stand 5 minutes or until thermometer registers 150° (medium-rare). **Yield:** 4 servings.

AGE OF ELEGANCE

Join four Brandon, Mississippi, hosts for a turn-of-the-century dinner that celebrates the language of flowers. Jan Harrell and fellow hosts Carol Swilley, Pauline Carroll, and Marianna Martin have naturally pulled out all the stops to turn back time with a leisurely, lavish Victorian dinner party.

VICTORIAN DINNER PARTY
Serves Eight

Cold Zucchini Soup
Fleur-de-lis Salad
Marinated Stuffed Filet of Beef
Mashed Potatoes With Crab Marinière
Sugar Snap Peas With Champagne Dressing
Watermelon Sorbet
Southern Custard Crêpe Cake

COLD ZUCCHINI SOUP

Prep: 40 minutes
Chill: 8 hours

4 medium zucchini, quartered and sliced
4 cups chicken broth
1 bunch green onions, chopped
1 teaspoon salt
1 teaspoon pepper
2 (8-ounce) packages cream cheese, cut into pieces and softened
1 tablespoon chopped fresh dill
1 (8-ounce) container sour cream
Garnish: chopped fresh chives

• **Combine** first 5 ingredients in a saucepan; cook over medium-high heat, stirring occasionally, 20 minutes. Add cream cheese and dill.
• **Process** mixture in batches in a blender until smooth. Stir in sour cream. Cover and chill 8 hours. Garnish, if desired. **Yield:** 9 cups.

Note: To lighten recipe, use fat-free chicken broth, reduced-fat cream cheese, and reduced-fat sour cream.

FLEUR-DE-LIS SALAD

Prep: 30 minutes

36 steamed jumbo fresh shrimp
6 avocados, cut into wedges
2 grapefruit, sectioned
1 (11-ounce) can mandarin orange sections, drained
12 cherry tomatoes
1 head Red Leaf lettuce
Rémoulade Sauce

• **Peel** shrimp; devein, if desired.
• **Arrange** shrimp and next 4 ingredients on lettuce-lined plates; serve with Rémoulade Sauce. **Yield:** 12 salad or 6 main-dish servings.

Rémoulade Sauce

Prep: 10 minutes

1 bunch green onions
1 celery rib, cut into 1-inch pieces
1 garlic clove
¼ cup loosely packed fresh parsley leaves
⅓ cup white vinegar
3 tablespoons hot Creole mustard
1 tablespoon paprika
½ teaspoon salt
¼ teaspoon pepper
⅔ cup olive oil

• **Pulse** first 4 ingredients in a food processor until chopped; add next 5 ingredients. With processor running, add oil in a slow, steady stream. **Yield:** 2¼ cups.

Note: If your market doesn't steam shrimp as a service, buy 3 pounds unpeeled, jumbo fresh shrimp. Cook in 9 cups boiling water 3 to 5 minutes or just until shrimp turn pink. Drain and rinse with cold water.

MARINATED STUFFED FILET OF BEEF

Prep: 30 minutes
Marinate: 2 hours
Bake: 1 hour and 10 minutes

2 (8-ounce) packages fresh
    mushrooms, sliced
1 bunch green onions, chopped
¼ cup chopped fresh parsley
1 teaspoon vegetable oil
½ cup soy sauce
⅓ cup dry white wine
2 garlic cloves, minced
2 tablespoons light brown sugar
2 tablespoons honey
1 tablespoon vegetable oil
1 (4-pound) beef tenderloin,
    trimmed
1 cup water

• **Sauté** first 3 ingredients in 1 teaspoon hot vegetable oil in a large skillet over medium-high heat 10 minutes or until all liquid is evaporated; cool.
• **Stir** together soy sauce and next 5 ingredients.
• **Make** a 1-inch-deep cut lengthwise down top of tenderloin; spoon mushroom mixture into cut.
• **Tie** tenderloin with cotton string at 1-inch intervals; place in a large shallow dish. Pour soy sauce mixture over top of tenderloin; cover and chill 2 to 8 hours, turning occasionally.
• **Remove** tenderloin from marinade, reserving marinade; place tenderloin on a lightly greased rack in a roasting pan. Add 1 cup water to roasting pan.
• **Bring** reserved marinade to a boil in a small saucepan over medium-high heat. Boil 1 minute.
• **Bake** tenderloin at 425° for 1 hour and 10 minutes or until a meat thermometer inserted in thickest portion registers 145° (medium-rare) to 160° (medium), basting occasionally with reserved marinade and covering with aluminum foil the last 30 minutes. Let stand 10 minutes before slicing. **Yield:** 10 to 12 servings.

MASHED POTATOES WITH CRAB MARINIÈRE

Prep: 25 minutes
Cook: 40 minutes

12 medium-size new potatoes,
    peeled and quartered (2½
    pounds)
¼ cup sour cream
1 cup butter, divided
½ teaspoon salt
½ teaspoon pepper
1½ ounces chopped black truffles
    (optional)
1 bunch green onions, diced
3 tablespoons all-purpose flour
2 cups milk
½ teaspoon salt
¼ teaspoon ground red pepper
⅓ cup dry white wine
1 egg yolk, beaten
1 pound fresh lump crabmeat,
    drained
Potato Baskets (optional; see
    recipe on next page)
Red bell pepper cups (optional)

• **Cook** potato in boiling water to cover 20 minutes or until tender; drain. Beat potato at medium speed with an electric mixer until smooth.
• **Stir** in sour cream, ½ cup butter, ½ teaspoon salt, pepper, and, if desired, truffles. Keep warm.
• **Melt** remaining ½ cup butter in a skillet over medium-high heat; add green onions. Sauté 2 minutes or until onions are tender.
• **Stir** in flour; cook, stirring constantly, 5 minutes. Gradually stir in milk.
• **Stir** in ½ teaspoon salt, red pepper, and wine. Reduce heat, and cook, stirring occasionally, 10 minutes or until mixture is thickened.
• **Stir** 1 cup hot mixture into beaten egg yolk; stir into remaining hot mixture. Cook, stirring often, 5 minutes. Add crabmeat, tossing gently.
• **Pipe** or spoon potato mixture evenly into Potato Baskets, if desired; top evenly with crab sauce. Place in bell pepper cups, if desired. **Yield:** 8 servings.

Potato Baskets

Prep: 1 hour and 20 minutes
Cook: 20 minutes

4 large baking potatoes
8 teaspoons cornstarch
Vegetable oil

• **Shred** potatoes in a food processor. Soak in water to cover 1 hour, draining and adding fresh water every 15 minutes. Drain well. Toss with cornstarch.
• **Pour** oil to a depth of 3 inches into a Dutch oven; heat to 375°. Dip a bird's-nest fryer into oil; drain. Arrange ⅔ cup potato mixture into lower basket; press upper basket onto potato to shape into a basket. Fry in hot oil 2 minutes or until golden; drain on paper towels. Repeat procedure 7 times with remaining potato mixture. **Yield:** 8 baskets.

Note: Substitute two wire-mesh strainers for bird's-nest fryer, if desired.

SUGAR SNAP PEAS WITH CHAMPAGNE DRESSING

Prep: 10 minutes
Chill: 1 hour

⅓ cup egg substitute
¼ cup champagne vinegar
2 teaspoons Dijon mustard
½ teaspoon salt
¼ teaspoon pepper
1 cup vegetable oil
3 pounds fresh sugar snap peas

• **Process** first 5 ingredients in a food processor 1 minute. With processor running, add oil in a slow, steady stream. Cover and chill at least 1 hour.
• **Cook** peas in boiling water to cover 3 minutes; drain. Plunge into ice water to stop the cooking process; drain. Serve with dressing. **Yield:** 12 servings.

WATERMELON SORBET

Prep: 15 minutes
Chill: 2 hours
Freeze: 1 hour

4 cups water
2 cups sugar
8 cups seeded, chopped watermelon
1 (12-ounce) can frozen pink lemonade concentrate, thawed and undiluted

• **Bring** 4 cups water and sugar just to a boil in a medium saucepan over high heat, stirring until sugar dissolves. Remove from heat. Cool.
• **Process** sugar syrup and watermelon in batches in a blender until smooth. Stir in lemonade concentrate. Cover and chill 2 hours. Pour mixture into freezer container of a 1-gallon electric freezer. Freeze according to manufacturer's instructions. **Yield:** 2½ quarts.

SOUTHERN CUSTARD CRÊPE CAKE

Prep: 40 minutes
Cook: 12 minutes
Chill: 9 hours

4 envelopes unflavored gelatin
4 cups milk
8 egg yolks
1⅓ cups sugar
¼ cup cornstarch
½ teaspoon salt
¼ cup butter, cut into pieces
2 tablespoons cream sherry
2 teaspoons vanilla extract
4 cups whipping cream, divided
1 cup fresh blueberries
1 cup fresh blackberries
1 cup fresh raspberries
Crêpes
4 to 6 tablespoons powdered sugar
Raspberry Sauce
Garnishes: sugared edible pansies, fresh mint sprigs

• **Sprinkle** gelatin over ½ cup milk in a saucepan; let stand 1 minute.
• **Whisk** remaining 3½ cups milk, egg yolks, and next 3 ingredients into gelatin mixture.
• **Cook** over medium heat, whisking often, until thickened. Remove gelatin mixture from heat.
• **Whisk** in butter, sherry, and vanilla. Cool 30 minutes; cover and chill.
• **Beat** 2 cups whipping cream at medium speed with an electric mixer until soft peaks form; fold into custard. Cover and chill 8 hours.
• **Toss** together blueberries, blackberries, and raspberries; set aside.
• **Stack** Crêpes, spreading custard evenly between layers and ending with a Crêpe.
• **Beat** remaining 2 cups whipping cream and powdered sugar at medium speed with an electric mixer until stiff peaks form.
• **Spread** sweetened whipped cream on top and sides of stacked Crêpes. Pipe a border around bottom of cake using a star tip. Chill at least 1 hour.
• **Serve** with Raspberry Sauce and berry mixture; garnish, if desired. **Yield:** 1 (6-inch) cake.

Crêpes

Prep: 10 minutes
Chill: 1 hour
Cook: 18 minutes

1¼ cups all-purpose flour
2 tablespoons sugar
¼ teaspoon salt
1½ cups milk
4 large eggs
3 tablespoons butter, melted

• **Process** all ingredients in a blender 30 seconds. Cover and chill 1 hour.
• **Place** a lightly oiled 6-inch crêpe pan or heavy skillet over medium heat until pan is hot.
• **Pour** 2 tablespoons batter into pan; quickly tilt pan in all directions so batter covers bottom.
• **Cook** 1 minute or until crêpe can be shaken loose from pan. Turn crêpe, and

cook 30 seconds. Place crêpe on a cloth towel to cool. Repeat procedure with remaining batter. **Yield:** 12 (6-inch) crêpes.

Raspberry Sauce

Prep: 10 minutes
Cook: 5 minutes
Chill: 2 hours

2 (14-ounce) packages frozen raspberries, thawed
1 cup sugar
1 tablespoon cornstarch
2 tablespoons raspberry liqueur

• **Press** raspberries through a fine wire-mesh strainer into a saucepan, discarding solids.
• **Stir** together sugar and cornstarch; stir into raspberry juice.
• **Cook** over medium-high heat, stirring constantly, until mixture boils.
• **Boil,** stirring constantly, 1 minute. Remove from heat; stir in liqueur. Cool. Cover and chill sauce 2 hours. **Yield:** about 3½ cups.

PARTY AT THE PETELOSES

When the Petelos family entertains, it's no small feast. Greek born and bred, Catherine and Angelo Petelos moved to Birmingham when they were nine and eleven, respectively. This cultural mix is evident in their food. Annual cookouts on Memorial Day, Fourth of July, and Labor Day overflow with Greek goodness and Southern charm. With about 80 family members and friends in attendance, there's a dish for everyone. You'll enjoy preparing some of the recipes that this family holds dear.

PASTITSIO

Pastitsio is a traditional Greek casserole made of pasta, beef, cinnamon, tomatoes, and a white sauce.

Prep: 45 minutes
Bake: 1 hour

8 ounces ziti, cooked
3 tablespoons butter or margarine
2 (3-ounce) packages shredded Parmesan cheese, divided
1½ pounds ground round
1 medium onion, diced
2 garlic cloves, minced
2 (8-ounce) cans tomato sauce
1½ teaspoons salt, divided
½ teaspoon ground cinnamon
¼ teaspoon pepper
½ cup butter or margarine
⅔ cup all-purpose flour
4 cups milk
2 large eggs

• **Toss** pasta with 3 tablespoons butter and ½ cup Parmesan cheese.
• **Cook** ground round, onion, and garlic in a large skillet over medium-high heat, stirring until beef crumbles and is no longer pink; drain.
• **Stir** in tomato sauce, 1¼ teaspoons salt, cinnamon, and pepper.
• **Melt** ½ cup butter in a heavy saucepan over low heat. Whisk in flour. Cook, whisking constantly, 1 minute.
• **Whisk** in milk; cook over medium heat, whisking constantly, until thickened and bubbly. Add remaining ¼ teaspoon salt. Remove from heat.
• **Whisk** eggs until thick and pale. Whisk about one-fourth milk mixture into eggs; add to remaining milk mixture, whisking constantly.
• **Spoon** pasta mixture into a greased 13- x 9-inch baking dish. Spoon beef mixture over pasta; sprinkle with remaining Parmesan cheese. Top with cream sauce.
• **Bake** at 350° for 1 hour or until golden. **Yield:** 8 to 10 servings.

Ann Mimikakis
Pelham, Alabama

SNOW COOKIES

These cookies, named for their powdered sugar coating, are a year-round dessert.

Prep: 1 hour
Bake: 30 minutes

1 (2-ounce) package slivered almonds
2 cups unsalted butter, softened
1 large egg
1 (16-ounce) package powdered sugar, divided
1 tablespoon vanilla extract
5 cups all-purpose flour
1 tablespoon baking powder
60 whole cloves (optional)

• **Pulse** almonds in a food processor until finely chopped.
• **Beat** butter at medium speed with a heavy-duty electric mixer until butter is creamy.
• **Add** egg, beating just until yellow disappears. Gradually add 1 cup powdered sugar, beating at low speed until blended; beat 1 minute. Add vanilla and almonds, and beat until blended.
• **Combine** flour and baking powder; gradually add to butter mixture, beating just until blended after each addition.
• **Pinch** off 1-inch pieces of dough; shape into crescents. Insert a clove into each cookie, if desired; place on ungreased baking sheets.
• **Bake** at 350° for 25 to 30 minutes; remove to wire racks to cool 30 minutes; roll in remaining sugar. **Yield:** 5 dozen.

Note: If not using a heavy-duty mixer, add 3 cups flour mixture to butter mixture, beating until smooth. Knead in remaining flour until dough is smooth and holds together.

Maria Latto
Charleston, South Carolina

GROVE PARK FAVORITES

The charming and historic Grove Park Inn in Asheville, North Carolina, shared this delightful menu with us. Just about any grilled entrée goes with it beautifully. These easy recipes will allow you to relax in no time—wherever you are.

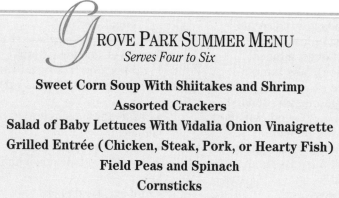

GROVE PARK SUMMER MENU
Serves Four to Six

Sweet Corn Soup With Shiitakes and Shrimp
Assorted Crackers
Salad of Baby Lettuces With Vidalia Onion Vinaigrette
Grilled Entrée (Chicken, Steak, Pork, or Hearty Fish)
Field Peas and Spinach
Cornsticks
Cream Cheese-Peach Tart

SWEET CORN SOUP WITH SHIITAKES AND SHRIMP
(pictured on page 190)

Prep: 10 minute
Cook: 1 hour

½ **pound unpeeled, medium-size fresh shrimp**
1 **leek, minced**
1 **small sweet onion, chopped**
¼ **cup olive oil, divided**
2 **garlic cloves, minced**
3 **cups fresh corn kernels, divided (about 7 ears)**
3 **cups chicken broth**
16 **small shiitake mushrooms, stems removed**
¼ **teaspoon salt**
¼ **teaspoon pepper**
Garnish: chopped fresh chives

• **Peel** shrimp, and devein, if desired. Set aside.

• **Sauté** leek and onion in 2 tablespoons hot oil in a Dutch oven 2 minutes; add garlic. Sauté 2 minutes. Add 2¼ cups corn kernels and chicken broth; bring to a boil. Reduce heat, and simmer 40 minutes. Remove from heat; cool slightly.
• **Process** half of corn mixture in a food processor or blender until smooth, stopping to scrape down sides; pour into a bowl. Repeat procedure with remaining corn mixture.
• **Sauté** mushrooms in remaining 2 tablespoons hot oil in Dutch oven over medium-high heat 5 minutes. Stir in salt and pepper; remove from Dutch oven.
• **Bring** pureed mixture to a boil in Dutch oven over medium-high heat, stirring often. Stir in remaining ¾ cup corn, mushrooms, and shrimp. Reduce heat; simmer 3 to 4 minutes or just until shrimp turn pink. Serve with crackers; garnish, if desired. **Yield:** about 8 cups.
Grove Park Inn
Asheville, North Carolina

SALAD OF BABY LETTUCES WITH VIDALIA ONION VINAIGRETTE
(pictured on page 191)

Prep: 10 minutes

Vidalia Onion Vinaigrette
8 **cups gourmet salad greens**
1 **cup freshly grated Asiago cheese ✱**
Garnish: cherry tomato halves

• **Toss** together Vidalia Onion Vinaigrette and salad greens; sprinkle evenly with cheese; garnish, if desired. **Yield:** 4 to 6 servings.

✱ Substitute 1 cup freshly grated Parmesan cheese for Asiago cheese, if desired.

Note: Asiago cheese is a semifirm Italian cheese found with specialty cheeses in large supermarkets.

Vidalia Onion Vinaigrette

Prep: 10 minutes

1 **large Vidalia onion, chopped**
1 **tablespoon vegetable oil**
½ **cup cider vinegar**
1 **tablespoon honey**
1 **tablespoon lemon juice**
1 **teaspoon Dijon mustard**
1 **teaspoon salt**
½ **teaspoon pepper**
¾ **cup vegetable oil**

• **Cook** onion in 1 tablespoon hot oil in a large skillet over low heat, stirring constantly, 20 minutes or until onion is caramel colored.
• **Process** onion, vinegar, and next 5 ingredients in a blender or food processor until smooth, stopping to scrape down sides. Turn blender on high; add ¾ cup vegetable oil in a slow, steady stream. **Yield:** 1½ cups.
Grove Park Inn
Asheville, North Carolina

FIELD PEAS AND SPINACH

(pictured on page 191)

Prep: 15 minutes
Cook: 45 minutes

4 bacon slices
1 medium onion, diced
3 cups shelled fresh field peas *
2½ cups water
½ teaspoon salt
½ teaspoon pepper
1 (10-ounce) package fresh
    spinach, torn

• **Cook** bacon in a Dutch oven over medium heat until crisp; remove bacon, reserving drippings in pan. Crumble bacon. Sauté onion in reserved drippings in Dutch oven 7 to 8 minutes or until tender. Add field peas and 2½ cups water; bring to a boil. Reduce heat, and simmer 30 minutes or until peas are tender; stir in salt and pepper.

• **Stir** in spinach; cook over medium heat 3 to 5 minutes or until spinach wilts. Drain. Sprinkle each serving with bacon. **Yield:** 4 to 6 servings.

∗ Substitute 1 (16-ounce) package frozen field peas for fresh, if desired.
Grove Park Inn
Asheville, North Carolina

CREAM CHEESE-PEACH TART

Prep: 40 minutes
Chill: 1 hour
Bake: 40 minutes

1 cup unsalted butter, softened
1¾ cups sugar, divided
3½ teaspoons vanilla extract,
    divided
2 large eggs, divided
2¾ cups all-purpose flour, divided
2 (8-ounce) packages cream
    cheese, softened
4 fresh peaches, peeled and sliced *

• **Beat** butter, ¾ cup sugar, and 1½ teaspoons vanilla extract at medium speed with an electric mixer until creamy; add 1 egg, beating until blended. Stir in 2½ cups flour.

• **Press** into bottom and up sides of a lightly greased removable bottom 11-inch tart pan, trimming excess pastry; cover and chill 1 hour.

• **Beat** cream cheese and ¾ cup sugar at medium speed until creamy; add remaining egg and remaining 2 teaspoons vanilla, and beat until blended.

• **Add** remaining ¼ cup flour, and beat until blended. Spread into pastry shell.

• **Toss** together peach slices and remaining ¼ cup sugar; arrange peach slices over cream cheese mixture.

• **Bake** at 400° for 35 to 40 minutes or until set. Cool on a wire rack. **Yield:** 1 (11-inch) tart.

∗ Substitute 1 (16-ounce) package frozen peach slices, thawed, for 4 fresh peaches, if desired.
Grove Park Inn
Asheville, North Carolina

SPICE POWER

Paprika is more than just a rusty-red addition to your spice rack. With a flavor ranging from mildly sweet to pungent and bold, paprika is a versatile—and essential—spice.

Try paprika with chicken, veal, mild cheeses, and shellfish for instant warmth and beautiful color. (And yes, it's still great for deviled eggs and goulash.)

PARMESAN-PAPRIKA POTATOES

Prep: 7 minutes
Bake: 50 minutes

¾ cup grated Parmesan cheese
⅓ cup all-purpose flour
3 tablespoons paprika
½ teaspoon pepper
8 small baking potatoes
½ cup butter or margarine, melted

• **Combine** first 4 ingredients in a large heavy-duty zip-top plastic bag; seal and shake to blend.

• **Cut** each potato into 8 wedges; place in bag. Seal and shake to coat. Arrange potato in a 13- x 9-inch pan; drizzle with butter.

• **Bake** at 375° for 20 to 25 minutes on each side or until potato is tender. Serve immediately. **Yield:** 6 to 8 servings.

MARINATED SHRIMP SALAD

This shrimp salad requires little more than a turn of the whisk and time to chill.

Prep: 20 minutes
Cook: 10 minutes
Marinate: 3 hours

2 quarts water
2½ pounds unpeeled, medium-size
    fresh shrimp
⅓ cup olive oil
⅓ cup white wine vinegar
⅓ cup Dijon mustard
2 tablespoons paprika
2 teaspoons sugar
½ teaspoon dried basil
½ teaspoon salt
¼ teaspoon freshly ground
    pepper
1 bunch green onions, chopped
2 celery ribs, chopped
2 garlic cloves, minced
8 cups mixed salad greens
Garnishes: lemon wedges,
    paprika

• **Bring** 2 quarts water to a boil; add shrimp, and cook 3 to 5 minutes or just until shrimp turn pink. Drain and rinse with cold water. Peel shrimp; devein, if desired. Chill.

• **Whisk** together olive oil and next 7 ingredients in a large bowl until blended; stir in green onions, celery, and garlic. Add shrimp, tossing to coat; cover and chill 3 hours.

• **Arrange** shrimp on salad greens; garnish, if desired. **Yield:** 8 servings.
Caroline Kennedy
Lighthouse Point, Florida

CHEESE BRICK

Prep: 1 hour and 10 minutes
Chill: 1 hour

2 (8-ounce) blocks Cheddar
    cheese
1 (8-ounce) package cream cheese,
    softened
1 (2-ounce) jar diced pimientos,
    undrained
½ cup chopped pecans
1 tablespoon mayonnaise
½ teaspoon garlic salt
½ teaspoon onion salt
½ cup paprika

• **Shred** Cheddar cheese, and let stand
at room temperature 1 hour.
• **Stir** together Cheddar cheese, cream
cheese, and next 5 ingredients; shape
into a rectangle, log, or ball; roll in paprika, coating evenly. Cover and chill at
least 1 hour. Serve with assorted crackers. **Yield:** 15 to 20 servings.

Regina Greer Cooper
Madison, Alabama

PAPRIKA PARTICULARS

■ Paprika is made by grinding the
tough pods of sweet red peppers.

■ Though Hungary is known for its
superior paprika, this versatile
spice actually originated in Spain.

■ Shop supermarkets for the
milder versions of paprika; try
ethnic markets for the more pungent varieties.

■ Purchase paprika in small
amounts and use it quickly, as it
rapidly loses flavor and aroma. A
dull brown color indicates that the
paprika is past its prime.

GARDEN TO GLASS

There's a soft rumble in the kitchen this
morning. It's the murmur of glass jars
rocking in a boiling-water bath, a sound
that heralds pickling season. Don't let it
scare you. Pickling is an easily mastered
art once you know the rules. Think of
the water bath as a way of safely tucking your pickled produce in for a long
nap. Turn to "From Our Kitchen to
Yours," page 180, for canning tips.

DILLED GREEN BEANS

Prep: 20 minutes
Process: 10 minutes

2 pounds green beans
7 hot red peppers *
7 garlic cloves, quartered
3½ teaspoons mustard seeds
3½ teaspoons dill seeds
5 cups white vinegar (5% acidity)
5 cups water
½ cup pickling salt

• **Pack** beans into hot jars, trimming to
fit ½ inch from top. Add 1 pepper, 1 garlic clove (quartered), ½ teaspoon mustard seeds, and ½ teaspoon dill seeds to
each jar.
• **Bring** vinegar, 5 cups water, and pickling salt to a boil; pour into each jar, filling to ½ inch from top. Remove air
bubbles; wipe jar rims. Cover at once
with metal lids; screw on bands.
• **Process** in a boiling-water bath 10
minutes. **Yield:** 7 pints.

* Substitute 1¾ teaspoons dried
crushed red pepper for hot red peppers,
if desired. Add ¼ teaspoon per jar.

Mona Cazes
Baton Rouge, Louisiana

SQUASH PICKLES

Prep: 1 hour and 25 minutes
Process: 20 minutes

6 cups sliced yellow squash
6 cups sliced zucchini
2 cups sliced onion
1 tablespoon pickling salt
3 cups white vinegar (5% acidity)
4½ cups sugar
1 medium-size green bell pepper,
    diced
2 teaspoons celery seeds
2 teaspoons mustard seeds

• **Combine** first 3 ingredients in a large
bowl; sprinkle with pickling salt, and let
stand 1 hour. Drain; pack into hot jars.
• **Bring** vinegar and next 4 ingredients
to a boil in a large saucepan. Pour hot
mixture into jars, filling to within ½ inch
from top. Remove air bubbles; wipe jar
rims. Cover at once with metal lids;
screw on bands.
• **Process** in a boiling-water bath 20
minutes. **Yield:** 7 pints.

Patricia Ann Hill
Elizabethton, Tennessee

PEACH PICKLES

Prep: 50 minutes
Stand: 8 hours
Process: 20 minutes

4 cups water
19 to 20 small peaches (6 pounds)
1 quart white vinegar (5%
    acidity)
6 cups sugar
1 tablespoon whole cloves
4 (2½-inch) cinnamon
    sticks

• **Bring** 4 cups water to a boil in a Dutch
oven. Remove from heat; add peaches,
and let stand 4 to 6 minutes. Drain
peaches; cool and peel.
• **Bring** vinegar and sugar to a boil in
Dutch oven; reduce heat, and simmer 15
minutes.
• **Place** cloves on a 6-inch square of
cheesecloth; tie with string. Add spice
bag and cinnamon to vinegar mixture.

- **Add** half of peaches, and cook 10 minutes. Remove peaches with a slotted spoon. Repeat procedure with remaining peaches.
- **Bring** syrup to a boil, and remove from heat.
- **Add** peaches; cover and let stand 8 hours. Remove peaches with a slotted spoon, and pack into hot jars. Remove and discard spice bag and cinnamon sticks.
- **Bring** syrup to a boil; pour over peaches, filling to ½ inch from top. Remove air bubbles; wipe jar rims. Cover at once with metal lids; screw on bands.
- **Process** in a boiling-water bath 20 minutes. **Yield:** 3 quarts.

Mrs. Curtis Lowery
Greenville, Alabama

PICKLED CANTALOUPE

Prep: 20 minutes
Process: 10 minutes

3 lemons, thinly sliced
2 cups water
2½ cups white vinegar (5% acidity)
3 cups sugar
7 (2-inch) cinnamon sticks
24 whole cloves
2 large cantaloupes, cut into bite-size pieces

- **Bring** first 6 ingredients to a boil in a large saucepan; reduce heat, and simmer 5 to 7 minutes.
- **Pack** cantaloupe pieces into hot jars; add hot syrup, filling to within ½ inch from top. Remove air bubbles; wipe jar rims. Cover at once with metal lids; screw on bands.
- **Process** in a boiling-water bath 10 minutes. **Yield:** 6 pints.

Carolyne M. Carnevale
Ormond Beach, Florida

TWO WAYS

These dishes offer delicious options—with meat and without. Just add bacon to Creamy Tortellini for a flavor variation. Either way, it's a delicious meal when paired with a salad of avocados and onion. Or make dinner an Asian-style feast with Cashew Fried Rice, ramen noodle soup, and egg rolls. Follow the chicken option for an even more substantial supper.

CREAMY TORTELLINI

Menu suggestion: Avocado-purple onion salad with Italian dressing

Prep: 28 minutes
Cook: 5 minutes

2 garlic cloves, minced
2 teaspoons olive oil
1 teaspoon white vinegar
9 ounces refrigerated cheese-filled tortellini, cooked
⅓ cup grated Parmesan cheese
¼ cup whipping cream
1 tablespoon chopped fresh parsley
¼ teaspoon salt
¼ teaspoon pepper

- **Sauté** garlic in hot oil in a skillet until tender; remove from heat. Stir in vinegar; toss with tortellini.
- **Add** cheese and next 4 ingredients; toss well. **Yield:** 4 servings.

Creamy Tortellini Carbonara: Toss 5 bacon slices, cooked and crumbled, with tortellini mixture.

Tracy Porter
Morristown, New Jersey

CASHEW FRIED RICE

Menu suggestion: Ramen noodle soup and egg rolls

Prep: 35 minutes
Cook: 12 minutes

2 large eggs, lightly beaten
2 tablespoons vegetable oil, divided
1 small onion, chopped
1 garlic clove, minced
½ teaspoon grated fresh ginger
1 (10-ounce) package frozen sweet green peas, thawed
5 cups cooked rice
⅛ teaspoon turmeric
¼ cup lite soy sauce
1 teaspoon sugar
¼ teaspoon dried crushed red pepper
½ cup chopped roasted cashews
¼ cup chopped green onions

- **Stir-fry** eggs in 1 tablespoon hot oil in a skillet 3 minutes. Remove eggs from skillet.
- **Heat** remaining oil in skillet; add onion and next 5 ingredients; stir-fry 3 minutes.
- **Whisk** together soy sauce, sugar, and red pepper. Add to skillet; stir-fry 5 minutes. Stir in eggs and cashews; top with green onions. **Yield:** 4 servings.

Chicken-Cashew Fried Rice: Cut 4 skinned and boned chicken breast halves into bite-size pieces. After cooking eggs, stir-fry chicken in 1 additional tablespoon hot oil 8 minutes. Add onion and next 5 ingredients. Continue with recipe as directed.

Patsy Bell Hobson
Liberty, Missouri

Tomatoes From the Vine

Whether you slice them or dice them, peel them or not, there is nothing like the juicy taste of summer tomatoes. These recipes are a delicious way of savoring their goodness without heating up your kitchen. Choose fragrant tomatoes that are heavy for their size and that yield to gentle pressure. Allow them to ripen at room temperature.

TOMATO-GRUYÈRE-BASIL SALAD
(pictured on page 187)

Prep: 10 minutes
Chill: 30 minutes

2 tomatoes
8 ounces Gruyère or smoked
   Gouda cheese
⅓ cup balsamic vinegar
⅓ cup olive oil
¼ cup soy sauce
2 garlic cloves, pressed
2 tablespoons chopped fresh
   basil
Mixed salad greens
¼ teaspoon freshly ground
   pepper

• **Cut** tomatoes into wedges; cut cheese into ½-inch cubes.
• **Toss** together tomato, cheese, and next 5 ingredients in a bowl. Cover and chill 30 minutes. Serve over salad greens, and sprinkle with pepper. **Yield:** 3 to 4 servings.

Nancy D. Matulich
Metairie, Louisiana

ZIPPY 'MATERS

Cider vinegar accounts for most of the zip in these chunky marinated tomatoes. Serve them for a tangy variation whenever the menu might merit sliced fresh tomatoes.

Prep: 5 minutes
Chill: 2 hours

5 large tomatoes
¼ cup thinly sliced onion
½ cup cider vinegar
2 tablespoons sugar
1 tablespoon olive oil
½ teaspoon celery seeds
¼ teaspoon salt
¼ teaspoon pepper

• **Cut** tomatoes into chunks.
• **Stir** together tomato and remaining ingredients; cover and chill 2 hours. **Yield:** about 8 cups.

Amy Aaron
Columbia, South Carolina

CLASSIC TOMATO GAZPACHO

Gazpacho originated in Spain, where it is thickened with bread.

Prep: 25 minutes
Chill: 8 hours

1 tablespoon butter or margarine
3 tablespoons olive oil, divided
5 cups (¾-inch) French bread
   cubes
4 garlic cloves, minced and
   divided
¾ teaspoon salt, divided
¾ teaspoon freshly ground pepper,
   divided
1½ pounds tomatoes
1 cucumber
½ onion
½ green bell pepper
1 (46-ounce) can vegetable juice
⅓ cup chopped fresh basil
2 tablespoons red wine vinegar

• **Melt** butter in 1 tablespoon oil in a large skillet over low heat; add bread cubes and half of garlic, and cook, stirring occasionally, until bread cubes are toasted. Remove from heat; sprinkle with ¼ teaspoon salt and ¼ teaspoon pepper. Place half of bread cubes in a food processor bowl; reserve remaining bread cubes.
• **Peel** and coarsely chop 1½ pounds tomatoes and cucumber; coarsely chop onion and bell pepper.
• **Add** vegetables and remaining 2 garlic cloves to bread cubes in processor; pulse until diced. Transfer mixture to a large bowl.
• **Stir** in remaining 2 tablespoons oil, remaining ½ teaspoon salt, remaining ½ teaspoon pepper, vegetable juice, basil, and vinegar.
• **Cover** and chill at least 8 hours. Serve gazpacho with reserved bread cubes. **Yield:** 16 cups.

COLD ITALIAN TOMATOES

Prep: 2 minutes
Chill: 8 hours

2 tomatoes, sliced
2 tablespoons olive oil
¼ teaspoon hot sauce
¼ cup chopped fresh basil
2 tablespoons grated Parmesan
    cheese
1 teaspoon coarsely ground pepper

• **Arrange** tomato slices in a dish.
• **Whisk** together olive oil and hot sauce; drizzle over tomato. Sprinkle with basil, cheese, and pepper. Cover and chill 8 hours. **Yield:** 3 to 4 servings.

Beth Baylis
Hattiesburg, Mississippi

A DROP OF HEAT

The temperature's rising outside—and so will your internal thermostat after trying these dishes. While hot sauce is often used as a condiment in the South, it is used here as an ingredient because of its low-calorie, flavor-boosting abilities.

GRILLED TOMATOES

A quick sizzle on the grill heats these Italian-inspired tomatoes just enough to serve alongside a deserving grilled entrée.

Prep: 5 minutes
Grill: 4 minutes

4 large tomatoes, cut in half
    crosswise
2 tablespoons olive oil
2 garlic cloves, minced
¼ cup chopped fresh basil
½ teaspoon salt
½ teaspoon pepper

• **Brush** cut sides of tomato halves with oil, and sprinkle evenly with garlic and remaining ingredients.
• **Grill,** covered with grill lid, over medium-high heat (350° to 400°) about 2 minutes on each side. Serve immediately. **Yield:** 8 servings.

FLANK STEAK SANDWICHES WITH APPLE BARBECUE SAUCE

Prep: 1 minute
Chill: 8 hours
Grill: 14 minutes

1 (1½-pound) flank steak
Apple Barbecue Sauce
6 onion rolls, split
6 tomato slices
Leaf lettuce
Purple onion slices (optional)
Coarsely ground pepper

• **Place** steak in a shallow dish or heavy-duty zip-top plastic bag; pour ½ cup Apple Barbecue Sauce over steak. Cover or seal, and chill 8 hours.
• **Remove** steak from marinade, discarding marinade.
• **Grill** steak, covered with grill lid, over medium-high heat (350° to 400°) 7 minutes on each side or to desired degree of doneness.
• **Cut** steak diagonally across the grain into thin strips. Serve on rolls with tomato, lettuce, and, if desired, onion. Drizzle with remaining Apple Barbecue Sauce; sprinkle with pepper. **Yield:** 6 servings.

Apple Barbecue Sauce

Prep: 4 minutes
Cook: 25 minutes

½ cup apple jelly
1 (8-ounce) can no-salt-added
    tomato sauce
¼ cup white vinegar
2 tablespoons light brown
    sugar
2 tablespoons water
1 teaspoon hot sauce
¼ teaspoon salt

• **Bring** all ingredients to a boil in a small saucepan, stirring until smooth. Reduce heat, and simmer, stirring occasionally, 20 to 25 minutes. **Yield:** 1⅓ cups.

Ethel Williams
Scottsbluff, Nebraska

♥ Per serving: Calories 469
Fat 15.2g Cholesterol 61mg
Sodium 375mg

GARDEN OMELET

Hot sauce gives new flavor dimension to this omelet and reduces the need for extra salt.

Prep: 8 minutes
Cook: 16 minutes

1 small tomato, seeded and
      chopped
1 small zucchini, chopped
1 small yellow squash, chopped
¼ cup chopped onion
¼ cup chopped green bell
      pepper
¼ cup sliced fresh mushrooms
Vegetable cooking spray
1 cup egg substitute
1 to 2 teaspoons hot sauce
¼ teaspoon salt
2 ounces reduced-fat sharp
      Cheddar cheese, shredded
1 tablespoon chopped fresh
      parsley

• **Sauté** first 6 ingredients in a 10-inch nonstick skillet coated with cooking spray over medium-high heat 9 minutes or until liquid evaporates; remove from skillet, and set aside. Wipe skillet clean.
• **Whisk** together egg substitute, hot sauce, and salt; pour into skillet coated with cooking spray. As mixture starts to cook, gently lift edges with a spatula, and tilt pan so uncooked portion flows underneath.
• **Spoon** vegetables onto egg; sprinkle with cheese. Fold in half, and transfer to a serving plate; sprinkle with parsley. **Yield:** 2 servings.

♥ Per serving: Calories 191
Fat 5.9g Cholesterol 18mg
Sodium 707mg

OVEN-FRIED CATFISH

Prep: 5 minutes
Chill: 2 hours
Bake: 14 minutes

6 (4-ounce) catfish fillets
¾ teaspoon salt
1 (2-ounce) bottle hot sauce
1 to 1½ cups yellow cornmeal
Vegetable cooking spray
Tartar Sauce

• **Sprinkle** fish with salt; place in a heavy-duty zip-top plastic bag. Pour in hot sauce; seal and chill 2 hours, turning occasionally.
• **Remove** fish from marinade; dredge in cornmeal. Place fish on a baking sheet coated with cooking spray.
• **Bake** at 425° for 10 minutes or until fish flakes with a fork. Broil 3 inches from heat (with electric oven door partially open) 4 minutes or until lightly browned. Serve with Tartar Sauce. **Yield:** 6 servings.

♥ Per serving: Calories 264
Fat 6g Cholesterol 66mg
Sodium 425mg

Tartar Sauce

Prep: 5 minutes
Chill: 2 hours

1 cup reduced-fat mayonnaise
1 tablespoon dill pickle relish
1 tablespoon chopped
      pimiento-stuffed olives
1 tablespoon capers
1 tablespoon grated shallots
1 tablespoon lemon juice
⅛ to ¼ teaspoon hot sauce

• **Stir** together all ingredients. Cover and chill 2 hours. **Yield:** 1¼ cups.

♥ Per tablespoon: Calories 36
Fat 3.7g Cholesterol 5mg
Sodium 90mg

BLACK-EYED PEA SALAD

Prep: 10 minutes
Chill: 2 hours

3 tablespoons red wine vinegar
2 tablespoons vegetable oil
2 tablespoons hot sauce
2 tablespoons chopped fresh
      cilantro
1 garlic clove, pressed
½ teaspoon salt
2 (15.5-ounce) cans black-eyed
      peas, rinsed and drained
1 medium-size purple onion,
      diced
1 medium tomato, seeded and
      diced
1 green bell pepper, diced
Curly leaf lettuce

• **Whisk** first 6 ingredients in a large bowl; add black-eyed peas and next 3 ingredients, tossing to coat. Cover and chill at least 2 hours. Serve on a lettuce-lined platter. **Yield:** 6 cups.

♥ Per cup: Calories 163
Fat 5.3g Cholesterol 0mg
Sodium 617mg

HOT SAUCE TIPS

There is an abundance of hot sauces on grocery store shelves. Here are some shopping tips.

■ Check sodium content if you are on a restricted diet. Sodium content ranges from 30 to 240 milligrams per teaspoon.

■ Heat intensities vary. Hot sauces are made from different peppers. The cayenne is hotter than the jalapeño; the habanero is hotter than the cayenne.

■ For testing purposes only, we used Tabasco hot sauce in these recipes.

Summer's Outdoor Best

Savor the refreshing flavors in this no-fuss menu. Welcome guests with a Lemon-Mint Spritzer while Garlic-Herb Steaks sizzle on the grill. Tabbouleh, a colorful bulgur wheat salad, can be prepared ahead.

Summer Get-Together
Serves Four

Garlic-Herb Steaks

Tabbouleh

Tomato Slices

Lemon-Mint Spritzer

Fudge Cake

GARLIC-HERB STEAKS
(pictured on page 150)

Find minced garlic in a jar in the produce area of your grocery store. To keep herbs fresh, swish the sprigs in cool water; wrap stems in a damp paper towel, and seal in a zip-top bag.

Prep: 10 minutes
Chill: 1 hour
Grill: 20 minutes

4 (4-ounce) beef tenderloin
    steaks
¼ teaspoon salt
¼ teaspoon freshly ground
    pepper
¼ cup minced garlic
1 tablespoon minced fresh
    rosemary

• **Sprinkle** steaks with salt and pepper; coat with minced garlic and rosemary. Cover and chill 1 hour.
• **Prepare** fire by piling charcoal or lava rocks on 1 side of grill, leaving other side empty; place rack on grill.
• **Arrange** steaks over empty side, and grill, covered with grill lid, over high heat (400° to 500°) 10 minutes on each side or until desired degree of doneness. **Yield:** 4 servings.

TABBOULEH
(pictured on page 150)

Prep: 40 minutes

2 cups bulgur wheat, uncooked
1 cup hot water
2 cups loosely packed fresh parsley
2 large tomatoes, diced
4 green onions, diced
2 garlic cloves, minced
¼ cup chopped fresh mint
½ cup lemon juice
2 tablespoons olive oil
1 teaspoon salt
¾ teaspoon pepper
Lettuce leaves

• **Stir** together bulgur and 1 cup hot water; let stand 30 minutes.
• **Drain** bulgur well; place in a bowl. Stir in parsley and next 8 ingredients. Cover; chill, if desired. Serve over lettuce leaves. **Yield:** 6 servings.

LEMON-MINT SPRITZER

Prep: 50 minutes

1 (12-ounce) can frozen pink
    lemonade concentrate,
    undiluted
¼ cup sugar
6 fresh mint sprigs, divided
1 lemon
1 (750-milliliter) bottle
    lemon-flavored sparkling
    mineral water
¾ cup vodka (optional)

• **Bring** concentrate, sugar, and 4 mint sprigs to a boil, stirring until sugar dissolves; boil 1 minute. Remove from heat; cool. Discard mint sprigs from syrup. Slice lemon; cut slices in half.
• **Place** remaining 2 mint sprigs and lemon slices in a pitcher; add mineral water. Add lemonade syrup and, if desired, vodka; stir. Serve over crushed ice. **Yield:** about 4½ cups.

Note: For testing purposes only, we used Perrier water.

Allison Mendosa
Houston, Texas

FUDGE CAKE
(pictured on page 150)

Prep: 20 minutes
Bake: 20 minutes

½ cup butter or margarine,
   softened
1 cup sugar
1 large egg
1 cup all-purpose flour
1 teaspoon baking powder
¼ teaspoon salt
½ cup cocoa
¾ cup milk
1 cup mint chocolate morsels
1 teaspoon vanilla extract
Mint Chocolate Frosting

• **Beat** butter at medium speed with an electric mixer until creamy. Add sugar; beat until fluffy. Add egg, beating well.
• **Combine** flour and next 3 ingredients; add to butter mixture alternately with milk, beginning and ending with flour mixture. Stir in morsels and vanilla. Pour into a greased and floured 8-inch square pan.
• **Bake** at 350° for 20 minutes or until a wooden pick inserted in center comes out clean. Cool in pan on a wire rack 10 minutes. Invert onto wire rack; cool. Spread with Mint Chocolate Frosting. **Yield:** 6 to 8 servings.

Mint Chocolate Frosting

Prep: 10 minutes

¾ cup mint chocolate morsels
½ cup butter or margarine,
   softened
2 cups powdered sugar
⅓ cup cocoa
¼ cup half-and-half
¼ teaspoon peppermint extract

• **Microwave** morsels in a 1-cup glass measuring cup at HIGH 1 minute or until melted, stirring twice.
• **Beat** butter and melted morsels at medium speed with an electric mixer until creamy.
• **Add** powdered sugar and cocoa; beat until blended. Add half-and-half and peppermint extract; beat until blended. **Yield:** 2 cups.

PERFECTLY SCALLOPED

Go for high flavor with scallops. Harvest them from the Gulf Coast waters of Florida or your nearest seafood market. The delicate taste and texture of small bay scallops stand up well to a variety of sauces; large sea scallops make easy kabobs. Turn to "From Our Kitchen to Yours" on page 180 for more tips on scallops.

MAPLE SCALLOPS

Prep: 5 minutes
Cook: 14 minutes

4 bacon slices, chopped
2 garlic cloves, minced
1 tablespoon all-purpose
   flour
¾ cup half-and-half
1 pound bay scallops, drained
¼ teaspoon salt
2 tablespoons chopped fresh
   parsley
¾ cup (3 ounces) shredded
   white Cheddar cheese,
   divided
2 tablespoons maple syrup
Garnish: fresh parsley sprigs

• **Cook** bacon in a nonstick skillet until crisp. Remove from skillet, reserving 1 tablespoon drippings. Add garlic, and sauté until tender.
• **Whisk** in flour; cook, whisking constantly, until lightly browned. Whisk in half-and-half; cook, whisking constantly, until thickened and bubbly.
• **Add** scallops; cook, stirring often, 5 minutes or until scallops are opaque. Remove from heat; stir in salt, parsley, ½ cup cheese, and maple syrup.
• **Spoon** mixture into 4 (6-ounce) custard cups; top with remaining ¼ cup cheese and bacon. Broil 6 inches from heat

(with electric oven door partially open) 1 minute or until cheese melts. Garnish with parsley, if desired. **Yield:** 4 main-dish servings or 6 appetizer servings.

SCALLOPS AND ANGEL HAIR PASTA

Prep: 20 minutes
Cook: 10 minutes

½ cup hot water
¼ cup chopped dried tomatoes
1 small onion, chopped
2 garlic cloves, minced
2 tablespoons olive oil
1 small green bell pepper, chopped
1 medium-size red bell pepper,
   chopped
1 pound bay scallops, drained
1 cup half-and-half
¼ teaspoon salt
¼ teaspoon dried crushed red
   pepper (optional)
8 ounces angel hair pasta, cooked
½ cup grated Parmesan cheese
   (optional)

• **Pour** ½ cup hot water over tomatoes. Let stand 10 minutes or until softened. Drain and set aside.
• **Sauté** onion and garlic in hot oil in a large skillet over medium heat until

tender. Add tomatoes and bell peppers; sauté 3 to 4 more minutes or until tender. Reduce heat to low; stir in scallops, half-and-half, salt, and, if desired, crushed red pepper. Cook, stirring often, 2 to 3 minutes or until scallops are opaque.

• **Toss** together pasta and scallop mixture. Sprinkle with Parmesan cheese, if desired. **Yield:** 4 servings.

Georgene Falcon
Alexandria, Virginia

GINGER SCALLOPS

Prep: 20 minutes
Cook: 15 minutes

2 pounds sea scallops, cut in half
¼ teaspoon salt
¼ teaspoon freshly ground pepper
2 tablespoons butter or margarine
4 green onions, chopped
1 tablespoon grated fresh ginger
½ cup chicken broth
½ cup dry white wine
1 teaspoon fresh lime juice
¾ cup whipping cream
2 medium-size tomatoes, peeled, seeded, and chopped
Hot cooked pasta shells

• **Rinse** scallops, and pat dry; sprinkle with salt and pepper.
• **Melt** butter in a large skillet over medium-high heat. Add green onions; sauté until tender.
• **Stir** in ginger and next 3 ingredients. Reduce heat to medium; add scallops. Cook, stirring often, 3 minutes or until scallops are opaque. Remove scallops; keep warm.
• **Bring** broth mixture to a boil; boil 10 minutes or until reduced by half. Stir in whipping cream; cook, stirring often, until thickened. Stir in tomato and scallops. Serve over pasta. **Yield:** 4 servings.

Caroline Kennedy
Lighthouse Point, Florida

PANNING FOR GOLD

If you are a typical seafood fan, you love scallops but have no idea how they are harvested. Take a trip to the little beach town of Steinhatchee, Florida, on the Gulf of Mexico, and you'll find out. It is one of the few places that permits recreational scalloping. (The season runs from July 1 to September 10.) Locals will assure you that anybody can do it—no special skills needed. The only requirement is a recreational saltwater fishing license from the state and a willingness to get wet.

If you envision ambling along water's edge and dipping them out by the handfuls, think again. At Hagen's Cove, a Steinhatchee favorite for wading, you'll learn that the proper way of gathering the beautiful shelled creatures is to tie a rope around your waist and around an inner tube on which floats a bucket. This keeps the bucket steady and your hands free to gather scallops as you walk through the water and pick your way through seaweed. You'll be just steps away from a luscious dinner. Panning for gold couldn't be more exciting.

But "panning" for scallops isn't always the best way to get a large catch. The water temperature and currents determine how far the scallops are found from shore. They could be just off the beach in four feet of water, or they could be offshore in twelve.

In this small Florida town, your best bet is to reserve a boat for a half-day run. For about $125 you'll have an experienced scalloper to instruct you in the intricacies of snorkeling and gathering. You'll learn how to don the gear—a snorkel, mask, and a mesh bag. Then you'll learn to jump off the back of the boat and float into a world of scallops.

Once in the water, you'll see scallops everywhere—nestled on the grassy bottom and moving jerkily through the water—brushing by you, with their seven sets of fluorescent blue-green eyes glowing and with their shells rapidly opening and closing. Usually you'll be able to pick them up easily and in no time fill your bag with the daily limit of two gallons.

It's little wonder the delicate mollusks cost so much, because shucking scallops is a tedious task that demands great patience. First, you should ice them so that they will open a bit. Then pry open the shells one by one to remove the white muscle inside with a grapefruit spoon. A bag of scallops yields a small bowl of shucked meat. But if you catch them yourself, you'll probably think they are the best scallops that anyone has ever eaten. Try the recipes on these pages for some of our favorite ways to serve these seafood gems.

Speedy Seafood

Joyce Taylor of the North Carolina State University Seafood Laboratory shares some recipes and tips for grilling seafood. If there's no time for marinating, Joyce suggests keeping it simple and quick. Brush a fillet with melted margarine, sprinkle it with salt and pepper, and place it on the grill for a few minutes.

MAHI-MAHI WITH LEMON MAYONNAISE

Prep: 10 minutes
Grill: 8 minutes

4 mahi-mahi fillets (1½ pounds) *
1 tablespoon vegetable oil
¼ teaspoon salt
¼ teaspoon pepper
Lemon Mayonnaise

• **Brush** fillets with oil; sprinkle with salt and pepper. Place in a lightly greased grill basket.
• **Grill,** covered with grill lid, over medium heat (300° to 350°) 4 minutes on each side or until fish flakes with a fork. Serve with Lemon Mayonnaise. **Yield:** 4 servings.

* Substitute 1½ pounds amberjack fillets for mahi-mahi, if desired.

Lemon Mayonnaise

Prep: 5 minutes

½ cup mayonnaise
1½ teaspoons grated lemon
      rind
1 tablespoon fresh lemon juice
¼ teaspoon salt
⅛ teaspoon ground red pepper

• **Stir** together all ingredients; cover and chill. **Yield:** ½ cup.

Joyce Taylor
The North Carolina State University
Seafood Laboratory

GRILLED GARLIC SHRIMP

Prep: 8 minutes
Chill: 20 minutes
Grill: 10 minutes

1 pound unpeeled, large fresh
      shrimp
¾ cup butter or margarine
10 garlic cloves, minced
2 tablespoons fresh lemon
      juice
1 teaspoon chopped fresh dill or
      ½ teaspoon dried dillweed
¼ teaspoon sugar
¼ teaspoon ground red pepper

• **Peel** shrimp; devein, if desired.
• **Melt** butter in a heavy saucepan over medium heat; add garlic, and sauté 1 minute. Stir in lemon juice and next 3 ingredients; bring to a boil. Reduce heat, and simmer 1 minute; remove from heat. Cool.
• **Add** shrimp to garlic mixture, stirring gently; chill 20 minutes.
• **Thread** shrimp onto skewers.
• **Grill,** covered with grill lid, over medium heat (300° to 350°) 5 minutes on each side or just until shrimp turn pink. **Yield:** 3 servings.

Joyce Taylor
The North Carolina State University
Seafood Laboratory

GRILLED HERBED GROUPER

Prep: 10 minutes
Grill: 16 minutes

1 (1½-pound) grouper fillet
2 teaspoons olive oil
½ teaspoon salt
¼ teaspoon pepper
1 cup fine, dry breadcrumbs
⅓ cup minced fresh or
      2 tablespoons dried
      parsley flakes
1 tablespoon minced fresh or
      1 teaspoon dried basil
1 tablespoon minced fresh or
      1 teaspoon dried thyme
**Garnishes: fresh basil sprigs, fresh
      thyme sprigs, lemon slices**

• **Brush** fillet with oil; sprinkle with salt and pepper.
• **Stir** together breadcrumbs and next 3 ingredients, and press onto all sides of fillet. Place fillet in a lightly greased grill basket.
• **Grill,** covered with grill lid, over medium heat (300° to 350°) 7 to 8 minutes on each side or until fish flakes with a fork. Garnish, if desired. **Yield:** 3 to 4 servings.

Joyce Taylor
The North Carolina State University
Seafood Laboratory

JOYCE'S SEAFOOD POINTERS

■ A hinged metal grill or fish basket makes cooking all seafood easier. Purchase them at discount or hardware stores.

■ Use a covered grill, if possible, for faster cooking and moist, tender seafood.

■ Never baste cooked fish or shellfish with marinade that has been used on raw seafood. You can contaminate the food with harmful bacteria.

■ Toss herbs such as bay leaves, basil, thyme, tarragon, or rosemary on hot coals. The herb will impart its flavor to the fish during grilling.

■ Most fish recipes that call for broiling or baking can also be grilled.

$\mathcal{S}$WEET SURRENDER

Bite-size desserts are always a treat, but particularly at parties where juggling a fork, a plate, and a cup may leave you crying, so to speak, over spilled punch. You'll find these festive nibblers ideal for brunches, showers, wedding receptions—any place where the emphasis is more on mingle than unmanageable.

BLACKBERRY SUPREMES

Prep: 20 minutes
Bake: 7 minutes

1 (15-ounce) package refrigerated piecrusts
⅓ cup water
½ cup sugar
2 tablespoons cornstarch
2 tablespoons butter or margarine
1 pint fresh blackberries
1 (3-ounce) package cream cheese, softened
2 tablespoons butter or margarine, softened
1 teaspoon vanilla extract
1 cup sifted powdered sugar
Powdered sugar (optional)

• **Unfold** piecrusts; press out fold lines with a rolling pin on a lightly floured surface. Cut piecrusts with a 2½-inch star-shaped cutter, and fit into lightly greased miniature muffin pans.
• **Bake** at 350° for 7 minutes or until golden. Remove from pans, and cool on wire racks.
• **Bring** ⅓ cup water and next 4 ingredients to a boil in a heavy saucepan over medium heat. Boil, stirring constantly, 1 minute; remove from heat.
• **Stir** together cream cheese and next 3 ingredients.
• **Spoon** blackberry mixture into tart shells; pipe or dollop with cream cheese mixture. Sprinkle with additional powdered sugar, if desired. **Yield:** 20 tarts.

Donna Donnell
Houston, Texas

TINY CARAMEL TARTS

Prep: 5 minutes
Cook: 25 minutes
Chill: 2 hours

2 cups sugar, divided
½ cup butter or margarine
6 tablespoons all-purpose flour
4 egg yolks
2 cups milk
Cream Cheese Pastry Mini Shells
  (see recipe on next page)
Whipped cream (optional)

• **Sprinkle** 1 cup sugar in a heavy skillet, and cook over medium heat, stirring constantly, until sugar melts and turns a light golden color. Stir in butter.
• **Whisk** together remaining 1 cup sugar, flour, egg yolks, and milk in a heavy saucepan; bring just to a simmer over low heat, whisking constantly.
• **Add** sugar mixture to flour mixture immediately, and cook, whisking constantly, until thickened. Cover; chill 2 hours. Spoon caramel into Cream Cheese Pastry Mini Shells; top with whipped cream, if desired. **Yield:** 6 dozen.

PASTEL SUGAR COOKIES

If time's short, substitute refrigerated sugar cookie dough.

Prep: 25 minutes
Chill: 1 hour
Bake: 6 to 8 minutes per batch

½ cup butter, softened
½ cup margarine, softened
1 cup sugar
1 large egg
1 teaspoon vanilla extract
3 cups all-purpose flour
1 teaspoon baking powder
⅛ teaspoon salt
Colored Sugar or sugar sprinkles

• **Beat** butter and margarine at medium speed with an electric mixer until creamy; gradually add 1 cup sugar, beating well.
• **Add** egg and vanilla, beating well.
• **Combine** flour, baking powder, and salt; gradually add to butter mixture, beating until blended. Cover and chill at least 1 hour or until dough is firm enough to handle.
• **Divide** dough in half; roll each portion to ⅛-inch thickness on a lightly floured surface. Cut dough into assorted shapes with floured cookie cutters; place on lightly greased baking sheets. Sprinkle with Colored Sugar.
• **Bake** at 350° for 6 to 8 minutes or until lightly browned. Cool on pans 1 minute; remove to wire racks to cool. **Yield:** about 6 dozen.

Colored Sugar

1 cup sugar
5 drops of desired liquid food coloring

• **Stir** together sugar and food coloring until blended; let dry, making sure there are no lumps. Store in an airtight container. **Yield:** 1 cup.

CREAM CHEESE PASTRY MINI SHELLS

Fill these delicate shells with any sweet custard.

Prep: 20 minutes
Bake: 10 to 12 minutes per batch

3½ cups all-purpose flour
1 (8-ounce) package cream cheese, softened
1¼ cups butter or margarine, softened

• **Stir** together all ingredients until blended.
• **Shape** dough into 72 (¾-inch) balls. Press dough balls into miniature muffin pans, forming pastry shells.
• **Bake** at 400° for 10 to 12 minutes. Remove from pans, and cool on wire racks. **Yield:** 6 dozen.

Note: For convenience, make baked pastry shells ahead and freeze in an airtight container. Thaw at room temperature.

Telia Johnson
Birmingham, Alabama

FROM OUR KITCHEN TO YOURS

DON'T GET BURNED AT THE GRILL

Keep kabob pieces from falling into the grill by resting them on a foil pan. Punch holes in the pan, and close the grill lid so that smoky goodness can surround the food. Turn the kabobs once during cooking.

A little wood can go a long way. After you soak a handful of hickory or mesquite chips to flavor your grilled food, put the wet wood on a foil pan. Rest the pan of wood chips on the hot coals.

You'll get a steady supply of smoke using much less wood. (Wood chips tossed directly on hot coals cause flames to flare and can impart a burned taste to food.)

SAFE MAYONNAISE

Many of you want to make your own mayonnaise but are concerned about the use of raw eggs. Here's our standard mayonnaise recipe using egg substitute. It's so good you probably won't taste the difference. It works great in a food processor as well as a blender and takes just 5 minutes to make.

HOMEMADE MAYONNAISE

2½ tablespoons white wine vinegar
¼ cup egg substitute
1½ tablespoons coarse-grained mustard
½ to ¾ teaspoon salt
½ teaspoon pepper
⅔ cup vegetable oil

• **Process** first 5 ingredients in a blender until smooth, stopping to scrape down sides. With blender running, add oil in a slow, steady stream, blending until thickened. **Yield:** 1 cup.

A PECK OF PICKLING TIPS

When you read the recipes on pages 170 and 171, heed these hints.

A boiling-water bath canner has a tight-fitting lid and a metal rack to hold the jars. If you don't have a canner, you can use any big metal container deep and large enough to submerge the jars. Remember, the container needs a tight-fitting cover and a rack to keep the jars off the bottom of the kettle.

Use only standard canning jars and lids for pickling; leftover food jars aren't safe to use. And make sure the lids have sealed properly before storing pickled food. When jars are sealed, the center of the lids should have a downward curve that you can feel.

Put labels and dates on your colorful jars and store them in a cool, dry place.

TWICE THE SPICE ISN'T NICE

When just a sprinkle is all you need, spice overload can mean disaster. To avoid an accidental downpour from that large, spoon-size closure on herb and spice containers, place a small piece of tape over the large opening. You'll still have easy access to the opening, but you won't sprinkle from it by mistake.

SUCCULENT SCALLOPS

The following tips will help you celebrate the delicate flavor of the recipes on pages 176-177.

■ Scallops can range in color from off-white to pale pink. Don't buy those that appear too white—they have excess water added and almost no flavor. Select scallops that smell sweet and have a moist sheen. Buy them from a seafood market that gets fresh shipments regularly. Most scallops come to the market frozen, so try not to refreeze them; they're especially susceptible to freezer burn.

■ Small bay scallops are sweeter and have a richer flavor than larger sea scallops. One pound of sea scallops contains about 30 pieces, while a pound of bay scallops has about 100 pieces.

■ Use small bay scallops in pasta sauces, risotto, or wherever flavor is more important than size. For grilling or broiling, sea scallops are easier to handle.

■ Pat scallops dry before you sauté them so they won't "water out" in the recipe.

AUGUST

Celebrated chef Emeril Lagasse often inspires the loyal viewers of his cooking show, and in "Emeril's Inspirations" we discover what inspires him: his friends. They share with us their stories and the recipes they serve him when he visits—Lemony Pecan-Crusted Snapper With Crabmeat Relish, Crickhollow Roast Pork, and Marcelle's Bouillabaisse. After a taste, you might also develop a passion for Louisiana cooking.

"Peach Appeal" helps you take advantage of the last of the juicy, right-off-the-tree summer peaches with Cream of Peach Soup and Easy Peach Cobbler. If you're looking for ways to serve other late-summer produce, turn to "Quick & Easy: Summer Vegetables" for old-fashioned recipes like Corn-and-Okra Medley and Squash Fritters.

A WELL-SEASONED SUPPER

Enjoy the brilliant goodness of herbs with this harvest of innovative, make-ahead recipes. They're served chilled—perfect for beating the heat and the clock. And for a real treat, add one more "ingredient" to the mix—the great outdoors.

GARDEN PARTY
Serves Eight

Herbed Cheesecakes
Dilled Summer Soup
Shrimp-and-Orzo Salad
Spicy Rosemary Aspic
Lemon Pound Cake With Mint Berries and Cream

HERBED CHEESECAKES

Prep: 25 minutes
Bake: 30 minutes
Chill: 8 hours

1 cup round buttery cracker crumbs
3 tablespoons butter or margarine, melted
2 (8-ounce) packages cream cheese, softened
1 (16-ounce) container sour cream, divided
2 (3-ounce) packages goat cheese
3 large eggs
¼ cup chopped fresh chives
2 tablespoons minced fresh thyme
Fresh spinach leaves
Garnish: fresh thyme sprigs

• **Stir** together cracker crumbs and butter; press evenly into bottoms of 4 (4-inch) springform pans.
• **Beat** cream cheese, 1 cup sour cream, and goat cheese at medium speed with an electric mixer until smooth. Add eggs, 1 at a time, beating until blended. Stir in chives and minced thyme, and pour into pans.
• **Bake** at 325° for 30 minutes or until almost set. Cool on a wire rack. Cover and chill 8 hours, or freeze up to 1 month.
• **Spread** tops evenly with remaining sour cream; remove from pans, and cut into wedges. Serve wedges on spinach leaves with assorted crackers. Garnish, if desired. **Yield:** 8 servings.

Note: Cheesecake may be baked in 1 (8-inch) springform pan; bake at 325° for 40 minutes.

DILLED SUMMER SOUP
(pictured on page 189)

Prep: 20 minutes
Cook: 15 minutes
Chill: 3 hours

2 small leeks, sliced
2 tablespoons vegetable oil
1½ pounds zucchini or yellow squash, sliced
3 cups chicken broth
1 cup half-and-half
1 (8-ounce) container sour cream
½ teaspoon salt
⅓ cup chopped fresh dill
Garnish: fresh dill sprigs

• **Sauté** leeks in hot oil in a Dutch oven until tender. Add zucchini and broth. Bring to a boil; cover, reduce heat, and simmer 8 to 10 minutes or until zucchini is tender. Remove from heat, and cool slightly.
• **Process** zucchini mixture in batches in a blender until smooth, stopping to scrape down sides.
• **Stir** in half-and-half and next 3 ingredients. Chill at least 3 hours. Garnish, if desired. **Yield:** 9 cups.

SHRIMP-AND-ORZO SALAD
(pictured on page 188)

Prep: 45 minutes
Cook: 15 minutes

2 bunches fresh asparagus
6 cups water
1½ pounds unpeeled, medium-size fresh shrimp
16 ounces orzo, cooked
1 (14-ounce) can artichoke hearts, drained and halved
1 small red bell pepper, coarsely chopped
½ cup shredded fresh basil
2 tablespoons chopped fresh oregano
Fresh Herb Vinaigrette
6 cups gourmet salad greens
Shaved Parmesan cheese

• **Snap** off tough ends of asparagus; arrange asparagus in a steamer basket over boiling water. Cover and steam 8 minutes or until crisp-tender. Plunge asparagus into ice water to stop the cooking process; drain and chill.

• **Bring** 6 cups water to a boil in a saucepan; add shrimp, and cook 3 to 5 minutes or just until shrimp turn pink. Drain and rinse with cold water. Peel shrimp; devein, if desired.

• **Combine** shrimp, orzo, artichokes, and next 3 ingredients in a large bowl; add Fresh Herb Vinaigrette, tossing well. Serve over salad greens with asparagus; top with Parmesan cheese. **Yield:** 8 servings.

Fresh Herb Vinaigrette

Prep: 15 minutes

½ cup olive oil
½ cup white wine vinegar
½ cup chopped fresh basil
3 tablespoons chopped fresh oregano
⅓ cup sliced green onions
2 garlic cloves, minced
½ teaspoon seasoning salt
½ teaspoon dried crushed red pepper
½ teaspoon sugar

• **Whisk** together all ingredients in a bowl. **Yield:** 1⅓ cups.

SPICY ROSEMARY ASPIC
(pictured on page 188)

Prep: 15 minutes
Chill: 4 hours and 45 minutes

1 cup chicken broth
2 envelopes unflavored gelatin
3 cups spicy vegetable juice
1 tablespoon lemon juice
1½ tablespoons minced fresh rosemary

• **Cook** broth and gelatin in a small saucepan over medium heat 5 minutes, stirring until gelatin dissolves.

• **Stir** in vegetable juice and lemon juice, and chill about 45 minutes or to consistency of unbeaten egg whites. Stir in rosemary. Pour mixture into 4 (1-cup)

Herbs are remarkable garden treasures. Lush, fragrant, healthful, packed with flavor— their natural beauty and culinary charisma have been adored throughout the ages, but never more so than at their peak of freshness. And with these recipes, summer never looked so good. For even more herb appeal, check out "From Our Kitchen to Yours" on page 208.

---

molds. Chill at least 4 hours. Unmold and cut each in half. **Yield:** 8 servings.

Note: Substitute 1 (4-cup) mold, if desired. Cut into eighths. Aspic has a soft texture, so do not substitute a square dish and cut into squares.

LEMON POUND CAKE WITH MINT BERRIES AND CREAM
(pictured on page 189)

Prep: 40 minutes
Bake: 1 hour

¼ cup sugar
¼ cup loosely packed mint leaves
¾ cup butter, softened
3 cups powdered sugar, divided
3 large eggs
1½ cups all-purpose flour
2½ cups whipping cream, divided
2 teaspoons grated lemon rind
2 tablespoons fresh lemon juice
1 (12-ounce) jar lemon curd
1 quart fresh strawberries, sliced
Garnish: fresh mint sprigs

• **Process** sugar and mint leaves in a food processor until blended.

• **Beat** softened butter at medium speed with an electric mixer 2 minutes or until creamy; gradually add 1½ tablespoons mint mixture and 2½ cups powdered sugar, beating 5 to 7 minutes.

• **Add** eggs, 1 at a time, beating just until yellow disappears. Add flour alternately with ½ cup whipping cream, beginning and ending with flour. Beat at low speed just until blended after each addition.

• **Stir** in lemon rind and lemon juice. Pour batter into an 8½- x 4½-inch greased and floured loafpan.

• **Bake** at 350° for 1 hour or until a wooden pick inserted in center comes out clean. Cool in pan on a wire rack 10 minutes. Remove pound cake from pan, and cool on wire rack.

• **Beat** remaining 2 cups whipping cream, ¼ cup powdered sugar, and 1 tablespoon mint mixture at medium speed with electric mixer until stiff peaks form. Fold in lemon curd.

• **Stir** together remaining mint mixture, remaining ¼ cup powdered sugar, and strawberries.

• **Serve** pound cake with lemon cream and strawberries. Garnish, if desired. **Yield:** 8 servings.

LOWCOUNTRY CLASSIC

Pilau (pih-LOW) is a traditional dish dear to the hearts of rice-loving coastal South Carolinians. Long-grain rice cooked with meat or seafood and other ingredients forms a one-pot meal or side dish. Red rice is one variation, and the soupy staple Chicken Bog is a close cousin. But Lowcountry cooks prefer their rice fluffy, with the grains separate. Try some of these ideas for a taste of the coast.

SHRIMP PILAU

Prep: 35 minutes
Cook: 35 minutes

1½ pounds unpeeled, medium-size fresh shrimp
½ cup chopped cooked ham
2 tablespoons vegetable oil
2 garlic cloves, minced
1 large green bell pepper, diced
1 medium onion, diced
1 (14½-ounce) can diced tomatoes
2 cups chicken broth
1 tablespoon Creole seasoning
1¾ cups uncooked long-grain rice

• **Peel** shrimp; devein, if desired.
• **Sauté** ham in hot oil in a Dutch oven over medium-high heat 2 minutes or until lightly browned.
• **Add** garlic, green pepper, and onion; sauté 3 minutes.
• **Stir** in tomatoes, broth, and Creole seasoning; cook 5 minutes.
• **Stir** in rice; cover, reduce heat, and simmer 20 minutes.
• **Arrange** shrimp evenly over rice in Dutch oven; cover and cook 5 minutes. Remove from heat, and let stand 5 minutes. **Yield:** 6 servings.

CHICKEN PILAU

Myrtle Gibson boosts the flavor of this mild dish by sprinkling plenty of chopped pepper on top.

Prep: 2 hours and 15 minutes
Cook: 20 minutes

1 (2½-pound) whole chicken
2 celery ribs, cut in half
2 carrots
1 medium onion
1½ quarts water
1 teaspoon salt
½ teaspoon garlic salt
½ teaspoon pepper
1 cup uncooked long-grain rice

• **Bring** first 8 ingredients to a boil in a Dutch oven. Reduce heat, and simmer 1 hour or until chicken is done. Remove from heat; let stand in broth 1 hour.
• **Remove** chicken, and cool slightly; reserve 1⅔ cups broth. Skin and bone chicken, and cut into bite-size pieces.
• **Bring** chicken, reserved broth, and rice to a boil in a large saucepan. Cover, reduce heat, and cook 20 minutes or until broth is absorbed and rice is tender. Remove from heat; let stand 5 minutes. Fluff with a fork. **Yield:** 4 servings.
Myrtle Gibson
Sumter, South Carolina

SAUSAGE PILAU

Prep: 15 minutes
Cook: 30 minutes

2 bacon slices, cut into ½-inch pieces
½ pound smoked pork sausage links, cut into ¼-inch slices
½ medium onion, chopped
¼ large green bell pepper, chopped
2 cups water
1 cup uncooked long-grain rice
1 teaspoon salt
¼ teaspoon paprika

• **Cook** bacon pieces in a Dutch oven over medium-high heat 4 minutes or until almost crisp.

• **Add** sausage, and cook 4 minutes or until browned; remove bacon and sausage, reserving 1 tablespoon drippings in pan.
• **Sauté** onion and bell pepper in hot drippings 2 minutes or until tender.
• **Add** bacon, sausage, 2 cups water, and next 3 ingredients; bring to a boil. Cover, reduce heat, and cook 20 minutes or until water is absorbed and rice is tender. Remove from heat, and let stand 5 minutes. **Yield:** 4 servings.
Michele Fipps
Johns Island, South Carolina

OKRA PILAU

Prep: 15 minutes
Cook: 30 minutes

8 bacon slices, diced
1½ cups sliced fresh okra *
1 large onion, chopped
1 green bell pepper, chopped
1½ cups uncooked long-grain rice
½ teaspoon salt
¼ teaspoon pepper
2 cups water

• **Cook** bacon in a large skillet until crisp; remove bacon, reserving 2 tablespoons drippings in skillet.
• **Sauté** okra, onion, and bell pepper in hot drippings over medium-high heat 5 minutes or until tender.
• **Stir** in rice and next 3 ingredients; bring to a boil. Cover, reduce heat, and simmer 20 minutes or until water is absorbed and rice is tender. Remove from heat; stir in bacon. Let stand 5 minutes. **Yield:** 4 servings.

* Substitute 1 (16-ounce) package frozen sliced okra for fresh, if desired.
Angela Jeffers
Johns Island, South Carolina

Savory Summer Pie,
page 159

Beef Salad Niçoise, page 159

Chicken Fajitas, page 158

Tomato-Gruyère-Basil Salad, page 172

187

*Shrimp-and-Orzo Salad, Spicy Rosemary
Aspic, pages 182 and 183*

*Lemon Pound Cake
With Mint Berries and
Cream, page 183*

*Dilled Summer Soup,
page 182*

*Sweet Corn Soup With
Shiitakes and Shrimp,
page 168*

*Salad of Baby Lettuces With
Vidalia Onion Vinaigrette,
Field Peas and Spinach,
Grilled Chicken, pages 168
and 169*

Raspberry Spritzers,
Lemony Ice Cream Pie, page 207

I CAN DO IT MYSELF

A cooking contest just for kids
Brought us many tasty bids.
They mixed and blended, stirred and baked.
Here are 17 great recipes you can make!

SMART STARTS

If it's breakfast that you're makin',
And you're tired of eggs and bacon,
Here are a few starters with new appeal.
Try these treats for your morning meal.

STUFFIN' MUFFIN

Finalist

Prep: 10 minutes
Cook: 4 minutes

2 teaspoons butter or margarine
1 large egg
1 tablespoon milk
⅛ teaspoon salt
1 English muffin, split and toasted
1 (1-ounce) cooked ham slice
1 (¾-ounce) process American
   cheese slice

• **Melt** butter in a small nonstick skillet
over medium heat. Whisk together egg,
milk, and salt; add to skillet. Cook, without stirring, until egg begins to set on
bottom. Draw a spatula across skillet to
form large curds.
• **Cook** until egg is thickened but still
moist (do not stir constantly). Fold egg
over to fit on muffin. Place egg on bottom
half of muffin; top with ham and cheese.
Cover with muffin top. **Yield:** 1 serving.
Ashley Walker, age 8
Cape Coral, Florida

> *"I can do it myself*
> *because my mom*
> *works two jobs and on*
> *Saturday mornings*
> *I let her rest and I fix her*
> *breakfast as a treat."*
> *Ashley Walker (age 8)*

OATMEAL IN A SLOW COOKER WITH ICE CREAM

Finalist

Prep: 5 minutes
Cook: 8 hours

3 cups milk
1 teaspoon butter or margarine,
   softened
1 cup uncooked regular oats
2 Granny Smith apples, peeled and
   chopped
Dash of salt
Pancake syrup
Vanilla ice cream
Garnish: fresh berries

• **Bring** milk to a boil in a heavy saucepan over medium-high heat, stirring
often. Remove from heat.
• **Grease** inside of slow cooker with
butter. Add hot milk, oats, apple, and
salt, stirring gently. Cook, covered, at
LOW 8 hours.
• **Serve** with syrup and ice cream; garnish, if desired. **Yield:** 2 to 3 servings.
Tara Martin, age 11
Phoenix, Arizona

BEST PANCAKES

Semifinalist

Prep: 5 minutes
Cook: 4 minutes per batch

2 cups self-rising flour
1 teaspoon sugar
1 large egg
1 cup milk
1 tablespoon vegetable oil
2 medium-size ripe bananas, mashed

• **Stir** together flour and sugar; make a well in center of mixture. Combine egg, milk, and oil; add to dry ingredients, stirring just until moistened. Stir in banana.
• **Pour** about ¼ cup batter for each pancake onto a hot, lightly oiled griddle. Cook pancakes until tops are covered with bubbles and edges look cooked; turn and cook other side. **Yield:** 12 (4-inch) pancakes.

Jonathan Ham, age 9
Mount Pleasant, South Carolina

EAGLE NEST EGG

Semifinalist

Prep: 5 minutes
Cook: 4 minutes

1 white sandwich bread slice
1 teaspoon butter or margarine
1 large egg
2 tablespoons hash brown potatoes
Salt

• **Cut** center from bread with a 2-inch round cutter. (Reserve center of bread for another use.)
• **Melt** butter in a small nonstick skillet over medium heat. Brush both sides of bread with melted butter; place in skillet. Crack egg into hole in bread. Spoon potatoes around egg. Sprinkle lightly with salt. Cook 2 minutes on each side or until egg is done and potatoes are browned. **Yield:** 1 serving.

Katelyn Ammons, age 8
Memphis, Tennessee

COOL FOR SCHOOL

After Mom packs your lunch with care,
Take these yummy treats anywhere.
One is wrapped and one is rolled.
One is warm, the other cold.

WESTERN WRAPS

Finalist

Prep: 20 minutes

½ (8-ounce) package cream cheese, softened
1 tablespoon taco sauce
4 (6-inch) flour tortillas
1 cup canned black beans, rinsed and drained
¼ cup real bacon pieces
½ small green bell pepper, diced
¼ cup (1 ounce) shredded Cheddar cheese

• **Stir** together cream cheese and taco sauce; spread mixture evenly on 1 side of tortillas. Top with black beans and next 3 ingredients.
• **Roll** tortillas tightly. Wrap in plastic wrap; chill. **Yield:** 4 wraps.

Tai-Tien Chan, age 10
Albany, California

"I can do it myself because it's more fun to make than bread sandwiches."
Tai-Tien Chan (age 10)

CINNAMON TOAST ROLLUPS

Finalist

Prep: 10 minutes
Bake: 12 minutes

¼ cup firmly packed light brown sugar
½ cup sugar
½ teaspoon ground cinnamon
1 (8-ounce) can refrigerated crescent rolls
¼ cup butter or margarine, melted

• **Stir** together first 3 ingredients.
• **Unroll** crescent rolls; brush with melted butter, and sprinkle evenly with sugar mixture.
• **Separate** dough into 8 triangles. Roll up each triangle, starting with shortest side; place on a lightly greased baking sheet.
• **Bake** at 350° for 10 to 12 minutes or until golden; remove to a wire rack to cool. To carry in a lunchbox, wrap in aluminum foil sandwich wrapper sheets. **Yield:** 8 rollups.

Samantha Bolf, age 8
Cadillac, Michigan

GOUDA LOVER'S CHICKEN SANDWICHES

Semifinalist

Prep: 10 minutes

1 (2½-pound) roasted whole
    chicken
1 (16-ounce) French bread
    loaf
¼ cup mayonnaise
1 (6-ounce) Gouda cheese round,
    cut into 12 slices
Lettuce
2 medium tomatoes, sliced
¼ cup honey mustard

• **Slice** chicken from bone; set aside.
• **Split** bread loaf horizontally; cut each
half crosswise into 4 pieces. Place, cut
side up, on a baking sheet.
• **Broil** bread 5 inches from heat (with
electric oven door partially open) until
lightly browned. Remove from oven.
• **Spread** 4 bread pieces with mayonnaise. Top each with desired amount of
chicken slices and 3 cheese slices.
(Reserve any remaining chicken for
another use.) Top each with lettuce and
tomato.
• **Spread** remaining bread pieces with
honey mustard. Place on top of sandwiches. To carry in lunchbox, wrap in
aluminum foil sandwich wrapper
sheets. **Yield:** 4 sandwiches.

Note: For hot sandwiches, top 4 bread
pieces with chicken and cheese, and
broil 2 to 3 minutes or until cheese
melts. Proceed as directed above; serve
immediately.

Sami Rivard, age 5
Danville, Kentucky

Winner Dinners

This fun pizza is no phony.
It's just made with macaroni.
If the pizza doesn't fill your tummy,
Try Poppy Seed Chicken—
It's really yummy.

MACA-PIZZA

Finalist

Prep: 25 minutes
Bake: 25 minutes

8 ounces hot cooked elbow
    macaroni
4 (1-ounce) process American
    cheese slices, cut into thin
    strips
2 large eggs, lightly beaten
1 teaspoon peanut oil
1 (7-ounce) jar pizza sauce
2 cups (8 ounces) shredded
    mozzarella cheese
1½ ounces sliced pepperoni

• **Stir** together macaroni and American
cheese in a large bowl until cheese
melts. Cool. Stir in eggs. Brush oil on a
12-inch pizza pan with sides. Spread
macaroni mixture evenly in pan.
• **Bake** at 350° for 10 minutes. Spread
with sauce; top with mozzarella cheese
and pepperoni. Bake 15 minutes or until
cheese melts. **Yield:** 1 (12-inch) pizza.

Taylor Keen, age 6
Decherd, Tennessee

POPPY SEED CHICKEN

Finalist

Prep: 15 minutes
Bake: 30 minutes

3 cups chopped cooked chicken
1 (10¾-ounce) can cream of
    chicken soup, undiluted
1 (10¾-ounce) can cream of
    mushroom soup, undiluted
1 (16-ounce) container sour cream
1 cup (4 ounces) shredded
    Cheddar cheese
3 tablespoons poppy seeds
36 saltine crackers, crushed
¼ cup butter or margarine, melted

• **Stir** together first 4 ingredients. Spread
half of mixture in a lightly greased 11- x
7-inch baking dish. Sprinkle with half of
cheese and 1 tablespoon poppy seeds.
Repeat layers. Top with cracker crumbs
and remaining 1 tablespoon poppy seeds;
drizzle with butter.
• **Bake** at 350° for 30 minutes or until
lightly browned. **Yield:** 6 to 8 servings.

Brett Ransom, age 10
Rome, Georgia

> *"I can do it myself
> because I know how to
> make a pizza."*
> Taylor Keen (age 6)

Neat Sweets

Root beer and marshmallows
Are always fun.
Try these desserts.
You can't like only one!

ROCKY ROAD PIZZA DESSERT

Winner

Prep: 10 minutes
Bake: 15 minutes

1 (5- to 6-inch) refrigerated pizza
   crust
¾ cup miniature marshmallows
¾ cup candy-coated peanut butter
   pieces
¼ cup chopped pecans

• **Place** crust on a baking sheet. Top with
marshmallows; sprinkle with candy and
pecans. Bake at 375° for 10 to 15 minutes.
Yield: 1 (6-inch) pizza.

Note: For testing purposes only, we used
Mama Mary's Pizza Crusts and Reese's
Pieces Candies.

> *Hunter Hubbs, age 5*
> *New Llano, Louisiana*

> *"I can do it myself
> because it's easy. I make
> it at MawMaw's house, so
> she can help me and I
> won't get burned."*
> *Hunter Hubbs (age 5)*

CARAMEL O'S

Semifinalist

Prep: 20 minutes
Cook: 3 minutes

1 (15.4-ounce) package caramel
   candies, unwrapped
3 tablespoons evaporated milk
1 cup chopped pecans
4 cups sweetened 3-grain
   apple-and-cinnamon cereal

• **Microwave** caramels in a microwave-
safe bowl according to package directions. Stir in milk until blended. Stir in
pecans and cereal.
• **Drop** mixture by rounded tablespoonfuls onto a lightly greased baking sheet.
Chill until firm. **Yield:** 3 dozen.

> *Daniel Keech, age 8*
> *Broken Arrow, Oklahoma*

ROOT BEER FLOAT CAKE

Winner

Prep: 20 minutes
Bake: 40 minutes

1 (18.25-ounce) package yellow
   cake mix
1 (12-ounce) bottle root
   beer
¼ cup vegetable oil
3 large eggs
Root Beer Glaze
Vanilla ice cream

• **Combine** first 4 ingredients in a large
bowl; beat mixture at low speed with an
electric mixer until dry ingredients are
moistened.
• **Beat** at medium speed 2 minutes.
Pour into a greased and floured 12-cup
Bundt pan.
• **Bake** at 350° for 35 to 40 minutes or
until a long wooden pick or skewer
inserted in center comes out clean.
• **Cool** in pan on a wire rack 15 minutes;
remove cake from pan, and cool completely on wire rack.

• **Pierce** top of cake at 2-inch intervals
with a long wooden pick. Pour Root
Beer Glaze evenly over cake. Cool completely before serving. Serve with ice
cream. **Yield:** 1 (10-inch) cake.

Root Beer Glaze

Prep: 2 minutes

½ cup powdered sugar
3 tablespoons root beer

• **Stir** together sugar and root beer until
smooth. **Yield:** about ¾ cup.

> *Eric Welander, age 10*
> *Richmond, Virginia*

> *"I can do it myself
> because I do a lot of
> cooking and know how to
> measure carefully.
> Cooking and eating is
> how I learned to really
> understand fractions."*
> *Eric Welander (age 10)*

CITRUS SMOOTHIE

Prep: 5 minutes

1 quart lime or orange sherbet,
   softened
1½ cups lemon-lime or orange-
   tangerine thirst quencher

• **Process** ingredients in a blender until
smooth. Serve immediately. **Yield:**
about 4 cups.

NO-BAKE BANANA PUDDING

Prep: 10 minutes
Chill: 30 minutes

1 (3.4-ounce) package vanilla
   instant pudding mix
½ cup sour cream
1¾ cups milk
48 vanilla wafers
2 medium bananas, sliced
Whipped cream or frozen whipped
   topping, thawed

• **Beat** first 3 ingredients at low speed
with an electric mixer 2 minutes or until
thickened.
• **Line** bottom and sides of a 1½-quart
bowl with vanilla wafers. Layer with half
of banana and one-third of pudding. Repeat layers, ending with pudding. Cover
and chill. Spread with whipped cream.
Yield: 6 servings.

BUNCH O' MUNCHIES

There are times in every day
When a growling stomach won't go away.
Only one thing keeps it quiet—
Snacking on a healthy diet.

CHOCO-PEANUT DELIGHTS

Finalist

Prep: 15 minutes

36 round buttery crackers,
   divided
¾ cup creamy peanut butter
1 large banana, sliced (optional)
1 cup (6 ounces) semisweet
   chocolate morsels

• **Spread** 18 crackers evenly with
peanut butter; top evenly with banana
slices, if desired. Cover with remaining
crackers.
• **Place** chocolate morsels in a heavy-
duty zip-top plastic bag; seal. Submerge
in hot water until chocolate melts. Snip
a tiny hole in 1 corner of bag, and drizzle
chocolate over snacks. Cool. **Yield:** 18
snacks.

Kathryn Holmen, age 6
Manassas, Virginia

> *"I can do it myself because it's so easy even a kid like me can make this treat."*
> Kathryn Holmen (age 6)

PIZZA ROLLUPS

Finalist

Prep: 10 minutes
Bake: 10 minutes

1 medium tomato, diced
5 (1-ounce) cooked ham slices,
   diced
1 small green bell pepper,
   diced
1 (8-ounce) can pineapple tidbits,
   drained
¼ cup almonds, chopped
4 (8-inch) flour tortillas
¼ cup pizza sauce
1 cup (4 ounces) shredded
   mozzarella cheese

• **Stir** together first 5 ingredients.
• **Brush** tortillas with pizza sauce.
Spread one-fourth of tomato mixture
down center of each tortilla; sprinkle
with cheese.

• **Roll** up, and place, seam side down, in
a lightly greased 13- x 9-inch pan.
• **Bake** at 350° for 10 minutes. **Yield:** 4
rollups.

Shavano Shaw, age 9
Miami, Florida

QUICK FIESTA DIP

This three-ingredient dip
uses convenience items to make
a fast, flavorful snack.

Prep: 5 minutes
Cook: 7 minutes

1 (9-ounce) package frozen corn
   niblets
1 (12-ounce) jar thick-and-chunky
   mild salsa
1 cup (4 ounces) shredded colby or
   Cheddar cheese
Tortilla chips or corn chips

• **Cook** corn according to package
directions; drain.
• **Pour** salsa into a 9-inch glass pieplate;
stir in corn. Cover with plastic wrap;
fold back a small section of wrap to
allow steam to escape.
• **Microwave** at HIGH 2 minutes or until
bubbly. Sprinkle cheese over salsa;
cover with plastic wrap. Let stand 5
minutes or until cheese is melted. Serve
with chips. **Yield:** 1½ cups.

$\mathscr{E}$MERIL'S INSPIRATIONS

When it comes to fine dining, superstar chef Emeril Lagasse certainly knows how to please. But so do the friends he calls his inspirations. Kick it up a notch with these recipes from the behind-the-scenes friends who've taught Emeril a thing or two about the good life.

LEMONY PECAN-CRUSTED SNAPPER WITH CRABMEAT RELISH

"Relish" is what South Louisianians call a chunky topping. Don't worry— no pickles are in sight.

Prep: 15 minutes
Cook: 14 minutes

4 (5- to 6-ounce) red snapper
　　fillets
3 tablespoons Emeril's Essence
　　(see recipe at right),
　　divided
2 cups all-purpose flour
½ cup toasted ground pecans
2 large eggs
1 cup milk
½ cup olive or canola oil
Lemon-Butter Sauce
Crabmeat Relish

• **Sprinkle** fillets evenly with 1 tablespoon Emeril's Essence. Set aside.
• **Combine** 1 cup flour and 1 tablespoon essence; set aside.
• **Combine** remaining 1 tablespoon essence, remaining 1 cup flour, and pecans.
• **Stir** together eggs and milk until well blended.

• **Dredge** fillets in flour mixture; dip in egg mixture, and dredge in pecan mixture, shaking off excess.
• **Fry** fillets in hot oil in a large ovenproof skillet about 3 minutes on each side. Place skillet in a 375° oven; bake 8 minutes or until browned and crisp.
• **Spoon** Lemon-Butter Sauce evenly on individual plates; add fillets, and top with Crabmeat Relish. **Yield:** 4 servings.

Lemon-Butter Sauce

Prep: 10 minutes
Cook: 18 minutes

1 cup dry white wine
3 lemons, peeled and quartered
6 to 8 garlic cloves, minced
1 teaspoon salt
½ teaspoon freshly ground
　　pepper
⅛ teaspoon Worcestershire
　　sauce
⅛ teaspoon hot sauce
½ cup whipping cream
¾ cup unsalted butter, sliced
1 tablespoon chopped fresh
　　parsley

• **Cook** first 3 ingredients in a nonaluminum saucepan over medium-high heat 5 minutes, whisking to blend lemons.

• **Stir** in salt and next 3 ingredients; cook 10 minutes or until texture of syrup.
• **Stir** in whipping cream; cook 1 minute. Reduce heat to low, and gradually whisk in butter.
• **Pour** mixture through a wire-mesh strainer into a bowl, discarding pulp. Stir in parsley; serve immediately. **Yield:** 2 cups.

Crabmeat Relish

Prep: 15 minutes

½ pound fresh lump crabmeat,
　　drained
½ cup pecan halves, toasted
4 green onions, chopped
2 tablespoons minced roasted
　　sweet red peppers
1 tablespoon lemon juice
¼ teaspoon salt
½ teaspoon pepper

• **Toss** together all ingredients. Cover and chill up to 8 hours. **Yield:** 2 cups.
Craig Borges
New Orleans Fish House
New Orleans, Louisiana

EMERIL'S ESSENCE

5 tablespoons sweet paprika
¼ cup salt
¼ cup garlic powder
2 tablespoons dried oregano
2 tablespoons dried thyme
2 tablespoons onion powder
2 tablespoons freshly ground
　　black pepper
2 tablespoons ground red
　　pepper

• **Stir** together all ingredients. Store in an airtight container up to 3 months. **Yield:** 1 cup.

Emeril Lagasse
New Orleans, Louisiana

> *"If I can walk away knowing I've inspired one*
> *person to start cooking, I'm happy."*
>
> Emeril Lagasse

Emeril Lagasse is the king of "New" New Orleans cuisine, the ruler of cooking-show airwaves, the CEO of six restaurants with 700 employees, and the boxer-paced host with the absolute most—from best-selling cookbooks to seasoning mixes.

But the one aspect of his life that gets lost in the media-blitz shuffle is his constant self-education about the people surrounding him. He's learned much about Louisiana, he says, from a few people "who've shown me a lot about life, hard work, and the importance of friendship.

"Of course, I have a tremendous respect for Ella Brennan," he says of the doyenne of New Orleans' Commander's Palace, where he made a name for himself. "She gave me polish—period," he says with his Fall River, Massachusetts, accent, now mingled nicely with the similar N'Awlins dialect. "Everybody knows Ella, or should know Ella. But maybe you didn't know about these guys," Emeril says, referring to farmer Dan Crutchfield, fish-seller Craig Borges, and Acadian culinary folklorist Marcelle Bienvenu.

HIGH ON THE HOG

A hundred miles from New Orleans, organic farmer Dan Crutchfield makes silk purses, so to speak, out of the hormone-free pork and other items he delivers weekly to Big Easy restaurateurs. "I like that more people are thinking healthier, wanting quality," he says, shooing away a few curious pigs straying about on his Jayess, Mississippi, farm, Crickhollow. "That makes me happy." Emeril feels the same way.

The chef has inspired Dan to experiment, and business has blossomed. Dan grows two acres of specialty produce (including heirloom tomatoes and baby vegetables). Another 22 acres are filled with grazing cattle and hogs. Another 16 are filled with pine trees (a future investment). "I'm just gettin' started at sowing my oats in this field," he says. "It's nice to have folks believe in you. It makes you believe in yourself."

FISHY BUSINESS

Craig Borges has been studying, smelling, and selling fish since he was a small-fry. His father sold fish, as did his grandfather. "Craig knows fish," says Emeril, one of his first customers. "He knows fish like no one else I know."

At the bustling New Orleans Fish House, a wholesale company Craig and cousin Billy Borges founded in 1990 (the same year Emeril opened his first restaurant, Emeril's), one might imagine it to be, well, fishy-smelling. Not so; it's as clean as a Gulf breeze. "To smell fish is to smell bad fish," says Craig, "and we don't sell bad fish. Once it comes out of the water, the clock starts ticking." And so does he, supplying the top restaurants in town with everything from shrimp to baby octopus.

"What gave me the courage to keep at this game was that Emeril believed in us from the start," Craig says. "He's a perfectionist; he's taught us to be, too. 'This is nice,' Emeril might say, assessing a fish. 'But I'm looking for something better.' Now I find myself saying the same thing."

MUSIC TO EMERIL'S EARS

With a French last name meaning "welcome," it's fitting that Marcelle Bienvenu's smile and her cozy home near Lafayette are just as inviting. Sipping a mint julep outside her St. Martinville cottage, Marcelle surveys the Bayou Teche setting: moss-draped oaks, small pier, husband Rock's fishing boat, a plaster alligator sunning near the water, an iron fish-fry skillet drying on a fence. The only thing missing is Acadian folk music. It comes in Marcelle's buttery voice and melodious laugh.

These days Marcelle—a respected food writer and historian (*Who's Your Mama, Are You Catholic, and Can You Make a Roux?* and its sequel) and contributor to several of Emeril's books—spends a lot of time testing recipes for him "and just being a friend—he's family now," she says.

Sharing a love of good food and good humor, they later worked together in 1996 on Emeril's second book, *Louisiana Real and Rustic.* "Marcelle's an excellent sounding board," he says. "Say, if I'm doing an eggplant dish and want to put bell pepper in it, she won't let me get off the page. 'It might be nice, Emeril, but most people wouldn't do that; it wouldn't be authentic,'" he mimics her saying. "That's the kind of thing we really believe in—preserving folklore. She's like filé powder to a great gumbo—beautiful."

For more on Marcelle Bienvenu, call (318) 394-7674; the New Orleans Fish House, (504) 821-9700; Crickhollow Farm, (601) 684-4940; and Emeril Lagasse, (504) 524-4241.

CRICKHOLLOW ROAST PORK

Prep: 20 minutes
Bake: 1 hour and 45 minutes

1 (4-pound) boneless pork
   roast
1 tablespoon minced garlic
1 tablespoon Emeril's Essence
   (see recipe on page 198)
2 tablespoons butter
6 slab bacon slices, rind removed
Crickhollow Barbecue Sauce

• **Rub** roast with garlic and Emeril's Essence.
• **Melt** butter in a large Dutch oven over medium-high heat.
• **Add** roast, and cook 4 to 5 minutes on each side or until browned. Wrap bacon over roast, and pour 2 cups Crickhollow Barbecue Sauce over top.
• **Bake** at 350° for 1 hour and 45 minutes or until a meat thermometer registers 160°. **Yield:** 12 servings.

Crickhollow Barbecue Sauce

Prep: 10 minutes

2 cups red wine vinegar
1 cup lime juice
½ cup dried parsley flakes
¼ cup olive oil
1 tablespoon Worcestershire
   sauce
1 teaspoon Emeril's Essence (see
   recipe on page 198)
1 teaspoon paprika
½ teaspoon pepper

• **Stir** together all ingredients. Store in refrigerator. **Yield:** 4 cups.

Dan Crutchfield
Jayess, Mississippi

MARCELLE'S BOUILLABAISSE

"Since my father loved to fish, our family enjoyed many fish dishes, but this is a personal favorite," Marcelle says. To "kick it up a notch," add a dash of Emeril's Essence (page 198) just before serving.

Prep: 20 minutes
Cook: 1 hour

1 pound unpeeled, medium-size
   fresh shrimp
2½ pounds trout or redfish fillets
1 teaspoon salt, divided
1 teaspoon ground red pepper,
   divided
3 medium-size yellow onions,
   coarsely chopped
2 medium-size green bell peppers,
   coarsely chopped
2 celery ribs, chopped
3 garlic cloves, minced
½ cup butter
2 (28-ounce) cans crushed
   tomatoes
4 bay leaves
½ cup dry white wine
2 tablespoons chopped fresh
   parsley

• **Peel** shrimp, and devein, if desired. Set aside.
• **Sprinkle** fish fillets with ½ teaspoon salt and ½ teaspoon red pepper; set aside.
• **Toss** together remaining ½ teaspoon salt, remaining ½ teaspoon red pepper, onion, and next 3 ingredients.
• **Melt** butter in a 6-quart Dutch oven over medium heat; remove from heat.
• **Arrange** half of fish fillets in Dutch oven; layer with half of vegetable mixture, half of tomatoes, and 2 bay leaves. Repeat procedure with remaining fish fillets, vegetable mixture, tomatoes, and bay leaves. Arrange shrimp on top; add wine.
• **Bring** mixture to a boil. Cover, reduce heat, and cook 1 hour. (Do not remove cover.) Sprinkle each serving with chopped parsley. **Yield:** 12 cups.

Marcelle Bienvenu
St. Martinville, Louisiana

FILL UP THE GRILL

Grilled Chicken and Vegetables gives a jump-start to other meals, though you fire up the grill only once.

To serve a hungry family of four, plan Grilled Chicken and Vegetables tonight and Grilled Chicken on Greens later in the week. Or duos can turn leftovers into Summer Open-Faced Sandwiches.

GRILLED CHICKEN AND VEGETABLES

Italian and sweet-and-sour dressings give Grilled Chicken and Vegetables its tang.

Prep: 10 minutes
Chill: 4 hours
Grill: 35 minutes

2 zucchini
2 yellow squash
2 red bell peppers
2 large sweet onions
1 (8-ounce) bottle light Italian
   dressing
1 (8-ounce) bottle sweet-and-sour
   dressing
½ cup dry white wine or chicken
   broth
¼ cup soy sauce
6 skinned and boned chicken
   breast halves

• **Cut** zucchini and yellow squash into ¼-inch-thick slices; cut bell peppers into 2-inch pieces, and cut onions into small wedges.
• **Combine** Italian dressing and next 3 ingredients; reserve ½ cup mixture to use later in the week. Cover and chill.
• **Place** chicken in a shallow dish or heavy-duty zip-top plastic bag; add 1¾ cups dressing mixture, turning to coat. Cover or seal; chill 4 to 8 hours.
• **Place** vegetables in a bowl; add remaining ½ cup dressing mixture, tossing to coat. Cover vegetables, and chill 2 hours.

• **Drain** vegetables, reserving marinade in bowl. Arrange vegetables in a grill basket.
• **Grill,** covered with grill lid, over medium-high heat (350° to 400°) 15 minutes or until tender. Return half of vegetables to bowl, and toss with reserved marinade; keep warm. Cover and chill remaining vegetables.
• **Drain** chicken; discard marinade.
• **Grill** chicken, covered with grill lid, over medium-high heat (350° to 400°) 10 minutes on each side or until done. Serve 4 pieces with warm vegetables. Cover and chill remaining chicken. **Yield:** 4 servings.

Robin Ball
Saluda, South Carolina

Grilled Chicken on Greens: Toss 4 cups mixed salad greens with ¼ cup reserved dressing mixture; arrange on individual plates. Cut remaining 2 grilled chicken breast halves into strips; cut 1 medium tomato into wedges. Place chicken and tomato on greens; drizzle with remaining ¼ cup reserved dressing mixture. **Yield:** 2 servings.

Summer Open-Faced Sandwiches: Cut 1 (12-inch) French bread loaf in half lengthwise; lightly toast bread. Drizzle cut sides with ¼ cup reserved dressing mixture. Layer each half with 1 large tomato, thinly sliced; half of remaining grilled vegetables; and remaining 2 grilled chicken breast halves, cut into strips. Top with 4 mozzarella cheese slices. Broil 5 inches from heat (with electric oven door partially open) 2 minutes. Or wrap in aluminum foil, and grill, covered with grill lid, over medium-high heat (350° to 400°) 8 minutes. Halve each portion. **Yield:** 2 servings.

UPTOWN GROUND

It's hard to beat a juicy burger for good, old-fashioned appetite satisfaction. Each of these ground beef creations layers a savory filling between two generous patties. No matter how you serve them—open-faced or even without buns—after one bite, you'll wonder why you waited so long to treat yourself to such bliss.

STUFFED SOUTHWESTERN-STYLE BURGERS

Prep: 20 minutes
Cook: 20 minutes

1 avocado
3 plum tomatoes, chopped
1 garlic clove, pressed
2 teaspoons lemon juice
1½ teaspoons salt, divided
1½ teaspoons pepper, divided
2 pounds lean ground beef
1 small onion, diced
2 teaspoons chili powder
1 (8-ounce) package Monterey Jack cheese with peppers, cubed
6 large sesame seed buns, toasted
Toppings: leaf lettuce, tomato slices, purple onion slices

• **Mash** avocado with a fork in a small bowl; stir in tomato, garlic, lemon juice, ½ teaspoon salt, and ½ teaspoon pepper. Set aside.

• **Combine** ground beef, onion, remaining 1 teaspoon salt, remaining 1 teaspoon pepper, and chili powder; shape into 12 patties.
• **Top** 6 patties with cheese cubes; cover with remaining patties, pressing edges to seal. Place on a rack in a broiler pan.
• **Broil** 5½ inches from heat (with electric oven door partially open) 10 minutes on each side or until beef is no longer pink. Serve in buns with desired toppings and avocado mixture. **Yield:** 6 servings.

La Juan Coward
Jasper, Texas

MUSHROOM-STUFFED HAMBURGER STEAKS

Prep: 15 minutes
Cook: 20 minutes

1 tablespoon butter or margarine
1 small onion, chopped
6 fresh mushrooms, sliced
2 pounds lean ground beef
½ medium potato, shredded
1 large egg, lightly beaten
¼ cup ketchup
1 tablespoon all-purpose flour
1 tablespoon Worcestershire
    sauce
½ teaspoon salt
½ teaspoon pepper
8 bacon slices

• **Melt** butter in a large skillet; add onion and mushrooms, and sauté over medium heat 2 to 3 minutes or until tender. Remove from skillet.
• **Combine** ground beef and next 7 ingredients in a large bowl; shape into 8 patties. Top 4 patties evenly with onion mixture; cover with remaining patties, pressing edges to seal. Wrap each with 2 bacon slices, securing with wooden picks. Place on a rack in a broiler pan.
• **Broil** 5½ inches from heat (with electric oven door partially open) 10 minutes on each side or until beef is no longer pink. **Yield:** 4 servings.

Eunice Oakley
Jay, Oklahoma

INSIDE OUT CHEESEBURGERS

Prep: 20 minutes
Cook: 32 minutes

2 pounds lean ground beef
1½ teaspoons salt
¾ teaspoon pepper
¼ cup Dijon mustard
6 (½-inch-thick) onion slices
6 (1-ounce) sharp Cheddar cheese
    slices
½ cup pickle relish
6 large sesame seed buns,
    toasted
Toppings: mayonnaise, mustard,
    leaf lettuce, tomato slices

• **Combine** first 4 ingredients in a large bowl; shape into 12 patties. Set aside.
• **Sauté** onion in a large nonstick skillet coated with cooking spray 10 minutes or until tender.
• **Top** 6 patties with onion, cheese, and relish; cover with remaining 6 patties, pressing edges to seal.
• **Cook** patties in batches in nonstick skillet over medium heat 8 minutes on each side or until beef is no longer pink. Serve in buns with desired toppings. **Yield:** 6 servings.

APPLE-BACON BURGERS

Prep: 20 minutes
Cook: 20 minutes

1 small onion, chopped
1 Granny Smith apple, chopped
½ teaspoon ground sage, divided
1 teaspoon olive oil
2 pounds lean ground beef
3 tablespoons white wine
    Worcestershire sauce
1 teaspoon salt
½ teaspoon pepper
12 bacon slices
4 hamburger buns, toasted

• **Sauté** onion, apple, and ¼ teaspoon sage in a small skillet in hot oil over medium-high heat 2 to 3 minutes or until tender. Set aside.
• **Combine** ground beef, remaining ¼ teaspoon sage, Worcestershire sauce, salt, and pepper in a large bowl. Shape into 12 patties. Top 6 patties evenly with apple mixture; cover with remaining 6 patties, pressing edges to seal. Wrap each with 2 bacon slices, securing with wooden picks. Place on a rack in a broiler pan.
• **Broil** 5½ inches from heat (with electric oven door partially open) 10 minutes on each side or until beef is no longer pink. Serve on buns. **Yield:** 6 servings.

Della Taylor
Jonesboro, Tennessee

SIZABLE SALADS

It's time for *the* neighborhood get-together, and your assignment is salad. These offerings range from 8 to 20 servings—all can be prepared in 30 minutes or less.

When planning a tossed salad for a crowd, a 1½-pound head of iceberg or romaine lettuce yields about 12 cups bite-size pieces. A ¾-pound bunch of spinach or a 1-pound bunch of leaf lettuce yields about 8 cups bite-size pieces. It takes 4½ quarts of tossed salad to serve 1½ cups to each of 12 guests.

GREEK VEGETABLE SALAD

Prep: 10 minutes
Chill: 2 hours

⅓ cup olive oil
3 tablespoons lemon juice
2 garlic cloves, pressed
1½ teaspoons dried oregano
½ teaspoon salt
¼ teaspoon pepper
4 medium tomatoes, cut into
    wedges
1 small cucumber, sliced
1 small zucchini, peeled, halved,
    and cut into thin strips
½ small purple onion, sliced and
    separated into rings
1 (14-ounce) can artichoke heart
    quarters, drained
14 pitted ripe olives, halved
1 (4-ounce) package crumbled feta
    cheese
Lettuce leaves

• **Whisk** together first 6 ingredients in a large bowl.
• **Add** tomato and next 5 ingredients, tossing well. Cover and chill at least 2 hours. Sprinkle with feta cheese; serve on lettuce leaves. **Yield:** 8 to 10 servings.

Summer Vegetables

Driving home from the beach, you used to be able to find lots of restaurants with mama's recipes. Now the interstates don't pass these places. But at home you can bring back the delicious dishes of yesterday. Just choose your favorites, spend a little time cooking, and enjoy one of the best things about summer—eating fresh vegetables.

RICH GREEN SALAD

Prep: 30 minutes

1 head iceberg lettuce, torn
1 bunch Green Leaf lettuce, torn
1 bunch Red Leaf lettuce, torn
1 pound carrots, sliced
3 yellow squash, sliced
3 large tomatoes, cut into wedges
2 zucchini, sliced
1 cucumber, peeled and sliced
1 (8-ounce) package sliced fresh mushrooms
3 hard-cooked eggs, sliced
1 (2.8-ounce) can French-fried onions
1 (5¼-ounce) package garlic croutons
1 (8-ounce) bottle Ranch-style dressing

• **Combine** first 12 ingredients in a large bowl. Toss with Ranch-style dressing; serve immediately. **Yield:** 20 servings.

Cathy Oestmann
Midland, Texas

ITALIAN GARDEN SALAD

Prep: 30 minutes
Chill: 2 hours

4 medium cucumbers, peeled and thinly sliced
2 medium-size sweet onions, cut into thin rings
6 plum tomatoes, thinly sliced
1 (8-ounce) block mozzarella cheese, cubed
1½ cups Italian dressing
¼ cup red wine vinegar
¼ cup water
½ teaspoon salt
½ teaspoon pepper

• **Combine** first 4 ingredients in a large bowl. Whisk together dressing and next 4 ingredients; pour over vegetable mixture, tossing to coat. Cover and chill at least 2 hours. **Yield:** 10 to 12 servings.

Patricia E. Brock
Palestine, Texas

CORN-AND-OKRA MEDLEY

Prep: 15 minutes
Cook: 25 minutes

4 ears fresh corn
½ pound fresh okra
4 bacon slices, chopped
1 small onion, chopped
½ cup water
1 to 1½ teaspoons chili powder
1 teaspoon beef bouillon granules
4 medium tomatoes, peeled and chopped

• **Cut** corn from cobs, and slice okra; set aside.
• **Cook** bacon in a large skillet over medium heat until crisp; remove bacon with a slotted spoon, reserving drippings in skillet.
• **Add** corn, okra, onion, and next 3 ingredients to skillet. Bring to a boil; cover, reduce heat, and cook 10 minutes.
• **Stir** in tomato; cover and cook 5 minutes. Stir in bacon. **Yield:** 8 servings.

Nell H. Amador
Guntersville, Alabama

SQUASH FRITTERS

Prep: 10 minutes
Cook: 10 minutes

2 medium-size yellow squash, grated
¼ cup diced onion
2 tablespoons diced green bell pepper
1 teaspoon brown sugar
1 teaspoon salt
1 tablespoon all-purpose flour
1 large egg, lightly beaten
2 teaspoons butter, melted
½ cup olive oil

• **Stir** together first 8 ingredients.
• **Heat** oil in a large heavy skillet. Drop mixture by tablespoonfuls into hot oil; fry in batches until golden, turning once. Drain on paper towels, and serve immediately. **Yield:** 4 to 6 servings.

Rubie M. Walker
Lynchburg, Virginia

EASY BLACK-EYED PEAS

Prep: 10 minutes
Cook: 45 minutes

2½ pounds fresh black-eyed or
    pink-eyed peas, shelled (3
    cups) *
3 cups water
2 large beef bouillon cubes
1 medium onion, chopped
½ (16-ounce) package kielbasa,
    sliced, browned, and drained
    (optional)

• **Bring** first 4 ingredients and, if desired, sausage to a boil in a saucepan.
Reduce heat; simmer 40 minutes or until
tender. Serve with Sweet Onion Relish
(see recipe below). **Yield:** 4 servings.

* Substitute 1 (16-ounce) package
frozen black-eyed or pink-eyed peas, if
desired. Reduce cooking time to 30 minutes or until tender.

Cheryl Hughes
El Dorado, Arizona

SWEET ONION RELISH

Prep: 12 minutes
Cook: 14 minutes

2 large sweet onions, chopped
1 tablespoon vegetable oil
¼ cup apple jelly
1½ teaspoons salt
½ teaspoon dried crushed red
    pepper

• **Sauté** onion in hot oil in a large skillet
over medium-high heat, stirring often,
10 minutes.
• **Add** remaining ingredients, stirring
until jelly melts. Serve relish with Easy
Black-eyed Peas (see recipe above).
Yield: 1¾ cups.

Janet Campbell
Mount Nebo, West Virginia

ℱRYING RIGHT

*Stir-frying is a great way to prepare light meals
because it requires little fat. Sesame and other
strong-flavored oils are often used because a small
amount imparts lots of flavor. These dishes get their
appeal from their flavor and their versatility—each
has a meat and a meatless version.*

BEEF-AND-VEGETABLE STIR-FRY

*This one-dish meal is complete
on a bed of hot cooked rice.*

Prep: 25 minutes
Cook: 10 minutes

1 pound fresh asparagus
12 ounces top round steak, cut
    into thin strips
3 tablespoons all-purpose
    flour
¼ cup lite soy sauce
¼ cup water
2 garlic cloves, minced
1 tablespoon dark sesame oil,
    divided
1 tablespoon hoisin sauce
¼ teaspoon dried crushed red
    pepper
4 small carrots, cut diagonally
    into ¼-inch-thick slices
1 small red bell pepper, cut into
    thin strips
½ cup sliced fresh mushrooms
5 green onions, cut into 1-inch
    pieces
2 cups hot cooked rice

• **Snap** off tough ends of asparagus; cut
spears into 1-inch pieces, and set aside.

• **Dredge** steak in flour; set aside.
• **Stir** together soy sauce, ¼ cup water,
garlic, 1 teaspoon sesame oil, hoisin
sauce, and crushed red pepper.
• **Heat** remaining 2 teaspoons oil in a
large skillet or wok over medium-high
heat 2 minutes.
• **Add** beef and carrot, and stir-fry 4 minutes. Add soy sauce mixture, and stir-fry
1 minute. Add vegetables, and stir-fry 3
minutes. Serve beef mixture over rice.
Yield: 4 servings.

❤ Per serving: Calories 357
Fat 7.8g Cholesterol 49mg
Sodium 665mg

Vegetable Stir-Fry: Omit round steak
and flour, and stir-fry vegetables as
directed above.

❤ Per serving: Calories 243
Fat 4.3g Cholesterol 0mg
Sodium 621mg

GLAZED STIR-FRY VEGETABLES

Prep: 15 minutes
Cook: 7 minutes

1 teaspoon chile oil
1 medium potato, peeled and cut into thin strips
3 cups broccoli flowerets
1 medium-size red bell pepper, cut into 1-inch pieces
2 tablespoons sugar
2 teaspoons cornstarch
½ teaspoon grated lemon rind
3 tablespoons fresh lemon juice
½ cup water

• **Heat** oil in a large skillet or wok over medium-high heat 2 minutes.
• **Add** potato, and stir-fry 2 minutes.
• **Add** broccoli and bell pepper; stir-fry 2 minutes or until crisp-tender.
• **Stir** together sugar and next 4 ingredients until smooth. Add to vegetables; stir-fry 1 minute or until thickened and bubbly. **Yield:** 4 servings.

Sara A. McCullough
Aualla, Texas

♥ Per serving: Calories 110
Fat 1.5g   Cholesterol 0mg
Sodium 22mg

Glazed Stir-Fry Vegetables and Chicken: Cut 4 (4-ounce) skinned and boned chicken breast halves into 1-inch pieces. Heat oil in a large skillet or wok over medium-high heat 2 minutes. Add chicken, and stir-fry 5 minutes or until done and lightly browned. Remove from skillet, and drain well on paper towels. Stir-fry vegetables without additional oil in skillet as directed. Return chicken to skillet when cornstarch mixture is added.

♥ Per serving: Calories 237
Fat 2.9g   Cholesterol 67mg
Sodium 97mg

WOK WISELY

Stir-frying dates back thousands of years when food had to be cooked quickly to preserve fuel. Because of the short cooking times, food retains texture, vitamins, and minerals. Here are some tips for stir-frying success.

■ Have all of the ingredients ready to go before you turn on the heat. To save even more time, chop the ingredients ahead of time and store in labeled zip-top plastic bags. In mere minutes, you can have a hot, home-made meal on the table.

■ Chop ingredients uniformly to ensure even doneness. Slice meat thinly so that it will cook quickly.

■ Plan to start cooking the rice, if needed, before you begin the stir-fry. It will be cooked and hot when the stir-fry is ready.

■ Make sure the oil is hot before you begin cooking so that the food will cook quickly.

■ Keep things moving. When stir-frying, stir constantly and briskly for even cooking.

■ Stir-fry the firmest vegetables first. Then add tender vegetables that require little cooking. Stir-fry only until the vegetables are crisp-tender. This will keep colors vibrant and nutrition high.

VEGETABLE MEDLEY STIR-FRY

Prep: 20 minutes
Cook: 8 minutes

2 medium shiitake mushrooms
1 tablespoon olive oil
½ cup sliced cabbage
½ cup chopped broccoli
½ cup chopped cauliflower
1 red bell pepper, chopped
1 zucchini, cut diagonally into ½-inch-thick slices
1 yellow squash, cut diagonally into ½-inch-thick slices
⅓ cup water
¼ cup orange juice
¼ cup lite soy sauce
2 garlic cloves, minced
2 teaspoons cornstarch
2 cups hot cooked rice
1 green onion, sliced

• **Remove** stems from mushrooms; reserve for another use. Thinly slice mushroom caps.
• **Heat** oil in a large skillet or wok over medium-high heat 1 minute.
• **Add** mushrooms, cabbage, and next 3 ingredients; stir-fry 3 minutes. Add zucchini and yellow squash, and stir-fry 3 minutes.
• **Stir** together ⅓ cup water and next 4 ingredients until smooth. Add to skillet; stir-fry 1 minute or until thickened and bubbly. Serve over rice. Sprinkle with green onion. **Yield:** 4 servings.

♥ Per serving: Calories 212
Fat 4.1g   Cholesterol 0mg
Sodium 552mg

Shrimp-and-Vegetable Medley Stir-Fry: Add 1 pound medium-size fresh shrimp, peeled and deveined, with corn-starch mixture; stir-fry as directed above or until shrimp turn pink.

♥ Per serving: Calories 296
Fat 5g   Cholesterol 166mg
Sodium 743mg

MIXED VEGGIE STIR-FRY

Prep: 15 minutes
Cook: 16 minutes

2 teaspoons hot pepper oil
2 garlic cloves, minced
2 carrots, thinly sliced
2 celery ribs, thinly sliced
3 tablespoons hoisin sauce
1 large sweet onion, cut in half and thinly sliced
1 large green bell pepper, cut into thin strips
1 small zucchini, sliced
1 small yellow squash, sliced
1 cup fresh broccoli flowerets
1 (8-ounce) package fresh mushrooms, sliced
1 tablespoon chopped fresh basil
2 tablespoons sherry (optional)

• **Heat** oil in a large skillet or wok over medium-high heat 2 minutes; add garlic and next 3 ingredients, and stir-fry 2 minutes.
• **Add** onion and next 3 ingredients, and stir-fry 5 minutes.
• **Add** broccoli and mushrooms, and stir-fry 3 minutes.
• **Stir** in basil and, if desired, sherry; stir-fry 4 minutes or until carrot is crisp-tender. **Yield:** 4 servings.

Note: For testing purposes only, we used Colavita pepperolio oil.

Kathy Seaberg
St. Petersburg, Florida

♥ Per serving: Calories 122
Fat 3.3g Cholesterol 0mg
Sodium 222mg

Mixed Veggie-and-Pork Stir-Fry: Cut 12 ounces lean boneless pork loin chops into thin strips. Heat oil in a large skillet or wok over medium-high heat 2 minutes; add pork, and stir-fry 6 minutes. Add garlic and next 3 ingredients, and proceed as directed above.

♥ Per serving: Calories 254
Fat 9.7g Cholesterol 51mg
Sodium 276mg

TUNNEL THROUGH CHOCOLATE

Who's ready for dessert? When it's chocolate cake, you won't have to ask twice, especially when it's tunneled with coconut and glazed with chocolate.

COCONUT-FUDGE CAKE

Prep: 30 minutes
Bake: 1 hour and 10 minutes

2¼ cups sugar, divided
1 cup vegetable oil
3 large eggs, divided
3 cups all-purpose flour
2 teaspoons baking soda
2 teaspoons baking powder
1½ teaspoons salt
¾ cup cocoa
1 cup brewed coffee or water
1 cup buttermilk
½ cup chopped pecans
2 teaspoons vanilla extract, divided
1 (8-ounce) package cream cheese, softened
½ cup flaked coconut
1 cup (6 ounces) semisweet chocolate morsels
Chocolate Glaze

• **Beat** 2 cups sugar, oil, and 2 eggs at high speed with an electric mixer 1 minute.
• **Combine** flour and next 4 ingredients; combine coffee and buttermilk. Add flour mixture and coffee mixture to oil mixture. Beat at medium speed 3 minutes.
• **Stir** in pecans and 1 teaspoon vanilla. Pour half of batter into a greased and floured 12-cup Bundt pan.
• **Beat** cream cheese at medium speed until fluffy; gradually add remaining ¼ cup sugar and remaining egg. Beat just until blended.
• **Stir** in remaining vanilla, coconut, and morsels; spoon over batter in pan, leaving a ½-inch border around center and edge. Top with remaining batter.

• **Bake** at 350° for 1 hour and 10 minutes or until a wooden pick inserted in center comes out clean. Cool in pan on a wire rack 15 minutes. Remove from pan; cool on wire rack. Drizzle with warm Chocolate Glaze. **Yield:** 1 (10-inch) cake.

Chocolate Glaze

Prep: 5 minutes
Cook: 8 minutes

2 tablespoons butter or margarine
1 cup powdered sugar
3 tablespoons cocoa
1 to 3 tablespoons hot water
2 teaspoons vanilla extract

• **Melt** butter in a saucepan over low heat; stir in sugar and remaining ingredients. **Yield:** about ½ cup.

Thelma Foley
Waynesbury, Kentucky

PEACH APPEAL

If you haven't had your fill of peaches this summer, there's still time. Farmers markets, roadside stands, and grocery stores have baskets of peaches ready to sweeten the end of the season—and these recipes are the perfect ways to show off their summery goodness.

EASY PEACH COBBLER

Prep: 15 minutes
Bake: 55 minutes

4 cups sliced peach (about 6 peaches)
1 cup sugar, divided
½ cup butter or margarine
¾ cup all-purpose flour
2 teaspoons baking powder
¾ cup milk
Vanilla ice cream

- **Combine** peach and ½ cup sugar; let stand 15 minutes or until a syrup forms.
- **Melt** butter at 350° in an 11- x 7-inch baking dish.
- **Stir** together remaining ½ cup sugar, flour, baking powder, and milk; pour mixture over melted butter. (Do not stir.) Spoon peach over mixture.
- **Bake** at 350° for 55 minutes. Serve warm cobbler with vanilla ice cream. **Yield:** 6 to 8 servings.

Bob Martin
Wilmington, North Carolina

CREAM OF PEACH SOUP

Prep: 15 minutes
Cook: 5 minutes
Chill: 2 hours

2 pounds ripe peaches (about 6 large)
¼ cup sugar
1 cup water
1 cup whipping cream
½ cup white wine
Grated rind of 1 lemon
Garnishes: chopped and sliced peach, fresh mint sprigs, chopped mint leaves

- **Dip** peaches, 1 at a time, into boiling water to cover 1 minute. Plunge peaches immediately into ice water to stop the cooking process; drain and slip skins off. Cut peaches into quarters.
- **Bring** sugar and 1 cup water to a boil in a large saucepan over medium heat. Reduce heat, and add peach quarters; cover and simmer 5 minutes. Cool.
- **Process** peach mixture in batches in a blender until smooth, stopping to scrape down sides.
- **Stir** together peach mixture, whipping cream, wine, and lemon rind; cover and chill. Garnish, if desired. **Yield:** 5 cups.

Sandi Pichon
Slidell, Louisiana

SHADES OF ADE

The tartness of lemonade quenches thirst on a hot day. With five ingredients or less, these citrus refreshers are guaranteed not to keep you in the kitchen. Lemony Ice Cream Pie is so easy, you can keep an extra one in the freezer for unexpected guests.

LEMONY ICE CREAM PIE
(pictured on page 192)

Prep: 10 minutes
Freeze: 2 hours

1 quart vanilla ice cream, softened
1 (6-ounce) can frozen lemonade concentrate, partially thawed
1 (9-inch) graham cracker crust
Garnishes: fresh raspberries, lemon slices, fresh mint sprigs

- **Stir** together ice cream and lemonade concentrate until blended. Spoon into crust, and freeze 2 hours or until firm. Garnish, if desired. **Yield:** 1 (9-inch) pie.

ALMOND-LEMONADE TEA

Serve with your favorite cookies.

Prep: 5 minutes

4 cups brewed tea, chilled
3 cups cold water
1 (6-ounce) can frozen lemonade concentrate, thawed
¼ cup sugar
1 teaspoon almond extract

- **Stir** together all ingredients in a large pitcher until sugar dissolves. Serve over ice. **Yield:** 2 quarts.

Theresa Mazoeh
Corpus Christi, Texas

RASPBERRY SPRITZERS
(pictured on page 192)

These treats are even cooler served with sprigs of fresh mint.

Prep: 5 minutes

1 (10-ounce) package frozen raspberries, thawed
1 (12-ounce) can frozen cranberry juice drink concentrate, thawed
1 (12-ounce) can frozen pink lemonade concentrate, thawed
2 (2-liter) bottles ginger ale, chilled

- **Process** raspberries in a blender until smooth. If desired, strain pureed raspberries, discarding seeds.
- **Combine** raspberry puree and concentrates in a 1½-gallon container. Stir in ginger ale just before serving. **Yield:** 5 quarts.

Emily Custer
West Valley City, Utah

PITCHER PERFECT

Make a citrus collar for your favorite glass pitcher by threading lemon slices onto clear nylon thread. Measure circumference of the pitcher's neck; cut a length of thread to match measurement plus three to four inches. Position string of lemon slices around pitcher, tying ends together to snugly hold lemons in place.

FROM OUR KITCHEN TO YOURS

HERB SAVVY

In "A Well-Seasoned Supper" (page 182), we pay tribute to summer's finest herbs with terrific recipes such as Herbed Cheesecakes and Dilled Summer Soup. Now let's focus on the herbs themselves.

In most cases, fresh herbs can be kept refrigerated, wrapped in lightly dampened paper towels inside a zip-top plastic bag, up to one week.

If you want to substitute fresh herbs for dried herbs, you can generally use three times the amount of fresh herbs as dried ones.

Here are some common herbs used in our recipes.

■ **Basil**'s flavor is a tasty blend of lemon, licorice, and cloves. It's especially nice with fresh tomatoes and in pasta sauces, and it's the main ingredient in pesto.

■ **Chives** are slender, hollow-stemmed flowering herbs with an onion-leek flavor. They enhance vegetables, omelets, salads, and soups. Add chopped chives to a dish just before serving to retain the herb's subtle flavor.

■ **Cilantro,** also known as Chinese parsley, is grown for its spicy-flavored foliage and for its seed called coriander. Cilantro is the leaf; coriander is the seed or powdered form of the herb. Use cilantro leaves in Southwestern, Mexican, and Asian dishes.

■ **Dill,** a delicate, feathery, flowering herb, perks up vegetables, fish, coleslaw, potato salad, and cream soups. It's also the main flavor in many pickles. Fresh dill loses its flavor when overheated; however, heat intensifies the flavor of dried dillweed.

■ **Mint,** a peppery, aromatic herb, is refreshing in both sweet and savory dishes, from tea to fruit to lamb. It has long been a symbol of hospitality. Mint julep, anyone?

■ **Oregano**'s bold, pungent flavor is a natural in tomato dishes and is vital to any good pizza or spaghetti sauce. This versatile herb is also used as a staple in Mexican and Mediterranean fare.

■ **Rosemary** adds a refreshing, robust lemon-pine flavor to breads, chicken, lamb, venison, and soups.

■ **Thyme**'s tiny leaves bring a nutty, lemony flavor to vegetable dishes, meat, poultry, and cream sauces.

TIPS AND TIDBITS

Healthy food doesn't have to be bland. Try these tips to make low-fat, low-calorie foods taste fabulous. For an extra kick, add a splash of (fresh) lemon or lime juice to vegetables, fish, or poultry before serving. Use frozen juice concentrate, thawed, as a sweetener in place of sugar.

■ Substitute fresh herbs for salt.

■ Stock up on herb-infused vinegars to pump up the flavor of marinades, dressings, and sauces.

■ Be bold: Increase your use of pungent spices such as ginger, hot paprika, ground cumin, ground red pepper, and fresh chile peppers.

WAYS OF THE GRAIN

Park your shopping cart on the rice aisle to examine the many varieties and flavors available. Take several kinds of rice home and experiment with them.

■ **Basmati** is a very long-grain, needle-shaped rice. The grains stay separate and firm. Serve it hot with roast beef or meat loaf.

■ **Brown rice** has been taken from the husk but not milled and polished. It takes about twice as long to cook, but its chewy texture and additional nutrients are worth it.

■ **Louisiana pecan rice,** a long-grain aromatic variety, has a nutty taste and aroma. This one is a great side for roasted chicken.

■ Buy **pearl rice,** a short-grain variety, for creamy puddings.

■ **Sticky rice** can be long- or short-grain. Try it steamed to accompany pork chops.

■ **Superfino** is the "Rolls Royce" of Italian Arborio rice for risotto. Once you try this one, you'll want to keep some on hand.

Buying rice in bulk can save money. However, if you don't use it regularly, it can get stale, take longer to cook, and sometimes be tough. Store rice in an airtight container away from light and moisture. While it looks pretty in glass canisters on countertops, the light robs rice of its flavor.

SEPTEMBER

September's harvest of golden honey reminds us of nature's ability to achieve perfection, and this month we applaud the efforts of wondrous honeybees in "Nature's Sweet Reward." Honey Ice Cream, Honey Graham Bread, and Honey-Apple Cake are some of our favorite ways to enjoy honey's amber warmth.

Glossy purple hues and delicious versatility make eggplant difficult to resist, and "Exquisite in Purple" presents recipes that feature this mild fruit. Eggplant Caviar, Spicy Eggplant, and Eggplant-Spinach Casserole provide you with the perfect ways to enjoy eggplant at its peak.

NATURE'S SWEET REWARD

In cakes and pies and even barbecue sauce, honey finds a place to shine. Sample this collection of showcase recipes. Then say a sweet thank you to Mother Nature.

HONEY-APPLE CAKE
(pictured on page 228)

Prep: 15 minutes
Bake: 1 hour

1 cup chopped pecans, divided
2 cups sugar
1 cup vegetable oil
¼ cup honey
3 large eggs
3 cups all-purpose flour
1 teaspoon baking soda
1 teaspoon salt
1 teaspoon ground cinnamon
¼ teaspoon ground nutmeg
1 teaspoon vanilla extract
3 cups peeled, chopped Golden
  Delicious apple
Honey Sauce
Vanilla ice cream (optional)

• **Grease** and flour a 12-cup Bundt pan; sprinkle bottom of pan with ¼ cup pecans. Set aside.
• **Beat** sugar, oil, and honey at medium speed with an electric mixer until well blended. Add eggs, 1 at a time, beating just until blended.
• **Combine** flour and next 4 ingredients. Gradually add to sugar mixture, beating at low speed just until blended.

• **Stir** in vanilla, remaining ¾ cup pecans, and apple. Spoon over pecans in pan.
• **Bake** at 350° for 55 to 60 minutes. Cool in pan on a wire rack 15 minutes; remove from pan, and place on wire rack over wax paper. Pour ½ cup Honey Sauce over warm cake. Cool.
• **Heat** remaining Honey Sauce, and serve with cake. Top with ice cream, if desired. **Yield:** 1 (10-inch) cake.

Honey Sauce

Prep: 5 minutes
Cook: 2 minutes

1 cup firmly packed brown sugar
½ cup butter or margarine
¼ cup honey
¼ cup milk

• **Bring** all ingredients to a boil in a medium saucepan over medium-high heat, stirring constantly; boil, stirring constantly, 2 minutes. **Yield:** 1½ cups.
Mary Beightol
Maryville, Tennessee

HONEY-APPLESAUCE SALAD DRESSING

Fragrant orange blossom honey is perfect for this fruit salad dressing.

Prep: 10 minutes

½ cup applesauce
½ cup honey
¼ teaspoon grated lemon rind
3 tablespoons fresh lemon juice
1 tablespoon white vinegar
½ teaspoon paprika
½ teaspoon salt
¼ teaspoon dry mustard
½ cup vegetable oil
1 tablespoon poppy seeds

• **Process** first 8 ingredients in a blender until smooth, stopping to scrape down sides. Turn blender on high; add oil in a slow, steady stream. Stir in poppy seeds. Serve over fresh fruit or spinach with apple and pear slices. **Yield:** about 2 cups.
Millie Givens
Savannah, Georgia

TEXAS BARBECUE SAUCE

Bold, distinct gallberry honey holds its own in this zesty sauce.

Prep: 5 minutes
Cook: 5 minutes

2 cups ketchup
½ cup white vinegar
½ cup honey
½ cup water
2 teaspoons dried crushed green
  pepper
1 tablespoon minced onion
2 tablespoons Worcestershire
  sauce
¼ teaspoon ground black pepper
Dash of garlic powder
Dash of ground red pepper

• **Bring** all ingredients to a boil in a large saucepan over medium-high heat, stirring often. Cool; store in refrigerator. **Yield:** 3½ cups.

Judy Laramy
Austin, Texas

HONEY GRAHAM BREAD
(pictured on page 228)

Prep: 50 minutes
Rise: 1 hour and 45 minutes
Bake: 35 minutes

2 (¼-ounce) envelopes active dry
   yeast
½ cup warm water (100° to 110°)
2 teaspoons sugar
3 cups whole wheat flour
1½ cups milk
½ cup honey
2 teaspoons salt
¼ cup butter or margarine,
   softened
2½ to 3 cups bread flour

• **Combine** yeast, ½ cup warm water,
and sugar in a 2-cup glass measuring
cup; let stand 5 minutes.
• **Beat** yeast mixture, 1½ cups whole
wheat flour, and next 4 ingredients at
medium speed with an electric mixer
until blended.
• **Stir** in remaining 1½ cups wheat flour.
Add bread flour, 1 cup at a time, beating
after each addition. Let stand 15 minutes.
• **Turn** dough out onto a lightly floured
surface, and knead 5 to 10 minutes or
until smooth and elastic. Place in a well-
greased bowl, turning to grease top.
• **Cover** and let rise in a warm place
(85°), free from drafts, 1 hour or until
doubled in bulk.
• **Punch** dough down, and divide into 2
equal portions. Shape each portion into
a loaf; place loaves into 2 greased 9- x 5-
inch loafpans.
• **Cover** and let rise in a warm place,
free from drafts, 30 to 45 minutes or
until doubled in bulk.
• **Bake** at 375° for 20 minutes; cover
loosely with aluminum foil, and bake 15
more minutes or until loaves sound hollow when tapped. Remove from pans,
and cool on wire racks. **Yield:** 2 (9-inch)
loaves.

Agnes L. Stone
Ocala, Florida

The pedigree of honey
Does not concern the bee
A clover, any time, to him is Aristocracy.

Emily Dickinson

Come September, we can thank
the tiny honeybee for delivering one
of nature's trophy harvests. After
spring and summer days spent
tirelessly buzzing from flower to
flower—through fields of clover
or groves of orange trees—the
industrious little insects give
up their golden treasure to their
keepers. To us belongs the simple
task of savoring the bounty.

BUZZ WORDS
■ The color and flavor of honey
depend on where bees harvest their
nectar. Expect light color and mild
flavor and aroma from clover,
orange blossom, and sourwood
honeys. Buckwheat honey boasts a
full-bodied flavor and deep color.

■ When you substitute honey for
sugar in a recipe, reduce any liquid
by ¼ cup and add ½ teaspoon baking soda for each cup of honey used.
Also, reduce oven temperature by 25
degrees to prevent overbrowning.

■ As an ingredient, honey absorbs
and retains moisture, which helps
delay the drying out of baked goods.

■ Store honey at room temperature.
If it crystallizes, remove the lid and
place the jar in a container of warm
water until the crystals dissolve.

■ For easy removal, coat your measuring cup with vegetable cooking
spray before measuring honey. The
honey will slide right out.

■ Honey can be toxic to infants
under one year of age.

BUSY BEES
Wondrous honeybees diligently
manufacture their product in one
of the world's most efficient facto-
ries—the beehive. For every pound
of honey, a hive of the four-winged
workers must fly more than 55,000
miles and tap more than 2 million
flowers.

■ The wings of honeybees stroke
11,400 times per minute to make
their distinctive buzz.

■ About one-third of our diet comes
from plants pollinated by insects.
The honeybee takes credit for 80
percent of this pollination.

■ A honeybee flies about 15 m.p.h.

■ It would take only 1 ounce of
honey to fuel a honeybee's flight
around the world.

■ The average worker honeybee
makes about 1/12 teaspoon of honey
in its lifetime.

APRICOT BUTTER
(pictured on page 228)

Prep: 10 minutes

½ cup butter or margarine, softened
¼ cup honey
¼ cup finely chopped dried apricots
½ teaspoon grated lemon rind

• **Beat** butter at medium speed with an electric mixer until fluffy; add remaining ingredients, beating until blended. Chill, if desired. **Yield:** ¾ cup.

Eleanor Conlon
Proctor, West Virginia

GRANOLA
(pictured on page 263)

Choose sweet, delicate Tupelo honey for this healthful cereal.

Prep: 10 minutes
Bake: 1 hour and 45 minutes

4 cups uncooked regular oats
1 cup sunflower seeds
½ cup whole almonds
½ cup sesame seeds
¾ cup wheat germ
1 (3.5-ounce) can flaked coconut
½ cup honey
⅓ cup vegetable oil
2 tablespoons water
1 cup dried apricots, coarsely chopped
1 cup raisins

• **Stir** together first 6 ingredients in a large bowl. Stir together honey, oil, and 2 tablespoons water; pour over oat mixture, tossing well.
• **Spread** mixture into a lightly greased 15- x 10-inch jellyroll pan.
• **Bake** at 225° for 1 hour and 45 minutes, stirring every 15 minutes.
• **Stir** in apricots and raisins. Cool completely. Store in an airtight container. **Yield:** 10 cups.

Stanlay Webber
Winston-Salem, North Carolina

HONEY-PECAN TART

Try the mellow taste of sourwood honey to complement the richness of this favorite.

Prep: 50 minutes
Freeze: 1 hour
Bake: 30 minutes

1 cup sugar
¼ cup water
1 cup whipping cream
¼ cup unsalted butter, cut into small pieces
¼ cup honey
½ teaspoon salt
2½ cups pecan halves, coarsely chopped
1 (15-ounce) package refrigerated piecrusts
2 teaspoons sugar, divided
½ (4-ounce) package bittersweet chocolate, chopped

• **Bring** 1 cup sugar and ¼ cup water to a boil in a medium-size heavy saucepan, stirring until sugar dissolves. Cover and boil over medium-high heat, without stirring, 8 minutes or until golden, swirling pan occasionally.
• **Remove** from heat, and gradually stir in whipping cream (mixture will bubble with addition of cream).
• **Add** butter, honey, and salt, stirring until smooth. Stir in pecans; simmer over medium heat, stirring occasionally, 5 minutes. Remove from heat; cool completely.
• **Unfold** 1 piecrust on a lightly floured surface; roll into an 11-inch circle. Fit into a 9-inch removable bottom tart pan. Trim edges. Freeze crust 30 minutes.
• **Spread** pecan mixture into crust. Unfold remaining piecrust, and roll into a 10-inch circle. Place crust over mixture, pressing into bottom crust to seal; trim edges. Sprinkle with 1 teaspoon sugar. Freeze 30 minutes.
• **Bake** at 400° for 30 minutes. Cool on a wire rack.
• **Place** chocolate in a small heavy-duty zip-top plastic bag; seal. Submerge in hot water until chocolate melts. Snip a tiny hole in 1 corner of bag; drizzle chocolate over tart. Sprinkle with remaining 1 teaspoon sugar. **Yield:** 1 (9-inch) tart.

Caroline Harris
Athens, Georgia

HONEY ICE CREAM

Prep: 5 minutes
Stand: 1 hour

2 quarts half-and-half
1½ cups honey
2 tablespoons vanilla extract

• **Stir** together all ingredients, and pour into freezer container of a 1-gallon electric freezer.
• **Freeze** according to manufacturer's instructions. Pack with additional ice and rock salt, and let stand 1 hour before serving. **Yield:** 3 quarts.

CHICKEN QUICK

When it comes to a fast meal from scratch, it's hard to beat chicken breast halves. Boned and skinned, they cook in 20 minutes or less; bone-in halves with skin require about 15 minutes more. Individually quick-frozen breast halves offer added convenience—no thawing necessary.

OVEN-FRIED CHICKEN

Prep: 15 minutes
Bake: 20 minutes

1¼ cups Italian-seasoned breadcrumbs
¼ cup grated Parmesan cheese
½ cup fat-free mayonnaise
½ teaspoon salt
½ teaspoon poultry seasoning
¼ teaspoon ground red pepper
8 skinned and boned chicken breast halves

• **Stir** together breadcrumbs and Parmesan cheese in a shallow dish.

- **Stir** together mayonnaise and next 3 ingredients.
- **Brush** both sides of chicken with mayonnaise mixture, and dredge in breadcrumb mixture. Place in an aluminum foil-lined 15- x 10-inch jellyroll pan coated with vegetable cooking spray.
- **Bake** at 425° for 20 minutes or until done. **Yield:** 8 servings.

J. A. Allard
San Antonio, Texas

CHICKEN CACCIATORE

Prep: 15 minutes
Cook: 45 minutes

4 bone-in chicken breast halves, skinned
2 tablespoons olive oil
1 green bell pepper, cut into rings
1 small onion, sliced
1 garlic clove, minced
1 (14½-ounce) can Italian-style stewed tomatoes
1 (6-ounce) can Italian-style tomato paste
¾ cup dry red wine or chicken broth
1 bay leaf
1 teaspoon dried Italian seasoning
Hot cooked spaghetti

- **Brown** chicken in hot oil in a Dutch oven over medium-high heat 5 minutes on each side. Remove chicken, reserving drippings in pan.
- **Add** bell pepper and onion to hot drippings, and sauté until tender.
- **Return** chicken to pan; add garlic and next 5 ingredients. Bring to a boil; cover, reduce heat, and simmer 45 minutes. Discard bay leaf. Serve over spaghetti. **Yield:** 4 servings.

Elaine C. Heintz
Staunton, Virginia

HONEY-GLAZED GRILLED CHICKEN

Prep: 15 minutes
Marinate: 8 hours
Grill: 12 minutes

½ cup honey
2 tablespoons soy sauce
2 tablespoons dry white wine
2 tablespoons lemon juice
2 green onions, minced
2 garlic cloves, minced
1 tablespoon minced fresh ginger
¼ teaspoon salt
¼ teaspoon pepper
6 skinned and boned chicken breast halves *
Garnish: green onion tops

- **Stir** together first 9 ingredients in a shallow dish; add chicken. Cover and chill 8 hours.
- **Remove** chicken from marinade, discarding marinade.
- **Grill** chicken, covered with grill lid, over medium-high heat (350° to 400°) 6 minutes on each side or until done. Garnish, if desired. **Yield:** 6 servings.

* Substitute 6 boneless pork chops for chicken, if desired.

Debbie Collard Estes
Vine Grove, Kentucky

CHICKEN BREASTS DIANE

Prep: 20 minutes
Cook: 10 minutes

4 skinned and boned chicken breast halves
½ teaspoon salt
¼ teaspoon pepper
1 tablespoon butter or margarine
1 tablespoon olive oil
4 green onions, chopped
¼ cup chicken broth
2 tablespoons lemon juice
2 tablespoons brandy or chicken broth
2 tablespoons Dijon mustard
3 tablespoons chopped fresh parsley
Hot cooked rice

- **Place** chicken between 2 sheets of heavy-duty plastic wrap; flatten to ¼-inch thickness using a meat mallet or rolling pin. Sprinkle with salt and pepper.
- **Melt** butter in oil in a skillet over medium-high heat; add chicken, and cook 2 minutes on each side or until done. Remove chicken, and keep warm. Reduce heat to medium.
- **Add** onions and next 4 ingredients to skillet; cook, whisking constantly, until bubbly. Stir in parsley. Pour over chicken; serve with rice. **Yield:** 4 servings.

Trish Zinsmeister
DeSoto, Texas

CRAVING BACON

Nothing beats the heady aroma of bacon sizzling in the skillet, a sign that a bountiful breakfast is on the way. But true bacon lovers crave it at any meal.

These recipes, from appetizers to side dishes to brunch favorites, feature bacon at its best.

BACON-SHRIMP BITES

Prep: 20 minutes
Cook: 10 minutes

40 unpeeled, large fresh shrimp
20 bacon slices
2 cups barbecue sauce

- **Peel** shrimp; devein, if desired.
- **Cut** bacon slices in half crosswise. Wrap bacon pieces around shrimp, and secure with wooden picks; place on a lightly greased rack in a broiler pan.
- **Broil** 6 inches from heat (with electric oven door partially open) 5 minutes on each side or until bacon is crisp.
- **Heat** barbecue sauce, and serve with shrimp. **Yield:** 40 appetizers.

Genie Usie
Bourg, Louisiana

LOADED CORNBREAD

Prep: 15 minutes
Bake: 28 minutes

1 (12-ounce) package frozen corn
   soufflé, thawed
1 (8½-ounce) package Mexican
   cornbread mix
1 cup (4 ounces) shredded
   Cheddar cheese
8 bacon slices, cooked and crumbled
2 green onions, minced
¼ teaspoon ground red pepper

• **Stir** together all ingredients until
blended. Pour into a greased 8-inch
square pan. Bake at 400° for 28 minutes
or until bread is lightly browned and a
wooden pick inserted in center comes
out clean. **Yield:** 9 servings.

SPICY RICE

Prep: 30 minutes
Cook: 11 minutes

¾ cup uncooked long-grain rice
2 cups water, divided
15 bacon slices
1 medium onion, chopped
2 celery ribs, thinly sliced
2 small carrots, thinly sliced
½ cup frozen sweet green peas,
   thawed
¼ teaspoon garlic salt
¼ teaspoon ground red pepper
¼ teaspoon seasoned pepper

• **Bring** rice and 1½ cups water to a
boil; cover, reduce heat, and simmer 20
minutes or until liquid is absorbed.
• **Cook** bacon in a large skillet until crisp;
drain bacon, reserving 2 tablespoons
drippings in pan. Crumble bacon.
• **Sauté** onion, celery, and carrot in hot
drippings over medium-high heat 3 minutes or until tender. Add peas, and sauté
3 minutes.
• **Stir** in rice, remaining ½ cup water,
bacon, and seasonings; cook 5 minutes
or until thoroughly heated. Serve immediately. **Yield:** 4 servings.

J. Marvin Smith
Palm Harbor, Florida

NASSAU GRITS

Prep: 45 minutes
Cook: 17 minutes

1 (12-ounce) package bacon, cut
   into 1-inch pieces
½ pound ground pork sausage
1 medium onion, diced
1 small green bell pepper, diced
1 garlic clove, minced
4 cups water
2 (14.5-ounce) cans diced
   tomatoes with basil, garlic,
   and oregano
½ teaspoon salt
½ teaspoon pepper
1½ teaspoons Worcestershire
   sauce
½ teaspoon hot sauce
1 cup uncooked regular grits

• **Cook** bacon and sausage in a Dutch
oven over medium heat 25 minutes, stirring until sausage crumbles and is no
longer pink and bacon is crisp. Drain
sausage and bacon, reserving 1 tablespoon drippings in pan.
• **Sauté** onion, bell pepper, and garlic in
hot drippings over medium heat 10 minutes or until tender.
• **Stir** in 4 cups water and next 5 ingredients; bring to a boil. Gradually stir in
grits; cover, reduce heat, and simmer,
stirring occasionally, 15 to 17 minutes or
until thickened. Stir in sausage and
bacon. **Yield:** 4 to 6 servings.

Diane Osborne
Columbus, Georgia

BACON BISCUIT CUPS

To reheat, wrap biscuit cups in foil. Bake at
350° for 10 minutes or until warm.

Prep: 10 minutes
Bake: 22 minutes

2 (3-ounce) packages cream
   cheese, softened
2 tablespoons milk
1 large egg
½ cup (2 ounces) shredded Swiss
   cheese
1 green onion, chopped
1 (10-ounce) can refrigerated
   flaky biscuits
5 bacon slices, cooked and crumbled

• **Beat** first 3 ingredients at medium
speed with an electric mixer until
blended. Stir in cheese and chopped
green onion. Set aside.
• **Separate** biscuits into 10 portions.
Pat each portion into a 5-inch circle, and
press on bottom and up sides of greased
muffin cups, forming a ¼-inch edge.
Sprinkle with half of bacon, and spoon
cream cheese mixture evenly on top.
• **Bake** at 375° for 22 minutes or until
set. Sprinkle with remaining bacon,
lightly pressing into filling. Remove immediately from pan, and serve warm.
Yield: 10 servings.

Note: For testing purposes only, we used
Hungry Jack Refrigerated Flaky Biscuits.

Mildred Bickley
Bristol, Virginia

BACON BITS

■ To help separate the slices,
remove bacon from the refrigerator
at least 30 minutes before cooking,
or microwave the bacon at HIGH 30
seconds.

■ If your recipe calls for diced
bacon, it's easier to cut when
the bacon is still semifrozen.

■ The thinner the bacon, the crispier
it becomes after frying.

■ Start bacon in a cold skillet,
and cook over medium heat to
minimize shrinkage; prick bacon
with a fork to reduce curling.

Source: *The Food Lover's Tiptionary*

CASSEROLE CONVENIENCE

Casseroles are a family cook's best friends—they're easy to prepare, ready to serve, and universally popular. They're also often loaded with heavy sauces or large quantities of cheese, ingredients that bring high taste and high calorie counts. This classic selection cuts calories while keeping taste intact.

CHICKEN-RICE CASSEROLE

Prep: 20 minutes
Bake: 1 hour

½ cup chopped celery
¼ cup chopped onion
2 garlic cloves, minced
Vegetable cooking spray
1 (8-ounce) package sliced fresh mushrooms
1 cup uncooked regular rice
1 (10¾-ounce) can reduced-sodium, reduced-fat cream of mushroom soup, undiluted
1 cup water
1 (8-ounce) can sliced water chestnuts, drained
3 tablespoons chopped fresh parsley
¼ cup dry sherry (optional)
6 bone-in chicken breast halves, skinned
½ teaspoon salt
½ teaspoon pepper

• **Sauté** first 3 ingredients in a large non-stick skillet coated with cooking spray over medium heat 5 minutes or until tender. Add mushrooms; sauté 2 minutes. Stir in rice, next 4 ingredients, and, if desired, sherry; spoon into a lightly greased 13- x 9-inch baking dish. Top with chicken. Sprinkle chicken with salt and pepper.
• **Bake,** covered, at 350° for 1 hour or until chicken is done. **Yield:** 6 servings.

♥ Per serving: Calories 320
Fat 3.1g Cholesterol 72mg
Sodium 489mg

LOW-FAT SPAGHETTI CASSEROLE

Prep: 25 minutes
Bake: 25 minutes

7 ounces uncooked spaghetti
⅓ cup grated Parmesan cheese
2 egg whites, lightly beaten
1 tablespoon margarine
1 (8-ounce) container nonfat cottage cheese
1 pound low-fat ground pork sausage
½ cup chopped onion
¼ cup chopped green bell pepper
1 garlic clove, minced
1 (14½-ounce) can no-salt-added stewed tomatoes
1 (6-ounce) can no-salt-added tomato paste
1 teaspoon sugar
1 teaspoon dried oregano
½ cup (2 ounces) shredded reduced-fat mozzarella cheese

• **Cook** spaghetti according to package directions, omitting salt; drain.
• **Toss** spaghetti with Parmesan cheese, egg whites, and margarine. Place in a lightly greased 8-inch square baking dish. Spread cottage cheese over spaghetti mixture.
• **Cook** sausage and next 3 ingredients in a large nonstick skillet over medium heat, stirring until sausage crumbles and is no longer pink. Drain and pat dry with paper towels. Wipe drippings from skillet with a paper towel. Return sausage mixture to skillet; stir in stewed tomatoes and next 3 ingredients.

• **Cook** over medium heat until thoroughly heated. Spoon over cottage cheese. Bake at 350° for 25 minutes. Sprinkle casserole with mozzarella cheese. **Yield:** 6 servings.

Karen C. Christiansen
Little Rock, Arkansas

♥ Per serving: Calories 409
Fat 16.4g Cholesterol 38.5mg
Sodium 813mg

BEEF, BEAN, AND CORNBREAD CASSEROLE

Prep: 25 minutes
Bake: 30 minutes

1 pound lean ground beef
1 cup chopped onion
2 garlic cloves, pressed
Vegetable cooking spray
2 (8-ounce) cans no-salt-added tomato sauce
2 (16-ounce) cans pinto beans, rinsed and drained
1 (4.5-ounce) can chopped green chiles, undrained
1 tablespoon chili powder
1½ teaspoons ground cumin
½ teaspoon dried oregano
1 (6-ounce) package cornbread mix

• **Cook** first 3 ingredients in a large saucepan coated with vegetable cooking spray over medium-high heat, stirring until beef crumbles and is no longer pink. Drain and pat dry with paper towels. Wipe drippings from skillet with a paper towel.
• **Return** beef mixture to skillet. Stir in tomato sauce and next 5 ingredients. Cover and cook over medium-low heat 10 minutes. Pour into a lightly greased 2-quart baking dish.
• **Prepare** cornbread batter according to package directions using fat-free milk. Pour over beef mixture.
• **Bake** at 400° for 30 minutes or until lightly browned. **Yield:** 6 servings.

♥ Per serving: Calories 577
Fat 18.3g Cholesterol 101mg
Sodium 802mg

SOUTHWESTERN CASSEROLE

Prep: 25 minutes
Bake: 33 minutes

1 onion, chopped
1 green bell pepper, chopped
1 jalapeño pepper, seeded and
     chopped
2 garlic cloves, minced
2 to 3 teaspoons chili powder
1 teaspoon dried oregano
Vegetable cooking spray
1 (10¾-ounce) can reduced-
     sodium, reduced-fat cream of
     mushroom soup, undiluted
1 (10¾-ounce) can reduced-
     sodium, reduced-fat cream of
     chicken soup, undiluted
1 (10-ounce) can diced tomatoes
     and green chiles, undrained
2¼ cups chopped cooked
     chicken
2 cups crumbled baked tortilla
     chips
5 tablespoons chopped fresh
     cilantro, divided
1 cup (4 ounces) shredded
     reduced-fat Cheddar
     cheese

• **Sauté** first 6 ingredients in a large non-stick skillet coated with cooking spray over medium heat 8 minutes.
• **Stir** in mushroom soup, next 4 ingredients, and 4 tablespoons cilantro; spoon mixture into a lightly greased 13- x 9-inch baking dish.
• **Bake,** covered, at 350° for 30 minutes or until bubbly.
• **Toss** remaining 1 tablespoon cilantro with cheese. Uncover casserole, and sprinkle with cheese mixture. Bake 3 more minutes. **Yield:** 8 servings.

Georgana Dettman
Wiemar, Texas

♥ Per serving: Calories 217
Fat 7.3g Cholesterol 52mg
Sodium 742mg

$\mathcal{B}$IG-TIME MUSHROOMS

The portobello mushroom has a kingly reputation—not just for its size, but for its versatility. Its earthy flavor and meaty texture make it ideal for grilling or roasting. It's also beautiful sliced atop pizzas and salads. See for yourself in these two good reasons to adore them.

PORTOBELLO-PINE NUT PIZZA

Prep: 20 minutes
Bake: 15 minutes

1 (12-inch) pizza crust
1 (6-ounce) can tomato
     paste
¼ cup water
2 teaspoons sugar
2 teaspoons balsamic vinegar
½ teaspoon dried Italian
     seasoning
¼ teaspoon dried crushed red
     pepper
1 garlic clove, pressed
2 medium portobello mushroom
     caps
3 tablespoons olive oil
1 small onion, thinly sliced
¼ cup dried tomatoes,
     chopped
2 tablespoons pine nuts
½ cup shredded Parmesan
     cheese
1 cup (4 ounces) shredded
     mozzarella cheese

• **Bake** pizza crust at 400° for 4 minutes.
• **Stir** together tomato paste and next 6 ingredients. Spread over pizza crust.

• **Brush** mushrooms with oil; place in a hot grill skillet or regular skillet. Cook 4 minutes on each side or until tender. Thinly slice; arrange on pizza.
• **Top** pizza with onion, tomatoes, and pine nuts. Sprinkle with cheeses.
• **Bake** at 400° for 15 minutes. **Yield:** 1 (12-inch) pizza.

GRILLED PORTOBELLO SALAD

Enjoy this salad with a sprightly Sauvignon Blanc.

Prep: 5 minutes
Marinate: 3 hours
Broil: 8 minutes

1 (8-ounce) bottle balsamic
     vinaigrette (1 cup), divided *
4 medium portobello mushroom
     caps
4 cups gourmet salad greens
½ cup chopped walnuts or pecans,
     toasted
¼ cup crumbled goat cheese

• **Combine** ½ cup balsamic vinaigrette and mushrooms in a heavy-duty zip-top plastic bag. Seal and chill 2 to 3 hours.

- **Drain** mushrooms well, and place on a baking sheet.
- **Broil** 5 inches from heat (with electric oven door partially open) 3 minutes; turn mushrooms over, and broil 5 more minutes or until tender.
- **Cut** mushrooms into thick slices, cutting to but not through opposite side.
- **Arrange** salad greens on individual plates; top with walnuts, goat cheese, and mushrooms.
- **Drizzle** evenly with remaining ½ cup vinaigrette. Serve with Parmesan cheese toast. **Yield:** 4 servings.

* Substitute 1 (8-ounce) bottle Italian dressing, if desired.

Note: For testing purposes only, we used Newman's Own Balsamic Vinaigrette.

Al Roberts
Amerigo Italian Restaurant
Ridgeland, Mississippi

PORTOBELLO PANACHE

■ Portobellos are mature versions of the crimino mushroom (related to the common white button variety). Their diameters range 3 to 6 inches.

■ For the best mild flavor, select mushroom caps that are smooth, light tan, and slightly rounded. As they age, they get darker and more wrinkled (better for chopping), and their flavor intensifies (a plus for mushroom lovers).

■ Refrigerate portobellos only in paper bags or wrapped in paper towels; plastic promotes moisture, which alters flavor.

■ Before cooking, lightly rinse or wipe portobellos with damp paper towels. Trim off the woody-flavored stems to add to soups or stews.

EXQUISITE IN PURPLE

Eggplant's mild flavor makes it fabulous in highly seasoned casseroles and sauces. So don't wait for a bumper crop; try these recipes year-round.

EGGPLANT-SPINACH CASSEROLE

Prep: 1 hour
Bake: 40 minutes

1 large eggplant
¾ cup buttermilk
2 cups Italian-seasoned breadcrumbs
½ cup vegetable oil, divided
2 (10-ounce) packages frozen chopped spinach, thawed and well drained
1 (15-ounce) container ricotta cheese
½ (8-ounce) container cream cheese with chives and onion
¼ teaspoon salt
¼ teaspoon pepper
1 (26-ounce) jar marinara sauce
1 cup (4 ounces) shredded Italian cheese blend

- **Peel** eggplant, and cut in half lengthwise; cut each half lengthwise into 6 very thin slices. Dip each slice in buttermilk, and dredge in breadcrumbs.
- **Sauté** 3 slices in 2 tablespoons hot oil in a large skillet over medium heat 3 to 4 minutes on each side or until tender and golden. Set aside to cool. Repeat procedure 3 times with remaining eggplant and oil. Stir together spinach and next 4 ingredients. Spread over eggplant; roll up, starting with a short side.
- **Pour** half of marinara sauce into a lightly greased 13- x 9-inch baking dish.
- **Arrange** eggplant rolls, seam side down, over sauce, and pour remaining sauce over rolls.
- **Bake,** covered, at 375° for 30 minutes. Uncover and sprinkle with cheese; bake 10 more minutes. **Yield:** 6 servings.

EGGPLANT CAVIAR
(pictured on page 225)

Prep: 20 minutes
Cook: 20 minutes

1 large onion, diced
1 green bell pepper, diced
2 garlic cloves, minced
¼ cup vegetable oil
1 medium eggplant, peeled and diced
4 plum tomatoes, peeled, seeded, and chopped
1 teaspoon salt
½ teaspoon pepper
1 teaspoon hot sauce
1 teaspoon Worcestershire sauce
½ cup dry white wine or chicken broth

- **Sauté** first 3 ingredients in hot oil in a skillet over medium-high heat 5 minutes. Add eggplant; sauté 10 minutes or until tender. Stir in remaining ingredients. Cook, stirring occasionally, 5 minutes or until liquid is absorbed. Serve warm, or chill up to 1 week. Serve with crackers or toasted pita triangles. **Yield:** about 3 cups.

Conley Barclay
Memphis, Tennessee

SPICY EGGPLANT

Prep: 10 minutes
Cook: 12 minutes

1 large eggplant
¼ cup olive oil or dark sesame oil
3 tablespoons balsamic vinegar
1 tablespoon sugar
¾ teaspoon salt
½ teaspoon dried crushed red pepper
2 tablespoons minced fresh parsley

- **Peel** eggplant; cut into 2- x ½-inch strips. Sauté in hot oil in a large skillet over medium-high heat 8 minutes or until browned. Add vinegar and next 3 ingredients; cook, stirring often, 1 to 2 minutes or until liquid is absorbed. Stir in parsley; serve immediately. **Yield:** 4 servings.

Caroline Kennedy
Newborn, Georgia

SUPPER CLUB CO-OP

Here's a novel idea: Instead of worrying about cooking for your family every night, form a cooperative to share the burden. One member will cook a meal on Monday, another will prepare the Tuesday meal, and so on. That way you'll have to cook only one day a week.

Of course, you'll be cooking in volume—enough for all of the families—but only once during the week. This idea isn't new for a group of Birmingham, Alabama, women. Each member prepares and delivers one weeknight meal. Here are a few of their recipes, along with reheating instructions and serving suggestions.

AMARILLO SQUASH

Deliver with roast beef, steamed rice, and rolls.

Prep: 36 minutes
Bake: 20 minutes

2 **pounds yellow squash, thinly sliced (8 cups)** *
1 **medium onion, chopped**
2 **tablespoons water**
2 **(8-ounce) containers sour cream**
1 **(4.5-ounce) can chopped green chiles, undrained**
1 **(2-ounce) jar diced pimiento, drained**
2 **cups (8 ounces) shredded Monterey Jack cheese**
½ **teaspoon salt**
¼ **teaspoon pepper**
1½ **cups crushed cheese-flavored tortilla chips**

• **Combine** first 3 ingredients in a lightly greased 11- x 7-inch baking dish. Cover with heavy-duty plastic wrap; fold back 1 corner to allow steam to escape.
• **Microwave** at HIGH 14 to 16 minutes or until squash is almost tender, stirring once. Drain well.
• **Stir** together sour cream, chiles, and next 4 ingredients in a large bowl. Stir in squash mixture.
• **Spoon** half of mixture into baking dish, and sprinkle with half of crushed chips. Repeat layers.
• **Bake** at 350° for 20 minutes. Cool, cover, and chill. To reheat, bake at 350° for 30 minutes or until thoroughly heated. **Yield:** 8 servings.

* Substitute 3 (1-pound) packages frozen sliced yellow squash, thawed, if desired. Omit microwave instructions. Sauté onion in a lightly greased nonstick skillet until tender; add squash, and proceed with directions.

Note: Squash mixture and crushed chips may be evenly divided and layered into 2 (9- x 5-inch) disposable aluminum containers.

Leigh Fran Jones
Indian Springs, Alabama

QUICHE LORRAINE

Deliver with fresh fruit.

Prep: 30 minutes
Bake: 50 minutes

1 **(9-inch) frozen deep-dish pastry shell**
1 **tablespoon Dijon mustard (optional)**
½ **pound bacon slices, cooked and crumbled**
2 **cups (8 ounces) shredded Swiss cheese** *
1½ **cups half-and-half or milk**
3 **large eggs**
¼ **to ½ teaspoon salt**
¼ **teaspoon ground nutmeg**
¼ **teaspoon ground red pepper**
¼ **teaspoon ground black pepper**

• **Bake** pastry shell at 425° for 8 to 10 minutes. Gently press down pastry, and cool. Brush with mustard, if desired, and sprinkle with bacon and cheese.
• **Whisk** together half-and-half and next 5 ingredients until blended; pour over bacon and cheese.
• **Bake** at 375° for 45 to 50 minutes or until a knife inserted in center comes out clean. Let stand 10 minutes. Cover and chill. To reheat, bake at 350° for 10 minutes or until thoroughly heated, or microwave individual servings on microwave-safe plates at HIGH for 30-second intervals until thoroughly heated. **Yield:** 4 to 6 servings.

* Substitute 2 cups (8 ounces) shredded cheese blend, if desired.

Caroline Grant
Homewood, Alabama

VEGETABLE-BEEF SOUP

Deliver with cornbread or crackers.

Prep: 18 minutes
Cook: 30 minutes

1 **pound ground chuck**
1 **medium onion, chopped**
1 **small green bell pepper, chopped**
1 **(15¼-ounce) can whole kernel corn, drained**
1 **(15-ounce) can mixed vegetables, drained**
1 **(14.5-ounce) can diced tomatoes, undrained**
1 **(11⅛-ounce) can Italian tomato soup with basil and oregano, undiluted**
1 **(10-ounce) can diced tomatoes with green chiles, undrained**
1 **(10-ounce) package frozen sliced okra**
1¼ **cups water**
1 **teaspoon salt**

• **Cook** first 3 ingredients in a Dutch oven over medium-high heat 10 minutes, stirring until beef crumbles and is no longer pink. Drain well. Add corn and remaining ingredients.
• **Bring** to a boil; cover, reduce heat, and simmer 30 minutes. To reheat, cook in a saucepan over low heat. **Yield:** 11 cups.

Melinda Goode
Birmingham, Alabama

ROLLED REUBEN SANDWICH

Deliver with potato chips and dill pickles.

Prep: 20 minutes
Bake: 30 minutes

½ **cup sauerkraut, drained**
1 **(10-ounce) can refrigerated pizza crust**
¼ **cup prepared mustard**
1 **teaspoon caraway seeds, divided**
½ **teaspoon garlic powder**
½ **pound thinly sliced corned beef ***
½ **cup (2 ounces) shredded Swiss cheese**
Cornmeal (optional)

• **Press** sauerkraut between paper towels to remove excess moisture.
• **Roll** pizza crust dough to a 10-inch square on a lightly floured surface.
• **Stir** together mustard, ½ teaspoon caraway seeds, and garlic powder; spread evenly over dough. Layer with corned beef, sauerkraut, and cheese.
• **Roll** up; pinch ends to seal. Fold ends under. Place on a lightly greased baking sheet sprinkled with cornmeal, if desired. Brush top with water; sprinkle with remaining ½ teaspoon caraway seeds.
• **Bake** at 350° for 30 minutes or until golden. Cool and wrap in aluminum foil; chill. To reheat, bake wrapped sandwich at 350° for 20 minutes. Cut into slices. **Yield:** 4 servings.

✳ Substitute ½ pound ham or turkey, if desired.

Leigh Fran Jones
Indian Springs, Alabama

EASY RED BEANS AND RICE
(pictured on page 226)

Deliver with a tossed green salad and French bread.

Prep: 15 minutes
Cook: 30 minutes

1 **pound smoked sausage, thinly sliced**
1 **medium onion, chopped**
1 **medium-size green bell pepper, chopped**
1 **garlic clove, minced**
1 **tablespoon vegetable oil**
3 **(15-ounce) cans red beans, rinsed and drained**
1 **(16-ounce) can tomato paste**
1 **(14½-ounce) can stewed tomatoes, undrained and chopped**
1½ **cups water**
¼ **teaspoon dried oregano**
¼ **teaspoon dried thyme**
¼ **teaspoon hot sauce**
1 **bay leaf**
Hot cooked rice

• **Sauté** first 4 ingredients in hot oil in a Dutch oven over medium-high heat 8 minutes or until vegetables are tender. Add beans and next 7 ingredients.
• **Bring** mixture to a boil; cover, reduce heat, and simmer 20 minutes. Discard bay leaf. Serve over rice. To reheat, microwave at MEDIUM (50% power) 3 to 5 minutes or until thoroughly heated. **Yield:** 8 servings.

Caroline Grant
Homewood, Alabama

CO-OP TIPS

You'll need to meet and plan at least one month of menus. Here are a few things to consider when organizing a co-op.

■ Decide the number of nights you want dinner delivered. This will determine the number of families in your co-op.

■ Set delivery times that are convenient for everyone involved.

■ Make the group aware of allergies, food likes and dislikes, and nutritional needs (low fat, reduced sodium, etc.).

After a one-month trial, get together again and ask these questions.

■ Is there enough food?

■ How is your family reacting to co-op dining?

■ Are the recipes satisfying for all members?

■ Is the delivery time right?

Now you are ready to plan several months of menus at a time.

LAUGHTER ON THE LAWN

Celebrate the end of a spectacular summer with this fitting finale of vibrant colors and refreshing flavors. Bake the dessert, chill the salads, and mix the lemonade in advance, and then wrap the sandwiches as you're packing for your favorite spot—a playground, a park, or your own backyard. We wish you a joyous close to a grand season.

END-OF-SUMMER MENU
Serves Six

Fresh-Squeezed Lemonade

Smoked Turkey, Mozzarella, and Blackberry Sandwiches

Sour Cream Coleslaw   Favorite Fruit Salad

Angel Fluff Brownies

FRESH-SQUEEZED LEMONADE

Prep: 20 minutes

1½ cups sugar
½ cup boiling water
1 tablespoon grated lemon rind
1½ cups fresh lemon juice (8 large lemons)
5 cups water

• **Stir** together sugar and ½ cup boiling water until sugar dissolves.
• **Stir** in lemon rind, lemon juice, and 5 cups water. Chill. Serve over ice. **Yield:** 8 cups.

Ginger Gentry
Soddy Daisy, Tennessee

SMOKED TURKEY, MOZZARELLA, AND BLACKBERRY SANDWICHES

If the balsamic blackberries are too tart for tots, you can serve them unmarinated on the side.

Prep: 10 minutes
Marinate: 30 minutes

2 cups fresh blackberries
⅓ cup balsamic vinegar
2 teaspoons sugar
1 teaspoon lemon juice
2 pounds smoked turkey slices
½ pound smoked mozzarella cheese slices
12 white or wheat sandwich bread slices, toasted
3 tablespoons minced fresh sage or 1 dried sage leaf, crushed

• **Toss** together first 4 ingredients; let stand 30 minutes.
• **Layer** turkey and cheese on 6 bread slices. Spoon blackberry mixture over cheese; sprinkle with sage. Top with remaining bread slices. **Yield:** 6 sandwiches.

Mike Singleton
Memphis, Tennessee

SOUR CREAM COLESLAW

Prep: 20 minutes

1 (16-ounce) container sour cream
2 tablespoons sugar
2 tablespoons white vinegar
2 to 3 teaspoons caraway or celery seeds
1 teaspoon salt
1 small head cabbage, shredded (15 cups)
½ medium-size green bell pepper, diced
3 tablespoons minced purple onion

• **Stir** together first 5 ingredients in a large bowl; add cabbage, bell pepper, and onion, tossing well. Cover and chill 8 hours, if desired. **Yield:** 11 cups.

Charlotte Bryant
Greensburg, Kentucky

FAVORITE FRUIT SALAD

Prep: 20 minutes
Chill: 1 hour

¾ cup orange juice
½ cup honey
1½ pints fresh strawberries, halved
1½ cups fresh raspberries
1½ cups fresh blueberries
2 oranges, peeled and sectioned
1½ cups honeydew melon balls
⅓ cup fresh mint leaves, chopped

• **Whisk** together orange juice and honey; add fruit and mint, tossing to coat. Cover and chill 1 hour. **Yield:** 8 cups.

Mary Pappas
Richmond, Virginia

ANGEL FLUFF BROWNIES

Mix in your favorite pudding flavors for fun variations.

Prep: 10 minutes
Bake: 25 minutes

1 (3.3-ounce) package chocolate instant pudding mix
⅔ cup sugar
½ cup all-purpose flour
2 large eggs
⅓ cup butter or margarine, melted
¼ cup whipping cream
1 teaspoon vanilla extract
½ cup chopped walnuts, toasted
Powdered sugar (optional)

• **Stir** together first 8 ingredients in a large bowl until blended.
• **Spoon** batter into a lightly greased 8- or 9-inch square pan.
• **Bake** at 350° for 25 minutes or until edges pull away from pan. Cool in pan on a wire rack.
• **Sprinkle** with powdered sugar, if desired. **Yield:** 16 brownies.

Joan Summers
Chattanooga, Tennessee

QUICK & EASY

APPETIZERS FROM THE FREEZER

Keeping a collection of appetizers in your freezer will instantly make you a successful and spontaneous host. Be sure to try the Parmesan Cheese Bites; we gave them our highest rating in our Test Kitchens. Take a batch to the next impromptu gathering, but be warned— it's hard to stop nibbling.

GARLIC PEPPER JELLY

Prep: 4 minutes
Cook: 10 minutes

2 (16-ounce) jars apple jelly
2 tablespoons dried parsley flakes
1 tablespoon pressed garlic
½ teaspoon dried crushed red pepper
4 teaspoons white vinegar

• **Melt** apple jelly in a medium saucepan over low heat, stirring often.
• **Stir** in parsley and next 3 ingredients. Pour into jars or freezer containers. Cool. Cover and freeze up to 6 months. (Jelly will not freeze solid.) Serve over cream cheese or Brie, or use as a basting sauce for chicken or pork. **Yield:** 3 cups.

Anne Stokes-Krusen
Nashville, Tennessee

PARMESAN CHEESE BITES

You can freeze baked cheese bites up to one month.

Prep: 20 minutes
Thaw: 8 hours
Bake: 15 minutes

1 cup all-purpose flour
⅔ cup grated Parmesan cheese
¼ teaspoon ground red pepper
½ cup butter or margarine, cut up
2 tablespoons milk

• **Stir** together first 3 ingredients in a medium bowl; cut in butter with a pastry blender until mixture is crumbly. (Mixture will look very dry.) Gently press mixture together with hands, working until blended and smooth (about 2 to 3 minutes).
• **Shape** dough into 2 (4-inch-long) logs. Wrap in plastic wrap, and place in an airtight container. Freeze up to 3 months.
• **Thaw** dough overnight in refrigerator. Cut into ¼-inch-thick slices, and place on a lightly greased baking sheet. Brush with milk.

• **Bake** at 350° for 12 to 15 minutes or until lightly browned. **Yield:** 32 appetizer servings.

Note: Dough may be rolled into a 10- x 8- x ¼-inch rectangle on a lightly floured surface. Cut lengthwise into 8 strips and crosswise into 4 strips, using a pastry wheel or knife and forming 32 pieces. Place on a lightly greased baking sheet; brush with milk, and bake.

Caryn Nabors
Gadsden, Alabama

GREEK OLIVE CUPS

Prep: 10 minutes
Bake: 15 minutes

1 cup chopped pecans, toasted
1 cup (4 ounces) shredded Cheddar cheese
1 cup chopped pimiento-stuffed olives
2 tablespoons mayonnaise
2 (21-ounce) packages frozen mini phyllo shells

• **Stir** together first 4 ingredients. Remove pastry cups from package, leaving them in tray.
• **Spoon** 1 teaspoon mixture into each pastry shell; place tray in a heavy-duty zip-top plastic bag, and freeze up to 1 month. Remove from tray, and place on a baking sheet. Let stand 10 minutes.
• **Bake** cups at 375° for 12 to 15 minutes or until thoroughly heated. Serve immediately. **Yield:** 30 appetizer servings.

Note: Olive cups may be baked after assembling at 375° for 12 minutes. Serve immediately.

Vikki D. Sturm
Rossville, Georgia

FOUR-LAYER CHEESE LOAF

To make two loaves, use two 7- x 3-inch loafpans. Mix ingredients as directed; divide mixtures in half, and follow layering procedure for each loaf.

Prep: 15 minutes
Thaw: 8 hours

1 (10-ounce) package frozen chopped spinach, thawed and drained
2 (8-ounce) blocks sharp Cheddar cheese, shredded
½ cup chopped pecans, toasted
½ cup mayonnaise
2 (8-ounce) packages cream cheese, softened and divided
¼ teaspoon salt
½ teaspoon freshly ground pepper
¼ cup chutney
¼ teaspoon ground nutmeg
Garnish: toasted chopped pecans

• **Line** a 9- x 5-inch loafpan with heavy-duty plastic wrap.
• **Press** spinach between layers of paper towels to remove excess moisture; set aside.
• **Stir** together Cheddar cheese, pecans, and mayonnaise; spread half of mixture evenly into prepared pan.
• **Stir** together spinach, 1 package cream cheese, salt, and pepper; spread evenly over Cheddar cheese layer.
• **Stir** together remaining package cream cheese, chutney, and nutmeg; spread evenly over spinach layer.
• **Top** loaf with remaining Cheddar cheese mixture. Cover and freeze up to 1 month. Thaw in refrigerator overnight. Garnish, if desired, and serve with assorted crackers. **Yield:** 25 appetizer servings.

Traci Storch
Hoover, Alabama

CHOPS OF DISTINCTION

You're in for a real treat with this adaptable menu. It's simple, satisfying, and just right for family meals or special guests. If pork chops aren't your preference, simply substitute four skinned and boned chicken breast halves and chicken broth for the beef broth.

A MENU AT HOME
Serves Four

Apple-Spinach Salad
Pork Chops in Onion Gravy
Mashed Potato Casserole
Dilled Carrots and Green Beans

APPLE-SPINACH SALAD
(pictured on page 264)

Prep: 10 minutes

2 (6-ounce) packages fresh baby spinach *
2 Granny Smith apples, chopped
½ cup salted cashews
¼ cup raisins or golden raisins
¼ cup sugar
¼ cup vegetable oil
2 tablespoons balsamic or apple cider vinegar
¼ teaspoon celery salt

• **Combine** first 4 ingredients in a serving bowl. Whisk together sugar and next 3 ingredients until well blended. Pour mixture over salad, tossing gently. Serve immediately. **Yield:** 4 to 6 servings.

* Substitute 1 (10-ounce) package regular fresh spinach, if desired.

The Andersons
Austin, Texas

PORK CHOPS IN ONION GRAVY
(pictured on page 264)

Prep: 10 minutes
Cook: 30 minutes

4 (1- to 1½-inch-thick) bone-in pork chops (about 2¼ pounds)
½ teaspoon salt
½ teaspoon pepper
2 tablespoons all-purpose flour
2 tablespoons vegetable oil
2 medium onions, cut in half and thinly sliced
½ cup beer or beef broth
½ cup beef broth
1 teaspoon cornstarch
2 tablespoons water

• **Sprinkle** pork chops with salt and pepper; coat evenly with flour, shaking off excess.
• **Cook** pork chops in hot oil in a heavy skillet over medium-high heat 3 minutes on each side.
• **Add** sliced onion, and cook 5 minutes, turning pork chops once.
• **Add** beer and beef broth; cover, reduce heat, and simmer 15 minutes or until pork chops reach desired degree of doneness. Remove pork chops, reserving onion mixture in skillet; keep pork chops warm.
• **Stir** together cornstarch and 2 tablespoons water until thoroughly blended; stir into onion mixture.
• **Cook** over medium-high heat, stirring constantly, 3 minutes or until gravy is thickened and bubbly. Spoon over pork chops, and serve immediately. **Yield:** 4 servings.

Clairiece Gilbert Humphrey
Charlottesville, Virginia

MASHED POTATO CASSEROLE
(pictured on page 264)

Prep: 20 minutes
Bake: 40 minutes

1 (22-ounce) package frozen
    mashed potatoes
½ teaspoon salt
¼ teaspoon pepper
2 large eggs, lightly beaten
1 (3-ounce) package cream cheese,
    softened
1 small onion, chopped
1 (2-ounce) jar diced pimiento,
    undrained
1 cup (4 ounces) shredded sharp
    Cheddar cheese

• **Prepare** potatoes according to package, adding ½ teaspoon salt and ¼ teaspoon pepper.
• **Stir** in eggs, cream cheese, and onion; fold in pimiento. Place mixture in a lightly greased 11- x 7-inch pan.
• **Bake,** covered, at 350° for 30 minutes. Uncover and sprinkle with cheese. Bake 10 more minutes. **Yield:** 6 servings.

Terry Anderson
Brooksville, Florida

DILLED CARROTS AND GREEN BEANS
(pictured on page 264)

Prep: 15 minutes
Cook: 15 minutes

1 pound fresh green beans, trimmed
½ pound whole baby carrots
½ teaspoon salt
½ teaspoon dried dillweed
1 cup water
2 tablespoons butter or margarine
2 tablespoons diced onion

• **Cook** first 5 ingredients in a saucepan over medium heat 8 to 10 minutes or until vegetables are crisp-tender. Drain. Remove from pan; keep warm. Melt butter in pan over medium heat; add onion. Sauté until tender. Add vegetables; toss gently to coat. **Yield:** 4 to 6 servings.

Kathy Hunt
Dallas, Texas

JEWEL OF A CAKE

Carrots are the delightful secret to this moist, flavorful cake. This one has a fresh twist: citrus in the frosting. Don't let the long list of ingredients keep you from making it. If time is at a premium, combine dry ingredients the day before; then assemble and bake the next day.

PECAN-CARROT CAKE

Prep: 15 minutes
Bake: 45 minutes

⅔ pound carrots, grated
1 cup water
¾ cup unsalted butter, softened
1½ cups sugar
½ cup firmly packed light brown
    sugar
4 large eggs
3 cups cake flour
1½ teaspoons baking powder
1¼ teaspoons baking soda
½ teaspoon salt
1½ teaspoons ground cinnamon
1½ cups buttermilk
1 teaspoon vanilla extract
1½ cups finely chopped pecans
Citrus Cream Cheese Frosting

• **Bring** carrot and 1 cup water to a boil in a medium saucepan. Cover, reduce heat, and simmer 15 minutes or until tender. Do not drain. Process carrot mixture in a blender or food processor until smooth, stopping to scrape down sides. Measure 1 cup puree; set aside.
• **Beat** butter and sugars at medium speed with an electric mixer until blended. Add eggs, 1 at a time, beating just until blended after each addition.
• **Combine** cake flour and next 4 ingredients. Combine carrot puree, buttermilk, and vanilla. Gradually add flour mixture to butter mixture alternately with carrot mixture, beginning and ending with flour mixture. Beat at low speed until blended after each addition. Stir in pecans. Spoon batter into a greased and floured 13- x 9-inch pan.
• **Bake** at 350° for 45 minutes or until a wooden pick inserted in center comes out clean. Cool in pan on a wire rack. Spread with Citrus Cream Cheese Frosting. **Yield:** 12 servings.

Note: Batter may be spooned evenly into 3 greased and floured 9-inch round cakepans. Bake at 350° for 30 minutes or until a wooden pick inserted in center comes out clean. Cool in pans 10 minutes. Remove from pans; cool on wire racks. Spread frosting between layers and on top and sides of cake.

Citrus Cream Cheese Frosting

Prep: 10 minutes

1 (8-ounce) package cream cheese,
    softened
½ cup unsalted butter, softened
1 tablespoon grated orange rind
1 tablespoon fresh orange juice
1½ teaspoons vanilla extract
1 (16-ounce) package powdered
    sugar

• **Beat** first 5 ingredients at medium speed with an electric mixer until blended; gradually add powdered sugar, beating until smooth. **Yield:** 2½ cups.

Marie A. Davis
Charlotte, North Carolina

From Our Kitchen to Yours

KEEP IT CLEAN

September is National Food Safety Education Month. The National Cattlemen's Beef Association and the International Food Safety Council want to help you stay safe and healthy with some simple but important guidelines. Here are several food safety steps you'll want to take.

■ Always wash your hands before preparing food and after activities such as handling pets. Use warm water to moisten hands; then apply soap and rub hands together for 20 seconds before rinsing.

■ Consider using paper towels to clean kitchen surfaces. If you use cloth towels, be sure to wash them frequently in the hot cycle of the washing machine.

■ Wash cutting boards in hot, soapy water, or run them through the dishwasher to disinfect.

Here is some additional advice during this important month.

■ Keep raw meats and vegetables well wrapped and separated.

■ Use a thermometer to be sure you cook food to its proper temperature.

■ Don't leave food resting on the stovetop for later use. Refrigerate it as soon as possible, and then reheat portions as needed.

The Beef Association and Food Safety Council also cite these top 10 most common food-safety mistakes.

1. Unwashed hands and utensils
2. Inadequate cooking time
3. Countertop thawing
4. Leftovers and doggie bags kept at room temperature
5. Unclean cutting board
6. Shared knife for raw meats and vegetables
7. Store-to-refrigerator lag time
8. Room-temperature marinating
9. Stirring and tasting with the same spoon
10. Hide-and-eat Easter eggs

For a free copy of "Plating It Safe," send a self-addressed, stamped envelope to "Plating It Safe," Dept. FC, National Cattlemen's Beef Association, 444 North Michigan Avenue, Chicago, IL 60611. To receive a free copy of "Cook It Safely," call 1-800-266-5762.

TIPS AND TIDBITS

Jo Carpenter of Lightfoot, Virginia, shares with us a creative tip that will help fruitcake bakers out of a sticky situation. Jo writes, "Instead of chopping candied fruit and fresh fruit peel with a knife and folding it into the batter, simply put the measured amount of sugar in your food processor, toss in the fruit, and pulse several times. It won't make any difference to the cake and will save you from a tedious and very sticky job."

Assistant Foods Editor Patty Vann shows how to be prepared for surprise guests by storing appetizers in the freezer (see page 221). Don't forget to pick up a medium-bodied white wine, such as a Pinot Gris or Sauvignon Blanc, to pair with the hors d'oeuvres. They're great appetizer partners. Don't overlook sparkling wines; they're not necessarily more expensive. Several good selections are available for $9 to $10.

FLOUR POWER

Ever have trouble sifting through the various flours? Here's help.

■ **All-purpose flour** is fine textured and comes in two basic forms—bleached and unbleached. The two are interchangeable. If either is labeled "enriched," vitamins A and D have been added. You can substitute 1 cup plus 2 tablespoons cake flour for each cup all-purpose flour.

■ **Bread flour** is a blend of 99.8 percent hard wheat flour, a bit of malted barley flour, and vitamin C or potassium bromate. This blend improves yeast activity, promotes elasticity, and is perfect for yeast breads.

■ **Whole wheat flour** contains wheat germ, which makes it higher in fiber, nutrients, and fat content. Because of its fat content, it should be stored in the refrigerator.

■ **Self-rising flour** is all-purpose flour with baking powder and salt added. To substitute all-purpose flour, put 1½ teaspoons baking powder and ½ teaspoon salt in a 1-cup measure; spoon in all-purpose flour, and level off with a knife. Substitute this for each cup self-rising flour.

Eggplant Caviar, page 217

Easy Brunswick Stew,
Buttermilk Cornbread, page 235

Easy Red Beans and
Rice, page 219

Garlic-and-Herb Stuffed Leg of Lamb served with your favorite wild rice blend and steamed baby carrots, page 241

Honey-Apple Cake, page 210;
Honey Graham Bread, page 211;
Apricot Butter, page 212

OCTOBER

Crisp autumn mornings deserve a big country feast, and "Farmhouse Breakfast" delivers just that. Take a leisurely break from today's busy lifestyle to enjoy hearty morning fare such as Ham Biscuits, Grits With Sausage, and Broccoli-Cheese Breakfast Casserole.

October ushers in cooler weather and the beginning of the holiday season. "Halloween Bites" provides plenty of tasty recipes for any spooky get-together. White Meringue Ghosts, Pumpkin Patch Cheese Balls, Breadstick Haystacks, and Apple Bobbing Punch will be hits with kids of all ages. For another October tradition, turn to "Feast on Oktoberfest," and enjoy some of this holiday's customary German recipes, including hearty Rouladen and decadent Shortcut Sachertorte.

THE BOUNTY OF BILTMORE

The Biltmore Estate's three restaurants—The Stable Café, The Bistro, and Deerpark—are supplied by the estate's bounty of wines, vegetables, herbs, and beef. Such abundance allows the Biltmore chefs to create innovative, fresh recipes. Try these dishes for a taste.

FRIED GREEN TOMATO NAPOLEONS

Wine suggestion: Château Biltmore Chardonnay

Prep: 1 hour and 25 minutes
Cook: 25 minutes

1 garlic bulb
1 tablespoon olive oil
1 large egg
½ cup buttermilk
¾ cup cornmeal
½ cup all-purpose flour
1 teaspoon salt
½ teaspoon pepper
4 medium-size green tomatoes, cut into ¼-inch-thick slices
1 cup vegetable oil
4 cups gourmet salad greens
Balsamic Vinaigrette
6 yellow pear or cherry tomatoes, halved
6 red pear or cherry tomatoes, halved
5 plum tomatoes, chopped
¼ cup chopped fresh parsley
Tomato Crostini
Garnish: fresh basil sprigs

• **Cut** off pointed end of garlic bulb; place on a piece of aluminum foil. Drizzle with olive oil, and fold foil to seal.

• **Bake** at 400° for 1 hour. Cool and peel 12 cloves; set aside. Reserve any remaining cloves for other uses.
• **Whisk** egg and buttermilk in a small mixing bowl.
• **Stir** together cornmeal and next 3 ingredients.
• **Dip** tomato slices in egg mixture, and dredge in cornmeal mixture, shaking off excess.
• **Heat** vegetable oil to 350° in a large skillet. Fry tomato slices, in batches, in hot oil 1 minute on each side; drain.
• **Toss** greens with Balsamic Vinaigrette. Arrange on individual plates.
• **Stack** tomato slices and pear tomatoes on plates. Sprinkle with chopped plum tomato, parsley, and peeled roasted garlic. Serve with Tomato Crostini. Garnish, if desired. **Yield:** 4 servings.

Balsamic Vinaigrette

Prep: 20 minutes

1 onion, diced
¼ cup olive oil
2 garlic cloves, minced
¼ teaspoon dried thyme
¼ teaspoon pepper
¼ teaspoon salt
1 bay leaf
¼ cup balsamic vinegar
2 teaspoons honey

• **Sauté** onion in hot oil in a nonstick skillet over medium-high heat 2 minutes. Add garlic and next 4 ingredients. Remove from heat; whisk in vinegar and honey. Discard bay leaf. **Yield:** ¾ cup.

Tomato Crostini

Prep: 20 minutes

¼ cup goat cheese
¼ cup cream cheese, softened
1 (6-inch) Italian bread shell
5 plum tomatoes, chopped
2 teaspoons chopped fresh herbs (parsley, thyme, basil, or rosemary)

• **Stir** together goat cheese and cream cheese; spread on bread shell. Cut into wedges; top with tomato and herbs. **Yield:** 4 servings.

Biltmore Estate
Asheville, North Carolina

LAMB CHOPS WITH MINTED APPLES
(pictured on page 261)

Wine suggestion: Château Biltmore Cabernet Sauvignon

Prep: 1 hour and 10 minutes
Bake: 45 minutes

1 garlic bulb
1 tablespoon olive oil
8 (2-inch-thick) lamb chops, trimmed
Biltmore Dry Rub
Minted Apples

• **Cut** off pointed end of garlic bulb, and place bulb on a piece of aluminum foil. Drizzle with oil; fold foil to seal.
• **Bake** at 400° for 1 hour. Cool and peel 12 cloves; set aside. Reserve any remaining cloves for other uses.
• **Sprinkle** lamb chops on both sides with Biltmore Dry Rub, and place on a lightly greased rack in a broiler pan.
• **Bake** lamb chops at 325° for 45 minutes or until a meat thermometer inserted into thickest portion registers 150° (medium-rare). Reserve ¼ cup

drippings for Minted Apples. Serve lamb with Minted Apples and peeled roasted garlic. **Yield:** 4 servings.

Biltmore Dry Rub

Prep: 10 minutes

3 **cups salt**
2 **tablespoons paprika**
2 **tablespoons onion powder**
2 **tablespoons ground celery seeds**
2 **tablespoons garlic powder**
2 **tablespoons pepper**
1 **tablespoon dried rosemary**
1 **tablespoon ground sage**
1 **tablespoon dried dillweed**

• **Stir** together all ingredients. Store in an airtight container up to 6 months. Use to season lamb, chicken, or steak. **Yield:** about 4 cups.

Minted Apples

Prep: 10 minutes
Cook: 12 minutes

3 **tablespoons butter**
2 **shallots, thinly sliced**
1 **garlic clove, minced**
2 **tablespoons sugar**
3 **Granny Smith apples, peeled and sliced**
⅓ **cup apple cider vinegar**
¼ **cup reserved lamb drippings or bacon drippings**
2 **tablespoons mint jelly**
2 **teaspoons chopped fresh mint**

• **Melt** butter in a large skillet over low heat; add shallots and garlic, and sauté until tender. Stir in sugar.
• **Add** apple; cook, stirring often, 3 minutes or until lightly caramelized.
• **Add** vinegar, drippings, and jelly; cook, stirring often, 6 to 8 minutes. Serve immediately, or chill and reheat before serving. Sprinkle with mint. **Yield:** 4 servings.

Biltmore Estate
Asheville, North Carolina

"Some chefs have an herb garden—we practically have a whole farmers market, seafood market, and meat market at our fingertips."

—Stephen Adams, Biltmore executive chef

SELF-SUFFICIENT FARM

The verdant vineyards, lush gardens, and magnificent château suggest Bordeaux, but it's the Blue Ridge Mountains that provide soil and setting to Biltmore Estate in Asheville, North Carolina. Its 73-acre vineyard is just as serious about wine as its French competition 4,000 miles away. It has the national and international awards to prove it—not to mention the backing of The Biltmore Company's annual revenue of almost $50 million.

George W. Vanderbilt's palatial 250-room home and 75-acre garden captivate more than 900,000 visitors yearly. But many of them don't realize that the Gilded Age estate is—put simply by its down-to-earth CEO, Bill Cecil Jr.—"just a big ol' working farm."

By adopting "vertical integration"—a business practice popular in Mr. Vanderbilt's day—his family not only could own a solid estate for generations but could also be sustained by their own beef, produce, and dairy foods.

The focal point of the estate's agricultural endeavors is its winery, which has earned Biltmore labels more than 135 medals. The wines, produced in the estate's 90,000-square-foot winery, include Merlot, Cabernet Sauvignon, Chardonnay, and many others. Sparkling wines in the French *méthode champenoise* style are also produced and distributed in seven Southeastern states.

"Our wine business is a way for us to look beyond our 8,500 acres—to share our strong connection with the land," says Jerry Douglas, vice president of The Biltmore Estate Wine Company.

The Biltmore's aquaculture work provides more than 60,000 rainbow trout throughout the year, some of which go to local markets. In addition, about 600 pounds of freshwater prawns are produced each summer.

Meanwhile, the Biltmore's Angus and Limousin cattle and Polled Dorset sheep provide more than 40,000 pounds of federally inspected meat to its three restaurants. Also thriving is the 10-acre market garden, which seasonally supplies more than 130 different herbs, greens, vegetables, and fruits to the eateries.

RISE AND SHINE

The Biltmore Company wants to do more than just wine and dine guests—it plans to attract even more visitors with a new 213-room Inn on Biltmore Estate, scheduled to open in spring 2001.

The $32 million hotel will feature a gourmet restaurant, lobby bar, library, exterior swimming pool, fitness room, and on-property activities. Its look will reflect the other estate structures.

For details about the hotel, call (828) 274-6333. For general Biltmore Estate information, call 1-800-543-2961, or visit the Web site at www.biltmore.com.

VEAL SCALLOPINI WITH SHIITAKES

Wine suggestion: Biltmore Estate's Cardinal Crest (a mild red blend)

Prep: 5 minutes
Cook: 25 minutes

1   cup all-purpose flour
1   teaspoon salt
½   teaspoon ground white pepper
2   pounds thinly sliced veal
½   cup olive oil
½   pound fresh shiitake
    mushrooms
¾   cup dry red wine
1½ tablespoons honey
2   teaspoons lemon juice
¾   cup water
¼   cup liquid vegetable broth
    concentrate
½   cup butter, cubed

• **Stir** together first 3 ingredients in a shallow bowl. Dredge veal in mixture.
• **Cook** veal, in batches, in about 1½ tablespoons hot oil at a time in a large nonstick skillet over high heat 1 minute on each side. Remove from skillet, reserving hot drippings in pan.
• **Add** mushrooms to hot drippings, and sauté 1 minute; remove from skillet, reserving drippings in pan.
• **Add** wine and next 4 ingredients to drippings; cook over medium heat 10 minutes, stirring to loosen particles from bottom. Gradually whisk in butter until blended.
• **Return** veal and mushrooms to skillet, stirring gently to coat. **Yield:** 6 servings.
Biltmore Estate
Asheville, North Carolina

FARMHOUSE BREAKFAST

In the past, mornings at a rural Southern home often meant simple food in huge quantities. Fried chicken or fish, grits, bacon, eggs, rice, pan-fried sweet potatoes, and a revolving door of hot, buttery biscuits were breakfast staples. Today, our lifestyles have changed, but that makes an occasional farm-style meal that much sweeter. Sample these recipes that capture the essence of breakfasts past.

BAKED POLENTA WITH CHEESE AND OKRA
(pictured on page 262)

Prep: 9 minutes
Cook: 1 hour and 15 minutes

4   cups water, divided
6   small fresh okra pods
1   cup uncooked quick-cooking
    grits
½   teaspoon salt
2   large eggs, lightly beaten
¼   cup butter or margarine, cut
    into pieces
1   (8-ounce) block sharp Cheddar
    cheese, cubed *

• **Bring** 2 cups water to a boil in a large saucepan over medium heat; add okra, and cook 10 minutes.
• **Remove** okra with a slotted spoon, reserving liquid in pan; cool okra slightly, and coarsely chop.
• **Add** remaining 2 cups water to reserved liquid; bring to a boil. Gradually stir in grits and salt, and return to a boil. Cover, reduce heat, and simmer 5 to 7 minutes. Gradually whisk about one-fourth of hot grits into eggs; add to remaining hot mixture, whisking constantly. Whisk in butter.
• **Stir** in okra and cheese. Spoon mixture into a lightly greased 11- x 7-inch baking dish.
• **Bake** at 350° for 55 to 60 minutes or until set. **Yield:** 6 servings.

* Substitute 2 (4-ounce) logs fresh goat cheese, crumbled, for Cheddar cheese, if desired.

Marilou Robinson
Portland, Oregon

GLAZED APPLES
(pictured on page 262)

Prep: 10 minutes
Cook: 20 minutes

4 large Granny Smith or Rome
   apples
½ cup apple juice
1 tablespoon lemon juice
¼ teaspoon ground ginger
¼ teaspoon ground cinnamon
¼ cup butter or margarine
½ cup sugar
Whipped cream (optional)

• **Core** apples, and cut each into ½-inch-thick rings.
• **Stir** together apple juice and next 3 ingredients.
• **Melt** butter in a large nonstick skillet over medium-high heat; cook apple rings, in batches, until browned on both sides. Return all apple rings to skillet; drizzle with juice mixture, and sprinkle with sugar.
• **Cover** and cook over medium heat 5 minutes or until tender and glazed. Serve warm with whipped cream, if desired. **Yield:** 6 to 8 servings.

Ardell W. Tregia
Merryville, Louisiana

HAM BISCUITS
(pictured on page 262)

Prep: 16 minutes
Bake: 10 minutes

1 (12-ounce) package ground ham
   sausage
⅓ cup shortening
2 cups self-rising flour
⅔ cup buttermilk

• **Cook** ham sausage in a large skillet over medium-high heat, stirring until it crumbles and is no longer pink. Drain well, and set aside.
• **Cut** shortening into flour with a pastry blender until crumbly; add buttermilk to flour mixture, stirring until dry ingredients are moistened.
• **Turn** dough out onto a lightly floured surface; knead 3 or 4 times.

• **Pat** or roll dough to ¼-inch thickness. Sprinkle sausage over dough, gently pressing into dough; cut with a 2½-inch round cutter. Place on lightly greased baking sheets.
• **Bake** at 450° for 8 to 10 minutes. **Yield:** 15 biscuits.

Note: For testing purposes only, we used Smithfield ham sausage.

GRITS WITH SAUSAGE

Prep: 20 minutes
Chill: 8 hours
Cook: 10 minutes

1 (16-ounce) package reduced-fat
   ground pork sausage
4½ cups water
1 teaspoon salt
1 cup uncooked regular grits
½ cup cornmeal
½ teaspoon pepper
Toppings: shredded Cheddar
   cheese, salsa

• **Cook** sausage in a skillet over medium-high heat, stirring until it crumbles and is no longer pink; drain.
• **Bring** 4½ cups water and salt to a boil in a large saucepan; add grits. Cover, reduce heat, and simmer, stirring occasionally, 10 minutes.
• **Stir** in sausage, cornmeal, and pepper; cook, stirring occasionally, 5 minutes. Spoon into a foil-lined 9- x 5-inch loaf-pan; cover and chill 8 hours.
• **Remove** loaf from pan; cut crosswise into ½-inch-thick slices.
• **Cook** slices, in batches, in a skillet coated with cooking spray over medium-high heat 5 minutes on each side or until browned. Serve with desired toppings. **Yield:** 8 servings.

Note: For testing purposes only, we used Smithfield 40% Lower Fat Sausage.

BROCCOLI-CHEESE BREAKFAST CASSEROLE

Use hot sausage in this dish if you'd like it on the spicy side. Mild sausage will flavor it for people of all ages.

Prep: 20 minutes
Bake: 45 minutes

½ pound ground pork sausage
1 small onion, chopped
1 (10-ounce) package frozen
   broccoli cuts, thawed
1½ cups (6 ounces) shredded
   three-cheese gourmet Cheddar
   cheese blend, divided
8 large eggs, lightly beaten
1 cup ricotta cheese
¼ cup milk
1 teaspoon pepper
½ teaspoon salt
1 plum tomato, thinly sliced

• **Cook** sausage and onion in a skillet over medium-high heat, stirring until sausage crumbles and is no longer pink; drain.
• **Toss** together sausage mixture, broccoli, and ½ cup cheese blend. Spoon mixture into a lightly greased 11- x 7-inch baking dish.
• **Stir** together ½ cup cheese blend, eggs, and next 4 ingredients; pour over broccoli mixture.
• **Sprinkle** casserole with remaining ½ cup cheese blend. Arrange tomato slices on top.
• **Bake** at 350° for 30 minutes; uncover and bake 15 more minutes. Let casserole stand 10 minutes before serving. **Yield:** 6 servings.

MUFFINS: HOT AND FRESH

Treat yourself to fresh baked goods the easy way—make some muffins. These small quick breads require minimal preparation and yield maximum enjoyment. For a breakfast treat, mix the dry ingredients the night before, and stir in the wet ingredients just before baking.

BASIC SWEET MUFFINS

Prep: 5 minutes
Bake: 20 minutes

1½ cups all-purpose flour
½ cup sugar
2 teaspoons baking powder
½ teaspoon salt
1 large egg
½ cup milk
¼ cup vegetable oil

• **Stir** together first 4 ingredients in a large bowl; make a well in center of mixture.
• **Stir** together egg, milk, and oil until blended. Add to dry ingredients, stirring just until moistened.
• **Spoon** batter into lightly greased muffin pans, filling two-thirds full.
• **Bake** at 400° for 18 to 20 minutes. Remove muffins from pans immediately. **Yield:** 1 dozen.

Apple Muffins: Add ¾ cup peeled, chopped apple; ¼ teaspoon ground cinnamon; and ¼ teaspoon ground nutmeg to dry ingredients. Proceed with recipe as directed.

Blueberry Muffins: Fold ¾ cup fresh or frozen blueberries, unthawed, into batter. Proceed with recipe as directed.

Date-Nut Muffins: Fold ½ cup chopped dates and ½ cup chopped pecans into batter. Proceed with recipe as directed.

PEPPERED CHEDDAR MUFFINS
(pictured on page 263)

Serve these spicy muffins warm or at room temperature with butter or apple butter.

Prep: 5 minutes
Bake: 20 minutes
Cool: 2 minutes

2 cups all-purpose flour
1 tablespoon sugar
1 tablespoon baking powder
½ teaspoon salt
½ to 1 teaspoon coarsely ground pepper
1 cup (4 ounces) shredded sharp Cheddar cheese
1¼ cups milk
1 large egg
2 tablespoons vegetable oil

• **Stir** together first 6 ingredients in a large bowl; make a well in center of mixture.
• **Stir** together milk, egg, and oil until blended. Add to dry ingredients, stirring just until moistened.
• **Spoon** batter into greased muffin pans, filling two-thirds full.
• **Bake** at 400° for 18 to 20 minutes or until tops are golden. Cool muffins in pans 2 minutes; remove from pans, and serve. **Yield:** 1 dozen.

Janice M. France
Louisville, Kentucky

STRAWBERRY MUFFINS

Prep: 15 minutes
Bake: 20 minutes

1 (10-ounce) package frozen sliced strawberries, thawed and undrained
2 cups all-purpose flour
⅔ cup sugar
1½ tablespoons baking powder
¾ teaspoon salt
⅔ cup milk
2 large eggs
⅓ cup vegetable oil
Strawberry Butter

• **Reserve** 2 tablespoons strawberries for Strawberry Butter.
• **Stir** together flour and next 3 ingredients in a large bowl; make a well in center of mixture.
• **Stir** together remaining strawberries, milk, eggs, and oil until blended. Add to dry ingredients, stirring just until dry ingredients are moistened.
• **Spoon** batter into greased muffin pans, filling two-thirds full.
• **Bake** at 375° for 20 minutes. Remove from pans immediately, and serve with Strawberry Butter. **Yield:** 14 muffins.

Strawberry Butter

Prep: 5 minutes

½ cup butter, softened
2 tablespoons reserved strawberries

• **Stir** together butter and strawberries until well blended. **Yield:** ½ cup.
René Ralph
Broken Arrow, Oklahoma

HOME-STYLE THE SLOW WAY

Sometimes we avoid preparing favorite dishes because of long cooking times and busy schedules. But with a slow cooker, you can create Easy Brunswick Stew and Hot-and-Spicy Black-Eyed Peas with little effort.

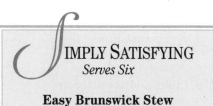

IMPLY SATISFYING
Serves Six

Easy Brunswick Stew
or
Hot-and-Spicy Black-Eyed Peas
Old-Fashioned Coleslaw
Buttermilk Cornbread

EASY BRUNSWICK STEW
(pictured on page 226)

Prep: 15 minutes
Cook: 6 hours and 30 minutes

1 large onion, chopped
1 celery rib, chopped
1 large green bell pepper, chopped
1 cup frozen sliced okra, thawed
4 cups frozen cubed hash browns, thawed
¾ pound barbecued pork, chopped
1 cup chopped cooked chicken
1 (14½-ounce) can diced tomatoes, undrained
1 (15-ounce) can tomato sauce
1 (15¼-ounce) can whole kernel corn with red and green peppers, drained
1 (15¼-ounce) can lima beans, drained
2 cups chicken broth
½ teaspoon salt
½ teaspoon pepper
¼ teaspoon Worcestershire sauce

• **Combine** all ingredients in a 5-quart slow cooker. Cook, covered, at HIGH 6 hours and 30 minutes. **Yield:** 14 cups.

Note: For testing purposes only, we used Ore-Ida Southern Style Potatoes and Texas BBQ Southern Style Pulled Pork Barbeque With Sauce.

HOT-AND-SPICY BLACK-EYED PEAS

Bake Buttermilk Cornbread after adding tomatoes and rice to the slow cooker.

Soak: 8 hours
Prep: 20 minutes
Cook: 8 hours and 30 minutes

1 (16-ounce) package dried black-eyed peas
4 green onions, chopped
1 red bell pepper, chopped
1 jalapeño pepper, diced
1 (3-ounce) package pepperoni slices, diced
2 cups hot water
1 chicken bouillon cube
½ teaspoon salt
¼ teaspoon ground red pepper
1 (14.5-ounce) can Mexican stewed tomatoes
¾ cup uncooked quick rice

• **Place** peas in a 5-quart slow cooker. Cover with water 2 inches above peas; let stand 8 hours. Drain.
• **Combine** peas, onion, and next 7 ingredients in slow cooker. Cover and cook at LOW 8 hours. Stir in tomatoes and rice; cook, covered, 30 minutes. **Yield:** 12 cups.

Julie Smith
Lawrenceville, Georgia

OLD-FASHIONED COLESLAW

Prep: 20 minutes

1 (10-ounce) package angel hair slaw cabbage
4 green onions, chopped
1 medium-size green bell pepper, chopped
1 medium tomato, seeded and chopped
3 tablespoons mayonnaise
½ teaspoon salt

• **Stir** together all ingredients. **Yield:** 6 servings.

Donna Taylor
Arab, Alabama

BUTTERMILK CORNBREAD
(pictured on page 226)

Prep: 5 minutes
Bake: 20 minutes

2 tablespoons vegetable oil
1 cup yellow cornmeal
1 tablespoon all-purpose flour
1½ teaspoons baking powder
¼ teaspoon baking soda
¼ teaspoon salt
1 cup buttermilk
1 large egg

• **Heat** oil in an 8-inch cast-iron skillet or muffin pans in a 450° oven 5 minutes.
• **Combine** cornmeal and next 4 ingredients in a medium bowl; make a well in center of mixture.
• **Stir** together buttermilk and egg; add to dry ingredients, stirring just until moistened. Pour into hot skillet.
• **Bake** at 450° for 20 minutes or until golden. **Yield:** 6 to 8 servings.

Mary Lynn Hanily
Tuscaloosa, Alabama

BEANS AND THINGS

You just can't beat beans for a stick-to-your-ribs meal that's easy on the budget. But beans don't have to stand alone these days. Creative cooks are using dried and canned varieties with vegetables and grains in tasty combinations. The flavors in these dishes are so rich you won't miss the meat.

PASTA WITH BEANS

Prep: 20 minutes
Cook: 20 minutes

1 (15-ounce) can tomatoes, undrained
1 onion, chopped
1 carrot, diced
2 garlic cloves, minced
2 tablespoons chopped fresh parsley
2 teaspoons chopped fresh or ¼ teaspoon dried basil
1 teaspoon dried oregano
¼ cup olive oil
1 teaspoon salt
½ teaspoon pepper
2 teaspoons sugar (optional)
1 (16-ounce) can cannellini or white kidney beans, rinsed and drained
8 ounces elbow macaroni, cooked
2 tablespoons butter or margarine
¼ cup shredded Parmesan cheese
Garnish: fresh basil sprigs

• **Drain** tomatoes, reserving ¼ cup liquid. Chop tomatoes.
• **Sauté** onion and next 5 ingredients in hot oil in a large skillet over medium-high heat until onion is tender.
• **Add** tomato, reserved liquid, salt, pepper, and, if desired, sugar. Cover, reduce heat, and simmer 10 minutes. Stir in beans; cover and simmer 10 minutes.

• **Toss** cooked macaroni with butter; top with bean mixture, and sprinkle with Parmesan cheese. Serve immediately with French bread. Garnish, if desired. **Yield:** 4 servings.

Karen C. Greenlee
Lawrenceville, Georgia

GARBANZO-BLACK BEAN MEDLEY

Prep: 25 minutes
Cook: 20 minutes

1 large onion, chopped
4 garlic cloves, minced
3 cups broccoli flowerets
2 cups sliced fresh mushrooms
1 (15½-ounce) can garbanzo beans, drained and rinsed
1 (15-ounce) can black beans, drained and rinsed
1 (14½-ounce) can diced tomatoes, undrained
1 teaspoon dried Italian seasoning
¾ teaspoon dried oregano
½ teaspoon dried thyme
1 teaspoon salt
½ teaspoon pepper
Hot cooked rice

• **Sauté** onion and garlic in a large skillet coated with cooking spray over medium heat 5 minutes or until tender.

• **Add** broccoli and mushrooms; cook, covered, 5 minutes. Stir in beans, tomatoes, and next 5 ingredients.
• **Bring** to a boil; cover, reduce heat, and simmer 5 minutes. Serve over rice. **Yield:** 6 main-dish servings or 12 side-dish servings.

LENTILS AND RICE

Garam masala [gah-RAHM mah-SAH-lah] is an Indian spice mix found in the spice section of large supermarkets or specialty shops.

Prep: 20 minutes
Cook: 30 minutes

1½ tablespoons butter or margarine
1 large onion, chopped
2 garlic cloves, minced
1 teaspoon grated fresh ginger
½ teaspoon ground turmeric
8 ounces dried red lentils
3 cups chicken broth
½ teaspoon salt
½ teaspoon garam masala
Hot cooked rice

• **Melt** butter in a large skillet over medium heat; add onion, garlic, and ginger. Sauté until golden.
• **Stir** in turmeric and lentils; cook, stirring occasionally, 1 to 2 minutes.
• **Stir** in broth; bring to a boil. Cover, reduce heat, and simmer 15 minutes.
• **Stir** in salt and garam masala; cover and simmer, stirring occasionally, 15 minutes or until lentils are tender and mixture is thickened. Serve with hot cooked rice. **Yield:** 6 servings.

Fran Pointer
Kansas City, Missouri

DAD GOES STIR CRAZY

Someone told Jim Mitchell of Homewood, Alabama, to take a wok—and that's just what he did. Several years ago, he took a cooking class, a gift from his wife, Sue, and their three kids. To Sue's delight, he's been wokking ever since.

"We love this kind of cooking because it's easy," she says. "And it's easy to do," Jim adds, "because I do all the work."

Here is a sampling of the best from Jim's busy kitchen, favorites among his hungry friends.

HOISIN SHRIMP

Prep: 15 minutes
Cook: 8 minutes

1 pound unpeeled, large fresh
   shrimp
2 tablespoons hoisin sauce
1 tablespoon rice wine vinegar
2 teaspoons sugar, divided
½ teaspoon salt
3 tablespoons peanut oil
6 green onions, cut into 1-inch
   pieces
1½ teaspoons minced fresh
   ginger
Hot cooked rice

• **Peel** shrimp; devein, if desired.
• **Stir** together hoisin sauce, vinegar, 1 teaspoon sugar, and salt.
• **Heat** oil in a large skillet or wok over high heat 2 minutes.
• **Add** shrimp, and stir-fry 2 minutes. Add remaining 1 teaspoon sugar, and stir-fry 30 seconds.
• **Add** green onions and ginger, and stir-fry 2 minutes. Add hoisin sauce mixture, and stir-fry 2 minutes. Serve over rice. **Yield:** 3 to 4 servings.

Jim Mitchell
Homewood, Alabama

MOO SHU PORK

Prep: 35 minutes
Cook: 13 minutes

10 dried wood ear mushrooms *
2 (4-ounce) boneless pork loin
   chops, trimmed
1½ teaspoons cornstarch
3 tablespoons soy sauce
2 tablespoons peanut or vegetable
   oil, divided
2 large eggs, lightly beaten
1 cup shredded napa cabbage
1 (8-ounce) can bamboo shoots,
   drained and chopped
½ cup sliced fresh mushrooms
2 green onions, cut into 1-inch
   pieces
9 moo shu pancakes
¼ cup hoisin sauce

• **Soak** wood ear mushrooms in hot water to cover 15 minutes or until soft; drain and slice. Set aside.
• **Freeze** pork chops 30 minutes or until firm. Remove from freezer, and cut into ⅛-inch-thick strips.
• **Toss** pork with cornstarch and soy sauce; set aside.
• **Heat** 1 tablespoon oil in a large skillet or wok at medium-high heat 2 minutes. Add eggs; stir-fry 1 minute or until done. Remove eggs from wok.
• **Add** remaining 1 tablespoon oil to skillet, and heat over medium-high heat 2 minutes. Add pork, and stir-fry 3 to 4 minutes or until done.
• **Add** wood ear mushrooms, cabbage, bamboo shoots, and fresh mushrooms. Stir-fry 2 to 3 minutes.
• **Add** eggs and green onions, and stir-fry 30 seconds. Spoon evenly down centers of pancakes; roll up. Serve with hoisin sauce. **Yield:** 8 servings.

* Substitute 1 cup sliced fresh mushrooms for wood ear mushrooms, if desired; omit soaking.

Note: Moo shu pancakes are small thin pancakes similar to flour tortillas. Find them in Asian markets and in some large supermarkets; they may be labeled as "moo shu shells" on the package.

Jim Mitchell
Homewood, Alabama

JIM'S CHICKEN AND VEGETABLES

Prep: 20 minutes
Cook: 10 minutes

4 to 6 dried black mushrooms
1 cup hot water
4 skinned and boned chicken
   breast halves
2 tablespoons cornstarch, divided
¼ cup lite soy sauce, divided
1½ tablespoons fermented black
   beans or soybean miso
1 tablespoon oyster sauce *
1 tablespoon dry sherry
1 teaspoon sugar
¼ cup vegetable or sesame oil,
   divided
1 large onion, chopped
2 to 3 garlic cloves, minced
6 cups shredded napa cabbage
2 tablespoons water

• **Soak** black mushrooms in 1 cup hot water 15 minutes; drain, reserving ¼ cup mushroom liquid. Chop mushrooms, and set aside.
• **Cut** chicken into ½-inch-thick strips; toss with 1 tablespoon cornstarch and 2 tablespoons soy sauce. Set aside.
• **Stir** together remaining 2 tablespoons soy sauce, reserved ¼ cup mushroom liquid, black beans, and next 3 ingredients with a fork, pressing to mash.
• **Heat** 2 tablespoons oil in a large skillet or wok over medium-high heat 2 minutes. Add chicken, and stir-fry 5 minutes or until done. Remove from skillet.
• **Heat** remaining 2 tablespoons oil in skillet over medium-high heat 2 minutes. Add onion; stir-fry 1 minute and 30 seconds. Add garlic; stir-fry 30 seconds.
• **Add** mushrooms; stir-fry 1 minute. Add chicken and cabbage; stir-fry 30 seconds. Make a well in center of mixture.
• **Stir** together remaining 1 tablespoon cornstarch and 2 tablespoons water until smooth. Add cornstarch mixture and bean mixture to skillet, and bring to a boil; boil 1 minute or until thickened. **Yield:** 4 servings.

* Substitute 1 tablespoon hoisin sauce for oyster sauce, if desired.

Jim Mitchell
Homewood, Alabama

SPRING ROLLS

Prep: 45 minutes
Cook: 4 minutes per batch

1 (½-ounce) package dried black
    mushrooms
1 (8-ounce) can bamboo shoots,
    drained
4 skinned and boned chicken
    breast halves
¼ cup lite soy sauce
1 tablespoon cornstarch
¼ cup peanut or vegetable oil
2 tablespoons lite soy sauce
1 tablespoon sesame oil
¼ teaspoon salt
½ teaspoon pepper
1 (8-ounce) package bean
    sprouts
1 tablespoon cornstarch
2 tablespoons water
1 (16-ounce) package spring or
    egg roll wrappers
1 large egg
2 tablespoons water
6 cups vegetable oil
Sweet-and-sour sauce

• **Soak** black mushrooms in hot water to cover 15 minutes; drain. Chop and set aside. Chop bamboo shoots, and set aside.
• **Cut** chicken into ¼-inch-thick strips; toss with ¼ cup soy sauce and 1 tablespoon cornstarch.
• **Heat** ¼ cup peanut oil in a Dutch oven or wok at medium-high heat 2 minutes. Add chicken; stir-fry 5 minutes or until done. Remove from Dutch oven; chop.
• **Stir** together 2 tablespoons soy sauce, 1 tablespoon sesame oil, salt, and pepper. Add to skillet with mushrooms, bamboo shoots, and bean sprouts, and stir-fry 2 minutes.
• **Stir** together cornstarch and 2 tablespoons water until smooth. Stir chicken and cornstarch mixture into mushroom mixture, and stir-fry 2 minutes or until thickened. Remove from heat.
• **Spoon** about ⅓ cup chicken mixture onto center of each wrapper. Fold 1 corner over filling, and fold both adjacent corners over filling.
• **Stir** together egg and 2 tablespoons water; brush remaining corner with egg mixture.
• **Roll** up, starting at opposite filled side; press edges of brushed corner to seal.
• **Pour** vegetable oil to a depth of 4 inches in Dutch oven or wok; heat to 375°. Fry rolls, a few at a time, 1 to 2 minutes on each side or until golden; drain on paper towels. Serve immediately with sweet-and-sour sauce. **Yield:** 18 rolls.

Jim Mitchell
Homewood, Alabama

WHAT'S IN THE WOK

■ Hoisin is a thick, spicy-sweet mixture of soybeans, garlic, chile peppers, and various spices. It can be found in Asian markets and in large supermarkets.

■ Wood ear mushrooms have a slightly crunchy texture and delicate flavor. Upon reconstituting, the dried variety increases 5 to 6 times in size.

■ Oyster sauce is a condiment made from a mixture of oysters, brine, and soy sauce.

■ Miso, also called bean paste, has the consistency of peanut butter and comes in several flavors, colors, and textures.

WRAP AND ROLL

Egg roll wrappers adapt well to pasta recipes, and when substituted for jumbo pasta shells and manicotti shells, the paper-thin sheets of dough can significantly reduce prep time. Look for the wrappers in the produce department of your supermarket.

SOUTHWESTERN WRAPS

Prep: 20 minutes
Bake: 30 minutes

1 (15-ounce) can tomato sauce
1 (4.5-ounce) can chopped green
    chiles
⅔ cup water
1 tablespoon chili powder
½ teaspoon dried oregano
½ teaspoon ground cumin
½ teaspoon garlic powder
1 tablespoon butter or margarine
1 large onion, chopped
½ green bell pepper, chopped
3 cups diced cooked chicken
1 (8-ounce) bottle Ranch-style
    dressing
¼ teaspoon pepper
1 (16-ounce) package egg roll
    wrappers
2 cups (8 ounces) shredded
    colby-Monterey Jack cheese

• **Bring** first 7 ingredients to a boil in a saucepan over medium heat, stirring often. Reduce heat, and simmer 5 minutes. Spread ½ cup tomato sauce mixture in bottom of a lightly greased 13- x 9-inch baking dish.
• **Melt** butter in a large skillet over medium-high heat; add onion and bell pepper. Sauté until tender; remove from heat. Stir in chicken, dressing, and pepper.
• **Spoon** about ¼ cup mixture just below center of each egg roll wrapper. Fold in left and right sides to partially enclose filling; fold up bottom edge, and roll up. Place, seam side down, in baking dish. Pour remaining tomato sauce mixture over rolls.
• **Bake** at 350° for 25 minutes. Sprinkle with cheese. Bake 5 more minutes or until cheese is melted. **Yield:** 6 to 8 servings.

Southwestern Stuffed Shells: Substitute 16 jumbo pasta shells, cooked, for egg roll wrappers.

Note: To lighten recipe, substitute no-salt-added tomato sauce, reduced-fat Ranch-style dressing, and low-fat Mexican cheese blend; omit butter or margarine, and use vegetable cooking spray.

Julia McLeod
Hendersonville, North Carolina

ULTIMATE CHILI CASSEROLE

Prep: 30 minutes
Bake: 50 minutes

1 small onion, chopped
1 garlic clove, minced
1 tablespoon vegetable oil
2 (10.5-ounce) cans chili without beans
1 (16-ounce) jar salsa
2 large eggs
1 (24-ounce) container cream-style cottage cheese, drained
1½ cups (6 ounces) shredded sharp Cheddar cheese, divided
12 egg roll wrappers

• **Sauté** onion and garlic in hot oil in a large skillet over medium-high heat until tender.
• **Stir** in chili and salsa; cook until thoroughly heated. Spoon half of chili mixture into a lightly greased 13- x 9-inch baking dish.
• **Stir** together eggs, cottage cheese, and 1 cup Cheddar cheese. Spoon about ¼ cup cheese mixture evenly on 1 side of each egg roll wrapper, and roll up. Place, seam side down, in baking dish.
• **Spoon** remaining chili mixture evenly over top, spreading to completely cover wrappers.
• **Bake,** covered, at 350° for 45 minutes. Uncover and sprinkle with remaining ½ cup Cheddar cheese; bake 5 more minutes or until cheese is melted. Let stand 5 minutes. **Yield:** 6 servings.

Chili Manicotti: Substitute 12 manicotti shells, cooked, for egg roll wrappers.

Note: To lighten recipe, substitute low-fat chili without beans, low-fat cottage cheese, and shredded reduced-fat Cheddar cheese.

Judy Perry
Spring, Texas

HOT SANDWICHES

These hearty sandwiches certainly qualify as meals in themselves. But for a robust appetite, add your favorite soup or salad.

To save time when a recipe calls for chopped cooked chicken, cook the meat on the weekend or while you're preparing dinner another night. Chop the chicken and freeze it in 1- or 2-cup portions. Another solution is frozen chopped cooked chicken from the grocery. Canned cooked chicken is also an option, but the texture is a little different. No matter the method you choose, be sure to try our Grilled Chicken 'n' Cheese Sandwiches on the next page. They rated high in our kitchens.

OPEN-FACED MEATBALL SANDWICHES

Prep: 20 minutes
Cook: 30 minutes

1 pound ground round
⅓ cup Italian-seasoned breadcrumbs
¼ cup shredded Parmesan cheese
¼ cup ketchup
1 large egg
1 tablespoon grated onion
2 garlic cloves, minced
½ teaspoon salt
¼ teaspoon pepper
1 (15-ounce) can Italian-style tomato sauce
1 (5.5-ounce) can spicy vegetable juice
3 hoagie rolls, split and toasted

• **Combine** first 9 ingredients; shape into 1-inch balls.
• **Brown** meatballs in a large skillet over medium heat; drain. Wipe skillet clean with a paper towel.

• **Add** tomato sauce and vegetable juice to skillet.
• **Cook** over medium heat, stirring often, 5 minutes. Return meatballs to skillet; cover and cook, stirring occasionally, 15 minutes or until meatballs are no longer pink. Spoon over rolls. **Yield:** 6 servings.

FAJITA PITAS

Prep: 25 minutes
Cook: 10 minutes

4 whole wheat pita bread rounds
1 (16-ounce) can refried beans
4 skinned and boned chicken breast halves, cut into strips
1 tablespoon fajita seasoning
3 tablespoons vegetable oil
1 large onion, cut into strips
1 large red bell pepper, cut into strips
1 (8-ounce) container sour cream
1 cup (4 ounces) shredded Cheddar cheese
1 tomato, diced
2 cups shredded lettuce

• **Cut** bread rounds in half; spread ¼ cup beans in each half. Wrap in aluminum foil.
• **Bake** at 350° for 10 minutes.
• **Toss** chicken with fajita seasoning. Sauté in hot oil in a skillet over medium-high heat 5 minutes.
• **Add** onion and bell pepper; sauté 3 minutes or until chicken is done. Spoon into pitas. Top with sour cream and remaining ingredients. **Yield:** 8 servings.

Shannon Gaudin
Shreveport, Louisiana

GRILLED CHICKEN 'N' CHEESE SANDWICHES

Prep: 30 minutes
Cook: 6 minutes

2 cups chopped cooked chicken
⅓ cup golden raisins
¼ cup slivered almonds, toasted
¼ cup diced celery
½ cup mayonnaise
12 (¾-ounce) Monterey Jack cheese slices
12 whole wheat bread slices
¼ cup butter or margarine, softened

• **Stir** together first 5 ingredients. Place 1 cheese slice on each of 6 bread slices; spread evenly with chicken mixture. Top with remaining cheese and bread slices. Spread half of butter evenly on 1 side of sandwiches.
• **Cook** sandwiches, buttered side down, in a nonstick skillet or griddle over medium heat about 3 minutes or until lightly browned. Spread remaining butter evenly on ungrilled sides; turn and cook 3 minutes or until lightly browned. **Yield:** 6 sandwiches.

Agnes Mixon
Ocala, Florida

CREAMED CHICKEN TOPPERS

Prep: 15 minutes
Cook: 5 minutes

1 (14½-ounce) can chicken broth
⅓ cup all-purpose flour
½ cup mayonnaise
2 cups chopped cooked chicken
½ cup frozen sweet green peas
1 (2-ounce) jar diced pimiento
¼ teaspoon salt
¼ teaspoon pepper
6 white bread slices, toasted

• **Whisk** broth gradually into flour in a saucepan; whisk over medium-high heat until mixture is thickened. Remove from heat; whisk in mayonnaise.

• **Add** chicken and next 4 ingredients; cook until thoroughly heated. (Do not boil.) Serve over bread. **Yield:** 6 servings.

Lorene Breland
Mathiston, Mississippi

JAZZING UP SPAGHETTI SAUCE

If you're searching for creative ways to perk up meats and vegetables—or simply don't have time to make spaghetti sauce from scratch—here is a variety of delicious recipes using prepared spaghetti sauces that are sure to get you cooking in the right direction.

CHICKEN CAPRESE WITH TOMATO-BASIL CREAM

Prep: 20 minutes
Bake: 30 minutes

⅔ cup soft breadcrumbs
⅓ cup crumbled feta cheese
1 tablespoon chopped fresh or 1 teaspoon dried basil
¼ teaspoon salt
¼ teaspoon pepper
3 tablespoons olive oil
2 tablespoons lemon juice
4 skinned and boned chicken breast halves
Tomato-Basil Cream
Garnishes: lemon slices, basil sprigs

• **Stir** together first 5 ingredients in a shallow bowl. Whisk together oil and lemon juice until blended. Dip chicken into oil mixture; dredge in breadcrumb mixture, pressing to coat. Place in a lightly greased 11- x 7-inch baking dish.
• **Bake** at 375° for 30 minutes or until chicken is done. Serve chicken with Tomato-Basil Cream; garnish, if desired. **Yield:** 4 servings.

Tomato-Basil Cream

Prep: 3 minutes
Cook: 5 minutes

1 cup spaghetti sauce
2 tablespoons whipping cream or light sour cream
1 tablespoon chopped fresh or 1 teaspoon dried basil

• **Cook** all ingredients in a small saucepan over low heat, stirring often, 5 minutes or until heated. **Yield:** 1 cup.

Lori Welander
Shelburne, Vermont

EGGPLANT SANDWICHES

Prep: 30 minutes
Broil: 15 minutes

2 small eggplants
2 cups Italian-seasoned breadcrumbs
¾ cup grated Parmesan cheese
3 large eggs
3 tablespoons water
Olive oil-flavored cooking spray
4 (6- to 8-inch) hard Italian rolls, split
1 (16-ounce) jar spaghetti sauce
1 cup (4 ounces) shredded mozzarella cheese

• **Cut** eggplants crosswise into ¼-inch slices.
• **Combine** breadcrumbs and Parmesan cheese. Whisk together eggs and water.
• **Dip** eggplant into egg mixture, and dredge in breadcrumb mixture. Place eggplant on baking sheets coated with cooking spray. Coat eggplant slices with cooking spray.
• **Broil** 12 inches from heat (with electric oven door partially open) 5 minutes on each side. Place eggplant evenly on roll halves, and place rolls on baking sheet. Top with spaghetti sauce, and sprinkle evenly with mozzarella cheese.
• **Broil** 3 to 5 more minutes or until cheese is melted and bubbly. **Yield:** 8 servings.

Agnes L. Stone
Ocala, Florida

RICE-STUFFED PEPPERS

Prep: 20 minutes
Bake: 50 minutes

4   medium-size green bell
       peppers
1   large onion, chopped
1   tablespoon olive oil
1   (16-ounce) jar spaghetti sauce,
       divided
1   cup cooked long-grain rice
1   cup vegetarian burger
       crumbles
2   tablespoons chopped fresh
       parsley
¼   teaspoon salt
¼   teaspoon pepper
¾   cup (3 ounces) shredded
       mozzarella cheese (optional)

• **Cut** off tops of bell peppers; remove seeds and membranes. Place bell pepper cups in a lightly greased 8-inch square baking dish. Remove stems from tops, and discard; chop bell pepper tops.
• **Sauté** chopped bell pepper and onion in hot oil in a large skillet over medium-high heat about 5 minutes. Remove from heat.
• **Stir** in 1½ cups spaghetti sauce and next 5 ingredients.
• **Spoon** mixture evenly into bell pepper cups. Top evenly with remaining ½ cup spaghetti sauce.
• **Bake,** covered, at 400° for 45 minutes. Uncover and sprinkle evenly with cheese, if desired; bake 5 more minutes or until cheese melts. **Yield:** 4 servings.

Note: For testing purposes only, we used Boca Burger Crumbles for vegetarian burger crumbles.

Karen C. Greenlee
Lawrenceville, Georgia

LEARNING ABOUT LAMB

Pity those beef lovers who consider lamb "wool on a stick." Lamb is, in fact, a meat of complex and succulent flavors. Leg of lamb lends itself to a variety of preparations—bone-in, boneless, or extravagantly rolled.

GARLIC-AND-HERB STUFFED LEG OF LAMB
(pictured on page 227)

Prep: 1 hour
Bake: 2 hours and 10 minutes

2   large garlic bulbs
2   tablespoons olive oil
2½ teaspoons salt, divided
2½ teaspoons pepper, divided
¼   cup olive oil
1   tablespoon fresh lemon juice
1   tablespoon minced shallots
1   (5- to 6-pound) leg of lamb,
       boned
3   tablespoons chopped fresh or
       1 teaspoon dried rosemary
3   tablespoons chopped fresh or
       1 teaspoon dried thyme
2   teaspoons grated lemon rind
Garnish: fresh rosemary sprigs

• **Cut** off pointed ends of garlic bulbs. Place each bulb on a piece of aluminum foil; drizzle evenly with 2 tablespoons olive oil, and sprinkle evenly with ½ teaspoon salt and ½ teaspoon pepper. Fold foil to seal.
• **Bake** at 425° for 30 minutes; cool. Squeeze pulp from garlic cloves; mash and set aside.
• **Whisk** together ¼ cup olive oil, lemon juice, and shallots; brush inside of lamb with half of oil mixture, and sprinkle with 1 teaspoon salt and 1 teaspoon pepper. Spread inside with mashed garlic, and sprinkle with rosemary, thyme, and lemon rind.
• **Roll** up lamb; tie with string at 1-inch intervals. Place on a rack in a roasting pan. Brush with remaining oil mixture. Sprinkle with remaining 1 teaspoon salt and remaining 1 teaspoon pepper.
• **Bake** at 425° for 25 minutes; reduce oven temperature to 350°, and bake 1 hour and 45 minutes or until a meat thermometer inserted into thickest portion registers 145°. Remove from oven, and let stand 15 minutes or until meat thermometer registers 150° (medium-rare). Serve with steamed baby carrots and your favorite wild rice blend. Garnish, if desired. **Yield:** 8 servings.

Edwina Gadsby
Great Falls, Montana

TEST KITCHENS TIP

"Remove all the fat and the fell (the thin white membrane covering the lamb) for the best flavor and the best aroma," suggests Vanessa McNeil.

ROAST LEG OF LAMB

Prep: 25 minutes
Bake: 1 hour and 30 minutes

1 (5- to 6-pound) leg of lamb
8 garlic cloves, sliced
1 cup shredded Parmesan cheese
⅓ cup chopped fresh parsley
1 teaspoon salt
1 teaspoon pepper

• **Cut** 1-inch-deep slits, 2 to 3 inches apart, into lamb. Insert a garlic slice into each slit.
• **Stir** together cheese, parsley, salt, and pepper; stuff 2 tablespoons mixture evenly into slits. Coat lamb with vegetable cooking spray. Press remaining cheese mixture onto lamb. Place lamb on a rack in a roasting pan.
• **Bake** at 350° for 1 hour and 30 minutes or until a meat thermometer inserted into thickest portion registers 145°. Remove from oven; let stand 10 to 15 minutes or until thermometer registers 150° (medium-rare). **Yield:** 6 servings.
Mrs. John Massey
Knoxville, Tennessee

LAMB EXTRAORDINAIRE

Prep: 25 minutes
Bake: 2 hours

½ cup minced fresh parsley
2 tablespoons garlic salt
2 tablespoons dried basil
1 tablespoon dried oregano
1 (5- to 6-pound) leg of lamb, boned
1 (8-ounce) pork tenderloin, trimmed
¼ cup olive oil
4 garlic cloves, pressed
1 teaspoon salt

• **Stir** together first 4 ingredients in a bowl; sprinkle 1 tablespoon mixture over inside of lamb. Place tenderloin in center of lamb.
• **Roll** up; tie with string at 1-inch intervals. Sprinkle with 1 tablespoon parsley mixture. Stir together oil, garlic, and salt; brush over lamb. Place, seam side down, in a roasting pan.

• **Bake** at 350° for 2 hours or until a meat thermometer inserted into thickest portion registers 160° (medium). Let meat stand 10 minutes before slicing. Cover and chill remaining parsley mixture to season other meat dishes. **Yield:** 8 servings.
Bess L. Rizzo
Deltona, Florida

FEAST ON OKTOBERFEST

The townspeople of Munich staged a storybook wedding on October 12, 1810, for Crown Prince Ludwig of Bavaria. That wedding feast has since spawned widespread Oktoberfests. Many communities in the South celebrate German heritage with rousing festivals and robust food.

In the spirit of tradition, we salute Oktoberfest with some favorite recipes from one of our readers, German native-turned-Southerner Brigitte Patterson of Peachtree City, Georgia.

ROULADEN

Prep: 45 minutes
Cook: 1 hour and 30 minutes

3 (1-pound) packages ½-inch-thick top round steaks
5 thick-cut bacon slices, diced
2 tablespoons Dijon mustard
1 small onion, chopped
⅓ cup dill pickle relish, drained
3 tablespoons butter or margarine
2 cups beef broth, divided
2 tablespoons all-purpose flour

• **Cut** steaks in half lengthwise. Place steak strips between sheets of heavy-duty plastic wrap, and flatten with a meat mallet or rolling pin to ¼-inch thickness.
• **Cook** bacon in a large skillet until lightly browned; drain.
• **Combine** bacon and next 3 ingredients; spread evenly on steak strips. Roll up each strip, starting with a short end; tie each roll with string or secure with wooden picks. Wipe skillet clean.
• **Melt** butter in skillet over medium heat; add steak rolls, and brown 3 minutes on each side.
• **Add** 1 cup broth. Reduce heat to low, and cook, covered, 1 hour and 30 minutes or until tender. Remove beef rolls, reserving drippings in skillet.
• **Whisk** together remaining 1 cup broth and flour until blended; whisk into hot drippings, and cook, whisking constantly, until thickened. Return beef rolls to skillet, and cook until thoroughly heated. **Yield:** 6 servings.
Brigitte Patterson
Peachtree City, Georgia

SPAETZLE

Spaetzle [SHPEHT-sluh] is served as a side dish much like potatoes, rice, or noodles and is usually accompanied by a sauce or gravy.

Prep: 10 minutes
Cook: 15 minutes

3 cups all-purpose flour
3 teaspoons salt, divided
⅛ teaspoon ground nutmeg
3 large eggs
¾ cup milk
2 quarts water
3 tablespoons butter or margarine
⅓ cup fine, dry breadcrumbs

• **Stir** together flour, 1 teaspoon salt, and nutmeg in a large bowl; make a well in center. Whisk together eggs and milk; gradually stir into dry ingredients, stirring until moistened. Let stand 10 minutes.
• **Divide** dough into thirds on a heavily floured surface. Flatten each portion to ¼-inch thickness, and cut with a wet knife into 4- x ⅛-inch pieces.
• **Bring** 2 quarts water and remaining 2 teaspoons salt to a boil in a Dutch oven.

Drop dough into water, and simmer 3 to 5 minutes or until dumplings float to surface. Remove with a slotted spoon.
• **Melt** butter in a large skillet over medium heat; add dumplings, and sauté 2 minutes on each side or until golden. Sprinkle with breadcrumbs, and serve spaetzle immediately. **Yield:** 6 to 8 servings.

Brigitte Patterson
Peachtree City, Georgia

CUCUMBERS IN SOUR CREAM

Prep: 15 minutes

5 salad cucumbers
1 (8-ounce) container sour cream
2 tablespoons balsamic vinegar
1 tablespoon chopped fresh dill
¼ teaspoon salt
½ teaspoon pepper

• **Peel** cucumbers, and cut into very thin slices. Whisk together sour cream and next 4 ingredients in a large bowl; stir in cucumbers. Serve immediately. **Yield:** 4 to 6 servings.

Brigitte Patterson
Peachtree City, Georgia

SHORTCUT SACHERTORTE

Prep: 25 minutes
Bake: 18 minutes

1 (18.25-ounce) package Swiss chocolate cake mix without pudding
3 large eggs
½ cup vegetable oil
1⅓ cups water
1 (10-ounce) jar seedless raspberry jam
½ cup whipping cream
1 cup semisweet chocolate mini-morsels
Garnishes: whipped cream, fresh raspberries, grated semisweet chocolate

• **Beat** first 4 ingredients at medium speed with an electric mixer 2 minutes.

Spoon batter into 3 greased and floured 8-inch round cakepans.
• **Bake** at 350° for 18 minutes or until a wooden pick inserted in center comes out clean. Cool in pans on wire racks 10 minutes. Remove from pans, and cool completely on wire racks.
• **Spread** jam between layers.
• **Microwave** whipping cream at HIGH 1 minute; add chocolate morsels, stirring until melted. Pour mixture over top of cake, using a spatula to spread dripping mixture around sides of cake. Garnish, if desired. **Yield:** 1 (3-layer) cake.

Brigitte Patterson
Peachtree City, Georgia

.

SIDES BY MARTHA

Nashville chef and cookbook author Martha Phelps Stamps looks forward to October's golden days. Like many of us, she catches fall fever and breathes deeply the cleaner, cooler air. She also rediscovers the simple joy of sampling the Earth's bounty, scouring farmers markets and her own garden for the season's best fruits and vegetables.

Ready to join her in savoring this goodness? Settle in for Martha's side dishes inspired by the bounty at hand.

BRAISED RED CABBAGE

Prep: 10 minutes
Cook: 25 minutes

¼ cup butter or margarine
1 medium onion, thinly sliced
½ medium red cabbage, thinly sliced (about 1¼ pounds)
¼ cup water
¼ teaspoon salt
¼ teaspoon ground white pepper
2 carrots, grated
2 tablespoons cider vinegar
½ teaspoon caraway seeds

• **Melt** butter in a large skillet over medium heat.
• **Add** onion, and sauté 5 minutes or until tender. Add cabbage; cook, stirring often, 2 minutes.
• **Add** ¼ cup water, salt, and pepper; cook, covered, 10 minutes or until cabbage is crisp-tender.
• **Stir** in carrot, vinegar, and caraway seeds; cook, uncovered, 5 minutes. Serve warm. **Yield:** 8 servings.

Note: This dish may be made up to a day in advance and reheated.

Martha Phelps Stamps
Nashville, Tennessee

SPICY KALE WITH TOMATOES

For a meatless main dish, Martha serves this combination over a generous helping of mashed potatoes.

Prep: 20 minutes
Cook: 40 minutes

2 bunches kale (about 1 pound)
1 medium-size purple onion, thinly sliced and separated into rings
3 tablespoons olive oil
4 garlic cloves, minced
1 teaspoon salt
1 (28-ounce) can whole tomatoes, undrained and coarsely chopped
1 (12-ounce) can beer
1 cup water
1 teaspoon red wine vinegar
1 tablespoon hot sauce

• **Remove** stems and discolored spots from kale; rinse with cold water, and drain. Tear into bite-size pieces.
• **Sauté** onion in hot oil in a Dutch oven over medium-high heat 3 minutes. Add kale, garlic, and salt; cook, stirring often, 2 minutes or until kale wilts. Add tomatoes and next 4 ingredients. Bring to a boil; cook, covered, 40 minutes or until kale is tender. Serve with a slotted spoon. **Yield:** 8 servings.

Martha Phelps Stamps
Nashville, Tennessee

MASHED SWEET POTATOES WITH CUMIN

Ground cumin provides a smoky flavor surprise in this vegetable classic.

Prep: 30 minutes
Bake: 45 minutes

4 sweet potatoes, peeled and
      cubed (about 3½ pounds)
2 medium-size purple onions,
      coarsely chopped
½ cup butter or margarine, cubed
1 teaspoon salt
½ teaspoon ground red pepper
2 tablespoons maple syrup
1 tablespoon lemon juice
1 teaspoon ground cinnamon
1 teaspoon ground cumin
½ cup chopped pecans, toasted

• **Combine** first 3 ingredients in a lightly greased 11- x 7-inch or shallow 2-quart baking dish; sprinkle with salt and red pepper. Bake, covered, at 375° for 40 to 45 minutes or until potato is tender. Remove from oven. Add syrup and next 3 ingredients; mash, leaving a few lumps. Sprinkle with pecans. **Yield:** 8 to 10 servings.

Note: To make ahead, cover and chill after baking and mashing. Remove from refrigerator; let stand 30 minutes. Bake at 375° for 30 minutes.

Martha Phelps Stamps
Nashville, Tennessee

HONEY-GLAZED ROASTED FALL VEGETABLES

Prep: 30 minutes
Bake: 40 minutes

3 medium beets
3 medium Yukon Gold or other
      thin-skinned potatoes
3 purple onions
¾ cup chicken broth
3 tablespoons olive oil
1 teaspoon salt
½ teaspoon pepper
3 medium turnips
2 tablespoons lemon juice
1½ tablespoons honey

• **Peel** first 3 ingredients; cut each into 8 wedges.
• **Toss** together vegetable wedges, broth, and next 3 ingredients in a large bowl. Spread wedges evenly in a 15- x 10-inch jellyroll pan; pour broth mixture over vegetables in pan.
• **Bake** at 375° for 20 minutes.
• **Peel** turnips; cut each turnip into 8 wedges. Add to baked vegetables, stirring to coat well; bake 20 more minutes or until liquid is absorbed.
• **Stir** together lemon juice and honey; add to vegetables, tossing well. **Yield:** 8 servings.

Note: To make ahead, chill vegetables after baking 40 minutes. Remove from refrigerator; let stand 30 minutes. Bake, covered, at 375° for 15 minutes; toss with lemon juice mixture.

Martha Phelps Stamps
Nashville, Tennessee

BAKED MACARONI WITH SPINACH

Prep: 45 minutes
Bake: 40 minutes

8 ounces elbow macaroni, cooked
1 teaspoon vegetable oil
1 pound broccoli, cut into
      flowerets
1½ teaspoons salt, divided
1 (6-ounce) package fresh baby
      spinach
2 tablespoons butter or margarine
½ medium onion, chopped
2 (8-ounce) packages mushrooms,
      quartered
2 tablespoons all-purpose flour
2 cups milk
2 cups (8 ounces) shredded sharp
      white Cheddar cheese, divided
1 cup whipping cream
½ teaspoon pepper
½ teaspoon ground nutmeg

• **Toss** macaroni with vegetable oil in a large bowl.
• **Cook** broccoli with 1 teaspoon salt in boiling water to cover 2 minutes or until crisp-tender; drain. Plunge into ice water to stop the cooking process, and drain.

• **Add** broccoli and spinach to macaroni in bowl.
• **Melt** butter in a medium saucepan over medium heat; add onion, and sauté until tender.
• **Add** mushrooms, and cook 5 minutes. Sprinkle with flour, stirring until blended. Gradually stir in milk; cook over medium heat, stirring constantly, 15 minutes.
• **Add** 1½ cups cheese, remaining ½ teaspoon salt, whipping cream, pepper, and nutmeg, stirring until cheese melts. Stir into macaroni mixture; spoon into a lightly greased 13- x 9-inch baking dish. Sprinkle with remaining ½ cup cheese.
• **Bake** at 375° for 40 minutes or until set. **Yield:** 8 to 10 servings.

Martha Phelps Stamps
Nashville, Tennessee

SIGNATURE SALAD DRESSINGS

A satiny, smooth salad dressing brings new life to your favorite leafy greens. Assemble these flavorful toppers in seven minutes or less using a whisk, blender, or food processor.

BLUE CHEESE DRESSING

Prep: 5 minutes
Chill: 1 hour

1 (5-ounce) can evaporated milk
1 cup mayonnaise
3 tablespoons lemon juice
1 (4-ounce) package crumbled
      blue cheese

• **Whisk** together first 3 ingredients until blended; stir in blue cheese. Cover and chill at least 1 hour. Serve on mixed salad greens or as a vegetable dip. **Yield:** 2 cups.

Ruth Bouldin
Murfreesboro, Tennessee

APRICOT DRESSING

Prep: 5 minutes

1 (8½-ounce) can unpeeled
     apricot halves, drained
1 (8-ounce) container sour cream
¼ cup honey
1 tablespoon lemon juice
⅛ teaspoon salt

• **Process** all ingredients in a blender until smooth, stopping to scrape down sides. Cover and chill, if desired. Serve over salad greens or fruit. **Yield:** 2 cups.
Charlotte Bryant
Greensburg, Kentucky

SOUTHWESTERN MAYONNAISE DRESSING

Prep: 5 minutes

1¼ cups mayonnaise
2 tablespoons orange juice
1 tablespoon white wine vinegar
¼ teaspoon chili powder
3 tablespoons chopped canned
     green chiles

• **Whisk** together first 4 ingredients in a small bowl until smooth; stir in green chiles. Cover and chill, if desired. Serve over mixed salad greens or as a dressing for chicken salad. **Yield:** 1½ cups.
Suzan L. Wiener
Spring Hill, Florida

SASSY FRENCH DRESSING

Prep: 5 minutes
Chill: 30 minutes

1 (8-ounce) can tomato sauce
½ cup vegetable oil
⅓ cup rice vinegar
1 tablespoon brown sugar
½ teaspoon salt
¼ teaspoon dry mustard
⅛ teaspoon garlic powder

• **Whisk** together all ingredients in a bowl until blended. Cover and chill at least 30 minutes; serve over mixed salad greens. **Yield:** 2 cups.
Johnsie Ford
Rockingham, North Carolina

CREAMY HONEY-DIJON SALAD DRESSING

Prep: 7 minutes
Chill: 8 hours

1½ cups mayonnaise
¼ cup honey
2 tablespoons minced onion
2 tablespoons lemon juice
1 teaspoon minced fresh parsley
1 teaspoon Dijon mustard

• **Process** all ingredients in a blender or food processor until smooth, stopping to scrape down sides. Cover and chill at least 8 hours. Serve over mixed salad greens or as a dip for chicken nuggets. **Yield:** 2 cups.
Joy Knight Allard
San Antonio, Texas

SALAD DRESSING MIX

Prep: 3 minutes

½ cup dried parsley flakes
¼ cup freeze-dried chives
1 tablespoon dried dillweed
¼ teaspoon salt
⅛ teaspoon pepper

• **Stir** together all ingredients, and store in an airtight container up to 6 months. **Yield:** ¾ cup.

Herbed Salad Dressing: Whisk together 2 tablespoons Salad Dressing Mix, ½ cup mayonnaise, and ½ cup buttermilk or sour cream. Cover; chill at least 2 hours. Serve over mixed salad greens or as a vegetable dip. **Yield:** 1 cup.
Nora Henshaw
Okemah, Oklahoma

HALLOWEEN BITES

Create a spooky landscape on your party table with a field of fall finger foods. If cheese balls are a favorite appetizer, try this shapely new version with a surprise inside. Goblins of all ages will love them.

PUMPKIN PATCH CHEESE BALLS

Prep: 25 minutes
Chill: 1 hour
Bake: 12 minutes

2 tablespoons pine nuts
½ cup butter or margarine,
     softened
4 drops of yellow liquid food
     coloring
2 drops of red liquid food coloring
1½ cups all-purpose flour
¼ teaspoon ground red pepper
1 (6-ounce) roll garlic cheese
1 (7-ounce) jar pimiento-stuffed
     olives, drained

• **Bake** pine nuts in a shallow pan at 350°, stirring occasionally, 5 minutes or until toasted; cool.
• **Stir** together butter and food colorings in a large bowl. Add flour and red pepper; cut in cheese with a pastry blender until mixture is blended. Shape into a large ball using hands.
• **Press** 1 tablespoon cheese mixture around each olive. Using dull side of a paring knife, score cheese balls with vertical lines to resemble pumpkins. Chill 1 hour.
• **Bake** on a parchment paper-lined baking sheet at 400° for 10 to 12 minutes or until golden.
• **Place** 1 pine nut into each cheese ball to resemble stem. Serve immediately or at room temperature, or freeze up to 1 month. **Yield:** about 3 dozen.

WHITE MERINGUE GHOSTS

Prep: 20 minutes
Bake: 2 hours
Stand: 8 hours

6 egg whites
½ teaspoon cream of tartar
¾ cup sugar
½ teaspoon almond extract
1 tablespoon semisweet chocolate
    mini-morsels
String Licorice (optional)

• **Beat** egg whites and cream of tartar at high speed with an electric mixer until foamy. Gradually add sugar, 1 table-spoon at a time, beating until stiff peaks form and sugar dissolves (2 to 4 minutes). Add almond extract; beat until blended.
• **Spoon** mixture into a zip-top plastic bag; snip a small hole in 1 corner, and pipe mixture into ghostly shapes on parchment paper-lined baking sheets.
• **Add** mini-morsels for eyes. If desired, cut licorice into 2-inch pieces. Firmly pinch ends together. Insert 1 in top of each ghost for a hanger.
• **Bake** at 200° for 2 hours. Turn oven off, and let meringues stand in closed oven with light on 8 hours. **Yield:** 16 meringues.

BREADSTICK HAYSTACKS

Prep: 10 minutes
Bake: 12 minutes

1 (11-ounce) can refrigerated
    breadsticks
Butter-flavored cooking spray
1 tablespoon dry Ranch-style
    dressing mix

• **Unroll** breadsticks. Cut each bread-stick in half crosswise, forming 3½-inch pieces; cut each portion in half length-wise, forming ½-inch strips. Place on lightly greased baking sheets. Coat with cooking spray, and sprinkle with dress-ing mix.
• **Bake** at 375° for 10 to 12 minutes or until lightly browned. Serve haystacks with spaghetti sauce. **Yield:** 4 dozen.

APPLE BOBBING PUNCH

Prep: 10 minutes
Chill: 3 hours

1 (32-ounce) bottle apple cider
1 (32-ounce) bottle cranberry
    juice drink
1 (16-ounce) jar whole crab
    apples, undrained
1 (6-ounce) can frozen orange
    juice concentrate, thawed
1 (6-ounce) can frozen lemonade
    concentrate, thawed
1 (1-liter) bottle ginger ale or
    lemon-lime soft drink, chilled

• **Stir** together first 5 ingredients. Chill. Stir in ginger ale just before serving. Serve over ice. **Yield:** 4 quarts.

Sweet Pairings

Cool days require special foods, and baked apples and pears fill the bill nicely. Enhance them with sugar, spices, and wines or fruit juices, and offer them as a surprise side dish or stylish dessert.

CRANBERRY APPLES

Prep: 25 minutes
Bake: 30 minutes

1½ cups sweet vermouth *
1½ cups apple cider
6 large Granny Smith or Rome
    apples
5 tablespoons sugar
6 tablespoons dried cranberries
½ teaspoon ground cinnamon
2 tablespoons butter or margarine,
    cut up
Vanilla ice cream (optional)

• **Boil** vermouth and cider in a saucepan about 40 minutes or until reduced to

1 cup. Core apples, cutting to but not through bottom ends; place in a lightly greased 11- x 7-inch baking dish. Fill each apple with 2 teaspoons sugar and 1 tablespoon cranberries. Pour vermouth mixture over apples.
• **Combine** remaining 1 tablespoon sugar and cinnamon; sprinkle evenly over apples. Dot apples with butter.
• **Bake,** covered, at 350° for 15 minutes. Uncover; bake 15 more minutes or until tender, basting occasionally. Serve with ice cream, if desired. **Yield:** 6 servings.

* Substitute 1½ cups apple cider for vermouth, if desired.

PEARS BLUE

Prep: 45 minutes
Bake: 35 minutes

1 (750-milliliter) bottle red
    Zinfandel or other red wine
3 tablespoons sugar
6 large firm Anjou pears
1 (3-ounce) package cream cheese,
    softened
⅓ cup crumbled blue cheese
6 tablespoons chopped walnuts,
    toasted

• **Boil** wine and sugar in a Dutch oven 20 to 25 minutes or until reduced to 1 cup.
• **Peel** pears. Remove top third of each pear, and set stemmed portions aside. Core pears, cutting to but not through bottom ends.
• **Place** pears, including top portions, in wine mixture; cover and simmer over medium heat 20 minutes or until tender. Drain and arrange cored pears in an 11- x 7-inch baking dish.
• **Stir** together cream cheese, blue cheese, and walnuts. Spoon mixture evenly in center of cored pears.
• **Bake,** covered, at 375° for 20 minutes; uncover and bake 15 more minutes. Place tops on pears just before serving. **Yield:** 6 servings.

TAFFY PECAN APPLES

Prep: 15 minutes
Bake: 1 hour

4 large Granny Smith or Rome
     apples
½ cup chopped pecans
½ cup firmly packed dark brown
     sugar
¼ teaspoon salt
¼ cup half-and-half

• **Core** apples, cutting to but not through
bottom ends; arrange in a lightly greased
9-inch square baking dish. Stir together
pecans and next 3 ingredients; spoon
into apples. Bake, covered, at 375° for
45 minutes; uncover and bake 15 more
minutes. Serve warm. **Yield:** 4 servings.

Note: Apples may be sliced and placed
in a lightly greased 11- x 7-inch baking
dish; spread pecan mixture over apple,
and bake at 375° for 30 to 35 minutes.
Mrs. John B. Wright
Greenville, South Carolina

STUFFED APPLES

Prep: 20 minutes
Bake: 45 minutes

4 large Granny Smith apples
¼ cup mincemeat
¼ cup golden raisins (optional)
2 tablespoons butter or margarine,
     cut up
¼ cup honey
¾ cup Madeira wine *
Vanilla ice cream or whipped topping

• **Core** apples, cutting to but not through
bottom ends. Fill apples evenly with
mincemeat and, if desired, raisins.
Arrange in a lightly greased 9-inch
square baking dish. Dot with butter, and
drizzle with honey. Pour wine into dish.
• **Bake** at 375° for 45 minutes or until
tender, basting often. Serve with ice
cream. **Yield:** 4 servings.

* Substitute ¾ cup apple juice, if desired.
Gwen Louer
Boynton Beach, Florida

CINNAMON, CLOVES & NUTMEG

Surround yourself with the aromas of cinnamon,
cloves, and nutmeg as desserts bake and ciders simmer.
Pairing these tastes with fresh produce, such as
acorn squash and bananas, captures the scents
and flavors of the season. These particular spices are
available ground or whole. For a more intense flavor,
buy them whole and grind them just before using.

SPICED BANANAS WITH RUM SAUCE

Prep: 5 minutes
Cook: 4 minutes

2 small ripe bananas
1 tablespoon butter or
     margarine
1 tablespoon brown sugar
2 tablespoons apple juice
     concentrate, thawed and
     undiluted
1 teaspoon vanilla extract
¼ teaspoon ground cinnamon
⅛ teaspoon ground allspice
2 tablespoons dark rum
1 cup vanilla reduced-fat frozen
     yogurt

• **Cut** bananas in half crosswise, and cut
halves lengthwise.
• **Melt** butter in a large nonstick skillet
over medium-high heat.

• **Add** brown sugar and next 4 ingredients; cook 30 seconds.
• **Add** banana pieces, and cook 1 minute
on each side.
• **Heat** rum in a small saucepan. Pour
over banana mixture. Ignite rum with a
long match, if desired; let flames die
down. Stir gently; top with yogurt. Serve
immediately. **Yield:** 2 servings.

♥ Per serving: Calories 357
Fat 7.9g Cholesterol 25mg
Sodium 137mg

WINTER SQUASH-SPICE BUNDT CAKE

Although this cake doesn't rise much, it is very moist.

Prep: 50 minutes
Bake: 45 minutes

1 (1½-pound) acorn squash
2¾ cups self-rising flour, divided
1 cup raisins
1 teaspoon ground cinnamon
1 teaspoon ground nutmeg
½ teaspoon ground cloves
1½ cups sugar
½ cup egg substitute
½ cup applesauce
¼ cup vegetable oil
Vegetable cooking spray
Powdered sugar (optional)

• **Cut** squash in half; discard seeds and membrane. Place squash halves, cut sides down, in an 11- x 7-inch baking dish. Add water to a depth of ¼ inch.
• **Bake** at 375° for 35 to 45 minutes or until tender; cool slightly.
• **Scoop** out and mash pulp; discard shells.
• **Toss** together ¼ cup flour and raisins. Set aside.
• **Combine** remaining 2½ cups flour, cinnamon, nutmeg, and cloves, and set aside.
• **Combine** squash pulp, sugar, and next 3 ingredients; stir in flour mixture until blended. Stir in raisins. Pour into a 12-cup Bundt pan coated with vegetable cooking spray.
• **Bake** at 350° for 45 minutes or until a wooden pick inserted in center comes out clean. Cool in pan on a wire rack 10 minutes. Remove from pan, and cool completely. Sprinkle with powdered sugar, if desired. **Yield:** 16 servings.

Joann Porter
Wallingford, Kentucky

♥ Per serving: Calories 227
Fat 3.9g Cholesterol 0mg
Sodium 287mg

HOT SPICED CIDER

Prep: 6 minutes
Cook: 20 minutes

2 quarts apple cider
½ cup molasses
4 lemon slices, cut in half
12 whole cloves
2 (2-inch) cinnamon sticks
¼ cup lemon juice
Garnishes: cinnamon sticks, lemon wedges, whole cloves

• **Bring** first 5 ingredients to a boil in a large saucepan over medium-high heat, stirring occasionally; reduce heat, and simmer 15 minutes.
• **Remove** cinnamon sticks and cloves with a slotted spoon; stir in lemon juice. Garnish, if desired. Serve immediately. **Yield:** 9 cups.

Valerie Stutsman
Norfolk, Virginia

♥ Per cup: Calories 163
Fat 0.5g Cholesterol 0mg
Sodium 16mg

STORING SPICES

■ Store spices in airtight containers in a cool, dark place up to six months. If keeping them longer than six months, store in the freezer.

■ Label each jar with date of purchase so you know when it's time to replace spices.

■ Alphabetize spice jars on the rack to make locating spices easier.

APPLE QUESADILLAS

Prep: 15 minutes
Cook: 24 minutes

4 medium Granny Smith apples, peeled and sliced
1 tablespoon lemon juice
¼ cup sugar, divided
Vegetable cooking spray
1 (8-ounce) package reduced-fat cream cheese, softened
1 (14-ounce) can fat-free sweetened condensed milk
1 teaspoon vanilla extract
8 (8-inch) fat-free flour tortillas
2½ tablespoons chopped pecans, toasted
½ teaspoon ground cinnamon

• **Toss** together apple, lemon juice, and 3 tablespoons sugar.
• **Cook** apple mixture in a large non-stick skillet coated with cooking spray over medium-high heat, stirring often, 5 minutes or until tender and golden. Remove apple mixture from skillet, and set aside. Wipe skillet clean.
• **Beat** cream cheese, condensed milk, and vanilla at medium speed with an electric mixer until smooth (2 minutes).
• **Place** 1 tortilla in skillet coated with cooking spray over medium heat; spread with about ¼ cup cream cheese mixture. Cook 1 minute or until filling bubbles. Spoon ¼ cup apple mixture on half of filling; sprinkle with about 1 teaspoon pecans. Fold tortilla in half; cook 30 seconds to 1 minute on each side until browned. Repeat procedure with remaining tortillas, fillings, and pecans.
• **Combine** remaining 1 tablespoon sugar and cinnamon; sprinkle mixture evenly over quesadillas. Cut each quesadilla into 3 wedges. **Yield:** 12 servings.

♥ Per serving: Calories 252
Fat 4.6g Cholesterol 15mg
Sodium 354mg

Something Nutty

Chocolate and dried fruit are the perfect complements to crunchy nuts in pies and tarts. Unsalted nuts are the best choice for baking. Bring out additional flavor and crispness by toasting nuts at 350° for 5 to 7 minutes. Before measuring, taste a few nuts to ensure peak freshness.

APRICOT-NUT TART

Prep: 30 minutes
Freeze: 2 hours
Bake: 40 minutes

1 **cup almonds**
1 **cup pecans**
1 **cup walnuts**
1½ **cups all-purpose flour**
1¼ **cups firmly packed light brown sugar, divided**
6 **tablespoons butter or margarine**
4 **large eggs, divided**
½ **cup dried apricots, diced**
½ **cup light corn syrup**
¼ **cup butter or margarine, melted**
2 **tablespoons apricot nectar**
1 **tablespoon vanilla extract**
1½ **teaspoons grated lemon rind**
Vanilla ice cream (optional)
Garnishes: toasted chopped almonds, pecans, walnuts

• **Chop** first 3 ingredients coarsely. Place in a shallow pan.
• **Bake** at 350° for 5 to 7 minutes or until toasted, stirring once. Set aside.
• **Pulse** flour, ¼ cup brown sugar, and 6 tablespoons butter in a food processor 7 or 8 times or until mixture is crumbly. Add 1 egg; pulse 4 or 5 times or until dough forms a ball.
• **Press** dough into bottom and up sides of an 11-inch tart pan with removable bottom. Freeze 2 hours.
• **Stir** together remaining 1 cup brown sugar, remaining 3 eggs, apricots, and next 5 ingredients. Stir in reserved toasted nuts, and pour into crust.
• **Bake** at 350° on bottom oven rack for 35 to 40 minutes or until set. Cool on a wire rack. Serve with ice cream, if desired. Garnish, if desired. **Yield:** 1 (11-inch) tart.

BLACK-AND-WHITE FUDGE PIE

Prep: 35 minutes
Bake: 50 minutes
Chill: 4 hours

1¼ **cups all-purpose flour, divided**
½ **cup ground walnuts**
⅓ **cup cocoa**
1¼ **cups sugar, divided**
½ **teaspoon salt, divided**
1 **cup butter or margarine, divided**
¼ **cup milk**
2 **teaspoons vanilla extract, divided**
4 **(1-ounce) bittersweet chocolate squares**
3 **large eggs, divided**
½ **cup chopped walnuts**
1 **(8-ounce) package cream cheese, softened**

• **Combine** 1 cup flour, ground walnuts, cocoa, ¼ cup sugar, and ¼ teaspoon salt; cut in ½ cup butter with a pastry blender until crumbly. Stir in milk and 1 teaspoon vanilla.
• **Press** into bottom and up sides of a 9-inch pieplate. Prick bottom and sides of piecrust with a fork.
• **Bake** at 425° for 10 minutes; cool completely on a wire rack.
• **Melt** remaining ½ cup butter and chocolate over low heat, stirring until smooth.
• **Beat** 2 eggs at medium speed with an electric mixer until blended. Add remaining ¼ cup flour, ⅔ cup sugar, and remaining ¼ teaspoon salt, beating until blended.
• **Stir** in melted chocolate mixture and chopped walnuts. Remove ½ cup batter; set aside. Spread remaining batter into piecrust.
• **Beat** cream cheese, remaining ⅓ cup sugar, remaining egg, and remaining 1 teaspoon vanilla until smooth.
• **Spread** mixture over chocolate batter. Spoon dollops of reserved chocolate batter over cream cheese mixture, and swirl batter gently with a knife.
• **Bake** at 325° for 35 to 40 minutes or until set, shielding with strips of aluminum foil, if necessary. Cool completely on a wire rack. Cover and chill 4 hours. **Yield:** 1 (9-inch) pie.

Kate Stewart Rovner
Plano, Texas

HARD-SHELL GUIDELINES

■ Purchase nuts from stores that sell in bulk and have a rapid turnover.

■ Shelled nuts should feel heavy for their size. Pack in airtight containers, and store in the refrigerator up to four months, or freeze up to six months.

■ Toasting nuts helps remove excess moisture.

FROM OUR KITCHEN TO YOURS

SWEET ORANGES

This month citrus growers' sweetest oranges are arriving in supermarkets. See what's available in a produce department near you. Here is a guide to different types.

■ **Hamlins** are thin-skinned, medium-size oranges. Roll one of these smooth, deep-yellow fruits between your palms for a juicy treat.

■ **Navels** are large, seedless fruits with thick skins. These are especially easy to peel and section.

■ **Temples** are considered to be Florida's best eating orange. Their skins zip off easily, and they smell as good as they taste.

■ **Valencias** are known for their juice. The smooth-skinned fruit is not easy to peel but it contains very few seeds.

■ **Tangelo** is a cross between a tangerine and a pomelo (Chinese grapefruit). This fruit has a light red-orange color, pebbly skin, and refreshing flavor.

When you're using oranges in recipes, here's a quick guide:

2 to 4 medium oranges = 1 cup juice
2 medium oranges = 1 cup bite-size pieces
1 medium orange = 10 to 12 sections
1 medium orange = 4 teaspoons grated peel

WE DO KNOW BEANS

The recommended daily requirement of folate for adults is 400 micrograms (mcg). One cup of cooked dried beans can have as much as 366 mcg of folate.

Dried beans are the best vegetable source of folate. The bean recipes on page 236 are delicious ways to get the valuable nutrient.

TIPS AND TIDBITS

■ Mary Allen Perry of our Test Kitchens staff sings the praises of parchment paper. "I love parchment for the fast cleanup; it doesn't smoke, you can reuse it, and, most importantly, food never sticks to it." Use it to line cakepans, form instant pastry tubes, and as a flavor barrier in claypot cooking. You'll find rolls of the crisp paper among the foil and plastic wrap on grocers' shelves.

■ Margaret Beam of Arlington, Virginia, sent us this good hint: When cooking soups that must be pureed, instead of transferring the soup to a food processor, simply use a handheld blender (milk shake maker). The soup doesn't leave the pot, preparation time is reduced, and cleanup is much easier.

■ T. Smythe Richbourg, of Cary, North Carolina, uses two of the same size pieplates to pack crumb crusts. Use one to press the crumbs into the other. "I use a back-and-forth rotating motion, the way kids imitate turning a car's steering wheel."

■ Peggy Smith, assistant foods editor, keeps all of her plastic storage containers smelling fresh. She stores each container with a clean, dry paper towel inside, which leaves containers free of odors. Try this, and your containers will both look and smell clean.

BEER PAIRINGS

Oktoberfest always puts beer in the spotlight. With so many types available, finding what you like can be overwhelming. When tasting, move from light to dark. Remember, food brings out the flavors in beer rather than the other way around.

■ Golden or blonde ale and American wheat ale are great thirst-quenchers with spicy food.

■ Amber ale is a good all-purpose beer for any food that isn't sweet. It complements soups, pizzas, sandwiches, and barbecue.

■ American brown ale is a natural with hamburgers and sausages.

■ Cream, sweet, or imperial stout takes its place as an after-dinner beer. It's made for chocolate and fruit desserts.

■ Dark lager or bock is perfect for the Oktoberfest menu on pages 242 and 243.

■ Fruit beers can be sweet or sour. Enjoy some of the sweet lambics, slightly effervescent fruity beers, at the end of a meal.

NOVEMBER

Slow down and savor the holidays—a time for family, close friends, and good food. Make Thanksgiving a memorable occasion with "A Beautiful, Bountiful Meal," a splendid feast planned with make-ahead convenience in mind.

Southerners share their favorite holiday recipes in the special section "Holiday Dinners®: Southerners Entertain" beginning on page 265. Celebrate the season in grand style with the large selection of sensational recipes, from Stuffed Tuscany Tenderloin to Merry Cranberry-Nut Yeast Scones to Chocolate Mousse Present. Gracious entertaining has never been so simple.

A BEAUTIFUL, BOUNTIFUL MEAL

Celebrate Thanksgiving with us in easygoing fashion, without fuss and fancy. It is a day to enjoy good food, good friends, and the good earth.

BOUNTIFUL THANKSGIVING FEAST
Serves Eight

Acorn Squash-Thyme Soup

Apple-Rosemary Roasted Turkey

Southern Rice Dressing (page 256)

Whole-berry Cranberry Sauce

Caramelized Onion-and-Pecan Brussels Sprouts

Rustic Breads

Cracked Caramel-Pumpkin Pie

ACORN SQUASH-THYME SOUP

Prep: 30 minutes
Bake: 30 minutes
Chill: 8 hours
Cook: 30 minutes

9 large acorn squash, divided
½ teaspoon salt
½ teaspoon pepper
2 medium leeks
¼ cup butter or margarine, divided
2 garlic cloves, minced
2 tablespoons fresh thyme leaves
5 cups chicken broth
1½ cups half-and-half
Garnish: 8 fresh thyme sprigs

• **Cut** a 1-inch slice from bottom of 8 squash, allowing squash to sit flat. Cut 1 inch below stems from tops; discard stems. Scoop out and discard seeds.
• **Sprinkle** squash with salt and pepper. Place, stem end up, in a lightly greased 15- x 10-inch jellyroll pan.
• **Bake** at 350° for 30 minutes or until tender. Cool slightly.
• **Scoop** out squash pulp, leaving ¼-inch-thick shells. Reserve pulp; place shells in plastic bags. Seal and chill 8 hours.
• **Peel** remaining 1 acorn squash. Scoop out and discard seeds; chop pulp.
• **Remove** and discard green tops from leeks. Cut white portions in half lengthwise; cut into ½-inch slices.
• **Melt** 2 tablespoons butter in a large Dutch oven over medium or medium-high heat; add chopped squash pulp, leeks, garlic, and 2 tablespoons thyme. Sauté 10 minutes.
• **Add** broth, and cook 30 minutes or until squash is tender.
• **Stir** in reserved baked squash pulp. Cool slightly.
• **Process** mixture, in batches, in a food processor or blender until smooth. Return to Dutch oven. Cover; chill 8 hours.
• **Stir** half-and-half into soup; cook until heated. (Do not boil.)
• **Melt** remaining 2 tablespoons butter in a large skillet. Add squash shells to skillet, bottom sides up, and cook 2 minutes or until edges are browned. Serve soup in shells, and garnish, if desired. **Yield:** 8 servings.

APPLE-ROSEMARY ROASTED TURKEY

Prep: 30 minutes
Bake: 4 hours and 20 minutes
Chill: 8 hours
Cook: 32 minutes

1 (12- to 13-pound) whole turkey
1 teaspoon salt
1½ teaspoons pepper, divided
2 Granny Smith apples, quartered
1 onion, quartered
8 fresh rosemary sprigs
2 fresh sage sprigs
1 (12-ounce) can frozen apple juice concentrate, thawed, undiluted, and divided
½ cup butter or margarine, melted
2 cups water
¼ cup all-purpose flour

• **Remove** giblets and neck from turkey, discarding giblets and reserving neck. Rinse turkey with cold water; pat dry.
• **Sprinkle** outside of turkey and cavity with salt and 1 teaspoon pepper; stuff cavity with apple, half of onion, and 6 rosemary sprigs. Loosen skin from turkey breast without detaching it; insert remaining 2 rosemary sprigs and sage beneath skin. Place turkey on a rack in a roasting pan.
• **Stir** together 1 cup apple juice concentrate and butter. Attach needle to

marinade injector, and fill with apple juice concentrate mixture according to directions. Inject marinade into turkey breast several times and into thighs and drumsticks.

• **Bake** at 425° for 20 minutes; reduce oven temperature to 350°, and bake 4 hours or until a meat thermometer inserted into turkey thigh registers 180°. Cover loosely with aluminum foil to prevent excessive browning, if necessary.

• **Remove** turkey from pan, reserving ½ cup drippings. Cool. Remove apple, onion, and rosemary from cavity, and discard; wrap turkey in plastic wrap, then aluminum foil. Chill 8 hours.

• **Bring** 2 cups water, remaining apple juice concentrate, turkey neck, and remaining half of onion to a boil in a saucepan; boil 15 minutes.

• **Pour** through a wire-mesh strainer into a measuring cup, discarding solids.

• **Heat** reserved drippings in a heavy saucepan over medium heat; whisk in flour until smooth.

• **Cook,** whisking constantly, 1 minute. Gradually add apple juice mixture, whisking constantly.

• **Cook,** whisking constantly, until thickened. Stir in remaining ½ teaspoon pepper. Cover and chill 8 hours. Reheat gravy, and serve warm with turkey and, if desired, whole-berry cranberry sauce. **Yield:** 12 servings.

Apple-Rosemary Turkey Breast: Substitute 1 (6-pound) bone-in turkey breast for whole turkey. Bake at 350° for 1½ hours; cover and bake 1 more hour or until meat thermometer registers 170°. **Yield:** 8 servings.

Note: Baste turkey with apple juice concentrate mixture every 30 minutes if marinade injector isn't available. See "From Our Kitchen to Yours" on page 296 for ordering information.

A day at the lake, surrounded by mellow colors and autumn's musky scent, reminds us that Thanksgiving is the harvest's fulfillment.

What better place than a lake retreat to savor the fabulous fall foliage and an unforgettable meal. Resolve to slow down, breathe deeply, and savor the holidays to come.

Plan ahead to make the occasion a holiday for the host, too. Here is a game plan for preparing this streamlined menu brimming with seasonal produce with a minimum of fuss. Turn the page to find a complete menu packing list for your trip.

AN EASY PLAN FOR SUCCESS
3 or 4 days ahead
■ Bake cornbread for dressing; prepare dressing, but do not bake. Cover and chill.

■ Thaw turkey in refrigerator, if necessary.

■ Prepare soup according to directions; process in blender, and chill. Seal squash shells in plastic bags, and chill. (Do not heat soup or brown cut sides of shells.)

1 day ahead
■ Bake turkey; prepare gravy. Remove apple, onion, and rosemary from cavity. Chill turkey and gravy.

■ Prepare and bake pie. (Do not add topping.) Cover and chill.

■ Slice onion and brussels sprouts for Caramelized Onion-and-Pecan Brussels Sprouts; seal in separate plastic bags, and chill.

2 hours before serving
■ Pour topping over pie; let stand at room temperature 2 hours.

1 hour and 15 minutes before serving
■ Remove dressing from refrigerator; let stand at room temperature 30 minutes. Bake, covered, at 350° for 45 minutes or until thoroughly heated.

35 minutes before serving
■ Remove turkey from refrigerator, and slice.

■ Prepare Caramelized Onion-and-Pecan Brussels Sprouts.

■ Reheat soup, and brown baked squash shells.

■ Reheat gravy.

Before serving dessert
■ Tap hard sugar topping on Cracked Caramel-Pumpkin Pie with back of a spoon to crack.

■ Prepare whipped cream.

CARAMELIZED ONION-AND-PECAN BRUSSELS SPROUTS

Prep: 15 minutes
Chill: 8 hours
Cook: 25 minutes

1 large onion
1 pound brussels sprouts
¼ cup butter or margarine
1 cup pecan pieces
1 teaspoon salt
½ teaspoon pepper

● **Cut** onion in half; thinly slice. Cut brussels sprouts in half; cut each half crosswise into thin slices. Place vegetables in separate plastic bags; seal. Chill 8 hours.
● **Melt** butter in a large heavy skillet over medium-high heat; add pecans. Sauté 5 minutes or until toasted. Remove from skillet. Add onion; cook, stirring often, 15 minutes or until caramel colored. Add pecans and brussels sprouts; cook about 3 minutes or until heated. Sprinkle with salt and pepper. **Yield:** 8 servings.

CRACKED CARAMEL-PUMPKIN PIE
(pictured on page 302)

Prep: 25 minutes
Bake: 40 minutes
Chill: 8 hours
Stand: 2 hours

½ (15-ounce) package
      refrigerated piecrusts
1 (14-ounce) can sweetened
      condensed milk
1 (15-ounce) can pumpkin
2 cups whipping cream, divided
2 large eggs, lightly beaten
2 egg yolks, lightly beaten
¼ cup firmly packed brown sugar
½ teaspoon pumpkin pie spice
3 tablespoons water
3 tablespoons corn syrup
⅓ cup sugar
Garnish: chopped pecans

● **Fit** piecrust into a 9-inch pieplate according to package directions; fold edges under, and crimp.
● **Cook** condensed milk in a medium-size heavy saucepan over medium-high heat, stirring constantly, 10 minutes or until thickened and bubbly. Remove from heat; stir in pumpkin.
● **Stir** in 1 cup cream and next 4 ingredients until smooth. Pour into crust. Bake at 350° on bottom oven rack for 40 minutes. Cool on a wire rack. Chill 8 hours.
● **Cook** 3 tablespoons water, syrup, and sugar in a small saucepan over medium heat, without stirring, until a candy thermometer registers 300° (hard-crack stage). Pour immediately over pie, and quickly spread with a metal spatula. Let stand 2 hours before serving.
● **Tap** hard sugar topping with back of a spoon to crack. Beat remaining cream at medium speed with an electric mixer until soft peaks form. Serve with pie. Garnish, if desired. **Yield:** 1 (9-inch) pie.

PACK FOR THE LAKE

In the cooler
Apple-Rosemary Roasted Turkey
Gravy
Southern Rice Dressing
Acorn Squash-Thyme Soup
Cracked Caramel-Pumpkin Pie
Squash shells (baked)
6 tablespoons butter
1 large onion
1 pound brussels sprouts
1 cup whipping cream
1½ cups half-and-half
Fresh thyme sprigs

For the dinner box
Rustic breads
1 (16-ounce) can whole-berry
      cranberry sauce (optional)
⅓ cup sugar
Salt and pepper
3 tablespoons corn syrup
1 cup pecan pieces
Beverages
Candy thermometer
Handheld electric mixer
Recipes for Acorn Squash-Thyme
      Soup, Caramelized Onion-and-
      Pecan Brussels Sprouts, and
      Cracked Caramel-Pumpkin Pie

DEEP-DISH TREASURES

Juicy berries and other fruit bubbling through a crisp, brown crust taste like sweet days at granny's house. Cobblers are homey desserts that don't have to look like a picture to be perfect.

PLUM COBBLER

Prep: 8 minutes
Bake: 1 hour

6 plums, sliced (about 2 pounds)
1½ cups sugar, divided
¼ teaspoon ground allspice
¾ cup water
1 tablespoon lemon juice
¼ cup butter or margarine,
      softened
1 cup all-purpose flour
2 teaspoons baking powder
¼ teaspoon salt
½ cup milk

● **Bring** plums, 1 cup sugar, and next 3 ingredients to a boil in a saucepan. Remove from heat.
● **Stir** together butter and remaining ½ cup sugar in a 2-quart baking dish until blended; stir in flour, baking powder, and salt. Stir in milk. Top with plum mixture.
● **Bake** at 375° for 1 hour or until golden. **Yield:** 6 to 8 servings.

Lynne McCrork
Orange Park, Florida

SWEET POTATO COBBLER

Prep: 1 hour and 30 minutes
Bake: 1 hour

6 or 7 medium-size sweet
    potatoes
1½ cups orange juice
½ cup sugar
¼ cup firmly packed light brown
    sugar
3 tablespoons all-purpose flour
¾ teaspoon salt, divided
½ teaspoon ground cinnamon
¼ teaspoon ground nutmeg
½ cup butter or margarine,
    divided
2 cups all-purpose flour
⅔ cup shortening
½ cup cold water
2 teaspoons sugar
Whipped cream (optional)

• **Pierce** sweet potatoes several times with a fork, and place on a baking sheet.
• **Bake** at 400° for 1 hour or until done; cool slightly. Peel and cut crosswise into ¼-inch-thick slices.
• **Place** sweet potato slices in a lightly greased 13- x 9-inch baking dish; add orange juice.
• **Stir** together ½ cup sugar, brown sugar, 3 tablespoons flour, ¼ teaspoon salt, cinnamon, and nutmeg. Sprinkle over sweet potato. Dot with 6 table-spoons butter.
• **Combine** 2 cups flour and remaining ½ teaspoon salt; cut in shortening with a pastry blender until mixture is crumbly.
• **Sprinkle** ½ cup cold water, 1 table-spoon at a time, evenly over surface, and stir with a fork until dry ingredients are moistened. Shape into a ball.
• **Roll** pastry into a 13- x 9-inch rectangle. Place over sweet potato mixture, sealing edges. Cut slits in top to allow steam to escape.
• **Microwave** remaining 2 tablespoons butter in a 1-cup glass measuring cup 30 seconds at HIGH or until melted. Brush butter over crust, and sprinkle with 2 teaspoons sugar.
• **Bake** at 400° for 1 hour or until golden. Serve warm with whipped cream, if desired. **Yield:** 8 servings.

Ellie Wells
Lakeland, Florida

COUNTRY APPLE COBBLER

Prep: 10 minutes
Bake: 40 minutes

1 cup sugar
¼ cup water
2 tablespoons instant tapioca
¼ teaspoon ground cinnamon
½ cup chopped walnuts
4 Granny Smith apples, peeled and
    thinly sliced (2 pounds)
1 cup all-purpose flour
½ teaspoon salt
1½ teaspoons baking powder
1½ cups (6 ounces) shredded
    sharp Cheddar cheese
½ cup butter or margarine, melted
½ cup milk
Whipped cream

• **Bring** first 5 ingredients to a boil in a saucepan, stirring constantly. Remove from heat; stir in apple. Pour into an 8-inch square pan.
• **Combine** flour and next 3 ingredients; stir in butter and milk. Spoon over apple mixture.
• **Bake** at 375° for 40 minutes. Serve cobbler with whipped cream. **Yield:** 6 to 8 servings.

Norma Cowden
Shawnee, Oklahoma

COBBLER CRUSTS

Fashion a lattice, seal the top with a solid crust, or drop in dumplings—any way you make cobbler crusts, they're good. If you like lots of crust, follow this tip: Bake several strips of crust before you assemble the cobbler, and distribute the crisp pieces throughout the filling before you add the top crust. The result is more crust in every juicy spoonful.

PEACH-APRICOT COBBLER

Prep: 25 minutes
Bake: 30 minutes

1 (29-ounce) can sliced peaches,
    undrained
1 (15¼-ounce) can apricot halves,
    undrained
1 cup sugar, divided
2 tablespoons cornstarch
1 tablespoon butter or margarine
1½ teaspoons ground cinnamon,
    divided
¼ teaspoon ground nutmeg
½ cup all-purpose flour
1 teaspoon baking powder
¼ teaspoon salt
2 tablespoons butter, softened
1 large egg, lightly beaten
1 cup whipping cream
2 tablespoons honey

• **Drain** peaches and apricots, reserving ½ cup juice from each.
• **Combine** ½ cup sugar and cornstarch in a saucepan. Add reserved juices; bring to a boil over medium heat.
• **Boil,** stirring constantly, 1 minute. Remove from heat.
• **Stir** in 1 tablespoon butter, ½ teaspoon cinnamon, nutmeg, and fruit. Spoon into a 1½-quart baking dish.
• **Combine** remaining ½ cup sugar, flour, baking powder, and salt; stir in 2 tablespoons butter and egg. Spoon over fruit mixture.
• **Bake** at 400° for 30 minutes.
• **Beat** whipping cream at medium speed with an electric mixer until foamy; gradually add honey and remaining 1 teaspoon cinnamon. Beat until soft peaks form. Serve with cobbler. **Yield:** 6 servings.

Adelyn Smith
Dunnville, Kentucky

CRANBERRY-APPLE COBBLER WITH CINNAMON BISCUITS
(pictured on page 301)

Prep: 40 minutes
Bake: 30 minutes

4 cups fresh or frozen
   cranberries
1¼ cups sugar, divided
⅓ cup maple syrup
5 Rome apples, peeled and
   sliced
3 tablespoons all-purpose
   flour
3 teaspoons ground cinnamon,
   divided
2 cups all-purpose flour
1 teaspoon baking powder
1 teaspoon baking soda
½ teaspoon salt
½ cup butter or margarine
¾ cup buttermilk
½ cup sliced blanched almonds
1 tablespoon sugar

• **Cook** cranberries, 1 cup sugar, and maple syrup in a nonaluminum saucepan over medium heat, stirring occasionally, 8 minutes or until berries pop.
• **Toss** together apple and 3 tablespoons flour; add to cranberry mixture. Stir in 1 teaspoon cinnamon; cool and set aside.
• **Combine** 2 cups flour, remaining ¼ cup sugar, baking powder, soda, and salt. Cut butter into flour mixture with a pastry blender until crumbly; add buttermilk, stirring until dry ingredients are moistened.
• **Turn** dough out onto a lightly floured surface sprinkled with 1 teaspoon cinnamon; knead 3 or 4 times.
• **Pat** dough to ¾-inch thickness; cut with a 2½-inch round cutter.
• **Pour** cranberry mixture into a 13- x 9-inch baking dish. Top with cinnamon biscuits.
• **Stir** together remaining 1 teaspoon cinnamon, sliced almonds, and 1 tablespoon sugar; sprinkle over cobbler.
• **Bake** at 400° for 30 minutes. **Yield:** 6 to 8 servings.

Rosemary Leicht
Bethel, Ohio

PLEASE PASS THE DRESSING

Most of us have memories of childhood Thanksgivings, memories of meals that included dressing— moist or dry, soft or firm, textured or smooth. This year, create something new for your family with these imaginative traditions from our readers.

SOUTHERN RICE DRESSING

Prep: 1 hour
Bake: 45 minutes

2 garlic bulbs
2 teaspoons olive oil
2 cups cooked regular rice
1 recipe Basic Cornbread,
   crumbled (see recipe on
   facing page)
1 (16-ounce) package ground
   pork sausage
3 tablespoons butter or
   margarine
1 medium onion, diced
1 medium-size red or green bell
   pepper, diced
1 large carrot, diced
½ cup chopped fresh parsley
1 tablespoon poultry seasoning
1½ tablespoons chopped fresh
   or 1 to 2 teaspoons rubbed
   sage
½ teaspoon salt
½ teaspoon pepper
4 cups chicken broth

• **Cut** off pointed ends of garlic bulbs; place garlic on a piece of aluminum foil, and drizzle with oil. Fold foil to seal. Bake at 350° for 45 minutes; cool. Squeeze pulp from garlic cloves into a large bowl. Add rice and cornbread.

• **Cook** sausage in a large skillet over medium heat, stirring until it crumbles and is no longer pink. Drain sausage on paper towels, and wipe skillet clean.
• **Melt** butter in skillet over medium-high heat.
• **Add** onion, bell pepper, and carrot; sauté 3 minutes or until tender.
• **Stir** sausage, vegetables, parsley, and next 4 ingredients into rice mixture. Add broth; stir to moisten. Spoon into a lightly greased 13- x 9-inch baking dish. Cover and chill 8 hours, if desired; remove from refrigerator, and let stand at room temperature 30 minutes.
• **Bake,** covered, at 350° for 45 minutes or until thoroughly heated. **Yield:** 12 servings.

Lisa Ferro
Woodlands, Texas

BASIC CORNBREAD

Prep: 10 minutes
Bake: 25 minutes

2 cups self-rising buttermilk white
    cornmeal mix
½ cup all-purpose flour
¼ cup butter or margarine, melted
1 large egg, lightly beaten
2 cups buttermilk

• **Heat** a well-greased 9-inch ovenproof skillet at 450° for 5 minutes.
• **Stir** together all ingredients in a bowl. Pour batter into hot skillet.
• **Bake** at 450° for 20 minutes or until golden. **Yield:** 1 (9-inch) cornbread (about 5 cups crumbled).

CRAWFISH-CORNBREAD DRESSING

Prep: 30 minutes
Bake: 1 hour

10 tablespoons butter or
    margarine
1 large onion, chopped
2 small green bell peppers, chopped
1 recipe Basic Cornbread, crumbled
    (see recipe above)
1 (16-ounce) package frozen
    peeled, cooked crawfish tails,
    thawed
2 cups chicken broth
2 large eggs, lightly beaten
¼ cup chopped fresh parsley
1 teaspoon ground white pepper
1 teaspoon ground red pepper
1 teaspoon ground black pepper

• **Melt** butter in a large skillet over medium-high heat; add onion and bell pepper, and sauté 4 to 5 minutes or until tender.
• **Stir** together vegetables, cornbread, and remaining ingredients in a large bowl until moistened. Spoon into a lightly greased 13- x 9-inch baking dish.
• **Bake** at 350° for 1 hour or until firm and golden. **Yield:** 12 servings.

FRUITED TURKEY DRESSING

Prep: 35 minutes
Stand: 2 hours
Bake: 30 minutes

½ cup raisins
½ cup cognac or frozen apple juice
    concentrate, thawed and
    undiluted
½ cup butter or margarine
2 medium onions, chopped
2 garlic cloves, minced
1 (16-ounce) package ground pork
    sausage
2 large Granny Smith apples,
    chopped
3 celery ribs, chopped
2 (8-ounce) packages stuffing
    croutons
3 cups chicken broth
2 large eggs, lightly beaten
½ cup chopped fresh parsley
1 tablespoon chopped fresh sage
1 teaspoon chopped fresh thyme
¼ teaspoon ground cloves
1 teaspoon salt
1 teaspoon pepper

• **Combine** raisins and cognac; let stand 2 hours.
• **Melt** butter in a large skillet over medium heat; add onion and garlic, and sauté 5 minutes or until tender.
• **Add** sausage, and cook, stirring until it crumbles and is no longer pink; drain and return to skillet.
• **Stir** in apple and celery, and cook, stirring occasionally, about 10 minutes. Transfer mixture to a large bowl.
• **Stir** in raisin mixture, croutons, and remaining ingredients until moistened. Spoon into a lightly greased 13- x 9-inch baking dish.
• **Bake,** covered, at 350° for 30 minutes. **Yield:** 12 servings.

Cathy Carazza
Sharpsburg, Georgia

CORNBREAD, SAUSAGE, AND PECAN DRESSING

Prep: 25 minutes
Bake: 30 minutes

1 (16-ounce) package ground
    pork sausage
1 large onion, chopped
2 large celery ribs, chopped
1 recipe Basic Cornbread,
    crumbled (see recipe at left)
1½ cups coarsely chopped
    pecans
¼ cup chopped fresh parsley
1½ cups chicken broth
¼ cup dry sherry or chicken
    broth
¼ cup milk
½ teaspoon salt
¼ to ½ teaspoon pepper
½ teaspoon dried thyme
¼ teaspoon ground nutmeg

• **Cook** sausage in a large skillet over medium heat, stirring until it crumbles and is no longer pink. Remove sausage, reserving 1 tablespoon drippings in skillet. Drain sausage on paper towels.
• **Sauté** onion and celery in hot drippings over medium-high heat until tender. Remove vegetables with a slotted spoon.
• **Combine** sausage, vegetables, cornbread, and remaining ingredients in a large bowl, stirring gently until moistened. Spoon into a lightly greased 13- x 9-inch baking dish.
• **Bake,** covered, at 350° for 30 minutes or until thoroughly heated. **Yield:** 12 servings.

Pauline Lanciotti
Morgantown, West Virginia

CORNY CORNBREAD DRESSING

Prep: 35 minutes
Bake: 35 minutes

2 tablespoons butter or margarine
6 white bread slices
½ cup butter or margarine
2 large onions, chopped
4 large celery ribs, chopped
3 cups chicken broth
2 recipes Basic Cornbread, crumbled (see recipe on previous page)
1 (16-ounce) can cream-style corn
2 cups corn chips, coarsely crushed
2 (16-ounce) cans hot tamales, cut into ½-inch slices
3 tablespoons chopped fresh or 1 tablespoon dried sage

• **Spread** 2 tablespoons butter evenly on bread slices; place on a baking sheet.
• **Bake** at 350° for 25 minutes or until crisp; cut into ½-inch cubes.
• **Melt** ½ cup butter in a large skillet over medium-high heat; add onion and celery, and sauté until tender.
• **Add** broth; bring to a boil. Pour mixture into a large bowl; stir in bread cubes and cornbread. Cover and let stand 20 minutes.
• **Fold** in corn and remaining ingredients. Spoon into 1 lightly greased 13- x 9-inch baking dish and 1 lightly greased 11- x 7-inch baking dish.
• **Bake** at 350° for 35 minutes or until golden. **Yield:** 20 servings.

Joyce K. French
Houston, Texas

HOLIDAY MENU

Here's a menu for eight that is sure to please. For starters, try delicious Cranberry Crackers. And just when everyone thinks you can't top this grand meal, there's the finale. Dazzle them with a two-ingredient Raspberry Sauce that adds sophistication to simple Sour Cream Pound Cake.

FESTIVE BUFFET
Serves Eight

Cranberry Crackers
Italian Bread Salad
Oven-Roasted Vegetables and Pork
Lemony Green Beans
Yeast Rolls
Sour Cream Pound Cake With Raspberry Sauce

CRANBERRY CRACKERS

Assemble these right before guests arrive to keep the crackers from becoming soggy.

Prep: 20 minutes
Chill: 3 hours

1 cup finely chopped fresh cranberries
2 green onions, thinly sliced
1 teaspoon seeded and minced jalapeño pepper
1½ tablespoons minced fresh cilantro
1½ teaspoons grated fresh ginger
2 tablespoons sugar
½ (8-ounce) package reduced-fat cream cheese, softened
1½ teaspoons orange juice
2 tablespoons finely chopped walnuts
16 wheat crackers or light shredded whole wheat wafers

• **Stir** together first 6 ingredients; cover and chill 2 to 3 hours.
• **Stir** together cream cheese and orange juice; stir in walnuts.
• **Spread** cream cheese mixture on crackers; top with cranberry mixture. Serve immediately. **Yield:** 16 appetizers.

Note: For testing purposes only, we used SnackWells Wheat Crackers.

Jean Roczniak
Rochester, Minnesota

♥ Per appetizer: Calories 46
Fat 2.1g Cholesterol 4mg
Sodium 70mg

ITALIAN BREAD SALAD

Prep: 20 minutes

10 (1-inch-thick) stale Italian bread
      slices, cut into 1-inch cubes
6 plum tomatoes, chopped
1 small purple onion, chopped
¼ cup chopped fresh or 1 teaspoon
      dried basil
¼ cup chopped fresh or 1 teaspoon
      dried oregano
Balsamic Dressing

● **Combine** first 5 ingredients. Add Balsamic Dressing; toss gently. Let stand 20 minutes before serving. **Yield:** 8 servings.

Balsamic Dressing

Prep: 5 minutes

¼ cup balsamic vinegar
2 tablespoons olive oil
¼ teaspoon salt
¼ teaspoon pepper

● **Whisk** together all ingredients in a bowl until well blended. **Yield:** ⅓ cup.
Karen Beckman
Santa Ana, California

♥ Per serving: Calories 165
Fat 4g Cholesterol 0mg
Sodium 304mg

OVEN-ROASTED VEGETABLES AND PORK

Prep: 20 minutes
Bake: 30 minutes

1½ pounds boneless pork
      tenderloins
Vegetable cooking spray
1 pound carrots, cut into 2-inch
      pieces
2 pounds new potatoes, halved
1 medium onion, cut into 6 wedges
1 tablespoon olive oil
2 teaspoons dried rosemary,
      crushed
1 teaspoon dried sage, crushed
¼ teaspoon salt
¼ teaspoon pepper

● **Brown** pork in a skillet coated with cooking spray over medium-high heat.
● **Place** pork in a roasting pan coated with cooking spray; arrange carrot, potato, and onion around pork.
● **Drizzle** pork and vegetables with olive oil; sprinkle evenly with rosemary and next 3 ingredients.
● **Bake** at 450° for 30 minutes or until a meat thermometer inserted into thickest portion of pork registers 165° and vegetables are tender, stirring vegetables occasionally. **Yield:** 8 servings.
Louise Bodziony
Gladstone, Missouri

♥ Per serving: Calories 234
Fat 4.8g Cholesterol 55mg
Sodium 143mg

LEMONY GREEN BEANS

Prep: 20 minutes
Cook: 18 minutes

2 pounds fresh green beans,
      trimmed
2 teaspoons grated lemon
      rind
3 tablespoons fresh lemon
      juice
1 tablespoon olive oil
½ teaspoon salt
½ teaspoon pepper
6 green onions, chopped
½ cup chopped fresh or 1 teaspoon
      dried basil

● **Cook** green beans in boiling water to cover 15 minutes; drain. Place beans in a large bowl.
● **Whisk** together lemon rind and next 4 ingredients. Pour mixture over beans. Add onions and basil, tossing to coat. **Yield:** 8 servings.

♥ Per serving: Calories 56
Fat 1.8g Cholesterol 0mg
Sodium 155mg

SOUR CREAM POUND CAKE WITH RASPBERRY SAUCE
(pictured on page 300)

Prep: 20 minutes
Bake: 45 minutes

Vegetable cooking spray
All-purpose flour
1 (18.25-ounce) package
      reduced-fat yellow cake mix
½ cup sugar
1 (8-ounce) container fat-free
      sour cream
1 cup egg substitute
¾ cup applesauce
1 teaspoon almond or vanilla extract
Raspberry Sauce
Garnishes: powdered sugar, fresh
      mint sprigs

● **Coat** a 12-cup Bundt pan with cooking spray, and sprinkle with flour, shaking to coat pan.
● **Beat** cake mix and next 5 ingredients at medium speed with an electric mixer 4 minutes. Spoon into pan.
● **Bake** at 325° for 45 minutes or until a wooden pick inserted in center comes out clean. Cool in pan on a wire rack 10 minutes. Remove from pan; cool on wire rack. Serve with Raspberry Sauce; garnish, if desired. **Yield:** 16 servings.

Raspberry Sauce

Prep: 5 minutes
Chill: 1 hour

4 (10-ounce) packages frozen
      raspberries, thawed
4 teaspoons sugar

● **Process** both ingredients in a blender until smooth. Pour through a wire-mesh strainer into a bowl, discarding seeds. Cover and chill 1 hour. **Yield:** 3 cups.
Catherine Lawler
Baton Rouge, Louisiana

♥ Per slice with 3 tablespoons sauce:
Calories 246
Fat 1.1g Cholesterol 0mg
Sodium 244mg

JUMP-START THE HOLIDAYS

Start planning this month to make December worry-free. Get out your slow cooker and prepare Steak Soup: Brown the meat, toss it in the slow cooker, and add remaining ingredients. Dinner is ready in 8 hours, and you won't even have to stir.

STEAK SOUP

Prep: 30 minutes
Cook: 8 hours

1 (2-pound) package top round
   steak, cut into 1-inch cubes
⅓ cup all-purpose flour
3 tablespoons vegetable oil
4 cups water
5 baking potatoes, cut into ½-inch
   cubes
3 carrots, sliced
2 small onions, chopped
1 celery rib, chopped
1 cup frozen sweet green
   peas
1 (16-ounce) can whole kernel
   corn, drained
1 (6-ounce) can tomato paste
2 tablespoons beef bouillon
   granules
1 to 2 teaspoons pepper

● **Toss** together steak and flour.
● **Brown** steak in hot oil in a large skillet over medium-high heat 5 to 6 minutes.
● **Stir** together browned steak, 4 cups water, and remaining ingredients in a 5-quart slow cooker. Cook, covered, at HIGH 8 hours or until vegetables are tender. **Yield:** 16 cups.

Delana W. Pearce
Lakeland, Florida

FREEZER SLAW

Prep: 30 minutes

1½ cups sugar
1 cup cider vinegar
3 (10-ounce) packages shredded
   angel hair cabbage slaw
1 large carrot, shredded
1 small green bell pepper, diced
1 teaspoon celery salt
1 teaspoon mustard seeds

● **Bring** sugar and vinegar to a boil in a small saucepan, stirring until sugar dissolves; cool.
● **Combine** cabbage and next 4 ingredients. Pour vinegar mixture over cabbage mixture, tossing to coat. Place in a large heavy-duty zip-top plastic bag or an airtight container, and freeze up to 3 months. Thaw in refrigerator before serving. **Yield:** about 6 cups.

Mrs. R. W. Nieman
Dunnellon, Florida

CINNAMON LOAVES

Prep: 15 minutes
Bake: 45 minutes

1 (18.25-ounce) package yellow
   cake mix with pudding
4 large eggs
¾ cup vegetable oil
¾ cup water
1 teaspoon vanilla extract
½ cup sugar
3 tablespoons ground cinnamon

● **Beat** first 5 ingredients at high speed with an electric mixer 3 minutes.
● **Pour** half of batter evenly into 2 greased and floured 8- x 3¾-inch disposable loafpans.
● **Stir** together sugar and cinnamon; sprinkle half of sugar mixture evenly over batter in loafpans.
● **Pour** remaining batter evenly into loafpans, and sprinkle evenly with remaining sugar mixture. Gently swirl with a knife.
● **Bake** at 350° for 45 minutes or until a wooden pick inserted in center comes out clean. Cool in pans on wire racks. Store in freezer, if desired. **Yield:** 2 loaves.

Linda J. Stewart
Cumming, Georgia

Miniature Cinnamon Loaves: Pour half of batter evenly into 5 greased and floured 5¾- x 3¼- x 2-inch disposable loafpans. Sprinkle evenly with half of sugar mixture. Pour remaining batter into pans; sprinkle with remaining sugar mixture. Swirl with a knife. Bake at 350° for 35 minutes or until a wooden pick inserted in center comes out clean.

Lamb Chops With Minted Apples, page 230

Glazed Apples, Ham Biscuits, Baked Polenta With Cheese and Okra, pages 232 and 233

Peppered Cheddar Muffins, page 234

Granola, page 212

(above right) Apple-Spinach Salad, page 222; (below) Pork Chop in Onion Gravy, Dilled Carrots and Green Beans, Mashed Potato Casserole, pages 222 and 223

SOUTHERNERS ENTERTAIN

Celebrations in the South always share graciousness and great food. Join us for an intimate family feast, an all-day brunch, an afternoon tea, and much more.

A SICILIAN CELEBRATION

In the home of Mabel and Santo Formica, cooking is both pleasure and passion. "You can learn a lot about our heritage when you sit down for a meal with us," says Santo. He and Mabel pride themselves on their authentic, yet easy, recipes. Join them in a taste trip to Italy.

SHRIMP DI SANTO

Prep: 20 minutes
Bake: 20 minutes

1½ **pounds unpeeled, medium-size fresh shrimp**
1½ **teaspoons dried granulated garlic**
1 **teaspoon seasoned salt**
¼ **cup olive oil**
1 **cup Italian Breadcrumb Mix**

● **Peel** shrimp, and devein, if desired; place in a large bowl.
● **Sprinkle** shrimp with garlic and seasoned salt, tossing to coat. Add olive oil, tossing well.
● **Sprinkle** with Italian Breadcrumb Mix, and toss to coat. Arrange shrimp in an even layer in an olive oil-greased 15-x 9-inch jellyroll pan.
● **Bake** shrimp at 400° for 20 minutes, stirring twice. Serve warm. **Yield:** 8 servings.

Italian Breadcrumb Mix

Prep: 5 minutes

⅔ **cup fine, dry breadcrumbs**
⅓ **cup grated Parmesan cheese**
2 **tablespoons chopped fresh parsley**
1½ **teaspoons dried granulated garlic**
½ **teaspoon pepper**

● **Stir** together all ingredients. Use mix for seasoning fish, chicken, or pork. **Yield:** about 1¼ cups.

Mabel and Santo Formica
Sherwood, Arkansas

CAESAR SALAD

Prep: 25 minutes

1 **garlic clove, halved**
2 **heads romaine lettuce, torn**
1 **(6-ounce) package seasoned croutons**
½ **cup extra-virgin olive oil**
¼ **cup egg substitute**
¼ **cup red wine vinegar**
2 **garlic cloves, minced**
1 **tablespoon Worcestershire sauce**
½ **cup grated Parmesan cheese**
1 **(2-ounce) can anchovies, drained**

● **Rub** sides of a wooden salad bowl with garlic halves. Add lettuce and croutons, tossing well.
● **Process** oil and next 6 ingredients in a blender until smooth, stopping to scrape down sides. Pour over lettuce mixture, tossing to coat. **Yield:** 6 to 8 servings.

Mabel and Santo Formica
Sherwood, Arkansas

MINI EGGPLANT CRÊPES WITH MARINARA SAUCE

Prep: 30 minutes
Stand: 1 hour
Bake: 25 minutes

2 medium eggplants
1 tablespoon salt
¼ cup olive oil
1 (15-ounce) container ricotta
    cheese
2 large eggs
½ cup (2 ounces) shredded
    mozzarella cheese
½ cup grated Parmesan cheese
2 tablespoons chopped fresh
    parsley
1 teaspoon garlic powder
½ teaspoon pepper
Marinara Sauce (see recipe at
    right)

● **Peel** eggplants, and cut into ¼-inch-thick slices; sprinkle with salt. Place in a large bowl; add water to cover. Let stand 1 hour. Drain eggplant; pat dry between paper towels.
● **Brown** eggplant, in batches, in hot oil in a large skillet over medium-high heat 1 minute on each side. Drain on paper towels.
● **Stir** together ricotta cheese and next 6 ingredients.
● **Place** 1 tablespoon mixture in center of each eggplant slice, and roll up.
● **Spread** half of Marinara Sauce in bottom of a lightly greased 13- x 9-inch baking dish.
● **Arrange** eggplant rolls, seam side down, over sauce; cover with remaining sauce.
● **Bake** at 375° for 25 minutes. **Yield:** 8 servings.

Mabel and Santo Formica
Sherwood, Arkansas

SICILIAN SECRETS FROM MABEL AND SANTO

■ Stir tubular pasta well when you first put it into the boiling water so that it won't stick to itself or the pan.

■ Fresh and dry herbs are based on a 3 to 1 ratio: 3 units fresh is equal to 1 unit dry.

■ If you can't use fresh garlic, use granulated garlic. The granules don't stick to each other like they do in garlic powder.

■ When a recipe calls for fresh tomatoes and it's not summer, use plum tomatoes.

■ A dollop of tomato sauce makes a nice contrast on a bed of pasta with pesto.

MARINARA SAUCE

Prep: 30 minutes
Cook: 20 minutes

1 medium onion, thinly sliced
3 garlic cloves, minced
3 tablespoons olive oil
2 (16-ounce) cans tomato sauce
1 (16-ounce) can crushed
    tomatoes
3 tablespoons chopped fresh parsley
1½ teaspoons dried oregano
1½ teaspoons dried basil
1 teaspoon salt
½ teaspoon pepper

● **Sauté** onion and garlic in hot olive oil in a large skillet 5 minutes; add tomato sauce and remaining ingredients. Reduce heat, and simmer, uncovered, 15 minutes. **Yield:** 2 cups.

Mabel and Santo Formica
Sherwood, Arkansas

OLIVES SCACIATI

Double this recipe for a dramatic presentation that will feed a large group.

Prep: 20 minutes
Chill: 8 hours

2 pounds large, unpitted green
    olives
2 cups ½-inch celery pieces with
    leaves
¾ cup extra-virgin olive oil
¼ cup red wine vinegar
2 tablespoons dried oregano
1 teaspoon pepper
¾ teaspoon dried crushed red
    pepper
6 garlic cloves, coarsely chopped

● **Wash** olives; drain. Gently pound each olive with a wooden mallet to open. (Don't mash, and don't remove pit.) Place olives and celery in a large bowl.
● **Whisk** together oil and next 5 ingredients until blended; pour over olive mixture, tossing to coat. Cover and chill 8 hours or up to 1 month. Serve at room temperature. **Yield:** 6 cups.

Mabel and Santo Formica
Sherwood, Arkansas

Holiday Dinners

ZUPPA INGLESE

Prep: 20 minutes
Cook: 16 minutes
Chill: 2 hours

2 cups half-and-half
3 egg yolks
¾ cup powdered sugar
5 tablespoons all-purpose
   flour
1 teaspoon grated lemon rind
½ cup whipping cream
1 (4-ounce) semisweet chocolate
   bar, chopped
1 (12-ounce) frozen pound cake,
   thawed
¼ cup blackberry brandy or
   light rum
Garnishes: sweetened whipped
   cream, chocolate shavings

● **Whisk** together first 4 ingredients in a heavy saucepan until blended.
● **Cook** over medium heat, whisking often, 15 minutes or until thickened. Stir in lemon rind, and set custard aside.
● **Combine** whipping cream and chocolate in a small glass bowl. Microwave at HIGH 1 minute; stir until smooth.
● **Cut** cake into thin slices, and sprinkle with brandy.
● **Layer** half of custard, half of cake, and half of chocolate mixture into 4 (10-ounce) compotes; repeat layers with remaining custard, cake, and chocolate mixture. Chill 2 hours. Garnish, if desired. **Yield:** 4 servings.

Mabel and Santo Formica
Sherwood, Arkansas

A FEAST FOR THE EYES

Clarissa McConnell of Orlando loves to entertain. One of her longtime acquaintances wrote to us, describing her as "a gourmet cook and table-setting artist." Here Clarissa shares one of her favorite appetizers—crab cakes.

CRAB CAKES
(pictured on page 298)

Prep: 25 minutes
Cook: 8 minutes

3 cups saltine cracker crumbs,
   divided
2 large eggs, lightly beaten
½ cup diced onion
3 tablespoons mayonnaise
1 tablespoon prepared mustard
2 teaspoons lemon juice
½ teaspoon salt
¼ teaspoon pepper
⅛ teaspoon ground red pepper
¼ teaspoon hot sauce
1 pound fresh lump crabmeat,
   drained
2 tablespoons butter or margarine
2 tablespoons vegetable oil
Lemon-Dill Mayonnaise
Red Bell Pepper Sauce
Garnishes: mixed salad greens,
   lemon slices, fresh parsley
   sprigs

● **Stir** together 2 cups cracker crumbs and next 9 ingredients; fold in crabmeat. Shape into 8 (3-inch) patties; dredge in remaining 1 cup cracker crumbs.
● **Melt** butter in oil in a large skillet over medium-high heat.
● **Add** crab cakes; cook 4 minutes on each side or until golden. Serve with Lemon-Dill Mayonnaise and Red Bell Pepper Sauce. Garnish, if desired. **Yield:** 8 appetizer or 4 main-dish servings.

Lemon-Dill Mayonnaise

Prep: 10 minutes
Chill: 1 hour

1 cup mayonnaise
2 teaspoons grated lemon
   rind
1 tablespoon lemon juice
¾ teaspoon dried dillweed
¼ teaspoon garlic powder
¼ teaspoon hot sauce (optional)

● **Stir** together first 5 ingredients and, if desired, hot sauce in a bowl. Cover and chill at least 1 hour. **Yield:** 1¼ cups.

Red Bell Pepper Sauce

Prep: 10 minutes
Cook: 15 minutes
Chill: 1 hour

1 red bell pepper
½ cup mayonnaise
2 teaspoons sherry
½ teaspoon garlic powder
½ teaspoon salt
¼ teaspoon pepper
¼ teaspoon hot sauce

● **Place** bell pepper on an aluminum foil-lined baking sheet.
● **Bake** at 450° for 15 minutes or until pepper is blistered, turning once.
● **Place** pepper in a heavy-duty zip-top plastic bag; seal. Let stand 10 minutes to loosen skin. Peel pepper; remove and discard seeds.
● **Process** pepper and ¼ cup mayonnaise in a food processor until smooth. Stir in remaining ¼ cup mayonnaise, sherry, and remaining ingredients. Cover and chill at least 1 hour. **Yield:** 1¼ cups.

Clarissa McConnell
Orlando, Florida

COME BY FOR BRUNCH

Donna Armstrong has a surefire way of seeing all her friends and acquaintances at least once a year—she throws an all-day brunch.

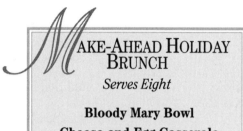

AKE-AHEAD HOLIDAY BRUNCH

Serves Eight

Bloody Mary Bowl

Cheese-and-Egg Casserole

Cheese Grits

Fresh Fruit

Wassail

BLOODY MARY BOWL

Prep: 10 minutes
Chill: 1 hour

1 (46-ounce) can vegetable juice
   cocktail
1 cup vodka
1 tablespoon prepared
   horseradish
3 tablespoons fresh lime juice
1 tablespoon Worcestershire
   sauce
Garnishes: lime slices, celery ribs

• **Stir** together first 5 ingredients in a large bowl; chill at least 1 hour. Serve over ice. Garnish, if desired. **Yield:** 7 cups.
Donna Armstrong
Mechanicsville, Virginia

CHEESE-AND-EGG CASSEROLE

Prep: 10 minutes
Chill: 8 hours
Bake: 30 minutes

3 cups seasoned croutons
15 large eggs
2 cups milk
1 teaspoon seasoned salt
1 teaspoon coarsely ground pepper
¾ teaspoon onion powder
2 tablespoons chopped fresh or
   frozen chives
1½ cups (6 ounces) shredded
   Cheddar cheese

• **Place** croutons in a 13- x 9-inch baking dish coated with cooking spray. Whisk together eggs and next 5 ingredients; stir in cheese. Pour over croutons. Cover and chill 8 hours, stirring once. Uncover casserole; stir. Bake at 350° for 30 minutes or until set. **Yield:** 8 to 10 servings.
Donna Armstrong
Mechanicsville, Virginia

WASSAIL

Prep: 15 minutes
Cook: 30 minutes

1½ cups sugar
¾ cup water
2 lemons, thinly sliced
3 oranges, thinly sliced
6 (2-inch) cinnamon sticks
1 quart pineapple juice
1 quart orange juice
3 cups dry white wine

• **Stir** together sugar and ¾ cup water in a large Dutch oven.
• **Add** lemon and orange slices and cinnamon sticks, squeezing fruit slices gently. Bring to a boil.
• **Boil,** stirring occasionally, 10 minutes or until syrup consistency.
• **Stir** in pineapple juice, orange juice, and wine; return to boil. Reduce heat; simmer 15 minutes.
• **Discard** fruit and cinnamon sticks. Serve warm. **Yield:** 12 cups.

Note: To prepare up to 1 week ahead, cool mixture, and freeze in an airtight container. Cook Wassail over low heat, stirring occasionally, until thoroughly heated.

Donna Armstrong
Mechanicsville, Virginia

SECRET TO SUCCESS

Donna, a Mechanicsville, Virginia, native, prepares egg casseroles the night before and chills them in chafing dish pans. "I always have one casserole on the table in a chafing dish, another in reserve on the gas grill at a low temperature, and another baking in the oven."

Complete this meal with make-ahead cheese grits and fresh fruit.

CHARITY BEGINS WITH FRIENDS

In Joplin, Missouri, 12 couples have been meeting for monthly dinner parties for more than 25 years. When Dot and Bob Willcoxon hosted the December dinner in their home, they asked each guest to bring a wrapped gift for a child and then donated the gifts to a local shelter for women and children. The following dinner menu is the perfect backdrop for a night celebrating the spirit of Christmas.

A GRACIOUS DINNER PARTY
Serves 8 to 10

Stuffed Tuscany Tenderloin

Creamy Risotto

Snap Peas With Roasted Garlic Dressing

Dinner Rolls

Apple-Cranberry Pie

STUFFED TUSCANY TENDERLOIN
(pictured on page 297)

Prep: 25 minutes
Bake: 50 minutes

1   onion, diced
2   tablespoons olive oil
½   pound fresh spinach, chopped
½   teaspoon salt
½   teaspoon freshly ground pepper
⅓   cup shredded Parmesan cheese
3   tablespoons drained and chopped dried tomatoes in oil
1   (4-pound) beef tenderloin, trimmed

● **Sauté** onion in hot oil in a skillet over medium heat until tender. Add spinach, salt, and pepper; sauté 1 minute. Remove from heat. Stir in cheese and tomato.
● **Cut** beef lengthwise down center, cutting to, but not through, bottom. Lay flat. Spoon spinach mixture down center. Fold tenderloin over mixture; tie with string at 1-inch intervals. (Tenderloin won't completely close.) Chill 2 hours, if desired.
● **Place** tenderloin, cut side up, on a rack in a roasting pan. Cover exposed filling with a strip of aluminum foil.
● **Bake** at 425° for 50 minutes or until a meat thermometer inserted into thickest portion registers 145° (medium-rare). Let stand 10 minutes before slicing. **Yield:** 10 servings.

Dot and Bob Willcoxon
Joplin, Missouri

SNAP PEAS WITH ROASTED GARLIC DRESSING
(pictured on page 1 and page 297)

Prep: 15 minutes
Cook: 5 minutes

4   cups fresh or frozen sugar snap peas
1   red bell pepper, sliced
1   purple onion, sliced
¼   cup Roasted Garlic Dressing
½   cup crumbled feta cheese
½   teaspoon salt
½   teaspoon pepper

● **Cook** first 4 ingredients in a skillet over low heat, stirring constantly, 5 minutes or until thoroughly heated. Remove from heat. Stir in remaining ingredients. Serve immediately. **Yield:** 8 to 10 servings.

Roasted Garlic Dressing

Prep: 1 hour

3   garlic bulbs
½   cup plus 3 tablespoons olive oil
¼   cup white wine vinegar
2   tablespoons Dijon mustard
¼   teaspoon salt
¼   teaspoon pepper

● **Cut** off pointed ends of garlic bulbs; place bulbs on a piece of foil. Drizzle with 3 tablespoons oil. Fold foil to seal.
● **Bake** at 350° for 40 minutes; cool.
● **Squeeze** pulp from cloves. Process pulp, remaining ½ cup oil, vinegar, and next 3 ingredients in a blender until smooth. **Yield:** 1 cup.

Dot and Bob Willcoxon
Joplin, Missouri

APPLE-CRANBERRY PIE
(pictured on page 1)

Prep: 20 minutes
Bake: 1 hour

¼   cup brandy or apple juice
1   cup dried cranberries
⅔   cup sugar
3   tablespoons all-purpose flour
¼   teaspoon ground allspice
2¼   pounds Granny Smith apples, peeled and thinly sliced
1   teaspoon vanilla extract
1   (15-ounce) package refrigerated piecrusts
Vanilla ice cream (optional)

● **Microwave** brandy in a microwave-safe bowl at HIGH 30 seconds; stir in dried cranberries. Cover and let stand 10 minutes.
● **Combine** sugar, flour, and allspice in a large bowl; stir in cranberry mixture, apple, and vanilla.
● **Stack** piecrusts, gently pressing together. Fit pastry into a 9-inch pieplate according to package directions; flute edges. Spoon apple-cranberry mixture into piecrust.
● **Bake** at 375° for 1 hour, shielding edges of crust with aluminum foil after 30 minutes to prevent excessive browning. Cool pie on a wire rack 1 hour. Serve with vanilla ice cream, if desired. **Yield:** 1 (9-inch) pie.

Dot and Bob Willcoxon
Joplin, Missouri

THANKSGIVING IN TEXAS

*Join Diane and Scott Sealy and their family in Dallas
for one of their favorite casual holiday meals.*

A CASUAL HOLIDAY MENU
Serves 8 to 10

Moist-and-Saucy Meat Loaf

Garlic-Cheese Grits

Corn Pudding

Spinach Casserole

Extra-Rich Chocolate Cake

GARLIC-CHEESE GRITS

*Prep: 35 minutes
Bake: 1 hour*

7   cups water
2   cups uncooked regular grits
3   large eggs, separated
1   (6-ounce) roll garlic cheese
¾   cup butter or margarine
2   teaspoons salt
¼   teaspoon ground red pepper

• **Bring** 7 cups water to a boil in a large saucepan; gradually stir in grits. Cover, reduce heat, and simmer, stirring occasionally, 10 minutes. Remove from heat; let stand 15 minutes. Stir in egg yolks and next 4 ingredients until smooth.
• **Beat** egg whites at high speed with an electric mixture until stiff peaks form. Fold into grits mixture. Spoon into a lightly greased 3-quart baking dish.
• **Bake** at 275° for 1 hour or until set. **Yield:** 12 servings.

*The Sealy Family
Dallas, Texas*

MOIST-AND-SAUCY MEAT LOAF

*Prep: 22 minutes
Bake: 1 hour*

2   pounds ground sirloin
1   onion, minced
1   green bell pepper, diced
¾   cup firmly packed brown sugar
½   cup crushed saltines (about 20)
2   large eggs, lightly beaten
¼   cup steak sauce
3   tablespoons ketchup
1   teaspoon salt
½   teaspoon garlic salt
Mustard Sauce
Tomato Sauce

• **Combine** first 10 ingredients; shape into a 14- x 8-inch loaf. Place on a lightly greased 15- x 10-inch jellyroll pan.
• **Brush** top of meat loaf with Mustard Sauce; pour Tomato Sauce over meat loaf. Bake at 375° for 1 hour or until loaf is no longer pink in center. Let stand 15 minutes; drain before serving. (Meat loaf will be soft in texture.) **Yield:** 8 to 10 servings.

Mustard Sauce

Prep: 1 minute

½   cup firmly packed light brown sugar
¼   cup prepared mustard

• **Stir** together sugar and mustard in a small bowl until mixture is smooth. **Yield:** ¾ cup.

Tomato Sauce

Prep: 2 minutes

1   cup canned crushed tomatoes
1   (8-ounce) can tomato sauce
¼   teaspoon salt
¼   teaspoon garlic salt
¼   teaspoon pepper

• **Stir** together all ingredients in a small bowl until mixture is blended. **Yield:** 2 cups.

*The Sealy Family
Dallas, Texas*

CORN PUDDING

*Prep: 10 minutes
Bake: 35 minutes*

4   (15¼-ounce) cans whole kernel corn, drained and divided
½   cup all-purpose flour
⅓   cup sugar
6   tablespoons butter or margarine, melted
2   tablespoons cornmeal
1½   cups milk
4   large eggs
½   teaspoon salt

• **Process** 1 can corn and next 7 ingredients in a blender or food processor until smooth, stopping to scrape down sides. Transfer to a bowl; stir in remaining corn.
• **Pour** mixture into a lightly greased 2-quart baking dish. Bake at 350° for 35 minutes or until set. **Yield:** 12 servings.

*The Sealy Family
Dallas, Texas*

SPINACH CASSEROLE

Prep: 20 minutes
Bake: 30 minutes

4 (10-ounce) packages frozen chopped spinach, thawed
¼ cup butter or margarine
½ onion, chopped
2 tablespoons all-purpose flour
1 (12-ounce) can evaporated milk
1 (6-ounce) roll jalapeño pepper cheese *
½ teaspoon garlic salt
½ teaspoon celery salt
1 teaspoon Worcestershire sauce
2 cups crushed round buttery crackers (about 56)
¼ cup butter or margarine, melted

• **Drain** spinach well, gently pressing between layers of paper towels.
• **Melt** ¼ cup butter in a large skillet over medium-high heat; add onion, and sauté until tender.
• **Add** flour; cook, stirring constantly, 1 minute.
• **Add** evaporated milk and next 4 ingredients, stirring until cheese melts.
• **Stir** in spinach. Spoon into a lightly greased 11- x 7-inch baking dish.
• **Stir** together cracker crumbs and ¼ cup melted butter; sprinkle over spinach mixture.
• **Bake** at 350° for 30 minutes or until bubbly. Let stand 5 minutes. **Yield:** 8 to 10 servings.

* Substitute 6 ounces mild Mexican loaf pasteurized prepared cheese product for jalapeño pepper cheese, if desired.
The Sealy Family
Dallas, Texas

A SUPPERTIME TRADITION

No one has to call the Sealys twice for supper. This family knows that when the dinner bell rings it's time to gather.

Diane Sealy's philosophy is simple: "In order to be loved, you have to show up." And for breakfast and dinner, throughout their childhood and youth, her four children showed up to share family meals.

"Sunday dinners were especially important," says Diane. "They were always casual, maybe burgers or chili, but that was the way we started off the new week."

The children also learned to cook. Daughter Lisa Sealy's specialties are cookies and pastries; Michael makes a mean boudin; Scotty hunts his own wild duck; and Amy and her husband, Warner McGowin, favor fried quail.

Today, despite separate homes and busy lives, they all manage to find their ways home several evenings each week for their family tradition.

EXTRA-RICH CHOCOLATE CAKE

Prep: 20 minutes
Bake: 25 minutes

2 cups all-purpose flour
2 cups sugar
¾ teaspoon baking soda
½ teaspoon salt
½ teaspoon ground cinnamon
1 cup water
½ cup vegetable oil
¼ cup butter or margarine
3 tablespoons cocoa
2 large eggs
½ cup buttermilk
1½ teaspoons vanilla extract
¼ cup strong brewed coffee
Chocolate Frosting
Chopped pecans (optional)

• **Stir** together first 5 ingredients.
• **Bring** 1 cup water and next 3 ingredients to a boil. Add to flour mixture, and beat at medium speed with an electric mixer until smooth.
• **Beat** eggs and next 3 ingredients at medium speed with electric mixer until blended. Stir into flour mixture. Pour into a greased and floured 15- x 10-inch jellyroll pan.
• **Bake** at 350° for 25 minutes or until a wooden pick inserted in center comes out clean. Cool in pan on a wire rack 10 minutes.
• **Spread** Chocolate Frosting over warm cake; cool completely in pan on a wire rack. Sprinkle with chopped pecans, if desired. **Yield:** 24 servings.

Chocolate Frosting

Prep: 10 minutes

½ cup butter or margarine
3 tablespoons cocoa
1 (16-ounce) package powdered sugar
6 tablespoons milk
1½ teaspoons vanilla extract
¼ teaspoon salt

• **Melt** butter with cocoa over low heat. Remove from heat; stir in powdered sugar and remaining ingredients until smooth. **Yield:** 3 cups.
The Sealy Family
Dallas, Texas

ONE WEEKEND, THREE PARTIES

This year, have your holiday parties all in one weekend. Just follow the lead of April Burt of Knoxville. Here she shares with us a menu for an entire weekend of festivities.

A WEEKEND OF MENUS

FRIDAY DINNER PARTY
Spiral-cut Baked Ham
Wild Rice-and-Cranberry Salad
Winter Bake
Rolls
Amaretto Cheesecake

SATURDAY BRUNCH
Breakfast Casserole
Potato Casserole
Wild Rice-and-Cranberry Salad
Assorted Cookies
Sweet Rolls

SUNDAY TEA PARTY
Ham Sandwiches on Whole Grain Bread With Mustard and Chutney
Beet-and-Pecan Sandwiches
Dried Tomato-and-Basil Sandwiches
Merry Cranberry-Nut Yeast Scones With Mock Devonshire Cream
Amaretto Cheesecake
Assorted Cookies

It's no surprise that when April Burt entertains for the holidays, afternoon tea is one of the events. April is known in the Knoxville area for her passion for teas. And not just any teas, but real English teas, complete with china pots and cups, silver trays, tiny sandwiches, and scones with cream. But a tea party is just the finishing touch to April's annual Christmas entertaining schedule.

April organizes all her gatherings during one weekend, allowing her to consolidate all the cooking and the heavy housecleaning.

WILD RICE-AND-CRANBERRY SALAD

This dish does double duty at the Friday night dinner party, with leftovers served at brunch. Depending on how many people you're serving at each event, prepare the recipe three or four times to have enough servings for the second party.

Prep: 45 minutes
Chill: 2 hours

1 **(6-ounce) package long-grain and wild rice mix**
1 **cup sweetened dried cranberries**
1 **cup fresh broccoli flowerets, chopped**
4 **green onions, chopped**
3 **celery ribs, thinly sliced**
1 **(2-ounce) jar diced pimiento, drained**
½ **cup sweet-and-sour dressing**
1 **cup dry-roasted peanuts**

• **Prepare** rice mix according to package directions; cool.
• **Combine** rice, cranberries, and next 4 ingredients; add dressing. Stir gently. Cover and chill at least 2 hours. Stir in peanuts just before serving. **Yield:** 6 to 8 servings.

Note: For testing purposes only, we used Ocean Spray Craisins for sweetened dried cranberries.

April Burt
Knoxville, Tennessee

Holiday Dinners

WINTER BAKE

Prep: 20 minutes
Bake: 35 minutes

1 medium rutabaga
1 medium butternut squash
2 large sweet potatoes
¼ cup olive oil
2 teaspoons crushed dried
     rosemary

● **Peel** vegetables, and cut into 1-inch cubes.
● **Toss** together vegetables and oil in a lightly greased 13- x 9-inch pan. Sprinkle with rosemary.
● **Bake** at 500° for 35 minutes or until tender. **Yield:** 10 to 12 servings.

April Burt
Knoxville, Tennessee

AMARETTO CHEESECAKE

Prep: 20 minutes
Bake: 40 minutes
Stand: 1 hour
Chill: 8 hours

2 cups sliced almonds,
     toasted
1 cup sugar, divided
¼ cup butter or margarine,
     melted
3½ (8-ounce) packages cream
     cheese, softened
1 teaspoon vanilla extract
2 large eggs
3 egg yolks
2 tablespoons all-purpose
     flour
⅓ cup whipping cream
⅓ cup amaretto
Garnishes: whipped cream,
     chopped toasted almonds

● **Process** 2 cups almonds in a food processor until ground; add ¼ cup sugar and butter, and process until blended.
● **Press** almond mixture into bottom and 1½ inches up sides of an aluminum foil-lined 9-inch springform pan.

● **Bake** at 400° for 10 minutes. Cool on a wire rack.
● **Beat** cream cheese, remaining ¾ cup sugar, and vanilla at medium speed with an electric mixer until smooth.
● **Add** 2 eggs and 3 egg yolks, 1 at a time, beating well after each addition.
● **Add** flour; beat until smooth.
● **Add** whipping cream and amaretto; beat until blended. Spoon mixture into prepared crust.
● **Bake** at 400° for 10 minutes. Reduce temperature to 350°, and bake 30 more minutes or until center is firm. Turn off oven. Let cheesecake stand in oven, with oven door closed, 30 minutes.
● **Remove** cheesecake from oven; cool in pan on a wire rack 30 minutes. Cover and chill 8 hours.
● **Invert** cheesecake onto a serving dish. Garnish, if desired. **Yield:** 12 to 14 servings.

April Burt
Knoxville, Tennessee

A WEEKEND OF CELEBRATION

April Burt holds her parties early in the holiday season for several reasons. "I like to have my parties early in December," she explains, "so I can get them out of the way."

She adds, "I always told my daughters that if they're frustrated with the way the house looks, throw a party. This puts everyone into high gear; the house will be spotless in no time."

This weekend of parties plan has another bonus. "It leaves me free to go to everyone else's parties later in the month," she adds with a laugh.

BREAKFAST CASSEROLE

Prep: 15 minutes
Chill: 8 hours
Stand: 30 minutes
Bake: 45 minutes

1 pound ground pork sausage ✻
10 white sandwich bread slices,
     cubed (6 cups)
1 (8-ounce) block sharp Cheddar
     cheese, shredded
6 large eggs
2 cups milk
1 teaspoon salt
1 teaspoon dry mustard
¼ teaspoon Worcestershire sauce

● **Cook** sausage in a skillet over medium heat, stirring until it crumbles and is no longer pink; drain well.
● **Place** bread cubes in a lightly greased 13- x 9-inch baking dish; sprinkle evenly with cheese, and top with sausage.
● **Whisk** together eggs and next 4 ingredients; pour evenly over sausage. Cover and chill 8 hours. Let stand at room temperature 30 minutes. Bake at 350° for 45 minutes or until set. **Yield:** 8 servings.

✻ Substitute 2 cups cubed cooked ham for sausage, if desired.

Note: Bake casserole after chilling 1 hour, if desired. Omit standing time, and bake as directed.

April Burt
Knoxville, Tennessee

Holiday Dinners

POTATO CASSEROLE

Prep: 15 minutes
Bake: 45 minutes

¾ cup butter or margarine,
   divided
1 (30-ounce) package frozen
   country-style hash browns,
   thawed
1 cup frozen mixed vegetables,
   thawed
1 (10¾-ounce) can cream of
   celery soup, undiluted
1 (8-ounce) container sour
   cream
1 cup (4 ounces) shredded
   Cheddar cheese
1 teaspoon salt
1 teaspoon pepper
2 cups cornflakes cereal,
   crushed

• **Heat** ½ cup butter in a 13- x 9-inch baking dish in a 350° oven 5 to 6 minutes or until melted.
• **Spread** hash browns over butter in dish; top with vegetables.
• **Stir** together soup and next 4 ingredients; spread over vegetables.
• **Heat** remaining ¼ cup butter in a saucepan over low heat until melted. Stir together crushed cornflakes and melted butter; sprinkle over casserole.
• **Bake** at 350° for 45 minutes. **Yield:** 10 to 12 servings.

Note: For testing purposes only, we used Bird's Eye Frozen Broccoli, Green Beans, Pearl Onions, and Red Peppers for frozen mixed vegetables.

April Burt
Knoxville, Tennessee

BEET-AND-PECAN SANDWICH SPREAD

Prep: 5 minutes

1 (8-ounce) package cream cheese,
   softened
½ cup coarsely chopped pecans
¼ cup canned beets, drained
2 tablespoons orange juice

• **Process** all ingredients in a food processor until smooth.
• **Spread** mixture between small white sandwich bread slices.
• **Cut** sandwiches into shapes. **Yield:** 1½ cups.

April Burt
Knoxville, Tennessee

DRIED TOMATO-AND-BASIL SANDWICHES

Prep: 30 minutes

½ (8-ounce) package cream
   cheese, cubed and softened
⅓ cup minced dried tomatoes in
   oil, well drained
2 tablespoons finely chopped
   walnuts
2 tablespoons shredded Parmesan
   cheese
12 very thin wheat sandwich bread
   slices
12 very thin white sandwich bread
   slices
¾ cup Basil Butter
Finely chopped walnuts (optional)

• **Beat** first 4 ingredients at medium speed with an electric mixer until blended.
• **Spread** cheese mixture evenly on 1 side of wheat bread slices. Spread 1 side of white bread slices evenly with Basil Butter. Press together spread sides of 1 wheat slice and 1 white slice. Repeat procedure with remaining bread slices.
• **Trim** crusts from sandwiches. Cut sandwiches with a 2-inch round cutter. Roll sides in walnuts, if desired. **Yield:** 2 dozen sandwiches.

Basil Butter

Prep: 20 minutes

½ cup butter or margarine,
   softened
½ cup loosely packed fresh basil
   leaves, chopped
¼ teaspoon sugar
½ teaspoon lemon juice

• **Stir** together all ingredients in a small bowl until well blended. Cover and chill. **Yield:** ¾ cup.

April Burt
Knoxville, Tennessee

MERRY CRANBERRY-NUT YEAST SCONES

Prep: 25 minutes
Chill: 1 hour
Bake: 10 minutes

¼ cup warm water (100° to 110°)
2 (¼-ounce) envelopes active dry
   yeast
2 teaspoons sugar
5 cups all-purpose flour
1 tablespoon baking powder
2 teaspoons salt
1 teaspoon baking soda
1 cup shortening
2 cups buttermilk
½ cup sweetened dried
   cranberries
½ cup chopped walnuts or pecans
Mock Devonshire Cream
Jelly (optional)

• **Stir** together first 3 ingredients in a 1-cup glass measuring cup; let stand 5 minutes.
• **Combine** flour and next 3 ingredients in a large mixing bowl.
• **Cut** shortening into flour mixture with a pastry blender until crumbly. Gradually add yeast mixture and buttermilk, stirring just until dry ingredients are moistened.
• **Stir** in cranberries and chopped walnuts. Cover and chill at least 1 hour or up to 48 hours.

- **Turn** dough out onto a lightly floured surface; knead 3 or 4 times. Pat to ½-inch thickness.
- **Cut** dough with a 2-inch round cutter, and place scones on ungreased baking sheets.
- **Bake** at 450° for 10 minutes or until golden. Serve hot with Mock Devonshire Cream and, if desired, jelly. **Yield:** 3½ dozen.

Note: For testing purposes only, we used Ocean Spray Craisins for sweetened dried cranberries.

Mock Devonshire Cream

Prep: 10 minutes

1 (8-ounce) package cream
   cheese, softened
½ cup unsalted butter, softened
1 (12-ounce) container
   frozen whipped topping,
   thawed

- **Beat** cream cheese and butter at high speed with an electric mixer until mixture is fluffy.
- **Add** whipped topping; beat at medium speed until blended. Cover and chill. **Yield:** 3 cups.

April Burt
Knoxville, Tennessee

Holiday Dinners
HOLIDAY ON THE HARBOR

Ann and Jim Edwards' view of life is reflected in the name of their Mount Pleasant, South Carolina, home, "O Be Joyful." And it's evident that this couple celebrates every day as joyously as they do the holidays. They love to entertain at their home with menus like this.

A SOUTH CAROLINA CELEBRATION
Serves Eight

Charleston Harbor Pickled Shrimp
Pimiento Cheese Spread
Cream of Leek Soup
Company Pork Roast
Rice Pilaf
Sunshine Carrots and Asparagus
Pandy's Biscuits
Chocolate Bread Pudding With Whiskey Sauce

CHARLESTON HARBOR PICKLED SHRIMP

Prep: 20 minutes
Chill: 8 hours

2 quarts water
1 pound unpeeled, medium-size
   fresh shrimp
3 tablespoons Creole
   seasoning
1 small onion, cut in half and
   sliced
1 green bell pepper, cut into thin
   strips
1 red bell pepper, cut into thin
   strips
1½ cups water
½ cup white vinegar
1 tablespoon salt

- **Bring** 2 quarts water to a boil in a Dutch oven; add shrimp and Creole seasoning to Dutch oven. Boil 2 minutes or just until shrimp turn pink; drain. Peel shrimp, and devein, if desired.
- **Place** shrimp in a bowl or jar. Top with onion and peppers.
- **Stir** together 1½ cups water, vinegar, and salt; pour over peppers. Cover and chill 8 hours. Drain before serving. **Yield:** 8 servings.

Ann and Jim Edwards
Mount Pleasant, South Carolina

Holiday Dinners

PIMIENTO CHEESE SPREAD

Prep: 15 minutes
Chill: 2 hours

2 (8-ounce) blocks sharp Cheddar
   cheese, shredded
1 (4-ounce) jar diced pimiento
1 cup mayonnaise
¾ cup chopped pecans, toasted
⅛ teaspoon salt
¼ teaspoon hot sauce

● **Stir** together all ingredients; cover and
chill at least 2 hours. Serve spread with
crackers or sliced fruit. **Yield:** 3 cups.
Ann and Jim Edwards
Mount Pleasant, South Carolina

CREAM OF LEEK SOUP
(pictured on page 298)

Prep: 20 minutes
Cook: 40 minutes

4 leeks
¼ cup butter or margarine
1 large onion, cut in half and sliced
3 pounds potatoes, peeled and cut
   into thin slices
5 cups chicken broth
2 teaspoons salt
2 cups milk
2 cups half-and-half
Garnishes: fresh chives, cracked
   black pepper

● **Discard** green tops from leeks. Cut
white portion of leeks into thin slices.
● **Melt** butter in a Dutch oven over
medium-high heat; add leeks and onion,
and sauté 5 minutes or until tender.
● **Stir** in potato, broth, and salt; bring to a
boil. Cover, reduce heat, and simmer 35
to 40 minutes. Cool slightly. Process, in
batches, in a food processor or blender
until smooth. Return to Dutch oven; stir
in milk and half-and-half.
● **Cook** over medium heat, stirring often,
until heated. (Do not boil.) Garnish, if
desired. **Yield:** about 5 quarts.
Ann and Jim Edwards
Mount Pleasant, South Carolina

SOUTH CAROLINA CELEBRATIONS

Entertaining has been a big part
of Ann and Jim Edwards' 47 years
together. Jim is the former governor
of South Carolina, former U.S. Secre-
tary of Energy, and now president
of the Medical University of South
Carolina. And, Ann says, "Jim is
exceedingly gregarious, so we've
always had people in our home."

At Thanksgiving the couple
entertains at their country home
near Huger, South Carolina. Children
Jim Jr. and Cathy bring their families, and Jim's siblings arrive from
all over the country.

"Jim is the second to the youngest
of five, but he's the patriarch," Ann
says. "His sisters and brothers come
from Pennsylvania, Georgia, and all
over with their families. It's like an
old-time Thanksgiving—we start
with hymns and thank the Lord for
our blessings."

This year's Christmas dinner is a
smaller, more formal event enjoyed
in the dining room of the couple's
1790s Sea Island-style home. Silver
serving pieces rest on the aged ma-
hogany sideboard, camellias from
the front yard grace the table, and
candles glow softly. The Edwards
have prepared a feast.

After Jim offers a toast, the con-
versation, eating, and fun continue
long into the evening. And, without
exception, the faces around the table
reflect the delight found in their love
of one another.

COMPANY PORK ROAST
(pictured on page 1 and page 299)

Prep: 15 minutes
Cook: 2 hours and 30 minutes

1 cup ketchup
½ cup water
¼ cup red wine vinegar
2 tablespoons dried onion
   flakes
1 tablespoon brown sugar
2 tablespoons vegetable oil
2 tablespoons Worcestershire
   sauce
1 teaspoon mustard seeds
1 teaspoon dried oregano
1 bay leaf
½ teaspoon salt
¼ teaspoon pepper
¼ teaspoon chili powder
2 (2½-pound) boneless pork loin
   roasts, trimmed
Garnishes: arugula, apple
   slices

● **Bring** first 13 ingredients to a boil in a
saucepan; reduce heat, and simmer 20
minutes. Discard bay leaf.
● **Prepare** fire by piling charcoal or lava
rocks on 1 side of grill, leaving the other
side empty. Place rack on grill.
● **Arrange** roasts over empty side of
grill, and grill, covered with grill lid, over
medium-high heat 2 hours and 30 minutes or until a meat thermometer inserted into thickest portion of roasts
registers 160°, basting every 30 minutes
with sauce.
● **Bring** remaining sauce to a boil, and
boil 1 minute. Slice pork roast; serve
with sauce. Garnish, if desired. **Yield:** 12
servings.
Ann and Jim Edwards
Mount Pleasant, South Carolina

Holiday Dinners

SUNSHINE CARROTS AND ASPARAGUS
(pictured on page 299)

A bright citrus glaze adds the "sunshine" to these crisp-tender carrots and asparagus.

Prep: 10 minutes
Cook: 12 minutes

2 pounds baby carrots
2 quarts water
1½ pounds thin, fresh asparagus spears
2 tablespoons sugar
2 teaspoons cornstarch
½ teaspoon salt
½ teaspoon ground ginger
½ cup orange juice
2 tablespoons butter or margarine

● **Cook** carrots in 2 quarts boiling water in a Dutch oven 5 minutes. Add asparagus, and boil 5 minutes; drain.
● **Combine** sugar and next 3 ingredients in a small saucepan.
● **Stir** in orange juice. Bring mixture to a boil, stirring constantly; boil, stirring constantly, 1 minute. Remove mixture from heat.
● **Add** butter, stirring until melted. Toss with carrots and asparagus. **Yield:** 8 servings.

Ann and Jim Edwards
Mount Pleasant, South Carolina

PANDY'S BISCUITS
(pictured on page 299)

An extra pinch of soda teams with self-rising flour to ensure a good rise for these flaky buttermilk biscuits.

Prep: 10 minutes
Bake: 12 minutes per batch

4 cups self-rising flour
½ teaspoon baking soda
⅔ cup shortening
2 cups buttermilk

● **Combine** flour and baking soda; cut in shortening with a pastry blender until crumbly.
● **Add** buttermilk, stirring just until dry ingredients are moistened.
● **Turn** dough out onto a lightly floured surface; knead 3 or 4 times.
● **Pat** or roll dough to ¾-inch thickness; cut with a 2-inch round cutter, and place on lightly greased baking sheets.
● **Bake** at 400° for 10 to 12 minutes. **Yield:** 2 dozen.

Ann and Jim Edwards
Mount Pleasant, South Carolina

CHOCOLATE BREAD PUDDING WITH WHISKEY SAUCE

Dessert doesn't get any better than this rich chocolate pudding drizzled with warm, buttery Whiskey Sauce.

Prep: 50 minutes
Bake: 1 hour and 45 minutes

¼ cup unsalted butter
7 cups French bread cubes
2 cups whipping cream
1 cup milk
8 (1-ounce) bittersweet chocolate squares, chopped
5 egg yolks, lightly beaten
⅔ cup firmly packed light brown sugar
1 teaspoon vanilla extract
Whiskey Sauce
Garnish: chocolate shavings

● **Melt** butter in a large heavy skillet over medium heat.
● **Add** bread cubes, and cook, stirring constantly, 3 minutes or until bread cubes are golden.
● **Transfer** to a lightly greased 13- x 9-inch baking dish.
● **Bring** whipping cream and milk to a boil over medium heat in skillet. Remove from heat, and whisk in chocolate until smooth.
● **Whisk** in egg yolks, brown sugar, and vanilla. Pour over bread cubes; let stand 30 minutes. Cover with aluminum foil;

cut 6 small holes in foil to allow steam to escape.
● **Place** baking dish in a roasting pan. Add hot water to pan to a depth of 1½ inches.
● **Bake** at 325° for 1 hour and 45 minutes or until set. Remove bread pudding from water, and cool 30 minutes on a wire rack. Serve warm with Whiskey Sauce. Garnish, if desired. **Yield:** 8 to 10 servings.

Whiskey Sauce

Prep: 10 minutes
Cook: 5 minutes

1½ cups milk
½ cup butter or margarine
1 cup sugar
3 tablespoons cornstarch
¼ cup water
½ cup bourbon

● **Cook** first 3 ingredients in a medium-size heavy saucepan over low heat, stirring often, until butter melts and sugar dissolves.
● **Combine** cornstarch and ¼ cup water, stirring until smooth. Add to butter mixture; stir in bourbon.
● **Bring** to a boil over medium heat, stirring constantly; boil, stirring constantly, 1 minute. **Yield:** 2¾ cups.

Ann and Jim Edwards
Mount Pleasant, South Carolina

Holiday Dinners

STANDING INVITATIONS

Some parties thrive on suspense and surprise; their unexpected invitations are part of the panache. Others are as predictable as the holidays themselves. These are gatherings of familiar faces at a traditional time. Here's a sampling of some long-standing events, the kind that keep folks coming back year after year.

A NEIGHBORHOOD ROMP

The Red Mountain Rompers playgroup hosts a party that draws together an entire Alabama community.

Each year, the group's parents purchase, wrap, and label presents especially for their own children, and then sneak them to the hosts, Ruth and William Varnell. "Gifts range from about $5 to $15," says Ruth, "but all must have immediate play value."

The Varnells erect a throne in their study, the perfect setting for kids to converge around Santa (a dad in disguise). Older kids, "Romper alums," play a special part in the fun, too, posing as mischievous elves who dig deep in Santa's bag and hand out gifts.

Neighbor Carolanne Roberts says, "We plan the party early in the evening so the kids are happy and fresh. There are always video cameras whirring and flashes popping—the president wouldn't get more attention! It's a nice way to keep in touch in this very tight-knit little community."

MULLED CRANBERRY CIDER
(pictured on page 301)

Prep: 5 minutes
Cook: 35 minutes

8 black peppercorns
6 whole allspice
6 whole cloves
2 (3-inch) cinnamon sticks
1 gallon apple cider
2 quarts cranberry juice drink

• **Place** first 4 ingredients on a 5-inch-square piece of cheesecloth, and tie with string.
• **Bring** cider and juice drink to a boil with spice bag in a Dutch oven. Partially cover, reduce heat, and simmer 30 minutes. Remove and discard spice bag before serving. Serve hot or cold. **Yield:** 1½ gallons.

Ruth and William Varnell
Birmingham, Alabama

CLEAR-THE-CUPBOARD COOKIES

Our Test Kitchens staff awarded these wonderful cookies its highest rating.

Prep: 20 minutes
Bake: 10 minutes per batch

1 cup shortening
1 cup sugar
1 cup firmly packed light brown sugar
2 large eggs
2 cups all-purpose flour
1 teaspoon baking soda
1 teaspoon baking powder
1 teaspoon salt
1 cup uncooked regular oats
1 cup flaked coconut
1 cup crisp rice cereal
1 teaspoon vanilla extract
1 cup chopped pecans, toasted (optional)

• **Beat** shortening at medium speed with an electric mixer until fluffy; add sugars, beating well. Add eggs, beating until blended.
• **Combine** flour and next 4 ingredients; gradually add to sugar mixture, beating after each addition.
• **Stir** in coconut, cereal, vanilla, and, if desired, pecans.
• **Drop** by tablespoonfuls onto baking sheets.
• **Bake** at 350° for 10 minutes or until lightly golden. Remove to wire racks to cool. **Yield:** 4½ dozen.

Ruth and William Varnell
Birmingham, Alabama

Holiday Dinners

THE BEST OF WHAT'S LEFT

No need to ditch half a bowl of left-over dip if you're a friend of Candy Ford of Louisville.

Candy explains, "It all started 12 years ago. My husband, Cary, and I were alone on New Year's, wondering what to do. I said, 'Why don't we make some chili and invite some friends?' So Cary's brother came with his wife and kids and whatever food they had left over—odds and ends, like a half-eaten box of candy."

Now more than 100 people come to the annual nonstop New Year's gathering. "It's the most casual party you'll go to during the holidays," she says.

HOT CHILI SUPPER

Prep: 20 minutes
Cook: 2 hours

2   pounds ground chuck
4   (15-ounce) cans tomato sauce
1   (30-ounce) can hot chili beans,
      undrained
2   (14½-ounce) cans diced
      tomatoes with green peppers
      and onions
1   large onion, diced
3   to 4 tablespoons chili powder
2   tablespoons dried oregano
1   teaspoon minced garlic
1   tablespoon paprika
2   to 3 teaspoons ground red pepper
Hot cooked spaghetti (optional)
Toppings: shredded Cheddar
      cheese, oyster crackers

● **Cook** ground beef in a Dutch oven over medium heat, stirring until it crumbles and is no longer pink; rinse and drain. Return to Dutch oven.
● **Add** tomato sauce and next 8 ingredients. Bring to a boil; reduce heat, and simmer, stirring occasionally, 2 hours. Serve over pasta, if desired, with toppings. **Yield:** 8 to 10 servings.

Candy Ford
Louisville, Kentucky

CHUNKY CHEESE QUESO

Prep: 15 minutes
Cook: 2 hours

1   pound ground hot pork sausage
1   (16-ounce) jar process cheese
      spread
1   (16-ounce) loaf pasteurized
      prepared cheese product,
      cubed
1   (20-ounce) jar hot salsa

● **Brown** sausage in a large skillet, stirring until it crumbles and is no longer pink; rinse and drain.
● **Stir** together sausage and remaining ingredients in a 2½-quart slow cooker.
● **Cover** and cook at LOW 2 hours or until cheese melts. Serve with tortilla chips. **Yield:** 6 cups.

Note: To cook on the stove-top, prepare sausage as directed above. Return to skillet; add remaining ingredients. Cook over low heat, stirring occasionally, 8 to 10 minutes or until cheese melts.

Candy Ford
Louisville, Kentucky

WARM-AND-SPICY SALSA

Prep: 10 minutes
Cook: 30 minutes

1   cup white vinegar
1   large onion, diced
2   celery ribs, diced
3   garlic cloves, pressed
3   (10-ounce) cans diced tomatoes
      and green chiles, undrained
1   (16-ounce) can crushed tomatoes
1   teaspoon salt
1   teaspoon sugar
½   teaspoon pepper

● **Bring** first 4 ingredients to a boil in a saucepan over medium heat; add remaining ingredients. Return to a boil, stirring occasionally. Serve warm with tortilla chips. **Yield:** 4½ cups.

Candy Ford
Louisville, Kentucky

EMMA'S CHRISTMAS LEGACY

Emma O'Hear began her Birmingham Christmas Eve tradition in 1935 as an act of kindness to friends during the Depression. Her daughter Susan Brown remembers, "They had a group of friends who didn't have children, so they'd invite them over for eggnog. By the time I married, my friends and their kids started coming."

Susan's grandchildren, the fourth generation, now attend along with their friends. "Once people are invited, they come each year; no one really drops out," she says.

Emma held the party at her home until she was in her late eighties. When Emma died two years ago Susan took the helm as host. "It's a lot of work," Susan admits, "but this is the easiest way to entertain a crowd. Plus, everyone who knows us sees it as a tribute to my mother, Emma."

CHEESE WAFERS

Prep: 40 minutes
Bake: 10 minutes per batch

2   cups (8 ounces) shredded sharp
      Cheddar cheese
1   cup butter or margarine,
      softened
2½   cups all-purpose flour
½   teaspoon ground red pepper
1   teaspoon Worcestershire sauce
1   teaspoon salt
2   cups crisp rice cereal

● **Beat** first 6 ingredients at medium speed with an electric mixer until blended; knead in cereal. Shape into 1-inch balls; arrange on baking sheets. Flatten each ball with a fork.
● **Bake** at 350° for 10 minutes or until lightly browned. Cool on a wire rack. **Yield:** 4 dozen.

Susan Brown
Birmingham, Alabama

SMART COOKIES

Pat Wine's holiday odyssey began 23 years ago, when she invited Fauquier County, Virginia, faculty pals for a winter vacation celebration.

"I baked a record 35 dozen cookies," she remembers. Since then, the fete for five has grown to an extravaganza for 100. Last year's cookie tally reached 332 dozen. "Once, I kept track of all the ingredients. I used 40 pounds of flour, 25 pounds of granulated sugar, 20 pounds of brown sugar, 19 pounds of margarine, and 8 dozen eggs.

"Of course," Pat continues, "the magic ingredient is love." Here are some favorites of the well-fed Fauquier County faculty.

OATMEAL COOKIES

Prep: 30 minutes
Bake: 11 minutes per batch

1¼ cups butter or margarine, softened
¾ cup firmly packed brown sugar
½ cup sugar
1 large egg
1 teaspoon vanilla extract
1½ cups all-purpose flour
1 teaspoon baking soda
½ teaspoon salt
1 teaspoon ground cinnamon
¼ teaspoon ground nutmeg
3 cups uncooked regular oats
1½ cups raisins

• **Beat** first 3 ingredients at medium speed with an electric mixer until creamy; add egg and vanilla, beating until blended.
• **Combine** flour and next 4 ingredients; gradually add to butter mixture, beating until blended. Stir in oats and raisins. Drop by rounded teaspoonfuls 2 inches apart onto ungreased baking sheets.

• **Bake** at 375° for 9 to 11 minutes. Cool 1 minute on baking sheets; remove to wire racks to cool. Freeze up to 6 months. **Yield:** 5 dozen.

Pat Wine
Warrenton, Virginia

RASPBERRY-ALMOND TARTS

Prep: 1 hour
Chill: 1 hour
Bake: 30 minutes

½ cup butter or margarine, softened
1 (3-ounce) package cream cheese, softened
1 cup all-purpose flour
⅓ cup seedless raspberry preserves
1 large egg
½ cup sugar
⅓ cup almond paste, crumbled
½ cup whole blanched almonds, coarsely chopped

• **Beat** butter and cream cheese at medium speed with an electric mixer until creamy; add flour, beating until blended. Cover and chill 1 hour.
• **Shape** pastry into 24 (1-inch) balls. Place balls in ungreased miniature (1¾-inch) muffin pans; press evenly into bottom and up sides.
• **Spoon** ½ teaspoon preserves into each tart.
• **Stir** together egg, sugar, and almond paste; spoon 1 teaspoon mixture over preserves, and sprinkle with chopped almonds.
• **Bake** at 325° for 25 to 30 minutes. Cool slightly in pans on a wire rack; remove from pans. Cool completely. Freeze up to 1 month, if desired. **Yield:** 2 dozen.

Pat Wine
Warrenton, Virginia

CHOCOLATE-COVERED CHERRY COOKIES

Prep: 22 minutes
Bake: 10 minutes per batch

1 (10-ounce) jar maraschino cherries
½ cup butter or margarine, softened
1 cup sugar
1 large egg
1½ teaspoons vanilla extract
1½ cups all-purpose flour
½ cup cocoa
¼ teaspoon baking powder
¼ teaspoon baking soda
¼ teaspoon salt
1 cup (6 ounces) semisweet chocolate morsels
½ cup sweetened condensed milk

• **Drain** cherries, reserving 3 teaspoons juice. Cut cherries in half, and set aside.
• **Beat** butter and sugar at medium speed with an electric mixer until creamy.
• **Add** egg, vanilla, and 2 teaspoons reserved cherry juice, beating until blended.
• **Combine** flour and next 4 ingredients; gradually add flour mixture to butter mixture, beating until blended after each addition.
• **Shape** dough into 1-inch balls, and place on ungreased baking sheets. Press center of each ball with thumb, and place 1 cherry half in indentation.
• **Cook** chocolate and milk in a small saucepan over low heat, stirring occasionally, until melted.
• **Stir** in remaining 1 teaspoon reserved cherry juice. Cool slightly. Spoon 1 teaspoon mixture over each cherry half.
• **Bake** at 350° for 10 minutes. Freeze up to 3 months. **Yield:** 6 dozen.

Pat Wine
Warrenton, Virginia

ʃWEET DREAMS

*Create a party with these scaled-down treats
from Elise Griffin Hughes of Atlanta. Select one
large dessert and three or four family favorites
sure to delight guests of all ages.*

CARAMEL-PECAN TRIANGLES

Prep: 40 minutes
Cook: 35 minutes
Bake: 25 minutes
Chill: 8 hours

4 cups firmly packed light brown
   sugar, divided
¾ cup unsalted butter,
   melted
2 large eggs
1 teaspoon vanilla extract
1 teaspoon bourbon (optional)
½ cup all-purpose flour
½ cup cocoa
1 teaspoon salt, divided
¾ cup unsalted butter
½ cup dark corn syrup
⅔ cup whipping cream
2 tablespoons vanilla extract
3½ cups pecan pieces, toasted

● **Line** a 13- x 9-inch pan with aluminum
foil; grease foil. Set aside.
● **Beat** 1 cup brown sugar, melted butter, eggs, 1 teaspoon vanilla, and if desired, bourbon at medium speed with an
electric mixer until smooth.

● **Combine** flour, cocoa, and ½ teaspoon salt. Gradually add to brown
sugar mixture, beating until blended.
Spread into prepared pan.
● **Bake** at 375° for 15 minutes. Cool on a
wire rack.
● **Bring** ¾ cup butter, syrup, remaining
3 cups brown sugar, and remaining ½
teaspoon salt to a boil, stirring constantly; boil, stirring constantly, until a
candy thermometer registers 250° (hard
ball stage). Remove from heat.
● **Stir** in whipping cream and 2 tablespoons vanilla until blended.
● **Stir** in pecans. Pour mixture over prepared crust.
● **Bake** at 375° for 25 minutes. Cool on a
wire rack; cover and chill 8 hours. Cut
into 12 squares; cut each square into 2
triangles. Store in refrigerator. **Yield:** 2
dozen.

Elise Griffin Hughes
Atlanta, Georgia

CHOCOLATE MOUSSE PRESENT
(pictured on page 304)

Prep: 20 minutes
Cook: 5 minutes
Freeze: 8 hours

3 (8-ounce) packages semisweet
   chocolate squares
¾ cup sugar
1 cup strong brewed coffee
½ cup bourbon
1 cup butter or margarine
2 cups whipping cream, whipped

● **Cook** first 5 ingredients in a heavy
saucepan over low heat, stirring until
smooth. Cool. Fold into whipped cream.
Spoon mousse into a plastic wrap-lined
9- x 5-inch loafpan. Cover; freeze 8 hours.
● **Invert** onto a plate; remove plastic
wrap. Decorate with ribbon and a rose to
resemble a wrapped package. Store in refrigerator; serve with additional whipped
cream, if desired. **Yield:** 10 servings.

Elise Griffin Hughes
Atlanta, Georgia

A DESSERT-LOVER'S DELIGHT

Elise Griffin Hughes of Atlanta has
a passion for food and a flair for
the unique. Guests frequently grace
her home, but her biggest entertaining challenge arrives each year
on the Saturday before Christmas.

Ten years ago, her Champagne
Dessert Party was born. It's not
your typical party. "Larger-than-
life" desserts are cut into festive
shapes and then placed on glass
trays. "The wow of larger homemade desserts is very effective,"
says Elise.

Holiday Dinners

GIANT APPLE NAPOLEON

Bake puff pastry the day before; assemble Napoleon the day of the party.

Prep: 30 minutes
Bake: 15 minutes
Chill: 30 minutes

1 (17¼-ounce) package frozen puff pastry sheets, thawed
1 large egg
1 tablespoon water
1 (3.5-ounce) package vanilla instant pudding mix
2 cups whipping cream
¼ cup butter or margarine
5 large Granny Smith apples, peeled and sliced
1 cup sugar
1 teaspoon ground cinnamon
Powdered sugar

• **Unfold** pastry sheets on baking sheets; press out fold lines. Stir together egg and 1 tablespoon water; brush on pastry sheets.
• **Bake** at 400° for 15 minutes or until golden. Cool on wire racks.
• **Beat** pudding mix and whipping cream at medium speed with an electric mixer 2 minutes. Cover and chill 30 minutes.
• **Melt** butter in a large skillet over medium heat. Add apple, sugar, and cinnamon. Cook, stirring constantly, 10 minutes or until tender; drain.
• **Spread** pudding over 1 pastry sheet; top with apple mixture. Place remaining pastry sheet over apple slices; sprinkle with powdered sugar. Gently cut into bars to serve. **Yield:** 8 servings.

Elise Griffin Hughes
Atlanta, Georgia

KEY LIME BARS WITH MACADAMIA CRUST

Prep: 45 minutes
Chill: 8 hours

2 cups all-purpose flour
½ cup firmly packed light brown sugar
⅔ cup chopped macadamia nuts
6 tablespoons butter, cubed
½ teaspoon salt
¾ cup sugar
½ cup Key lime juice
1 envelope unflavored gelatin
2 tablespoons Key lime juice
1 (14-ounce) can sweetened condensed milk
1 teaspoon grated lime rind
2½ cups whipping cream, whipped
Garnish: grated lime rind

• **Process** first 5 ingredients in a food processor until finely ground. Press mixture into a greased aluminum foil-lined 13- x 9-inch pan.
• **Bake** at 350° for 20 minutes or until golden. Cool on a wire rack.
• **Heat** ¾ cup sugar and ½ cup lime juice over low heat, stirring until sugar dissolves. Remove from heat, and set aside.
• **Sprinkle** gelatin over 2 tablespoons lime juice in a medium bowl; stir gelatin mixture, and let stand 3 to 5 minutes.
• **Add** hot mixture, stirring until gelatin dissolves.
• **Whisk** in sweetened condensed milk and 1 teaspoon grated lime rind.
• **Place** bowl in a larger bowl filled with ice; whisk mixture 10 minutes or until partially set.
• **Fold** lime mixture into whipped cream. Pour evenly over prepared crust; cover and chill 8 hours. Cut into diamond shapes. Garnish, if desired. **Yield:** 24 bars.

Elise Griffin Hughes
Atlanta, Georgia

MINT CHEESECAKE BITES

Here's an easy way to bake and serve cheesecake for a crowd. You'll love the chocolate cookie crust.

Prep: 30 minutes
Bake: 35 minutes
Chill: 8 hours

3 cups cream-filled chocolate sandwich cookie crumbs (40 cookies)
½ cup butter or margarine, melted
4 (8-ounce) packages cream cheese, softened
1 cup sugar
4 large eggs
1½ teaspoons peppermint extract
6 drops of green liquid food coloring
½ cup semisweet chocolate morsels
1 teaspoon shortening

• **Stir** together cookie crumbs and butter; press mixture into bottom of an aluminum foil-lined 13- x 9-inch pan.
• **Bake** at 350° for 10 minutes. Cool on a wire rack.
• **Beat** cream cheese and sugar at medium speed with an electric mixer until creamy.
• **Add** eggs, 1 at a time, beating just until blended after each addition.
• **Stir** in peppermint extract and food coloring. Spread cream cheese mixture over prepared crust.
• **Bake** at 300° for 35 minutes or until set. Cool on a wire rack. Cover; chill 8 hours.
• **Place** chocolate morsels and shortening in a small heavy-duty zip-top plastic bag; seal. Submerge bag in hot water until chocolate melts; gently knead until mixture is smooth.
• **Snip** a tiny hole in 1 corner of plastic bag; drizzle chocolate over cheesecake in a crisscross pattern, if desired. Cut into squares. **Yield:** 24 servings.

Elise Griffin Hughes
Atlanta, Georgia

GIFTS TO SHARE

Nothing is more welcome than a gift from your kitchen, and these recipes are tailored for holiday gift-giving. Make Bean Soup Mix, package it in decorative Christmas bags, and attach the recipe for the soup. Or stir up a batch of Cinnamon Rolls a month ahead, place them in disposable pans, and store in the freezer.

BEAN-CHICKEN SOUP

Prep: 38 minutes
Cook: 2 hours

2 cups Bean Soup Mix
2 quarts water
2 cups chopped cooked chicken
1 large onion, chopped
1 garlic clove, minced
1 chicken bouillon cube
1 teaspoon salt
½ teaspoon pepper
1 (14½-ounce) can diced tomatoes
1 (10-ounce) can diced tomatoes
   and green chiles

● **Place** Bean Soup Mix in a Dutch oven; add water to cover, and let stand 30 minutes. Drain.
● **Bring** soup mix, 2 quarts water, and next 6 ingredients to a boil in Dutch oven. Cover, reduce heat, and simmer 1 to 1½ hours.
● **Stir** in diced tomatoes and tomatoes with chiles; return to a boil. Cover and simmer 30 minutes or until beans are tender, adding more water, if necessary. **Yield:** 9 cups.

Bean Soup Mix

Prep: 5 minutes

1 (14-ounce) package barley
1 (16-ounce) package dried red
   beans
1 (16-ounce) package dried pinto
   beans
1 (16-ounce) package dried
   lentils
1 (16-ounce) package dried
   black-eyed peas
1 (16-ounce) package dried black
   beans
1 (16-ounce) package dried navy
   pea beans
1 (16-ounce) package dried great
   Northern beans
1 (16-ounce) package dried green
   split peas

● **Combine** all ingredients in a large bowl. Store in an airtight container. **Yield:** 19 cups.

Anna T. Rucker
Norfolk, Virginia

GARLIC JELLY

This tangy-sweet, garlic-inspired jelly tastes great with cream cheese and crackers.

Prep: 24 minutes
Stand: 24 hours
Cook: 52 minutes
Process: 5 minutes

½ cup finely chopped garlic
2 cups white wine vinegar
3 cups water
1 (1¾-ounce) package powdered
   pectin
5½ cups sugar
¼ teaspoon vegetable oil
2 drops of green liquid food
   coloring (optional)

● **Bring** garlic and vinegar to a boil in a 2-quart saucepan; reduce heat, and simmer 15 minutes. Pour into a glass bowl; cover and let stand 24 hours.
● **Pour** vinegar mixture through a wire-mesh strainer into a 2-cup glass measuring cup, pressing garlic with the back of a spoon to squeeze out liquid; discard solids.
● **Bring** vinegar mixture, 3 cups water, and pectin to a boil in a 5-quart saucepan, stirring constantly.
● **Add** sugar; return to a boil, stirring constantly.
● **Add** oil; boil, stirring constantly, 2 minutes. Remove mixture from heat, and skim off foam with a metal spoon. Add food coloring, if desired.
● **Pour** hot jelly into hot, sterilized jars, filling to ¼ inch from top; wipe jar rims. Cover at once with metal lids, and screw on bands.
● **Process** in boiling water bath 5 minutes. Use on grilled chicken, pork, and lamb, or serve with cream cheese and crackers. **Yield:** 7 (½-pint) jars.

Sylvia Stocksbury
Maryville, Tennessee

CINNAMON ROLLS

If you give Cinnamon Rolls before baking, double the Glaze recipe and include about ¼ cup in a small zip-top plastic bag with each gift. Add instructions to place the bag in hot water, snip a corner, and then drizzle over baked rolls.

Prep: 35 minutes
Rise: 1 hour and 30 minutes
Bake: 25 minutes

½ cup instant potato flakes
1 cup water
2 (¼-ounce) envelopes active dry yeast
2 cups warm water (100° to 110°)
9½ to 10 cups all-purpose flour, divided
5 large eggs, lightly beaten
1 cup sugar
1 cup shortening, melted
1 tablespoon salt
½ cup butter or margarine, softened
1⅓ cups firmly packed light brown sugar
4 teaspoons ground cinnamon
½ cup chopped pecans, toasted
½ cup raisins (optional)
Glaze

• **Stir** together potato flakes and 1 cup water in a microwave-safe bowl. Microwave at HIGH 3 minutes; stir.
• **Combine** yeast and 2 cups warm water in a 2-cup glass measuring cup; let stand 5 minutes.
• **Combine** mashed potatoes, 4 cups flour, eggs, and next 3 ingredients in a 6-quart bowl.
• **Stir** in yeast mixture until blended. Gradually stir in remaining 5½ to 6 cups flour until a soft dough forms.
• **Cover** and let rise in a warm place (85°), free from drafts, 1 hour or until doubled in bulk.
• **Divide** dough in half. Roll each portion on a lightly floured surface into an 18- x 15-inch rectangle. Spread each with ¼ cup butter; sprinkle each with ⅔ cup brown sugar, 2 teaspoons cinnamon, ¼ cup pecans, and, if desired, ¼ cup raisins.
• **Roll** up, jellyroll fashion, starting at a long edge. Cut each roll into 1-inch-thick slices. Arrange in 4 (13- x 9-inch) pans or 8 (8-inch) square pans.

• **Cover** and let rise in a warm place (85°), free from drafts, 30 minutes or until doubled in bulk.
• **Bake** at 375° for 25 minutes or until golden. Drizzle with Glaze. **Yield:** about 3 dozen.

Note: Freeze unbaked rolls, if desired. To bake, remove from freezer, and thaw in refrigerator 8 hours. Bake as directed.

Glaze

Prep: 5 minutes

2 cups powdered sugar
2 tablespoons milk
2 tablespoons water
1 teaspoon vanilla extract
2 tablespoons cream cheese, softened
2 tablespoons butter or margarine, softened

• **Whisk** together first 4 ingredients until blended; add cream cheese and butter, whisking until smooth. **Yield:** 1 cup.
Carolyn Saxon
Jesup, Georgia

APRICOT-CHEESE CRESCENTS

Prep: 27 minutes
Chill: 8 hours
Bake: 15 minutes

2 cups all-purpose flour
½ teaspoon salt
1 cup butter or margarine, cut up
1 (12-ounce) container small-curd cottage cheese
1 (6-ounce) package dried apricots
½ cup water
1 cup sugar, divided
1 egg white, lightly beaten
¾ cup finely chopped almonds

• **Stir** together flour and salt; cut in butter with a pastry blender until crumbly. Stir in cheese until blended. Shape into 1-inch balls. Cover; chill 8 hours.
• **Bring** apricots and ½ cup water to a boil in a saucepan; cover, reduce heat, and simmer 15 minutes. Remove from heat; cool 10 minutes.

• **Process** apricot mixture and ½ cup sugar in a food processor until smooth, stopping to scrape sides.
• **Pat** each ball on a lightly floured surface into a 2½-inch circle. Spoon 1 teaspoon apricot mixture in center of each circle. Fold circles in half, pressing edges to seal. Place on lightly greased baking sheets. Brush with egg white. Stir together remaining ½ cup sugar and almonds; sprinkle over crescents.
• **Bake** at 375° for 12 to 15 minutes or until lightly browned. **Yield:** 3½ dozen.
Ellie Wells
Lakeland, Florida

TOUGH AND TENDER

The old-fashioned way to serve rutabagas is simply cubed and steamed with salt, pepper, and a pat of butter. These recipes show off the yellow-fleshed root at its best.

GLAZED RUTABAGA

Prep: 15 minutes
Cook: 28 minutes

¼ cup water
5 tablespoons butter or margarine, divided
1 large rutabaga, peeled and cut into 1-inch pieces
½ cup firmly packed brown sugar
½ teaspoon grated orange rind
½ cup fresh orange juice
¼ teaspoon ground nutmeg
Pinch of salt

• **Bring** ¼ cup water and 2 tablespoons butter to a boil in a large skillet over medium-high heat. Add rutabaga, stirring to coat. Reduce heat; cover and simmer 20 minutes or until slightly tender. Drain.

• **Melt** remaining 3 tablespoons butter in skillet over medium heat; stir in brown sugar and next 4 ingredients. Add rutabaga, stirring to coat. Cook, stirring often, 8 minutes. **Yield:** 4 to 6 servings.

GREEK-ROASTED RUTABAGA

Prep: 10 minutes
Bake: 50 minutes

1 **large rutabaga, peeled and cut into 2-inch pieces ***
¼ **cup olive oil**
1 **tablespoon dried oregano**
1 **tablespoon lemon juice**
1 **teaspoon Greek seasoning**
½ **teaspoon salt**
⅛ **teaspoon pepper**

• **Toss** together all ingredients, and spread into a lightly greased 15- x 10-inch jellyroll pan.
• **Bake** at 450° for 25 minutes; stir mixture, and bake 25 more minutes. **Yield:** 6 to 8 servings.

* Substitute 10 medium potatoes, cut into 2-inch chunks, for rutabaga, if desired. Bake at 450° 10 minutes; stir and bake 30 more minutes.

Karen C. Greenlee
Lawrenceville, Georgia

RUTABAGA-CABBAGE SKILLET

Prep: 20 minutes
Cook: 26 minutes

3 **bacon slices**
1 **large rutabaga, peeled and cut into 1-inch pieces**
½ **teaspoon salt**
¼ **teaspoon pepper**
Pinch of sugar
2 **cups water**
1 **large head cabbage, coarsely chopped**
½ **teaspoon cornmeal mix**

• **Cook** bacon in a large Dutch oven until crisp. Remove bacon, reserving

drippings in pan. Crumble bacon, and set aside. Add rutabaga and next 4 ingredients to drippings in pan.
• **Bring** mixture to a boil. Reduce heat to medium, and cook, covered, 20 minutes. Uncover and return to a boil; stir in cabbage.
• **Cook** 5 minutes or until rutabaga is tender. Sprinkle with cornmeal mix; stir until blended. Cook 1 more minute. Sprinkle with bacon. **Yield:** 6 servings.

Mattie H. Scott
Birmingham, Alabama

FRIED RUTABAGA

Soak: 2 hours
Prep: 30 minutes
Cook: 5 minutes

2 **large rutabagas, peeled and sliced**
1 **large egg**
¾ **cup milk**
1 **teaspoon white vinegar**
1 **cup all-purpose flour**
1 **cup cornmeal**
½ **teaspoon baking powder**
¼ **teaspoon salt**
¼ **teaspoon pepper**
Vegetable oil
Salt

• **Soak** rutabaga in salted water to cover 2 hours. Drain.
• **Whisk** together egg, milk, and vinegar until blended.
• **Stir** together flour and next 4 ingredients. Dip rutabaga slices in egg mixture; dredge in flour mixture.
• **Pour** oil to a depth of 2 inches into a Dutch oven; heat to 375°. Fry rutabaga, in batches, in hot oil until browned. Drain on paper towels. Sprinkle with additional salt. **Yield:** 6 to 8 servings.

Helen Stone
Jewett, Texas

MINCEMEAT AND SPICE

Fans of mincemeat pie will enjoy this simplified version. Sugar-tossed pecans replace the traditional pastry, and ice cream is a vital ingredient. This pie is ready for the freezer in 30 minutes.

MINCEMEAT ICE CREAM PIE

Prep: 30 minutes
Freeze: 8 hours

1¾ **cups finely chopped pecans**
1 **tablespoon sugar**
2 **tablespoons butter or margarine, melted**
1 **(9-ounce) package dry mincemeat**
½ **cup water**
1 **quart vanilla ice cream, softened**
1 **tablespoon grated orange rind**
¼ **teaspoon ground cinnamon**
¼ **teaspoon ground ginger**
⅛ **teaspoon ground allspice**
Garnishes: toasted chopped pecans, ground cinnamon

• **Stir** together first 3 ingredients; press into bottom of a well-greased 9-inch pieplate.
• **Bake** at 350° for 10 minutes. Cool on a wire rack.
• **Bring** mincemeat and ½ cup water to a boil in a small saucepan; boil 3 minutes. Cool. Spread mixture into crust.
• **Stir** together ice cream and next 4 ingredients; spread over mincemeat. Freeze 8 hours. Remove from freezer, and let stand 20 minutes before serving. Garnish, if desired. **Yield:** 1 (9-inch) pie.

Eileen Bodoh-Kalupa
Milwaukee, Wisconsin

EASY OVEN MEALS

Oven-prepared meals allow you to focus on other activities. Marmalade Baked Chicken and Vegetable-Cheese Medley team for an easy meal. The next night, use the leftover chicken as a substitute for shrimp in Shrimp-and-Vegetable Oven Omelet.

VEGETABLE-PASTA OVEN OMELET

Add a tossed garden salad and Italian bread to make a well-rounded supper.

Prep: 30 minutes
Bake: 30 minutes

3 dried tomatoes in oil
1 small onion, chopped
½ red bell pepper, diced
3 garlic cloves, minced
2 tablespoons olive oil
1 small zucchini, diced
1 (3-ounce) package cream cheese, softened
7 ounces vermicelli, cooked
6 large eggs
¾ cup shredded Parmesan cheese, divided
¾ cup milk
1 teaspoon dried Italian seasoning
½ teaspoon salt
¼ teaspoon pepper

● **Drain** dried tomatoes well, pressing between layers of paper towels; chop tomatoes.

● **Sauté** onion, bell pepper, and garlic in hot oil in a nonstick 12-inch ovenproof skillet 5 minutes or until vegetables are tender.
● **Add** tomato and zucchini, and sauté 3 minutes.
● **Stir** in cream cheese until melted. Add pasta; toss to coat.
● **Whisk** together eggs, ½ cup Parmesan cheese, milk, and next 3 ingredients in a bowl. Pour egg mixture over pasta mixture in skillet.
● **Bake** at 375° for 25 to 30 minutes or until set.
● **Sprinkle** omelet with remaining ¼ cup shredded Parmesan cheese. Let omelet stand 10 minutes before serving. **Yield:** 8 servings.

Dolores C. Suedel
Ridgeland, Mississippi

Shrimp-and-Vegetable Oven Omelet: Toss 2 cups chopped cooked shrimp with pasta mixture. Continue as directed above.

MARMALADE BAKED CHICKEN

Prep: 10 minutes
Bake: 1 hour and 30 minutes

1 (5- to 6-pound) whole chicken
1 cup orange marmalade
2 tablespoons Worcestershire sauce
4 teaspoons Old Bay seasoning
2 teaspoons minced onion
1 tablespoon chopped fresh parsley

● **Remove** giblets from chicken, and discard. Rinse chicken with cold water, and pat dry. Tuck wingtips under bird, and tie legs, if desired.
● **Place** bird, breast side up, on a rack coated with vegetable cooking spray, and place rack in a roasting pan.
● **Stir** together orange marmalade and next 3 ingredients; pour mixture over chicken in pan.
● **Sprinkle** chicken evenly with parsley.
● **Bake** chicken at 350° for 1 hour and 30 minutes or until done, basting chicken occasionally with pan juices. **Yield:** 6 to 8 servings.

Deena J. Powell
North Wales, Pennsylvania

COOK'S TIPS

■ If you substitute pans for baking dishes, the baking times may be longer.

■ Cook pasta ahead of time, tossing it with a little oil so that it doesn't get sticky.

■ Line pan with aluminum foil, and spray foil with vegetable cooking spray before baking chicken.

VEGETABLE-CHEESE MEDLEY

Prep: 13 minutes
Bake: 25 minutes

2 cups baby carrots
2 cups broccoli flowerets
2 cups cauliflower flowerets
½ cup butter or margarine
1 medium onion, chopped
2 garlic cloves, minced
1 cup (4 ounces) shredded
      mozzarella cheese
½ cup shredded Parmesan
      cheese
¾ teaspoon pepper

• **Place** carrots in a heavy-duty zip-top plastic bag; seal. Place in a microwave-safe dish. Cut several slits in bag.
• **Microwave** at HIGH 2 minutes; add broccoli and cauliflower, and seal bag. Microwave at HIGH 2 minutes or until vegetables are tender.
• **Melt** butter in a skillet over medium heat; add onion and garlic, and sauté 5 minutes.
• **Arrange** one-third of vegetables in a lightly greased 2-quart baking dish.
• **Spoon** one-third of onion mixture over vegetables.
• **Stir** together cheeses; sprinkle ½ cup cheese mixture over onion mixture, and sprinkle with one-third of pepper. Repeat layers twice.
• **Bake** at 350° for 25 minutes. **Yield:** 4 to 6 servings.

Nancy Woodall
Bellaire, Texas

THE LURE OF LENTILS

Don't overlook the lowly lentil, often called "the poor man's meat." The tiny, dried discs are a nutritional powerhouse and are very affordable. Delicious in soup, lentils easily overcook in other dishes if they're not in the hands of a watchful cook. Make sure they become soft and tender but retain their shape.

LENTIL BURRITOS

Prep: 45 minutes
Bake: 10 minutes

1 cup dried lentils
4 cups water
1 small onion, chopped
1 large green bell pepper,
      chopped
1 tablespoon vegetable oil
1 cup (4 ounces) shredded
      Cheddar cheese
16 (7-inch) flour tortillas
1 (8-ounce) can tomato sauce with
      roasted garlic
1 teaspoon ground cumin
1 tablespoon green taco
      sauce
1 teaspoon cornstarch
Toppings: sour cream, guacamole

• **Simmer** lentils in 4 cups water in a saucepan over medium heat 20 minutes or until tender; drain, reserving 1 cup liquid.
• **Sauté** onion and bell pepper in hot oil in a large skillet over medium-high heat 5 minutes or until tender. Remove from heat; stir in lentils and cheese.
• **Spoon** mixture evenly down centers of tortillas, and roll up. Place in a lightly greased 13- x 9-inch baking dish.
• **Bring** ¾ cup reserved liquid, tomato sauce, cumin, and taco sauce to a boil in a saucepan.
• **Stir** together remaining ¼ cup reserved liquid and cornstarch until smooth.

• **Stir** cornstarch mixture into sauce mixture; cook over medium heat, stirring often, 10 minutes. Pour sauce over burritos.
• **Bake** at 350° for 10 minutes or until thoroughly heated. Serve with desired toppings. **Yield:** 8 servings.

Karen C. Greenlee
Lawrenceville, Georgia

CHEESY PASTA AND LENTILS

Prep: 20 minutes
Cook: 1 hour and 10 minutes

1½ cups dried lentils
1 onion, chopped
3½ cups water
½ teaspoon salt
¼ teaspoon pepper
2 (15-ounce) cans chunky
      garlic-and-herb tomato
      sauce
2 carrots, thinly sliced
2 celery ribs, sliced
1 green bell pepper, chopped
8 ounces rotini, cooked
2 tablespoons chopped fresh
      parsley
1 cup (4 ounces) shredded
      Cheddar cheese

• **Bring** first 5 ingredients to a boil in a Dutch oven over medium-high heat. Cover, reduce heat, and simmer 40 minutes. Add tomato sauce and next 3 ingredients; bring to a boil. Cover, reduce heat, and simmer 20 minutes or until vegetables are tender.
• **Stir** in pasta and parsley. Sprinkle each serving with Cheddar cheese. **Yield:** 6 servings.

LENTIL SPREAD

Prep: 30 minutes

¼ cup dried lentils
¾ cup water or chicken broth
1 tablespoon lemon juice
1 teaspoon sesame oil
¼ teaspoon salt
¼ teaspoon ground red pepper
1 to 2 garlic cloves, pressed
Toasted sesame seeds (optional)

• **Bring** lentils and water to a boil in a small saucepan; partially cover, reduce heat, and simmer 20 minutes or until tender. Drain.
• **Process** lentils, lemon juice, and next 4 ingredients in a food processor until smooth, stopping to scrape down sides. Cover and chill up to 3 days, if desired.
• **Sprinkle** top of spread with toasted sesame seeds, if desired. Serve spread with crackers or assorted raw vegetables. **Yield:** ¾ cup.

TEX-MEX LENTILS

Prep: 15 minutes
Cook: 1 hour and 40 minutes

3½ cups dried lentils
7 cups water
1 (16-ounce) can Mexican-style stewed tomatoes, undrained
2 (6-ounce) cans tomato paste
½ cup uncooked bulgur wheat
2 tablespoons chili powder
2 teaspoons salt
½ teaspoon pepper
½ teaspoon dried thyme
3 garlic cloves, pressed
1 medium onion, chopped
1 tablespoon red wine vinegar
Shredded taco cheese blend

• **Bring** lentils and 7 cups water to a boil in a Dutch oven. Cover, reduce heat, and simmer 30 minutes.
• **Add** tomatoes and next 8 ingredients; cover reduce heat, and simmer, stirring occasionally, 1 hour.
• **Stir** in vinegar; sprinkle each serving with cheese. **Yield:** 10 cups.

BIG, BOLD CHEESES

As adults, many of us have grown to love the tangy bite of Parmesan, feta, Asiago, and blue cheese. These recipes highlight the rich flavors of these bold cheeses.

BLUE CHEESE TERRINE WITH TOMATO-BASIL VINAIGRETTE

For an hors d'oeuvre, serve the terrine with toasted baguette slices.

Prep: 30 minutes
Broil: 10 minutes
Chill: 8 hours

2 red bell peppers, cut in half
2 yellow bell peppers, cut in half
6 ounces blue cheese, crumbled
2 (8-ounce) packages cream cheese, softened
Tomato-Basil Vinaigrette
Mixed salad greens

• **Place** bell pepper halves, cut sides down, on an aluminum foil-lined baking sheet.
• **Broil** 5 inches from heat (with electric oven door partially open) 8 to 10 minutes or until bell peppers look blistered.
• **Place** bell peppers in a heavy-duty zip-top plastic bag; seal and let stand 10 minutes to loosen skins. Peel peppers; remove and discard seeds. Pat dry with paper towels.
• **Beat** cheeses at medium speed with an electric mixer until smooth.

• **Spread** half of cheese mixture in a plastic wrap-lined 8- x 4-inch loafpan. Top with 4 pepper halves. Spread remaining cheese mixture over peppers; top with remaining pepper halves. Cover and chill 8 hours.
• **Unmold** onto a serving dish; drizzle with Tomato-Basil Vinaigrette. Serve terrine on mixed salad greens. **Yield:** 10 to 12 servings.

Tomato-Basil Vinaigrette

Prep: 5 minutes

¼ cup white wine vinegar
1 tablespoon Dijon mustard
1 teaspoon salt
½ teaspoon pepper
1 teaspoon lemon juice
½ cup olive oil
6 plum tomatoes, peeled, seeded, and diced
¼ cup chopped fresh basil

• **Whisk** together first 5 ingredients in a small bowl. Gradually whisk in oil. Stir in tomato and basil. **Yield:** 2 cups.

WINTER HERB GARDEN SCALLOPED POTATOES

Prep: 35 minutes
Bake: 1 hour and 15 minutes

6   small russet potatoes
2   tablespoons butter or
      margarine
¼   cup chopped purple onion
3   tablespoons chopped dried
      tomato
2   garlic cloves, minced
2   tablespoons all-purpose
      flour
2   cups whipping cream
½   cup milk
½   (8-ounce) package cream
      cheese, softened
2   tablespoons chopped fresh
      chives
2   tablespoons chopped fresh
      parsley
1   teaspoon chopped fresh
      rosemary
1   teaspoon salt
¼   teaspoon pepper
½   cup grated Asiago cheese
½   cup shredded Parmesan
      cheese

● **Peel** potatoes, and cut into ⅛-inch-thick slices. Set aside.
● **Melt** butter in a large skillet over medium heat.
● **Add** onion, tomato, and garlic; sauté until tender.
● **Add** flour, stirring until blended. Gradually add whipping cream, milk, and cream cheese, stirring until smooth.
● **Stir** in chives and next 4 ingredients; cook, stirring constantly, 3 minutes.
● **Combine** potato and cream sauce in a lightly greased 11- x 7-inch baking dish.
● **Bake,** covered, at 375° for 1 hour. Sprinkle with Asiago and Parmesan cheeses; bake, uncovered, 15 more minutes or until potato is tender. **Yield:** 6 to 8 servings.

Miriam Baroga
Fircrest, Washington

TUSCAN FETA SALAD SANDWICH

Prep: 9 minutes
Chill: 2 hours

⅔   cup vinaigrette
½   teaspoon dried oregano
      leaves, crushed
½   teaspoon dried basil,
      crushed
½   teaspoon pepper
1   (8-inch) round sourdough
      bread loaf (about 16 ounces)
2   cups shredded romaine
      lettuce
1   large tomato, sliced
1   (4-ounce) package crumbled feta
      cheese
1   medium cucumber, sliced
½   medium-size purple onion,
      sliced
¼   cup sliced ripe olives

● **Whisk** together first 4 ingredients.
● **Cut** bread in half horizontally. Scoop out inside of bread halves, leaving 2-inch shells; brush inside with 3 tablespoons vinaigrette mixture.
● **Layer** lettuce and tomato in bottom half of bread, brushing tomato with remaining vinaigrette mixture.
● **Layer** cheese and next 3 ingredients over tomato. Cover with top half of bread. Cover with plastic wrap; chill 2 hours. (Place a large plate on top of sandwich, weighting it down with cans, if necessary, to compress sandwich.) Cut into wedges to serve. **Yield:** 4 to 6 servings.

PARTY PUNCHES

Flavor-boosting spices, citrus juices, and fresh mint make these easy sipping beverages festive. The helpful shortcuts and early preparation tips make any celebration a breeze.

FRUIT SPARKLE

Prep: 10 minutes
Cook: 20 minutes
Chill: 3 hours

3½   cups water, divided
⅔   cup sugar
2   (3-inch) cinnamon sticks
12   whole cloves
1   (6-ounce) can frozen pineapple
      juice concentrate, thawed and
      undiluted
1   (6-ounce) can frozen orange
      juice concentrate, thawed and
      undiluted
¼   cup lemon juice
1   (1-liter) bottle ginger ale,
      chilled

● **Bring** 1½ cups water and next 3 ingredients to a boil; reduce heat. Simmer 15 minutes. Pour through a wire-mesh strainer into a large bowl, discarding spices.
● **Process** remaining 2 cups water, pineapple and orange juice concentrates, and lemon juice in a blender 1 minute or until frothy. Stir into syrup mixture. Chill 3 hours.
● **Stir** in ginger ale just before serving. Serve over ice. **Yield:** 2 quarts.

Marie Davis
Charlotte, North Carolina

CHAMPAGNE BLOSSOM PUNCH

Prep: 5 minutes

⅓ cup frozen orange juice
    concentrate, thawed and
    undiluted
¼ cup frozen lemonade
    concentrate, thawed and
    undiluted
1 (750-milliliter) bottle dry white
    wine, chilled
1 (750-milliliter) bottle
    champagne, chilled

● **Stir** together all ingredients. Serve immediately over ice. **Yield:** 6⅔ cups.

Note: For testing purposes only, we used Riesling for dry white wine.

Marge Killmon
Annandale, Virginia

CRANBERRY PUNCH

Prep: 25 minutes
Chill: 2 hours

2 cups cranberry juice drink
2 tablespoons chopped fresh
    mint
1 (16-ounce) can jellied cranberry
    sauce
1 (1-liter) bottle ginger ale,
    chilled

● **Bring** cranberry juice drink and mint to a boil in a saucepan; remove from heat. Cover and let stand 15 minutes. Pour through a wire-mesh strainer into a blender; discard mint.
● **Add** cranberry sauce. Process until smooth. Chill 2 hours. Stir in ginger ale just before serving over ice. **Yield:** 2 quarts.

Janie Wallace
Seguin, Texas

LEBANON LEGACY

Lots of grandmothers reside in Lebanon, Kentucky, but the town only knows one Mammow. And for 111 progeny and scores of fond friends, great-great-grandmother Aileen Ferrell fixes everyone's favorite meals. Here we share her irresistible Potato Rolls and her festive Cranberry Salad; both are Ferrell family traditions.

POTATO ROLLS

Prep: 15 minutes
Stand: 11 hours
Bake: 10 minutes per batch

1 large potato, peeled and
    chopped
1 (¼-ounce) envelope active dry
    yeast
1 cup shortening
⅔ cup sugar
2 teaspoons salt
4½ cups all-purpose flour,
    divided

● **Cook** potato in boiling water to cover 10 minutes or until tender. Drain, reserving 1 cup liquid; set potato aside.
● **Heat** reserved 1 cup liquid to 100° to 110° in a small saucepan. Sprinkle with yeast; stir and let stand 5 minutes.
● **Mash** potato in a large bowl with a potato masher or fork; stir in yeast mixture, shortening, sugar, and salt. Let stand at room temperature 2 hours. Gradually add 4 cups flour, stirring to make a soft dough.
● **Place** dough in a well-greased bowl, turning to grease top. Cover and chill 8 hours.
● **Punch** dough down; turn out onto a surface sprinkled with remaining ½ cup flour, and knead 4 or 5 times. Roll to ½-inch thickness, and cut with a 2½-inch round cutter. Place on lightly greased baking sheets.

● **Cover** and let rise in a warm place (85°), free from drafts, 1 hour or until doubled in bulk.
● **Bake** at 400° for 10 minutes or until golden. **Yield:** 5 dozen.

Aileen Ferrell
Lebanon, Kentucky

CRANBERRY SALAD

Prep: 50 minutes
Chill: 8 hours

1 (12-ounce) package fresh
    cranberries
1 cup sugar
1 (8-ounce) can crushed
    pineapple, undrained
1 (3-ounce) package raspberry
    gelatin
1 envelope unflavored gelatin
½ cup cold water
1 (15-ounce) can mandarin orange
    sections, undrained
2 large celery ribs, diced
1 medium Granny Smith apple,
    diced
½ cup finely chopped pecans,
    toasted
1 cup miniature marshmallows

● **Process** cranberries and sugar in a food processor until cranberries are coarsely chopped. Add pineapple, and pulse 3 times.
● **Sprinkle** raspberry gelatin and unflavored gelatin over ½ cup cold water in a large saucepan; stir and let stand 1 minute.
● **Cook** over low heat, stirring until gelatin dissolves (about 2 minutes).
● **Stir** in cranberry mixture, oranges, and next 3 ingredients. Cool to room temperature.
● **Stir** in marshmallows, and pour into a 13- x 9-inch pan. Cover and chill 8 hours. **Yield:** 8 servings.

Aileen Ferrell
Lebanon, Kentucky

EYE OF ROUND ROASTS

The secret to juicy, flavorful, cut-with-a-fork meat is all in the cooking. The eye of round has less marbling (layers of fat distributed in the meat), so you need to cook it in liquid, covered, for an extended period of time over low heat.

SWEET-AND-SOUR POT ROAST

Prep: 22 minutes
Bake: 3 hours

1 (4-pound) eye of round roast
1 tablespoon vegetable oil
2 medium onions, thinly sliced
¼ cup sugar
¼ cup honey
⅓ cup lemon juice
1 teaspoon salt
¼ teaspoon pepper
¼ teaspoon ground cloves

• **Brown** roast on all sides in hot oil in a large Dutch oven. Add onion and remaining ingredients.
• **Bake,** covered, at 300° for 3 hours or until tender. **Yield:** 8 to 10 servings.

Jodie McCoy
Tulsa, Oklahoma

EASY BANQUET ROAST

Prep: 10 minutes
Bake: 4 hours

1 (4-pound) eye of round roast
½ teaspoon garlic salt
½ teaspoon pepper
4 medium onions, quartered
3 (10¾-ounce) cans beefy mushroom soup, undiluted
1 (16-ounce) package baby carrots
2 pounds new potatoes

• **Sprinkle** roast with garlic salt and pepper, and place in a roasting pan. Add onion. Pour soup over roast.
• **Bake,** covered, at 325° for 2 hours and 30 minutes to 3 hours; add carrots and potatoes. Bake, covered, 1 more hour. Serve roast with sauce. **Yield:** 8 to 10 servings.

Sonya S. Spencer
Sandersville, Georgia

SPICY MARINATED EYE OF ROUND

Prep: 5 minutes
Chill: 8 hours
Bake: 4 hours and 15 minutes

1 (3- to 5-pound) eye of round roast
3 sweet onions, sliced
½ teaspoon salt
¼ teaspoon pepper
Spicy Sauce

• **Place** roast in a roasting pan, and add onion. Sprinkle with salt and pepper.
• **Bake,** covered, at 325° for 3 hours and 30 minutes. Cool and thinly slice.
• **Place** roast in an ovenproof container; add Spicy Sauce. Cover; chill 8 hours. Remove from refrigerator; let stand 30 minutes.
• **Bake** at 350° for 45 minutes or until thoroughly heated. Serve roast with mashed potatoes, if desired. **Yield:** 8 to 10 servings.

Spicy Sauce

Prep: 15 minutes
Cook: 1 hour

2 cups ketchup
2 cups water
2 large sweet onions, sliced
⅓ cup red wine vinegar
¼ cup firmly packed brown sugar
2 tablespoons Worcestershire sauce
1 teaspoon dry mustard
1 teaspoon dried oregano
1 teaspoon pepper
½ teaspoon garlic powder
½ teaspoon chili powder
½ teaspoon ground cloves
¼ teaspoon ground nutmeg
¼ teaspoon hot sauce
1 bay leaf

• **Bring** all ingredients to a boil in a Dutch oven over medium heat; reduce heat to low. Simmer 1 hour. Cool. Discard bay leaf. **Yield:** 7 cups.

Denise Schwartz
Brighton, Michigan

Slow Cooker Spicy Marinated Eye of Round: Cut roast in half; sprinkle with salt and pepper. Place roast and onion slices in a 5-quart slow cooker. Stir together ingredients for Spicy Sauce; pour over uncooked roast. Cook roast at HIGH 9 hours; remove roast. Cool slightly, and cut into thin slices. Return slices to slow cooker, and cook 1 more hour.

MARINATED BEEF KABOBS WITH VEGETABLES

Cutting the roast into cubes and marinating it overnight tenderizes the meat and reduces the cooking time.

Prep: 27 minutes
Marinate: 8 hours
Grill: 16 minutes

1 cup white wine vinegar
1 cup vegetable oil
⅓ cup soy sauce
1 tablespoon dried rosemary
1 tablespoon dried thyme
1 teaspoon dry mustard
1 teaspoon salt
1 teaspoon pepper
½ teaspoon Worcestershire sauce
2 garlic cloves, pressed
1 (3½-pound) eye of round roast, cut into 1½-inch cubes
12 small whole onions
1 pound large whole mushrooms
2 green bell peppers, cut into 1½-inch pieces

• **Stir** together first 10 ingredients; reserve ½ cup marinade, and chill. Pour remaining marinade into a large heavy-duty zip-top plastic bag.
• **Add** meat cubes; seal and chill 8 hours. Drain, discarding marinade.
• **Thread** meat and vegetables onto 12-inch skewers.
• **Grill,** covered with grill lid, over medium-high heat 16 minutes, basting with reserved ½ cup marinade and turning often. **Yield:** 8 to 10 servings.

Barkley Shreve
Mobile, Alabama

A JUICY SECRET

Take a fresh look at oranges. They are excellent traveling companions, cloaked in sturdy skin that keeps them juicy and flavorful for days. Oranges are also extremely nutritious; a medium fruit supplies 120 percent of our daily need for vitamin C, as well as healthy amounts of folate and fiber.

Use oranges in various sweet and savory dishes. The tart rind provides a boost to frostings, salad dressings, chicken, and seafood dishes. The juice can be added to many of these same recipes for natural sweetness.

TORTELLINI IN CITRUS BROTH

Prep: 5 minutes
Cook: 13 minutes

1 large orange
3 (14½-ounce) cans beef broth
2 teaspoons chopped fresh or ½ teaspoon dried basil
1 (9-ounce) package refrigerated garlic-and-cheese tortellini or cheese ravioli

• **Peel** orange rind with a vegetable peeler, and finely chop rind. Squeeze juice into a Dutch oven. Add chopped rind, broth, and basil.
• **Bring** to a boil over medium heat; cover, reduce heat, and simmer 5 minutes. Stir in tortellini; cook 8 minutes. **Yield:** 4 servings.

SHRIMP IN ORANGE SAUCE

Prep: 50 minutes
Cook: 18 minutes

2 quarts water
2 pounds unpeeled, large fresh shrimp
¼ cup butter or margarine
1 small onion, diced
2 teaspoons grated orange rind
1 cup fresh orange juice
2 tablespoons orange liqueur or orange juice
¼ cup whipping cream
½ teaspoon salt
¼ teaspoon pepper
1 tablespoon chopped fresh parsley
6 French bread slices, toasted

• **Bring** 2 quarts water to a boil; add shrimp, and cook 3 to 5 minutes or just until shrimp turn pink. Drain and rinse with cold water. Peel shrimp; devein, if desired.
• **Melt** butter in a large skillet over medium heat; add onion, and sauté until tender. Stir in orange rind and next 5 ingredients, and cook 6 to 8 minutes or until slightly thickened. Stir in shrimp, and cook 2 minutes or until thoroughly heated. Sprinkle with parsley, and serve over French bread. **Yield:** 6 servings.

David H. Darst
Tallahassee, Florida

MARBLED LOAVES
WITH ORANGE GLAZE

Prep: 25 minutes
Bake: 50 minutes

4 large eggs, separated
1½ cups sugar
1 cup butter or margarine,
      softened and divided
5 cups all-purpose flour,
      divided
1 teaspoon baking soda,
      divided
2 teaspoons cream of tartar,
      divided
½ cup milk
1 cup firmly packed brown sugar
½ cup molasses
1½ teaspoons ground allspice
1½ teaspoons ground cinnamon
1½ teaspoons ground nutmeg
½ cup buttermilk
Orange Glaze

• **Beat** egg whites and 1½ cups sugar at medium speed with an electric mixer about 3 minutes or until foamy; add ½ cup butter, beating until blended.
• **Combine** 2½ cups flour, ½ teaspoon baking soda, and 1 teaspoon cream of tartar; add to butter mixture alternately with milk, beginning and ending with flour mixture. Beat at low speed just until blended after each addition. Set batter aside.
• **Beat** egg yolks and brown sugar at medium speed with electric mixer.
• **Add** remaining ½ cup butter, beating until blended.
• **Stir** in ½ cup molasses.
• **Combine** remaining 2½ cups flour, remaining ½ teaspoon baking soda, remaining 1 teaspoon cream of tartar, and spices.
• **Add** to brown sugar mixture alternately with buttermilk, beginning and ending with flour mixture. Beat at low speed just until blended after each addition.
• **Drop** batters by spoonfuls, alternating dark and light next to each other, into 2 greased and floured 9- x 5-inch loafpans. Gently swirl light and dark batters together with a knife.
• **Bake** loaves at 350° for 45 to 50 minutes or until a wooden pick inserted in center comes out clean. Cool in pans on wire racks 10 minutes, and remove from pans to wire racks.
• **Drizzle** Orange Glaze over warm loaves; cool completely on wire racks. **Yield:** 2 loaves.

Orange Glaze

Prep: 5 minutes

1 cup powdered sugar
1 teaspoon grated orange rind
⅓ cup fresh orange juice
¼ teaspoon orange extract

• **Stir** together all ingredients until smooth. **Yield:** ⅔ cup.

Sharon McCullar
Shreveport, Louisiana

ORANGE-GLAZED
CORNISH HENS

Serve these savory, beautiful birds at a dinner party or as a change of pace for Thanksgiving.

Prep: 30 minutes
Bake: 1 hour and 30 minutes

6 (1½-pound) Cornish hens
1 teaspoon salt
1 teaspoon pepper
Sausage Stuffing
½ cup water
2 large eggs, lightly beaten
1 cup orange marmalade
¼ cup orange juice
3 tablespoons honey
1 tablespoon lemon juice
¼ teaspoon ground ginger
Garnishes: orange slices, fresh
      parsley sprigs

• **Rub** hens with salt and pepper; spoon 3 tablespoons Sausage Stuffing into each hen cavity. Tie legs together, if desired. Place hens on a rack in an aluminum foil-lined roasting pan.
• **Stir** ½ cup water and eggs into remaining stuffing, and spoon into a lightly greased 13- x 9-inch baking dish. Cover and set aside.
• **Stir** together orange marmalade, juice, and next 3 ingredients in a small saucepan. Cook mixture over medium heat, stirring constantly, 5 minutes or until orange marmalade is melted.
• **Bake** hens at 350° for 30 minutes; brush evenly with orange sauce, and bake 20 more minutes. Brush again with orange sauce, and cover loosely with aluminum foil.
• **Bake** Cornish hens and stuffing casserole 40 minutes, uncovering stuffing after 30 minutes. Garnish, if desired. **Yield:** 6 servings.

Sausage Stuffing

Prep: 15 minutes
Cook: 10 minutes

1 pound ground pork sausage
3 small onions, chopped
6 green onions, chopped
4 celery ribs, chopped
1 cup coarsely chopped walnuts,
      toasted
1 (8-ounce) package herb-
      seasoned stuffing mix
1 (16-ounce) package cornbread
      stuffing mix
1 cup dry white wine or chicken
      broth
2 (14½-ounce) cans chicken
      broth
2 teaspoons poultry seasoning
½ teaspoon salt

• **Cook** first 4 ingredients in a Dutch oven over medium-high heat, stirring until sausage crumbles and is no longer pink. Drain well; return to pan.
• **Stir** in walnuts and remaining ingredients. **Yield:** 12 cups.

H. W. Asbell
Tallahassee, Florida

ORANGE-APPLE TURNOVERS

Prep: 25 minutes
Bake: 10 minutes

4 small Granny Smith apples
1½ teaspoons grated orange rind,
     divided
2 tablespoons fresh orange juice,
     divided
3 tablespoons brown sugar
3 tablespoons butter or
     margarine
1 teaspoon ground cinnamon
1 (15-ounce) package refrigerated
     piecrusts
¼ cup powdered sugar

• **Peel** and chop apples. Combine apple, 1 teaspoon orange rind, 1 tablespoon orange juice, and next 3 ingredients in a medium saucepan.
• **Cook** over medium heat, stirring occasionally, 10 to 15 minutes or until apple is soft. Cool.
• **Unfold** piecrusts, and stack together on a lightly floured surface. Roll into a 14- x 9-inch rectangle; cut pastry into 8 equal rectangles.
• **Spoon** apple mixture evenly into centers of rectangles. Starting with a short side, fold dough over filling. Press edges with a fork to seal, and prick tops.
• **Place** turnovers on an aluminum foil-lined baking sheet.
• **Bake** at 450° for 10 minutes or until golden. Cool.
• **Stir** together powdered sugar, remaining ½ teaspoon grated orange rind, and remaining 1 tablespoon fresh orange juice. Drizzle over turnovers. **Yield:** 8 turnovers.

Charlotte Bryant
Greensburg, Kentucky

GRANDMOTHER'S GINGERBREAD GATHERING

For Gwyn Huffman Willbanks, grandson Trey's arrival in 1985 sparked a cherished tradition.

"As a grandmother, I wanted to begin the Christmas season by spending a day with family," says Gwyn.

From this wish has grown "Gingerbread Day," an annual event Gwyn hosts for cookie baking, storytelling, carol singing, and lots of hugs. It is without question Gwyn's favorite day of the year. The Willbanks grandchildren and grandnieces and nephews look forward each November to receiving their invitations to join Gwyn, affectionately known as "Ditty."

Gwyn says keeping things simple and focusing on enjoyment of time together are keys to a successful gathering. Here she shares her Gingerbread Men recipe.

GINGERBREAD MEN

Prep: 30 minutes
Bake: 12 minutes per batch

2¼ cups sugar
¾ cup water
⅓ cup dark corn syrup
1½ tablespoons ground ginger
1¼ tablespoons ground
     cinnamon
2 teaspoons ground cloves
1¼ cups butter or margarine
1 tablespoon baking soda
1 tablespoon water
6 cups all-purpose flour
Decorations: sugar crystals, red
     cinnamon candies, assorted
     decorator frosting tubes

• **Cook** first 6 ingredients in a medium saucepan over medium heat, stirring until sugar dissolves. Add butter, stirring until melted.
• **Combine** baking soda and 1 tablespoon water; stir into sugar mixture. Pour sugar mixture into a bowl, and gradually add flour, beating at medium speed with a heavy-duty electric mixer until blended.
• **Divide** dough into thirds. Roll one-third of dough to ⅛-inch thickness on a lightly floured surface. Cut with a 5½-inch gingerbread man cutter, and place on lightly greased baking sheets.
• **Bake** at 350° for 10 to 12 minutes. Cool 1 minute on pan; remove cookies to wire racks, and cool completely. Repeat procedure with remaining dough. Decorate as desired. **Yield:** 3 dozen.

Gwyn Huffman Willbanks
Pearland, Texas

GINGERBREAD JOY

With guidelines for her annual gingerbread afternoon, Gwyn encourages grandmothers everywhere to host a memorable cookie caper.

■ Invite children only for the baking activity. Parents appreciate having extra holiday shopping time alone. Ask parents to return for supper, songs, and show-and-tell of each child's handiwork.

■ Plan an activity or custom that can become part of each year's gathering. Gwyn adds a single wooden toy each year to a collection she began at her first gathering.

■ Measure and mix cookie ingredients before children arrive. Ask another adult to assist children with rolling, baking, and decorating cookies. Let children take turns in the kitchen.

■ Don't forget the focus of the season. Read the Christmas story. Ask youngsters to tell or reenact the story for their parents or help arrange figures in a nativity scene.

TOP-RATED CHEESECAKE

*Georgia Kinney of Greensboro, North Carolina, has
a passion for developing desserts. Her Praline-Crusted
Cheesecake is so exceptional, our Test Kitchens awarded
it our highest rating. Sample a buttery cookie-and-praline
crust beneath a dense, creamy filling.*

PRALINE-CRUSTED CHEESECAKE
(pictured on page 303)

*Prep: 38 minutes
Bake: 1 hour and 40 minutes
Chill: 8 hours*

2 cups crushed shortbread
   cookies (about 28 cookies)
3 tablespoons butter or margarine,
   melted
4 Pralines, coarsely crumbled
5 (8-ounce) packages cream
   cheese, softened
1¾ cups sugar
2 tablespoons all-purpose
   flour
1½ teaspoons vanilla
   extract
4 large eggs
2 egg yolks
⅓ cup whipping cream
1 teaspoon grated lemon rind
2 (8-ounce) containers sour
   cream
⅓ cup sugar
Garnish: crumbled Pralines

● **Combine** cookie crumbs and butter.
Press into bottom and up sides of a
greased 10-inch springform pan.
● **Bake** at 350° for 8 minutes. Cool on a
wire rack.
● **Sprinkle** 4 coarsely crumbled Pralines over crust.
● **Beat** cream cheese at medium speed
with a heavy-duty electric mixer until
creamy. Gradually add 1¾ cups sugar,
flour, and vanilla, beating until smooth.
● **Add** 4 eggs and 2 egg yolks, 1 at a time,
beating just until yellow disappears.
● **Stir** in whipping cream and grated
lemon rind. Pour into crust. Place springform pan on an aluminum foil-lined baking sheet.
● **Bake** at 350° on lower oven rack 10
minutes. Reduce oven temperature to
325,° and bake 1 hour and 20 minutes or
until almost set. Cool cheesecake on a
wire rack 1 hour.
● **Stir** together sour cream and ⅓ cup
sugar; spread over cheesecake.
● **Bake** at 325° for 10 minutes. Cool on a
wire rack. Cover and chill 8 hours. Remove sides of pan. Garnish, if desired.
Yield: 12 servings.

Pralines

*Prep: 20 minutes
Cook: 13 minutes*

Butter
¾ cup firmly packed light brown
   sugar
¾ cup sugar
¾ cup half-and-half
3 tablespoons butter or margarine
1¼ cups coarsely chopped pecans
½ teaspoon vanilla extract

● **Butter** bottom of a heavy 3-quart saucepan. Cook brown sugar and next 3 ingredients in saucepan over low heat, stirring
constantly, until sugars dissolve and butter melts. Stir in pecans. Bring to a boil
over medium heat; cook, stirring occasionally, 6 to 8 minutes or until a candy
thermometer registers 238° (soft ball
stage). Remove from heat.
● **Stir** in vanilla, and let stand 3 minutes.
Beat mixture with a wooden spoon 3
minutes or until mixture begins to
thicken. Working rapidly, drop by tablespoonfuls onto wax paper. Let stand
until firm. **Yield:** 1 dozen.

*Georgia Kinney
Greensboro, North Carolina*

CHEESECAKE TIPS

Reap the rewards of success by
following these tips for this recipe.

■ Use a 10-inch springform pan;
bake on a foil-lined baking sheet.

■ Before adding the sour cream
topping, let the cheesecake cool
1 hour.

■ To simplify this recipe, you can
substitute packaged pralines. If
you have a hard time finding them,
try this mail-order source: Aunt
Aggie De's Pralines, P.O. Box
27008, Austin, TX 78755; call toll-
free at 1-888-772-5463.

FROM OUR KITCHEN TO YOURS

BUTTER UP

The Land O' Lakes Holiday Bakeline shares the following facts about butter:

- Salted and unsalted butter are interchangeable in baking recipes.

- Butter absorbs odors easily. To prevent the transfer of odors to butter, place it in an airtight container in a separate compartment in the refrigerator.

- Use butter by the recommended date printed on the package, or freeze in airtight containers up to six months.

- Melting butter releases and enhances its unique flavor. Watch butter closely to ensure that it doesn't burn.

- To soften butter quickly, cut it into chunks and leave it at room temperature, or place the stick between two sheets of wax paper and hit with a rolling pin.

- Butter and margarine are both 80 percent fat, but butter's source of fat is pure cream. Margarine is made from oil.

- Butter and margarine both have 100 calories and 11 fat grams per tablespoon.

- Light butter is a good low-fat topping on vegetables or as a table spread, but it is not recommended for baking.

- It takes 21 pounds (10 quarts) of whole milk to make 1 pound of butter.

For additional baking tips and information, call the Bakeline; the toll-free number is 1-800-782-9606.

TIPS AND TIDBITS

Vie Warshaw of our Test Kitchens staff steams vegetables in gallon-size heavy-duty zip-top plastic bags in the microwave. She fills the bag and pierces it with a fork for vents. Baby carrots are perfectly done when cooked on HIGH for 4 minutes; broccoli and cauliflower are ready in 2 minutes. Try tossing the vegetables with a little butter for a quick side dish—and there's no steamer to clean.

Here's a tip from our Cooking School: Use flour-dusted plastic wrap or sandwich bags as "gloves" when working with sticky dough.

TURKEY POINTERS

Time, space, and the number you expect to feed will help you select the right turkey for your family feast. If you have room in your freezer, buy and store a frozen turkey. Plan to thaw the bird, unwrapped, in the refrigerator, allowing one day for every 5 pounds.

Or choose a fresh turkey. The never-frozen birds are available a week or so before the big day. Expect to pay about 20 cents more per pound for fresh, but the savings in time and space may make it your best buy.

To decide how large a turkey you need to buy, allow ¾ to 1 pound per person; if you want leftovers, allow 2 pounds per person.

Apple-Rosemary Roasted Turkey, in the Thanksgiving feast menu on page 252, gets its flavor from the inside out. Vanessa McNeil of our Test Kitchens used an internal-external stainless steel baster with injector needle to season the meat with apple juice and melted butter. Williams-Sonoma offers the baster-injector for $12; call 1-800-541-2233.

For more information and recipes, call the Reynolds Turkey Tips Line, open 24 hours a day from November 1 through December 31; the toll-free number is 1-800-745-4000.

CAN-DO CRANBERRIES

Jan Moon, another whiz from our Test Kitchens staff, created a delicious alternative for when you want the taste and texture of homemade cranberry sauce but don't have time. Start with a can of whole-berry cranberry sauce; stir in the zest of 1 lemon, 2 tablespoons fresh lemon juice, and a 3-inch piece of fresh ginger, grated.

DRESSING SPOONS

Dressings and stuffings have special spoons designed to serve them. The 8-inch-long handle gives neat and easy access to the delicious side dish stuffed inside the turkey.

Although old ornate spoons are not a necessity, they do add history and beauty to the holiday table. If you have one, pull it out and use it—whether your dressing is inside or outside the bird. The next time you're browsing antique shops be on the lookout for dressing spoons.

Don't worry if you can't find a dressing spoon in your particular silver pattern; serving pieces that have different patterns work well together.

Stuffed Tuscany Tenderloin and Snap Peas With Roasted Garlic Dressing served with creamy risotto, page 269

Cream of Leek Soup,
page 276

Crab Cakes, page 267

*(above) Pandy's Biscuits, page 277;
(below) Company Pork Roast and
Sunshine Carrots and Asparagus served
with rice pilaf, pages 276 and 277*

Sour Cream Pound Cake With
Raspberry Sauce, page 259

Mulled Cranberry
Cider, page 278

Cranberry-Apple Cobbler With
Cinnamon Biscuits, page 256

*Cracked Caramel-Pumpkin
Pie, page 254*

Praline-Crusted Cheesecake,
page 295

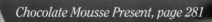
Chocolate Mousse Present, page 281

DECEMBER

Feast on 15 fabulous award-winning recipes in "Simply the Best," our third-annual Holiday Recipe Contest. From appetizers like Crab Cakes With Maui Sauce to sensational sweets like Fudge Truffle-Pecan Tart, each winner promises a delicious dish you'll want to add to your file of favorites. Your only dilemma should be which one you'll try first.

Traditional holiday layer cakes—fruit-filled Lane cake, rich Italian cream cake, and velvety chocolate cake—get a makeover in "Holiday Cakes in Less Time." These tempting desserts provide all of the made-from-scratch flavor of the originals but take half the time to prepare.

HOLIDAY CAKES IN LESS TIME

These simplified versions of holiday layer cakes blend the best of traditional flavors with the ease of cake mixes. The results are delicious desserts that take half the time to prepare.

HOLIDAY LANE CAKE
(pictured on cover)

Prep: 17 minutes
Bake: 20 minutes

1 (18.25-ounce) package white
    cake mix
3 large eggs
1¼ cups buttermilk
¼ cup vegetable oil
Nutty Fruit Filling
1 (7.2-ounce) package fluffy white
    frosting mix
½ cup boiling water
Holly Leaves
Assorted red candies
Fruit-shaped candies (optional)
Candy Bow
White sugar crystals

• **Beat** first 4 ingredients at medium speed with an electric mixer 2 minutes. Pour cake batter evenly into 3 greased and floured 8-inch round or square cakepans.
• **Bake** at 350° for 15 to 20 minutes or until a wooden pick inserted in center comes out clean. Cool in pans 10 minutes on wire racks. Remove from pans, and cool completely on wire racks.
• **Spread** Nutty Fruit Filling between layers. Set aside.
• **Beat** frosting mix and ½ cup boiling water at low speed with an electric mixer 30 seconds. Scrape down sides of bowl, and beat at high speed 5 to 7 minutes or until stiff peaks form.

• **Spread** frosting on top and sides of cake. Arrange Holly Leaves on cake to resemble a wreath. Arrange candies for berries; place Candy Bow on wreath. Sprinkle cake with sugar crystals. **Yield:** 1 (3-layer) cake.

Nutty Fruit Filling

Prep: 15 minutes
Cook: 12 minutes

½ cup butter or margarine
8 egg yolks
1 cup sugar
1 cup chopped pecans, toasted
1 cup chopped sweetened dried
    cranberries
1 cup flaked coconut
½ cup diced red or green candied
    cherries
⅓ cup orange juice

• **Melt** butter in a heavy saucepan over low heat. Whisk in egg yolks and sugar; cook, whisking constantly, 11 minutes or until mixture thickens. Stir in remaining ingredients. Cool. **Yield:** 3½ cups.

Holly Leaves

Prep: 20 minutes
Cook: 1 minute
Stand: 12 hours

1 (14-ounce) package green candy
    melts
⅓ cup light corn syrup

• **Microwave** candy in a microwave-safe bowl at MEDIUM (50% power), stirring once, 1 minute or until melted. Stir in corn syrup. Place in a zip-top plastic bag; seal and let stand 8 hours.
• **Knead** 2 to 3 minutes or until soft (about 12 times). Turn out onto a surface dusted with powdered sugar. Roll to 1/16-inch thickness.
• **Cut** with 1-inch and 2-inch holly leaf-shaped cutters. Score leaves with a knife. Place on wax paper and over sides of an inverted cakepan for a curved shape. Let stand 3 to 4 hours. Store in an airtight container up to 3 days, if desired. **Yield:** 8 dozen.

Candy Bow

Prep: 25 minutes
Cook: 1 minute
Stand: 8 hours and 30 minutes

1 (14-ounce) package red candy
    melts
⅓ cup light corn syrup

• **Microwave** candy in a microwave-safe bowl at MEDIUM (50% power), stirring once, 1 minute or until melted. Stir in corn syrup. Place in a zip-top plastic bag; seal and let stand 8 hours.
• **Knead** 2 to 3 minutes or until soft (about 12 times). Turn out onto a surface dusted with powdered sugar. Roll to 1/16-inch thickness.
• **Cut** into 6 (12- x ½-inch) strips and 1 (½-inch) square with a fluted pastry cutter. Place ends of 2 strips together to form loops. Shape each loop into a heart. Place tops of hearts together to form half of bow. Place ends of 2 strips together to form 2 more loops.
• **Place** each on top of bow half. Wrap ½-inch square around center of bow. Place bow on side of an inverted cakepan.
• **Place** ends of remaining 2 strips under center of bow. Shape into streamers, placing on sides of cakepan. Let dry at least 30 minutes. Store in an airtight container up to 3 days. **Yield:** 1 bow.

Note: For testing purposes only, we used M&M's and Skittles for assorted red candies. Swiss Petite Fruit may be added to wreath, if desired.

EASY PERFECT CHOCOLATE CAKE

Prep: 5 minutes
Bake: 25 minutes
Chill: 1 hour

1 (18.25-ounce) package devil's
    food cake mix with pudding
3 large eggs
1¼ cups water
½ cup vegetable oil
Whipped Cream Filling
Creamy Chocolate Frosting

• **Beat** first 4 ingredients at medium speed with an electric mixer 2 minutes. Pour batter into 2 greased and floured 9-inch round cakepans.
• **Bake** at 350° for 25 minutes or until a wooden pick inserted in center comes out clean. Cool in pans on wire racks 10 minutes; remove from pans, and cool completely on wire racks. Cover and chill 1 hour.
• **Spread** Whipped Cream Filling between layers. Spread Creamy Chocolate Frosting on top and sides of cake. Store in refrigerator. **Yield:** 1 (2-layer) cake.

Whipped Cream Filling

Prep: 5 minutes

1 cup whipping cream
¼ cup powdered sugar
1 teaspoon vanilla extract

• **Beat** all ingredients at medium speed with an electric mixer until stiff peaks form. **Yield:** about 2 cups.

Creamy Chocolate Frosting

Prep: 28 minutes
Cook: 5 minutes

1 cup (6 ounces) semisweet
    chocolate morsels
½ cup half-and-half
1 cup butter or margarine
2½ cups powdered sugar

• **Cook** first 3 ingredients in a heavy saucepan over medium heat, stirring until chocolate melts. Remove from heat; cool 15 minutes. Stir in sugar.

• **Place** pan in ice; beat at medium speed with an electric mixer about 8 minutes or until thickened and of spreading consistency. **Yield:** 3 cups.

QUICK ITALIAN CREAM CAKE

Prep: 10 minutes
Bake: 17 minutes
Chill: 2 hours

1 (18.5-ounce) package white cake
    mix with pudding
3 large eggs
1¼ cups buttermilk
¼ cup vegetable oil
1 (3½-ounce) can flaked coconut
⅔ cup chopped pecans, toasted
3 tablespoons rum (optional)
Cream Cheese Frosting

• **Beat** first 4 ingredients at medium speed with an electric mixer 2 minutes. Stir in coconut and pecans. Pour batter into 3 greased and floured 9-inch round cakepans.
• **Bake** at 350° for 15 to 17 minutes or until a wooden pick inserted in center comes out clean. Cool in pans on wire racks 10 minutes. Remove from pans, and cool completely on wire racks. Sprinkle layers evenly with rum, if desired; let stand 10 minutes.
• **Spread** frosting between layers and on top and sides of cake. Chill 2 hours before slicing. **Yield:** 1 (3-layer) cake.

Cream Cheese Frosting

Prep: 10 minutes

1 (8-ounce) package cream cheese,
    softened
½ cup butter or margarine,
    softened
1 (16-ounce) package powdered
    sugar
1 cup chopped pecans, toasted
2 teaspoons vanilla extract

• **Beat** cream cheese and butter at medium speed with an electric mixer until smooth. Gradually add powdered sugar, beating until light and fluffy. Stir in pecans and vanilla. **Yield:** 4 cups.

YOU SAY POTATO

Consider the spud, our most versatile vegetable, for your family's next casual meal. For easy entertaining, serve several toppings in a baked potato bar.

You'll savor the way these recipes make a meal that's wholesome but never humdrum.

CRAB-STUFFED POTATOES

This superior spud received our Test Kitchens' highest rating.

Prep: 10 minutes
Bake: 15 minutes

4 large baking potatoes, baked
½ cup butter or margarine
½ cup whipping cream
2 cups fresh crabmeat, drained and
    flaked
1 cup (4 ounces) shredded
    Cheddar cheese
1 tablespoon grated onion
1½ teaspoons salt
Paprika

• **Cut** a 1-inch-wide strip from top of each baked potato. Carefully scoop out pulp, leaving shells intact.
• **Mash** potato pulp with butter and whipping cream; stir in crabmeat and next 3 ingredients. Spoon evenly into shells, and place on a baking sheet. Sprinkle with paprika.
• **Bake** at 425° for 15 minutes. **Yield:** 4 servings.

Denise Bagnall
Ashland, Virginia

SHRIMP-AND-MUSHROOM STUFFED POTATOES

For a thrifty alternative to fresh shrimp, substitute a flaked mild fish.

Prep: 20 minutes
Bake: 20 minutes

1 pound peeled, small fresh shrimp
6 cups water
1 (3-ounce) package crawfish, shrimp, and crab boil-in-bag mix
8 large baking potatoes, baked
2 tablespoons butter or margarine
1 small onion, chopped
4 green onions, chopped
1¼ cups sliced fresh mushrooms
½ cup chopped green bell pepper
1¼ cups half-and-half
¾ cup (3 ounces) shredded Cheddar cheese, divided
¾ teaspoon salt
½ teaspoon coarsely ground pepper
¼ cup Italian-seasoned breadcrumbs
¼ cup grated Parmesan cheese

• **Devein** shrimp, if desired.
• **Bring** 6 cups water and boil-in-bag mix to a boil in a Dutch oven. Add shrimp; cook 3 minutes or just until shrimp turn pink. Drain and rinse with cold water.
• **Cut** a 1-inch-wide strip from top of each baked potato. Carefully scoop out pulp, leaving shells intact. Mash pulp.
• **Melt** butter in a large skillet over medium heat; add onion and next 3 ingredients, and sauté 5 minutes.
• **Add** half-and-half; cook, stirring often, 2 minutes. Stir in mashed potato pulp, shrimp, ½ cup Cheddar cheese, salt, and pepper. Spoon into shells, and place on a baking sheet.
• **Sprinkle** evenly with remaining ¼ cup Cheddar cheese, breadcrumbs, and Parmesan cheese.
• **Bake** at 350° for 20 minutes. **Yield:** 8 servings.

Betz Guice
Baton Rouge, Louisiana

BROCCOLI BAKERS

Prep: 10 minutes
Bake: 30 minutes

4 large baking potatoes, baked
¼ cup diced broccoli
½ cup (2 ounces) shredded Cheddar cheese
4 bacon slices, cooked and crumbled
2 green onions, chopped
½ cup sour cream
¼ cup milk
1 teaspoon salt

• **Cut** a 1-inch-wide strip from top of each baked potato. Carefully scoop out pulp, leaving shells intact.
• **Mash** pulp. Stir in remaining ingredients. Spoon into shells, and place on a baking sheet.
• **Bake,** covered, at 400° for 30 minutes. **Yield:** 4 servings.

Kristi Montero
Florence, Alabama

TATER TRICKS

■ Store potatoes in slightly raised bins in a cool, dark, well-ventilated place up to a week—never in a plastic bag or in the refrigerator.

■ Don't squander the skins! The cortex of the potato, just below the peel, holds one-third of its nutrients.

■ Always prick the skin before baking to avoid a dangerous buildup of steam.

■ Don't wrap baking potatoes in foil or they'll be soggy and steamed. Do oil the skin before baking for better flavor and appearance.

■ Boil potatoes for about 5 minutes before baking to cut the baking time in half.

CREAMY CHEESE-AND-CHIVE POTATOES

Experiment with a variety of flavored soft spreadable cheeses such as spinach or vegetable blends.

Prep: 25 minutes
Bake: 20 minutes

4 large baking potatoes, baked
2 tablespoons butter or margarine
1 shallot, chopped
2 garlic cloves, minced
3 tablespoons chopped fresh chives, divided
⅔ cup sour cream
1 (5.5-ounce) container garlic-and-herb soft spreadable cheese
1 teaspoon prepared horseradish
¼ teaspoon ground white pepper

• **Cut** a 1-inch-wide strip from top of each baked potato. Carefully scoop out pulp, leaving shells intact. Mash pulp.
• **Melt** butter in a small skillet over medium heat; add shallot and garlic, and sauté 2 minutes.
• **Stir** together potato pulp, shallot mixture, 1 tablespoon chives, and next 4 ingredients. Spoon into shells, and place on a baking sheet.
• **Bake** at 350° for 20 minutes. Sprinkle with remaining 2 tablespoons chives. **Yield:** 4 servings.

Note: For testing purposes only, we used Alouette Garlic et Herbes Gourmet Spreadable Cheese.

Miriam Baroga
Fircrest, Washington

Creamy Chive-and-Gorgonzola Stuffed Potatoes: Substitute 2 ounces crumbled Gorgonzola cheese for soft spreadable cheese; increase sour cream to 1 cup.

CHILDREN MAKE IT MAGICAL

Your entire family will find these nibbles hard to resist, especially when they're made with little hands. Big brothers and sisters can help measure ingredients or assist in a quick stir, if needed. Colorful bags and ribbons add a personal touch for gift-giving.

MAGIC REINDEER FOOD

Sprinkle some of this outside on Christmas Eve, and watch your children's faces when they see just crumbs left in the morning.

Prep: 17 minutes

2 (24-ounce) packages vanilla
   candy coating
3 cups mini pretzels
1 (12-ounce) can cocktail peanuts
1 (14.25-ounce) package frosted
   toasted oat O-shaped cereal
1 (12-ounce) package crisp rice
   cereal squares
1 (16-ounce) package holiday
   candy-coated chocolate pieces
Red and green sugars

• **Place** candy coating in a glass container, and microwave at HIGH 2½ minutes or until melted, stirring once.
• **Combine** pretzels and next 3 ingredients in a large bowl; add melted candy coating, tossing to coat.
• **Stir** in chocolate pieces. Spread mixture onto wax paper, and sprinkle with sugars. Let stand 30 minutes. Break into pieces. **Yield:** 25 cups.

Jackson Moon
Birmingham, Alabama

ELF BISCUITS

Prep: 10 minutes
Bake: 12 minutes

1 (5⅓-ounce) package graham
   crackers (1 sleeve crackers)
¾ cup butter or margarine
½ cup sugar
1 cup chopped pecans or almonds

• **Arrange** 11 whole crackers on an ungreased 15- x 10-inch jellyroll pan.
• **Bring** butter, sugar, and pecans to a boil in a medium saucepan; boil 2 minutes. Pour mixture on crackers, spreading quickly to cover.
• **Bake** at 300° for 12 minutes. Remove crackers to wax paper to cool. Cut biscuits with a knife along perforations. **Yield:** 44 biscuits.

RUDOLPH COOKIES

Prep: 45 minutes

4 (1-ounce) chocolate candy
   coating squares
96 pretzel sticks
1 (16-ounce) package peanut
   butter sandwich cookies
64 green, blue, or brown candy-
   coated chocolate pieces
32 red candy-coated chocolate
   pieces or red cinnamon
   candies

• **Microwave** chocolate candy coating in a small shallow glass dish at HIGH 3 minutes, stirring once.
• **Place** 2 pretzel sticks in peanut butter filling of each sandwich cookie, making large antlers. Break remaining pretzel sticks in half; place 1 half pretzel stick next to each longer pretzel stick, forming smaller antlers.
• **Dip** 1 side of green chocolate pieces in melted candy coating, and place on cookies for eyes. Dip 1 side of red chocolate pieces in candy coating; place on cookies for noses. **Yield:** 32 cookies.

Note: For testing purposes only, we used Nabisco brand Nutter Butter peanut butter sandwich cookies.

GOLDEN NORTH POLE NUGGETS

Prep: 5 minutes
Cook: 2 minutes and 30 seconds

1 (10-ounce) package peanut
   butter morsels
2 tablespoons shortening
1½ cups thin pretzel sticks
1 (6-ounce) package plain
   fish-shaped crackers

• **Combine** peanut butter morsels and shortening in a large glass bowl; microwave at HIGH 2½ minutes, stirring once. Gently stir in pretzel sticks and crackers.
• **Drop** mixture by tablespoonfuls onto wax paper. Let stand 30 minutes or until firm. **Yield:** 2 dozen.

SIMPLY THE BEST

Join us as we savor 15 award-winning recipes—dazzling to down-home—from our third-annual Holiday Recipe Contest.

GREAT BEGINNINGS

Open a festive evening with one of these sensational starters.

CRAB CAKES WITH MAUI SAUCE

Grand Prizewinner

Julie DeMatteo serves her stellar crab cakes as an appetizer or an entrée. "I created the crab cakes after enjoying an interesting Asian variation at a popular Northeast seafood eatery," says Julie. She then developed her own take on this seafood favorite.

Prep: 20 minutes
Cook: 12 minutes

8 ounces fresh lump crabmeat, drained
¼ cup soft breadcrumbs
2 tablespoons minced shallots
2 tablespoons minced fresh parsley
1 tablespoon minced fresh basil
2 tablespoons Dijon mustard
1 tablespoon lemon juice
1 teaspoon minced fresh ginger
1 teaspoon dark sesame oil
½ teaspoon salt
½ teaspoon coarsely ground pepper
1 large egg, lightly beaten
¼ cup butter or margarine, divided
6 cups loosely packed fresh spinach leaves
Maui Sauce

• **Stir** together first 12 ingredients, and shape into 12 patties.
• **Melt** 2 tablespoons butter in a large nonstick skillet over medium heat. Add crab cakes, and cook 5 minutes on each side or until golden. Remove from skillet, and keep warm.
• **Add** spinach to skillet, and sauté 1 to 2 minutes or until wilted. Stir in remaining 2 tablespoons butter.
• **Spoon** Maui Sauce onto 4 individual plates, and top evenly with crab cakes. Spoon spinach mixture around crab cakes. Serve immediately. **Yield:** 4 appetizer servings.

Maui Sauce

Prep: 5 minutes
Cook: 10 minutes

1 cup pineapple juice
¼ cup rice wine vinegar
1 teaspoon soy sauce
3 tablespoons mayonnaise

• **Bring** juice and vinegar to a boil in a small saucepan over medium-high heat. Boil 8 to 10 minutes or until mixture is reduced by half.
• **Stir** in soy sauce, and cool slightly.
• **Whisk** in mayonnaise until smooth. Serve warm. **Yield:** ¾ cup.

Julie DeMatteo
Clementon, New Jersey

TORTILLA SOUP

Runner-up

Prep: 20 minutes
Cook: 30 minutes

4 (6-inch) corn tortillas, cut into 1-inch pieces
1 large onion, chopped
4 to 6 garlic cloves, minced
2 tablespoons dried cilantro
3 tablespoons vegetable oil
2 cups chopped cooked chicken
2 quarts chicken broth
1 (14.5-ounce) can stewed tomatoes, undrained and chopped
1 (10-ounce) can diced tomatoes and green chiles
1 tablespoon ground cumin
1 bay leaf
½ teaspoon pepper
4 to 8 (6-inch) corn tortillas, cut into ¼-inch strips
½ cup vegetable oil
2 cups (8 ounces) shredded Monterey Jack or mozzarella cheese
Avocado slices (optional)

• **Sauté** first 4 ingredients in 3 tablespoons hot vegetable oil in a Dutch oven 5 minutes.
• **Add** chicken and next 6 ingredients. Bring to a boil; reduce heat, and simmer 30 minutes. Discard bay leaf.
• **Fry** tortilla strips in ½ cup hot oil in a large skillet until crisp. Drain on paper towels. Sprinkle fried strips and cheese over each serving. Top with avocado, if desired. **Yield:** 14 cups.

Susan Cearley
Tennyson, Texas

CHICKEN-AND-BRIE QUESADILLAS WITH CHIPOTLE SALSA

Runner-up

Prep: 15 minutes
Stand: 1 hour
Bake: 10 minutes

2   cups chopped plum tomato (about 8)
1   small onion, chopped
3   garlic cloves, minced
3   tablespoons fresh lime juice
2   teaspoons minced canned chipotle chiles in adobo sauce
½   teaspoon salt
5   green onions, minced and divided
½   cup chopped fresh cilantro, divided
1   cup finely chopped cooked chicken
1   (4.5-ounce) can diced green chiles, drained
8   (7-inch) flour tortillas
8   ounces Brie, trimmed and diced

• **Stir** together first 6 ingredients, ¼ cup green onions, and ¼ cup cilantro. Let salsa stand 1 hour.
• **Stir** together remaining green onions, remaining ¼ cup cilantro, chicken, and diced green chiles.
• **Arrange** 4 tortillas on a large baking sheet coated with vegetable cooking spray. Top evenly with cheese, chicken mixture, and remaining tortillas, pressing down slightly.
• **Bake** at 425° for 8 to 10 minutes or until cheese melts. Cut into wedges, and serve immediately with salsa. **Yield:** 12 appetizer servings.

Note: Freeze remaining chipotle chiles in adobo sauce, if desired.

Mary Lou Cook
Welches, Oregon

BY POPULAR DEMAND

Every family has its favorite holiday recipes—the solid traditions they look forward to sharing. Our top three Family Favorites offer a great start for creating new great-tasting traditions, both savory and sweet.

AMARETTO-WALNUT BROWNIES

Grand Prizewinner

"Soaking the walnuts in almond liqueur gives a distinctive flavor surprise," says Tina. "And instead of icing the brownies, I simply dust them with powdered sugar." Either way—plain or fancy— these fudgy squares are some of the best ever.

Soak: 6 hours
Prep: 15 minutes
Bake: 35 minutes

1   cup coarsely chopped walnuts, toasted
½   cup almond liqueur
1   cup butter
8   (1-ounce) unsweetened chocolate squares
5   large eggs
3⅓   cups sugar
¼   cup Swiss mocha instant coffee mix
1   tablespoon vanilla extract
1⅔   cups all-purpose flour
⅛   teaspoon salt

• **Soak** chopped walnuts in liqueur 4 to 6 hours. Drain, discarding liqueur.
• **Melt** butter and chocolate in a heavy saucepan over low heat. Beat eggs, sugar, and Swiss mocha mix at medium-high speed with an electric mixer 8 minutes. Gradually add chocolate mixture, beating at low speed until blended. Gradually add vanilla, flour, and salt, beating until blended. Stir in walnuts. Pour into a lightly greased foil-lined 13- x 9-inch pan.

• **Bake** at 350° for 30 to 35 minutes. Cool on a wire rack. Cut into squares. **Yield:** 15 brownies.

Note: For testing purposes only, we used International Coffees Suisse Mocha.

Tina Hoover
Olathe, Kansas

SAUSAGE, SPINACH, AND BEAN SOUP

Runner-up

Prep: 25 minutes
Cook: 25 minutes

8   ounces ground Italian sausage *
1   teaspoon olive oil
5   garlic cloves, minced
½   teaspoon dried crushed red pepper
2   (10-ounce) packages fresh spinach, torn
2   (15-ounce) cans cannellini beans, undrained
3   cups chicken broth
¼   cup unsalted butter
½   cup freshly shredded Parmesan cheese
2   plum tomatoes, diced
2   tablespoons chopped fresh parsley
¼   teaspoon salt
¼   teaspoon pepper

• **Brown** sausage in hot oil in a Dutch oven over medium-high heat 10 minutes, stirring until it crumbles and is no longer pink. Add garlic and red pepper; sauté 2 minutes. Add spinach; sauté 2 minutes or until wilted.
• **Stir** in beans, and cook 1 minute. Add broth, and bring to a boil. Add butter, cheese, tomato, and 1 tablespoon parsley. Cook until thoroughly heated. Stir in salt and pepper. Sprinkle servings evenly with remaining 1 tablespoon parsley. **Yield:** about 10 cups.

* Substitute 8 ounces Italian sausage, casings removed, for ground Italian sausage, if desired.

Alisa S. Decatur
Centreville, Virginia

ROSEMARY ROASTED TURKEY

Runner-up

Prep: 30 minutes
Bake: 4 hours

1 (14-pound) bone-in turkey
1 (¾-ounce) package fresh
 rosemary sprigs, divided
¼ cup salt
1 tablespoon pepper
1½ tablespoons paprika
2 tablespoons dried rosemary,
 crushed
11 garlic cloves, pressed
2 tablespoons grated lemon rind
 (4 large lemons)
2 large yellow onions, cut into
 1½-inch chunks
⅔ cup fresh lemon juice
¼ cup unsalted butter, melted
1 (750-milliliter) bottle white
 Zinfandel or dry white wine,
 divided
2 (12-inch) cheesecloth squares
1 cup orange juice

• **Remove** giblets and neck from turkey,
and discard. Rinse turkey with cold
water; pat dry. Loosen skin from turkey
breast without detaching it; carefully
place 2 rosemary sprigs under skin. Set
remaining rosemary sprigs aside.
• **Combine** salt and next 3 ingredients;
sprinkle turkey inside and out with mixture. Sprinkle garlic and lemon rind in
turkey cavity; stuff with onion and remaining rosemary sprigs.
• **Place** turkey, breast side up, in a large
shallow roasting pan, tucking wingtips
under. Pour lemon juice over turkey.
• **Stir** together butter and 1 cup wine in
a large bowl. Add cheesecloth; let stand
until liquid is absorbed. Place cheesecloth over turkey, covering entire bird.
• **Bake** at 325° for 30 minutes.
• **Add** remaining 2 cups wine and orange
juice to pan, and bake 3 hours and 30
minutes or until a meat thermometer inserted into thigh registers 180°, basting
every 30 minutes with pan juices.
Moisten cheesecloth with pan juices to
remove easily. Let stand 20 minutes before carving. **Yield:** 12 to 15 servings.

Faith Elliott
McKinney, Texas

EASYGOING ENTRÉES

Our One-Dish Entrée winners make it
possible for you to forget grand plans and
time-consuming menus in favor of sim-
pler, just-as-satisfying fare. Gear down
with any one of these top three recipes.

HEARTY TEX-MEX SQUASH-CHICKEN CASSEROLE

Grand Prizewinner

*This winning one-dish entrée
boasts a world of flavor and great
heritage. "I inherited my love of creating
new family-style dishes from both my
mother and grandmother, the 'queens
of substitution,'" Cathy says.*

Prep: 45 minutes
Bake: 35 minutes

1 (10-ounce) package frozen
 chopped spinach, thawed
3 medium-size yellow squash,
 thinly sliced
1 large red bell pepper, cut into
 ½-inch pieces
1 yellow onion, thinly sliced
2 tablespoons peanut oil
3 cups shredded cooked chicken or
 turkey
12 (6-inch) corn tortillas, cut into
 1-inch pieces
1 (10¾-ounce) can cream of celery
 soup, undiluted *
1 (8-ounce) container sour
 cream *
1 (8-ounce) jar picante sauce
1 (4.5-ounce) can chopped green
 chiles, undrained
1 (1.4-ounce) envelope fajita
 seasoning
2 cups (8 ounces) shredded sharp
 Cheddar cheese, divided *

• **Drain** spinach well, pressing between
paper towels to remove excess moisture.

• **Sauté** squash, bell pepper, and onion
in hot oil in a large skillet over medium-
high heat 6 minutes or until tender. Remove from heat.
• **Stir** in spinach, chicken, next 6 ingredients, and 1½ cups cheese. Spoon into
a lightly greased 13- x 9-inch baking dish.
• **Bake** at 350° for 30 minutes. Sprinkle
with remaining ½ cup cheese, and bake
5 more minutes. **Yield:** 6 to 8 servings.

* Substitute reduced-sodium, reduced-
fat cream of celery soup, light sour
cream, and reduced-fat sharp Cheddar
cheese, if desired.

Catherine D. Boettner
Charleston, Tennessee

SAVANNAH SEAFOOD PARMESAN

Runner-up

Prep: 45 minutes
Bake: 30 minutes

1 pound unpeeled, large fresh
 shrimp
1 cup water
½ cup butter or margarine
2 garlic cloves, minced
½ cup all-purpose flour
3 cups half-and-half
⅓ cup dry white wine or chicken
 broth
1 (8-ounce) bottle clam juice *
2 tablespoons cocktail sauce
¾ teaspoon Old Bay seasoning
½ teaspoon salt
¼ teaspoon pepper
1½ cups freshly grated Parmesan
 cheese, divided
1 cup fresh lump crabmeat,
 drained
1 (4-ounce) jar diced pimiento,
 undrained
2 teaspoons chopped fresh or
 ½ teaspoon dried thyme
16 ounces bow tie pasta, cooked

• **Peel** shrimp, reserving shells; devein
shrimp, if desired. Chill.
• **Bring** reserved shrimp shells and 1
cup water to a boil in a medium saucepan; reduce heat, and simmer, uncovered, 2 minutes.

- **Pour** stock through a wire-mesh strainer into a measuring cup, discarding shells.
- **Melt** butter in saucepan over medium heat; add garlic, and sauté 2 minutes.
- **Whisk** in flour until smooth.
- **Cook,** whisking constantly, 1 minute. Gradually whisk in shrimp stock and half-and-half until smooth.
- **Add** wine, clam juice, and next 4 ingredients to pan.
- **Cook,** whisking constantly, 5 minutes or until thickened and bubbly.
- **Stir** in shrimp, ¾ cup cheese, and next 3 ingredients.
- **Combine** sauce and pasta, tossing to coat. Spoon into a lightly greased 13- x 9-inch baking dish, and sprinkle with remaining ¾ cup cheese.
- **Bake** at 350° for 25 to 30 minutes or until bubbly. **Yield:** 8 to 10 servings.

* Substitute ¾ cup chicken broth for clam juice, if desired.

Mary Louise Lever
Rome, Georgia

APPLE-BACON STUFFED CHICKEN BREASTS

Runner-up

Prep: 14 minutes
Cook: 20 minutes

2 bacon slices, diced
½ cup peeled, chopped Granny Smith apple
½ cup dried cranberries, divided
1 tablespoon fine, dry breadcrumbs
½ teaspoon poultry seasoning
½ teaspoon ground cinnamon
4 skinned and boned chicken breast halves
2 tablespoons butter or margarine
1 cup apple juice
2 tablespoons apple brandy or apple juice
¼ teaspoon salt
2 teaspoons cornstarch
1 tablespoon water
¼ cup coarsely chopped pecans
2 tablespoons chopped fresh parsley

- **Cook** bacon in a large skillet over medium heat until crisp; remove bacon, reserving 1 tablespoon bacon drippings in skillet.
- **Sauté** chopped apple in reserved drippings over medium-high heat 4 minutes. Remove from heat.
- **Stir** in bacon, ¼ cup cranberries, and next 3 ingredients.
- **Cut** a 3½-inch-long horizontal slit through thickest portion of each chicken breast half, cutting to, but not through, other side, forming a pocket. Stuff apple mixture evenly into each pocket. Wipe skillet clean.
- **Melt** butter in skillet over medium heat. Add chicken.
- **Cook** chicken 8 to 10 minutes on each side or until done. Remove chicken, and keep warm.
- **Add** remaining ¼ cup cranberries, apple juice, apple brandy, and salt to skillet. Stir together cornstarch and 1 tablespoon water until smooth; stir into juice mixture.
- **Cook,** stirring constantly, 1 minute or until thickened.
- **Spoon** sauce over chicken; sprinkle chicken with pecans and parsley. **Yield:** 4 servings.

Priscilla Yee
Concord, California

ALL-STAR SIDE DISHES

"Vegetables often get overlooked during menu planning," says Grand Prizewinner Helen Wolt. "For a truly memorable meal, I try to serve a vegetable dish that carries its own weight with the other dishes I'll be serving."

Helen's recipe for Savory Spinach-Gorgonzola Custards will become a new holiday favorite, as will the other two side-dish winners: Divine Macaroni and Cheese and Potato-Horseradish Gratin With Caramelized Onions.

SAVORY SPINACH-GORGONZOLA CUSTARDS

Grand Prizewinner

These custards hold their own on a plate with roast beef, turkey, or pork. "If you prefer a single casserole, try baking the mixture in a square baking dish instead of individual custard cups," says Helen.

Prep: 40 minutes
Bake: 40 minutes

½ cup frozen chopped spinach, thawed
1 tablespoon butter or margarine
1 tablespoon olive oil
2 large onions, cut in half and thinly sliced
2 teaspoons brown sugar
5 ounces crumbled Gorgonzola cheese (about ⅔ cup) *
3 large eggs
1½ cups half-and-half
¼ teaspoon salt
¼ teaspoon ground nutmeg
⅛ teaspoon pepper

- **Drain** spinach well, pressing between paper towels to remove excess moisture.
- **Melt** butter in a large skillet over medium heat; add oil and onion, and sauté 5 minutes.
- **Stir** in sugar; cook, stirring occasionally, 20 minutes or until onion is caramel colored. Reserve ¼ cup onion. Spoon remaining onion into 6 lightly greased 6-ounce custard cups; sprinkle with cheese.
- **Whisk** together eggs and next 4 ingredients until blended. Stir in spinach. Spoon evenly over cheese; place custard cups in a 13- x 9-inch pan. Add hot water to pan to a depth of 1 inch.
- **Bake** at 350° for 30 to 40 minutes or until almost set. Remove cups from pan. Let stand 10 minutes; unmold and top with reserved onion. **Yield:** 6 servings.

* Substitute 1 (4-ounce) package crumbled blue cheese, if desired.

Note: Savory Spinach-Gorgonzola may be baked in a lightly greased 9-inch square baking dish.

Helen Wolt
Colorado Springs, Colorado

DIVINE MACARONI AND CHEESE

Runner-up

Prep: 30 minutes
Bake: 27 minutes

2 tablespoons butter or margarine
2 garlic cloves, pressed
1½ cups milk
1 cup shredded Parmesan cheese, divided
1 (8-ounce) package cream cheese, softened
1 (8-ounce) package mascarpone cheese
1 (4-ounce) package crumbled Gorgonzola cheese
1 teaspoon salt
1 teaspoon ground white pepper
¼ teaspoon ground nutmeg
1 (10-ounce) package frozen chopped spinach, thawed and well drained (optional)
16 ounces penne pasta, cooked
1 cup soft breadcrumbs

• **Melt** butter in a Dutch oven over medium heat; add garlic, and sauté until tender.
• **Add** milk, and cook until thoroughly heated. Gradually stir in ½ cup Parmesan cheese and next 6 ingredients until smooth.
• **Stir** in spinach, if desired. Add pasta, tossing to coat; spoon into a lightly greased 13- x 9-inch baking dish.
• **Bake** at 400° for 7 minutes. Remove from oven; sprinkle with remaining ½ cup Parmesan cheese and breadcrumbs. Reduce oven temperature to 350°.
• **Bake** at 350° for 20 minutes. **Yield:** 8 servings.

Raleigh McDonald Hussung
Brentwood, Tennessee

POTATO-HORSERADISH GRATIN WITH CARAMELIZED ONIONS

Runner-up

Prep: 1 hour and 25 minutes
Bake: 1 hour and 10 minutes

2½ pounds medium baking potatoes
1 teaspoon salt, divided
1 teaspoon pepper, divided
2 cups half-and-half
½ cup cream-style horseradish
¼ cup butter or margarine
2 large onions, thinly sliced
1 teaspoon sugar
1 tablespoon balsamic vinegar
1 cup (4 ounces) shredded Swiss cheese
¼ cup chopped fresh parsley, divided

• **Cook** potatoes in boiling water to cover 20 minutes or until almost tender. Drain and cool slightly.
• **Peel** potatoes, and cut into ¼-inch-thick slices.
• **Arrange** potato slices in a lightly greased 13- x 9-inch baking dish. Sprinkle with ½ teaspoon salt and ½ teaspoon pepper.
• **Stir** together half-and-half and horseradish, and pour over potato.
• **Bake,** covered, at 400° for 40 minutes.
• **Melt** butter in a large skillet over medium heat.
• **Add** onion, remaining ½ teaspoon salt, and remaining ½ teaspoon pepper; cook, stirring occasionally, 20 minutes.
• **Add** sugar, and cook, stirring occasionally, 5 to 8 minutes or until onion is caramel colored.
• **Stir** in vinegar, and cook 2 minutes or until liquid evaporates. Remove from heat, and cool 5 minutes. Fold in cheese and 2 tablespoons parsley.
• **Uncover** potato; top with onion mixture. Reduce oven temperature to 350°.
• **Bake** at 350° for 30 minutes. Let stand 5 minutes, and sprinkle gratin with remaining 2 tablespoons parsley. **Yield:** 8 servings.

Gilda Lester
Wilmington, North Carolina

SWEET REWARDS

Desserts hold honored places as centerpieces at a holiday feast. Serve these top-notch confections as part of your celebration.

FIG CAKE

Grand Prizewinner

"Fig Cake's snowy icing and spicy flavor make it a perfect choice for the holidays. The fig preserves add a sweet moistness," says Susan.

Prep: 20 minutes
Bake: 40 minutes

3 large eggs
1 cup sugar
1 cup vegetable oil
½ cup buttermilk
1 teaspoon vanilla extract
2 cups all-purpose flour
1 teaspoon baking soda
1 teaspoon salt
1 teaspoon ground cinnamon
½ teaspoon ground cloves
½ teaspoon ground nutmeg
1½ cups fig preserves
½ cup applesauce
1 cup chopped pecans, toasted
Cream Cheese Frosting

• **Beat** first 3 ingredients at medium speed with an electric mixer until blended. Add buttermilk and vanilla, beating well.
• **Combine** flour and next 5 ingredients; gradually add to buttermilk mixture, beating until blended.
• **Fold** in fig preserves, applesauce, and pecans. (Batter will be thin.) Pour batter into 2 greased and floured 8-inch round cakepans.
• **Bake** at 350° for 35 to 40 minutes or until a wooden pick inserted in center comes out clean. Cool on wire racks 10 minutes; remove from pans, and cool completely on wire racks.

- **Spread** Cream Cheese Frosting between layers and on top and sides of cake. Store in refrigerator. **Yield:** 1 (2-layer) cake.

Cream Cheese Frosting

Prep: 5 minutes

1½ (8-ounce) packages cream cheese, softened
5 tablespoons butter, softened
2 teaspoons vanilla extract
2 cups powdered sugar

- **Beat** cream cheese, butter, and vanilla at medium speed with an electric mixer until smooth. Gradually add powdered sugar, beating at low speed just until blended. (Do not overbeat, or frosting will be too thin.) **Yield:** about 3½ cups.

Note: For testing purposes only, we used Braswell's Pure Fig Preserves. Coarsely chop figs, if necessary.

Susan Conley
Natchez, Mississippi

TOASTED ALMOND-BUTTER CAKE

Runner-up

Prep: 25 minutes
Bake: 22 minutes

½ cup butter or margarine, softened
½ cup shortening
2 cups sugar
5 large eggs, separated
2¼ cups all-purpose flour
1¼ teaspoons baking soda
1 cup plus 2 tablespoons buttermilk
1 teaspoon almond extract
½ teaspoon vanilla extract
½ teaspoon butter flavoring
1 cup flaked coconut
1 cup slivered almonds, toasted and chopped
Cream Cheese Frosting
½ cup slivered almonds, toasted (optional)

- **Beat** butter and shortening at medium speed with an electric mixer until creamy. Gradually add sugar, beating well. Beat in egg yolks, 1 at a time.
- **Combine** flour and baking soda; add to butter mixture alternately with buttermilk, beginning and ending with flour mixture. Beat at low speed until blended after each addition.
- **Stir** in flavorings, flaked coconut, and chopped almonds.
- **Beat** egg whites at high speed with electric mixer until stiff peaks form; fold into batter.
- **Pour** into 3 greased and floured 9-inch round cakepans.
- **Bake** at 350° for 20 to 22 minutes or until a wooden pick inserted in center comes out clean.
- **Cool** cake layers in pans on wire racks 10 minutes; remove from pans, and cool on wire racks.
- **Spread** Cream Cheese Frosting between layers and on top and sides of cake. Sprinkle with ½ cup slivered almonds, if desired. **Yield:** 1 (3-layer) cake.

Cream Cheese Frosting

Prep: 5 minutes

1 (8-ounce) package cream cheese, softened
½ cup butter or margarine
6 cups powdered sugar
1 teaspoon vanilla extract

- **Beat** cream cheese and butter at medium speed with an electric mixer until creamy; gradually add powdered sugar, beating until blended. Stir in vanilla. **Yield:** 4 cups.

Mrs. Roby Love
Siloam, North Carolina

FUDGE TRUFFLE-PECAN TART

Runner-up

Prep: 10 minutes
Bake: 20 minutes

½ cup butter or margarine, softened
¾ cup firmly packed light brown sugar
3 large eggs
2 cups (12 ounces) semisweet chocolate morsels, melted
2 teaspoons vanilla extract, divided
½ cup all-purpose flour
1 cup finely chopped pecans
2 teaspoons instant coffee granules
Chocolate Tart Shell
2 cups whipping cream
¼ cup sugar

- **Beat** butter and brown sugar at medium speed with an electric mixer until blended; add eggs, beating well. Stir in melted chocolate, 1 teaspoon vanilla, and next 3 ingredients. Pour into Chocolate Tart Shell.
- **Bake** at 375° for 20 minutes. Cool on a wire rack 30 minutes.
- **Beat** whipping cream at high speed until foamy; gradually add ¼ cup sugar, beating until soft peaks form. Stir in remaining 1 teaspoon vanilla. Serve with warm tart. **Yield:** 1 (10-inch) tart.

Chocolate Tart Shell

Prep: 5 minutes
Bake: 6 minutes

1¼ cups chocolate graham cracker crumbs
⅓ cup butter or margarine, melted

- **Combine** both ingredients; press into bottom of a 10-inch tart pan.
- **Bake** at 350° for 6 minutes. Cool on a wire rack. **Yield:** 1 (10-inch) tart shell.

Note: For testing purposes only, we used Nabisco Honey Maid Chocolate Graham Crackers.

Mari G. Chandler
Anniston, Alabama

POTLUCK GATHERINGS

Potluck suppers allow more time for fellowship because everyone shares the responsibilities. Prepare dishes that can be made ahead and heated before serving. Add your own touch by placing food on an attractive serving platter and enhancing it with a garnish—and remember to bring serving pieces.

WILD RICE-AND-ROASTED VEGETABLE SALAD

Prep: 25 minutes
Cook: 1 hour
Bake: 30 minutes

2 cups vegetable broth
½ cup uncooked wild rice, rinsed
½ cup bulgur wheat
1 cup boiling water
1 pound fresh asparagus
1 bunch green onions
1 small yellow bell pepper
1 small red bell pepper
2 medium carrots
2 tablespoons olive oil
Dressing

● **Bring** broth to a boil in a medium saucepan.
● **Stir** in wild rice. Cover, reduce heat, and simmer 1 hour or until rice is tender. Drain rice, reserving ¼ cup broth for Dressing.
● **Soak** bulgur in 1 cup boiling water 45 minutes; drain.
● **Snap** off tough ends of asparagus. Cut asparagus and green onions into 1-inch pieces; cut bell peppers and carrots into thin strips.
● **Toss** vegetables with olive oil; spread vegetables evenly into a 15- x 10-inch jellyroll pan.
● **Bake** at 450° for 30 minutes.
● **Toss** together roasted vegetables, wild rice, bulgur, and Dressing. Serve warm or cold. **Yield:** 8 to 10 servings.

Dressing

Prep: 5 minutes

¼ cup reserved vegetable broth
¼ cup balsamic vinegar
¼ cup olive oil
1 teaspoon Dijon mustard
½ to 1 teaspoon salt
¼ teaspoon pepper

● **Whisk** together all ingredients. Cover and chill, if desired. **Yield:** ¾ cup.

Joan H. Ranzini
Waynesboro, Virginia

SEASONED CHICKEN

Prep: 10 minutes
Bake: 35 minutes

2 cups cornflakes cereal, crushed
¾ cup grated Parmesan cheese
1 (0.4-ounce) envelope buttermilk Ranch-style dressing mix
6 skinned and boned chicken breast halves
¼ cup butter or margarine, melted

● **Stir** together first 3 ingredients in a shallow dish. Dip chicken in butter; dredge in cornflake mixture. Place in a lightly greased 13- x 9-inch baking dish.
● **Bake** at 350° for 30 to 35 minutes or until done. **Yield:** 6 servings.

Sandra Barnett
Hoover, Alabama

CRANBERRY SALSA

Store tightly wrapped unpeeled ginger in the freezer up to six months.

Prep: 10 minutes
Chill: 1 hour

1 (15-ounce) can pineapple tidbits
½ cup diced fresh cranberries
3 green onions, diced
¼ cup diced dates
1½ tablespoons honey
1 teaspoon lemon juice
1¼ teaspoons minced fresh ginger
¼ teaspoon ground red pepper (optional)

● **Stir** together first 7 ingredients and, if desired, pepper. Cover and chill at least 1 hour. Serve with ham or turkey. **Yield:** 1½ cups.

Clark Huey
Altus, Oklahoma

POTLUCK REMINDERS

■ Know the food preferences of your group. It's helpful to tell people in advance what you would like for them to bring.

■ Place entrées and side dishes apart from desserts and beverages for easier serving.

■ To ensure that the lines flow smoothly, allow ample room on both sides of the table.

■ If your serving dishes aren't disposable, put your name on the bottom with freezer tape and a marking pen.

■ Ask for volunteers to help clean up. Extra hands can work in record speed.

WARM WINTER SOUPS

Bone-chilling cold calls for rib-sticking soup. It's just the thing to thaw that wintery chill. These hearty soups are simple to make using timesaving canned and frozen foods. Just add crusty bread, a leafy salad, and you've got the makings for a satisfying meal.

To remove fat and improve flavor, make soups and stews a day ahead and chill overnight. Allow fat to congeal; then simply skim it off the top.

SPINACH-TORTELLINI SOUP

Prep: 10 minutes
Cook: 20 minutes

1 (14½-ounce) can chicken broth
4 cups water
2 extra-large vegetable bouillon cubes
1 (10-ounce) package frozen chopped spinach, unthawed
2 (14½-ounce) cans stewed tomatoes, undrained
1 garlic clove, minced
2 (9-ounce) packages refrigerated cheese-filled tortellini
½ cup (2 ounces) refrigerated shredded Parmesan cheese

● **Bring** first 3 ingredients to a boil in a Dutch oven over medium-high heat.
● **Add** spinach, tomatoes, and garlic; return to a boil.
● **Stir** in tortellini, and cook 5 minutes. Sprinkle each serving with cheese. **Yield:** 16 cups.

Note: For testing purposes only, we used Knorr Vegetable Bouillon Cubes.

Lauren Wedewer
Jacksonville, Florida

CHILLY NIGHT CHILI

Serve your favorite cornbread or cornsticks with this hearty cold-weather chili.

Prep: 15 minutes
Cook: 45 minutes

2 pounds lean ground beef
1 large onion, diced
1 (28-ounce) can diced tomatoes, undrained
2 (8-ounce) cans tomato puree
2 (16-ounce) cans kidney beans, undrained
1 (4.5-ounce) can chopped green chiles
1 cup water
2 garlic cloves, minced
2 tablespoons chili powder
2 teaspoons salt
2 teaspoons ground cumin
1 teaspoon pepper
Hot cooked rice
Toppings: shredded Cheddar cheese, sour cream, sliced ripe olives

● **Cook** ground beef and onion in a Dutch oven over medium-high heat, stirring until beef crumbles and is no longer pink. Drain beef mixture, and return to Dutch oven.
● **Add** tomatoes and next 9 ingredients to Dutch oven.
● **Bring** chili mixture to a boil; reduce heat, and simmer 45 minutes. Serve over rice with desired toppings. **Yield:** 8 to 10 servings.

Joy Kloess
Birmingham, Alabama

POLISH SAUSAGE SOUP

Kielbasa is a smoked sausage sold in links—it is also known as Polish sausage.

Prep: 10 minutes
Cook: 35 minutes

1 (16-ounce) package kielbasa sausage, cut into ¼-inch-thick slices
2 (15-ounce) cans kidney beans, undrained
2 (14½-ounce) cans chicken broth
1 (15-ounce) can tomato sauce
1 (14½-ounce) can diced tomatoes, undrained
1 (24-ounce) jar picante sauce
2 (4.5-ounce) cans sliced mushrooms, drained
1 small head cabbage, shredded
1 medium onion, chopped
1 medium-size green bell pepper, chopped
1½ teaspoons chili powder

● **Brown** sausage in a Dutch oven over medium-high heat; drain on paper towels, and wipe Dutch oven clean with a paper towel. Return browned sausage to Dutch oven.
● **Add** beans and remaining ingredients to Dutch oven.
● **Bring** sausage mixture to a boil; reduce heat, and simmer 30 minutes. **Yield:** 20 cups.

Lilann Hunter Taylor
Savannah, Georgia

CALL ON CAULIFLOWER

Although cauliflower is available year-round, fall and winter are its peak seasons. Look for white or creamy colored heads with tight, firm flowerets. Once purchased, the vegetable will keep in the refrigerator up to one week.

CHEDDAR CAULIFLOWER

Prep: 25 minutes
Cook: 30 minutes

1 cauliflower, broken into
   flowerets
3 tablespoons butter or
   margarine
3 tablespoons all-purpose
   flour
1½ cups milk
⅔ cup (2.6 ounces) shredded
   Cheddar cheese
1 tablespoon chopped pimiento
1 teaspoon salt
¼ teaspoon celery salt
¼ teaspoon pepper
1 (3½-ounce) can French-fried
   onions, crushed and divided

• **Arrange** cauliflower in a steamer basket over boiling water. Cover and steam 10 minutes or until crisp-tender. Place in a lightly greased 2-quart baking dish.
• **Melt** butter in a heavy saucepan over low heat; whisk in flour, whisking until smooth.
• **Cook,** whisking constantly, 1 minute. Gradually whisk in milk; cook over medium heat, whisking constantly, until thickened and bubbly. Add cheese and next 4 ingredients, stirring until cheese melts. Stir in 1½ cups crushed onions, and pour mixture over cauliflower.
• **Bake** at 350° for 25 minutes. Sprinkle with remaining crushed onions, and bake 5 more minutes. **Yield:** 6 servings.

Kay C. Cooper
Madison, Alabama

CRUNCHY CAULIFLOWER SURPRISE

Prep: 15 minutes
Bake: 25 minutes

1 large cauliflower, broken into
   flowerets
1 (10¾-ounce) can cream of
   chicken soup, undiluted
1 (8-ounce) container sour cream
¼ teaspoon pepper
1 celery rib, diced
½ small onion, diced
1 cup (4 ounces) shredded sharp
   Cheddar cheese
1 (5-ounce) can chunk chicken in
   water, rinsed and drained
   (optional)
1 (5½-ounce) package Cheddar-
   and-sour cream potato chips,
   crushed (about 2 cups)

• **Cook** cauliflower in boiling water to cover 10 minutes or until crisp-tender; drain.
• **Stir** together soup, sour cream, and pepper in a large bowl. Stir in cauliflower flowerets, celery, onion, shredded cheese, and, if desired, chicken.
• **Spoon** mixture into a lightly greased 13- x 9-inch baking dish. Sprinkle with potato chips.
• **Bake** at 350° for 25 minutes. **Yield:** 8 servings.

Note: For testing purposes only, we used Ruffles Cheddar and Sour Cream Potato Chips.

Teresa Hubbard
Russellville, Alabama

OVEN-FRIED CAULIFLOWER

Prep: 15 minutes
Bake: 1 hour

1 cup light mayonnaise
1 medium cauliflower, broken into
   flowerets
1 cup Italian-seasoned
   breadcrumbs

• **Place** mayonnaise in a large heavy-duty zip-top plastic bag. Add cauliflower; seal and shake to coat.
• **Place** breadcrumbs in a large heavy-duty zip-top plastic bag.
• **Add** half of cauliflower mixture; seal and shake to coat. Spread in a single layer onto a lightly greased baking sheet. Repeat with remaining cauliflower mixture and breadcrumbs.
• **Bake** cauliflower at 350° for 1 hour. **Yield:** 8 servings.

Geri Lucas
Greensboro, North Carolina

CAULIFLOWER SOUP

Prep: 30 minutes
Cook: 8 minutes

2 cups cauliflower flowerets
4 celery ribs, diced
3 carrots, chopped
1 (10¾-ounce) can cream of
   chicken soup, undiluted
1 cup milk
4 ounces pasteurized prepared
   cheese product, cubed
¼ teaspoon salt
¼ to ½ teaspoon pepper
Paprika

• **Arrange** cauliflower, celery, and carrot in a steamer basket over boiling water. Cover and steam 10 minutes or until crisp-tender; drain.
• **Cook** soup and milk in a large saucepan over medium heat, stirring occasionally, 5 minutes. Stir in cheese until melted. Add vegetables, salt, and pepper; cook until thoroughly heated. Sprinkle with paprika. **Yield:** 4 cups.

Irma Fleming
Village Mills, Texas

FLAVORFUL MEMORIES

Storyteller and author Lorraine Johnson-Coleman of Savannah pays tribute to members of her family and community and keeps family history alive through stories of food and fun. Here she shares recipes for tea cakes and for green beans.

OLD-FASHIONED TEA CAKES

Prep: 15 minutes
Chill: 1 hour
Bake: 8 minutes per batch

½ cup butter, softened
1 cup sugar
2 large eggs
2½ cups all-purpose flour
2 teaspoons baking powder
½ teaspoon ground nutmeg
1 tablespoon milk

• **Beat** butter at medium speed with an electric mixer until creamy; gradually add sugar, beating well.
• **Add** eggs, beating until blended.
• **Combine** flour, baking powder, and nutmeg; add to butter mixture alternately with milk, beginning and ending with flour mixture. Beat at low speed just until blended after each addition.
• **Divide** dough in half; cover with plastic wrap, and chill 1 hour.
• **Roll** half of dough to ¼-inch thickness on a lightly floured surface. Cut with a 2¼-inch round cutter, and place on greased baking sheets. Repeat procedure with remaining half of dough.
• **Bake** at 350° for 8 minutes. (Cookies will be pale.) Cool on wire racks. **Yield:** 3½ dozen.

Lorraine Johnson-Coleman
Savannah, Georgia

LORRAINE'S GREEN BEANS

Prep: 20 minutes
Cook: 1 hour and 15 minutes

5 cups water
1 (14½-ounce) can chicken broth
2 smoked turkey wings (1½ pounds)
1 small onion, minced
2 teaspoons salt
½ teaspoon pepper
⅛ teaspoon baking soda
3 pounds fresh green beans, trimmed

• **Bring** first 7 ingredients to a boil in a Dutch oven; cover and boil 30 minutes.
• **Add** beans; return to a boil. Cover, reduce heat, and simmer 30 to 45 minutes or until tender. **Yield:** 8 servings.

Lorraine Johnson-Coleman
Savannah, Georgia

LORRAINE'S WORDS

Lorraine's storytelling is favorite holiday entertainment for her children. Here is one of her stories about learning to cook.

Aunt Maribelle never taught me how to cook collard greens. So I took some initiative and fixed them myself for Thanksgiving (one year when I was too young to know any better). Don't you want to give me points for bravery?

I'd been eating a lot of salad that year and mistakenly assumed that cleaning one green leaf was just like cleaning any other. What I didn't know was while you can just rinse lettuce, you've got to scrub collards or they remain as gritty as the dirt outside. Enthusiastic but ignorant, I seasoned and cooked a big pot of dirty greens.

Of course Aunt Maribelle was the first person to sit at the table to sample the offerings. After one taste, she frowned and said, "Girl, all this sand in here is like having dinner on the beach!"

While I'm a really good cook now, I've never been allowed to cook anything else for the big family gatherings. I'm relegated to cleaning the fish. . . .Little did Aunt Maribelle know I'd watched and paid attention to her every move in the kitchen for years. I can do wonderful things with fresh vegetables.

We love green beans—the way they tasted years ago in Farmville, North Carolina—so I serve them often. I use smoked turkey wings instead of ham hocks or salt pork, since we're trying to do healthier cooking. Try this simple recipe [Lorraine's Green Beans] for a taste of the good ole days.

OUT OF THE SHELL

The old adage to avoid oysters during months spelled without an "R" comes from the fact that oysters spawn during those warm months. While soft and less flavorful then, they're safe to eat. But in fall and winter, oysters are plump, firm, and full of flavor. Now's the time to serve oysters.

OYSTER BISQUE

Prep: 10 minutes
Cook: 23 minutes

2 pints fresh oysters, undrained
¼ cup butter or margarine
1 medium-size green bell pepper, chopped
1 medium onion, chopped
1 (8-ounce) package sliced fresh mushrooms
¼ cup all-purpose flour
1 teaspoon salt
1 teaspoon pepper
⅛ teaspoon ground nutmeg
⅛ teaspoon paprika
2 cups whipping cream
¼ cup dry white wine or
    2 tablespoons dry sherry
Oyster crackers

• **Drain** oysters, reserving 1 cup liquid. Set oysters and liquid aside.
• **Melt** butter in a Dutch oven over medium-high heat; add bell pepper and onion, and sauté 7 minutes or until tender. Add mushrooms; sauté 5 minutes.
• **Stir** in flour and next 4 ingredients. Reduce heat to medium, and cook, stirring constantly, 3 minutes. Gradually stir in reserved liquid and whipping cream; cook 5 minutes or until thickened and bubbly.
• **Stir** in oysters, and cook 3 minutes or until oysters begin to curl. Stir in wine. Serve bisque with oyster crackers. **Yield:** about 7 cups.

FRIED OYSTERS

Prep: 20 minutes
Chill: 2 hours
Cook: 20 minutes

2 pints fresh oysters, rinsed and drained
1 large egg, lightly beaten
1½ cups saltine crumbs (1 sleeve crackers)
1 cup ketchup
1 tablespoon prepared horseradish
⅛ teaspoon hot sauce (optional)
Canola oil

• **Dip** oysters in egg, and dredge in cracker crumbs. Place on a pan in a single layer, and chill 2 hours, if desired.
• **Stir** together ketchup, horseradish, and, if desired, hot sauce; cover and chill ketchup mixture.
• **Pour** oil to a depth of 1 inch in a Dutch oven; heat to 350°.
• **Fry** oysters, in batches, 3 to 4 minutes or until golden. Drain on paper towels. Serve immediately with sauce. **Yield:** 6 to 8 servings.

Kathleen Wissinger
McGaheysville, Virginia

OYSTER-AND-CHICKEN CASSEROLE

Prep: 45 minutes
Bake: 30 minutes

2 tablespoons butter or margarine
1 (8-ounce) package sliced fresh mushrooms
2 cups chopped cooked chicken
3 cups cooked long-grain rice
1 cup frozen sweet green peas, thawed
1 (2-ounce) jar diced pimiento, drained
⅓ cup butter or margarine
⅓ cup all-purpose flour
1 (14½-ounce) can chicken broth
1 cup whipping cream
½ teaspoon salt
½ teaspoon pepper
1 (12-ounce) container fresh oysters, well drained
2 tablespoons butter or margarine, melted
1 cup soft breadcrumbs

• **Melt** 2 tablespoons butter in a large skillet; add mushrooms, and sauté until tender; drain well.
• **Return** mushrooms to skillet; add chicken and next 3 ingredients.
• **Melt** ⅓ cup butter in a heavy saucepan over low heat; whisk in flour until smooth. Cook, whisking constantly, 1 minute. Gradually whisk in broth and whipping cream; cook over medium heat, whisking constantly, until thickened and bubbly.
• **Stir** in salt and pepper. Add to chicken mixture, stirring gently.
• **Spoon** half of chicken mixture into a lightly greased 13- x 9-inch baking dish. Top with oysters and remaining chicken mixture.
• **Stir** together 2 tablespoons melted butter and breadcrumbs; sprinkle over casserole.
• **Bake** at 350° for 30 minutes or until bubbly. **Yield:** 8 servings.

SCALLOPED OYSTERS

Prep: 13 minutes
Bake: 45 minutes

2 pints fresh oysters, undrained
2 cups whipping cream
¼ cup butter or margarine, melted
¼ teaspoon hot sauce
1 (10-ounce) package oyster
    crackers, crushed
1 cup Italian-seasoned
    breadcrumbs
1 small sweet onion, diced
2 garlic cloves, pressed
3 bacon slices, cooked and
    crumbled
½ teaspoon salt
½ teaspoon pepper

● **Drain** oysters, reserving ½ cup liquid. Set oysters aside.
● **Stir** together reserved liquid, whipping cream, butter, and hot sauce.
● **Combine** cracker crumbs and next 6 ingredients. Place 3 cups cracker mixture on bottom of a lightly greased 13- x 9-inch baking dish. Top with half of oysters and half of cream mixture. Repeat procedure with remaining cracker mixture, oysters, and cream mixture.
● **Bake** at 375° for 45 minutes. **Yield:** 8 to 10 servings.

Kelly Rhinehart
Homer, New York

IN YOUR WINEGLASS

Muscadet wines are classically paired with shellfish, particularly oysters, because of the wines' light and dry style. Each true bottle of Muscadet has an oyster tag on the neck to ensure it's the real thing. Have the wine buyer in your local market help select these for you. Cheers.

GREAT DRINKS, GRAND HOTELS

While there's no place quite like home for the holidays, some of the South's grand hotels offer a cozy welcome and seasonal libations. One is served chilled, two will warm you, and all are spirited and delicious. Enjoy them as a toast to good times, wonderful friends, and togetherness.

HOT APPLE PIE

Top off a holiday visit to Dallas' Melrose Hotel with this comforting drink in The Library.

Prep: 5 minutes
Cook: 6 minutes

1 quart apple cider
⅔ cup vanilla-and-orange flavored
    brandy
4 (3-inch) cinnamon sticks
Sweetened whipped cream
    (optional)

● **Heat** cider in a medium saucepan over medium heat 5 to 6 minutes.
● **Stir** in brandy. Place cinnamon sticks in 4 mugs. Pour cider mixture into mugs; top with sweetened whipped cream, if desired. **Yield:** 4⅔ cups.

Note: For testing purposes only, we used Tuaca for vanilla-and-orange flavored brandy.

The Melrose Hotel
Dallas, Texas

CHRISTMAS BLOSSOM

Those who visit The Cloister at Sea Island, Georgia, enjoy that state's trademark fruit in this smooth concoction. The Cloister's year-round favorite drink, the Peach Blossom, becomes a Christmas Blossom during the holidays.

Prep: 10 minutes

2 cups fresh or frozen peach slices
¼ cup sugar
¾ cup vodka
3 tablespoons peach schnapps
Ice cubes
Garnish: fresh mint sprigs

● **Process** first 4 ingredients in a blender until smooth.
● **Add** ice cubes to mixture in blender to 5-cup level; process until smooth. Pour into glasses; garnish, if desired. Serve immediately. **Yield:** 4¼ cups.

The Cloister
Sea Island, Georgia

THE PEABODY PEPPERMINT PATTI

This grown-up hot chocolate is a perfect cold-weather drink, and the Peabody's elegant Lobby Bar in Memphis is a great place to enjoy it.

Prep: 5 minutes
Cook: 10 minutes

4 (1-ounce) envelopes hot
    chocolate mix
4 cups boiling water
¼ cup peppermint schnapps
Sweetened whipped cream
    (optional)

● **Empty** all envelopes of hot chocolate mix into a large heatproof pitcher.
● **Add** 4 cups boiling water to pitcher, stirring until hot chocolate mix dissolves; stir in peppermint schnapps.
● **Pour** mixture into mugs; top each serving with whipped cream, if desired. **Yield:** 4½ cups.

The Peabody Hotel
Memphis, Tennessee

Seasonal Salad Sensations

Celebrate the cold snap with produce that stays perky once the mercury falls. The time is ripe for serving these salads, all featuring fruits and vegetables that taste wonderfully fresh all winter.

ROASTED RED PEPPER-AND-GREEN BEAN SALAD

Prep: 15 minutes
Cook: 10 minutes
Chill: 8 hours

1½ pounds fresh green beans, trimmed
½ cup red wine vinegar
1 tablespoon olive oil
1 teaspoon ground cumin
1 teaspoon freshly ground pepper
½ teaspoon salt
½ cup chopped fresh cilantro
1 (8-ounce) package sliced fresh mushrooms
1 (15-ounce) jar roasted sweet red peppers, drained and cut into strips

● **Arrange** green beans in a steamer basket over boiling water. Cover and steam 10 minutes or until crisp-tender. Drain and rinse with cold water.
● **Whisk** together vinegar and next 5 ingredients in a large bowl until blended.
● **Add** green beans, mushrooms, and red peppers, tossing to coat. Cover and chill 8 hours. **Yield:** 8 servings.

Jean Roczniak
Rochester, Minnesota

SPAGHETTI SQUASH SALAD

Prep: 20 minutes
Cook: 18 minutes
Chill: 2 hours

1 (2-pound) spaghetti squash
3 tablespoons white or regular balsamic vinegar
2 teaspoons olive oil
¼ teaspoon salt
¼ teaspoon freshly ground pepper
12 cherry tomatoes, halved
1 green bell pepper, chopped
2 green onions, thinly sliced
2 tablespoons capers
2 tablespoons chopped fresh cilantro

● **Pierce** squash with a fork. Place in a microwave-safe pieplate. Microwave at HIGH 7 minutes. Turn squash over, and microwave 11 more minutes or until tender. Cool. Cut squash in half; discard seeds, and remove spaghetti-like strands with a fork, discarding shells.
● **Whisk** together vinegar and next 3 ingredients in a large bowl; add squash, tomato, and remaining ingredients. Toss to coat. Cover and chill at least 2 hours. **Yield:** 6 to 8 servings.

Barbara Sherrer
Bay City, Texas

HARVEST SALAD WITH CIDER VINAIGRETTE

Prep: 30 minutes
Chill: 1 hour

2 red pears, chopped
1 tablespoon lemon juice
¾ cup dried apricots, cut into thin strips
¾ cup dried figs, cut into thin strips
½ cup golden raisins
1 small purple onion, thinly sliced
1 cup diced jícama
Cider Vinaigrette
1 (6-ounce) package fresh spinach leaves
½ cup coarsely chopped walnuts or pecans, toasted
1 (4-ounce) package crumbled Gorgonzola or blue cheese

● **Toss** together chopped pear and lemon juice in a medium bowl.
● **Add** apricots and next 5 ingredients, tossing well. Cover and chill 1 hour or overnight.
● **Arrange** spinach on individual plates; top evenly with pear mixture. Sprinkle salad with walnuts and cheese. **Yield:** 6 servings.

Cider Vinaigrette

Prep: 5 minutes

3 tablespoons cider vinegar
1 garlic clove, pressed
1 teaspoon Dijon mustard
½ teaspoon sugar
⅓ cup olive oil

● **Whisk** together first 4 ingredients; gradually whisk in oil until blended. **Yield:** ½ cup.

Ronda Carman
Houston, Texas

WELCOME YOUR GUESTS

Along with heartwarming greetings to holiday guests, tuck a favorite Christmas book and a plate of Special Mints in the guest bedroom or offer fruit and Parmesan Twists for the late-night snacker.

SPECIAL MINTS

To decorate mints, gently press candy sprinkles into mints before drying. Store leftover frosting, covered, in the refrigerator up to 30 days. Freeze mints between layers of wax paper up to 12 months.

Prep: 40 minutes
Stand: 7 hours

1 cup butter, softened
1 (2-pound) package powdered sugar
¼ cup whipping cream
2 drops of spearmint oil
2 drops of peppermint oil
Green paste food coloring
Red paste food coloring
½ cup ready-to-spread vanilla frosting

● **Beat** butter at medium speed with an electric mixer until creamy; gradually add powdered sugar, beating until blended.
● **Add** whipping cream and oils, beating until smooth.
● **Divide** mixture in half; color 1 half with green food coloring and the other half with red food coloring. Set 2 tablespoons pink mint mixture aside.
● **Roll** mint mixtures to ¼-inch thickness on wax paper. Cut with holly leaf and other assorted 1-inch Christmas cutters. Place on wax paper-lined baking sheets.
● **Roll** reserved pink mixture into tiny balls; gently press onto holly leaf mints to resemble berries. Let stand 6 hours or until firm.

● **Spoon** frosting into a small heavy-duty zip-top plastic bag. Snip a tiny hole in 1 corner of bag, and decorate mints as desired. Let stand 1 hour or until firm. Store in an airtight container. **Yield:** 8 dozen.

Susan C. Richardson
Vienna, Georgia

PARMESAN TWISTS

Freeze these twists in an airtight container two to three months, if desired.

Prep: 20 minutes
Chill: 30 minutes
Bake: 15 minutes per batch

½ cup butter or margarine, softened
1 cup shredded Parmesan cheese
1 (8-ounce) container sour cream
2 cups all-purpose flour
2 teaspoons dried Italian seasoning
1 egg yolk
1 tablespoon water
2 tablespoons sesame seeds

● **Beat** butter at medium speed with an electric mixer until creamy. Add cheese and sour cream, beating until blended.
● **Combine** flour and Italian seasoning. Gradually add to butter mixture, beating at low speed until blended. Cover and chill 30 minutes.
● **Turn** dough out onto a lightly floured surface; knead 3 or 4 times. Divide dough in half. Roll half of dough into a 12- x 6-inch rectangle. Cut into 6- x ½-inch strips.
● **Stir** together egg yolk and 1 tablespoon water; brush over breadsticks. Sprinkle with 1 tablespoon sesame seeds. Twist strips; place on lightly greased baking sheets. Repeat with remaining dough, egg wash, and sesame seeds.
● **Bake** at 350° for 15 minutes or until golden. Freeze up to 3 months, if desired. **Yield:** 4 dozen.

Elizabeth A. Crawley
New Orleans, Louisiana

BLACK GOLD

Most people consider truffles exotic, expensive, and European. In reality, truffles are more accessible, affordable, and sometimes Southern. The wrinkled little fungus thrives in pecan groves in Georgia and Texas. A few North Carolina tobacco farmers are devoting some of their acreage to planting trees that—if truffles grow at their base—will generate four or five times the income from tobacco.

While whole fresh truffles sell for $300 to $500 per pound, you can experience their essence for just a few dollars in oils, buttery spreads, and sauces. A small amount adds character to a recipe without breaking your budget. Store truffle-infused oils and spreads in airtight containers in the refrigerator up to five weeks. Taste nature's most extravagant ingredient in the recipe below.

For a catalog of truffle products, call Urbani USA at 1-800-281-2330, or visit www.urbani.com.

BLACK TRUFFLE BRUSCHETTA

Prep: 5 minutes
Bake: 35 minutes

3 garlic cloves
Olive oil
6 thick French baguette slices
¼ teaspoon salt
¼ teaspoon pepper
⅛ teaspoon black truffle olive oil

● **Place** garlic on a piece of aluminum foil; drizzle with olive oil, and fold foil to seal.
● **Bake** at 400° for 30 minutes; cool garlic, and mash.
● **Bake** baguette slices on a baking sheet at 400° for 5 minutes. Sprinkle warm bread with salt and pepper. Spread evenly with mashed garlic, and brush with black truffle olive oil. Serve immediately. **Yield:** 6 servings.

PARTY PICKUPS

These high-flavored morsels make use of lean meat and other low-fat and fat-free products readily available in supermarkets. They will excite your palate while keeping calories in check and taste at a premium.

OVEN-FRIED SHRIMP WITH MARMALADE DIP

Prepare dip ahead, and chill. The shrimp are best served straight from the oven.

Prep: 12 minutes
Chill: 20 minutes
Bake: 15 minutes

6　unpeeled, jumbo fresh shrimp
　　(½ pound)
1　teaspoon grated orange
　　rind
½　cup fresh orange juice
¼　teaspoon dried crushed red
　　pepper
½　cup fine, dry breadcrumbs
½　teaspoon garlic pepper
　　seasoning
1　(4-ounce) container egg
　　substitute
Vegetable cooking spray
Marmalade Dip

• **Peel** shrimp, leaving tails on. Butterfly shrimp by making a deep slit lengthwise down the back from the large end to the tail, cutting to, but not through, the inside curve of shrimp. Rinse and pat dry.
• **Combine** orange rind, orange juice, and crushed red pepper in a shallow dish or heavy-duty zip-top plastic bag; add shrimp. Cover or seal, and chill 20 minutes.
• **Remove** shrimp from marinade, discarding marinade.
• **Combine** breadcrumbs and garlic pepper seasoning. Dip shrimp in egg substitute, and dredge in breadcrumb mixture. Place on a baking sheet coated with vegetable cooking spray.
• **Bake** at 350° for 15 minutes or until done. Serve with Marmalade Dip. **Yield:** 2 servings.

Marmalade Dip

Prep: 4 minutes

½　cup orange marmalade
2　teaspoons lite soy sauce
½　to 1 teaspoon prepared
　　horseradish

• **Stir** together all ingredients in a bowl. **Yield:** ½ cup.

♥ Per shrimp and 1 tablespoon dip:
Calories 149
Fat 1.7g　Cholesterol 58mg
Sodium 242mg

SHRIMP-STUFFED MUSHROOMS

Purchase steamed shrimp at the supermarket. Stuff mushrooms ahead, but bake just before serving.

Prep: 35 minutes
Bake: 20 minutes

12　large fresh mushrooms
　　(1 pound)
Butter-flavored cooking spray
½　cup chopped cooked shrimp
⅓　cup Italian-seasoned
　　breadcrumbs
¼　cup fat-free, low-sodium
　　chicken broth
¼　teaspoon salt
⅛　teaspoon ground red pepper
1　tablespoon grated Parmesan
　　cheese (optional)

• **Remove** stems from mushrooms; chop stems.
• **Spray** mushroom caps with cooking spray.
• **Stir** together chopped mushrooms, shrimp, and next 4 ingredients.
• **Spoon** evenly into mushroom caps, and sprinkle evenly with cheese, if desired. Place on a lightly greased rack in a broiler pan.
• **Bake** at 375° for 20 minutes. **Yield:** 12 appetizers.

Betsy Cochran
Midlothian, Virginia

♥ Per serving: Calories 29
Fat 0.7g　Cholesterol 14mg
Sodium 154mg

REFRESHING DILL DIP

Prep: 10 minutes
Chill: 1 hour

1　(8-ounce) package fat-free
　　cream cheese, softened
½　cup fat-free Ranch-style
　　dressing
1　medium cucumber, peeled,
　　seeded, and chopped
2　tablespoons minced fresh onion
1½　teaspoons dried dillweed

● **Beat** cream cheese and dressing at medium speed with an electric mixer until smooth.

● **Stir** in cucumber, onion, and dillweed. Cover and chill 1 hour. Serve with raw vegetables. **Yield:** 2 cups.

Johnsie Ford
Rockingham, North Carolina

♥ Per tablespoon: Calories 14
Fat 0g   Cholesterol 1mg
Sodium 73mg

SWEET-AND-SOUR MEATBALLS

Meatballs may be thoroughly cooked without sauce and frozen. Thaw and reheat with sauce.

Prep: 45 minutes
Cook: 19 minutes

¾ **pound extra-lean ground beef**
¾ **pound ground turkey**
1 **small onion, minced**
¼ **cup egg substitute**
½ **cup Italian-seasoned breadcrumbs**
¾ **cup ketchup**
⅓ **cup white vinegar**
¼ **cup low-sodium Worcestershire sauce**
3 **tablespoons sugar**
2 **teaspoons dry mustard**

● **Combine** first 5 ingredients; shape mixture into 1-inch balls. Brown meatballs, in batches, in a large nonstick skillet over medium-high heat. Remove meatballs from skillet; wipe skillet clean.

● **Stir** together ketchup and next 4 ingredients in skillet; bring to a boil. Add meatballs; reduce heat, and simmer 5 minutes or until meatballs are no longer pink. **Yield:** 3½ dozen.

Sharon Anderson
Franklin, Tennessee

♥ Per meatball: Calories 46
Fat 1.8g   Cholesterol 11mg
Sodium 106mg

FESTIVE CROSTINI

Toast bread, and prepare cheese and tomato mixtures ahead. Assemble just before serving to avoid soggy bread.

Prep: 45 minutes
Bake: 12 minutes

½ **(3-ounce) package dried tomatoes**
1½ **cups boiling water**
1 **(16-ounce) baguette, cut into ½-inch-thick slices**
2 **garlic cloves, divided**
½ **(8-ounce) package fat-free cream cheese, softened**
1 **(4-ounce) package crumbled feta cheese**
1 **(2.5-ounce) can sliced ripe olives, drained**
¼ **cup chopped fresh parsley**

● **Soak** tomatoes in 1½ cups boiling water 30 minutes; drain. Chop tomato, and set aside.

● **Place** bread slices on a baking sheet.

● **Bake** at 400° for 10 to 12 minutes or until toasted.

● **Cut** 1 garlic clove in half. Rub bread slices with cut sides of garlic.

● **Stir** together cream cheese and feta cheese until blended. Spread about 1 teaspoon cream cheese mixture evenly on bread slices.

● **Mince** remaining garlic clove. Stir together minced garlic, tomato, olives, and parsley. Spoon over cream cheese mixture. **Yield:** 30 appetizers.

♥ Per serving: Calories 87
Fat 1.9g   Cholesterol 4mg
Sodium 247mg

CHICKEN AND DUMPLINGS

These new chicken and dumplings recipes are as delicious as the old-fashioned version; however, we've streamlined them using readymade biscuit dough, biscuit mix, or flour tortillas. Because the preparation and cooking times are longer than most of our quick-and-easy recipes, we've provided "Quick Tips" that can help you save time.

CHICKEN AND POTATO DUMPLINGS

Prep: 25 minutes
Cook: 1 hour

1 (4-pound) whole chicken, cut up
8 cups water
1 teaspoon salt
1½ teaspoons poultry seasoning
¼ teaspoon pepper
1 (10¾-ounce) can cream of chicken soup, undiluted
2 tablespoons dried minced onion
1½ cups biscuit mix
½ cup instant potato flakes
⅔ cup milk

● **Bring** first 5 ingredients to a boil in a Dutch oven; cover, reduce heat, and simmer 45 minutes or until chicken is tender.
● **Remove** chicken, reserving broth in Dutch oven. Cool chicken and broth.
● **Skim** fat from broth. Skin, bone, and cut chicken into bite-size pieces; set chicken aside.

● **Whisk** soup and minced onion into broth; bring to a boil.
● **Stir** together biscuit mix, potato flakes, and milk until blended.
● **Turn** dough out onto a heavily floured surface; roll or pat dough to ¼-inch thickness. Cut into ½-inch strips.
● **Pinch** off ½-inch pieces from strips, and drop, 1 at a time, into boiling broth; add chicken. Cover, reduce heat, and simmer, stirring occasionally, 15 minutes. **Yield:** 6 servings.

Quick Tip: Substitute 8 cups chicken broth for water; reduce salt to ¼ teaspoon. Proceed with recipe using 3 to 4 cups chopped cooked chicken.

Lisa Kinsley
Greensboro, North Carolina

BISCUIT DUMPLINGS AND CHICKEN

Prep: 15 minutes
Cook: 45 minutes

4 bone-in chicken breast halves, skinned (3 pounds)
6 cups water
1 tablespoon Creole seasoning
1 (11-ounce) can refrigerated biscuits

● **Bring** first 3 ingredients to a boil in a Dutch oven; cover, reduce heat, and simmer 30 to 35 minutes or until chicken is tender. Remove chicken, reserving broth in Dutch oven; let chicken cool. Bone and cut chicken into bite-size pieces.
● **Place** biscuits on a floured surface; roll or pat biscuits to ⅛-inch thickness. Cut biscuits into thirds.
● **Bring** broth to a boil. Drop biscuits, 1 at a time, into boiling broth; add chicken. Cook, stirring occasionally, 10 minutes. **Yield:** 4 servings.

Quick Tip: Substitute 6 cups reduced-sodium chicken broth for water; use 3 cups chopped cooked chicken.

Anita Emory
Vincent, Alabama

CHICKEN IN A HURRY?

It's easy to prepare chopped cooked chicken to keep in your freezer. Arrange 3 celery ribs, cut into 4-inch pieces; 2 carrots, sliced; and 1 medium onion, sliced, in a lightly greased 13- x 9-inch pan. Top with 6 skinned and boned chicken breast halves. Sprinkle chicken with ½ teaspoon salt and ¼ teaspoon pepper. Bake, covered, at 400° for 25 to 30 minutes or until chicken is done. Cool chicken slightly; chop and store in plastic bags in freezer. Discard vegetables. Reserve liquid, if desired.

CHICKEN AND TORTILLA DUMPLINGS

Strips of flour tortillas make wonderfully easy dumplings.

Prep: 15 minutes
Cook: 1 hour and 10 minutes

6   chicken leg quarters (5 pounds)
8   cups water
2   celery ribs, chopped
1   small onion, chopped
2   chicken bouillon cubes
1½ teaspoons salt
1   teaspoon pepper
1   (10¾-ounce) can cream of
      chicken soup, undiluted
1   (15-ounce) package 8-inch flour
      tortillas

● **Bring** first 7 ingredients to a boil in a large Dutch oven; cover, reduce heat, and simmer 45 minutes or until chicken is tender. Remove chicken, reserving broth in Dutch oven. Let chicken and broth cool.
● **Skin,** bone, and cut chicken into bite-size pieces; set aside. Skim fat from broth. Add soup to broth; bring to a boil.
● **Cut** tortillas into 2- x 1-inch strips. Add strips, 1 at a time, to briskly boiling broth. Add chicken, reduce heat, and simmer 10 minutes, stirring occasionally to prevent dumplings from sticking. **Yield:** 6 servings.

Quick Tip: Substitute 8 cups chicken broth for water; omit bouillon cubes, reduce salt to ½ teaspoon. Proceed with recipe using 3 to 4 cups chopped cooked chicken.

Kathryn Burkhalter
Bruce, Florida

GET A HEAD START

Sunday Roast Beef, with its long baking time, serves as a terrific weekend entrée. Turn leftovers into Quick Beef Stroganoff or Barbecue Beef Sandwiches later in the week. At around $1.25 per serving (or less if bought on special), a boneless rump roast doesn't waste a penny.

SUNDAY ROAST BEEF

Prep: 15 minutes
Bake: 5 hours

1   (5½-pound) boneless rump
      roast
1   teaspoon salt
1   teaspoon pepper
1   garlic clove, cut into 3 slices
1⅓ cups all-purpose flour, divided
3   tablespoons olive oil
7   cups water, divided
½   cup sweet pickle juice
½   cup ketchup
1   tablespoon prepared mustard
1   tablespoon Worcestershire
      sauce
1   teaspoon chili powder

● **Rub** roast with salt and pepper. Cut three slits in roast; insert garlic slices. Coat roast with ⅓ cup flour.
● **Brown** roast on all sides in hot oil in a Dutch oven.
● **Stir** together 6 cups water and next 5 ingredients; pour over roast.
● **Bake,** covered, at 350° for 5 hours or until tender.
● **Remove** roast from Dutch oven; keep warm. Whisk together remaining 1 cup flour and remaining 1 cup water. Whisk flour mixture into drippings; cook over medium heat, stirring constantly, until thickened. Serve with roast. **Yield:** 8 to 10 servings.

Anita Paxton
Isola, Mississippi

QUICK BEEF STROGANOFF

Prep: 20 minutes
Cook: 15 minutes

½   pound cooked roast beef, cut
      into strips
¼   cup diced onion
2   cups water
1   large beef bouillon cube
1   (10¾-ounce) can cream of
      chicken soup, undiluted
1   (13.25-ounce) can mushroom
      stems and pieces, drained
1   (8-ounce) container sour cream
12 ounces egg noodles, cooked

● **Bring** first 4 ingredients to a boil in a medium saucepan. Reduce heat; simmer, stirring occasionally, 5 minutes. Stir in soup and mushrooms; cook, stirring often, 5 minutes. Stir in sour cream, and serve over noodles. **Yield:** 4 servings.

Becky Bish
Oklahoma City, Oklahoma

BARBECUE BEEF SANDWICHES

Prep: 15 minutes
Cook: 30 minutes

1   bacon slice, cut into 1-inch pieces
1   medium onion, chopped
½   cup ketchup
½   cup apple juice
1   tablespoon white vinegar
1   teaspoon prepared mustard
1   teaspoon Worcestershire sauce
½   teaspoon salt
⅛   teaspoon pepper
3   tablespoons sugar
12 ounces cooked roast beef,
      thinly sliced
4   kaiser rolls, split

● **Cook** bacon in a saucepan over medium-high heat 3 to 4 minutes; add onion. Sauté 3 to 5 minutes or until bacon is crisp. Stir in ketchup and next 6 ingredients; bring to a boil. Cover, reduce heat, and simmer, stirring occasionally, 15 to 20 minutes. Stir in sugar and beef. Serve warm on rolls. **Yield:** 4 servings.

Johnsie Ford
Rockingham, North Carolina

FROM OUR KITCHEN TO YOURS

HOLIDAY CAKE DECORATING

The holly leaves on our Holiday Lane Cake (page 306) are very easy to make. Roll candy and corn syrup mixture to ¹⁄₁₆-inch thickness. Cut with 1-inch and 2-inch holly leaf-shaped cutters. Score leaves with a knife. Place on wax paper and over sides of an inverted cakepan for curved shape. Let stand 3 to 4 hours.

Look for spearmint and peppermint oils in drugstores and kitchen shops, or you can order from Sweet Celebrations—call 1-800-328-6722.

SOMETHING EXTRA

When you bake Holiday Lane Cake you'll have eight egg whites left over. Don't throw them away. Vanessa McNeil of our Test Kitchens staff whipped up a sweet recipe—Dream Drops. If you don't have time to make these immediately, refrigerate the unbeaten egg whites in an airtight container for up to four days, or freeze them up to six months. To freeze, place one in each section of an ice-cube tray. Pop out the frozen cubes, and store in freezer bag. Thaw completely in the refrigerator overnight before using.

DREAM DROPS

Prep: 20 minutes
Bake: 30 minutes
Stand: 2 hours and 30 minutes

8 egg whites
1½ cups sugar
1 cup (6 ounces) semisweet
    chocolate morsels, melted

● **Beat** egg whites at high speed with an electric mixer until foamy.
● **Add** sugar, 1 tablespoon at a time, beating until stiff peaks form and sugar dissolves. Drop by ¼ cupfuls onto parchment paper-lined baking sheets.
● **Bake** meringues at 250° for 30 minutes. Turn oven off, and let baked

meringues stand in oven with oven door closed 30 minutes.
● **Spread** a thin layer of chocolate on flat sides of meringues. Let stand on wax paper 2 hours or until chocolate is firm. **Yield:** 2 dozen.

TIPS AND TIDBITS

Cake mixes are today's shortcut for scratch ingredients. You'll get the best results from the mixes when you follow these helpful hints.

■ Mixing too long at too high a speed may result in a low-volume cake that shrinks while it cools.

■ Loosely cover a frosted cake and store up to two days at room temperature, or store tightly covered up to one week in the refrigerator. Cakes with custard or whipped cream filling or topping must be stored in refrigerator. These don't freeze well.

■ Cake mixes usually produce very tender cakes, so cool at least 10 minutes before removing from pans.

For additional tips on cake mix success, read *The Cake Mix Doctor,* by Anne Byrn (Workman Publishing, $14.95 paperback, $23.95 hardcover). "Left untouched, cake mixes can be ho-hum," says Anne. "But with a dash of creativity, a tub of richness, and a cupful of inspiration, they turn out wonderful creations."

CHEERS

Handle sparkling wines properly to pour a perfect glass every time.

■ Champagne is ready to drink when it leaves the winery, so there's no need to buy in bulk for aging. Be sure to store bottles on their sides to keep the corks moist and retain their elasticity.

■ Three to four hours on the top shelf of the fridge is all sparkling wines need to reach the ideal serving temperature of 43° to 48°. Or, 20 to 30 minutes in an ice bucket or sink with half ice/half water will work. Don't put them in the freezer.

■ To open, remove the foil and the twisted wire hood. Keep a finger over the cork, and point the bottle away from you at a 45-degree angle. Grasp the cork with a towel; twist the bottle—not the cork—and you'll feel the cork loosening.

■ Tall, thin glasses are designed for sparkling wines. They guide the bubbles, concentrate the aromas, and hold the carbonation longer.

■ For 15 guests, have at least seven bottles—two for a champagne punch, two for sparkling wine drinkers, and three bottles for toasting.

■ You'll know the sugar content of champagnes by their names: Brut or Natural is the driest; Extra Dry is less dry than Brut; Sec is sweet; and Semi-Sec is even sweeter. Spumante is another sweet, fruity sparkling wine.

■ Taste hints of spice and full fruit flavors in Domaine Carneros Brut Vintage 1994. It's wearing a Millennium label. Read about it at www.domaine.com or call (707) 257-0101.

Southern Living®
COOKING SCHOOL
BONUS SECTION

Each spring and fall, the Southern Living *Cooking School experts set the stage in more than 15 cities for an entertaining and informative cooking show. They share timesaving tips for busy cooks, ideas for entertaining, up-close-and-personal cooking demonstrations, and easy-to-prepare recipes.*

This bonus section offers a sample of some of the most popular Cooking School recipes. From King Ranch Chicken to Apple Pie With Warm Cinnamon Crème, these delicious dishes are sure to become new family favorites.

SOUTHWESTERN ROUNDUP

The high-flavored ingredients that make up Southwestern dishes are combinations from Spanish explorers, American pioneers, and American Indians. Choose a new dish and bring the delectable tastes of this region into your own kitchen.

KING RANCH CHICKEN

Prep: 35 minutes
Bake: 40 minutes
Stand: 5 minutes

4 skinned and boned chicken breast halves
¼ teaspoon salt
¼ teaspoon pepper
2 tablespoons butter
1 green bell pepper, chopped
1 medium onion, chopped
2 (10-ounce) cans ROTEL Diced Tomatoes and Green Chiles
1 (10¾-ounce) can cream of mushroom soup, undiluted
1 (10¾-ounce) can cream of chicken soup, undiluted
12 (6-inch) corn tortillas, cut into quarters
2 cups (8 ounces) shredded Cheddar cheese

• **Sprinkle** chicken breast halves with salt and pepper; place in a lightly greased 13- x 9-inch baking dish.
• **Bake** at 325° for 20 minutes or until done; cool. Coarsely chop chicken.

• **Melt** butter in a large skillet over medium heat; add bell pepper and onion, and sauté until crisp-tender. Remove from heat; stir in chicken, tomatoes and green chiles, and soups.
• **Place** one-third of tortilla quarters in bottom of a lightly greased 13- x 9-inch baking dish; top with one-third of chicken mixture, and sprinkle evenly with ⅔ cup cheese. Repeat layers twice, reserving last ⅔ cup cheese.
• **Bake** at 325° for 35 minutes; sprinkle with reserved cheese, and bake 5 more minutes. Let stand 5 minutes before serving. **Yield:** 6 to 8 servings.

THREE-CHEESE CHICKEN ENCHILADAS

Prep: 45 minutes
Bake: 25 minutes

2 medium onions, chopped
2 garlic cloves, pressed
3 tablespoons vegetable oil
4 cups chopped cooked chicken
2 (14½-ounce) cans Mexican-style stewed tomatoes
1 (4.5-ounce) can chopped green chiles, drained
½ teaspoon salt
2 tablespoons chopped fresh or 2 teaspoons dried cilantro
4 ounces goat CHEESE, crumbled
24 (6-inch) flour tortillas
2 cups half-and-half
1 teaspoon chicken bouillon granules
2 cups (8 ounces) shredded Monterey Jack CHEESE
2 cups (8 ounces) shredded Cheddar CHEESE

• **Sauté** onion and garlic in hot oil in a Dutch oven over medium-high heat until tender. Stir in chicken and next 3 ingredients. Bring to a boil; reduce heat, and simmer, stirring occasionally, 15 minutes. Stir in cilantro and goat cheese.

• **Spoon** about ¼ cup chicken mixture down center of each tortilla; roll up tortillas, and place, seam side down, in 2 lightly greased 13- x 9-inch baking dishes.

• **Heat** half-and-half and bouillon granules in a large saucepan over low heat until granules dissolve. Pour mixture over tortillas.

• **Bake,** covered, at 350° for 10 minutes; uncover and bake 10 more minutes. Sprinkle with shredded cheeses, and bake 5 more minutes. Serve with Spanish rice. **Yield:** 12 servings.

SPICY BEEF AND BLACK BEANS

Prep: 15 minutes
Bake: 35 minutes

2 (10-ounce) cans ROTEL Mexican Diced Tomatoes and Green Chiles, drained
2 (15-ounce) cans black beans, rinsed and drained
1 medium onion, diced
2 garlic cloves, minced
1 pound boneless beef sirloin, thinly sliced
2 cups (8 ounces) shredded Monterey Jack cheese with peppers
Hot cooked yellow rice

• **Stir** together first 4 ingredients. Layer half of beef in a lightly greased 11- x 7-inch baking dish, and top with half of tomato mixture. Repeat procedure.

• **Bake** at 350° for 30 minutes. Sprinkle with cheese, and bake 5 more minutes. Serve over rice. **Yield:** 4 servings.

FIERY STEAK WITH PIMIENTO CHEESE SALSA

Prep: 15 minutes
Marinate: 4 hours
Grill: 12 minutes

1 (2-ounce) bottle hot sauce
½ to 1½ cups beer
1 (1-gallon) HEFTY OneZip Slider Bag
1 (1½-pound) beef top loin strip steak, trimmed
2 cups (8 ounces) four-cheese blend shredded cheese
3 tablespoons mayonnaise
1 (2-ounce) jar diced pimiento, drained
2 green onions, minced
3 tablespoons minced pickled jalapeño pepper

• **Combine** hot sauce and beer in slider bag; add steak. Seal bag, turning to coat. Chill 4 hours, turning occasionally.

• **Process** cheese and mayonnaise in a food processor until blended.

• **Stir** in pimiento, green onions, and pickled jalapeño pepper. Cover and chill 2 hours.

• **Remove** beef from marinade, discarding marinade.

• **Grill,** covered with grill lid, over high heat (400° to 500°) 5 to 6 minutes on each side or until desired degree of doneness. Cut into thin strips, and serve with pimiento cheese salsa. **Yield:** 4 to 6 servings.

ORANGE-AVOCADO SALAD

Prep: 15 minutes

1 orange, peeled and sectioned
½ large CALIFORNIA AVOCADO, peeled and sliced
½ small purple onion, sliced and separated into rings (optional)
2 cups torn leaf lettuce
Sweet-and-sour dressing

• **Arrange** orange sections, avocado slices, and, if desired, onion on lettuce. Drizzle evenly with sweet-and-sour dressing. **Yield:** 2 servings.

PRALINE-APPLE PIE

Prep: 15 minutes
Bake: 1 hour and 30 minutes
Cool: 1 hour

1 (3-pound, 1-ounce) package frozen MRS. SMITH'S Deep Dish Special Recipe Apple Pie
¼ cup butter
1 cup firmly packed brown sugar
⅓ cup whipping cream
1 teaspoon vanilla extract
1 cup powdered sugar
¾ cup chopped pecans, toasted

• **Remove** plastic overwrap from pie. Open center hole; cut 4 to 6 slits in top crust. Place pie on an aluminum foil-lined baking sheet.

• **Bake** at 375° for 1 hour and 20 minutes to 1 hour and 30 minutes, shielding edges with aluminum foil after 1 hour. Cool 1 hour.

• **Bring** butter, brown sugar, and whipping cream to a boil in a 2-quart saucepan over medium heat, stirring often. Boil 1 minute; remove from heat. Whisk in vanilla and powdered sugar until smooth. Pour praline mixture slowly over pie, spreading to cover. Top with pecans. **Yield:** 8 servings.

DINNER IN THE FAST LANE

At the end of the day, when time is short and appetites are large, these recipes put dinner on the table in record speed. We've taken favorite traditional recipes and streamlined them, using convenience products as well as common pantry ingredients.

ROASTED VEGETABLE-MEAT LASAGNA

Prep: 25 minutes
Bake: 50 minutes
Stand: 10 minutes

1 (40-ounce) package frozen STOUFFER'S Family Style Favorites Lasagna with Meat Sauce *
1 large sweet onion, sliced
1 red bell pepper, quartered
1 medium zucchini, sliced
2 small yellow squash, sliced
2 garlic cloves, peeled
3 tablespoons olive oil
½ teaspoon salt
½ teaspoon coarsely ground pepper
¼ cup chopped fresh basil
1 cup (4 ounces) Italian shredded cheese blend
Garnish: fresh basil leaves

• **Thaw** lasagna in microwave at MEDIUM (50% power) 15 to 20 minutes. Transfer to a lightly greased 11- x 7-inch baking dish, pressing gently into dish.
• **Toss** together onion and next 7 ingredients. Arrange vegetables in a single layer in a large pan.
• **Bake** vegetables at 500° for 20 minutes. Cool slightly.
• **Remove** skin from red bell pepper. Coarsely chop vegetables, and mince garlic; toss with chopped basil. Spread mixture over lasagna; top with cheese.
• **Bake** at 375° for 30 minutes or until thoroughly heated. Let stand 10 minutes. Garnish, if desired. **Yield:** 6 servings.

* Substitute 2 (20-ounce) packages frozen STOUFFER'S Family Style Favorites Lasagna with Meat Sauce, if desired.

PECAN CHICKEN

Prep: 12 minutes
Bake: 18 minutes

4 skinned and boned chicken breast halves
2 tablespoons honey
2 tablespoons GREY POUPON Dijon Mustard
2 tablespoons finely chopped pecans

• **Place** chicken between 2 sheets of heavy-duty plastic wrap, and flatten to ¼-inch thickness using a meat mallet or rolling pin.
• **Stir** together honey and Dijon mustard; spread on both sides of chicken, and dredge in pecans.
• **Arrange** chicken in a lightly greased 8-inch square baking dish.
• **Bake** at 350° for 15 to 18 minutes or until done. **Yield:** 4 servings.

PORK PICCATA

Prep: 15 minutes
Cook: 10 minutes

2 (¾-pound) pork tenderloins
1 (1-gallon) HEFTY OneZip Slider Bag
½ cup all-purpose flour
½ teaspoon salt
¼ teaspoon pepper
3 tablespoons olive oil
½ cup dry white wine
½ cup lemon juice
3 tablespoons butter or margarine
¼ cup chopped fresh parsley
1½ tablespoons capers
Hot cooked fettuccine

• **Cut** each tenderloin into 6 (2-ounce) medaillons. Place in slider bag; flatten to ¼-inch thickness using a meat mallet or rolling pin.
• **Combine** flour, salt, and pepper; dredge pork in flour mixture.
• **Cook** half of pork in 1½ tablespoons hot oil in a large skillet over medium heat about 2 minutes on each side or until lightly browned. Remove from skillet; keep warm. Repeat procedure with remaining pork and oil.
• **Add** white wine and lemon juice to skillet; cook until thoroughly heated.
• **Add** butter, chopped parsley, and capers to skillet, stirring until butter is melted. Arrange pork medaillons over fettuccine; drizzle with wine mixture. **Yield:** 6 servings.

HAMBURGERS TERIYAKI

Prep: 10 minutes
Grill: 8 minutes

¼ cup KIKKOMAN Soy Sauce
¼ cup honey
2 garlic cloves, pressed
1 teaspoon ground ginger
⅓ cup mayonnaise
2 pounds ground beef
½ teaspoon salt
¼ teaspoon pepper
6 sesame seed buns

- **Stir** together first 4 ingredients. Stir 2 teaspoons soy sauce mixture into mayonnaise, and set aside.
- **Combine** ⅓ cup soy sauce mixture, beef, salt, and pepper; shape into 6 patties. Brush with remaining soy sauce mixture.
- **Grill,** without grill lid, over medium-high heat (350° to 400°) 4 minutes on each side or until beef is no longer pink.
- **Coat** cut sides of buns with vegetable cooking spray, and grill, cut side down, 2 minutes. Spread buns evenly with mayonnaise mixture, and fill with patties. **Yield:** 6 servings.

DIJON-HONEY DRESSING

Prep: 5 minutes

1 cup mayonnaise
¼ cup GREY POUPON Dijon
     Mustard
¼ cup honey
2 tablespoons vegetable oil
¾ teaspoon cider vinegar
⅛ teaspoon onion salt
⅛ teaspoon ground red pepper

- **Process** all ingredients in an electric blender until smooth. Cover and chill thoroughly. **Yield:** 1¼ cups.

ICED CAPPUCCINO

Prep: 10 minutes

1 cup DOMINO Granulated Sugar
½ cup cocoa
½ cup instant coffee granules
1 cup hot water
6 cups cold milk
1 tablespoon vanilla extract
¼ cup almond liqueur or ⅛
     teaspoon almond extract
     (optional)
1 pint vanilla ice cream or ice
     cubes

- **Whisk** together first 4 ingredients in a large saucepan until smooth. Bring to

a boil over medium heat, whisking constantly; boil, whisking constantly, 2 minutes. Remove mixture from heat. Cool slightly.
- **Stir** in 6 cups cold milk, vanilla, and, if desired, liqueur. Cover and chill up to 2 days, or pour each serving immediately over ¼ cup ice cream or ice cubes. **Yield:** 8 cups.

KEY LIME PIE WITH MINTED TROPICAL SALSA

Prep: 15 minutes
Thaw: 2 hours

1 (2-pound, 7-ounce) package
     frozen MRS. SMITH'S
     Restaurant Classics Key
     Lime Pie
½ cup chopped refrigerated
     mango slices
½ cup chopped refrigerated
     papaya slices
1 small star fruit, sliced
½ cup sliced strawberries
1 kiwifruit, peeled and sliced
2 tablespoons minced fresh
     mint
¼ cup lime juice from
     concentrate
3 tablespoons powdered
     sugar

- **Remove** pie from carton, and discard plastic overwrap. Thaw pie, covered, in refrigerator 1½ to 2 hours.
- **Toss** together mango and next 7 ingredients. Chill, if desired.
- **Serve** salsa with a slotted spoon over Key lime pie. **Yield:** 8 servings.

AUTUMN GATHERINGS

Create delicious new traditions when family and friends celebrate special days this fall. Planning a menu from this group of timesaving entrées and sides guarantees you a shorter stint in the kitchen. A make-ahead cheesecake or a berry sauce served over your favorite pound cake sweetens your chances of hosting the most carefree party ever.

DIJON-ROSEMARY LAMB CHOPS

Prep: 10 minutes
Cook: 32 minutes

¼ cup GREY POUPON Dijon
     Mustard
8 lamb chops (4 pounds)
1 tablespoon chopped fresh or
     dried rosemary, crushed
All-purpose flour
2 tablespoons olive oil
1 cup dry white wine, divided
½ cup whipping cream
Salt and pepper

- **Spread** Dijon mustard over lamb chops; sprinkle with rosemary. Dredge lamb chops in flour, shaking to remove excess.
- **Brown** chops in hot oil in a large skillet over medium-high heat. Reduce heat to medium; cover and cook 10 minutes.
- **Turn** lamb chops over, and add ¼ cup wine. Cook 10 minutes or to desired degree of doneness. Remove from pan, and keep warm.
- **Add** remaining ¾ cup wine to pan drippings, stirring to loosen particles from bottom. Cook, stirring occasionally, 10 minutes or until liquid is reduced to about 1 cup. Stir in whipping cream; simmer 2 minutes. Season with salt and pepper to taste. Serve sauce with lamb chops. **Yield:** 4 servings.

BONUS SECTION

GARLIC-HONEY MARINATED PORK LOIN

Prep: 10 minutes
Marinate: 8 hours
Bake: 1 hour and 40 minutes

¾ cup lemon juice
¾ cup honey
6 tablespoons KIKKOMAN Soy
     Sauce
3 tablespoons dry sherry
6 garlic cloves, minced
1 (3- to 3½-pound) boneless pork
     loin roast
Garnishes: fresh parsley sprigs,
     sage leaves, lemon wedges

• **Combine** first 5 ingredients in a large shallow dish; add roast. Cover and chill 8 hours, turning occasionally.
• **Bake** at 325° for 1 hour and 40 minutes or until a meat thermometer inserted in thickest portion registers 160°. Garnish, if desired. **Yield:** 10 servings.

GOURMET GREEN BEAN GRATIN

Prep: 10 minutes
Bake: 25 minutes

2 (9-ounce) packages frozen
     STOUFFER'S Green Bean
     Mushroom Casserole
1½ cups shredded Parmesan
     cheese
1 (10-ounce) package frozen
     baby brussels sprouts in
     butter sauce, thawed and
     quartered
1 (14-ounce) can quartered
     artichoke hearts, drained
½ cup mayonnaise
2 tablespoons lemon juice
⅛ to ¼ teaspoon ground red
     pepper
2 tablespoons sliced almonds

• **Thaw** green bean mushroom casseroles in microwave at MEDIUM (50% power) 4 to 5 minutes.
• **Combine** ¾ cup Parmesan cheese and next 5 ingredients.

• **Spread** cheese mixture in bottom of a lightly greased 11- x 7-inch baking dish. Sprinkle with ½ cup cheese, and spread green bean mushroom casserole on top.
• **Sprinkle** with remaining ¼ cup cheese and sliced almonds.
• **Bake** at 350° for 20 to 25 minutes. **Yield:** 6 to 8 servings.

BLACK-AND-WHITE CHEESECAKE

Prep: 35 minutes
Bake: 1 hour
Chill: 8 hours

1⅓ cups DOMINO Granulated
     Sugar, divided
⅓ cup butter, melted
1½ cups chocolate wafer
     crumbs
1 cup slivered almonds, toasted
     and chopped
4 (8-ounce) packages cream
     cheese, softened
¼ cup almond liqueur
1 teaspoon vanilla extract
4 large eggs
4 (1-ounce) semisweet chocolate
     squares, melted

• **Stir** together ⅓ cup sugar and next 3 ingredients; press firmly onto bottom and 1 inch up sides of a 9-inch springform pan.
• **Bake** at 350° for 10 minutes.
• **Beat** cream cheese at medium speed with an electric mixer until creamy; gradually add remaining 1 cup sugar, beating well.
• **Stir** in liqueur and vanilla.
• **Add** eggs, 1 at a time, beating until blended after each addition. Reserve 1½ cups batter, spooning remaining batter into crust.
• **Stir** melted chocolate into reserved 1½ cups batter.
• **Spoon** chocolate batter into a heavy-duty zip-top plastic bag; snip a tiny hole in 1 corner of bag.
• **Insert** tip of bag ½ inch into center of vanilla batter; squeeze enough of chocolate batter to form a 2-inch circle.

• **Squeeze** remaining batter evenly into 6 (1½-inch) circles around edge of chocolate mixture.
• **Bake** at 350° for 1 hour or until center is almost set. Cool in pan on a wire rack. Cover and chill at least 8 hours. **Yield:** 10 to 12 servings.

Note: For testing purposes only, we used KEEBLER Chocolate Wafers.

TEA-BERRY SAUCE

Prep: 30 minutes

2 quarts fresh raspberries
1 cup water
2 LIPTON Cup Size Tea Bags
1½ cups sugar
2 tablespoons cornstarch
¼ cup butter
2 teaspoons vanilla extract

• **Bring** raspberries and 1 cup water to a boil in a saucepan over medium-high heat; reduce heat, and simmer 5 minutes. Add tea bags; cover and steep 5 minutes. Remove tea bags with a slotted spoon, squeezing gently.
• **Pour** berry mixture through a wire-mesh strainer into a 2-cup measuring cup; press berry mixture firmly against sides of strainer with back of a spoon to squeeze out juice. Discard pulp and seeds. Measure juice. If more than 1 cup, boil juice to reduce to 1 cup.
• **Combine** sugar and cornstarch in a small saucepan; gradually stir in 1 cup juice until smooth. Bring to a boil over medium heat, stirring constantly; boil 1 minute. Remove from heat; stir in butter and vanilla. Cover and chill. Serve over pound cake or vanilla ice cream. **Yield:** 2⅔ cups.

SIP AND SAMPLE

Our collection of stylish snacks and beverages offers sure-fire culinary ammunition for facing holiday entertaining. Crabmeat Puffs are a delicious nibbler for any occasion. And if you keep the makings of Cider Tea in your pantry, you'll be ever-ready to offer guests a warm welcome.

CRABMEAT PUFFS

Prep: 45 minutes
Bake: 12 minutes

1 (17¼-ounce) package frozen puff pastry sheets
1 (6-ounce) can lump crabmeat, drained *
1 cup (4 ounces) shredded mild Cheddar cheese
1 (3-ounce) package cream cheese, softened
2 green onions, chopped
2 teaspoons Worcestershire sauce
¼ teaspoon hot sauce
1 (1-gallon) HEFTY OneZip Slider Bag
1 large egg
1 tablespoon water

• **Thaw** pastry sheets at room temperature 30 minutes.
• **Unfold** each pastry sheet onto a lightly floured surface, and roll into a 15- x 9-inch rectangle; cut each rectangle into 15 (3-inch) squares.
• **Combine** crabmeat and next 5 ingredients in slider bag.
• **Knead** crabmeat mixture until all ingredients are combined. Cut tip off 1 corner of bag; pipe about 2 teaspoons crabmeat mixture into center of each pastry square.
• **Whisk** together egg and 1 tablespoon water, and brush on pastry edges. Fold corners of pastry to center, pinching edges to seal. Place pastry bundles on baking sheets.
• **Bake** at 400° for 12 minutes or until golden. **Yield:** 30 appetizer servings.

* Substitute 1 cup finely chopped cooked chicken for canned crabmeat, if desired.

CIDER TEA

Prep: 13 minutes

3 cups boiling water
4 LIPTON Cup Size Tea Bags
3 cups apple cider
3 tablespoons honey
Garnish: orange slices

• **Pour** 3 cups water over tea bags. Cover and steep 8 minutes; remove bags with a slotted spoon, squeezing gently. Stir in cider and honey. Serve warm or over ice. Garnish, if desired. **Yield:** 6 cups.

AVOCADO-CORN SALSA

Prep: 20 minutes
Chill: 2 hours

4 ears fresh yellow corn *
¾ cup water
1 medium tomato, chopped
1 jalapeño pepper, seeded and chopped
¼ cup chopped red bell pepper
¼ cup chopped purple onion
¼ cup chopped fresh cilantro
¼ cup white wine vinegar
2 tablespoons lime juice
½ teaspoon salt
3 small CALIFORNIA AVOCADOS, peeled and chopped

• **Cut** corn kernels from cobs into a saucepan.
• **Add** ¾ cup water, and bring to a boil. Cover, reduce heat, and simmer 6 to 7 minutes. Drain and place in a bowl.
• **Stir** in tomato and next 7 ingredients. Gently stir in avocado. Cover and chill 2 hours. Serve with tortilla chips or grilled fish or chicken. **Yield:** about 6 cups.

* Substitute 2½ cups frozen whole kernel corn for fresh corn, if desired.

PERFECTLY RIPE

If the avocados you find in the supermarket appear too firm for immediate use, place them in a paper bag with a bruised apple. Let stand for a couple of days at room temperature. Store ripe avocados in the refrigerator up to five days.

BEEF ON A STICK

For four main-dish servings, serve with reserved marinade over rice.

Prep: 40 minutes
Grill: 5 minutes

½ pound flank steak
2 tablespoons sesame seeds
2 tablespoons sesame oil
⅔ cup KIKKOMAN Lite Soy Sauce
4 green onions, thinly sliced
2 garlic cloves, crushed
¼ cup sugar
1 tablespoon ground ginger
¼ cup dry sherry
½ teaspoon pepper

• **Freeze** steak partially; cut diagonally across the grain into ⅛-inch-thick slices.
• **Bake** sesame seeds in a shallow pan at 350°, stirring occasionally, 3 minutes or until toasted. Cool.
• **Whisk** together sesame seeds, sesame oil, and next 7 ingredients. Reserve half of mixture. Pour remaining mixture into a heavy-duty zip-top plastic bag; add steak. Seal and chill 30 minutes, turning occasionally.
• **Remove** steak from marinade, discarding marinade; thread onto skewers.
• **Grill,** covered with grill lid, over medium heat (300° to 350°) 1½ to 2½ minutes on each side. Serve with reserved soy sauce mixture. **Yield:** 8 appetizer servings.

MOCK TEA SANGRÍA

Prep: 25 minutes
Chill: 2 hours

1 (10-ounce) package frozen raspberries, thawed
3 cups water
⅓ cup sugar
1 LIPTON Family Size Tea Bag
2 cups red grape juice
1 lemon, sliced
1 lime, sliced
1 (16-ounce) bottle orange soft drink, chilled *

• **Process** raspberries in a blender or food processor until smooth, stopping to scrape down sides. Pour through a fine wire-mesh strainer into a large container, discarding seeds. Set aside.
• **Bring** 3 cups water and sugar to a boil in a saucepan, stirring often. Remove from heat; add tea bag. Cover and steep 5 minutes.
• **Remove** tea bag with a slotted spoon, squeezing gently; cool tea mixture.
• **Stir** together raspberry puree, tea mixture, grape juice, and lemon and lime slices. Chill.
• **Stir** in orange soft drink, and serve immediately over ice. **Yield:** 9 cups.

* Substitute 1 cup orange juice and 1 cup lemon-lime soft drink, if desired.

CHILI-CHEESE SPREAD

Prep: 10 minutes

1 (8-ounce) package cream CHEESE, softened
1 (1¾-ounce) envelope chili seasoning mix
3 tablespoons salsa
1 cup chopped pecans
2 cups (8 ounces) finely shredded Monterey Jack CHEESE, divided

• **Beat** first 3 ingredients at medium speed with an electric mixer until smooth.
• **Stir** in pecans and 1 cup cheese.
• **Divide** mixture in half; shape each portion into a log or ball. Roll each in remaining cheese. Wrap in plastic wrap, and cover with aluminum foil. Freeze up to 3 months, if desired. Thaw at room temperature just before serving. Serve with crackers. **Yield:** 3 cups.

CASUAL COMBOS

You'll have ideal weeknight fare when you pair satisfying soup with flavorful sandwiches. Try Pecan Crispies or Apple Pie With Warm Cinnamon Crème for dessert. Preparing soup the day before you serve it allows the flavors to mellow.

CREAMY GREEN BEAN, MUSHROOM, AND HAM CHOWDER

Prep: 10 minutes
Cook: 45 minutes

1 (11-ounce) package frozen STOUFFER'S Potatoes au Gratin
2 (9-ounce) packages frozen STOUFFER'S Green Bean Mushroom Casserole
3 cups chicken broth, divided
3 tablespoons all-purpose flour
1 carrot, thinly sliced
1 medium onion, chopped
1 teaspoon vegetable oil
2 cups chopped cooked ham
½ teaspoon pepper
3 cups milk

• **Thaw** potatoes au gratin in microwave at MEDIUM (50% power) 6 to 7 minutes; set aside.
• **Thaw** 2 packages green bean mushroom casserole in microwave at MEDIUM (50% power) 10 to 12 minutes, and set aside.
• **Stir** together ¼ cup broth and flour until smooth.
• **Sauté** carrot and onion in hot oil in a Dutch oven until tender. Add potatoes, green bean mushroom casserole, remaining 2¾ cups broth, ham, and pepper. Bring to a boil; gradually stir in flour mixture and milk.
• **Return** to a boil; cover, reduce heat, and simmer 10 minutes. **Yield:** about 2½ quarts.

BONUS SECTION

CHICKEN-AVOCADO DAGWOODS

Mash avocados the clean and easy way. Place halves in a heavy-duty zip-top plastic bag; seal and squeeze.

Prep: 10 minutes

8 sourdough bread slices, toasted
2 tablespoons mayonnaise
8 purple onion slices
4 (1-ounce) Monterey Jack or provolone cheese slices
8 bacon slices, cooked
8 lettuce leaves
8 (¼-inch-thick) roasted chicken breast slices
8 tomato slices
2 CALIFORNIA AVOCADOS, peeled and mashed
⅛ teaspoon salt
⅛ teaspoon pepper

• **Spread** 1 side of toast slices with mayonnaise; top 4 slices evenly with onion slices and next 5 ingredients. Spoon avocado on top. Sprinkle with salt and pepper. Top with remaining toast slices, and serve immediately. **Yield:** 4 servings.

SPICY VEGETABLE SOUP

Prep: 10 minutes
Cook: 32 minutes

1 pound ground beef
1 cup chopped onion
2 garlic cloves, pressed
1 (30-ounce) jar chunky spaghetti sauce with mushrooms and peppers
1 (10½-ounce) can beef broth, undiluted
2 cups water
1 cup sliced celery
1 teaspoon sugar
1 teaspoon salt
½ teaspoon freshly ground pepper
1 (10-ounce) can ROTEL Diced Tomatoes and Green Chiles
1 (16-ounce) package frozen mixed vegetables

• **Cook** first 3 ingredients in a large Dutch oven over medium heat, stirring until meat is crumbled and no longer pink. Drain and return to Dutch oven.
• **Add** spaghetti sauce and next 6 ingredients. Bring to a boil; cover, reduce heat, and simmer, stirring often, 20 minutes. Stir in tomatoes and chiles and mixed vegetables; return to a boil. Cover and simmer 10 minutes. Serve with toasted bread triangles. **Yield:** 12 cups.

GRILLED SPINACH FONDUE SANDWICHES

For best results, coat the baking sheets with butter-flavored cooking spray.

Prep: 10 minutes
Bake: 20 minutes

1 (10-ounce) package frozen chopped spinach, thawed and drained
½ cup dry sherry
1½ cups (6 ounces) shredded Swiss CHEESE
2 tablespoons mayonnaise
¼ teaspoon salt
¼ teaspoon pepper
¼ teaspoon ground nutmeg
8 (1-inch-thick) French bread slices

• **Cook** spinach and sherry in a small saucepan over medium-high heat 4½ minutes or until liquid evaporates.
• **Combine** spinach mixture, cheese, and next 4 ingredients. Spread on 4 bread slices; top with remaining slices.
• **Place** sandwiches on a lightly greased baking sheet. Lightly grease bottom of another baking sheet; place, coated side down, on sandwiches.
• **Bake** at 475° for 15 to 20 minutes or until golden. Serve immediately. **Yield:** 4 sandwiches.

PECAN CRISPIES

Prep: 20 minutes
Bake: 15 minutes

½ cup butter, softened
½ cup shortening
2 cups firmly packed DOMINO Light Brown Sugar
2 large eggs
2½ cups all-purpose flour
½ teaspoon baking soda
¼ teaspoon salt
1 cup chopped pecans

• **Cream** butter and shortening at medium speed with an electric mixer; gradually add sugar, beating until fluffy. Add eggs; beat until blended. Add flour, soda, and salt; beat until blended. Stir in pecans.
• **Drop** by level tablespoonfuls 2 inches apart onto lightly greased baking sheets.
• **Bake** at 350° for 12 to 15 minutes. Cool slightly on baking sheets; remove to wire racks to cool. **Yield:** 3 dozen.

APPLE PIE WITH WARM CINNAMON CRÈME

Prep: 5 minutes
Bake: 1 hour and 30 minutes
Cook: 8 minutes

1 (3-pound, 1-ounce) package frozen MRS. SMITH'S Deep Dish Special Recipe Apple Pie
5 egg yolks
½ cup sugar
2 cups half-and-half
1 teaspoon ground cinnamon
2 teaspoons vanilla extract

• **Remove** plastic overwrap from pie. Open center hole; cut 4 to 6 slits in top crust. Place on a foil-lined baking sheet.
• **Bake** at 375° for 1 hour and 20 minutes to 1 hour and 30 minutes, shielding edges with aluminum foil after 1 hour.
• **Bring** egg yolks and next 3 ingredients to a boil in a medium saucepan over medium heat, whisking constantly.
• **Remove** from heat; whisk in vanilla. Cool. Serve with pie. **Yield:** 8 servings.

METRIC EQUIVALENTS

The recipes that appear in this cookbook use the standard United States method for measuring liquid and dry or solid ingredients (teaspoons, tablespoons, and cups). The information on this chart is provided to help cooks outside the U.S. successfully use these recipes. All equivalents are approximate.

METRIC EQUIVALENTS FOR DIFFERENT TYPES OF INGREDIENTS

A standard cup measure of a dry or solid ingredient will vary in weight depending on the type of ingredient. A standard cup of liquid is the same volume for any type of liquid. Use the following chart when converting standard cup measures to grams (weight) or milliliters (volume).

Standard Cup	Fine Powder (ex. flour)	Grain (ex. rice)	Granular (ex. sugar)	Liquid Solids (ex. butter)	Liquid (ex. milk)
1	140 g	150 g	190 g	200 g	240 ml
¾	105 g	113 g	143 g	150 g	180 ml
⅔	93 g	100 g	125 g	133 g	160 ml
½	70 g	75 g	95 g	100 g	120 ml
⅓	47 g	50 g	63 g	67 g	80 ml
¼	35 g	38 g	48 g	50 g	60 ml
⅛	18 g	19 g	24 g	25 g	30 ml

USEFUL EQUIVALENTS FOR LIQUID INGREDIENTS BY VOLUME

¼ tsp			=	1 ml
½ tsp			=	2 ml
1 tsp			=	5 ml
3 tsp =	1 tbls	= ½ fl oz	=	15 ml
	2 tbls	= ⅛ cup = 1 fl oz	=	30 ml
	4 tbls	= ¼ cup = 2 fl oz	=	60 ml
	5⅓ tbls	= ⅓ cup = 3 fl oz	=	80 ml
	8 tbls	= ½ cup = 4 fl oz	=	120 ml
	10⅔ tbls	= ⅔ cup = 5 fl oz	=	160 ml
	12 tbls	= ¾ cup = 6 fl oz	=	180 ml
	16 tbls	= 1 cup = 8 fl oz	=	240 ml
	1 pt	= 2 cups = 16 fl oz	=	480 ml
	1 qt	= 4 cups = 32 fl oz	=	960 ml
		33 fl oz	=	1000 ml = 1 l

USEFUL EQUIVALENTS FOR DRY INGREDIENTS BY WEIGHT

(To convert ounces to grams, multiply the number of ounces by 30.)

1 oz	=	¹⁄₁₆ lb	=	30 g
4 oz	=	¼ lb	=	120 g
8 oz	=	½ lb	=	240 g
12 oz	=	¾ lb	=	360 g
16 oz	=	1 lb	=	480 g

USEFUL EQUIVALENTS FOR LENGTH

(To convert inches to centimeters, multiply the number of inches by 2.5.)

1 in				=	2.5 cm	
6 in	= ½ ft			=	15 cm	
12 in	= 1 ft			=	30 cm	
36 in	= 3 ft	= 1 yd	=	90 cm	
40 in				=	100 cm	= 1 m

USEFUL EQUIVALENTS FOR COOKING/OVEN TEMPERATURES

	Fahrenheit	Celsius	Gas Mark
Freeze Water	32° F	0° C	
Room Temperature	68° F	20° C	
Boil Water	212° F	100° C	
Bake	325° F	160° C	3
	350° F	180° C	4
	375° F	190° C	5
	400° F	200° C	6
	425° F	220° C	7
	450° F	230° C	8
Broil			Grill

MENU INDEX

This index lists every menu by suggested occasion.
Recipes in bold type begin on the page number noted.
Suggested accompaniments are in regular type.

SIMPLE MENUS

(continued)

COOL SUMMER MENU
Serves 6
page 162

Smoked Oyster Mousse	Assorted Crackers
Grilled Corn Salsa	Tortilla Chips

Apricot-Chicken Salad
Iced Tea

GROVE PARK SUMMER MENU
Serves 4 to 6
page 168

Sweet Corn Soup With Shiitakes and Shrimp
Assorted Crackers
**Salad of Baby Lettuces
With Vidalia Onion Vinaigrette**
Grilled Entrée (chicken, steak, pork, or hearty fish)
Field Peas and Spinach
Cornsticks
Cream Cheese-Peach Tart

END-OF-SUMMER MENU
Serves 6
page 220

**Fresh-Squeezed Lemonade
Smoked Turkey, Mozzarella, and
Blackberry Sandwiches
Sour Cream Coleslaw
Favorite Fruit Salad
Angel Fluff Brownies**

SIMPLY SATISFYING
Serves 6
page 235

**Easy Brunswick Stew or
Hot-and-Spicy Black-Eyed Peas
Old-Fashioned Coleslaw
Buttermilk Cornbread**

WHEN COMPANY IS COMING

SUPPER FOR SIX
Serves 6
page 70

**Southern Fresh Fruit Punch
Goat Cheese Dumplings With
Roasted Bell Pepper Vinaigrette
Roasted Chicken With Poblano
Vinaigrette and Corn Pudding
Steamed Sugar Snap Peas**
Poppy Seed Rolls
Molded French Cream

SPRING BARBECUE
Serves 8
page 104

**Pork Chops With Tangy Barbecue Sauce
Dill Potato Salad**

Marinated Vegetables	**Molasses Baked Beans**

**Barbecue Bread
Tropical Ice**

MEXICAN MENU
Serves 8
page 160

Herbed Garbanzo Bean Spread
Assorted Crackers
**Jalapeño Grilled Pork
Minted Fruit Toss
Mexican Cornbread
Aztec Gold**
Ice Cream

A GRACIOUS DINNER PARTY
Serves 8 to 10
page 269

Stuffed Tuscany Tenderloin
Creamy Risotto
Snap Peas With Roasted Garlic Dressing
Dinner Rolls
Apple-Cranberry Pie

A SOUTH CAROLINA CELEBRATION
Serves 8
page 275

**Charleston Harbor Pickled Shrimp
Pimiento Cheese Spread
Cream of Leek Soup
Company Pork Roast**
Rice Pilaf
**Sunshine Carrots and Asparagus
Pandy's Biscuits
Chocolate Bread Pudding
With Whiskey Sauce**

MENUS FOR SPECIAL OCCASIONS

A SPRING CELEBRATION
Serves 4
page 55
Wild Rice-Shrimp Salad
Asparagus and Tomatoes With
Herb Vinaigrette
Orange-Pecan Muffins

FLAVORFUL FIESTA
Serves 6 to 8
page 119
Colorful Salsa
Creamy Guacamole
Tortilla Chips
Taco-Chicken Skewers
Mexican Pizza
Mock Margaritas

VICTORIAN DINNER PARTY
Serves 8
page 164
Cold Zucchini Soup
Fleur-de-lis Salad
Marinated Stuffed Filet of Beef
Mashed Potatoes With Crab Marinière
Sugar Snap Peas With Champagne Dressing
Watermelon Sorbet
Southern Custard Crêpe Cake

SUMMER GET-TOGETHER
Serves 4
page 175
Garlic-Herb Steaks
Tabbouleh
Tomato Slices
Lemon-Mint Spritzer
Fudge Cake

GARDEN PARTY
Serves 8
page 182
Herbed Cheesecakes
Dilled Summer Soup
Shrimp-and-Orzo Salad
Spicy Rosemary Aspic
Lemon Pound Cake
With Mint Berries and Cream

BOUNTIFUL THANKSGIVING FEAST
Serves 8
page 252
Acorn Squash-Thyme Soup
Apple-Rosemary Roasted Turkey
Southern Rice Dressing
Whole-berry Cranberry Sauce
Caramelized Onion-and-Pecan Brussels Sprouts
Rustic Breads
Cracked Caramel-Pumpkin Pie

FESTIVE BUFFET
Serves 8
page 258
Cranberry Crackers
Italian Bread Salad
Oven-Roasted Vegetables and Pork
Lemony Green Beans
Yeast Rolls
Sour Cream Pound Cake
With Raspberry Sauce

MAKE-AHEAD HOLIDAY BRUNCH
Serves 8
page 268
Bloody Mary Bowl
Cheese-and-Egg Casserole
Cheese Grits
Fresh Fruit
Wassail

A WEEKEND OF MENUS

FRIDAY DINNER PARTY
page 272
Spiral-cut Baked Ham
Wild Rice-and-Cranberry Salad
Winter Bake   Rolls
Amaretto Cheesecake

SATURDAY BRUNCH
page 272
Breakfast Casserole
Potato Casserole
Wild Rice-and-Cranberry Salad
Assorted Cookies   Sweet Rolls

SUNDAY TEA PARTY
page 272
Ham Sandwiches on Whole Grain Bread
With Mustard and Chutney
Beet-and-Pecan Sandwiches
Dried Tomato-and-Basil Sandwiches
Merry Cranberry-Nut Yeast Scones
With Mock Devonshire Cream
Amaretto Cheesecake   Assorted Cookies

RECIPE TITLE INDEX

This index alphabetically lists every recipe by exact title.
All microwave recipe page numbers are preceded by an "M."

MONTH-BY-MONTH INDEX

This index alphabetically lists every food article and accompanying recipes by month.
All microwave recipe page numbers are preceded by an "M."

GENERAL RECIPE INDEX

This index lists every recipe by food category and/or major ingredient.
All microwave recipe page numbers are preceded by an "M."

Favorite Recipes Journal

Jot down your family's and your favorite recipes for quick and handy reference. And don't forget to include the dishes that drew rave reviews when company came for dinner.

RECIPE	SOURCE/PAGE	REMARKS